DATE DUE

DEMCO 38-296

CONTEMPORARY MUSICIANS

Explore your options!
Gale databases offered in
a variety of formats

DISKETTE/MAGNETIC TAPE
Many Gale databases are available on diskette or magnetic tape, allowing systemwide access to your most-used information sources through existing computer systems. Data can be delivered on a variety of mediums (DOS-formatted diskette, 9-track tape, 8mm data tape) and in industry-standard formats (comma-delimited, tagged, fixed-field)

CD-ROM
A variety of Gale titles are available on CD-ROM, offering maximum flexibility and powerful search software.

The information in this Gale
publication is also available in some
or all of the formats described here.
Your Gale Representative
will be happy to fill you in.

ONLINE
For your convenience, many Gale databases are available through popular online services, including DIALOG, NEXIS, DataStar, ORBIT, OCLC, Thomson Financial Network's I/Plus Direct, HRIN, Prodigy, Sandpoint's HOOVER, The Library Corporation's NLightN, and Telebase Systems.

GALE NET
A number of Gale databases are available on an annual subscription basis through GaleNet, a new online information resource that features an easy-to-use end-user interface, the powerful search capabilities of BRS/SEARCH retrieval software and ease of access through the World-Wide Web.

For information, call

GALE
1-800-877-GALE

ISSN 1044-2197

CONTEMPORARY MUSICIANS

PROFILES OF THE PEOPLE IN MUSIC

BRIAN ESCAMILLA,
Editor

VOLUME 16
Includes Cumulative Indexes

GALE

STAFF

Brian Escamilla, *Editor*

Frank V. Castronova *Associate Editor*

Barbara Carlisle Bigelow, Rich Bowen, Carol Brennan, Susan Windisch Brown, John Cohassey, Louise Mooney Collins, Ed Decker, Lisa Fredricks, Kevin Hillstrom, Daniel Hodges, Simon Glickman, Ondine E. Le Blanc, John Packel, Jim Powers, Joseph M. Reiner, Joanna Rubiner, Julia Rubiner, Pamela L. Shelton, Sonya Shelton, B. Kimberly Taylor, Christopher B. Tower,*Contributing Editors*

Neil E. Walker, *Managing Editor*

Marlene S. Hurst, *Permissions Manager*
Margaret A. Chamberlain, Maria Franklin, *Permissions Specialists*
Diane Cooper, Michele Lonoconus, Maureen Puhl, Susan Salas, Shalice Shah, Kimberly F. Smilay, Barbara A. Wallace, *Permissions Associates*
Sarah Chesney, Edna Hedblad, Margaret McAvoy-Amato, Tyra Y. Phillips, Lori Schoenenberger, Rita Velaquez, *Permissions Assistants*

Mary Beth Trimper, *Production Director*
Shanna Philpott Heilveil, *Production Assistant*
Cynthia Baldwin, *Product Design Manager*
Barbara J. Yarrow, *Graphic Services Supervisor*
Randy Bassett, *Image Database Supervisor*
Pamela A. Hayes, *Photography Coordinator*
Willie Mathis, *Camera Operator*

Cover illustration by John Kleber

This book is printed on acid-free paper that meets the minimum requirements of American National Standard for Information Sciences—Permanence Paper for Printed Library Materials, ANSI Z39.48-1984.

This book is printed on recycled paper that meets Environmental Protection Agency Standards.

ISBN 0-8103-9317-4
ISSN 1044-2197

10 9 8 7 6 5 4 3 2 1

Contents

Introduction

Fills the Information Gap on Today's Musicians

Contemporary Musicians profiles the colorful personalities in the music industry who create or influence the music we hear today. Prior to *Contemporary Musicians,* no quality reference series provided comprehensive information on such a wide range of artists despite keen and ongoing public interest. To find biographical and critical coverage, an information seeker had little choice but to wade through the offerings of the popular press, scan television "infotainment" programs, and search for the occasional published biography or exposé. *Contemporary Musicians* is designed to serve that information seeker, providing in one ongoing source in-depth coverage of the important names on the modern music scene in a format that is both informative and entertaining. Students, researchers, and casual browsers alike can use *Contemporary Musicians* to meet their needs for personal information about music figures; find a selected discography of a musician's recordings; and uncover an insightful essay offering biographical and critical information.

Provides Broad Coverage

Single-volume biographical sources on musicians are limited in scope, often focusing on a handful of performers from a specific musical genre or era. In contrast, *Contemporary Musicians* offers researchers and music devotees a comprehensive, informative, and entertaining alternative. *Contemporary Musicians* is published twice yearly, with each volume providing information on more than 80 musical artists and record-industry luminaries from all the genres that form the broad spectrum of contemporary music—pop, rock, jazz, blues, country, New Age, folk, rhythm and blues, gospel, bluegrass, rap, and reggae, to name a few—as well as selected classical artists who have achieved "crossover" success with the general public. *Contemporary Musicians* will also occasionally include profiles of influential nonperforming members of the music community, including producers, promoters, and record company executives. Additionally, beginning with *Contemporary Musicians 11,* each volume features new profiles of a selection of previous *Contemporary Musicians* listees who remain of interest to today's readers and who have been active enough to require completely revised entries.

Includes Popular Features

In *Contemporary Musicians* you'll find popular features that users value:

- **Easy-to-locate data sections:** Vital personal statistics, chronological career summaries, listings of major awards, and mailing addresses, when available, are prominently displayed in a clearly marked box on the second page of each entry.

- **Biographical/critical essays:** Colorful and informative essays trace each subject's personal and professional life, offer representative examples of critical response to the artist's work, and provide entertaining personal sidelights.

- **Selected discographies:** Each entry provides a comprehensive listing of the artist's major recorded works.

- **Photographs:** Most entries include portraits of the subject profiled.

- **Sources for additional information:** This invaluable feature directs the user to selected books, magazines, and newspapers where more information can be obtained.

Helpful Indexes Make It Easy to Find the Information You Need

Each volume of *Contemporary Musicians* features a cumulative Musicians Index, listing names of individual performers and musical groups, and a cumulative Subject Index, which provides the user with a breakdown by primary musical instruments played and by musical genre.

Available in Electronic Formats

Diskette/Magnetic Tape. *Contemporary Musicians* is available for licensing on magnetic tape or diskette in a fielded format. Either the complete database or a custom selection of entries may be ordered. The database is available for internal data processing and nonpublishing purposes only. For more information, call (800) 877-GALE.

Online. *Contemporary Musicians* is available online through Mead Data Central's NEXIS Service in the NEXIS, PEOPLE and SPORTS Libraries in the GALBIO file.

We Welcome Your Suggestions

The editors welcome your comments and suggestions for enhancing and improving *Contemporary Musicians*. If you would like to suggest subjects for inclusion, please submit these names to the editors. Mail comments or suggestions to:

The Editor
Contemporary Musicians
Gale Research
835 Penobscot Bldg.
Detroit, MI 48226-4094
Phone: (800) 347-4253
Fax: (313) 961-6599

America

Folk-rock band

Photograph by Melodie Gimple, courtesy of American Gramaphone

Attracting a huge audience with their soft-rock sound, America released a string of popular hits in the 1970s. They adhered to their original pop formula over the next two and a half decades, even as the music scene evolved into harder-edged rock in the late 1970s and one of the trio's original members left to pursue solo interests. Although some critics have faulted the band in the past for their ultramellow sound, their recordings have often been cited for their fine harmonies and superior production.

Gerry Beckley, Dewey Bunnell, and Dan Peek—all sons of U.S. Air Force officers stationed in the United Kingdom—met while in high school in London in 1967. They began playing and writing music together and, with two other friends, formed an acoustic folk-rock quintet called Daze after graduation. Peek enrolled in college, then returned a year later; meanwhile, the two other members of Daze left the band for good. When Peek returned, the remaining threesome—he, Beckley, and Bunnell—decided to continue on as an acoustic trio and started to seek out club work.

Rock promoter Jeff Dexter, who managed a popular London club called the Roundhouse, was very impressed when the group auditioned for him. He began booking them as an opening act for many established bands who played at his club, including Pink Floyd. Now calling themselves America, the trio landed a contract with Warner Bros. in 1970—partly because Dexter was good friends with Ian Samwell, one of the record company's producers. America began recording songs for its first album at Trident Studios in London, working with Dexter and Samwell. Their first single, "A Horse with No Name," gave them instant fame as it soared to Number Three on the U.K. pop charts. America was soon likened to a softer version of Crosby, Stills and Nash, and Bunnell's vocals bore more than a passing resemblance to those of Neil Young.

The group's base of fans grew after they performed on a North American tour with the Everly Brothers. Soon after their return to England, America's debut million-selling single rose up the U.S. charts to Number One. Their self-titled debut album also made it to the top of the American LP charts. Soon to follow were two more Top Ten singles, "I Need You" and "Ventura Highway."

Changing their base of operations, the band self-produced and recorded their next two albums in the United States. They returned to London when their next three singles failed to crack the Top 30, then began working with famed Beatles producer George Martin. Martin collaborated regularly with the group through 1979. America enjoyed consistent success with their soft rock sound during much of the 1970s, with the singles "Tin

For the Record . . .

Original members included **Gerry Beckley** (born September 12, 1952, in Texas), vocals, guitar; **Dewey Bunnell** (born January 19, 1952, in Yorkshire, England), vocals, guitar; and **Dan Peek** (born November 1, 1950, in Panama City, FL; left group, 1977), vocals, guitar.

Formed acoustic folk-rock quintet called Daze in London, 1970; changed named to America and signed contract with Warner Bros., 1970; released first single, "A Horse with No Name," and debut album, *America*, 1972; toured North America with the Everly Brothers, 1972; first worked with producer George Martin, 1972; released *History: America's Greatest Hits*, 1975; became duo when Peek left group for a solo career in Christian music, 1977; signed with Capitol, 1980; returned to charts after long absence with "You Can Do Magic," 1982; vocalists on soundtrack for animated feature *The Last Unicorn*; released *Hourglass* on American Gramaphone, 1994.

Selected Awards: Grammy award for best new artist, 1972.

Addresses: *Record company*—American Gramaphone, 9130 Mormon Bridge Rd., Omaha, NE 68152.

generated a major hit with "You Can Do Magic," which made it to Number Eight on the U.S. charts in 1982. Written by songwriter-producer Russ Ballard, the song was the first of their Top Ten hits not to be written by a member of the group. Ballard worked on and off with the duo as a producer from this point on. Beckley and Bunnell also began writing songs with actor Bill Mumy, who as a child had starred in the television series "Lost in Space" in the 1960s.

In the late 1980s and early 1990s, America continued to perform and often toured with acts such as Stephen Stills, Three Dog Night, and the Beach Boys. After another change of record companies, the band released *Hourglass*, their eighteenth album, on American Gramaphone in 1994. Straying from their past practice of writing songs individually, Bunnell and Beckley made a pointed effort to collaborate on the songwriting process from the very beginning for this recording. Featured contributors to the album included Carl Wilson of the Beach Boys and Mannheim Steamroller's Chip Davis.

Whether their uncompromisingly mellow melodies continue to find an audience in the late 1990s and beyond remains to be seen. Clearly, the duo has no intentions of surprising its audience. As Beckley stated in the American Gramaphone press kit, "We stay very true to form. America's music has always been acoustic, lyrical, harmonious and accessible. Nothing way to left, or way to the right."

Selected discography

Singles; on Warner Bros., except as noted

"A Horse with No Name," 1972.
"I Need You," 1972.
"Ventura Highway," 1972.
"Don't Cross the River," 1973.
"Tin Man," 1974.
"Lonely People," 1974.
"Sister Golden Hair," 1975.
"You Can Do Magic," Capitol, 1982.

Albums; on Warner Bros., except as noted

America, 1972.
Homecoming, 1973.
Hat Trick, 1973.
Holiday, 1974.
Hearts, 1975.
History: America's Greatest Hits, 1975.
Hideaway, 1976.

Man," "Lonely People," and "Sister Golden Hair" all making the Top Ten in the States.

After a personal religious awakening, Dan Peek left the group in 1977 to pursue a solo career in Christian music. Beckley and Bunnell decided to carry on as a duo and continued to be a popular concert attraction even though their new songs made little impact. *Silent Letter,* their first studio album without Peek and final collaboration with Martin, only made it to Number 110 on the U.S. album charts in 1979.

Despite decreasing success, Beckley and Bunnell refused to shift their musical direction. "I remember one recording session in the 1970s where our producer suggested 'Why don't we put a disco beat here?'" said Bunnell in an American Gramaphone press kit. "But that wasn't what America was all about. Our core group of fans just weren't going to buy us going country or disco."

In 1980 America switched record labels, signing with Capitol. After a six-year absence from the charts, they

Harbor, 1977.
View from the Ground, Capitol, 1982.
Hourglass, American Gramaphone, 1994.

Sources

Bronson, Fred, *The Billboard Book of Number One Hits,* Billboard, 1988.

The Guinness Encyclopedia of Popular Music, Volume 1, edited by Colin Larkin, Guinness, 1992.

Hardy, Phil, and Dave Laing, *Encyclopedia of Rock,* Schirmer Books, 1987.

The Penguin Encyclopedia of Popular Music, edited by Donald Clarke, Viking, 1989.

Rees, Dafydd, and Luke Crampton, editors, *Rock Movers & Shakers,* ABC/CLIO, 1991.

Additional information for this profile was obtained from American Gramaphone publicity materials.

—Ed Decker

Dallas Austin

Rap artist, producer, songwriter

As one of the most sought-after songwriters and producers in contemporary music, 25-year-old Dallas Austin is in select company. His name is mentioned in the same sentence as legendary producers Phil Spector and Berry Gordy, and any artist looking for an Austin signature tune must be willing to write a $75,000 check for his services. Personally responsible for over 15 million records sold, there is no shortage of artists willing to hand over such a sum because Austin possesses a musical Midas touch, turning nearly everything he touches to platinum rather than gold. Austin has produced and written for Boyz II Men, Madonna, and TLC in addition to working with performers signed to his own label, Rowdy Records, based in Austin's hometown of Atlanta, Georgia.

As an adjunct to Rowdy Records, in 1992 Austin opened Dallas Austin Recording Projects, a production facility whose sound rooms have hosted Illegal and Ya'll So Stupid, two rap acts on the Rowdy label. Austin also has A&R (Artists and Repertoire) deals in place with EMI and Motown Records, allowing him to scout and sign talent for those labels as well as his own. After eight years in the business, Austin has reached the top of the profession and has been recognized by *Billboard* magazine as a top songwriter and producer in both R&B and pop music. With the corporate structure established to sign, produce, and release records the way he wants, Austin plans to concentrate on acts more alternative than those

he has worked with previously. "I want it to be, like, a real creative, artsy label. I'm not going to say it's not to make money, but it's not geared toward commercial acts. I'll see a guy playing a saxophone on the corner with a guy with bongos and give him a record deal, you know," he told the *Los Angeles Times*.

Austin represents a growing number of streetwise producers churning out hits for big-name artists in a manner that hearkens back to Motown's heyday. Sean "Puffy" Combs and Teddy Riley are fellow members of this informal conglomeration of hitmakers and have crafted successful tunes for Michael Jackson, the Notorious B.I.G., and a host of other chart-topping hip-hop and R&B artists. They share a friendly rivalry that raises the stakes for each successive project, pressing them to produce better and better songs for stars from contemporary music's short list. Combs told *Newsweek,* "When I heard Dallas's track for "Creep," [written and produced by Austin for TLC's 1995 release, *CrazySexyCool*] I said, 'Damn, I've got to come strong for TLC.' We push each other to do better." Like Combs and Riley, Austin grew up listening to R&B and witnessed the birth of rap and hip-hop in the early Eighties. Austin credits his brother for introducing him to a steady flow of new music as well as schooling him in the virtues of long-established artists. "The whole time I was growing up I was into music. My brother always had bands, so I was like the little kid that they'd tell to get out. I loved George Clinton, Earth, Wind & Fire, I listened to a lot of Chili Peppers...," Austin recalled in the *Los Angeles Times*.

Born in Columbus, Georgia, Austin would stay up late into the night playing along with recordings by his favorite performers on a keyboard. While this wee-hour apprenticeship served Austin well in the successful career that followed, his teachers found him tardy and generally inattentive. Austin told *Newsweek,* "I would get to school at 10 or 11 and the teachers would give me grief so I would just leave." He dropped out of high school during his junior year but his musical penchant quickly led to a job in the business, manning the lights for Atlanta's Princess and Starbreeze. Shortly thereafter, Austin moved from behind the lights to the stage after being asked to play keyboards for the group.

Austin then met Michael Bivins, a former member of the rap/R&B group New Edition, who moved Austin to the production booth to work with former Klymaxx singer Joyce Irby. Austin helped Irby craft "Hey Mr. D.J." and the song became a modest hit. On the heels of this success, he went to work for Motown acts Boyz II Men and another Atlanta-based act, Another Bad Creation (ABC), leaving more hit singles in his wake. He was responsible for ABC's "Iesha" and "Playground," two

For the Record . . .

Born 1971 in Columbus, GA; raised, along with one brother, by mother after father left family; moved to Atlanta neighborhood of Highland Place in 1983; *Education:* Attended M.D. Collins and Lakeshore High School; dropped out at age 17.

Began career as lightshow supervisor for Atlanta act Princess and Starbreeze; became keyboardist for same group; signed to La Face Records at age 17 as performer; produced single for Joyce Irby, formerly of Klymaxx; moved on to produce for Boyz II Men, TLC, Madonna, Lionel Richie; started Rowdy Records and Dallas Austin Recording Projects in Atlanta, early 1990s.

Selected awards: Named *Billboard* Producer of the Year, 1991; placed second in *Billboard*'s 1995 Top Ten Pop Songwriters of the Year and first in Top Ten R&B Songwriters of the Year.

Addresses: *Record company*—Rowdy Records, 75 Marietta Street, 6th floor, Atlanta, GA, 30305.

songs that helped spring the group to national prominence. With Boyz II Men, Austin wrote and produced eight of the ten songs on the R&B group's multiplatinum debut, *Cooleyhighharmony.*

Austin's musical prowess also brought attention from Antonio "L.A." Reid, an executive with Arista Records, after Austin's own demo tape crossed his desk. Then only 17, Austin signed a contract with Reid as a performer for Reid's Atlanta-based LaFace Records. LaFace had recently signed an all-female Atlanta trio now widely known as TLC. With Austin's help, their 1992 debut, *Oooooooohhh ...On the TLC Tip,* went platinum and established the group as one of the hottest acts in music of the Nineties. He wrote and produced "Ain't 2 Proud 2 Beg" and "What About Your Friends," with the former reaching platinum status and the latter going gold. Austin grew up with two TLC members in his College Park neighborhood in Atlanta. He told Atlanta's *Journal and Constitution,* "I knew Tionne from the skating rink, and Rozonda ...so I pretty much had a feel for TLC and what they were like already." Austin continued to work with TLC for the group's 1995 release, *CrazySexyCool,* writing and producing the wildly successful single, "Creep."

Between working as a freelance producer and managing his label and production studio, Austin is a member of a rock and R&B band, Highland Place Mobsters. The association dates back to 1983, when the preteen Austin moved from Columbus to the Atlanta neighborhood of Highland Park. With the Mobsters, Austin displays his more cutting-edge musical tastes, rebuking his mainstream commercial pedigree. The group's 1992 album *1746DCGA3005,* while definitely showing a much different musical side to Austin, did not sell. He told the *Journal and Constitution,* "I didn't expect people to get it because it was way out there. Most good stuff doesn't really sell a lot anyway." While an unexpected comment from a producer responsible for millions of purchased records, it reflects Austin's competitive edge over his competition. "My gift is knowing what other people could like," he remarked to the *Journal and Constitution.*

Selected discography

(With Highland Place Mobsters) *1746DCGA3005,* LaFace Records, 1992.

As producer

Another Bad Creation, *Coolin' At the Playground Ya-Know* (contains "Playground" and "Iesha"), Motown Records, 1991.
Boyz II Men, *Cooleyhighharmony,* Motown Records, 1991.
Madonna, *Bedtime Stories* (contains "Secret"), Maverick Records, 1994.
TLC, *Oooooooohhh... On the TLC Tip* (contains "Ain't 2 Proud 2 Beg" and What About Your Friends"), LaFace Records, 1991.
TLC, *CrazySexyCool* (contains "Creep"), LaFace Records, 1994

Sources

Billboard, June 3, 1995.
Journal and Constitution (Atlanta), June 6, 1993.
Los Angeles Times, December 6, 1992.
Newsweek, May 8, 1995.
Rolling Stone, August 24, 1995.
Schwann Spectrum, Winter 1995.

Additional information obtained from Rowdy Records publicity material, 1995.

—*Rich Bowen*

Babes in Toyland

Rock band

Nearly every description of Babes in Toyland includes some form of the characterization "girl group." The three women who make up the band, however, prefer to be called a "rock band," rather than a "female rock band." In fact, there is nothing traditionally feminine in their aggressive, post-punk sound, which inspired the Riot Grrrls movement, a cadre of mostly young women who have set out to prove, among other things, that gender had nothing to do with the quality of music.

Though Babes in Toyland is considered a Minneapolis band, its history actually began in a small town in Oregon, where a high school student named Katherine Bjelland became best friends with a troubled California transplant named Courtney Love. After graduating from high school, Bjelland and Love briefly attended college. They then moved to San Francisco, where Katherine became known as Kat. They hadn't planned to form a band—though Bjelland had started teaching herself how to play guitar when she was 19. But when Bjelland, Love, and their friend Jennifer Finch (who would go on

Photograph by Bill Phelps, © 1995 Reprise Records

For the Record . . .

Members include **Lori Barbero** (born November 27, 1961, in Minneapolis, MN), drums; **Kat Bjelland** (born December 9, 1963, in Salem, OR; married Stuart Spasm [a musician], 1992; divorced, 1994), vocals, guitar; and **Maureen Herman** (born July 25, 1965, in Philadelphia, PA), bass. Former members include bassists Courtney Love and Michelle Leon.

Band formed in Minneapolis, 1987; Leon replaced Love, 1988; Herman replaced Leon, 1992; released debut album, *Spanking Machine*, Twin/Tone, 1990; signed with Reprise Records and released *Fontanelle*, 1992; toured with Lollapalooza summer festival, 1993; appeared in, and contributed to soundtrack of, film *SFW* and contributed "The Girl Can't Help It" to soundtrack of film *Reform School Girls*, both 1994.

Addresses: *Record company*—Reprise Records, 3300 Warner Blvd., Burbank, CA 91505.

to join L7) caught an all-female punk band at a club one night, they decided to pick up instruments and give it a try. The three friends formed the band Sugar Baby Doll. But Bjelland soon decided to oust Love from the trio, effectively breaking up the band.

Minneapolis Beginnings

Remarkably, Bjelland and Love remained friends after this contentious event, deciding to pursue their musical careers in Minneapolis. By the end of 1987, they had met a cocktail waitress named Lori Barbero. Bjelland convinced Barbero that she could become a drummer. With Barbero on drums, Bjelland on guitar and vocals, and Love on bass, the first incarnation of Babes in Toyland was born. The name came from the Victor Herbert operetta (and 1961 Disney film), but as Bjelland would later explain in interview after interview, "Boys and girls are all babes in the universe."

A few months later, Bjelland once again kicked her longtime friend out of the band. Michelle Leon replaced Love on bass. Leon had only casually played her boyfriend's bass guitar, but she was eager to join the band. "It felt so right from the very first," she told Neal Karlen in his book *Babes in Toyland*. "I didn't want to just be in some band—I needed to be in this band. Though none of us knew how to read music, and Lori and I'd

never really played our instruments, it was like we could understand the beat of each other's pulses."

The trio's friendship grew so close that they began to think of themselves as sisters. By then Babes in Toyland had made a name for themselves playing the Minneapolis club circuit. In 1990 they released their first LP, *Spanking Machine*, on Twin/Tone, a respected independent label based in Minneapolis. Shortly thereafter, Tim Carr, a representative of Warner Bros. Records, happened to see the band play in New York. A few months later, Carr signed them to a record contract. The band left on a European tour almost immediately.

Near Breakup and a Love-Hate Relationship

Babes in Toyland spent most of 1991 on the road expanding their fan base. Then, as they were preparing to go into the studio to record their first album for Reprise, a subsidiary of Warner Bros., Leon decided to quit the band. Refusing to squander the momentum they had gained on tour by simply letting the band disintegrate, Barbero and Bjelland recruited yet another bass player, Maureen Herman. Herman, who had been playing bass for Cherry Rodriquez in Chicago, knew the other Babes from when she had lived in Minneapolis. To solidify the new lineup, Babes in Toyland continued to perform before beginning recording sessions.

Bjelland married Stuart Spasm of the Australian punk band Lubricated Goat a few weeks before the release of Babes in Toyland's first major-label album. The record was called *Fontanelle*, a reference to the soft spot on a newborn's head.

In the meantime, Love had formed the band Hole and married Kurt Cobain, singer, guitarist, and songwriter for Nirvana, which would become enormously popular. Love took advantage of her new prominence to start a feud with Bjelland over who had started the "kinder-whore" look that both women favored—tattered baby-doll dresses, little-girl shoes, garish makeup, and wildly messy hair. Babes in Toyland responded with a staged combat between Bjelland and photographer Cindy Sherman, imitating Love, in the band's first video, "Bruise Violet." The media war ultimately served to promote Babes in Toyland as much as Love.

At the end of the *Fontanelle* tour, Bjelland announced that she and her husband were moving to Seattle to form a new project, thus dissolving Babes in Toyland. But four days later, after a long, heart-to-heart talk with Barbero, Bjelland changed her mind about the band, if not Seattle. After Bjelland relocated west, she and Seattle resident Love reconciled. In the press, Love—

notoriously prone to overblown pronouncements—often stated that the original lineup of Babes in Toyland, with her on bass, could have become the next Beatles.

The current lineup of Babes in Toyland hadn't been doing too badly either: *Spin* named *Fontanelle* one of the year's Top 20 albums, and Jon Pareles of the *New York Times* listed Babes in Toyland among 1992's most notable groups.

Movies, Books, and MTV

In 1993 Babes in Toyland experienced another career surge, releasing an EP titled *Pain Killers,* which included a live version of "Bruise Violet." MTV's hit show *Beavis and Butt-head* started incorporating the "Bruise Violet" clip into its video segments, which increased the band's exposure and album sales. That summer Babes in Toyland joined the renowned Lollapalooza summer festival tour.

The following year the trio had a hand in the film *SFW,* playing themselves as well as recording the picture's title song. Not satisfied with this foray into filmdom, however, Babes in Toyland also cut a cover of Little Richard's "The Girl Can't Help It" for the movie *Reform School Girls.* Neal Karlen helped to further hype the band with his account of their story in his book *Babes in Toyland: The Making and Selling of a Rock and Roll Band.* And later in the year, the trio's version of "Calling Occupants of Interplanetary Craft" appeared on *If I Were a Carpenter,* a well-received homage to the 1970s pop band the Carpenters.

Before the recording of the band's next album, Bjelland divorced Spasm and returned to Minneapolis. In early 1995 Babes in Toyland released *Nemesister.* The LP included the corrosively catchy first single, "Sweet 69," and singular covers of disco stalwart Sister Sledge's "We Are Family," former Raspberry Eric Carmen's 1975 hit "All By Myself," and blues singer Billie Holiday's "Deep Song."

Over the years Babes in Toyland have developed a solid band chemistry and a distinctive musical identity. "We are not regular musicians," Barbero told *Billboard.* "We don't read and write music; we just do our own thing."

Selected discography

Spanking Machine, Twin/Tone, 1990.
Fontanelle, Reprise, 1992.
Pain Killers (EP), Reprise, 1993.
(Contributors) *If I Were a Carpenter,* A&M, 1994.
Nemesister, Reprise, 1995.

Sources

Books

Karlen, Neal, *Babes in Toyland: The Making and Selling of a Rock and Roll Band,* Times Books/Random House, 1994.
The Trouser Press Record Guide, edited by Ira A. Robbins, Collier, 1992.

Periodicals

Billboard, July 10, 1993; September 4, 1993; March 18, 1995.
Entertainment Weekly, July 16, 1993; July 23, 1993; April 28, 1995.
Rolling Stone, April 18, 1991; May 18, 1995; June 15, 1995.
Stereo Review, November 1993; December 1994.
Wilson Library Bulletin, December 1994.

Additional information for this profile was obtained from Reprise Records press materials, 1995.

—Sonya Shelton

Bad Brains

Punk, reggae band

When Bad Brains first introduced their frenetic take on rock and roll to audiences in 1978, the music world was experiencing the birth of a stripped-down, speeded-up phenom in the genre known as punk rock. The Ramones, the Clash, and the Buzzcocks, all seminal bands, were screaming their way into the music scene just as Bad Brains began playing small clubs and parties in their hometown of Washington, D.C. Since that time, punk rock in its many faces has found its way to larger and more diverse audiences, as multi-platinum acts such as Green Day, the Offspring, and the Red Hot Chili Peppers can attest. Guitarists such as Vernon Reid of Living Colour and Jane's Addiction founder and later Chili Pepper Dave Navarro pay tribute to Bad Brains' guitarist Dr. Know and his textured, blazing style through both word and deed. As one of punk rock's originators, Bad Brains helped to set the tone for hundreds of bands that followed their raucous, screeching lead.

After flirting with major-label notoriety for 18 years, the band stood poised on the verge of major exposure with the release of their 1995 album, *God of Love*, on

Photograph by Suzan Carson, MICHAEL OCHS ARCHIVES/Venice, CA

Formed 1979, in Washington, D.C.; original members include **Earl Hudson** (born December 17, 1957, in Alabama; left band, 1989; rejoined band, 1995), drums; **H.R.** (born Paul Hudson, February 11, 1956, in London, England; left band, 1989; rejoined band, 1995), vocals; **Darryl Jenifer** (born October 22, 1960, in Washington, D.C.), bass; and **Dr. Know** (born Gary Miller, September 15, 1958, in Washington, D.C.), guitar; later members include **Mackie Jayson** (born May 27, 1963, in New York City), drums; and **Israel Joseph-I** (born Dexter Pinto, February 6, 1971, in Trinidad), vocals.

Began as fusion jazz band; changed direction following exposure to first wave of English punk rock and began playing Washington clubs in late Seventies. Relocated to New York City in 1981; independently released single "Pay to Cum" in 1981; recruited by ROIR and released self-titled cassette that has sold over 60,000 copies; released *Rock For Light* in 1983 on PVC Records and produced by Ric Ocasek, formerly of the Cars; turned down major-label contract offers from Elektra and Island and chose to record on independent labels including SST, PVC, and Caroline; H.R. left band in 1989 to pursue solo career and play in reggae band, Human Rights, replaced by Israel Joseph-I; drummer Earl Hudson left band in 1989, replaced by Mackie Jayson; signed first major-label contract with Epic Records and released *Rise* in 1993; record sold poorly and band was dropped by Epic; H.R. and Earl rejoined band in to release 1995's *God of Love* on Maverick Records.

Addresses: *Record company*—Maverick Entertainment, 8000 Beverly Boulevard, Los Angeles, CA 90048.

Madonna's respected Maverick label. The album was produced by Ric Ocasek, formerly of the Cars, who had also produced the Brains' 1986 LP *I Against I* after being duly impressed with a powerful on-stage performance one night. Following a career as noted for its break-ups and reformations almost as much as its music, the four original members rejoined in 1995 to put together an album that would finally actualize the kind of potential that persuaded Bad Brains' original producer Ron St. Germain to tell the *Washington Post,* "They were without a doubt the best hard-core/speed metal band in the world." While the album sold moderately well, the on-stage antics of Bad Brains' lead singer, H.R., a.k.a. Paul Hudson, garnered the bulk of the media attention.

During the 1995 tour in support of the latest release, a violent run-in with fans in mid-performance landed H.R. in jail in Lawrence, Kansas. Maverick management posted bail, but not before some show dates had to be canceled. The tour then moved to Montreal, Quebec, where H.R. attacked Bad Brains' manager Anthony Countey backstage before the show, breaking his nose then winding up in jail yet again after officials found marijuana in his pocket when H.R. crossed the border back into the States. The band's relationship with both management and amongst themselves spiraled into chaos, especially after neither his bandmates nor his label posted H.R.'s bail after the second incident. Touring at the time with the Beastie Boys, several more dates were canceled while Bad Brains and its management took time to reflect on what had happened and determine its effect on the band's future. Certainly an unfortunate turn of events, it was not an unfamiliar scenario for a band that has flirted with success many times throughout its controversial and celebrated career.

Bad Brains first took shape when the four shared a Forrestville, Maryland, house. Comprised of H.R. and his brother, Earl Hudson, joined by Darryl Jenifer and Dr. Know (born Gary Miller), the group originally termed their musical enterprise Mind Power. They found inspiration in early punk records but set themselves apart by an affinity for the steady rhythms of reggae combined with lyrics driven by strong faith in Rastafarianism. The four attended a Bob Marley concert and the 1978 experience helped chart a course that would take the band into unknown musical territory. Hudson told *Rolling Stone,* in typical Bad Brains parable-speak, that the concert "was like a vision. I guess it was the season for things, the season for knowing."

Aside from reggae, the four found themselves drawn to fusion jazz and funk. Bassist Darryl Jenifer explained to the *Phoenix Gazette,* "We were into Mahavishu, Brand X, Return to Forever, Stevie Wonder, and we took that progressive jazz influence and grafted it onto the aggressiveness and revolutionary sounds of punk rock and reggae." Such diversity in their influences combined with strong musicianship made Bad Brains a well-respected band among their peers as well as an act not to be missed in the D.C. area. Their first single, "Pay to Cum," vaulted the foursome from local standouts to touring professionals in 1981.

It turned out to be a very good break, as the band found few Washington clubs willing to book them after a riot nearly erupted during one show. In response, the Brains recorded the tongue-in-cheek "Banned in D.C." and set their sights on bigger and better gigs. Club dates in New York led to a stint in Europe and set the stage for releases on the California-based, now-defunct alternative label, SST Records, as well as producer Ron St. Germain's own label, ROIR (Reach Out International Records).

While major labels courted Bad Brains, most notably Elektra in 1988 after the release of cult classic and Ric Ocasek-produced *I Against I* in 1986, H.R. and the other members rebuffed the corporate overtures, choosing to remain an indie-label band. That all changed in 1989 when H.R. departed to pursue more reggae-based ventures with a band he dubbed Human Rights. Chuck Moseley of Faith No More took over Bad Brains' vocals and New Yorker Mackie Jayson replaced drummer Earl Hudson, who had also left in 1989. Moseley then departed in 1992, with his spot taken over by Trinidad-born Rastafarian Israel Joseph-I. The original Brains migrated to different parts of the world—Earl Hudson to Cologne, Germany; H.R. to Los Angeles; Dr. Know and Jenifer to Woodstock, New York—but Jenifer, Dr. Know, Jayson and Joseph-I got together in 1992 to sign Bad Brains' first major-label deal. This new incarnation released *Rise* on Epic Records and industry watchers assumed the album would catapult Bad Brains to platinum-selling greatness. However, the record flopped and Epic dropped the band.

Were it not for the insistence of Beastie Boys' guitarist Adam Yauch, Bad Brains might have stopped making records and forever retained their underground status. During a 1994 Beastie Boys performance at the Lollapalooza tour stop in Los Angeles, H.R. visited with Yauch backstage and made several important points about the state of the alternative music industry and Bad Brains' past impact—and possible future—within it. Yauch's articulated convictions worked: H.R. agreed to put the original line-up back together, and Joseph-I gracefully stepped aside. Bad Brains' sophisticated equilibrium takes as its fulcrum the member's deep spirituality, and they attributed their 1995 comeback to the plan of Jah. "We re-formed to have fun and let people know the god of love is the heavenly father and heavenly mother together as one," H.R. told *Rolling Stone*. Although marred by troubles early in 1995, past history suggests that Bad Brains will continue to patch things back up to record and play together, and—depending on H.R.'s ability to avoid trouble—finally reach the level of success so many think they deserve.

Selected discography

Bad Brains (EP), Alternative Tentacles, 1982.
Bad Brains (cassette, contains "Pay to Cum"), ROIR, 1982.
Rock for Light, PVC, 1983.
I Against I, SST, 1986.
Live, SST, 1988.
With the Quickness, Caroline, 1989.
Attitude—The ROIR Sessions, Relativity/ROIR/Important, 1989.
The Youth Are Getting Restless, Caroline, 1990.
Rock For Light (re-issue), Caroline, 1991.
Spirit Electricity, SST, 1991.
Rise, Epic, 1993.
God of Love, Maverick Records/Warner Bros., 1995.

Sources

Books

The New Rolling Stone Encyclopedia of Rock and Roll, edited by Romanowski, George-Warner, Pareles, Fireside/Rolling Stone Press, 1995.

Periodicals

Boston Globe, May 16, 1995,.
Chicago Tribune, May 26, 1995.
Gazette (Montreal), May 16, 1995; May 17, 1995.
Guitar Player, October 1995.
Kansas City Star, July 22, 1995; July 27, 1995.
New York Times, July 9, 19959.
Phoenix Gazette, June 5, 1995.
RIP, August 1995.
Rolling Stone, June 29, 1995.
Seattle Times, May 26, 1995.
Times-Picayune (New Orleans), July 14, 1995.
Washington Post, July 30, 1995.

—Rich Bowen

Ginger Baker

Photograph by Howard Waggner, Archive Photos

Ginger Baker found his way into the Rock 'n' Roll Hall of Fame by playing the drums with a degree of proficiency and expression matched by few others. He first gained fame in the late 1960s with Eric Clapton and Jack Bruce as Cream, a now-legendary band that infused blues and jazz into rock and roll, producing an original and deeply textured sound. In its two-year existence, the English trio sold over 15 million records and played to adoring crowds and critical acclaim. Baker had much to do with the band's success—and likewise much to do with the band's demise.

Baker began as an aspiring jazzman and found himself a rock demigod. His brisk, purely businesslike approach caused him problems with his fellow musicians, and drug dependency cast a dark shadow over his career and his relationships. But since the late 1980s, the 50-year-old-plus father of three has straightened out his personal life, rekindled his interest in jazz, and enjoyed several successful solo and ensemble projects.

Born the son of a bricklayer, Baker dreamed as a youth of athletic rather than musical greatness. At the age of 15, he was a champion cyclist, winning a club title and courting aspirations of further success. But music eventually captured his attention. His first instrument, the trumpet, was soon replaced by a pair of drumsticks. Early on, Baker hoped to become a jazz drummer, playing on London's traditional jazz scene in the late 1950s and early 1960s.

After-school Jamming

Baker's after-school hours were spent jamming with noted jazz musicians Acker Bilk and Terry Lightfoot, as well as sitting in with several others. The bebop sound was his early focus. "When I was at school, I was listening to Max Roach, Philly Joe Jones, Art Blakely, Elvin Jones. Then I was in a trad jazz band, and they wanted me to play the Baby Dodds parts, so they gave me all these records to listen to. That was a complete revolution to me, 'cause all of a sudden you can see where Max and these guys came from. That had an enormous effect, which still comes out," Baker told *Musician.*

Baker's early experience with bebop and traditional jazz honed his technique and helped him acquire an impeccable sense of rhythm. His energetic phrasing makes him more than a timekeeper, giving him more creative impact than many drummers—jazz or otherwise. He told *Down Beat,* "When Philly Joe Jones heard me play in London, he came up to me and said, 'Man, you really tell a story when you play.' That's the biggest compliment I've ever had, because I loved Philly Joe Jones. Playing drums is the same as playing a horn. You're saying something musically."

After several stints drumming with London jazz outfits, Baker joined Alexis Korner's Blues Inc. The offer was extended following the departure of Charlie Watts, who left to join Mick Jagger, Keith Richards, Bill Wyman, and Brian Jones of the Rolling Stones in 1962. With Blues Inc., Baker played with bassist Jack Bruce. The two eventually joined the Graham Bond Trio and then merged with Clapton to form Cream.

Stardom and Its Aftermath

Baker's experience with jazz and R&B brought Cream to unknown levels of musicianship and technical ability in the rock world. Baker and Bruce provided an intricate,

blues-oriented rhythm for Clapton's guitar work. Of Clapton, Baker commented in *Musician*, "Man he used to just go for it. Incredible things were happening, timewise. The first time we got together, we played for hours and hours. No two gigs were ever the same." Though the band formed in 1966 with immediate success, tension between members would force their split-up just two years later.

Baker developed a fondness for heroin early in his career, and this mounting addiction expedited Cream's end. "I was an evil person back then.... I was a junkie and didn't know fear," Baker told *People*. Jack Bruce and lyricist Pete Brown wrote most of Cream's material, while, much to Baker's chagrin, Clapton was generally regarded as the band's frontman. "What really riles me is that most people thought that Cream was Eric Clapton's band. Not only do I not get much financial reward for the whole thing, I don't get any credit from either of the other two, which is really why I don't speak to them very much," he noted in *Down Beat*.

Clapton and Baker remained together for another project, Blind Faith. Together with Steve Winwood (guitar, vocals, and keyboards) and Rick Grech (bass), Blind Faith formed in 1969, debuting before 100,000 fans in London's Hyde Park. A huge-selling album prompted European and American tours. Dissension in the band and Baker's growing substance abuse problems caused a split that same year, though not before the group scored two hits in the States, "Can't Find My Way Home" and "Presence of the Lord." Concerning the demise of Blind Faith, Baker explained to *People*, "I got messed up with drugs again and had a long holiday to get straight. When I got back to England, Steve told me Eric had run off to form Derek and the Dominos."

Stumbles Both Personally and Professionally

After Blind Faith, Baker formed Ginger Baker's Air Force, a big band complete with horns, percussion, and a few woodwinds. The jazz-rock ensemble recorded two albums with various lineups and limited success. Notably, the band showcased Baker's growing interest in African music; he even invited African percussionists to join them for guest performances. Ginger Baker's Air Force disbanded when acclaim and interest waned. In the wake of his musical setbacks, the drummer once again struggled with his addiction to heroin and his ongoing business troubles.

Chief among Baker's financial downturns was a recording studio he financed near Lagos, Nigeria, the first professional recording studio in West Africa. Baker moved to Nigeria and opened the studio after visiting

Africa with Air Force percussionist Remi Kabaka. The venture turned sour, and Baker returned to England, though not before Paul McCartney recorded his hit album *Band on the Run* there in 1973.

Back on British soil, Baker joined up with the Gurvitz brothers, Paul and Adrian, to form Baker-Gurvitz Army. The group put out two jazz-rock records before disbanding. Though Baker worked on several projects with other musicians, including Atomic Roosters, Hawkwind, and Ginger Baker's Nutters, results were generally discouraging.

A downward spiraling career and personal misfortunes sent Baker deeper into heroin addiction. Tax troubles with the English government combined with drug use sent him to Italy in 1982 to recuperate. After settling in a small village in southern Italy, Baker worked on an olive farm and rarely played the drums. Music became less important while he shook his heroin habit. "I had to get out," he told the *Boston Globe* of the London scene. "All the people I knew were junkies. If I had stayed I was going to wind up dead." Two years passed while Baker learned to live drug-free. His recovery was not easy—with as many as 29 relapses by his own count—but it was ultimately successful.

Reemerges with New Recordings and Interests

While in Africa, Baker picked up the sport of polo and has since been an avid practitioner. His love for the game was a significant factor in his decision to leave Italy, where polo was not a popular sport. After a brief stay in England, Baker left for the United States in the mid-1980s. His first stop was Los Angeles, where he operated a drum school and pursued music for the first time in nearly a decade. Arriving on American shores without strong musical contacts, Baker's agent suggested he place an ad in the music section of a trade journal to meet other musicians. While Baker himself was wary of the plan, it proved a success. Baker returned to the studio and appeared on *Album* by Public Image Ltd. in 1985 at the insistence of producer Bill Laswell.

Baker rejoined forces with ex-Cream bassist Jack Bruce in 1989. Their jazz-rock collaboration was capped by an album and a tour. In addition to guest appearances with alternative acts such as Primal Scream, Baker brought new vigor to a career in jeopardy with solo efforts such as *Horses and Trees* and *Middle Passage*. Also at this time, Baker began to work with bassist Chris Goss and guitarist Googe under the name Masters of Reality. *Going Back Home*, a jazz record released in 1994 with Bill Frisell and Charlie Haden together as the Ginger Baker Trio, confirmed his mastery of the drums.

Baker's notoriety was cemented in 1993 with Cream's induction into the Rock 'n' Roll Hall of Fame. The ceremony including a much-anticipated reunion with Clapton and Bruce to play "Sunshine of Your Love" and other legendary Cream songs, the first and only Cream reunion as of 1995. Baker has since relocated to Colorado, competing in polo matches whenever possible and tending his horses on a small farm outside of Denver.

Musically, Baker engaged in a project with Jack Bruce known as BBM (Baker, Bruce, and guitarist Gary Moore), while furthering his jazz interest with the Ginger Baker Trio. Free from drugs, he has become an in-demand musician, surprising his critics—many of whom predicted he would die an early death. With respected recordings deftly showcasing his jazz sensibilities, he reentered the spotlight in the early 1990s.

Selected discography

With Cream; on Atco, except as noted

Disraeli Gears, 1967.
Fresh Cream, 1968.
Wheels of Fire, 1968.
Goodbye, 1969.
The Best of Cream, 1969.
Live Cream, 1970.
Live Cream, Volume 2, 1972.
Off the Top, Polydor, 1972.
Heavy Cream, Polydor, 1973.
The Best of Live Cream, Springboard, 1975.
Early Cream, Springboard, 1978.
The Very Best of Cream, Polydor, 1995

With others

(With Blind Faith) *Blind Faith*, Atco, 1969.
(With Ginger Baker's Air Force) *Air Force*, Atco, 1970.
(With Ginger Baker's Air Force) *Air Force 2*, Atco, 1970.
(With Fela Kuti) *Fela Ransom-Kuti and Africa '70 with Ginger Baker*, Signpost, 1972.
(With Baker-Gurvitz Army) *Baker-Gurvitz Army*, Janus, 1975.
(With Baker-Gurvitz Army) *Elysian Encounter*, Atco, 1975.
(With Baker-Gurvitz Army) *Hearts on Fire*, Atco, 1976.
(With Fela Kuti) *Kuti and Africa*, Sire, 1980.
(With Masters of Reality) *Masters of Reality*, Delicious Vinyl/ Island, 1990.
(With Masters of Reality) *Sunrise on the Sufferbus*, Chrysalis, 1993.

Solo releases

Stratavarious, Polydor, 1972.
Ginger Baker at His Best, Polydor, 1972.

Eleven Sides of Baker, Sire, 1977.
Horses and Trees, Celluloid, 1986.
Middle Passage, Axiom, 1991.
Going Back Home, Atlantic, 1994.

Sources

Books

All Music Guide, edited by Michael Erlewine, Chris Woodstra, and Vladimir Bogdanov, Miller Freeman Books, 1994.
The Penguin Encyclopedia of Popular Music, edited by Donald Clarke, Viking Books, 1989.
The Rolling Stone Encyclopedia of Rock & Roll, edited by John Pareles and Patricia Romanowski, Rolling Stone Press/Summit Books, 1983.

Periodicals

Boston Globe, December 26, 1988.
Calgary Herald, June 6, 1993.
Denver Post, January 20, 1995.
Down Beat, November 1990; October 1994.
Los Angeles Times, December 19, 1989; May 26, 1990; November 3, 1991; January 14, 1993.
Musician, May 1995.
New York Newsday, December 9, 1989.
People, June 19, 1989; January 25, 1993.
Rocky Mountain News (Denver, CO), June 17, 1994.
Rolling Stone, October 20, 1994.
Spectrum Guide, summer 1995.

—*Rich Bowen*

Bix Beiderbecke

Cornetist

Archive Photos/Frank Driggs Collection

Though he died in near-obscurity at age 28, cornetist Bix Beiderbecke has been hailed as the first important white musician in jazz. Long portrayed, in books and film, as a reckless paragon of the flaming youth of the roaring twenties, scholars have spent decades dispelling the Beiderbecke myth. "Bix didn't let anything at all detract his mind from that cornet," later related by friend and musical mentor, Louis Armstrong, in *Hear Me Talkin' To Ya*, "his heart was in it all the time." Compelled by the path of the self-taught artist, Beiderbecke succeeded, through gift of perfect pitch, analytic memory, and inventive wit, in fusing many elements of the world of the riverboat jazz horn with modern European harmonic ideas—a creative vision which antedated the modern jazz movement by two decades.

The second son of German middle class immigrants, Leon Bix Beiderbecke was born on March 10, 1903, in Davenport, Iowa. His father, owner of the East Davenport Lumber and Coal Company and his mother, an accomplished pianist, viewed Bix's early efforts to play piano as part of a well-rounded cultural education. Gifted with an accurate musical ear, Bix, by age three, started picking out simple melodies on the piano; in kindergarten, he impressed his teacher by directly reproducing vocal melodies on the class piano. Weekly private lessons by Professor Charles Grade did little to instill the discipline of sight-reading into the talented young Beiderbecke, who frustrated his instructor by playing his entire lessons by ear. The local paper took notice of Bix's piano talent by declaring him, as quoted in *Bix: Man and Legend*, a "Seven-Year-Old-Boy Musical Wonder."

Early Life In Davenport

In Davenport, Beiderbecke absorbed his parent's middle class values and the free form world of riverboat life, filled with the music of traveling jazz bands and riverboat pipe organs. After World War I, his older brother Charles brought several 78-rpm sides by the Original Dixieland Jazz Band—a five-piece white New Orleans ensemble who made the first jazz recordings in 1917. As a high school freshman, Beiderbecke became drawn to the sound of the ODJB's trumpeter Nick LaRocca. Given a tarnished, silver-plated cornet from a friend, he learned—left-handed and using the wrong fingering—LaRocca's trumpet lines note-by-note by slowing down the turntable speed of the family's phonograph. Keeping his private study of cornet a secret, he continued to play piano, and started a small band which performed at tea dances and Friday afternoon appearances in the school gym. Also at this time, he performed with Neal Buckley's Novelty Orchestra and the Plantation Jazz Orchestra on the stern-wheeler *Majestic*.

Born Leon Bix Beiderbecke, March 10, 1903, in Davenport, Iowa; died of lobar pneumonia in Queens, New York; son of Bismark, (a business owner) and Agatha; Lake Forest Academy November 1921-May 1922; attended University of Ohio a as "unclassified" student, February 2-20, 1925.

Began playing piano around age 3; by age 7 established local reputation as gifted pianist; started playing cornet in high school and started small ensemble; at Forest Academy founded Cy-Bix Orchestra 1921; October 1923 joined Wolverines at Stockton Club, near Hamilton, Ohio; recorded with Wolverines at Gennett studio February and May 1924; Wolverines open at Cinderella Ballroom, New York City, October, 1924; worked with Jean Goldkette November-December 1924; January 1925 recorded Gennett session under own name: Bix and His Rhythm Jugglers; joined Goldkette-managed band, Breeze Blowers, in Island, Lake, Michigan; 1925 worked with Frankie Trumbauer in St. Louis; played summer season with Trumbauer at Hudson Lake, Indiana; worked with Goldkette until September 1927; performed a short stint with Adrian Rollini big band; October 1927-1929 performed with Paul Whiteman Orchestra; worked briefly with Casa Loma Orchestra 1930; 1931 played universities date with various pick-up bands; fictional account of Beiderbecke's life, *A Man With a Horn*, by Dorothy Baker published in 1938; a film, *Young Man With a Horn*, starring Kirk Douglas, released in 1950.

Disillusioned over their son's interest in an "unrespectable" art form and his failing high school grades, Bismark and Agatha Beiderbecke sent Bix to Lake Forest Academy—a strict boarding school located thirty-five miles north of Chicago. With the school's close proximity to the city, Beiderbecke's parents, wrote Studhalter and Evans in *Bix: The Man and the Legend*, "had unwittingly furnished him an ideal launching pad into the very life from which they most wished to protect him." After arriving at Lake Forest in September 1921, Beiderbecke auditioned for the school orchestra on cornet and earned a reputation as a versatile pianist. By October he joined forces with saxophonist Samuel "Sid" Stewart, and drummer Walter Ernest "Cy" Welge, in forming the Cy-Bix Orchestra.

In November 1921 Beiderbecke visited Chicago and stopped in at a near-north side club, Friar's Inn, on Wabash and Van Buren, to listen to the New Orleans

Rhythm Kings. Led by trumpeter Paul Mares and featuring clarinetist Leon Roppolo and trombonist George Brunies, the NORK's greatly inspired Beiderbecke who, after his return to Lake Forest, sought to incorporate their musical ideas into the Cy-Bix Orchestra. Apart from off-campus work with his own band, he played shows in Chicago with Caldwell's Jazz Jesters and sat-in with the NORK's. Poor grades and increasing off-campus activity led to Beiderbecke's expulsion from Lake Forest in May 1922.

No longer pressured to complete a formal education, Beiderbecke, left Lake Forest for Chicago and rehearsed with a revue band of Marty Bloom. Before the engagement opened, however, his father brought him back to Davenport. While in Davenport, he took a summer job with Bill Grimm's Varsity Five on the lake boat *Michigan City*, and performed with Sid Stewart at the White Lake Yacht Club, in White Lake, Michigan. Later that summer, he played at a resort with pianist Bud Hatch in Delavan, Wisconsin. In *Bix: Man and Legend*, Hatch recalled the group's effort to play dixieland tunes: "On choruses, we'd give out with the melody the first time around, and from then on it would be every man for himself. This is where Bix really shone—I can state emphatically that he was considerably ahead of the period in his conception, especially of harmony."

New York, New York

Following the summer resort season of 1922, Beiderbecke arrived back in Davenport, only to depart once again with the eight-piece band of Pee Wee Rank's "Royal Harmonists of Indiana" for a job at the Alhambra Room in Syracuse, New York. Afterward, Beiderbecke and fellow bandmember Wayne "Doc" Hostetter set out for New York City to hear the Original Dixieland Jazz Band. Determined to sit-in with the ODJB, the young Davenport cornetist prodded his mentor, trumpeter Nick LaRocca, who finally allowed Beiderbecke to take the stage with the group. "Bix's first week in New York dissolved into chaos of sitting-in, running to catch taxis and trains to auditions which somehow never materialized," wrote Sudhalter and Evans in *Bix*, "and more bootlegged booze than the 19-year-old Iowan had ever consumed in one brief period of time."

Without musical employment, Beiderbecke went back to Davenport where his father demanded he work, as a bill collector and weighing clerk, at the family coal and lumber business. Quickly tiring of his job, Beiderbecke once again left for Chicago. In Chicago, he landed work with tenor saxophonist Dale Skinner's band at the Valentino Inn. Band members were impressed with the cornetist's improving style. "The awkwardness of

[Beiderbecke's] style was all but gone," wrote Studhalter and Evans in *Bix*. "The tone had taken on a lustre, and there were times when ideas would tumble out with a flow which made even [Paul] Mares sound stodgy." From the Valentino Inn he returned to the lake boat circuit.

"Bix didn't let anything at all detract his mind from that cornet, his heart was in it all the time."
—Louis Armstrong

At the end of the lake boat season in the fall of 1923, Beiderbecke went home to Davenport, where he got an offer to join clarinetist Hartwell's band at a rough roadhouse, the Stockton Club, near Hamilton, Ohio. As informal music director, Beiderbecke ran through arrangements four bars at a time. The band's limited repertoire included Jelly Roll Morton's "Wolverine Blues," which reportedly gave rise to the band's name, the Wolverines. As Max Harrison pointed out in the liner notes to *Bix Beiderbecke and the Chicago Cornets*, the Wolverines "were the first white jazz band of consequence to be composed entirely of non-Orleans men." The band's tenure at the Stockton Club soon ended, however, when a raucous crowd caused the burning of the club on New Years Eve, 1923.

In January 1924, the band took a job at Doyle's Dancing Academy in Cincinnati. "It wasn't an all-star band," wrote Richard Hadlock in *Jazz Masters of the Twenties*, "but the Wolverine Orchestra had a total impact as impressive as the New Orleans Rhythm Kings themselves. The group strived for an ensemble blend, and the brilliance of Beiderbecke's lead cornet gave the entire unit a surprising amount of class, as well as rhythmic force and melodic content." The band's increasing reputation in the Midwest led to a one-day recording session for the Gennett label on February 18, 1924, in Richmond, Indiana. The band recorded and released two standards from the Original Dixieland Jazz Band's repertoire—"Jazz Me Blues," and "Fidgety Feet"—which Richard Hadlock described, in *Jazz Master's of the Twenties*, as classic performances, "relaxed, in the manner of the New Orleans Rhythm Kings ... in 4/4 time rather than in the jerky 2/4 'cut' time that mars ODJB recordings."

As opposed to the critical acceptance of their recordings, the Wolverines failed to attract a large following at Doyle's. Breaking their contract, the band left the club and, through the connections of Hoagy Carmichael, the band took up residence at Indiana University, playing for fraternity dances. *In Frontiers of Jazz* saxophonist George Johnson told how the band "played many a jam session at the fraternity house packed twice to capacity, and Bix's efforts would produce shouts, the reverberations from which have crumbled any but a stone house."

On May 6, 1924, the band returned to the Gennett studio for its second recording date. The Gennett session included Carmichael's "Riverboat Shuffle," two selections from the ODJB and the NORK's, and Charley Davis' "Copenhagen." On all the selections, wrote Richard Hadlock in *Jazz Masters of the Twenties*, "Bix shows sharp improvement in his playing and confidence over the February session and reveals a predilection for blues phrasing that may have been a result of his enthusiasm at that time for King Oliver's band."

On September 12, 1924, the Wolverines opened at the Cinderella Ballroom in New York City. Four days later, the band entered the Gennett's New York Studio and recorded "Sensation," and "Lazy Daddy"—numbers, wrote Max Harrison in the liner notes for *The Chicago Cornets*, that "mark a further advance, the scope of [Beiderbecke's] invention growing, the ideas being more varied, yet tightly knit." On October 8, 1924, the band turned out two more Gennett sides, "Tia Juana" and "Big Boy," featuring his cornet and "Debussy-esque" piano work, but Bix left the Wolverines two days later.

Joined Goldkette in Detroit

In November 1924, Beiderbecke joined the Detroit-based orchestra of French-born pianist, bandleader, and booking company owner Jean Goldkette. Based in the elegant Graystone Ballroom, the Goldkette Orchestra enjoyed immense popularity as one of the Midwest's most talented ensembles. Added as a third trumpet in the brass section, Beiderbecke's poor music reading skills relegated him to the role of soloist. When the band attended a Victor recording session at the Detroit Athletic Club, Beiderbecke's deficient reading ability put him at odds with engineer Eddie T. King who disdained hot-style jazz. After hearing the young cornetist's sixteen-bar solo on "I Don't Know," he demanded Beiderbecke be taken off the session. Despite his respect for Beiderbecke's talented solo work, Goldkette eventually dismissed the young cornetist in December 1924.

In January 1925, Beiderbecke led a Gennett session under his own name, "Bix and his Rhythm Jugglers," with Goldkette members Tommy Dorsey, Don Murray, and Paul Mertz. To complete his high school education, he then enrolled at the University of Iowa as "unclassi-fied" student, taking required courses and music class-es. Unable to reconcile himself to the university's ac-ademic requirements, he dropped out after eighteen days, and traveled to New York and Chicago. In July 1925, he was rehired by Goldkette to perform in one of his ensembles led by trumpeter Nat Natoli. While per-forming with Natoli at a White Lake, Michigan resort, Beiderbecke landed a more promising job with another Goldkette-managed band, The Breeze Blowers, at near-by Island Lake.

In August 1925, Beidebecke arrived in St. Louis to join saxophonist Frankie Trumbauer's band at the Arcadia Ballroom, a "hanger-like wooden building" on Olive Street. Also recruited by Trumbauer, St. Louis clarinetist Charles "Pee Wee" Russell quickly befriended Beider-becke. "They found they both had been influenced by the recordings of the Original Dixieland Jazz Band," noted Robert Hilbert in *Pee Wee Russell*. "They also shared an interest in contemporary symphonic music, especially compositions by Stravinsky, Debussy, and Ravel, finding unusual harmonies and progressions pleasing to the ear at a time when most musicians and the general public dismissed such as 'ugly.'"

The summer of 1926 Beiderbecke and Russell per-formed in another Goldkette-managed Trumbauer unit at The Blue Lantern in Hudson Lake, Indiana. That fall, Trumbauer was invited by Goldkette and his partner Charlie Horvath to lead their first-string unit. As Trum-bauer explained in *Hear Me Talkin' To Ya*, "Charley Horvath made me an offer to conduct the Goldkette at Detroit, and when I mentioned bringing Bix with me, he wasn't sold on the idea, as he explained that Bix was around Detroit for some time and nothing happened. I refused the offer unless Bix could come along; so Charley reconsidered and told me I would have to be responsible for him, as he did not think it would work." In October 1926 Beiderbecke joined the all-star Gold-kette orchestra in New York to record the tune "Idoliz-ing," arranged by Bill Challis. During the same year, Beiderbecke recorded dates for OKeh under Frankie Trumbauer's name, cutting such classic titles as "Trum-bology," "Clarinet Marmalade," "Ostrich Walk," "River-boat Shuffle," "I'm Coming Virginia," and the twenties jazz masterpiece "Singin' the Blues." A session for OKeh also included Bix's best known solo piano com-position "In A Mist."

Paul Whiteman's Society Orchestra

After Goldkette's orchestra temporarily disbanded in September 1927, Beidebecke played a brief stint with bass saxophonist Adrian Rollini. In October of the same year, he joined the four-man trumpet section of the Paul Whiteman Orchestra. Bix's forty-five sides with the Whiteman band vary from his obscurity in the brass section to solos filled with his trademark phrasing and bell-like tone. Years of bootleg liquor and hard years on the road put him in state of poor health. Given time to recuperate, he took time off from the Whiteman orches-tra (November 1928 to March 1929). Though he re-turned to the band in California in May 1929, four months later, health problems led him to return to Davenport.

In 1930 Beidebecke was back in New York, jobless and in ill health. "A couple of record sessions with Hoagy Carmichael were thrown together," wrote Hadlock in *Jazz Masters of the Twenties*, "but Bix was no more than a spector of his old self." Early in 1931 he turned down an offer to rejoin Whiteman. Returning to New York, he played pick-up jobs with Benny Goodman and the Dorsey brothers at university dances, and briefly worked with the Casa Loma Orchestra. On August 6, 1931, Beiderbecke died, from complications of lobar pneu-monia, in the ground floor room of his apartment in Queens, New York.

Chicago saxophonist Bud Freeman voiced the senti-ments of many musicians when he stated, in *Crazeolo-gy*, "If Bix Beiderbecke had lived longer he would have become one of America's greatest composers." De-spite his lack of formal training, Beidebecke did emerge as one of the first jazzmen to attempt to bridge the worlds of jazz and European expressionism. In his cornet and piano work, he contributed in expanding the melodic and harmonic structure of jazz. Beiderbecke's influence can be heard in the trumpeter styles of Red Nichols, Bunny Berigan, and Rex Stewart, and within the stylings of later trumpeters who sought to explore the midrange tones of the instrument.

Selected discography

Bix Beiderbecke and the Wolverines, Riverside.
The Bix Beiderbecke Story, Vols, 1,2,3, Columbia.
The Bix Beiderbecke Legend, RCA Victor.
Bix Beiderbecke and The Chicago Cornets, Milestone.
Bix Beiderbecke Volume 1, Singin' The Blues, Columbia, 1990.
The Indispensable Bix Beiderbecke, RCA.

Collections
Big Band Jazz: From the Beginnings to the Fifties, Smithso-nian Collection of Recordings, 1983.

Sources

Freeman, Bud, *Crazeology: The Autobiography of a Jazzman*, University of Illinois Press, 1989.

Frontiers of Jazz, second edition, edited by Frank de Toledano, Ungar Pub. Co., 1962.

Hadlock, Richard, *Jazz Masters of the Twenties*, Da Capo, 1988.

Hilbert, Robert, *Pee Wee Russell: The Life of a Jazzman*, Oxford University Press, 1993.

Kennedy, Rick, *Jelly Roll, Bix, and Hoagy: Gennett and the Birth of Recorded Jazz*, Indiana University Press, 1994.

Shapiro, Nat and Nat Hentoff, *Hear Me Talkin' To Ya: The Story of Jazz as Told to the Men Who Made it*, Dover Publications, 1955.

Studhalter, Richard M., and Philip R. Evans, with William Dean Myatt, *Bix: The Man and the Legend*, Schirmer Books, 1974

Additional information: Liner notes by Max Harrison to *Bix Beiderbecke and the Chicago Cornets*.

—*John Cohassey*

Belly

Rock band

Eric Boehlert, writing in *Billboard,* described the phenomenally successful sound of Belly as "fuzzy guitars, big bouncy hooks, cryptic narratives, and alluring vocals." The quartet—composed of two women and two brothers—comes with an impressive alternative music resume that belies the breezy, almost poplike accessibility of their work. Leader Tanya Donelly cut her musical teeth in the much-lauded Throwing Muses of the 1980s; bassist Gail Greenwood is a veteran of two bands; and brothers Chris and Tom Gorman, respectively drummer and guitarist for Belly, served time in Verbal Assault.

With the release of Belly's debut album, *Star,* in early 1993, the band was virtually an overnight success; the record sold well beyond expectations and earned the reluctant alternative superstars two Grammy award nominations. Named with one of Donelly's favorite words, Belly takes some of its melodic cues from the weavy, dreamlike sounds of the Muses—but fuses that with a finely tuned standard pop-song construction. Such a blend of alternative ethos with Top 40 suitability set the

Photograph by Stephen DiRado, © Sire Records Company

For the Record . . .

Members include **Fred Abong** (left group, 1993; replaced by **Gail Greenwood** [born c. 1960]), bass and vocals; **Tanya Donelly** (born c. 1967), guitar and vocals; **Christopher Gorman** (worked earlier as a television production assistant), drums and percussion; and **Thomas Gorman** (studied architecture at Carnegie Mellon University), guitar and piano.

Donelly formed Throwing Muses with stepsister Kristin Hersh, 1981; also a founding member of the Breeders; left Throwing Muses, 1991, and formed Belly with Chris and Tom Gorman and Fred Abong; Greenwood joined Belly in 1993 after stints in the Dames and Boneyard.

Selected Awards: Grammy nominations for best new artist and best alternative album of 1993 for *Star*.

Addresses: *Record company*—Sire Records, 75 Rockefeller Plaza, 20th Floor, New York, NY 10019-6989.

group at the forefront of a nineties-era trend that promised mainstream success for other, similarly contemporary-sounding alternative acts.

"More than anything else, the folks in Belly resemble hip graduate students," remarked *Rolling Stone* writer Jancee Dunn after interviewing them. "They're well spoken, well read, funny. They are mindful of the truth (and consequences) of fame and dismissive of the myth of celebrity." Donelly grew up in Newport, Rhode Island, in a liberal household united when her father married the mother of a young girl her own age. Close friends before the marriage, Donelly and stepsister Kristin Hersh grew up in a free-spirited family that encouraged creativity. By the time they were teenagers, they had taught themselves how to play guitar and were writing songs in their room. In 1981, still high-schoolers, they formed Throwing Muses and by the time they graduated were local celebrities on Newport's burgeoning alternative music scene.

Joining Forces

Throwing Muses was signed to 4AD when Donelly was nineteen, and the act went on to earn a place in the indie rock hall of fame, putting out several critically acclaimed—if commercially unsuccessful—albums and paving the way for later female-fronted bands. Yet the muse behind the Muses was really Hersh's own person-

al demons, and hence the artistic territory belonged to her alone; other members contributed only nominally to the band's output.

Eventually Donelly began to seek another outlet for her own creative impulses. She found one in 1990 when she became a founding member of the Breeders with Kim Deal of the Pixies; she left Throwing Muses for good in 1991. Fortuitously, two brothers she had known in Newport, Chris and Tom Gorman, contacted Donelly soon after and asked if she was interested in working with them. The trio recruited Muses bass player Fred Abong and went into the studio to record their debut album, 1993's *Star*.

Launched with the single "Feed the Tree," *Star* was an immediate hit on the college charts, then broke through to a more mainstream pop-alternative audience on the so-called "modern rock" radio format. Belly's debut sold 450,000 copies in just under two years, rose to Number 59 on the *Billboard 200*, became the longest-ranking Number One album on the *Gavin Report's* alternative charts—and established Donelly's own creative credentials.

Donelly in Front

"Donelly sings like someone who's been around the block on more than one supporting tour—telling her tales with the savvy and sensuality of a world-weary ingenue," noted Chris Mundy in *Rolling Stone*. In a later review of *Star*, Kevin Ransom declared that Belly's leader and her cohorts "render a haunting, avant-folk-rock sound that provides sonic and psychic space for Donelly's surreal meditations on birth, mortality and sexuality." And Jas Obrecht, writing for *Guitar Player*, asserted that "among a galaxy of early-'90s alternative releases, few shone brighter than *Star*. Haunting avant folk-rock, Belly's debut set longevity records on college charts and established Donelly as a brilliant, albeit quirky, songwriter."

Indeed, much was made about Donelly's ability to shine as frontperson on her own, and critics often saw a thread of resemblance in Belly's quirky lyrical style with the unconventionalities of her former band. "As she wrestles with truths that can sometimes transcend language, Donelly favors oblique images and phonetic intrigue over narrative," noted Ransom, while *Village Voice* contributor Gina Arnold observed, "Donelly's adept at marshalling the most fragmentary emotion into an entire song." References to dreams, Shakespeare, folklore, and other founts of inner wisdom crop up frequently in Belly's lyrics. "I try not to be purposefully obscure. But whatever comes out, I tend to trust that it means something," Donelly told Boehlert. She noted in a talk with *Interview*'s Nils Bernstein that songwriting is a constant companion for her. "Snippets come at inconvenient times—in the middle of a conversation, at the bank, at tollbooths—whenever I'm in danger of losing a song forever. Words pick on me; they think it's funny," she said.

Continued Acclaim for Sophomore Effort

After being nominated for two Grammy awards—best alternative album and best new artist of 1993—Belly toured extensively in support of their debut, playing nearly 200 shows in 15 different countries. They also contributed a cover of "Are You Experienced?"—one of the more well-received tracks—to a 1993 Jimi Hendrix tribute album. When the time came to record their sophomore effort in early 1994, Belly's alternative star status helped them land assistance from eminent producer Glyn Johns, who had albums by the Rolling Stones and the Who on his production resume. The group headed down to the Compass Point Studios in the Bahamas to record it. "Though it seems really glamorous to record on a tropical island, Nassau is actually kind of boring, which helps you focus on your work," Donelly said of the experience in a press release.

The result of that focus was *King*, released early in 1995 with the first single "Now They'll Sleep." Overall, the record exhibits a harder, less pop-kindled side to Belly. "The album is tighter, leaner, more aggressive than *Star*," observed Dunn in *Rolling Stone*. "*King* has a timeless, complete feel to it, each song flowing smoothly into the next." Obrecht averred, "Folk-rock anxiety, '60s pop sparkle, and garage-band raucousness reign supreme on *King*," and, like Belly's first effort, the release "is ... awash with topsy-turvy lullabies, midnight confessions, strange, sweet harmonies, and exhilarating guitar tones."

Praise came easily for Donelly's voice, a "crystalline soprano ... alternately conveying vulnerability and determination," remarked Parke Puterbaugh in *Stereo Review*. Jen Fleissner, writing for *Spin*, declared *King* "a remarkable record.... When Donelly turns the lights down low for a ballad or two, she evokes Led Zeppelin or, at the very least, Kate Bush, back when she sang about bank robbers and magician's assistants."

Reporters have often remarked on the camaraderie and lack of self-absorbed "star" quality evident during encounters with Belly. The brothers Gorman provide balance to the dynamic personalities of Donelly and Greenwood, who likes to compare her bass-playing style to that of '80s rocker Billy Squier. Drummer Chris Gorman also moonlights as the graphic artist for the band, putting together the artistic packaging for their first two releases. Tom Gorman attempted to explain the quartet's dynamic in *Interview* magazine: "We don't really all have equal say in all things, but we've figured out what we all do best and have allowed a delegation of roles. For the most part our tastes and goals are similar, so we don't have to vote on things, we just do it. Call it an unconscious democracy."

Belly appears to have real staying power in the music business—a power built on talent, not gimmick. "To her credit, Donelly has consistently steered clear of crassly marketing her physical attributes, a ploy for which she certainly has the looks," remarked Gina Arnold in the *Village Voice*. Coasting toward mainstream success through alternative music—after spending many years on its fringes—has given Donelly a unique perspective, as she explained to Boehlert in *Billboard*. "It bothers me when bands will say, 'As soon as this starts to feel like a job, I'm outta here, man.' It's like ... what are you talking about? It is a job. It's a great job."

Selected discography

Star, Sire/Reprise, 1993.
(Contributors) *Stone Free: A Tribute to Jimi Hendrix*, Reprise, 1993.
King, Sire/Reprise, 1995.

Sources

Billboard, December 24, 1994; March 11, 1995.
Guitar Player, March 1995.
Interview, April 1995.
Rolling Stone, February 4, 1993; April 15, 1993; April 20, 1995.
Spin, March 1995.
Stereo Review, July 1995.
Village Voice, March 7, 1995; June 6, 1995.

Additional information for this profile was taken from promotional material provided by Sire/Reprise Records.

—*Carol Brennan*

Tony Bennett

Singer

Tony Bennett, the man who left his heart in San Francisco, experienced a sparkling resurgence in both popularity and record sales 40 years after first making his name in the entertainment business. Bennett, who was 57 years old when MTV first hit the airwaves, found an unlikely new audience in the younger flannel-clad generation and resurfaced with his familiar grace intact. Highlighting his return to music's inner circle, Bennett shared the stage with the Red Hot Chili Peppers at the 1993 MTV Music Awards. It seems that the definition of hip has evolved to include martinis, skinny ties, and torch songs—in short, all things Bennett. Even though he was once well-known for his criticism of rock music and its culture of delinquence, he embraced its audience with a performance on MTV's *Unplugged,* singing with Elvis Costello, k.d. lang, Lemonheads heartthrob Evan Dando, and J. Mascis of the prototype grunge band Dinosaur Jr. When asked by the *Observer* to explain his popularity with fans born two decades after his 1951 recording debut, he remarked "They see me as a guy who's never given in, like a fighter who never took a dive. And I think they like me because I don't try to do what they do, and because I sing in an honest way."

Urged into the alternative arena by his son and manager, Danny, Bennett was at first wary of the new turn his career was taking. "I was playing Carnegie Hall or the Merv Griffin resorts and then he had me going on Letterman, and I finally said, 'What are you doing?' But he said he knew something that I didn't realize. And what he knew is that there is a huge audience that likes me even more than their parents," Bennett told Salt Lake City's *Tribune.* Danny Bennett sensed a growing tolerance for musical styles dynamically opposed to the screaming guitars and pounding drums that marked the tastes of the MTV set. His suspicion proved correct when *Spin* magazine publisher Bob Guccione, Jr. published an editorial piece that affirmed the merits of traditional crooners, Bennett included, and their silken voices. Danny Bennett commented to the *Chicago Tribune,* "We are living at a time when young people are expanding their horizons. It's a time when Frank Sinatra can share the top of the charts with Pearl Jam." He pushed his father toward a younger audience with appearances on *The Late Show with David Letterman, SCTV,* and even *The Simpsons.* Danny also capitalized on the knowledge that members of the Red Hot Chili Peppers were closet Bennett fans. He arranged a meeting between the group and his father and the result was a brief tour, with Bennett's halcyon vocal musings opening for the Chili Peppers' frenetic, bass-driven rock.

When Bennett's *The Art of Excellence* hit the music stores in 1986, few would have predicted that two Grammy Awards were in the near future. Danny Bennett

Born Anthony Dominick Benedetto, August 13, 1926, in Astoria, Queens, NY; son of an Italian grocer and American seamstress; married Patricia Beech, 1952 (divorced, 1971); married Sandra Grant, 1971 (divorced, 1984); children: Danny (Bennett's manager) Daegal, Antonia, and Joanna.

Career began in New York City's Greenwich Village nightclubs at the start of the 1950s; appeared in Pearl Bailey's reviews at the Greenwich Village Inn; discovered by Bob Hope and brought to New York's Paramount Theater; landed Columbia recording contract, 1951; quickly rose to fame as one of America's best practioners of the torch song; early hits included "Because of You," "I Won't Cry Anymore," and "Blue Velvet"; recorded "I Left My Heart In San Francisco" in 1961; song became a worldwide hit; released over 80 albums on Columbia Records before departing label in 1971; started Improv Records; toured actively around the world; retained son, Danny, as manager in 1979; career picked up with appearances on television shows *The Late Show with David Letterman, SCTV,* and *The Simpsons*; re-signed by Columbia Records in 1985; released string of successful albums beginning with *The Art of Excellence* (1986); also an accomplished painter; works shown worldwide and have sold for as much as (U.S.) $40,000.

Selected awards: Received Grammy Awards in 1993 for *Steppin Out,* in 1992 for *Perfectly Frank,* and in 1962 for *I Left My Heart In San Francisco.*

Addresses: *Home*—New York, NY. *Record company*—Columbia Records/Sony Music Entertainment, 550 Madison Ave., New York, NY 10022-3211.

and Columbia, however, had a hunch. *Perfectly Frank* and *Steppin' Out* captured Grammy Awards, the music business's most coveted honors, in 1992 and 1993, respectively. The first covered lesser-known Frank Sinatra songs and the second paid tribute to songs sung by Fred Astaire in his movies. Both records captured the svelte Bennett style, unchanged over the years. Though some critics diminish Bennett's resurrection as a kitsch-laden fad among younger music listeners and the growing lounge music scene as pure camp, Columbia vice-president of marketing Jay Krugman feels otherwise. He told *Billboard,* "This is no novelty, but a real artist spanning the decades, permeating the culture. His stature and sales perspective will continue to spread

from the more traditional older audience to the MTV demo." And when the word "comeback" was used to describe his recent career history, Bennett demurely remarked to the *New York Times,* "Comeback? What comeback?... I never went anywhere."

Strictly speaking, Bennett is correct. Though the 1970s proved to be a difficult period for artists of Bennett's ilk, he never gave up touring and still logs 200 days a year on the road. "When I stopped recording," Bennett told the *Washington Post,* "I also stopped all the deadlines, and I suddenly had the freedom to think about performing, to take that energy and concentrate on what I have to do to entertain people." The only change for Bennett was the size of the room in which he performed—he retained his urbane charm and velvet delivery. Danny took over his father's management duties in 1979 with some thoughts on how to bring in a new audience and the pieces began falling into place. By 1995, Bennett was never in greater demand. "Today's young people are the most enthusiastic audience I've ever had," he told *Good Housekeeping,* "and all I'm doing is what I've always done—sing good songs."

Showed Early Artistic Aspirations

Born to an Italian-born father and American mother, Bennett was raised in Astoria, Queens, a borough of New York City. Early on, Bennett was not the family's strongest prospect for a career in entertainment. His older brother John was a member of Metropolitan Opera Boys' Chorus and showed potential as an opera singer. Tony Bennett lightheartedly remarked to the *Washington Post,* "It was that whole Italian family pride, y'know—'he's an opera singer, this is serious.' How could I compete?" While his father worked as a grocer and his mother as a seamstress, Bennett showed a propensity for painting and drawing and a knack for imitating comedy acts he heard on radio such as Al Jolson and Eddie Cantor. The family's joviality quickly ended, though, after the death of Bennett's father when Bennett was only nine. Young Tony was sent to live with an uncle while his mother recuperated from the passing of her husband. The boy proved an unwelcome addition to his uncle's household and was forced to sleep on the floor and given unpleasant tasks. When his mother was ready to receive him, he happily returned to his Astoria neighborhood and attended New York's High School for the Industrial Arts, where he anticipated a career in commerical art.

When Bennett graduated, he joined the Army's 63rd Infantry Division and saw combat action in Germany in World War II. The war, as was the case for a generation of men and women, had a dramatic effect on the young

New Yorker with hopes of a career in entertainment. "I saw men die there.... All the innocence goes out of you," he remarked to the *Observer.* Furthering his distaste for military life was a run-in with a sergeant who took a dislike toward Bennett after he had Thanksgiving dinner with a black soldier. Bennett was demoted, then given the duty of recovering bodies from mass graves left by the Germans. Despite his dislike of military service, Bennett remained for a second tour, this time as an entertainer, to sing for the troops still stationed in Europe at war's end.

"Today's young people are the most enthusiastic audience I've ever had and all I'm doing is what I've always done—sing good songs."

Bennett returned from Europe to New York and set out to build a career in show business. In addtion to taking singing lessons on the G.I. Bill, he found a job as a singing waiter at the Pheasant Tavern in Astoria, Queens, and adopted the stage name Joe Bari. Working for $15 a week, Bennett told *Life,* was a wonderful experience. "I loved the job. I figured, if I do this for the next 20 years, fine. I get to sing." Though Bennett's work satisfied his professional aspirations, his mother felt that he could do better and she implored her son to find more lucrative employment. Since falling to the status of lower-middle-class after Bennett's father's death, the family needed every dollar. Bennett satisfied his mother's concerns and found a job as an elevator operator at a New York hotel, but he also continued working toward his own goal.

Performing in nightclubs in Greenwich Village in New York were the likes of Billie Holiday, Stan Getz, Charlie Parker, and the little-known Joe Bari. Bennett worked hard on the club circuit, first grabbing attention by placing second to Rosemary Clooney on Arthur Godfrey's *Talent Scouts,* a variety show in the same vein as Ed McMahon's *Star Search.* That effort resulted in an invitation from Pearl Bailey to perform at her Greenwich Village Inn. Bari caught his next break when Bob Hope saw his act and brought him to the Paramount Theater to join Hope's show. Bennett's name, though, caused Hope some concern. "Just before I'm going on," Bennett told *Life,* "Hope tells me the name's no good. He asks what my real name is. I say Anthony Benedetto. That doesn't do it for him either. So he goes out and and

says to the audience, "And here's this new singer, Tony Bennett!" He had to introduce me twice, 'cause I didn't know who he was talking about."

Saw Both Sides of Fame

In 1951, again with Bob Hope's assistance, Bennett landed a recording contract with Columbia. Just months later, Bennett's "Because of You" rocketed to number one on the U.S. charts. Quick to follow were two more hits, "I Won't Cry Anymore" and "Blue Velvet." Bennett rapidly became one of the most popular American singers and a member of the illustrious "brat pack." With Frank Sinatra and Sammy Davis, Jr., Bennett immortalized the romantic era of American music with dozens of albums and hundreds of performances worldwide. Bennett also found time to marry Patricia Beech in 1952. Their relationship lasted 20 years before ending in divorce with Bennett on the road most of the time and constantly in the spotlight. A second marriage to Sandra Grant in 1971 met with the same fate. As he told London's *Daily Mail,* "The adulation put pressure on my marriages. I got too much too soon. It takes a long time to learn to live with the helium in the brain and you just kind of float away. You need lead weights to hold you down."

After a brief lull brought on by the onset of rock and roll and its new stars—with Buddy Holly and Elvis leading the way—his career was in need of a boost. What transpired in 1962 was a renewed explosion in Bennett's popularity after the release of what would become Bennett's signature song, "I Left My Heart in San Francisco." He told the *Washington Post,* "I've sung it for presidents and royalty, and I've been invited all over the world. It's sustained me right through the years and to hear that reaction every night when I sing it...." The rock and roll revolution, though, could not be assuaged forever and Bennett hit a professional and personal low in the early 1970s.

The Painter

In 1971 Clive Davis, Columbia's president, urged Bennett to bring his style in line with the rock and roll artists who were beginning to dominate pop audiences. After releasing over 80 albums for the label based on a simple strategy of quality material and his own voice, Bennett refused. Davis reportedly told him, "No one who leaves this label is ever heard from again," wrote Robert Sullivan in *Life.* As rock and roll flourished and Beatlemania swept the United States, however, Bennett considered updating his act. He confessed to *Life,* "I asked Count Basie if I should try rock. Basie told me in that sly, wise way of his, 'Why change an apple?'"

Dark days in Bennett's professional career mirrored a steady downturn in his personal life. Alcohol and drug use conspired with changing musical tastes to leave Bennett behind. Without a recording contract, Bennett spent his time on the road. Late one night during a stay in Las Vegas and still awake from a post-performance party, Bennett gazed down from his hotel terrace and noticed a man walking the streets. The moment proved to be an epiphany for the bleary-eyed singer. "It was like a light bulb went off in my head. Very quickly I came to realize all I needed to make me happy was a drumroll, a band, and some people who want me to sing," Bennett told *Good Housekeeping.* "Looking back, I know I grew up only when I was already in my forties."

Giving up the trappings of stardom and staying true to his talent, Bennett managed a most unlikely return to grace. With his companion, Susan Crow, a jazz agent, Bennett spends those few days when he is not on the road at their New York apartment, reading voraciously and painting. For his second art form, he retains his given name, Anthony Benedetto, and carries brushes, canvas, and an easel on the road with him. Bennett's works have sold for $40,000, and are shown in both major and minor galleries. The father of four children continues to devote himself to both his painting and music with no indication that he will give up either any time soon. Bennett told the *Saturday Evening Post,* "The great jazz-blues singer Joe Williams told me once, 'What people don't realize about you is not that you want to sing. You have to sing.'"

Selected discography

Released on Columbia Records

Treasure Chest of Songs, 1955.
Tony, 1957.
Blue Velvet, 1959.
To My Wonderful One, 1960.
I Left My Heart in San Francisco, 1963.
I Wanna Be Around, 1963.
16 Most Requested Songs, 1986.
Bennett/Berlin, 1987.
Tony Bennett Jazz, 1987.

The Movie Song Album, 1989.
Astoria, 1990.
Forty Years: The Artistry of Tony Bennett, 1991.
The Art of Excellence, 1992.
Perfectly Frank, 1992.
The Essence of Tony Bennett, 1993.
Steppin' Out, 1993.
In Person! With Count Basie and His Orchestra, 1994.
Unplugged, 1994.
Here's to the Ladies, 1995.

Released on Roulette Records

Count Basie Swings, Tony Bennett Sings, 1958.
Bennett and Basie Strike Up the Band, 1961.

Sources

Books

All Music Guide, edited by Michael Erlewine, Chris Woodstra, and Vladimir Bogdanov, Miller Freeman Books, 1994.
Guinness Encyclopedia of Popular Music, edited by Colin Larkin, Guinness Publishing, 1992.

Periodicals

Billboard, October 21, 1995.
Chicago Tribune, June 5, 1994.
Daily Mail (London), May 7, 1993.
Good Housekeeping, April 1995.
Independent (London), May 19, 1994.
Irish Times (Dublin), May 14, 1993.
Life, February 1995.
Los Angeles Times, November 26, 1995.
Maclean's, August 1, 1994.
New York, August 22, 1994.
New York Times, May 1, 1994.
Observer (London), March 5, 1995.
Orlando Sentinel, February 12, 1995.
Salt Lake Tribune, May 4, 1994.
Saturday Evening Post, January/February 1995.
Washington Post, June 30, 1991.

—Rich Bowen

Matraca Berg

Singer, songwriter

AP/Wide World Photos

M atraca (pronounced "Muh-tray-suh") Berg ventured to *The Phoenix* in 1994, "I am what you call an artist in search of herself in public." A successful songwriter who has co-written hits for Reba McEntire, Trisha Yearwood, Patty Loveless, and others, Berg struggled for several years as a recording artist; the strict confines of country radio kept her in limbo. Nonetheless, she took her pop-blues-country hybrid to pop radio and found an eager audience. "At her best," proclaimed Stewart Francke in *CD Review,* "she blends the sensuality of urban blues and soul with the wit and immediacy of rock." Geoffrey Himes of *Country Music* called her "typical of the new Nashville woman who refuses to be the passive victim anymore—of either callous lovers or conservative Music Row producers."

She was born in Nashville in 1963 and raised by her mother, Icee, a nurse who had harbored dreams of a musical career. "My mother was real spunky," Matraca related to *The Tennessean.* "She had a hard life, because you know she had me out of wedlock. We had a father [Ron Berg] around for a little while. But for the most part she raised me on her own. She was tough when she had to be. She didn't pull any punches with me." Her very musical family included an aunt who sang backup, and a steel-guitarist uncle. "I could not have avoided country music and Nashville if I tried," she maintained to *Phoenix* writer Chris Flisher. "It's in my blood. I knew I wanted to write at a very early age. I was eight or nine when I became obsessed with my aunt's piano. That's when I recall first wanting to write songs."

The voices of a couple of influential women also played a large role in her development. "You have to understand that there weren't many female role models to draw from in this town back then, as far as singer-songwriters playing guitar," she told *Billboard.* "Bobbie Gentry and Dolly Parton. It was pretty limited, and Dolly was the first big impression I ever had as a female songwriter."

Co-Wrote #1 Hit at Age 18

Her mother's connections in Nashville's Music Row were sufficient to introduce Matraca to some of the town's most gifted tunesmiths. "When I was growing up, Nashville had a very Bohemian vibe," she noted in a publicity profile. The "outlaw" sensibility of less mainstream country music was another important early influence. "It wasn't the way people expected it to be," Berg added. "There were those polished, polite country stars. But if you were able to see the inside, you knew that there were all these other things, this whole other world that was about creativity and *great* songwriting."

Matraca's obsession with songwriting bore fruit when she was 18. "Faking Love," a song she'd co-written with Bobby Braddock, became a number-one hit for T. G. Sheppard and Karen Brooks. She recalled in *The Tennessean* the bittersweet experience of listening to the song on the car radio with Icee: "We pulled over and Mom looked at me and she said, 'Tell me what it is like.' I just wanted to give it to her so badly." Unfortunately, Icee Berg was claimed by cancer before two years went by.

Meanwhile Matraca continued to write steadily for other artists—though always in collaboration. "I don't write by myself," she insisted to Flisher. "I can, but I am my own worst enemy. I am just too self-critical and a lot of times I just find that I have a lot of loose ends that just need someone else to tie together." Once the ends were tied, these songs became chart successes for country stars like McEntire, Yearwood, Patty Loveless, and Suzy Bogguss, among others. In a field dominated by men, Berg composed songs for female recording artists that managed to balance a blunt acknowledgement of women's experiences with a universal emotional reach. Though a gifted vocalist, she trusted her singing voice less than she did her writing voice. "I didn't sing. I was really shy," she averred in *The Tennessean*. "I just didn't feel like I was any good. Besides, I didn't want the stigma of being a 'chick singer.' I wanted to be a songwriter. I wanted respect."

Debut "Vindicated" Despite Poor Sales

Eventually, however, Berg's voice earned some attention of its own. An executive at the Nashville offices of RCA Records who heard her singing on a song demo intended for superstar Wynonna Judd signed her to a recording deal. Berg's debut, *Lying to the Moon*, was produced by Nashville vets Wendy Waldman and Josh Leo and released in 1991. It was a little too eccentric for country radio, however, and despite some very favorable reviews was rapidly consigned to obscurity. Even the critics weren't unanimous, in fact, and some seconded Berg's contention that she was still finding her voice. *Country Music* reviewer Himes, for example, felt that the album "spread on the self-pity a little too thick to win much sympathy from an audience." Alanna Nash of *Stereo Review*, on the other hand, felt the recording "established Berg as a writer far too talented and insightful to settle for country formula."

Even so, half the songs on *Lying* were covered by other artists. The title track, for instance—which *Request* dubbed a "magnificently twilit ballad"—was recorded by Yearwood. The acclaimed British vocalist Dusty Springfield and country star Pam Tillis also released their own versions of songs from *Lying*, which, Berg told *Bone* magazine, had thus "been vindicated."

Even so, the commercial misfire of her recording debut marked the beginning of a difficult period for the singer-songwriter, during which she recorded another country album that wasn't released and twice embarked on projects she didn't complete. These difficulties were counterbalanced by some happier events, however; she married musician Jeff Hanna in 1993, sang backup for superstar singer-songwriter Neil Young, and had a small role in the film *Made in Heaven*. It soon became clear that Berg was ready to broaden her appeal.

Grace Showed Wider Range

"It's taken me a couple of years to get used to the idea of being a recording artist and being out there in front of people," Berg averred in the *Chicago Tribune* in 1994. "It's much easier to hide behind a song." By the time of this admission she had moved from the country division of RCA to pop and recorded another album—this time in Los Angeles. The result, *The Speed of Grace*, showed her bluesier side and was unfettered by the firm genre rules of country radio. *Billboard* speculated on the singer's potentially diverse audience in a review of the *Grace* single "Guns In My Head," which was released on a 5-song EP: "Topical without being heavy-handed, [the] single has a maturity and depth that will initially make inroads on AC [Adult Contemporary] stations—though it has an aggressive vibe that will play equally well on album rock airwaves."

At the same time, *Grace* allowed Berg to pay tribute to her roots, covering Dolly Parton's classic "Jolene" and reworking her own "Lying to the Moon." Critics largely agreed that her new approach suited her better. *Rolling Stone* declared that her "singing is even more impressive than her songs. She doesn't have a big voice, but she makes little things mean a lot through expressive phrasing and exquisite attention to detail." *Rolling Stone* critic Don McLeese had some reservations about the "high-toned romantic melodrama" of her songs, but other critics were unabashedly positive. "Berg's sultry voice seeps through a bluesy, sometimes rocking mix of tunes that exudes a sharper edge and darker mood than anything she's written before," noted *Miami Herald* reviewer Mario Tarradell, who added that the singer-songwriter "has matured nicely." Alanna Nash wrote in *Stereo Review* that *Grace* was "occasionally uneven," but called it "nonetheless an impressive album that begs repeated plays."

"I guess it's more pop and adult contemporary, or whatever they call it," Berg said of the album in the *Boston Globe*. It was clear, however, that she had little use for labels and categories; this may have been a factor in her departure from RCA a bit later. And despite the fulfillment of a higher-profile recording career and a happy domestic life, Berg expressed her continuing devotion to sad songs. "Certain writers draw from happiness," she told *Phoenix* writer Flisher. "I draw more from the dark side of myself, and I think those songs represent me the best. I seem to be most comfortable there. Besides, I love those old weepy country ballads. I think they are so cool."

Selected discography

Released on RCA Records

Lying to the Moon, 1991.
The Speed of Grace (includes "Guns in My Head," "Lying to the Moon," and "Jolene"), 1994.
guns in my head...and others (5-song EP), 1994.

Sources

Billboard, July 23, 1994; September 3, 1994.
Bone, May 1994.
Boston Globe, June 3, 1994.
CD Review, July 1994.
Chicago Tribune, June 17, 1994.
Country Music, March 1994.
Miami Herald, June 16, 1994.
Phoenix, June 10, 1994.
Request, December 1993.
Rolling Stone, May 19, 1994.
Stereo Review, June 1994.
Tennessean, March 12, 1994.

Additional information was provided by publicity materials from Mike Crowley Artist Management, 1996.

—*Simon Glickman*

Björk

Singer

Photograph by Dina Alfano, Gamma-Liaison Network

On the outside, many describe singer Björk Gundmundsdottir with metaphors like innocent fairy, Icelandic pixie, and playful sprite. On the inside, Björk describes herself as a single mother who has had to fight hard for what she has and what she wants. Mike Bieber described Björk in *Audio* as "waifish and cute on the outside, but a chanteuse with a demon seed, nails-on-blackboard voice."

Mim Udovitch of *Rolling Stone* gave Björk the title of "The World's Only Cheerful Techno Icelandic Surrealist." Björk prides herself on the contradictions. She says her three obsessions are life, death, and sex, and her philosophy is that she supports the beautiful side of anarchy. Born in Reykjavik, Iceland in 1965, Björk was the only child of Gudmundur, an electricians' union chief, and Hildur, a homeopathic doctor and martial arts teacher. At the age of one, Björk's parents divorced, and Björk lived with her mother. When Björk turned five years old, her mother enrolled her in music school. Six years later, she released her first self-titled solo album. The 11-year-old's LP contained a mixture of Icelandic pop tunes and made her vaguely famous in her home country.

When Björk entered her teenage years, her taste and style of music took a different turn. Punk rock and new wave had made their mark on Iceland, and Björk responded by forming a number of different bands. At 13 years old, she had formed Exodus; at 14, Tappi Tikarrass; and at 18, KUKL. Björk and her then boyfriend Thor Eldon developed into a radical, anti-establishment, punk/Gothic rock combination. When KUKL transformed into The Sugarcubes, it became the launchpad for Björk's music career. At the same time, her personal life took a step to the next level: Björk married Thor in 1986 and became pregnant. Continuing with her rebellious edge, she performed on Icelandic TV wearing a shirt that read "Like A Virgin" and left her pregnant midriff exposed. Reportedly, her appearance caused one of the show's viewers to suffer a heart attack. She later gave birth to her son, Sindri.

The Sugarcubes signed with Elektra Records in 1988, and even though Björk and Thor had just split up, the band embarked on a worldwide tour. Over the next four years, Björk released three albums with The Sugarcubes that all received worldwide success. In 1990 she recorded a compilation of songs from the 1950s and '60s with a group of Icelandic jazz virtuosos. Two years later, The Sugarcubes disbanded. Björk decided to drop her last name and pursue a solo career in order to fulfill her urge to express her own songs. At the end of 1992, she moved to London, England, and began working on *Debut*.

For the Record . . .

Born Björk Gundmundsdottir, November 21, 1965, in Reykjavik, Iceland; daughter of Gudmundur (electricians' union chief) and Hildur (homeopathic doctor and martial arts teacher); married Thor Eldon, 1986; divorced, 1988; children: (son) Sindri.

Released first solo album at age 11; performed with several bands during teenage years; (with others) formed theatrical/rock ensemble KUKL, mid-1980s; formed The Sugarcubes, summer, 1986; signed with Elektra Records, 1986; released three albums, 1986-92; released first international solo LP, *Debut*, on Elektra, 1993.

Addresses: *Record company*—Elektra Records, 75 Rockefeller Plaza, New York, NY 10019.

"The Sugarcubes were a party band," Björk told Dev Sherlock in *Musician*. "They were about us getting hilariously drunk and simply having this permission to travel around the world because some foreigner liked us and decided that we were brilliant. It was a social band and the music reflected that. Whereas with my own record, all the songs I wrote in my home after midnight, when I'm on my own. And it's very kinda private and intimate."

Elektra Records released *Debut*, Björk's first international solo album, in July of 1993. The album ended up selling more than two and a half million copies worldwide and spawned five successful singles—"Human Behavior," "Venus As A Boy," "Big Time Sensuality," and "Violently Happy." Björk explained her lyrical inspiration to *Billboard*: "The lyrics for *Debut* were taken from my diaries over a 10-year period. It took me ages to decide to do that record. I finally figured out that I have the right to be selfish."

The following year, Björk once again ignited television controversy. The Independent Television Commission forced MTV Europe to move Björk's video for "Violently Happy" into late-night time slots. The video showed Björk mutilating a doll with scissors, and the ITC considered the video too violent for daytime audiences.

Before Björk released her next album, she made another mark on the music scene as a songwriter instead of a performer. She cowrote the number one dance hit "Bedtime Stories" for Madonna's album of the same name. "I wrote the lyrics with Madonna in mind," Björk told Brett Atwood in *Billboard*. "The lyrics just sort of

popped into my head. I thought of a collection of words that I have always wanted to hear Madonna say, 'Let's get unconscious, baby.' Then, I formed the song around those phrases."

In 1995 Björk released her next album, titled *Post*, which she wrote and coproduced with a number of other musicians, including trip-hop star and ex-Massive Attack member, Tricky, Howie Bernstein of Mo' Wax, and Graham Massey of the techno band 808 State. Björk recorded the album in Compass Point in Nassau, the Bahamas and finished it in London, England. *Post* debuted on the *Billboard* album charts at number 32, and the single "Army of Me" appeared as the lead track for the film *Tank Girl*.

Björk described the concept behind *Post* as a letter home to Iceland, which also explains the title. At the same time, many of her lyrics describe her friends' point of view rather than her own. "Most of my songs are written in the first person, from the point of view of my best friends," Björk explained to Jon Savage in *Interview*. "I find it ten times easier to express my friends' feelings than my own. If I write about myself, I usually write in the third person. It just feels natural."

The year 1995 not only launched another album for Björk, it also brought with it two lawsuits. A songwriter sued Björk for copyright infringement in February, and the case was dismissed in June. Then, a British music publisher sought royalties for a sample she used on *Post*. They reached a settlement by August. Björk wrote it off as another result of her success. "When people think you're rich, they just try anything," she said in *People*. "If they washed your socks six years ago, they send you a bill for $100,000."

With a career in music that started when she was just 11 years old, Björk has made her mark using contradictions as her striking tool. As long as she has something to sing, she plans to continue doing it for the rest of her life, whether or not she sells albums. She explained her view of the future to Jon Savage in *Interview*: "If I have any vision of my life, I think I'll be singing until I die, about 90 years old.... I could just as well move to a little island and live by the ocean and just be the village singer or whatever. Singing on Friday and Saturday nights, writing tunes for the rest of the week. That's my role."

Selected discography

With The Sugarcubes, on Elektra

Life's Too Good (includes "Birthday"), 1986.
Here Today, Tomorrow, Next Week, 1989.

Stick Around for Joy, 1992.
It's-It (dance remixes), 1992.

Solo, on Elektra

Debut (includes "Human Behavior," "Venus As A Boy," "Big Time Sensuality," and "Violently Happy"), 1993.
Post (includes "Army of Me"), 1995.

Sources

Audio, October 1993.
Billboard, July 17, 1993; October 14, 1993; June 4, 1994; May 13, 1995.
Entertainment Weekly, July 9, 1993; June 23, 1995; June 30-July 7, 1995.
Interview, June 1995.
Musician, May 1994.
People, June 19, 1995; September 25, 1995.
Rolling Stone, June 10, 1993; September 2, 1993; September 16, 1993; November 17, 1994; June 29, 1995; July 13-27, 1995.
Time, August 2, 1993; November 7, 1994; August 14, 1995.

Additional information for this profile was obtained from Elektra Records press information, 1995.

—*Sonya Shelton*

Blue Öyster Cult

Rock band

Blue Öyster Cult is sometimes referred to as the first heavy metal band; the group is even credited by some with coining the term "heavy metal" (note the early use of the unpronounced umlaut in a band's name). The New York-based ensemble formed in the late 1960s, originally as an alternative to the slick corporate rock of the era. After releasing several acclaimed albums during the 1970s, Blue Öyster Cult's popularity began to wane, their music seemingly eclipsed by younger, more bombastic heavy metal acts.

Beginning in the 1980s, a series of personnel changes and contractual difficulties conspired to keep Blue Öyster Cult from releasing new material, but a boost from novelist Stephen King in the the early 1990s helped put the band back in the public eye. King wanted to use Blue Öyster Cult's biggest hit, "(Don't Fear) The Reaper," on the soundtrack for a television version of one his books. The band's label, however, refused to comply with King's request. So a deal was struck with another label to re-record the Cult's biggest hits. The result was the 1994 release *Cult Classic*, which contained the

MICHAEL OCHS ARCHIVES/Venice, CA

original, analog-recorded songs remastered with digital technology. Reviewing the compilation for *Rolling Stone,* Matt Diehl noted, "At their best, BOC create distinctive hard rock that betrays a bitter core, couching perverse, apocalyptic lyrics in deceptively catchy compositions."

Blue Öyster Cult's origins stretch back to late-1960s Long Island, New York. Two of the members, drummer Albert Bouchard and guitarist Donald Roeser, were students at Clarkson College of Technology. They became members of a cover band called The Disciples. Bouchard also began playing in an act called The Lost and Found, where he met future Blue Öyster Cult vocalist Eric Bloom. The Disciples changed their name to The Travesty, and Bouchard and Roeser tried unsuccessfully to relocate the band to New York City.

Bouchard then headed to Chicago, where he met poet, performance artist, and future punk singer Patti Smith. Meanwhile, Roeser became friends with Sandy Pearlman, then a writer for the influential rock magazine *Crawdaddy.* Roeser also befriended Richard Meltzer. When Bouchard returned from Chicago he formed Soft White Underbelly. Pearlman and Meltzer served as a management/production team and wrote songs for the band, which had also thought of calling itself "Cow."

First Performance Disastrous

Soft White Underbelly played numerous gigs around Long Island, recruiting Allen Lanier on keyboards, Eric Bloom on vocals, and finally, Bouchard's younger brother Joe on bass. Eventually they won an opening slot at New York's Fillmore East on a bill with Jethro Tull and Jeff Beck. Unfortunately, their performance was disastrous. A name change seemed to be in order. They first rechristened themselves Oaxaca, then the Stalk-Forrest Group. As the latter they recorded an album for Elektra Records that was never released. Signing with Columbia Records in late 1971 proved more fruitful; their debut release, *Blue Öyster Cult,* appeared in January of 1972. Their ultimate moniker was based on a recipe for Blue Point oysters, discovered by Pearlman.

Many of the songs on *Blue Öyster Cult* were written by the bandmembers along with Pearlman and Meltzer. Pearlman also served as co-producer with Murray Krugman. This key behind-the-scenes lineup would remain intact for most of the decade. Early in their career, Blue Öyster Cult had adopted the band's trademark imagery—the symbol for Kronos, or Saturn, in white on a field of black. Such mythological-based iconography would be copied by legions of both big-league and backwater heavy metal acts for years to come. Also during these initial years, Blue Öyster Cult were frequently billed as a support act for Alice Cooper, an early-1970s "metal" act famous for incorporating blood, gore, and live snakes into his theatrical stage show.

Between tours, Blue Öyster Cult recorded a number of albums for Columbia, including *Tyranny* and *Mutation* and *Secret Treaties.* A live record, *On Your Feet or On Your Knees,* was released in February of 1975, but it was not until the band's fourth studio effort that Blue Öyster Cult achieved their breakthrough success. That record, 1976's *Agents of Fortune,* contained the seemingly sinister, slightly hypnotic hit "(Don't Fear) The Reaper." The song was interpreted by some as containing a pro-suicide message. Nonetheless, by the fall of 1976 the album had sold over a million copies; it would remain on the charts for 35 weeks. Patti Smith, by then the girlfriend of keyboardist Allen Lanier, sang on one of the cuts she and Lanier co-wrote, "The Revenge of Vera Gemini."

Outlandish Live Shows

Blue Öyster Cult followed the success of *Agents of Fortune* with *Spectres,* released in late 1977. A song written by Roeser, "Godzilla," became that disc's biggest hit. During their tours in support of these albums, the band introduced a mind-bending laser light show, one of the first outlandish spectacles of the rock concert experience. Rumors began circulating that fans were going blind as a result of the near-half-a-million-dollar technology. The displays were viewed as satanic by conservatives, and due to the controversy some arenas would not allow the laser equipment to be installed. The band eventually capitulated to the naysayers and abandoned the light shows.

Spectres was followed by another live recording, 1978's *Some Enchanted Evening.* Blue Öyster Cult then headed to California to record another studio effort. *Mirrors,* released in June of 1979, was the first work not produced by Pearlman and Krugman. The band played with Black Sabbath for a series of dates promoted as the "Black and Blue" tour, and a concert film of the same name appeared in 1981. "Burnin' for You," a Top 40 hit, was the standout single from 1981's *Fire of an Unknown Origin.*

From there things seemed to go downhill for the band. Drummer Albert Bouchard was a no-show for a tour date in England; he was replaced by a roadie named Rick Downey. Most of the gigs recorded for yet another live album, 1982's *Extraterrestrial Live,* featured Downey's contributions, as did *The Revolution by Night,* released in October of 1983. Downey left the band in 1985; more personnel changes followed. Both Joe Bouchard and Lanier had left the group by the time *Club Ninja* was issued in 1986.

Imaginos Marked by Discord

Imaginos, released in 1988, would be Blue Öyster Cult's last studio album; it was a record plagued by upheaval. A "concept" work exploring the idea that occult forces had caused World War I, *Imaginos* would ultimately be viewed by many fans as a solo project by Albert Bouchard. Bouchard had briefly rejoined the group around 1985 (as did Lanier permanently the following year). But the original drummer again severed his relationship with his former bandmates and longtime producer/manager

Pearlman over *Imaginos.* The record had started out in the early 1980s as a group project. Nonetheless, Bouchard ended up contributing most of the musical content and sang on all of the tracks, intending to release *Imaginos* as a solo album after leaving the group. But the label was dissatisfied with the outcome, and Pearlman managed to have the vocals redone by Bloom and Roeser. Bouchard eventually went on to form the avant-garde, New York City-based Brain Surgeons with his wife, rock journalist Deborah Frost.

Some saw a connection between *Imaginos's* content and the writings of early-twentieth-century science fiction novelist H. P. Lovecraft—not surprisingly also one of horror writer Stephen King's influences. When King attempted to win permission to use "(Don't Fear) The Reaper" on the soundtrack to his TV miniseries *The Stand,* a contractual dispute resulted in 1994's *Cult Classic,* a remastering of Blue Öyster Cult's biggest hits. In fact, changes in band personnel during the 1980s had been compounded by long-unresolved contractual problems with the band's label.

By the mid-1990s Blue Öyster Cult—then a quintet featuring Bloom, Lanier, and Roeser—seemed to be content to tour occasionally for the benefit of die-hard enthusiasts. At one point the band even sold T-shirts that proclaimed "On Tour Forever." But an active fan club and a wealth of information and discussion on on-line computer services kept the Blue Öyster Cult mythos alive and well—the latter a fittingly "plugged in" development that seemed to support rock critic Dave Marsh's assessment of them in his book *The Heart of Rock and Soul* as "the world's brainiest heavy metal band."

Selected discography

On Columbia/CBS Records, except where noted

Blue Öyster Cult, 1972.
Tyranny and Mutation, 1973.
Secret Treaties, 1974.
On Your Feet or on Your Knees, 1975.
Agents of Fortune, 1976.
Spectres, 1977.
Some Enchanted Evening, 1978.
Mirrors, 1979.
Cultosaurus Erectus, 1980.
Fire of Unknown Origin, 1981.
Extraterrestrial Live, 1982.
The Revolution by Night, 1983.
Club Ninja, 1986.
Imaginos, 1988.
Career of Evil: The Metal Years (compilation), 1990.

On Flame with Rock and Roll (compilation), 1990.
Cult Classic (compilation), Herald Records, 1994.
Workshop of the Telescopes, Columbia/Legacy, 1995.

Sources

Books

Marsh, Dave, *The Heart of Rock and Soul: The 1001 Greatest Singles Ever Made,* New American Library, 1989.
The Penguin Encyclopedia of Popular Music, edited by Donald Clarke, Viking, 1989.
The Rolling Stone Encyclopedia of Rock & Roll, edited by Jon Pareles and Patricia Romanowski, Rolling Stone Press/ Summit Books, 1983.

Periodicals

Rolling Stone, February 9, 1995.
BAM, December 15, 1995.

Additional information for this profile was obtained from the Blue Öyster Cult Frequently Asked Questions page on the Internet.

—Carol Brennan

James Brown

Singer, bandleader

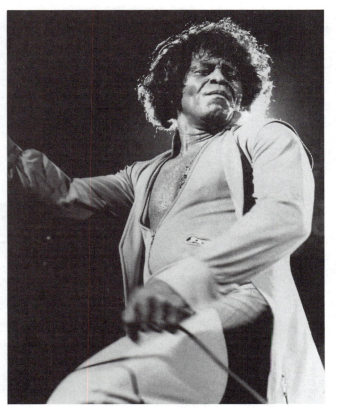

Photograph by David Corio, MICHAEL OCHS ARCHIVES/Venice, CA

In the book about his life, *Living in America*, James Brown told the author, "I never try to express what I actually did," regarding his influence on the American soul scene. "I wouldn't try to do that, 'cause definition's such a funny thing. What's put together to make my music—it's something which has real power. It can stir people up and involve 'em. But it's just something I came to hear."

The music that James Brown heard in his head—and conveyed to his extraordinary musicians with an odd combination of near-telepathic signals and vicious brow-beating—changed the face of soul. By stripping away much of the pop focus that had clouded pure rhythm and blues, Brown found a rhythmic core that was at once primally sexual and powerfully spiritual. Shouting like a preacher over bad-to-the-bone grooves and wicked horn lines, he unleashed a string of hits through the 1960s and early 1970s; he was also a formative influence on such rock and soul superstars as Parliament-Funkadelic leader George Clinton, Rolling Stones frontman Mick Jagger, Prince, and Michael Jackson, among countless others.

By the late 1970s, however, Brown's career was waning, and he was plagued by demands for back taxes, a nagging drug problem, and a combative relationship with his third wife. In 1988 he went to prison after leading police on a high-speed chase. And even as the advent of hip-hop has made him perhaps the most sampled artist in the genre, he has had frequent scrapes with the law since his release in 1991. Even so, his legacy—as bandleader, singer, dancer, and pop music visionary—is assured.

Brown was born in the South—sources vary, but generally have him hailing from Georgia or South Carolina—and grew up in Augusta, Georgia, struggling to survive. At the age of four, he was sent to live with his aunt, who oversaw a brothel. Under such circumstances, he grew up fast; by his teens he drifted into crime. In the words of Timothy White, who profiled the singer in his book *Rock Stars*, "Brown became a shoeshine boy. Then a pool-hall attendant. Then a thief." At 16 he went to jail for multiple car thefts. Though initially sentenced to 8-16 years of hard labor, he got out in under four for good behavior. After unsuccessful forays into boxing and baseball, he formed a gospel group called the Swanees with his prison pal Johnny Terry.

"The Hardest-Working Man in Show Business"

The Swanees shifted toward the popular mid-1950s doo-wop style and away from gospel, changing their name to the Famous Flames. Brown sang lead and played drums; their song "Please, Please, Please"—a

Born May 3, 1933, in Barnwell, SC (some sources say Augusta, GA, or Pulaski, TN); married three times (divorced twice, third wife died); children: six (son Teddy died c. 1970s).

Held various jobs before being incarcerated in Alto Reform School, Toccoa, GA, 1949-52; boxer and semi-professional baseball player, c. 1953-55; sang in gospel group that came to be known as the Famous Flames, 1955, then began playing R&B music; group changed name to James Brown and the Famous Flames and released Federal single "Please, Please, Please," 1956; signed to Smash label, 1964; Famous Flames quit; Brown signed to Polydor Records and released *Hot Pants*, 1971; charged with tax evasion, 1975; appeared in film *The Blues Brothers*, 1980; sang "Living in America" for *Rocky IV* soundtrack, 1986; signed to CBS records and released *Gravity*, 1986; recorded "Gimme Your Love," duet with Aretha Franklin, 1988; arrested after high-speed chase and sentenced to prison, 1988; performed and lectured as part of prison work-release program, 1990; Rykodisc released 4-CD career retrospective *Star Time*, 1991; charged with two counts of domestic violence, mid-1990s; signed to Scotti Bros. Records; new label released *Universal James*, 1993, and *The Great James Brown: Live at the Apollo, 1995*.

Selected awards: Grammy Awards for best R&B recording for "Papa's Got a Brand New Bag," 1965, and for best male R&B performance for "Living in America," 1987; inducted into Rock 'n' Roll Hall of Fame, 1986.

Addresses: *Record company*—Scotti Bros. Records, 2114 Pico Blvd., Santa Monica, CA 90405. *Production company*—New James Brown Enterprises, 1217 West Medical Park Rd., Augusta, GA 30909.

and released a string of mostly instrumental albums, on which he often played organ.

Brown's declamatory style mixed a handful of seminal influences, but his intensity and repertoire of punctuating vocal sounds—groans, grunts, wails, and screams—came right out of the southern church. His exhortations to sax player Maceo Parker to "blow your horn," and trademark cries of "Good God!" and "Take it to the bridge!" became among the most recognizable catchphrases in popular music. The fire of his delivery was fanned by his amazingly agile dancing, without which Michael Jackson's fancy footwork is unimaginable. And his band—though its personnel shifted constantly—maintained a reputation as one of the tightest in the business. Starting and stopping on a dime, laying down merciless grooves, it followed Brown's lead as he worked crowds the world over into a fine froth. "It was like being in the army," William "Bootsy" Collins—who served as Brown's bassist during the late 1960s—told *Musician,* adding that the soul legend "was just a perfectionist at what he was doing." Brown adopted a series of extravagant titles over the years, but during this period he was known primarily as "The Hardest-Working Man in Show Business."

"Guts"—and an Iron Hand

At the same time, Brown's harshness as a leader meant that bandmembers were constantly facing fines for lateness, flubbed notes, missed cues, violating his strict dress code, or even for talking back to him. His musicians also complained of overwork and insufficient pay, and some alleged that Brown took credit for ideas they had developed. The singer-bandleader's temper is legendary; as trombonist Fred Wesley told *Living in America* author Cynthia Rose, "James was bossy and paranoid. I didn't see why someone of his stature would be so defensive. I couldn't understand the way he treated his band, why he was so *evil.*"

Charles Shaar Murray ventured in his book *Crosstown Traffic* that "playing with James Brown was a great way to learn the business and to participate in the greatest rhythm machine of the sixties. It was a very poor way to get rich, to get famous, or to try out one's own ideas." Even so, the group—which included, at various times, funk wizards like Maceo Parker, guitarist Jimmy Nolen, and drummer Clyde Stubblefield—reached unprecedented heights of inspiration under Brown. "He has no real musical skills," Wesley remarked to Rose, "yet he could hold his own onstage with any jazz virtuoso—because of his guts."

The increasingly militant stance of many black activists in the late 1960s led Brown—by now among an elite

wrenchingly passionate number in which Brown wailed the titular word over and over—was released as a single in 1956 and became a million-seller. By 1960 the group had become the James Brown Revue and was generating proto-funk dance hits like "(Do the) Mashed Potato." Deemed the "King of Soul" at the Apollo Theater, New York's black music mecca, Brown proceeded over the ensuing years to burn up the charts with singles like "Papa's Got a Brand New Bag," "I Got You (I Feel Good)," "It's a Man's Man's Man's World," "Cold Sweat," "Funky Drummer," and many others. In the meantime, he signed with the Mercury subsidiary Smash Records group of influential African Americans—to flirt with the "Black Power" movement. Even so, the singer generally counseled nonviolence and won a commendation from President Lyndon B. Johnson when a broadcast of his words helped head off a race riot. He was also saluted by Vice-President Hubert Humphrey for his pro-education song "Don't Be a Dropout." Brown's music did begin to incorporate more overtly political messages, many of which reiterated his belief that black people needed to take control of their economic destinies. He was a walking example of this principle, having gained control of his master tapes by the mid-1960s.

> "What's put together to make my music—it's something which has real power. It can stir people up and involve 'em."

The year 1970 saw the release of Brown's powerful single "(Get Up, I Feel Like Being a) Sex Machine," a relentless funk groove featuring several hot young players, notably Bootsy Collins and his brother Phelps, aka "Catfish." Brown soon signed with Polydor Records and took on the moniker the "Godfather of Soul," after the highly successful mafia movie The Godfather. Further refining his hard funk sound, he released hits like "Get on the Good Foot," "Talking Loud and Saying Nothing," and "Soul Power." With the 1970s box-office success of black action films—known within the industry as "blaxploitation" pictures—Brown began writing movie soundtracks, scoring such features as Slaughter's Big Rip-Off and Black Caesar.

Taxes, Tragedy, and Trouble

James Brown may have been one of the biggest pop stars in the world—the marquees labeled him "Minister of New New Super Heavy Funk"—but he was not immune to trouble. In 1975 the Internal Revenue Service claimed that he owed $4.5 million in taxes from 1969-70, and many of his other investments collapsed. His band quit after a punishing tour of Africa, and most tragically, his son Teddy died in an automobile accident. Brown's wife later left him, taking their two daughters.

By the late 1970s, the advent of disco music created career problems for the Godfather of Soul. Though he dubbed himself "The Original Disco Man (a.k.a. The Sex Machine)," he saw fewer and fewer of his singles charting significantly. Things improved slightly after he

appeared as a preacher in the smash 1980 comedy film The Blues Brothers, and he demonstrated his importance to the burgeoning hip-hop form with Unity (The Third Coming), his 1983 EP with rapper Afrika Bambaataa. But Brown's big comeback of the 1980s came with the release of "Living in America," the theme from the film Rocky IV, which he performed at the request of star Sylvester Stallone. The single was his first million-selling hit in 13 years. As a result, Brown inked a new deal with CBS Records; in 1986 he was inducted into the Rock 'n' Roll Hall of Fame. "Living in America" earned him a Grammy Award for best R&B performance by a male artist.

Jailed After 1988 Chase

Through it all, Brown had been struggling with substance abuse, despite his participation in the President's Council against Drugs. His and his third wife Adrienne's use of the drug known as PCP or "angel dust" led to frequent encounters with the law; in May of 1988 he faced charges of assault, weapons and drug possession, and resisting arrest. In December he was arrested again after leading police on a two-state car chase and was sentenced to six years in State Park Correctional Facility in Columbia, South Carolina. His confinement became a political issue for his fans, and Brown was ultimately released in early 1991. "We've got lots of plans," the soul legend declared to Rolling Stone, adding that the experience "has opened James Brown's eyes about things he has to do." He later announced plans to tape a cable special with pop-rap sensation M.C. Hammer.

That same year saw the release of Star Time, a four-CD boxed set that meticulously collected Brown's finest moments; much of which had never been released on compact disc before. The project's release date was set to coincide with the 35th anniversary of "Please, Please, Please." Brown, meanwhile, set to work on a new album, Universal James, which included production by British soul star Jazzie B. "It'll be the biggest album I ever had," he declared to Spin, though this was not to be the case. The 1990s did, however, reveal just how influential James Brown's work had been in rap and hip-hop circles: hundreds of his records were sampled for beats, horn stabs, and screams; the group Public Enemy, which had taken its name from one of his singles, often elaborated on the political themes he had raised.

Meanwhile—thanks in part to his participation in The Blues Brothers and the use of his music in feature films like Good Morning, Vietnam—Brown emerged as a "classic" mainstream artist. Indeed, Time magazine listed 32 appearances of "I Got You (I Feel Good)" in films, movie trailers, and television commercials, and this list was probably not exhaustive. In 1993 the people of Steamboat Springs, Colorado, christened the James Brown Soul Center of the Universe Bridge. The following year a street running alongside New York's Apollo Theater was temporarily named James Brown Blvd., and he performed at Radio City Music Hall; superstar actress Sharon Stone sang "Happy Birthday" to him on the occasion of his 61st. "I'm wherever God wants me to be and wherever the people need for me to be," he told the *New York Times*.

Unfortunately, his troubles were not at an end. In December of 1994, he was charged with misdemeanor domestic violence after yet another conflagration with Adrienne. And on October 31, 1995, Brown was once again arrested for spousal abuse. He later blamed the incident on his wife's addiction to drugs, stating in a press release, "She'll do anything to get them." Just over two months later, Adrienne died at the age of 47 after undergoing cosmetic surgery.

Brown's penchant for survival and the shining legacy of his work managed to overshadow such ugly incidents. "No one in the world makes me want to dance like James Brown," wrote producer and record executive Jerry Wexler—one of the architects of modern soul—in his book *Rhythm and the Blues*. "I came from nothing and I made something out of myself," Brown commented in a *New York Times* interview. "I dance and I sing and I make it happen. I've made people feel better. I want people to be happy." The Godfather of Soul released a new live album in 1995.

Selected discography

On King, except where noted

"Please, Please, Please," Federal, 1956.
Live at the Apollo, 1963.
Pure Dynamite! Live at the Royal, 1964.
Showtime, Smash, 1964.
Grits and Soul, Smash, 1965.
Papa's Got a Brand New Bag, 1965.
James Brown Plays James Brown Yesterday and Today, Smash, 1965.
James Brown Plays New Breed, Smash, 1966.
It's a Man's Man's Man's World, 1966.
Handful of Soul, 1966.
Raw Soul, 1967.
Live at the Garden, 1967.
James Brown Plays the Real Thing, Smash, 1967.
Cold Sweat, 1967.
I Can't Stand Myself, 1968.
I Got the Feelin', 1968.
James Brown Plays Nothing But Soul, Smash, 1968.

Say It Loud—I'm Black and I'm Proud, 1969.
Gettin' Down to It, 1969.
James Brown Plays and Directs the Popcorn, Smash, 1969.
It's a Mother, 1969.
Sex Machine, 1970.
Super Bad, 1970.
Sho Is Funky Down Here, 1971.

On Polydor, except where noted

Hot Pants, 1971.
Revolution of the Mind, 1971.
Soul Classics, 1972.
There It Is, 1972.
Black Caesar, 1973.
Slaughter's Big Rip-Off, 1973.
Soul Classics, Volume 2, 1973.
The Payback, 1973.
Hell, 1974.
Reality, 1974.
Sex Machine Today, 1975.
Everybody's Doin' the Hustle and Dead on the Double Bump, 1975.
Hot, 1975.
Get Up Offa That Thing, 1976.
Bodyheat, 1976.
Mutha's Nature, 1977.
Jam/1980s, 1978.
Take a Look at Those Cakes, 1978.
The Original Disco Man, 1979.
(With Afrika Bambaataa) *Unity (The Third Coming)*, Tommy Boy, 1983.
(Contributor) *Rocky IV* (soundtrack; performs "Living in America"), 1986.
Gravity, CBS, 1986.
I'm Real, CBS, 1988.
Aretha Franklin, *Through the Storm* (appears on "Gimme Your Love"), Arista, 1988.
Star Time (4-CD boxed set), Rykodisc, 1991.
Universal James, Scotti Bros., 1993.
The Great James Brown: Live at the Apollo, 1995, Scotti Bros., 1995.

Sources

Books

Brown, James, *The Godfather of Soul*, 1990.
Murray, Charles Shaar, *Crosstown Traffic: Jimi Hendrix and the Rock 'n' Roll Revolution*, St. Martin's, 1989.
Rees, Dafydd, and Luke Crampton, *Rock Movers & Shakers*, ABC/CLIO, 1991.
Rose, Cynthia, *Living in America: The Soul Saga of James Brown*, Serpent's Tail, 1990.
Wexler, Jerry, *Rhythm and the Blues*, Knopf, 1993.
White, Timothy, *Rock Stars*, Stewart, Tabori & Chang, 1984.

Periodicals

Augusta Chronicle (Augusta, GA), April 30, 1995.
Entertainment Weekly, December 23, 1994.
Los Angeles Times, September 10, 1994; December 10, 1994.
Musician, November 1994, .
New York Times, April 13, 1994.
Oakland Press (Oakland County, MI), November 4, 1995; January 7, 1996.
Rolling Stone, April 18, 1991.
Spin, December 1992; December 1993.
Time, April 25, 1994; May 16, 1994.

Additional information for this profile was taken from Scotti Bros. publicity materials, 1995.

—Simon Glickman

Betty Buckley

Singer, songwriter, actress

AP/Wide World Photos

Critics like to call Betty Buckley the underground diva, primarily because the most significant work of her career is unfamiliar to those who do not frequent Broadway theaters. Many consider hers the finest voice on the contemporary American stage, yet most people think of her fondly as television's favorite stepmom, Abby Bradford of the late Seventies ABC-TV hit *Eight is Enough.* Yet Buckley's Tony award-winning performance as Grizabella in the Broadway production of *Cats* made the song "Memory" an American classic, and the Texas-born actress's replacement of Glenn Close in Andrew Lloyd Webber's *Sunset Boulevard* had the press talking for months. With all of these accomplishments Betty Buckley is still not a household name, but much of that was her own decision.

Betty Lynn Buckley was born in Fort Worth on July 3, 1947, where her aunt began giving her dance lessons at age three. By five she was singing in the church choir, but her father, a fundamentalist Christian, strongly discouraged Buckley from a performance career. Ironically, her mother, a former singer and dancer, encouraged Betty. Although she'd initially planned to be a rodeo star—and was already quite good—at 13 Betty listened raptly to every note of Judy Garland's live Carnegie Hall album and was inspired. In college, Buckley competed in the 1966 Miss Fort Worth pageant and won. Although she was only a runner-up in the subsequent Miss Texas contest, the producers of the Miss America show were so impressed by her voice they asked her to sing during the television broadcast from Atlantic City.

At 21 Buckley graduated from Texas Christian University with a degree in journalism to please her father. After a Miss America USO tour and while working as a teen reporter for the Forth Worth paper, an agent asked her to come to New York. Within two hours of her arrival she was auditioning for her first Broadway musical. When asked how long she'd been in town by those involved in what would become the smash hit *1776,* the novice just cast as Martha Washington responded, "What time is it?" From there Buckley went on to star in the London company of *Promises, Promises,* where she was nominated by the London critics for Best Musical Performer. She later replaced Jill Clayburgh for a two-and-a-half-year run as Catherine in Bob Fosse's *Pippin,* then went on to critical raves starring in Gretchen Cryer's off-Broadway feminist play *I'm Getting My Act Together and Taking It on the Road.*

Just before leaving Texas Buckley met Peter Flood, whom she would marry in 1972. She admits now that it was mostly to ease pressure from her parents and she and Flood divorced in 1974, but the two remained friends. The time was also a period of pain and emotional confusion for Buckley. She began seeing a psychiatrist and

Born July 3, 1947, in Fort Worth, TX, daughter of Ernest (a former Air Force colonel turned engineering professor) and Betty Bob (in theater public relations, former singer and dancer) Buckley. Married Peter Flood, 1972 (divorced, 1974). *Education:* Journalism degree from Texas Christian University, c. 1968.

Began performing in Fort Worth productions during adolescence; singing and acting debut on Broadway in *1776*, 1969-70; other Broadway performances include *Pippin*, 1973-75, *Cats*, 1982-84, *The Mystery of Edwin Drood*, 1985-86, *Song And Dance*, c. 1987, *Carrie*, 1988, and *Sunset Boulevard*, 1995—; off-Broadway productions include *I'm Getting My Act Together and Taking it on The Road*, 1981, and *Juno's Swans*, 1985; starred in London companies of *Promises, Promises*, 1970-71, and *Sunset Boulevard*, 1994-95; made feature film debut in *Carrie*, 1976; other film roles include *Tender Mercies*, 1983, *Wild Thing*, 1987, *Another Woman*, 1988, *Frantic*, 1988, *Rain Without Thunder*, 1993, *Wyatt Earp*, 1994, and *Ride for Your Life*, 1995; television debut, *Eight is Enough*, ABC-TV, 1977; acting teacher, c. 1971—.

Selected Awards: Tony Award as Best Featured Actress in a Musical for *Cats*, 1982; honorary Doctorate of Fine Arts from Marymount Manhattan College, 1995.

Addresses: *Management*—Abrams Artists, 420 Madison Avenue, 14th Floor, New York, NY 10017.

also started what would develop into a lifelong study of world religion, eastern philosophy, and meditation.

Television Debut in Eight Is Enough

Buckley was doing film voice replacement work for director Brian De Palma when he offered her the role of the gym teacher in *Carrie*, her first film. The sympathetic character attracted the attention of Lorimar Studios and they asked Buckley to replace the late Diana Hyland, an actress who recently passed away from cancer after the spring try-out of a new ABC drama called *Eight is Enough*. Although she had never considered television before, the offer was more money than she could refuse, so Buckley signed on as Abby Bradford. Work on television was a struggle at first: it wasn't easy for a 29-year-old actress to step into an already-established television family, and this medium's production was not like that of musical theater—to Buckley doing television seemed to have a factory-like quality to it. And besides, as she told Paul Wontorek in *TheaterWeek*, "They tried to lock me in the kitchen and put me in muumuus....In the beginning, it was a real struggle to make her hip. They wanted me to be like something from the '50s."

As a child of the 1960s, and as a performer, Buckley felt almost destined to have trouble with drugs and alcohol. During her time in Hollywood she lived at the famed Chateau Marmont, becoming close with another of the hotel's famous residents, actor and comedian John Belushi. They took drugs together, but it was watching Belushi's descent into hell that eventually made her realize she did not have to follow suit. After her first two years on *Eight is Enough*, Buckley cleaned up. When the show was canceled after four years, Buckley was simultaneously saddened and elated. Although many suggested she was doomed to play mothers all her life, she promptly proved them wrong by playing Robert Duvall's nasty country singer ex-wife in the Academy Award-winning film *Tender Mercies;* Buckley also performed the film's Oscar-nominated song "Over You."

The *Cats* Meow

In 1982 Buckley auditioned for the part of Grizabella in *Cats*, Andrew Lloyd Webber's musical adaptation of a book of poems by T.S. Eliot. "They wanted someone who conveyed vulnerability," Buckley explained to Paul Buetel in *Southwest Airlines Magazine.* "They felt I conveyed health and well-being, which is funny, because that's what I've always *tried* to convey. But I knew I had the ability to play that part." Buckley won the role and won a Tony Award in 1983 for her performance. Her rendition of the song "Memory" is regarded by many as the quintessential version.

Buckley left *Cats* during the peak of its run; after a year and a half it was time to move on. She did several films for television and an Off-Broadway appearance in *Juno's Swans*. In 1985 Buckley took on the roles of three different characters in Joseph Papp's New York Shakespeare Festival production of *The Mystery of Edwin Drood*, a play within a play based on an unfinished novel of Charles Dickens. "After *Cats* I was looking for something lighter and more joyful," she told *USA Today*'s Richard David Story. "Grizabella is a very sad creature, and she took her toll on me. I said, 'Enough death, dying and rejection. I want to have fun....[In *Drood*] I play a sort of English music-hall actress who impersonates a young man who himself is actually playing an old seafaring captain." The show promptly moved on to Broadway and once again Buckley was a hit.

Taking time off from Broadway for a while, Buckley tried her hand at the cabaret/nightclub circuit. Performing an eclectic bunch of songs—including several of her own creation—Buckley wowed audiences. Praised for her exquisite voice, moving song interpretation, and general ease with an audience, one critic, in the *Daily Advertiser*, thought "so comfortable was the evening that when [Buckley] walked off stage at intermission, I almost expected her to ask, 'Can I get you anything while I'm up?'" The accolades were unanimous.

The Road To Norma

In 1988 Buckley had what she considered the best working experience of her life thus far, but what also constituted Broadway's costliest flop ever: *Carrie,* a musical version of the best-selling Stephen King novel and also Buckley's first role on celluloid. It was also an eight-million-dollar disaster. Ever since the movie version, Buckley had ached to sink her teeth into the role of Carrie's unbalanced mother. As has often been the case in her career, Buckley's work was praised by all who saw it, while the play around her was trashed by critics. The play's brief run still won her a nomination for Best Actress in a Musical from the Outer Critics' Circle, however. Buckley spent the next several years honing her craft in prolonged engagements of her one-woman cabaret show, constantly delighting audiences and receiving rave reviews for both Carnegie Hall and road tour performances. She also appeared in television and several feature films including Roman Polanski's *Frantic,* Woody Allen's *Another Woman,* and Kevin Costner's *Wyatt Earp.*

In the mid-1990s Buckley became a figure in the media hype surrounding Andrew Lloyd Webber's stage version of *Sunset Boulevard.* The to-and-fro involving Lloyd Webber and the leading ladies in his adaptation of the 1950 Billy Wilder film gave the press fodder for over a year. Patti LuPone originated the role of Norma Desmond, unhinged former silent movie queen first played by Gloria Swanson, in London. When she found she would not be playing the role in its American debut in Los Angeles as promised, she quit. Buckley, whom many had thought would be considered for the role in the first place, replaced LuPone in London and won rave reviews as well as a nomination for the Laurence Olivier Award for Best Actress in a Musical.

Film star Glenn Close took over the Desmond role for *Sunset Boulevard*'s Los Angeles debut, and moved with it to Broadway, where her stage histrionics won her acclaim and a Tony. When Close left the show, Buckley was asked to take over, and the media was ready to pounce. But the show's producers smoothed the way with critics and theatergoers for an easy transition, and the new opening night starring Buckley was an overwhelming success—the audience leapt to its feet twice during the show, and cast members actually stepped out of character to applaud her. "Buckley is, bottom line, absolutely sensational as the musicalized Norma Desmond," wrote Robert Osborne in *The Hollywood Reporter,* "the best yet in fact, and I've seen 'em all....she has a voice that is one of the wonders of the world. In addition, she acts the role with great style, pizzazz and, above all, intelligence." Only Vincent Canby of the *New York Times,* an avowed Close/Desmond fan, had trouble buying Buckley's softer, more human version of Norma. Some industry-watchers actually considered Buckley's extraordinary talent a problem, making it suddenly apparent just how mediocre a show Lloyd Webber's *Sunset Boulevard* was when dimmed by the light of her performance.

Betty Buckley has spent a lifetime in the musical theater, on television, and in films. She has worked strenuously at her craft and has often purposefully chosen to take the road less likely to lead to the stardom, and it seems to have paid off. Forty-seven years old when she first took up the reigns of Norma Desmond, Buckley she felt as if she were just then getting her true chance. As she told Randall Short of *New York,* "I feel like this racehorse that's been dying for a big race. A really good, fast little racehorse. And finally the heavy hitters are putting their money on me."

Selected discography

(With others) *1776* (original cast recording), Columbia, 1969.
(With others) *Cats* (original cast recording), Geffen, 1983.
(With others) *The Mystery of Edwin Drood* (original cast recording), Polygram, 1986.
Betty Buckley, Rizzoli, 1987.
Children Will Listen, Sterling, 1993.
With One Look, Sterling, 1994.
Betty Buckley—The London Concert, Sterling, 1995.

Sources

American Film, June 1991.
American Record Guide, September 1992.
Arizona Daily Star (Tucson), September 12, 1992.
Back Stage, June 21, 1991; April 24, 1992.
Bay Area Reporter (San Francisco), October 28, 1988.
Berkshire Eagle, June 27, 1992.
Billboard, October 21, 1995.
Chatelaine, May 1988.
Chicago Tribune, May 6, 1993.
City Life (Scottsdale), April 16, 1986.

Commonweal, April 8, 1988.

Daily Advertiser (Lafayette), October 4, 1986.

Daily News (New York), April 27, 1980; May 17, 1983; June 11, 1990; June 29, 1990; July 23, 1995.

Daily Variety, July 24, 1995.

Dallas Morning News, November 1, 1984; December 7, 1990; July 10, 1992; September 17, 1995.

Drama-Logue, April 23, 1987.

Entertainment Weekly, August 25, 1995.

Florida Times Union (Jacksonville), January 31, 1984.

Fort Worth Star-Telegram, January 26, 1986; December 6, 1990; December 8, 1990.

Gannett Westchester Newspapers, May 12 1988.

Gay Chicago Magazine, May 13, 1993.

Glamour, March 1993.

Hollywood Reporter, July 25, 1995.

Library Journal, March 1, 1991; January 1993.

Los Angeles Herald Examiner, February 10, 1981.

Los Angeles Times, June 30, 1983.

Maclean's, March 14, 1988.

Nation, June 4, 1988.

National Catholic Reporter, December 2, 1988.

National Review, August 15, 1994.

New Leader, June 27, 1988.

New York, June 10, 1985; October 24, 1988; June 22, 1992; July 24, 1995; August 7, 1995.

New York Newsday, June 8, 1995; September 11, 1995.

New York Post, February 27, 1987; June 14, 1990; June 29, 1995; July 6, 1995; July 21, 1995.

New York Times, August 23, 1985; June 15, 1990.

New Yorker, March 21, 1988; May 23, 1988; November 21, 1994.

Newsweek, March 7, 1988; May 23, 1988; June 22, 1992; July 31, 1995.

Parade, July 2, 1995.

People, March 7, 1988; February 13, 1989; March 7, 1994; September 4, 1995.

Playbill, July 17, 1993; August 31, 1995.

Playboy, February 1993.

Premiere, February 1990.

Press Journal (New York), July 5, 1990.

Publishers Weekly, February 1, 1991; June 7, 1991.

Scranton Times, October 14, 1990.

Show Music, Fall 1993.

Southwest Airlines Magazine, July 1983.

TheaterWeek, July 29, 1991; June 29, 1992; July 17, 1995; August 7, 1995.

Time, March 14, 1988; May 23, 1988; May 30, 1988.

Tube View, July 15, 1981.

Up and Coming, November 1988.

USA Today, August 22, 1985; February 26, 1988; July 6, 1995; July 21, 1995.

Variety, March 2, 1988; May 18, 1988; October 12, 1988; February 1, 1989; March 29, 1989; February 14, 1990; July 4, 1990; March 1, 1993; October 18, 1993; April 25, 1994.

Vegetarian Times, October 1984.

Washington Post, April 28, 1983.

Wilson Library Bulletin, April 1991.

Additional information for this profile was provided by Richard Kornberg & Associates publicity materials, 1995 and a Reuter newswire report of June 23, 1988.

—Joanna Rubiner

Butthole
Surfers

Punk band

In the turbulent atmosphere of the so-called "alternative" music scene of the 1980s and early 1990s, countless groups have come and gone, self-destructing noisily under the frictions of fame and touring, or being quietly extinguished by lack of interest from the recording establishment. One band which seems to have overcome these pressures by completely ignoring them is the Butthole Surfers. Relentlessly uncompromising as their name would suggest, the Texas band has been a mainstay of the underground music circuit for over 15 years, performing concerts legendary for their loud dissonance, graphic visual decor, and on-stage mayhem, while releasing albums, alternately chaotic and sharply focused, that are paeans to the skewed reality of the punk psychedelia movement. Without significant airplay or mainstream acceptance, the Butthole Surfers have carved a unique niche for themselves as perhaps one of the most widely known bands never to have appeared on a sales chart or on a top-100 list.

Of all the places for such a corrosively non-conformist act to have sprung from, there could hardly have been

Photograph by Suzan Carson, MICHAEL OCHS ARCHIVES/Venice, CA

For the Record . . .

Members include **Gibson "Gibby" Haynes** (born c. 1958 in Dallas, TX; vocals), **Paul Leary** (born c. 1958 in San Antonio, TX; guitar), **Jeff Pinkus** (born c. 1958 in New York City; bass), **Jeff "King" Coffey** (born c. 1963 in Midland, TX; drums). Former members include **Quinn Matthews**, bass (left group in 1982); **Scott Matthews**, drums (left group in 1982 and was replaced by Jeff Coffey); **Bill Jolly**, bass (left group in 1984 and was replaced by **Terence Smart**, bass, left group in 1985 and was replaced by Jeff Pinkus); and **Teresa Taylor**, drums (left group in 1989).

Group formed in 1980, performed in Texas; toured in California, late 1981; released first album on Jello Biafra's Alternative Tentacles label (San Francisco), 1983; left Alternative Tentacles and signed with Touch and Go (Chicago), 1984; released first Touch and Go album, *Psychic, Powerless, Another Mans Sac*, 1984; appeared on Lollapalooza tour in 1990; signed with Capitol Records, 1991; released first Capitol album, *Independent Worm Saloon*, in 1993.

Addresses: Group—Austin, TX. *Agent*—International Creative Management, New York, NY. *Record label*—Capitol Records, New York, NY.

a more unlikely locale than the campus of Trinity University, a small liberal arts college in San Antonio, Texas. Here in 1977 ex-high school basketball star turned accounting major Gibson "Gibby" Haynes became friends with fellow business student Paul Leary, based on their mutual love of loud, raucous heavy metal bands such as Grand Funk Railroad and Black Sabbath. The two kept in contact after they graduated; Leary, a stockbroker-in-training, worked toward his MBA, while Haynes, voted "accounting student of the year" by his graduating class, toiled over spreadsheets at the firm of Peat Marwick. In 1980, however, evidently unenthused by the prospect of business careers, the two quit their jobs to devote themselves full-time to music, buying amplifiers with the remainder of Leary's student loan. Attracted by the flourishing punk/heavy metal scene of the time, they formed a group featuring Haynes as vocalist, Leary on lead guitar, and, after experimenting with several different line-ups, brothers Quinn and Scott Matthews on bass and drums.

Billed as The Dick Clark 5 for their first performance, the group appeared throughout Texas, performing under a number of different names, including The Dick Gas 5,

Vodka Family Winstons, Ashtray Baby Heads, and Nine Foot Worm Makes Own Food. At a 1981 gig for which they had been booked as The Bleeding Skulls, the band was mistakenly introduced as the Butthole Surfers, a lyric from one of their songs. Leary and Haynes were taken with the cheerfully obscene image and adopted the name as the group's permanent title, thus christening—and in a sense defining—what would become one of the most notorious club acts of the 1980s. The same concert also netted the newly dubbed Butthole Surfers $150, instilling in them the conviction that they could support themselves as musicians. Piling their instruments, equipment, and Leary's faithful pit bull, Mark Farner, into a 1977 Chevrolet Nova with the back seat ripped out, the band headed out to California, determined to stake their claim in its thriving music scene.

First Discovered by Jello Biafra

This initial Butthole Surfers' tour would exemplify the nomadic lifestyle they were to lead for much of the next decade. Wandering up and down the West Coast, the group begged club owners for gigs, garnering appearances here and there on sympathy alone. In the winter of 1981 when they appeared at the San Francisco club Tool and Die, Jello Biafra, leader of one of the premier punk bands of the time, the Dead Kennedys, was in the audience. Biafra liked what he saw and invited them to play shows with his band; more importantly, he signed them with his independent label, Alternative Tentacles. Despite these initial prospects of success, the band returned to Texas in 1982 and broke up. In order to record their first album, Leary and Haynes had to enlist the help of a variety of musicians, finally settling on Jeff "King" Coffey on the drums and Bill Jolly on bass as a permanent line-up for touring. Almost of equal importance, the band also purchased its first set of strobe lights, acquired for $50 from an ex-con, and began to put together the elements for their radically unique live stage act.

In 1983 the Butthole Surfers recorded a second and last album on Alternative Tentacles, with Teresa Taylor, sister of King Coffey, seconding him on drums. These first recordings, though notable for abrasive songs such as "The Shah Sleeps in Lee Harvey's Grave," were simply two among any number of similar albums from the many independent labels and punk bands of the time. Nonetheless, the group had begun to develop a public presence, largely because of the buzz generated by its chaotic concerts, and on the strength of incessant touring, they slowly established themselves as a force on the alternative music scene. Driving an assortment of clapped-out vehicles, including a van that caught fire and exploded in Athens, Georgia, the band spent the next several years almost constantly on the road, exposing themselves—often literally—to a wide range of audiences. The touring lifestyle was far from glamorous. Nourished on junk food bought at convenience stores, they slept wherever they could, nursing chronic cases of the flu from nights spent on cold floors; a high point in this period was when they made enough money to buy sleeping bags. In the process, however, they attracted a steady following of devotees and a reputation as a band that pushed live performance to its extremes.

Darkly Atmospheric Concerts

The fundamental appeal of the Butthole Surfers sprang from the darkly Bacchanalian, almost nightmarish, ambience created by their concerts. The often surreal atmosphere they surrounded themselves with was not intended so much to complement the bands' playing as to distract attention from it; as Paul Leary confessed in *Rip,* "We wanted to do something to cover up our musical ineptness." That "something" took the form of belching smoke machines, banks of cheap strobe lights, and old elementary-school movie projectors showing graphic depictions of such diverse subjects as penis reconstructive surgery, automobile wrecks, and marine life, to name a few, on a backdrop behind the barely visible band. The Surfers' efforts at audience distraction were heightened by the wild gyrations of a nude dancer named Kathleen who appeared regularly with the band after unexpectedly jumping on stage at a concert at New York's Danceteria club. The band members were also obsessed with pyrotechnics, often lighting parts of the stage or themselves on fire at some point in their concerts; a favorite stage prop of Haynes was a broken cymbal which he would fill with lighter fluid and then beat frantically with a drum-stick to send a fireball shooting up into the air.

Against this Dante-esque background, the Butthole Surfers ground out their trademark songs, savage, often inaudible, heavy metal-influenced dirges that were prototypes for the sound and fury of the "grunge" movement of the late 1980s and early '90s. The compositions themselves tended to be formless, prolonged meditations on dysfunctionality, full of harsh images howled at top volume by Haynes. As a counter-point to Gibby's cathartic wailing, a demented Paul Leary thrashed out power chords on his guitar, frantically working its tremolo bar to elicit cacophonous moans and screeches from the instrument. Behind the two frontmen, the band's sound was underpinned by the churning bass of Bill Jolly—succeeded in 1984 by Terence Smart and in 1985 by Jeff Pinkus—and the relentless drumming of Coffey and Taylor.

The band's reckless, no-holds-barred performing style often provoked an equally extreme reaction from their audience, an effect which they seemed to actively encourage as a key component to the chaotic ambience they were trying to establish. This was especially evident in the confrontational and wildly uninhibited stage presence of their physically imposing lead singer. At times, Butthole Surfers' concerts would degenerate into brawls between Haynes and any number of audience members and on one occasion, a concert in Canada, he was stabbed in the arm by a fan who apparently took offense at a song containing the lyrics "crippled midget lesbian boy." This kind of incident, coupled with the band's name—which most radio DJs refused to pronounce on air—did nothing to endear the group to record executives from major labels; throughout much of the 1980s, in spite of their reputation as an underground cult favorite, they were ignored by the mainstream music industry. Eventually they signed with Touch and Go, an independent label based in Chicago, whose management adopted a laissez-faire attitude towards the band's excesses and actually kept them afloat with strategic advances or by wiring money when their touring vehicles broke down.

> *"We wanted to do something to cover up our musical ineptness."*
> —Paul Leary

In return, the band recorded extensively, releasing seven albums from 1984 to 1989. They were characterized by the same focusless, primal energy the band unleashed in its live performances, and became underground classics. This creative frenzy largely took place in the dark confines of a boarded-up house on the outskirts of Austin, Texas, that served as the group's base in between tours. Paul Leary, although he had little prior experience as a producer, was responsible, through a process of trail and error, for the band's unique sound. Virtually all of the albums were recorded using a variety of discarded or second-hand equipment that the Surfers had accumulated in their travels, and the groups' limited budget often necessitated elaborate improvisations. In one instance, all of the drum tracks were done one-by-one because the group only had a single microphone with which to record them.

These prolonged and highly experimental studio sessions spawned distinctly original work, often recyclings of various musical genres stretched beyond recognition. The group enhanced the spontaneous feel of their recordings by distorting and mixing in seemingly random "found sounds," such as radio talk show chatter, Middle Eastern singing, and in one instance, a herd of cows recorded near their house. Perhaps the Butthole Surfers' most well-known work from this period was *Locust Abortion Technician*, released in 1987, a grab-bag of ambient noise and punk psychedelia that a *Melody Maker* critic described—admiringly—as a "sub-blues sewer." An equally favorable reaction greeted the more ethereal *Hairway to Steven*, which appeared the following year.

Wide Exposure at Lollapalooza

As the 1980s wound to a close, the Butthole Surfers went into a temporary hibernation, no doubt exhausted by the frenetic pace they had kept up throughout the decade, and severely curtailed their touring schedule. Teresa Taylor quit the band, while her brother, Pinkus, Haynes, and Leary devoted their energies to side projects such as starting their own labels, producing other groups' records, or dabbling in video technology and computer graphics. In 1990 the group toured again on a limited basis; among the venues they performed was alternative music's wildly successful low-budget traveling road-show, Lollapalooza. In an ironic twist, the Butthole Surfers, often appearing in daylight at the festival and without the usual panoply of projections, smoke, and strobe lights, enjoyed some of the widest public exposure they had ever had. Among the many in the audience impressed by their performance were record executives, and in 1991, they signed with Capitol Records. In a sign of the band's evolving fortunes, their first album on Capitol, *Independent Worm Saloon,* was produced—on a vastly larger budget than they were accustomed to—in a Northern California studio under the guidance of ex-Led Zeppelin bassist John Paul Jones. As of the mid-1990s, they continued to work on recording projects, albeit without the services of Jeff Pinkus, who left the group in 1994.

The Butthole Surfers' persona would seem to have been toned down from the excesses of the mid-1980s, their wild onstage antics and frenzied audience response perhaps overshadowed by the massive success of other groups, such as Nirvana and Nine Inch Nails, that emerged from the same creative ferment of the alternative music movement. However their songs, if more tightly produced since then, have lost none of their edge. The final track on *Worm Saloon*, for example, begins with a 30-second vomiting sequence. As they have since their debut, the group continues their odyssey through the changing American musical landscape, not expressing any specific destination or goal, and improvising, borrowing, adapting anything that seems in sync with their vision of the world. That this vision is often bleak, impenetrable, and a reflection of the chaos of the human condition, is perhaps the essential factor in the band's continuing appeal, coupled with a unique sound that music critic Simon Reynolds evocatively described in a *Melody Maker* article as "one part giant surge of flesh, one part holy revelation." Few who have experienced a Butthole Surfers' concert would disagree.

Selected discography

Brown Reason to Live, Alternative Tentacles, 1983.
Live PCP Pep, Alternative Tentacles, 1984.
Psychic, Powerless, Another Mans Sac, Touch and Go, 1984.
Cream Corn From The Socket of Davis, Touch and Go, 1985.
Rembrandt Pussyhorse, Touch and Go, 1986.
Locust Abortion Technician, Touch and Go, 1987.
Hairway to Steven, Touch and Go, 1988.
Widowermaker! Touch and Go, 1989.
PIOUHGD, Rough Trade, 1991.
Independent Worm Saloon, Capitol Records, 1993.
The Whole Truth and Nothing Butt, Trance Syndicate, 1995.

Sources

Details, May 1993.
Guitar Player, July 1993; June 1995.
Melody Maker, May 10, 1986; April 23, 1988; October 1, 1988; December 8, 1990; March 6, 1993.
Mix, August 1995.
Musician, March 1993.
Rip, August 1994.
Rolling Stone, June 24, 1993.
Side, November 1993.
Spin, June 1993.
Variety, August 27, 1994.

Additional material provided by Capitol Records publicity, March 1993. Special thanks to Jeff "King" Coffey.

—Dan Hodges

C + C Music Factory

Contemporary dance group

In 1991 the musical equation, "Rock + Soul + Funk + Pop + Techno = C + C Music Factory," flashed across C + C Music Factory's first video, *Gonna Make You Sweat (Everybody Dance Now)* and was printed on their first album. The Cs in the group's moniker stand for Robert Clivilles and David Cole, the originators, producers, and driving force behind C + C Music Factory.

The producing duo created the group, not as a band, but as a vehicle for new and rotating musicians who follow the musical equation. Clivilles and Cole shaped the sound and image of the group mostly from the other side of the microphones, like well-known producer Phil Spector did in the 1960s. They also played drums, percussion, and keyboards, wrote all the songs, and arranged the music. "We want to use this project as a means of discovering and introducing new talent to the industry," Clivilles told *Billboard.* "This will not be a factory in the sense of cranking out the same old thing over and over again, but rather a factory where untapped talent is always being developed. In *no* way, shape, or form is this going to *sound* like an assembly line."

Photograph by Bob Grant, Archive Photos/Fotos International

For the Record . . .

Formed and led by **Robert Clivilles**, producer, and **David Cole** (died January 24, 1995), producer/keyboards. Members have included: **April Allen**, vocals; **Vic Black** (born Victor Latimer, Brooklyn, NY), vocals; **Zelma Davis** (born in Liberia, West Africa), vocals; **Sheree Hicks**, vocals; **Kera Trotter**, vocals; **Martha Wash**, vocals; **Fred "Freedom" Williams** (born in Brooklyn, NY), vocals; **Audrey Wheeler**, vocals.

Robert Clivilles and David Cole formed collaboration, 1985. Signed to Columbia Records as venue to expose new artists; released *Gonna Make You Sweat*, 1991. Cole died of complications resulting from spinal meningitis, 1995. Signed to MCA Records as Clivilles's own project, released *C + C Music Factory*, 1995.

Addresses: *Record company*—MCA Records, 70 Universal City Plaza, Universal City, CA 91608.

Clivilles and Cole met in New York, where they both worked at Better Days nightclub in 1985. Cole played live keyboards, adding music and sound effects on top of the records Clivilles spun as the DJ. As they got to know each other, they decided to become a production/songwriting team. Two years later, they released their first production—"Do It Properly" by the performers who billed themselves as 2 Puerto Ricans. The song instantly became an underground dance club hit. "We were born in dance music," David Cole told Jay Cocks in *Time.* "We are disco babies." Added Robert Clivilles, "They tried to kill disco, and it's back. They just call it dance music now."

Fired Up Factory Machines

By the end of the 1980s, Clivilles and Cole had produced several club and pop hits for A&M Records subsidiary Vendetta Records. Their list of smashes included Seduction's crossover hit "Two To Make It Right." When the head of Vendetta, Larry Yasgar, moved to Columbia Records, he introduced the production team to the label's president, Don Ienner. In 1991 Columbia Records released C + C Music Factory's first LP, *Gonna Make You Sweat.* The first artists behind the group included rapper Freedom Williams and singers Martha Wash and Zelma Davis. The album sold more than 6.5 million copies worldwide and spawned several major hit singles, including "Gonna Make You Sweat

(Everybody Dance Now)," "Here We Go," and "Things That Make You Go Hmmmm...."

Martha Wash, the signature voice behind the group's first single "Gonna Make You Sweat," challenged C + C Music Factory's success by filing two lawsuits against Clivilles and Cole. First, Wash alleged that the team hadn't credited her properly on the album, then she complained that they didn't include her in the video, supposedly because of her weight. Cole and Clivilles took the lawsuits and the attacks as gracefully as they could, while promoting Zelma Davis, the other female vocalist, as much as possible. In the video, Davis mouthed the words originally sung by Wash, causing many to question her honesty and validity as a singer for the group. "We've always been in Martha's corner," Cole told *Time.* "Her [latest] gripe is that she wasn't in the video. She sued us the day after she did the [vocal] session! If someone is trying to burn your house down, do you invite them for dinner?"

C + C Music Factory continued promoting the album on the Club MTV Tour, along with Bell Biv DeVoe, Tony! Toni! Tone!, Gerardo, Color Me Badd, and Tara Kemp. In 1992 the group won five awards at the American Music Awards, including dance music single, dance artist, new dance artist, best pop rock group, and favorite new pop artist.

Dissension in the Ranks

As their creation took off in sales and popularity, Cole and Clivilles released *Greatest Remixes Vol. 1,* a collection of singles including two C + C Music Factory songs and new versions of songs already performed by various artists. In response to Clivilles and Cole taking the credit for the success of the group, Freedom Williams left C + C Music Factory in a bitter split. Like Martha Wash, he filed a lawsuit against the producing duo claiming damages totaling $10 million. Williams charged them with breach of contract and failure to pay royalties for publishing, merchandising, and recording. "Robert and David did not give me the talent I have, or create my appearance," Williams told *Billboard.* "Those were things that I brought to the project. C + C Music Factory was a joint effort that we could all be proud of, but all of that is behind me now."

Cole and Clivilles continued producing music and cultivating artists outside of their own project. In 1993 they won the Album of the Year Grammy Award for *The Bodyguard* soundtrack. By the following year, they had settled their lawsuits with Martha Wash, and she appeared alongside Zelma Davis and Audrey Wheeler on *Anything Goes!* Davis and Wash also both appeared on the video for the single "Do You Wanna Get Funky." The trio of singers called Trilogy replaced Freedom Williams' post on vocals. "We asked Freedom to work on the new album, and he said no," Clivilles told *Billboard* after the release of *Anything Goes!*. "But Trilogy defines today's vibe the way Freedom defined the vibe of the first album's time."

Death Strikes a Blow

Tragedy hit the C + C Music Factory collective on January 24, 1995. David Cole died of complications resulting from spinal meningitis, sending a wave of shock and uncertainty into the future of the group. The act's recording contract with Columbia had also expired several days after Cole's death, which added to the rumors of the group's demise. Columbia created even more sparks by releasing a remix of the groups previous hits in a compilation called *The Ultimate*. "We actually knew the label was going to drop us before David died," Clivilles told *Billboard*. "There is no connection between the two events. Our final word on the subject is that we're glad to have had the success we did with Columbia. Time to move on."

Clivilles did move on to MCA Records and continued to oversee C + C as a sole proprietor. One week after Columbia released *The Ultimate*, Clivilles released "I'll Always Be Around," the first single from his initial effort without Cole. "It was always David's and my intention for C + C Music Factory to be an ongoing source of exposing new talent," Clivilles told *Billboard*. "I couldn't let that dissolve with David's passing. We worked way too hard to get to the point where the C + C name carried weight in the music industry to let it slip away."

On December 5, 1995, *C + C Music Factory* was released on MCA Records. Clivilles produced, wrote, recorded, and mixed the album at his own studio, C&C's House of Sound in New York City. The new talents included Vic Black and the female trio A.S.K. M.E., which included April Allen, Sheree Hicks, and Kera Trotter. (A.S.K. M.E. stands for April, Sheree, and Kera Moving Everybody.) *C + C Music Factory* also included

guest appearances from rappers Greg Nice, Charlie Brown, and Doug Phat.

After 13 years together, Clivilles insisted on continuing Cole's memory and inspiration by keeping the machines moving in C + C Music Factory. Clivilles stated the fact in the group's MCA biography: "People are going to hear David's inspiration in it, because, damn it, we'd been together for 13 years! It's a style we created. Now that I have to do this by myself, I think you're always going to hear a piece of David in it. That's just the way it is."

Selected discography

Gonna Make You Sweat, Columbia, 1991.
Greatest Remixes Vol. 1, Columbia, 1992.
Anything Goes!, Columbia, 1994.
The Ultimate, Columbia, 1995.
C + C Music Factory, MCA Records, 1995.

Sources

Billboard, March 2, 1991; June 15, 1991; August 31, 1991; November 30, 1991; February 8, 1992; June 13, 1992; May 29, 1993; April 2, 1994; July 2, 1994; July 9, 1994; July 16, 1994; February 4, 1995; March 4, 1995; October 28, 1995.
Entertainment Weekly, March 6, 1992; August 12, 1994; October 6, 1995.
New York Times, October 30, 1991; November 3, 1991.
Newsweek, March 18, 1991.
People Weekly, August 22, 1994.
Seattle Times, December 18, 1991; January 28, 1992; January 29, 1995; September 7, 1995.
Spin, October 1994.
Teen, February 1992.
Time, April 29, 1991.

Additional information for this profile was obtained from MCA Records press material, 1995.

—*Sonya Shelton*

J. J. Cale

Singer, songwriter, guitarist

Photograph by Anton Corbijn, courtesy of Virgin Records

Although J.J. Cale has a staunch, almost cultish following, his most enduring legacy is a sound few know he pioneered, and a group of classic rock songs few know he wrote. Cale originated the bluesy, minor-key "Tulsa sound" imitated by the likes of Eric Clapton and Mark Knopfler and wrote the Clapton hits "After Midnight" and "Cocaine." He has had his music recorded by Lynyrd Skynyrd, Larry Carlton, Chet Atkins, Freddie King, and numerous others. However, Cale also has a respectable 11 solo albums to his own name, which have sold steadily through the various musical trends between 1972 and 1995.

Cale began his career with the assumption that music would never pay the bills. He played country, Western swing, and rock and roll in bars throughout the 1950s purely for the love of it. Supplementing his income with odd jobs like that of cook, elevator boy, and flower deliverer, Cale performed nights with his band Johnnie Cale and the Valentines. A self-taught guitarist, Cale continued to learn from recordings and other musicians. He mastered blues and jazz guitar on his own and then went to Nashville in 1959 with the hope of becoming a country singer. He toured with the Grand Ole Opry road company, but couldn't make it as a frontman.

In 1964 Cale followed two musician friends, pianist Leon Russell and bassist Carl Radle, to Los Angeles. Cale had played with the two in Tulsa and resumed the relationship in L.A. clubs. When Russell opened his Skye Hill studio, Cale got on-the-job experience as a studio engineer, developing skills he would use throughout his career. At the time, Cale also played with Delaney and Bonnie and produced and engineered albums for various groups. In 1968 he cut an album with some friends, calling themselves the Leathercoated Minds. Titled *A Trip Down the Sunset Strip,* the album featured several psychedelic pop songs, including "Eight Miles High," "Mr. Tambourine Man," and "Sunshine Superman," with the addition of a few instrumental pieces. The same year, Cale returned to Tulsa to write songs and cut demos.

Financial success for Cale waited until 1970 when Eric Clapton recorded "After Midnight," a song Cale had penned. It reached the Top 20 and assured Cale of recognition in the music industry. Soon after, he began working on his debut album. Shelter Records released *Naturally* in 1971, and the album has become a rock classic. The track "Crazy Mama" rose to Number 22 on the charts, and the album's commercial success settled Cale into a steady recording career.

With the money from *Naturally,* Cale moved to Nashville and built a 16-track studio he called Crazy Mama's. Over the next decade Cale wrote and recorded six more

For the Record . . .

Born c. 1938 in Tulsa, OK.

In the late 1950s and 1960s pioneered, with Leon Russell, the "Tulsa sound," a laid-back country-blues mix; achieved recognition in 1970 when Eric Clapton recorded his song "After Midnight"; in 1972 released his debut album *Naturally;* wrote and recorded prolifically throughout the 1970s and early 1980s; had further success with songs recorded by other artists, including "Cocaine" and "I'll Make Love to You Anytime" (both recorded by Clapton) and "Call Me the Breeze" and "Bringing It Back" (both recorded by Lynyrd Skynyrd); slowed his recording and touring pace considerably in the late 1980s and early 1990s, releasing an album *every few years* and performing only a few weeks a year.

Addresses: *Home*—San Diego, CA. *Record company*—Virgin Records, 338 North Foothill Rd., Beverly Hills, CA 90210.

albums for Shelter Records, most of which he produced himself in his studio. These albums followed in the footsteps of *Naturally,* which had a subtle, bluesy style. Most Cale songs were written in a minor key and used only two or three chord changes; occasionally Cale tossed in a faster, country-influenced piece. This style became Cale's signature, a fact he, perhaps not too seriously, has railed against. "I'd like to change," Cale told Dan Forte in an interview for *Musician* in 1981, "but you know what? You can't. Once you become, let's say, famous, you become stylized. You have to have a trademark, a bag, right? Up to that time you can imitate, you can be whoever you want to be. But once you're famous, it's really strange—you can't get out of your own bag."

Cale attributes that "bag" to his efforts to find a niche in the 1970s. When Cale started making songwriting and album deals in the 1970s, hard rock was the latest style. Rather than jump on the bandwagon, Cale took the opposite approach. "Rock 'n' roll in the late '60s and '70s, everybody was really standing on it," Cale explained to *Musician* in 1990. "But there was a hole in there, and I was trying to figure out how to make recordings and not get into anyone else's bag, so I kind of underplayed, and there wasn't anybody really underplaying at that time."

The strategy seemed to work. Cale's albums, such as the 1974 release *Okie* and 1981's *Shades,* found a moderate-sized audience, and his songwriting talents were being used by a number of artists. Although Cale's albums sold enough to ensure future contracts, they never broke into the upper strata of the charts. Cale attributed this lukewarm popularity to the rough condition of his recordings, which for the most part he produced and engineered himself. Because he saw his albums primarily as demos for his songwriting, he felt they did not need the slickness required to make them popular on the radio.

Cale worked prolifically for a decade, recording eight albums between 1972 and 1983. However, once Cale had achieved moderate fame and fortune, he backed away from what he considered a too-hectic career. In 1983 Cale got out of his contract with Mercury Records and into what he called "semi-retirement." With steady money coming in from his songs "Call Me the Breeze," "After Midnight," and "Cocaine," Cale stopped recording for several years.

Cale returned in 1990 with *Travel-Log,* which he described to *Musician* in 1990 as "basically the same old music, it's just that I'm a little fresher now because I've had a rest." *Travel-Log,* released by Silvertone/BMG, was well received, and Cale followed it at a relatively slow pace with *Number 10* in 1992. Two years later, Cale finished his 11th album, *Closer to You,* which had the familiar "Tulsa sound" and rough finish of his previous albums. However, Virgin had hopes that Closer to You would benefit from the trend toward rougher, lo-fi recordings and would reach a wider audience than Cale's recordings usually did.

Cale himself seemed unconcerned about his album's fate with the public. "I just try to get my music out to other musicians who need new material, rather than to the public, like the record company wants me to," Cale told Jim Bessman for *Billboard* in 1994. "I never polish my albums—when somebody records my songs, they're generally more accessible to the public than my records are." And because he never expected to make a living with music, Cale has said he is happy with how his career has gone. "I'm still in business, even if I never got up in the big time," he explained to Bessman. "But that's a kind of blessing. I thought I'd be selling shoes by now." Having spent several decades doing what he loves most, J.J. Cale has been content to influence rock rather than capture the spotlight himself.

Selected discography

(As the Leathercoated Minds) A Trip Down the Sunset Strip, Viva, 1968.
Naturally, Shelter, 1972.
Really, Shelter, 1973.

Okie, Shelter, 1974.
Troubadour, Mercury, 1976.
5, Shelter, 1980.
Shades, Shelter, 1981.
Grasshopper, Mercury, 1982.
#8, Mercury, 1983.
Special Edition, Mercury, 1984.
Travel-Log, Silvertone/BMG, 1990.
Number 10, Silvertone/BMG, 1992.
Closer to You, Virgin, 1994.

Sources

Billboard, July 16, 1994.
Entertainment Weekly, August 26, 1994.
Guitar Player, March 1990; June 1990.
Musician, July 1981; November 1990; November 1994.
Rolling Stone, August 20, 1981; June 20, 1982; February 22,
    1990.
Spin, December 1994.

Additional information for this profile was provided by Virgin
Records publicity materials, 1994.

—Susan Windisch Brown

Sheila Chandra

Singer

Photograph by Sheila Rock, courtesy of Real World Records

Born in London, England of Indian parents, Sheila Chandra did not greatly identify with her Indian origins as a youth. Yet her ethnic heritage would later play a great role in her vocal work. Like most adolescents she wanted to assimilate into the culture that surrounded her—and perhaps had little choice—attending a British school in which no Asians of any sort were enrolled aside from Chandra and her sister. Thus as a teenager, influential years for many pop singers, Sheila Chandra's musical consumption consisted of British pop and soul hits.

Chandra's exposure to show business began early. For two years, beginning at age 13, she starred in a popular British Broadcasting Corporation TV series called "Grange Hill." Then, at age 16, she joined with Steve Coe and Martin Smith to form Monsoon, a band intent on making Asian pop fusion music with a largely acoustic sound. Monsoon's first single, "Ever So Lonely" broke into the British top ten and was followed quickly by another single, "Shakti (The Meaning of Within)" which also sold well. No doubt Chandra's strikingly exotic appearance added to public interest.

While Monsoon's label, Mercury/Phonogram, "felt that they [Monsoon] should continue to remake the hits they just made," as Joe Compton wrote in *Dirty Linen* magazine in 1993, the band wasn't interested. They were determined to explore and experiment with Indian sounds and so the label association ended. However, Coe, Martin and Chandra stuck together and would make five Sheila Chandra solo LPs. The albums appeared on Coe and Chandra's Indipop label, which had been formed for that purpose.

All this took place before Chandra turned 20. The first Indipop album was the aptly-titled *Out On My Own* in 1983, which reached the top 40 in Scandinavia. Thereafter came *Quiet,* followed by *Nada Brahma* and *The Struggle* in 1985. These albums featured the usual Western instruments, alongside traditional Indian instrumentation—for example sitar, clay pot-shaped drums and the somewhat bongo-like drums called tablas. By the time of *Quiet,* all traces of Chandra's incarnation as Monsoon's vocalist had disappeared. This album featured little in the way of lyrics, consisting rather of *bols* music, a traditional South Indian form that consists of singing the rhythmical notes assigned to the tablas, which, in India, only the men perform.

The demanding pace of Chandra's early TV work, followed by her work with Monsoon and then a spate of the four solo albums led to a decision by Coe and Chandra, who married in 1985, to withdraw for a time. They moved to the famed and lovely Lake District of England. There, Chandra dedicated herself to some of

For the Record . . .

Born 1965, London, England, of Indian parents.
Found success as a teenager, starring in a popular BBC-TV show. At age 17, began performing with a largely acoustic band Monsoon, which delivered Indian-influenced pop and made several strong-selling singles. Monsoon split with record company, Mercury/Phonogram, in 1982. Chandra along with her eventual husband and fellow Monsoon member Steve Coe, went on to record a number of solo Sheila Chandra albums on their own label, Indipop. In the early 1990s Chandra moved to the Real World label, recording *Weaving My Ancestor's Voices* and *Zen Kiss*. In 1995, Real World re-issued Sheila Chandra's Indipop albums.

Addresses: *Record company*—Real World/Caroline 114 West 26th Street, New York, NY 10001.

the reflection and growth she had been singing about. When she emerged with *Roots and Wings* in 1989, the content reflected the listening Chandra had been doing to sources as varied as eastern European singing, southeast Asian song and, of course, classical Indian music—though she shunned Indian film or pop music.

Celtic music also now seemed an influence on Chandra as evidenced by her rendition of "Lament of McCrimmon" on *Roots and Wings.* This taste for folk music of the British Isles continued into her 1993 album *Weaving My Ancestor's Voices,* which included the song "Donalogue" and also the British folksong "Enchantment." Chandra found some lyrics in both these songs demeaning to women and did not hesitate to rewrite the words to fit her idea of a more proper vision. Folk music is a music that evolves to reflect the culture, Chandra reasoned, and this justified modernizing. Chandra not only found influence in the old songs of Britain but also in its current female bards, such as June Tabor, Maddy Prior and Sandy Denny.

Chandra's attention to more widespread cultural influences did not mean abandonment of her Indian *bols* singing, but she would now play with that tradition, improvising non-traditional patterns, for instance. In *Zen Kiss,* which appeared in 1994, her *bols* singing had evolved considerably. As Iris Brooks wrote in *Rhythm Music Magazine* in 1994, "the bols serve only as starting points, to which Chandra adds a multitude of other vocal sounds: bird songs, counting in Hindi and Finnish, parodies of commercial advertisements and elocution exercises and snippets of nonsense syllables." Yet,

Brooks concluded, these pieces were not simply "world scat improvisations," but sounded like carefully assembled sampling work. However, Chandra did not use studio-sampling techniques. On this point, Brooks notes, Sheila Chandra calls these works "post-sampling compositions" and explained that "I wouldn't have written them if I hadn't heard what people are doing with samplers."

In 1992 Chandra joined that year's WOMAD tour, her first real work as a stage performer, and drew the attention of Peter Gabriel's label, Real World. Garbed in traditional dress and wearing the *bindi,* a dot of color on the forehead that marks one's status as a married woman in Indian culture, Chandra often knelt on a cushion while singing, the force of her performance giving rise to a series of expressive gestures. That year she worked on the album *Weaving My Ancestor's Voices,* which incorporated the sound of her minimally accompanied live performance.

Riding the crest of the 1990s strong interest in world music, her album quickly became the best seller in the Real World arsenal and attracted many U.S. fans, particularly on the west coast. New elements or influences present in this sound, which depended less on backing tapes and other musicians, included Andalusian, Moorish, and Arabic music. Yet Chandra's song structures were more clearly Western. Following the album, *Zen Kiss,* in 1995 Real World reflecting interest in Chandra and the label's commitment to her work, reissued all of Chandra's original Indipop recordings.

Selected discography

Ever So Lonely, Phonogram, 1982 (a single).
Third Eye, Phonogram, 1983.
Out On My Own, Indipop, 1984.
Quiet, Indipop, 1984.
The Struggle, Indipop, 1985.
Nada Brahma, Indipop, 1985.
Roots and Wings, Indipop, 1990.
Silk, Indipop, 1990 (a sampler of earlier recordings).
Weaving My Ancestors' Voices ,Real World, 1993.
The Zen Kiss, Real World, 1994.

Sources

Periodicals

Dirty Linen, February/March, 1993.
Pulse!, September, 1995.
Rhthym Music Magazine, Number 7, 1994.

Additional information was obtained from Caroline Records publicity materials.

—*Joseph M. Reiner*

The Chenille Sisters

Folk group

The Chenille Sisters insist that they *are* sisters, it's just that they have different parents. Their voices blend like siblings—à la the Andrew, Boswell, and McGarrigle sisters—and their music is very reminiscent of the sound of those girl groups. Their own moniker shows their identification with sister bands, as well as with groups like the Nylons and the Chiffons: they've memorialized chenille, the soft and nubby fabric of bathrobes and grandmothers' bedspreads. Related or not, these three women have slowly and carefully made a name for themselves—first across the Midwest and then throughout the nation—as hilarious and talented songstresses.

The Chenilles are Cheryl Dawdy, Connie Huber, and Grace Morand. They hail from Ann Arbor, Michigan, where they still live when they're not touring, which they seem to do constantly. Dawdy began her music career as a "folkie," writing ballads and performing in coffee houses. By day she was a library assistant at the University of Michigan. Huber, an accomplished guitar player and percussionist, sang with rock and country-

Photograph by Ameen Howrani, courtesy of Donna Zajonc Management

For the Record . . .

Members include **Cheryl Dawdy**, vocals; **Connie Huber**, vocals and guitar; and **Grace Morand**, vocals.

Band formed in Ann Arbor, MI, 1985. Performed on *Prairie Home Companion* radio show, 1985; released *The Chenille Sisters* on their own Frou-Frou Records label, 1986; signed by Red House Records, 1988.

Selected awards Parents' Choice Gold Award and National Association of Independent Record Distributors (NAIRD) Children's Recording of the Year, both 1990, for *1,2,3, for Kids*.

Addresses: *Record company*—Red House Records, P.O. Box 4044, St. Paul, MN 55104. *Management*—Donna Zajonc Management, P.O. Box 7023, Ann Arbor, MI 48107.

western bands. Her day job was as a speech therapist. Morand, a hair stylist by profession, performed in musicals and studied opera in her spare time.

Huber and Dawdy had once worked together on a show, and later Morand and Huber started up a little band for fun. They performed Motown hits, Bonnie Raitt covers, and the like, but when they decided they wanted to sing Aretha Franklin's "Respect," Huber insisted she couldn't do the "Sock-it-to me" backing vocals by herself. They recruited Dawdy and on March 17, 1985, gave their first performance. The threesome settled on their name, as Morand told *Dirty Linen*, because "we ended up deciding that we wanted to be sisters. We felt that we had a natural blend of voices and we shared the same vision. We wanted to be the "'Something' Sisters," and chenille is comfy and down-home and pokes fun at established older groups."

Big Break on *Prairie Home Companion*

During the early years of their career, the Chenilles were considered a lesser imitation of those other established groups. But their live shows were so well loved by Ann Arbor audiences that their reputation kept growing. This gave them the confidence to make a homemade tape and send it off to Garrison Keillor's *Prairie Home Companion* radio show. The long shot paid off: they were invited to appear in the first of several live spots from the *Prairie Home Companion* listening audience. As a re-

sult, the Chenilles recorded their own album with loans from investor-friends. *The Chenille Sisters* was released on their own Frou-Frou Records label in 1986.

In 1988 the Chenilles were signed by the small but prestigious Red House Records label. That same year, they released their second album, *At Home with the Chenille Sisters*. "Although some have casually dismissed the Chenilles as a conglomeration of the best ideas of better artists, they are beginning to move as peers into the ranks of those same performers," wrote Harmen Mitchell in the *Ann Arbor News*. "The Chenilles may have gotten attention initially by mingling a wide array of girl-group harmonies with the pseudo-sarcastic wit of Seattle's Uncle Bonsai and New York's Christine Lavin, but there is evidence on their new album that a great deal of effort is being exerted to move the group beyond its reliance on the wit of others, in order to spotlight their own songwriting and arranging talents."

Singing for Kids

Mitchell wasn't the only one to recognize the Chenilles' growth. The group's next recording represented their first foray into children's music. *1,2,3, for Kids* received the coveted 1990 Parents' Choice Gold Award, was named Children's Recording of the Year by the National Association of Independent Record Distributors (NAIRD), and went on to become one of Red House Records' biggest selling recordings ever. "The Chenilles pulled out all the stops ... creating an irresistible recording that works on many levels," wrote D. L. Mabery in *Raising Minnesota*. "Quite unlike children's singers that arrange their songs with enough sugar coating to induce diabetes, the Chenilles keep an ear on today's pop music." *1,2,3, for Kids* even inspired an *Utne Reader* contributor to write: "These women may be Michigan's best contribution to music since Motown blew out for the coast."

The *Washington Post's* Geoffrey Himes found the Chenilles' fourth album, *Mama, I Wanna Make Rhythm*, "their most ambitious outing yet. With their peppy, unapologetic odes to "Chocolate" and "Big Hair" and their transformation of the lyric "La-la-la-la Bamba" into "Listen to Your Mama," they should satisfy their old fans' demands for laughs. Yet it's the more straightforward songs where the Chenilles show the most growth." A *Boston Herald* reviewer, however, did not agree. "When the Chenilles switch gears and get serious, they're lost. Their acoustic-based sound isn't distinctive enough to carry serious songs about lost love and depression. When [they] play for comedy, they soar. But when the subject is soap-opera drama, these sisters sink."

The year 1992 saw the release of the Chenilles' second children's album, *The Big Picture and Other Songs for Kids. Detroit News* contributor Ellyce Field called it "the kind of recording you'll want to swipe from your kids and play on your way to work." In addition to their kids' concerts, the Chenille Sisters began a PBS radio show called *Read to Me,* sponsored by the Borders Books and Music store chain. This serialized book review program, launched in 1995, takes young people on a journey through the pages of selected children's titles, with each four-minute segment devoted to a different book.

Back in the grown-up sphere, the Chenilles continued to branch out, releasing *Whatcha Gonna Swing Tonight?* in 1992. Backed by James Dapogny's Chicago Jazz Band, with whom the Chenilles had been touring on and off for years, the trio sings a combination of better and lesser known swing era favorites like "Goody-Goody," "Sentimental Journey," "Nagasaki," and "Little White Lies." Grover B. Proctor, Jr., of the *Saginaw News* found that "the combination of Dapogny's musical history tour of the first 50 years of jazz with the Chenille's original, hip, witty, harmonic commentaries on modern life was just too wonderful not to love." *Rapport* declared, "This is very special!"

Makin' Rhythm

In 1994 the Chenilles were "back to their same old goofy, lovable selves with their seventh album, *True to Life,*" according to the *Philadelphia Inquirer.* "In a word, 'fantastic!'" enthused *Victory Review.* "These three voices can melt your heart.... You can never guess what might come next on this album, but you listen, laugh, cry and wait. Just like reading a good book, you look forward to the next chapter."

In 1995 the Chenilles were the subject of a PBS television special called *The Chenille Sisters: Makin' Rhythm.* This exposure helped them along the road to reaching the ultimate goal that Morand voiced in *Dirty Linen:* "We want to keep doing what we are doing but on a much larger scale.... We wouldn't mind being—I don't want to say a household word, I don't think we wanted to be mainstream like Madonna or Michael Jackson—but there is an alternative audience out there who we haven't yet reached, and I think that we can." The fact that, while visiting Ann Arbor, American first family members Hillary and Chelsea Clinton asked reporters, "Isn't this where the Chenilles are from?," suggests that they're definitely a common enough name in *some* households.

Selected discography

On Red House Records, except as noted

The Chenille Sisters, Frou-Frou Records, 1986.
At Home with the Chenille Sisters, 1988.
1,2,3, for Kids, 1990.
Mama, I Wanna Make Rhythm (includes "Chocolate," "Big Hair," and "Listen to Your Mama"), 1991.
The Big Picture and Other Songs for Kids, 1992.
Whatcha Gonna Swing Tonight? (includes "Goody-Goody," "Sentimental Journey," "Nagasaki," and "Little White Lies"), 1992.
True to Life, 1994.
Haute Chenille, 1995.

Sources

Ann Arbor News (Ann Arbor, MI), December 9, 1988; December 10, 1988.
Billboard, January 14, 1989.
Boston Herald, April 26, 1991.
CD Review, December 1989.
Chicago Tribune, February 3, 1989.
Columbus Dispatch, March 13, 1995.
Detroit News, December 16, 1988; October 9, 1992.
Dirty Linen, February 1995.
Edmonton Journal (Edmonton, Alberta, Canada), October 31, 1992.
Evening Observer (Dunkirk/Fredonia, NY), April 3, 1992.
Folk Roots, August 1989.
Janesville Gazette, April 27, 1995.
Kennebec Journal (Augusta, ME), October 10, 1992.
Milwaukee Journal, March 3, 1989.
Muskegon Chronicle (Muskegon, MI), June 27, 1994.
People, February 13, 1989; September 2, 1991.
Philadelphia Inquirer, August 27, 1993; December 2, 1994.
Raising Minnesota, April 1990.
Rapport, January 1993.
Saginaw News (Saginaw, MI), June 14, 1993.
San Francisco Bay Guardian, August 9, 1989.
School Library Journal, September 1990.
Sing Out, February 1995.
Utne Reader, January 1991.
Victory Review, January 1995.
Washington Post, January 13, 1989; May 7, 1991; December 2, 1994.

Additional information for this profile was taken from a United Press International release dated January 27, 1989, and from Red House Records publicity materials, 1992 and 1994.

—Joanna Rubiner

Cinderella

Rock band

The career path of the Philadelphia/southern New Jersey heavy metal act Cinderella seems to have been stolen right out of a rock and roll fairy tale. The bar band was discovered by Jon Bon Jovi (when he was at the height of his own popularity with his hard rock band, Bon Jovi), and Cinderella's 1986 debut, *Night Songs,* would sell 30 million copies worldwide within a three-year span—without a hit single. This was a first in rock music history. "More than anything, Cinderella was the right band at the right time," wrote *Newsday* critic John Milford. He called the band "an '80s version of Aerosmith that arrived just in front of a flood of acts (from Guns N' Roses to Metallica) [who] subsequently combined to give hard rock and/or heavy metal immense commercial clout."

The actual origins of Cinderella are somewhat murky. It is certain, however, that vocalist and guitarist Tom Keifer played in a number of cover bands up and down the East Coast bar circuit, and for a time he was so destitute he slept in his Plymouth Duster, ate boxed grits, and pilfered from a cornfield in the area. By 1985

Photograph by Barry Morgenstein, Gamma-Liaison Network

he had settled in Philadelphia and was working with fellow aspiring musician Eric Brittingham. The two delivered film to developing outlets during the day and rehearsed and gigged together by night. In order to break out of the go-nowhere bar scene of Philadelphia and South Jersey, Keifer and Brittingham knew they would have to come up with original material, not just perform endless covers of Led Zeppelin and Black Sabbath tunes like their competition. Slowly they built up a repertoire of original material; eventually they became the house band at a bar called the Galaxy in South Jersey. They also ventured often into Philadelphia to play at a club called the Empire.

Discovered by Jon Bon Jovi

One night in 1985, Cinderella found themselves playing at a bar where Jon Bon Jovi was in the audience. The singer liked what he heard and told this to the person at PolyGram Records who had kickstarted Bon Jovi's career. The rocker urged label representative Derek Shulman to search for the demo tape that Cinderella had sent PolyGram. Shulman located it in the New York office, gave it a listen, and soon PolyGram approached Cinderella with contract in hand—but with one stipulation. The label didn't like the band's drummer and guitarist, forcing Keifer and Brittingham to can them. Drummer Fred Coury and guitarist Jeff LaBar signed on as replacements and Cinderella headed into the studio.

The result was Cinderella's debut album, *Night Songs*, released in 1986. A collection of power-chord rockers with a few ballads sandwiched in between, the rapid success of the record surprised almost everyone. Cinderella seemed to have entered the fray just as musical tastes were taking a new direction, reflected in the heavy metal mass-marketed to teens via MTV. A video of the track "Shake Me" introduced the band to legions of young fans, who in turn bought the album in droves. The relatively unknown band also managed to get airplay on album-oriented rock stations. Keifer and his bandmates did their part to spur sales with record store appearances and radio interviews. The results were apparent—at one point *Night Songs* was selling 50,000 to 60,000 copies a week.

Huge Sales and Elaborate Tours

"Cinderella is a straightforward hard-rock band, the most unfashionable genre in rock-and-roll," wrote *Chicago Tribune* writer Ken Tucker as *Night Songs* held court on the charts. "Cinderella's tunes are more melodic than most hard-rock material—and unlike many such outfits, lead singer Keifer actually sings well, with range and expression—but the music has the volume and aggressiveness that the young, predominantly teenage hard-rock audience craves." Cinderella was paired with established metal acts such as Bon Jovi, AC/DC, and David Lee Roth, hitting the road steadily for much of the year following their debut in order to build up a loyal fan base.

In the summer of 1988 Cinderella released their sophomore effort, *Long Cold Winter*. It generally recreated the successful formula of the debut, but with a bit more of a bluesy feel injected into it. In less than half a year the record had sold 25 million copies globally. More extensive touring followed, and by 1989 the group was headlining near-sell-out shows. Cinderella had reached the apex of heavy-metal stardom. Getting equipment from venue to venue required six trucks and an enormous crew. The band's live show included a fake snowfall, which drifted down for the rendition of *Long Cold Winter*'s title track; at the onset of another number, Keifer and the grand piano he was playing were gently lowered onstage. *Billboard* writer Scott Brodeur saw the show in Philadelphia, noting some technical flaws in the overall production. Yet Brodeur declared that the band "was able to overcome those awkward moments," and "on crunchy rockers like ... 'Nobody's Fool,' Keifer's wheeze-till-ya-bleed vocals and blues-based guitar runs cut through sharply."

Cinderella took a break after the *Long Cold Winter* dates. Keifer constructed a 24-track home studio and spent months experimenting with it. This sharpened his production skills, and by the time Cinderella went into the studio to record their third album, Keifer had already laid down the backbone of *Heartbreak Station*. The record marked a departure for the band, one that seemed to aim for pure hard rock, with much less of the metal thunder. Keifer even augmented his electric guitar with a series of instruments that included mandolin, slide guitar, mandocello, and dobro. He also utilized his extensive collection of vintage electric guitars for the recording sessions.

The title track from *Heartbreak Station* was produced with the help of one of Cinderella's idols, former Led Zeppelin bassist John Paul Jones. He arranged and conducted a 30-piece orchestra for the cut, and "Jones' touch [invested] a dramatic tension reminiscent of his former band," wrote Peter Cronin in *Musician.* With this record, "eagerness to grow as a band and increased studio savvy helped Cinderella strip away several layers of pretense," Cronin opined, going so far as to compare the song "Heartbreak Station" to the classic 1969 Rolling Stones tune "Love in Vain." John Leland of *Newsday* also remarked on the change of direction for the band. "After years of playing bland, generic lite-metal fluff ... the group sounds revitalized by its turn toward generic bluesy boogie," he wrote. Leland went on to call the album "all twang and pedal steel guitar and lofty American myth." *Heartbreak Station,* he concluded, "is rigidly formal, but the forms are right, and Cinderella plays them with the conviction of the young."

Heavy Metal Wanes, Sales Decline

Cinderella's new sound appealed to an audience that was also maturing, as evidenced by declining heavy metal sales. After only a few weeks, the album had entered *Billboard's* pop Top 20 and the first single, "Shelter Me," climbed quickly, despite the critical disparagement that frequently met the band. "I can pick up a snooty magazine and read a review written by one guy," Keifer told Cronin in *Musician.* "That's one person. Who cares? We're the ones that have to be happy with what we're playing." Unfortunately, by 1994 the band's fan base had begun to decline in earnest. The band released *Still Climbing,* another slice of the more bluesy side of rock and roll, but it received little attention. Hair bands, as Cinderella and its ilk were called, had all but fallen out of fashion. The emergence of the heavy "grunge" sound spearheaded in Seattle had rung the genre's death knell at the decade's dawn.

By the mid-1990s little had been heard from Cinderella; reports intimated that they had broken up and that Keifer was planning to pursue a solo career. To his credit, Keifer had always seemed ready to stretch the boundaries of the style in which Cinderella worked. "I don't ever want to come out with an album that people press play and say, 'Oh, that again,'" Keifer had told *Billboard* writer Elianne Halbersberg in 1991. "I want to always grow and maintain the attitude and energy that they like about us in the first place. It's real important to me that we not repeat ourselves, but always move on. The bands I loved—Zeppelin, the Stones—never stood in one place. I hope we always keep people pleasantly surprised."

Selected discography

On Mercury/PolyGram Records

Night Songs, 1986.
Long Cold Winter, 1988.
Heartbreak Station, 1991.
Still Climbing, 1994.

Sources

Amusement Business, March 25, 1989.
Billboard, May 20, 1989; January 26, 1991.
Chicago Tribune, October 16, 1986.
Entertainment Weekly, December 2, 1994.
Los Angeles Times, April 29, 1989.
Musician, February 1991; March 1991.
Newsday (Long Island, NY), April 28, 1989; December 16, 1990.
People, March 4, 1991.

—Carol Brennan

Collective Soul

Rock band

Photograph by Evan Agostini, Gamma-Liaison Network

As Collective Soul's recognition moved beyond their hometown of Stockbridge, Georgia, the media and the record industry said the band came up out of nowhere—they were an overnight success. But their lead singer and guitarist, Ed Roland, knows their "overnight success" was more than 12 years in the making.

Ed Roland and his brother, guitarist Dean Roland, grew up in a very strict household. Their father, Eddie Roland, was a southern Baptist minister, while their mother, Lynette, taught children with special needs. Until the boys became teenagers, the only rock n' roll they heard came from Elvis Presley and Jerry Lee Lewis records. But Eddie Roland often used music to minister to his church, and his sons Ed and Dean both became interested in playing guitar.

After graduating from high school, Ed Roland moved to Boston for a year to study at the renowned Berklee School of Music. When he returned to Stockbridge, he landed a job at a local recording studio, which he used to record his own music during the studio's off-hours. In the late 1980s, Roland, lead guitarist Ross Childress, and drummer Shane Evans played in a band called Marching Two Step.

In 1992 Roland, Childress, and Evans left Marching Two Step to form a new group called Collective Soul. They named the band after a concept from the classic novel The Fountainhead by Ayn Rand. Even before the days of Marching Two Step, Roland had sent demo tapes to every major label, hoping for a break. Year after year, he received rejections. In November of 1992, Collective Soul played a showcase for several of the big record companies—still to no avail. "We had done all these conventions, and had record people flying to see us, and no one took interest," Ed Roland told RIP magazine. "Basically, I had just had enough of the whole thing. So I told the guys, 'I'm dissolving the band—I do not want to do it anymore.'"

Radio Sparked Recognition

Roland spent the first three months of 1993 sequestered in the basement studio of his manager's house. He had decided that if he couldn't make it as a performer after 12 years of trying, he would attempt to get a publishing deal and sell his songs to other artists. He recorded a brand new set of songs for his demo and started sending them out.

While he was shipping out the demos, he went ahead and sent a copy to Georgia State University's radio station, WRAS, under the name Brothers and Brides.

For the Record . . .

Members include **Ross Childress**, lead guitar; **Shane Evans**, drums; **Dean Roland**, guitar; **Ed Roland**, vocals and guitar; and **Will Turpin**, bass guitar.

Band formed in Stockbridge, GA, in 1992, and disbanded until mid-1993. Debut album, *Hints Allegations and Things Left Unsaid*, released independently, 1993; rereleased on Atlantic Records, 1994. First single, "Shine," spent eight weeks at Number One on the AOR charts. *Collective Soul* released on Atlantic, 1995.

Selected Awards: Billboard Music Award for best rock song, 1996, for "December."

Addresses: *Record company*—Atlantic Records, 9229 Sunset Blvd., Los Angeles, CA 90069.

The station started playing the song "Shine," and Roland's project began to gain local attention. In September and October of 1993, he got Evans, Childress, his brother Dean, and longtime friend and bassist Will Turpin together for some live performances. By the end of the year, the band decided to stay together and record under the name Collective Soul. They added three of the songs they recorded in Marching Two Step to Roland's existing demo and released the CD *Hints Allegations and Things Left Unsaid* on the independent Rising Storm label.

Once again, Collective Soul sent their new CD to major record labels and received more rejections. But they also shipped the album to radio stations all over the country. Soon, many other radio stations joined WRAS in playing "Shine," and the band's popularity skyrocketed.

Shock and Success

By February of 1994, Atlantic Records had signed the band to a record contract. Atlantic remixed the CD and released it on their label just two months later, eliminating only one of the original songs. "Shine" became a gold single and spent eight weeks on top of the AOR charts. Roland's 12-year effort had come to fruition. "We were very shocked," he said in the band's press bio. "I was hoping to sell 10-20,000 records, just enough to make a real Collective Soul album."

The group spent the next few months touring and in August of 1994 celebrated a week of career excitement.

"It was probably the biggest week of our lives," Roland recalled in the press packet interview. "Wednesday we played in Toronto and got presented our Canadian platinum record. Friday we played Woodstock '94—sharing the stage with some of our favorite bands. The following Monday we started our opening tour with Aerosmith. And two days later we were certified platinum in the States. It was like one big blur.... I woke up Thursday morning shaking, asking myself, 'What's gonna happen today?'"

The whirlwind kept going throughout the rest of 1994. Collective Soul released the single "Breathe" in October. The band performed on *The Late Show with David Letterman* even though Roland's guitar amp had blown up before they went on. And they recorded a new song called "Gel" for *The Jerky Boys* film soundtrack.

Collective Collaboration

The group decided to self-title their second album—which was released in the spring of 1995—since they saw it as their first "official" album as a band. *Hints* compiled Ed Roland's songs, but *Collective Soul* represented the entire group's effort. The band's megahit, "December," showcased their musical versatility. "'December' is a much moodier song [than 'Shine']," Roland explained in the band's press biography. "We wanted people to know that there's a different side to us." The song went on to capture the *Billboard* Music Award for best rock song.

After the release of *Collective Soul*, the band hit the touring circuit once again, opening for rock veterans Van Halen. Two months later, they went out on their own, headlining smaller venues as the success of their first "official" album soared. Though a few members of the press predicted Collective Soul would be a "one-hit wonder" with "Shine," the group had proved them wrong. After a dozen years of working for their success, the band wasn't about to give up that easily—nor did they take it for granted. "When I start feeling down, I feel like I'm being selfish because there are so many people out there who wish they could be doing what we're doing," noted Roland. "I worked hard to be in this position for many years, and I'm very thankful to be here. I won't take it for granted. It could be a lot worse."

Selected discography

Hints Allegations and Things Left Unsaid, Rising Storm, 1993, reissued, Atlantic, 1994.
Collective Soul, Atlantic, 1995.

Sources

Billboard, May 14, 1994; October 1, 1994.

Bone, May 1995.

Detroit Free Press, May 6, 1994.

Entertainment Weekly, May 27, 1994; March 17, 1995.

Guitar, June 1995; July 1995.

Musician, December 1994.

RIP magazine, September 1994.

Rolling Stone, July 14, 1994; December 29, 1994-January 12, 1995; June 15, 1995.

Sassy, July 1995.

Seattle Times, June 24, 1994.

Stereo Review, June 1995.

Additional information for this profile was obtained from Atlantic Records press material, 1995.

—Sonya Shelton

Sean "Puffy" Combs

Producer, record company executive

AP\Wide World Photos

Sean "Puffy" Combs bends the ear of the rap and hip-hop community with intriguing releases, combining his production savvy with relentless promotion. The 24-year-old Combs runs Bad Boy Entertainment, a division of Arista Records, and stands behind several gold and platinum artists, chief among them the Notorious B.I.G., Craig Mack, and Mary J. Blige. His reputation among his R&B peers is that of an aggressive promoter with an ear for the street and the music created there. Despite his impressive credits, Combs's stature was threatened following nine deaths at an event he had organized. While the tragedy threatened to forever mar his career, Combs turned the setback around, emerging as a sought-after producer of hit singles and videos, ready to bring his efforts to a wider audience.

Combs earned notice in New York's hip-hop scene at the age of 19. He landed an internship at Uptown Records after being recommended by local rapper Heavy D. Uptown, affiliated with MCA Records, was then headed by Andre Harrell, himself an ex-rapper with the group Dr. Jekyll and Mr. Hyde. Combs's tenure as an intern was brief—roughly three months—before he was selected to head Uptown's Artists & Repertoire (A&R) department, a prestigious posting as this is the department that discovers and signs talent. "He was cool and energetic and I brought him in. He learned fast," remarked Curt Woodly, former head of A&R at Uptown, in the *New York Times.* As chief of A&R, Combs managed talent and helped artists choose and produce their releases. He also became known as a fiery and obstinate young man, making a few enemies along the way.

Deadly Accident Threatens Career

His musical interests not satiated by his work at the label, Combs also staged hip-hop parties in Manhattan clubs, something he had been doing since his days at Howard University in Washington, D. C. It was one of these events that brought Combs down in a matter of minutes. Combs arranged a charity basketball game with teams composed of rap and hip-hop stars to be played in a City College of New York (CCNY) gym in December, 1991. Anxious party-goers, unsure that they would be able to enter the already crowded venue, stormed the entrance. Nine were killed in the crush of bodies. When one man lost consciousness near Combs, he quickly began attempts to revive him. "His eyes were going to the back of his head. I could feel his death going inside of me," he told *Newsday.*

While an ensuing mayoral investigation dispensed blame to police, City College officials, Combs, his staff, and the crowd itself, Combs took the brunt of the blow. Media attacks centered on the fact that Combs had not insured the event, as required by his contract with CCNY, and that adequate security was not made available. Combs retreated to his Mt. Vernon, New York, home, depressed and angry over the event. He told *Newsday*, "It's hard to teach people to respect each other. All the security in the world won't achieve that. That has to come from inside."

Opportunity Followed Disaster

Combs was shuffled out of Uptown with a leave of absence that became permanent nearly a year after the CCNY incident. The split was difficult for Combs, who had come to view Harrell as more a mentor than a boss. Harrell had filled a role for Combs that had been vacant since his father was killed when he was three. He confided to *Rolling Stone*, "I was fired. It was like the old sensei [teacher] rejecting the student." The student, though, proved he had learned enough, signing a deal just two weeks later with Arista Records to form Bad Boy Entertainment. With Combs as president and his mother, Janice, acting as owner, Bad Boy was responsible for bringing new energy to a style of music already known for its intensity. "I like things harsh and basically different to the ear. I'm trying to think about what's not out there but still give you that same feel and vibe of the way kids are moving," he told *Rolling Stone*.

Bad Boy scored big with releases by cutting-edge performers Craig Mack and the Notorious B.I.G. Reportedly, Mack was homeless, subsisting on Long Island when Combs discovered him performing in a Manhattan club. B.I.G. was selling drugs and making demo tapes in a basement before one of them reached Combs. It is this ability to scour the streets for talent that sets Combs and Bad Boy apart from other labels. Combs is among an elite group of hip-hop producers and promoters with similar ties to large labels who have

succeeded in bringing new acts to prominence. These include Teddy Riley, Dallas Austin, and Jermaine Dupri. "Of course the record companies offer them these [custom] labels, because it's a cheap way to get the talent they couldn't find," commented Motown Records chairman Clarence Avant in *Newsweek* of Combs and his fellow hip-hop entrepreneurs

Maintained Street Connection

This sort of characterization aside, Combs sees himself and his company as a direct outlet for urban hip-hop. "I'm a student of the culture that I make music for. It's important to go out and vibe with the kids—to see what they're groovin' to and how they groove to it," he explained in *Billboard*. *Billboard* rap columnist Havelock Nelson told the *New York Times*, "He's one of the best young executives who is rolling with the big guys. Right now Puffy has his finger on the pulse of the music industry. Older executives could learn a lot from him." Bad Boy's offices are, in fact, graced by genuine hip-hop devotees, many straight from the street and hoping to bring the next rap superstar to the public eye. Surrounding himself with a young, aggressive staff brings fresh blood into the business and allows Combs to pass on to others the opportunities he had at Uptown.

While managing a burgeoning record label, producing hit records, and making videos, the ambitions Combs has also tried to break into acting. He is nonetheless best known as a top producer in a world that reveres producers nearly as much as artists. Bad Boy Entertainment planned to boost production to four projects a year by 1996. The success of singer Faith Evans in late 1995, facilitated by a well-organized label campaign, suggested that the company was keeping to its development schedule—and that Sean "Puffy" Combs was still on the rise.

Selected discography

As producer

Jodeci, *Forever My Lady*, Uptown, 1991.
Mary J. Blige, *What's the 411?*, Uptown, 1993.
Jodeci, *Diary of a Mad Band*, Uptown, 1993.
Mary J. Blige, *My Life*, Uptown, 1994.
Craig Mack, *Project: Funk Da World*, Bad Boy, 1994.
The Notorious B.I.G., *Ready to Die*, Bad Boy, 1994.
Raymond Usher, "Think of You," LaFace, 1994.
Faith Evans, *Faith*, Bad Boy, 1995.

Also producer of records by Supercat, 7669, Keith Sweat, and Caron Wheeler, among others.

Sources

Billboard, January 25, 1992; May 20, 1995.

Newsday (New York, NY), January 3, 1992; January 6, 1992; January 15, 1992; January 16, 1992.

Newsweek, May 8, 1995.

New York Times, January 5, 1992; January 16, 1992; November 6, 1994.

Rolling Stone, April 20, 1995.

Source, January 1995.

Schwann Spectrum, Summer 1995.

Washington Post, December 31, 1991.

—*Rich Bowen*

Julian Cope

Singer, songwriter

Photograph by Ed Sirrs, © 1994 American Recordings

In the mid-1990s, after almost two decades in the music business, Julian Cope had progressed from up-and-coming New Wave prankster to photogenic power-pop hero to a thought-provoking emeritus of the alternative era. His particular brand of songwriting, first honed in his early days fronting the Teardrop Explodes and later evidenced in the prolific releases of his solo career, has often found little appreciation outside of his native Great Britain; record companies have also run into difficulty trying to market Cope's talents. *Details* contributor Tom Hibbert called him "the last remaining Great English Eccentric of Rock" and likened him to Pink Floyd's forgotten founding member, the drug-soaked but brilliant Syd Barrett—a comparison that crops up frequently in discourses on Cope. *Chicago Sun-Times* music writer Jim DeRogatis described Cope's body of work as the meeting point of "psychedelia and punk. His songs are full of droning, otherworldly melodies and wistful lyrics," exemplified in the late 1960s works of the Beatles and Rolling Stones. "But," DeRogatis contended, "they also have the edgy energy of punks from the 13th Floor Elevators to the Sex Pistols."

Cope first ventured onto the exploding punk scene in England while a college student in Liverpool. In 1977 he formed a group called the Crucial Three along with Ian McCulloch, who went on to fame as the frontman for Echo and the Bunnymen. Cope's first live appearance was with the band at a Liverpool club in late 1978. By this time they had taken a new name from a comic book— the Teardrop Explodes. Their first record, *Kilimanjaro,* was released in late 1980 in England on Mercury Records and debuted the following year in the United States. Like much of Cope's early work, it was hailed by the British music press, sold well in England and Europe, but was virtually ignored in the American market.

First Solo Effort

Additionally, the excesses of the rock 'n' roll lifestyle began to take their toll on the Teardrop Explodes. "Everybody thinks, 'Oh, the Teardrop Explodes, they got famous and then they went mad,'" Cope told Hibbert in *Details.* "The Teardrops went mad *way* before they were famous." Cope became infamous himself for wild stage pranks that once included piercing his abdomen with a fractured microphone stand. The Teardrop Explodes disbanded in 1983 while working on their third record. Cope went solo, taking the band's drummer and guitarist with him when he recorded 1984's *World Shut Your Mouth.*

Cope had already written much of the material on *World Shut Your Mouth* for the aborted Teardrop Explodes album. Adam Sweeting of *Melody Maker* reviewed the

For the Record . . .

Born October 1957, in Deri, South Wales; married with children; wife's name, Dorian. *Education:* Studied education and drama in Liverpool, England, late 1970s.

Singer, songwriter, performer, recording artist, and author. Formed first band, the Crucial Three, 1977; renamed themselves the Teardrop Explodes, 1978; first live performance in Liverpool, England, November 1978; first single, "Sleeping Gas," released on Zoo Records, February 1979; signed with Mercury Records, c. 1979; began solo career, 1984, with release of *World Shut Your Mouth;* signed with Island Records, c. 1986; signed with American Recordings, 1994.

Addresses: *Home*—Wiltshire, England. *Record company*—American Recordings, Inc., 3500 W. Olive Ave., Suite 1550, Burbank, CA 91505.

solo effort and observed: "Spanning the sublime and the ridiculous with the ease of the truly uncritical, Julian Cope flies on (among other things) instinct, instability and incense." Sweeting decried some of the cuts for their lyrical silliness but noted, "The best bits of "World" do at least reaffirm Cope's addiction to the life-enhancing properties of pop fantasy (aural opiates)."

Later that year, Cope released his second solo album, *Fried.* On it, he let his quirky brilliance run full-throttle, prompting *Melody Maker* reviewer Steve Sutherland to call it "positively Shakespearean," adding, "all of it bristles with the exaggerated paranoia that transforms the most banal daily occurrence into something sinister and symbolic." Cope's convoluted takes on life—apparent on "Reynard the Fox" and "Sunspots"—were combined in a collection of tracks that Sutherland called "a greater variety of gorgeous tunes than any other album this year (his earlier 'World Shut Your Mouth' included)." Still, *Fried* garnered scant attention in the United States.

Signed with Island

Little was heard from Cope for the next year or so until the Island Records issue of the EP *World Shut Your Mouth* in late 1986, which coincided with Cope's signing with the label. Shortly thereafter, in 1987, *Saint Julian* was released in Britain. Cope finally made a name for himself in the States when the record reached American

shores. (*Saint Julian* includes the track "World Shut Your Mouth"—the first time the song appeared on a full-length album, despite the 1984 work of the same name.) Less verbally daunting and more melodic than his past efforts, the release received major media attention as well as considerable MTV airplay.

During the years off from recording and touring that preceded *Saint Julian,* the flamboyant Cope pulled himself together emotionally, focused his energies in a new direction, and gave up some of his experiments with mind-altering chemicals. He told *Melody Maker's* Helen FitzGerald: "It's the inevitable white Western male coming back down off his secluded, womb-like mountaintop and charging back into town with all the answers." *Rolling Stone* reviewer Parke Puterbaugh declared that nearly all of *Saint Julian's* cuts "hurtle forward with a concise sense of mission and barely containable energy.... He delivers feverish visions about God, death, sex and the universe, with a kind of cosmic giggle underlying it all."

Cope's next effort was 1988's *My Nation Underground,* whose first single was the love-obsession-tinged track "China Doll." The record, as noted in *The Trouser Press Record Guide,* shares similarities with *Saint Julian* in its accessibility, with the singer-songwriter "striking a brilliant balance between his dual personae as serious artiste and preening pop star." However, Cope's follow-up, *Skellington,* marked a return to his former sound, perhaps in part because the work was actually recorded around 1984. The collection of previously unreleased, mostly acoustic tunes showcased Cope's earlier trademark loopiness and penchant for wacky lyrics.

Cope claims that *Skellington* had not been issued in 1984 because he felt it too closely resembled *Fried,* but some industry insiders speculated that his label executives in England refused to issue the record because *Fried* failed commercially. On *Skellington,* Cope resurrected two tunes he had written for the Crucial Three— "Robert Mitchum," a paean to the macho American film star, and "Out of My Mind on Dope and Speed," a chronicle of self-abuse. Bob Stanley reviewed *Skellington* for *Melody Maker* and called it "classic Cope gobbledegook ... set to the sparest acoustic guitar/organ backing. And, of course, it's marvelous."

Cope's next full-length release was 1991's *Peggy Suicide.* The 75-minute recording was conceived as the initial installment in a series of concept albums, a lament against the environmental indignities inflicted upon the planet by civilization. Two tracks are diatribes against the pollution and the havoc wreaked by the automobile—and another relates Cope's experience swimming in the ocean with a dolphin—but the work also includes some straightforward pop tunes. "The best songs," wrote *Washington Post* contributor Mark Jenkins, "achieve an admirably relentless garage-rock groove." A *Stereo Review* panel slotted *Peggy Suicide* as one of the best recordings of the summer of 1991, and the critique lauded Cope's "bluesy, long-form psychedelia.... What keeps his kite from tearing loose and floating away is his grounding in the more succinct song structures of pop, the evocative type practiced by pioneers of the late Sixties."

Made a Statement with Concept Albums

The next installment in Cope's concept-album series was *Jehovahkill*, released in late 1992. By this time Cope had also embarked on a side project that began to consume his spare time—an investigation of the ancient stone monuments scattered around the British Isles, primitive monoliths of which Stonehenge is the most famous example. *Jehovahkill* is peppered with references to the stones, and *Spin* writer Ivan Kreilkamp called Cope's obsession "distressingly Spinal Tap—one would think no post-*Smell the Glove* rocker would dare to invoke ancient agronomic Druids as spiritual predecessors. But that's Cope's style." The lyrical content of *Jehovahkill* also touches on spirituality and contemporary religions as well as culturally determined gender roles.

Lengthy liner notes to *Jehovahkill* written by Cope attempt to explain some of his thoughts about the ancient peoples of the British Isles, the cross as a religious symbol, and the monoliths he was investigating. Despite the critical acclaim, however, Island Records unceremoniously dropped Cope soon after *Jehovahkill*'s U.K. release. He had just sold out a number of British tour dates, and the record stood at Number 20 on the charts there. "I had a lot of problems getting *Peggy Suicide* out the way that I wanted it," Cope told DeRogatis in the *Chicago Sun-Times,* "and with *Jehovahkill* they were even more hesitant.... I think people have a lot of preconceptions about what's difficult and what's obvious. I hear a lot of stuff that sounds like Nirvana nowadays, and I'm sure that *Nirvana* was a really difficult album until it sold 6 million copies."

During his time between labels—while several record companies were courting him—Cope worked on *The Modern Antiquarian,* his book about the stone monuments of the British Isles. He also issued two works through a mail-order company he founded called Ma-Gog Records. Eventually Cope signed with American Records, and the label execs were happy to let him have full control over his music. The result was 1994's *Autogeddon,* the third release in Cope's epic environmental opus. Cope took the title from a Heathcote Williams poem predicting the end of the world by auto emissions.

Autogeddon is filled with such tracks as "s.t.a.r.c.a.r." and "I Gotta Walk," in which Cope rails against the gasoline culture but acknowledges that he himself is part of the problem; apparently, this realization was what spurred him to write the songs. Cope told Craig Rosen of *Billboard* that he and his wife had been traveling a lot in their Range Rover, searching for "all the mystical sights in the world before some developer builds on top of them," and that inspired him to write *Autogeddon.* "You can be the most right-on person in the world, but by the mere fact that you exist you are killing something. There's no easy answers." *Pulse!* writer Scott Schinder called the record "a feral, deeply-felt epic that's a consistently riveting listen."

By mid-1995 Cope was working on an autobiography as well as a new album titled *Twenty Mothers*. His endurance in the alternative music industry and his distinct identity seemed to herald a promising future. And American Recordings seemed thrilled to have Cope on their roster of artists. "My dream is for Julian to have a 10-record catalog with American Recordings," label honcho Mark Geiger told *Billboard.* "If American can do anything for Julian, it is to explain to the world the history of Cope and how vital and important he is."

Selected discography

With the Teardrop Explodes

Kilimanjaro, Mercury, 1980.
Wilder, Mercury, 1981.
Piano (compilation), 1990.
Everybody Wants to Shag the Teardrop Explodes (compilation with previously unreleased material), Fontana, 1990.

Solo albums

World Shut Your Mouth, Mercury, 1984.
Fried, Mercury, 1984.
World Shut Your Mouth (EP), Island, 1986.
Saint Julian, Island, 1987.
My Nation Underground, Island, 1988.
Skellington, Island, 1989.
Droolian, Island, 1990.
Peggy Suicide, Island, 1991.
Floored Genius (compilation), Island, 1992.
Jehovahkill, Island, 1992.
Rite, K.A.K., 1993.
The Skellington Chronicles, K.A.K., 1993.
Queen Elizabeth, K.A.K., 1994.

Autogeddon, American, 1994.
Floored Genius 2: The Best of the BBC Sessions, 1983-91, Island, 1994.
Twenty Mothers, American, 1995.

Sources

Books

The Trouser Press Record Guide, 4th edition, edited by Ira Robbins, Collier Books, 1991.

Periodicals

Billboard, May 18, 1991; December 19, 1992; January 16, 1993; July 2, 1994.
Chicago Sun-Times, March 21, 1993.
Details, January 1993; March 1993.

Entertainment Weekly, August 12, 1994.
Independent, September 24, 1992; January 28, 1993.
Melody Maker, February 18, 1984,; November 1, 1986; July 8, 1989; February 3, 1990.
New York Times, June 29, 1991.
Pulse!, September 1994.
Rolling Stone, May 21, 1987; June 4, 1987; June 16, 1994; October 20, 1994.
Spin, May 1993.
Stereo Review, August 1991; October 1993.
Times (London), May 24, 1991; January 23, 1993.
Vox, September 1992.
Washington Post, June 26, 1991.

Additional information for this profile was obtained from promotional material provided by Mercury Records and American Records.

—*Carol Brennan*

Elizabeth Cotten

Singer, guitarist

M aking her debut as a folk singer at age 67, Elizabeth "Libba" Cotten played an important role in the folk-music revival of the 1950s with her unique style of guitar playing. "Freight Train," a song that she wrote when she was 12, is considered a folk classic, and her songs have been recorded by artists such as the Grateful Dead, Taj Mahal, and Peter, Paul, and Mary. Larry Sandberg and Dick Weissman wrote in *The Folk Music Sourcebook*, "Cotten has cultivated the most graceful and dignified of all finger-picking styles." As was noted in the *Penguin Encyclopedia of Popular Music*, "with elements of ragtime and gospel, [Cotten's] picking style became standard in folk guitar playing."

While Cotten's songs have been compared to the works of Mississippi John Hurt, John Jackson, and John Spence, her style of playing was truly her own. "Although influenced by others that she had heard, Elizabeth was a true, original source, going back to the turn of the century," said Dana Klipp, Cotten's accompanist in her later years, in *Acoustic Guitar*. "She was a link to that authentic style.... Her style of playing left-handed on

UPI/Corbis-Bettmann

For the Record . . .

Born January 5, c. 1892 (sources differ on exact year), in Chapel Hill, NC; died June 29, 1987, in Syracuse, NY; daughter of George and Louisa (Price) Nevills; married Frank Cotten (divorced); children: Lillie.

Wrote classic folk song "Freight Train" at age 12; worked as domestic servant and held other odd jobs; hired by musicologists Ruth Crawford Seeger and Charles Seeger, 1940s; recorded first album, *Elizabeth Cotten*, on Folkways label, 1957; secured partial rights to "Freight Train," 1957; performed in public for first time (with Mike Seeger), 1959; appeared at numerous folk festivals, including Newport Folk Festival, 1964; Smithsonian Festival of American Folklife, 1968-71, 1975; Washington Blues Festival, 1978; performed in Grass Roots Series video, *Old Time Music*, 1974; was guest performer at the Kennedy Center, Washington, D.C., 1975; appeared in "Me and Stella" documentary on PBS, 1977; was named the city's first "Living Treasure" after moving to Syracuse, NY, 1978; appeared at Carnegie Hall, New York, NY, 1978; toured with Taj Mahal in the U.S. and Europe, 1980s.

Selected awards: Burl Ives Award from National Folk Association, 1972; National Heritage Fellowship from National Endowment for the Arts, 1984; Grammy Award for best traditional folk music recording for *Elizabeth Cotten Live!*, 1985.

a right-handed guitar was unique, producing a sound unlike anything a right-handed player could simulate. This technique gives her music a softer, almost classical sound. A combination of her unparalleled technique and her custom of using light strings contribute to her sound."

Never Took a Lesson

Cotten grew up in a musical family in an area of North Carolina with a solid tradition of blues and church music. Her mother sang, and her uncles played the fiddle and banjo. By age seven Cotten would often sneak into her brother's room while he was at work and strum his homemade banjo. Not knowing the standard way to play the instrument, she strummed it with her left hand and held the frets with her right. "Say I'm a musician if you want to, but I didn't know one chord from another," said the entirely self-taught Cotten, according to *The Washingtonian*.

When her brother left home and took his instrument along, the 11-year-old Cotten quit school so that she could go to work and earn enough money to buy a guitar. She purchased her first instrument, a Stella Demonstrator guitar from Sears Roebuck, for $3.75. As with the banjo, Cotten played the guitar left-handed, further developing her method of picking that used just two fingers. She practiced relentlessly, much to the chagrin of her family. "My mother said, 'Now if you don't put that thing down, I'm gonna git ya,'" she was quoted as saying in *U.S. News & World Report*. "'I gotta get to sleep and to work in the mornin'.' And I just keep everybody awake all night. Lord have mercy. I was a nuisance."

Soon after learning to play the guitar, Cotten composed her famed "Freight Train" composition. Before long she could play a wide range of tunes that incorporated a variety of genres. "Influenced by the guitarists of the time, traveling musicians, medicine shows, minstrel shows, and local musical styles, Cotten developed an extensive repertoire of standards, dance tunes, and rags," according to Linda Demmerle in *Acoustic Guitar*.

Marriage at age 15, followed by the birth of a daughter a year later, diverted Cotten's focus away from her music. Her musical career eventually came to a complete halt, due to the influence of officials at her church who wanted her to devote herself more to religion. When she realized that religious songs were not nearly as enjoyable as the music she had been playing for years, she stopped playing her guitar altogether.

Chance Meeting Sparked Career

Cotten worked as a domestic servant in Chapel Hill, New York, and other places for much of her adult life. In 1947, following her divorce, she moved to Washington, D.C., so she could be closer to her daughter. While there, she took a job selling dolls in Landsburgh's Department Store, where a chance meeting changed her life forever. After finding a lost little girl named Peggy Seeger, she returned the child to her mother, Ruth Crawford Seeger. Ruth Seeger showed her thanks by offering Cotten a job as a domestic servant for her household. Little did Cotten know that both Ruth Seeger and her husband, Mike, were musicologists, and the parents of future folk-singing legend Pete Seeger.

At the time of Cotten's hiring, Ruth Seeger was compiling a collection of folk songs for her children. Cotten would often borrow Peggy Seeger's guitar and practice during her spare time, but it wasn't until the early 1950s that her talent became known to Mike and Ruth Seeger. Nicknaming her "Libba," the Seegers eagerly brought

Cotten into their musical fold. Mike Seeger first introduced her to the recording studio in 1952, producing her first album in 1957. She had her performing debut along with Mike Seeger at Swarthmore College in 1959 when she was a 67-year-old grandmother. Acclaim for her first recording resulted in her being invited to numerous folk and blues festivals in the years that followed, as a surging interest in folk music swept the country.

Cotten's "Freight Train," which had lain dormant in her repertoire for many decades, became the subject of a legal dispute in the 1950s. After Peggy Seeger had gone to England and performed the song, it was heard and recorded by Nancy Whiskey. Seeger had recorded the song for two men who then took credit for it, and it became a number-five hit in the United Kingdom. When the song, as recorded by Charles McDevitt, hit the top 40 in the U.S., Cotten heard it on the radio and began to wonder what was going on. With the help of Pete Seeger and after numerous court cases, Cotten was granted one-third of the credit for the song in 1957. In the early 1960s the song was also recorded by Peter, Paul, and Mary.

Became Mainstay on Folk Circuit

After her discovery Cotten became a fixture on the folk circuit. Starting in 1963 she performed solo in concert, and she appeared often at major festivals such as the Newport Folk Festival. Over the years Cotten was on the same bill with noted performers such as John Hurt, Skip James, John Estes, Muddy Waters, and Otis Spann. From the late 1960s to early 1970s she also appeared at the American Folklife Festival in Washington, D.C. Cotten was a guest performer at the Kennedy Center in Washington, D.C. in a performance of native American music, and in 1978 she performed at Carnegie Hall in New York City.

Like many folk musicians, Cotten improvised often and seldom played a song the same way twice. She enjoyed audience participation, frequently requesting that everyone sing along with her. Her straightforward, honest delivery on stage was a testament to her passion for her music. "I just love to sing," she said, according to *The Washingtonian*. "I love to get up before people and let 'em hear what I can do."

Refusing to slow down with age, Cotten maintained an active performance schedule into the 1980s and even went on an American and European tour with the group Taj Mahal when she was 90. Dana Klipp joined her in 1984, after Cotten began having difficulties with her hands that limited her guitar playing. Cotten gave her final performance at City College in New York City's Harlem in February of 1987, just four months before her death. "[Cotten] was an inspiration," said Klipp in *Acoustic Guitar*. "She endured and overcame hardships to share her music."

Selected compositions

"Freight Train."
"Washington Blues."
"Shake, Sugaree."
"Oh Babe, It Ain't No Lie."

Selected discography

Elizabeth Cotten (now retitled *Freight Train and Other North Carolina Folk Songs and Tunes*), Folkways, 1957.
Elizabeth Cotten Volume 2: Shake Sugaree, Folkways, 1967.
Elizabeth Cotten Volume 3: When I'm Gone, Folkways, 1975.
Elizabeth Cotten Live!, Arhoolie, 1985.

Sources

Books

Clarke, Donald, editor, *The Penguin Encyclopedia of Popular Music*, Viking, 1989.
Larkin, Colin, editor, *The Guinness Encyclopedia of Popular Music, Volume 1*, Guinness Publishing, 1992.
Santelli, Robert, *The Big Book of Blues*, Penguin, 1993.
Sandberg, Larry, and Dick Weissman, *The Folk Music Sourcebook, New, Updated Edition*, Da Capo, 1989.
Smith, Jessie Carney, editor, *Notable Black American Women*, Gale, 1992.

Periodicals

Acoustic Guitar, January/February 1995.
New York Times, June 30, 1987.
Syracuse Herald-Journal, June 29, 1995.
The Washingtonian, March 1989.
U.S. News & World Report, February 13, 1989.

—Ed Decker

The Cramps

Punk band

The Cramps have been a fixture on the fringes of the punk-alternative scene for almost two decades, and the band has long been heralded for their blend of rockabilly-style guitar noise and screwball humor. Often called the original progenitors of the musical genre known as "psychobilly," they think they may have even coined the term themselves. With their seminal 1976 debut EP, *Gravest Hits,* the Cramps attempted to explain their unique inner vision: "While the jackhammer rhythms of punk were proliferating in NYC, the Cramps dove into the deepest recesses of the rock 'n' roll psyche for the most primal of all rhythmic impulses—rockabilly—the sound of Southern culture falling apart in a blaze of shudders and hiccups," they stated in the album's liner notes. "The Cramps also picked and chose amongst the psychotic debris of previous rock eras—instrumental rock, surf, psychedelia, and sixties punk. And then they added the junkiest element of all—themselves."

The Cramps formed in the New York City area around 1976 with original members Lux Interior on vocals and Poison Ivy Rorschach and Bryan Gregory on guitar; behind the drum kit sat Miriam Linna. Interior and Rorschach were natives of Cleveland, Ohio, and later married. Of the lack of a bassist, Rorschach explained years later to *New York Newsday* writer Ira Robbins, "We weren't trying to do anything radical. None of us wanted to play bass. We collect a lot of old records, and if they have bass on 'em I can't hear it. It didn't seem essential." The combination of the two females, Rorschach and Linna, already made the Cramps unique in the testosterone-fueled Greenwich Village punk scene. But their particular brand of campy theatrical excess and undress combined with ear-splitting sonics gave them an edge the more cerebral bands couldn't muster.

Gravest Hits helped usher in the Cramps' cult following among music aficionados. The band was invited to open for the Police during their 1979 U.K. tour, with Linna replaced on drums by Nick Knox. In a 1979 profile for *Melody Maker,* writer Penny Kiley called them "America's rockabilly solution to the New Wave."

Taking Excess to New Heights

By this time the Cramps were known for outrageous onstage theatrics and a retro-outré look that seemed to combine the punk ethos with trash-culture tack. References to B-movies and a slightly sadomasochistic air infiltrated both lyrics and performance—an inevitability, so Rorschach explained in *Melody Maker:* "You can't separate music and other cultural things; what we do isn't just music. Everything I ever saw on TV, everything

For the Record . . .

Original members include **Bryan Gregory**, guitar; **Lux Interior** (born in Cleveland, OH; married Poison Ivy Rorschach), lead vocals; **Miriam Linna**, drums; and **Poison Ivy Rorschach** (born in Cleveland, OH; married Lux Interior), guitar. Later members include **Slim Chance**, bass; **Candy Del Mar**, bass; **Harry Drumdini**, drums; **Nick Knox**, drums; and **Congo Powers**, bass.

Band formed in New York City, c. 1976.

Addresses: *Record company*—The Medicine Label, 75 Rockefeller Plaza, 21st Floor, New York, NY 10019.

I ever ate, everything I heard on the radio is an influence. We're celebrating pop culture." In the same spirit, the band was one of the earliest to exploit the then-new medium of video to fully bring their unique vision to fans, filming a four-minute takeoff on the classic '50s-era horror film as promotional material back in the late '70s.

Sometime in the '80s the Cramps' lead guitarist dropped the "Rorschach" and became known as Poison Ivy. Meanwhile, husband and creative partner Interior earned a reputation for sporting latex and stiletto heels onstage. As *Chicago Tribune* contributor Greg Kot pointed out, "This yin-yang relationship ... [is] far from a traditional one: with the male as sex object and the female as lead guitarist, it subverts decades of rock stereotyping." More albums followed throughout the '80s—*Songs the Lord Taught Us* marked the Cramps' debut on IRS Records in 1980, prompting *Rolling Stone* reviewer Dave Marsh to liken them to "an otherworldly culture that's been developing rock & roll along parallel musical lines but utterly divergent social ones." *Psychedelic Jungle* followed a year later, marked by the defection of guitarist Bryan Gregory and the addition of Congo Powers on bass.

The Frenzy Continued

In 1984 IRS issued *Bad Music for Bad People,* a collection of previously released material from *Gravest Hits* and *Songs the Lord Taught Us* added to other tracks that had only been available as British imports. MTV news personality Kurt Loder—still writing record reviews for *Rolling Stone* at the time—was a big fan of the Cramps during this era. Critiquing *Bad Music for Bad People,* Loder declared, "This is rock & roll the way it never really was on the radio, but the way you always dreamed it could be."

Such dreams never translated into financial success, however. For many years much of the vinyl output by the band was self-financed; Interior and Ivy would then try to sell the finished product to record labels. *A Date with Elvis* was the Cramps' fifth release and third full-length album. The creative inspiration behind the 1986 work was the media madness over what would have been Elvis Presley's fiftieth birthday the year before. As Ivy explained to Kiley in *Melody Maker,* "It's our tribute album to Elvis.... Elvis has always been on our mind but he was especially on our mind last year because it was just like national Elvis year or something."

A Date with Elvis met with some criticism for its uninhibited lyrics in songs like "Hot Pool of Womanhood" and "Cornfed Dames." Simon Reynolds reviewed it for *Melody Maker* and found "few surprises here, none of the little touches of musical radicalism" that surfaced on the Cramps' earlier releases, and lampooned the more misogynist tracks as displaying "a relentlessly crude, stunted view of sex." Ivy, whose stage garb of bustiers and other provocative apparel belied her creative and decision-making status in the quartet, dismissed charges of sexism. "I think it's an unbelievable joke people saying we're sexist.... I create this music. I co-write these songs, how can I be sexist? Sexism to me is when you're blinded to seeing certain people and the accomplishments of certain people because you've got them tuned out. Paying attention to a girl isn't sexist at all, that's just animal."

Riding Out the Storms of Controversy

During the late 1980s the Cramps took a hiatus from releasing new material, although imports and compilations appeared intermittently. Soured deals and lawsuits provided additional distractions. For 1990's *Stay Sick!,* the band—now joined by bass replacement Candy Del Mar—kept up their own unique blend of covers of obscure rockabilly tunes and female-worshiping originals like "Bikini Girls with Machine Guns" and "Journey to the Center of a Girl." Evelyn McConnell gave it an enthusiastic review in *Rolling Stone,* noting "Rorschach's guitar is all burr and bristle; the ghost of Roy Orbison hiccups and growls through Interior as though the singer were swallowing hot tar in hell."

More lineup changes followed the release of *Stay Sick!.* Del Mar left, replaced by Slim Chance; longtime drummer Nick Knox also exited and Harry Drumdini took over. Both new members played on the Cramps' 1994 release *FlameJob,* their major-label debut after signing with the Medicine label, a division of Warner Bros. The band seemed at ease at their new corporate home. "Some labels in the past said, 'We don't have a pigeon-hole for you' or 'You should be doing a rave record' or 'You should give your multitrack to a DJ and let him make a new mix out of it'—all these horrible ideas," Interior told *Boston Globe* writer Jim Sullivan. "We had to spend a lot of time in the past saying, 'No, no, no, no...' feeling like we were from Mars because of it."

FlameJob boasted the usual psychobilly vortex of the Cramps with tracks like "Swing the Big Eyed Rabbit," "Sado County Auto Show," and "Ultra Twist." *Rolling Stone* reviewer Paul Evans noted that this psychobilly twang and the Cramps' original trash-culture ethos had become familiar musical territory for several other contemporary acts, like White Zombie. In the months between 1994 and 1995, the Cramps played several successful shows in major cities. Journalist Lorraine Ali reviewed their sold-out concert for the *Los Angeles Times* and asserted that their "enthusiasm, coupled with its freakish edge, is the key to the band's longevity."

A refusal to capitulate, despite the many obstacles encountered over the years in a notoriously fickle industry, may also have played a part in the Cramps' success; in the 1994 interview with Sullivan for the *Boston Globe,* Interior offered a reason why he and Ivy never decided to call it quits: "Probably we would have if we knew something else to do that was as fun."

Selected discography

Gravest Hits (EP), Illegal Records, 1976.
Songs the Lord Taught Us, IRS/A&M, 1980.
Psychedelic Jungle, IRS, 1981.
Bad Music for Bad People, IRS/A&M, 1984.
A Date with Elvis, Big Beat, 1986.
Psychedelic Jungle/Gravest Hits, IRS/A&M, 1989.
Stay Sick!, Enigma, 1990.
Look Mom No Head, Restless, 1992.
FlameJob, Medicine, 1994.

Sources

Billboard, August 20, 1994; October 15, 1994; November 19, 1994.
Boston Globe, November 18, 1994.
Chicago Tribune, November 13, 1994.
Guitar Player, March 1983; December 1994.
Los Angeles Times, January 30, 1995.
Melody Maker, June 9, 1979; February 22, 1986; March 29, 1986.
New York Newsday, November 25, 1994.
Rolling Stone, July 24, 1980; March 15, 1984; May 3, 1990; March 9, 1995.
Variety, January 19, 1977.

Additional information for this profile was taken from promotional material provided by the Medicine Label.

—*Carol Brennan*

Creedence Clearwater Revival

Rock band

Creedence Clearwater Revival (CCR) endured a long career, but the band enjoyed only a few short years in rock's limelight before internal dissension broke them apart. Led by the vocally powerful John Fogerty, CCR released now-classic hit records in the late 1960s and early 1970s—songs whose popular lifespan is closing out its third decade. "At a time when the rock audience had already divided into antagonistic sub-groups—hardcore rock and roll fans vs hardcore freaks, high school kids vs college students, AM vs FM—Creedence kept us all, dominating Top 40 radio while continuing to be acknowledged as 'serious' by the industry/media/fan cabal that arbitrates such matters," wrote Ellen Willis in *The Rolling Stone Illustrated History of Rock and Roll.* To honor the longevity of their music and their impact on contemporary rock, the group was inducted into the Rock and Roll Hall of Fame in 1993.

CCR began as the Blue Velvets in the early 1960s in El Cerrito, California, primarily as an instrumental act, with members John Fogerty, Stu Cook, and Douglas Clifford. Fogerty's brother, Tom, soon began joining their

Archive Photos

practice sessions and eventually became a full member of the group. The act was renamed the Golliwogs in 1964 after signing with San Francisco-based Fantasy Records; they didn't know about the name change until their first single came off the press. As the Golliwogs, the quartet had a minor San Francisco-area hit with a song called "Brown-Eyed Girl" but found neither fame nor fortune in pandering to the tastes of the general teenage public, who at the time were keen on peppy tunes from British bands.

Around 1967 Fantasy Records became the property of Saul Zaentz, an employee of the label familiar with the Golliwogs' work. Zaentz asked them if they'd like to do some more recording—and also suggested another change of name. The band settled on Creedence Clearwater Revival, taken from the name of an acquaintance and a beer commercial.

Burning Up the Charts

With the new moniker came a change of direction. Fogerty and the others focused on the kind of music they really wanted to play. The result was a more earthy sound, one that seemed to find a niche in the burgeoning rock 'n' roll scene around San Francisco in the late 1960s.

In the new studio sessions, this shift in style yielded "Suzie Q," a cover of a Dale Hawkins tune. The song became CCR's first hit. Released in the fall of 1968, the eight-minute track was recorded with a specific outlet in mind—San Francisco's avant-garde rock station KMPX. "I told the other guys that the quickest way we could get on the radio, therefore get more exposure and get this thing going was to specifically go in and record an arrangement of 'Suzie Q' that could get played on that station," Fogerty remembered in *Rolling Stone.* The plan worked and the song charted at Number 11.

A string of other hit singles followed, as well as a prolific five albums of original material in the space of two years. CCR's first single to reach Number One was "Proud Mary," released in January of 1969 and a staple of cover bands ever since. Like the rest of the group's output, the song was written, composed, and arranged by Fogerty. He also directed much of the studio work and made creative decisions for the band, a position of authority that he had to struggle to maintain when CCR finally became a success.

After the release of their first album, 1968's *Creedence Clearwater Revival,* the group began working on a follow-up almost immediately. However, while completing that album, titled *Bayou Country,* "we had a real confrontation," Fogerty admitted years later to *Rolling Stone* contributor Michael Goldberg. "Everybody wanted to sing, write, make up their own arrangements, whatever, right? This was after ten years of struggling. Now we had the spotlight.... I said to the other guys, 'If we blow it, the spotlight's going to move over there to the Eagles or somebody.' I didn't want to go back to the carwash."

The Politics of Rock 'n' Roll

Major acclaim followed for CCR in the early 1970s. Although their sound was rootsy, it was also hook-laden and lyrically assured; within months the group had become a major presence on rock and Top 40 radio. They played Woodstock in August of 1969, but had the unfortunate luck to go on in the middle of the night after a long set by the Grateful Dead. Fogerty, recalling the festival in a *Rolling Stone* interview with James Henke, remembered how excited they were—and then came the realization: "Wow, we got to follow the band that put half a million people to sleep.... These people were out; no matter what I did they were gone. It was sort of like a painting of a Dante scene, just bodies from hell, all intertwined and asleep, covered with mud." CCR did not appear in the film documentary or the live recordings of Woodstock.

Perhaps because of their mainstream success, CCR remained outsiders of sorts among the counterculture scenemakers of their era. Unlike other bands, they eschewed drugs and the rock 'n' roll lifestyle, although they did sport the obligatory long hair and beards. Like other bands, they were outspoken opponents of the war of Vietnam, but coming from a working-class background put a different perspective on their political opinions. Fogerty had put in time in the reserves and kept his fingers crossed that he would not be shipped overseas until his discharge papers arrived. He was perplexed by the animosity that many members of his generation held for the soldiers who returned from Southeast Asia. "I literally witnessed longhaired people walking through airports spitting at soldiers, and I just thought, 'How stupid! He just got caught, and you didn't,'" he told Henke.

These convictions surfaced when Fogerty penned "Fortunate Son" one day in less than a half hour. With its chorus of "It ain't me / It ain't me / I ain't no fortunate son," the song spoke of the ease with which sons of the wealthy and powerful were escaping the draft and the war in Vietnam. Released in November of 1969, the single reached Number Three and was included on the album *Willy and the Poor Boys*. Other politically minded songs followed, like "Who'll Stop the Rain," but despite the integrity behind their music, critics often lambasted CCR for their commercial success.

Tensions Took Their Toll

Dissension within the band proved to be a bigger problem, however, and one that began to surface in their records. "Their sixth album, *Pendulum,* released in December 1970, included what Creedence watchers took to be some tentative concessions to Art—stuff like improvised organ music," wrote Willis in *The Rolling Stone Illustrated History of Rock and Roll*, but it was really the result of a more democratic creative process. Fogerty's leadership was waning, in part because of the effort it took to stay there. "I was not popular in my own band," Fogerty said in the interview with Goldberg. "I gave in 'cause I got tired, and that's what they wanted." As a result, CCR's final album together as a band—1972's *Mardi Gras*—took almost a year to complete. The record "wasn't bad, just mediocre. Its rock was softened and countrified," wrote Willis.

By the time *Mardi Gras* hit record stores, Tom Fogerty had left CCR to pursue an unsuccessful solo career, and by the end of 1972 CCR had permanently disbanded. John Fogerty began his own project, the Blue Ridge Rangers, and put out a solo release in 1975. However, legal problems with CCR's label, Fantasy Records, kept Fogerty busy for the next two decades. Because of the difficulties, he steadfastly refused to perform any of CCR's hits, although fans clamored for them. Finally, at a Vietnam veterans' benefit concert in 1987, Fogerty

played them again, prompted in part by something vintage rocker Bob Dylan had said to him. If Fogerty kept refusing to resurrect his own songs, Dylan teased, the public would forever equate "Proud Mary" with Tina Turner, who covered the song in the early 1970s. "It was a very high point in my life," Fogerty said of the 1987 concert in the *Rolling Stone* interview with Henke. "Musically and even, I guess, nostalgically. Just because of what all those tunes meant to all those people in the audience. You know, we're all part of that generation, and it meant something to all of us."

Selected discography

Singles; on Fantasy

"Suzie Q," September 1968.
"I Put a Spell on You," November 1968.
"Proud Mary," January 1969.
"Bad Moon Rising," May 1969.
"Lodi," May 1969.
"Green River," August 1969.
"Commotion," August 1969.
"Fortunate Son," November 1969.
"Traveling Band," January 1970.
"Who'll Stop the Rain," January 1970.
"Up Around the Bend," April 1970.
"Run Through the Jungle," April 1970.
"Looking Out My Back Door," August 1970.
"Long As I Can See the Light," August 1970.
"Have You Ever Seen the Rain," January 1971.
"Hey Tonight," January 1971.
"Sweet Hitch Hiker," July 1971.
"Someday Never Comes," May 1972.
"I Heard It Through the Grapevine," January 1976.

Albums; on Fantasy

Creedence Clearwater Revival, 1968.
Bayou Country, 1969.
Green River, 1969.
Willy and the Poor Boys, 1969.
Cosmo's Factory, 1970.
Pendulum, 1970.
Mardi Gras, 1972.
Creedence Gold, 1973.
Chronicle, Vol. 1, 1976.
Royal Albert Hall Concert, 1980.
Chronicle, Vol. 2, 1986.

Solo albums by John Fogerty

Blue Ridge Rangers, Fantasy, 1973.
Centerfield, Warner Bros, 1985.
Eye of the Zombie, Warner Bros, 1986.

Sources

Books

Nite, Norm N., and Ralph M. Newman, *Rock On: The Illustrated Encyclopedia of Rock 'n' Roll—The Modern Years: 1964-Present*, Crowell, 1978.

Willis, Ellen, "Creedence Clearwater Revival," in *The Rolling Stone Illustrated History of Rock and Roll*, edited by Jim Miller, revised and updated edition, Random House, 1980.

Periodicals

Billboard, March 19, 1994.

Rolling Stone, November 5, 1987; September 8, 1988; February 4, 1993.

—*Carol Brennan*

The Cult

Rock band

For much of their recording career during the 1980s the Cult reveled in the heavy metal thunder of the late 1960s and early 1970s. When asymmetrical haircuts and drum machines were in, the band sported long hippie locks and songs rife with then-passe guitar solos. "The big rock sound they created for themselves a decade ago now fits snugly within the Nirvana-Pearl Jam-Soundgarden zeitgeist of the '90s," *Spin* contributor Steve Appleford observed in a 1995 article. But critical acclaim for the Cult never matched their fans' adoration. By the time grunge swept into alternative fashion in the early 1990s, the band was somehow too far behind, too overproduced, too serious. As their fortunes dwindled, tensions escalated within the group; an already bad situation was exacerbated by substance abuse problems. Record, then ticket sales fell off, and after only two scheduled dates into an American tour, the Cult disbanded in the spring of 1995.

The Cult formed from the ashes of two bands in the north of England in the early 1980s. Ian Astbury was a singer in the Southern Death Cult, while Billy Duffy played

Photograph by Anette Aurell, © 1994 Sire Records Company

guitar in an outfit called Theater of Hate. The two found common ground in the rejection of the then-current musical trends exemplified by bands like Depeche Mode and Bauhaus, preferring instead the thundering vintage style of Led Zeppelin and Free—acts almost nobody professed to liking at that time.

Early gigs together as Death Cult, and later just the Cult—which coalesced when Jamie Stewart and Les Warner signed on—attracted fans, but the British music press was merciless. Rock critics could not understand why a band would look backward in time for inspiration at a moment when so much new was happening in music, and Astbury tried, often unsuccessfully, to explain the Cult in rambling, nearly incomprehensible interviews.

The Rock Niche

Despite the journalistic snipes, the Cult built up a solid fan base in the U.K. before hitting it big with their American debut, *Love,* also their first full-length LP. When it hit American shores in late 1985—after a 19-week stint on the British charts with the single "She Sells Sanctuary"—*Rolling Stone* contributor David Fricke dismissed it as "just leaden Zeppelin." But stateside sales for the record were phenomenal, as were concert grosses when the Cult arrived for tour dates. Astbury's divine rock-god looks also seemed to be part of the equation for success. "Pop hits, platinum albums, and surging crowds suddenly launched Astbury into the role of the beautiful young sex deity, a new [flamboyant Doors frontman] Jim Morrison on the scene with photo spreads in Vogue," wrote Appleford in *Spin.*

The band went into the studio in 1986 to record a second album, but they were forced to scrap almost the entire effort. "Three quarters of the way through, these bad

vibes started rearing themselves," Duffy explained to *Melody Maker* contributor Carol Clark about the creative process. "It was like an unspoken thing. It just wasn't right." To remedy the situation, the Cult enlisted the talents of production prodigy Rick Rubin, who had already made a name for himself with behind-the-boards work for the Beastie Boys and Run D.M.C. Soon the band was rerecording in the New York City studio founded by Jimi Hendrix. The result was *Electric,* released in 1987 to both critical acclaim and explosive sales buoyed by the success of the track "Love Removal Machine." *Rolling Stone* reviewer Robin J. Schwartz asserted the record "swaggers, crunches and howls all right, but it does so with irreverence." As in the band's previous work, Astbury and Duffy remained the creative personnel, cowriting all the songs except a cover of Steppenwolf's "Born to Be Wild."

The Wrong Path

However, the success of *Electric*—and well-attended concert dates in support of it—began to take their toll on the band. In Vancouver, British Columbia, Astbury was arrested after tussling with security forces; in Texas, he faced charges of onstage obscenity. The singer seemed to heading down the very road already traversed by Jim Morrison. "The pressure manifested itself in many ways," he said of the disastrous 1987 tour a few years later in an interview with *Rolling Stone* reporter Michael Goldberg. "Alcohol was one. Self-destructive behavior was another. Arrests. Fornication. After we finished, there was nothing left."

Despite the problems—and the growing animosity rumored between Astbury and Duffy—the Cult headed back into the studio to record yet another successful album, 1989's *Sonic Temple.* Some personnel changes had taken place, with Matt Sorum replacing Les Warner on drums. Iggy Pop expressed his admiration for the band by guesting on backing vocals for one track, and cuts like "Fire Woman" and "Edie (Ciao Baby)" were instant hits; the record went platinum. Kim Neely of *Rolling Stone* felt *Sonic Temple* merged the band's earlier stylistic incarnations—the psychedelic aspect of *Love* with the bare-bones thunder of *Electric*—and noted in a review that "the best moments artfully embrace the two distinct musical styles that have marked the Cult's finest work, and its worst moments simply make you wonder why the band didn't stick to one or the other."

When it came time to tour again, Astbury and Duffy seemed to have kicked their bad habits, and the band looked to be back in business. But things soon went downhill. Like so many reviewers, Appleford deemed

Ceremony, released in 1991, "disastrous, irrelevant, and unheard," noting that the band's perennial substance abuse problems seemed to have been a factor in the album's failure. After a few years on hiatus, more personnel changes occurred: Sorum was replaced by a former jazz drummer, Scott Garrett, while Stewart's bass slot was taken by Craig Adams, an old friend of Astbury and Duffy. Together the new formation worked on a more enigmatic release, 1994's *The Cult*, recorded in Vancouver with producer Bob Rock.

Rebirth and Death of a Band

"Gone are the old gothic rock-star costumes, the helmets of perfect long hair, the pounds of jewelry," Appleford said of the Cult's new incarnation. "There is nothing left to distract from the music, which roars on the new album ... like an assault on their own bad reputation." Astbury reflected on his difficult family life as a teenager and the superstar treatment he received during the band's heyday in the mid-1980s, telling Appleford that much of his self-destructive behavior stemmed from those two sources. The singer admitted he had come to terms with some of his demons, and the slaying was helped in part by writing cathartic songs for *The Cult* like "Gone."

By early 1995 Astbury and Duffy had worked through some of their problems. Yet *The Cult* was not doing well in stores and received only scant critical attention for an act of their standing. North American tour dates were announced, and the group played two shows in April before Beggars Banquet, their label in the U.K., announced that they had disbanded. "It really was more of an Ian thing," an anonymous source at the company told *Melody Maker*. "He broke down and couldn't muster the stamina to carry on." The company asserted that scheduled shows had been sold out, but the magazine hinted that ticket sales had been dismal. Astbury and Duffy reportedly planned to pursue work on their own separate musical projects.

Selected discography

On Sire/Reprise

Love, 1985.
Electric, 1987.
Sonic Temple, 1989.
Ceremony, 1991.
The Cult, 1994.

Sources

Billboard, October 29, 1994.
Melody Maker, February 26, 1983; March 5, 1983; October 26, 1985; April 12, 1986; January 24, 1987; April 22, 1995; April 29, 1995.
Rolling Stone, February 13, 1986; July 2, 1987; June 1, 1989; July 13, 1989; December 29, 1994.
Spin, March 1995.
Vogue, March 1986.

Additional information for this profile was obtained from promotional material provided by Sire/Reprise Records.

—Carol Brennan

Dead Can Dance

Rock duo

Dead Can Dance have been included in a wide variety of musical subgenres within rock. Due to their name, image, and electronic-drum-driven ethereal sound, many defined the band as part of the dark, gothic style when they began to achieve notice in the early 1980s. Indeed, the media have called the work of Dead Can Dance everything from "world music" to "unclassifiable."

Brendan Perry and Lisa Gerrard, the core of Dead Can Dance, have said their creations come from pure inspiration. "No two people ever make the same music naturally, not if they're really honest with their music," Perry told Ann Marie Aubin in *Strobe.* "What we try to do is draw very deep inside us, in regions that are normally connected with the subconscious ... a willful immersion in trance-like states and improvisation, then bring down a whole gamut of influences we don't really have conscious control over."

Perry and Gerrard met in 1980 in Melbourne, Australia. They decided to name their project Dead Can Dance

Photograph by Dennis Keeley, © 1994 Warner Bros. Records Inc.

For the Record . . .

Members include **Lisa Gerrard** and **Brendan Perry**.

Duo formed in Melbourne, Australia, 1980; signed to 4AD label; released self-titled debut album, 1984; released U.S. debut, *A Passage in Time,* Rykodisc, 1992; signed to 4AD/Warner Bros. and released *Into the Labyrinth,* 1993.

Addresses: *Record company*—4AD/Warner Bros. Records, 3300 Warner Blvd., Burbank, CA 91505.

after a ritual mask from New Guinea. "The mask, though once a living part of a tree, is dead," Perry explained in *Time.* "Nevertheless, it has, through the artistry of its maker, been imbued with a life force of its own."

After writing music together for a few years, the duo decided to move to London, where they signed a recording contract with the 4AD label. In March of 1984 Dead Can Dance released their self-titled debut. The album's cover depicted a ritual mask from New Guinea. This first LP led to their classification as a "morbid goth" band, to which the two objected strenuously.

In the fall of that year, Dead Can Dance recorded a 12-inch EP called *Garden of the Arcane Delights.* The duo also contributed two songs to the debut of another band, This Mortal Coil. Word began to spread about Dead Can Dance, and their next album, *Spleen and Ideal,* reached Number Two on the British independent charts. The guitars and gothic rock sound of their debut had transformed into a more ethereal keyboard-based style, which was further distinguished by acoustic instrumentation—cellos, timpani, and trombone.

With a full band behind them, Perry and Gerrard spent most of 1986 performing around the world. They also contributed two songs, "Frontier" and "The Protagonist," to the 4AD compilation record and video *Lonely Is an Eyesore.* They released their third full-length album, *Within the Realm of a Dying Sun,* the following year. This time, the duo placed all the songs featuring Perry's vocals on one side of the LP and those featuring Gerrard on the other. Immediately thereafter, the two artists secluded themselves in their thirteenth-floor council flat in London to record their next album, releasing *The Serpent's Egg* in early 1988.

Later that year, the duo wrote the score for the Agustin Villarongas film *El Nino De La Luna* (Moonchild). Ger-

rard also made her acting debut in the picture. The project launched another career for Gerrard and Perry, who would go on to write other scores for both film and theater productions.

The two journeyed into another musical realm with their next album, *Aion.* Rather than use contemporary instruments alone, they incorporated reproductions of instruments used to create the music of the early Renaissance, the stylistic influence of which also made its way onto the recording. Perry and Gerrard spent most of 1991 working in Ireland. Among the projects completed there was Dead Can Dance's performance of Gerrard's score for a production of Sophocles's *Oedipus Rex.*

In 1992 Dead Can Dance made their U.S. recording debut when the independent Rykodisc label released *A Passage in Time,* a compilation of songs from the duo's previous albums plus two new songs, "Bird" and "Spirit." Without the support of major-label distribution and promotion, Dead Can Dance still managed to sell 60,000 records in the U.S. by the end of the year. The duo had already formed an underground fan base in the U.S. through imports of their earlier albums.

Dead Can Dance had another LP ready for release in 1993. By then 4AD Records had signed a distribution deal with Warner Bros. Records, which inspired the band to reteam with the previously independent label. With this powerhouse behind the album, *Into the Labyrinth* sold more than half a million copies worldwide. The album featured a song called "How Fortunate the Man with None," in which Perry set words from Bertoldt Brecht's play *Mother Courage* to music. The only other time the Brecht estate had granted permission for anyone to do such a thing was in 1963.

With *Into the Labyrinth,* Dead Can Dance received even more exposure in the U.S. "Dead Can Dance taps the ecstatic power of Middle Eastern devotional music, Gregorian chant, and Celtic canticle to forge a mesmerizing sound that seems to transcend centuries and cultures," wrote Guy Garcia in *Time.* Gerrard explained the band's approach to *Strobe:* "Now the relationship with the work is so percussive and rhythmical and so heartbeat-connected. It's just remembering to be a child. It's going back before the things that influenced you, being able to arrive at the before state. That's what music does to people— it takes them to a place before any of this, before the indoctrination of society over the things that happen or could have happened."

Dead Can Dance also maintained its music in the visual arena with another film. The critically acclaimed arthouse picture *Baraka* featured the song "The Host of the

Seraphim," from 1988's *Serpent's Egg.* Gerrard and Perry also included scenes from the film in their video for "Yulunga (Spirit Dance)," the first clip from *Into the Labyrinth.*

In the fall of 1993, Dead Can Dance toured for the first time in three years, selling out shows all over the world. The duo played their complex arrangements with the assistance of five additional musicians. At the end of the tour, they played two private shows at the Mayfair Theatre in Santa Monica, California. A 77-minute concert film resulted from the two performances, parts of which where interspersed with interview segments featuring Perry and Gerrard. *Toward the Within* was released as both a video and concert CD in October of 1994. Two-thirds of the material on the live release had never been recorded.

In late 1994, Perry and Gerrard began working on solo projects, though they had no intention of ending their relationship as Dead Can Dance. Perry told *Time* that Dead Can Dance made records to exorcise their demons, and that they "still have a lot of demons to exorcise."

Selected discography

Dead Can Dance, 4AD, 1984.
Garden of the Arcane Delights (EP), 4AD, 1984.
Spleen and Ideal, 4AD, 1985.
Within the Realm of a Dying Sun, 4AD, 1987.
The Serpent's Egg, 4AD, 1988.
Aion, 4AD, 1990.
A Passage in Time, Rykodisc, 1992.
Into the Labyrinth (includes "How Fortunate the Man with None), 4AD/Warner Bros., 1993.
Toward the Within, 4AD/Warner Bros., 1994.

Also contributed "Frontier" and "The Protagonist" to compilation *Lonely Is an Eyesore,* 4AD.

Sources

Books

The Trouser Press Record Guide, edited by Ira A. Robbins, Collier, 1992.

Periodicals

Billboard, October 9, 1993; September 17, 1994.
Entertainment Weekly, October 15, 1993; October 28, 1994.
New York Times, November 22, 1990; October 30, 1993.
Rolling Stone, July 14, 1994; February 23, 1995.
Seattle Times, February 16, 1995.
Strobe, November/December 1993.
Time, January 24, 1994.

Additional information for this profile was obtained from 4AD/Warner Bros. Records press materials, 1995.

—*Sonya Shelton*

Dokken

Rock band

The quartet of rockers known as Dokken, named after founder, vocalist, and guitarist Don Dokken, achieved a phenomenal level of success during the heavy metal blitz of the 1980s. Much of the Los Angeles-based group's star status was the result of the tenacity of Don Dokken, who had the foresight to predict that legions of teenagers would appreciate—and buy—records featuring thundering guitar assaults woven around songs about everyday life and love. "Dokken also created one of the darker metal sounds around, combining the classic metal of bands such as Black Sabbath with a new intelligence and a raunchy American-metal sound," added Brenda Herrmann in the *Chicago Tribune.* Although often vilified by the American rock press, the band was validated by several platinum-selling records and sell-out tours both at home and abroad during much of the 1980s.

Dokken founder Don Dokken grew up in a poorer section of Venice, California, a circumstance he credits as influencing his musical tastes. He played in a number of local hard rock bands and cut a record called *Hard*

AP/Wide World Photos

Luck Woman in 1980. Released on Hard Records, a label he had started up himself, the effort soon became lost among the plethora of New Wave acts then receiving attention: suddenly bands that sounded like the Knack and the Police were getting booked into local bars. "Wimp music was in," Dokken recalled, still fuming, in an interview with Dennis Hunt of the *Los Angeles Times.* "It was cool to stand real still on stage and be nerdy-looking. It was in to be a geek. I had real long hair then. I didn't fit in with the wimps." Dokken moved to West Germany to get his career started. "Rock 'n' roll was still happening there," he asserted.

Assembling the Band

In Europe, Dokken met others who had heard his first record and liked it. One of them was Dieter Dierics, who went on to become the producer of the Scorpions' million-selling LPs of the 1980s. Another appreciative listener was a talent scout for Elektra Records. Dierics loaned Dokken his studio to cut a record for the big label, but at this point he needed a band. Dokken mined talent from a Los Angeles act called Exciter, who had once been his club scene rivals. Exciter guitarist George Lynch had written a song for the demo tape, and Elektra urged Dokken to try him out; additionally, drummer Mick Brown didn't want to join the new band without his friend

Lynch. But the acrimony between the two guitar players--Dokken and Lynch--was undeniable, and it would serve to both fuel and hinder the band's success for the next decade.

To complete the lineup, Dokken needed a bass player and recruited Peter Baltes, the German-born member of a heavy metal act called Accept. As the newly formed Dokken, the quartet cut their record in Dierics's studio. It was released in Europe in 1982 and the following year hit the U.S. market as *Breaking the Chains* on Elektra. Baltes returned to Accept after his studio work with Dokken was complete. He was replaced by Jeff Pilson. By late 1983, *Breaking the Chains* was making a respectable appearance on the *Billboard* charts.

In 1984 Dokken released *Tooth and Nail,* a quintessential heavy metal opus produced by Tom Werman. Thundering guitars cranked against songs with lyrics about problematic women; the occasional softer ballad balanced things out. *People* contributor David Hiltbrand noted that Dokken seemed to be trying to position themselves as a live act, and "consequently, most of the record is made up of bombastic, febrile tunes," although Hiltbrand did concede that some tracks from *Tooth and Nail* "contain a smattering of melody while showing off Don Dokken's powerful voice."

Tumultuous Relationships

Dokken's third release, *Under Lock and Key* was produced by Neil Kernon and Michael Wagener. The 1986 work was another straightforward studio rock effort that sold millions and allowed the group to head back out on the road. By this time, Dokken's style of loud, dynamic heavy metal was becoming more popular; the rise of groups like Bon Jovi, Ratt, and Poison began to cut in on the turf that Dokken had already staked out. Other problems also plagued the band. The volatile personalities within Dokken were clashing. Bandmembers fought during recording sessions, and the rivalry between Dokken and Lynch was evident even to fans, according to *Los Angeles Times* reporter Hunt. "It's something you can see on stage," he reported. "Often it's like they're playing in two different groups. In a strange way, watching them not interact is part of the fun of a Dokken concert."

Dokken undertook another serious, extensive European tour to support *Under Lock and Key,* selling out nearly 40 shows spread over a dozen countries during the first half of 1986. At the time, terrorist incidents and anti-American sentiments were running high in Europe. "You would see slogans like `Yankees go home' spray-painted all over the place, particularly in Spain and

Italy," Dokken told *Chicago Tribune* reporter Lynn Van Matre. He also noted the anti-American, anti-Ronald Reagan stance apparent in the media and recalled, "We definitely encountered anti-American vibes in restaurants and hotels."

Back in the States, Dokken cut a fourth album, 1987's *Back for the Attack.* In a review for the *Los Angeles Times,* John Voland compared it with their previous release, which was notable for having a bit more relaxed, marketable sound. On *Back for the Attack,* "more of the band's salad-days metallic grind is back," Voland opined, and termed "Lost behind the Wall," "Cry of the Gypsy," and "Kiss of Death" (an anti-AIDS song) "standout tracks." The record made it into the Top 20, and the group toured the United States again, this time opening for Aerosmith.

Dokken next released a double live album, 1989's *Beast from the East,* but the long-simmering tensions within the band had finally split them asunder, seemingly for good. Don Dokken refused to concede defeat, however, and reformed with new members. He recruited Baltes again for bass, then another European named John Norum (formerly the guitarist for the metal act Europe) on guitar, joined by Billy White, a young Texan, and finally Mikkey Dee on drums.

Guitarist White was only twenty years old when he joined Dokken, and his recruitment was the stuff of which rock legends are generated. "I was recording at Bobby Blotzer's home studio," Dokken recalled for *Chicago Tribune* writer Herrmann. (Blotzer was then a member of Ratt.) "I just pulled a used cassette from a box. When I played it back, there was this guitar player, and he was just burning—it was very psychotic, really." Dokken called the telephone number on the tape and talked to White. "I didn't tell him who I was, but when I asked who he liked, he said Dokken. So I sent him an airplane ticket to come try out."

Return to Original Lineup

By this time Dokken had switched labels from Elektra to Geffen and with the new band recorded their debut for the label, *Up from the Ashes.* To prepare for the stress of touring, Dokken forced all the bandmembers to share a house with him in suburban Los Angeles. However, the new band was short-lived, and little was heard from Dokken—either Don or the band—for the first half of the

1990s. But in late 1994, a sold-out acoustic show was held at a club in L.A.—with all the original members. It was Dokken's first gig together since breaking up six years before, and a live album was cut from the session.

Early in 1995, Dokken toured Japan, while the live record began climbing the charts back in the States. Next, they embarked on a U.S. tour--playing mainly to crowds in small venues--and released a full-length comeback album titled *Dysfunctional.* After fifteen on-and-off years together, the bandmembers seemed to have mellowed a bit—and realized that their potential audience never goes away. By 1995 the "wimp" music of the original New Wave phenomenon had shaken hands with the metal mania of the 1980s, all of it remixed, repackaged, and resold to teenagers as "alternative." In the summer of 1995 the reformed band played a Florida festival along with Tesla and Bush. "By the end of the show the whole crowd was just really into it," Dokken bassist Pilson told *Amusement Business* reporter Athena Schaffer. "I could tell that we won over a lot of the so-called alternative fans. It was really an alternative festival, but I could see that these young kids could really grasp what we were doing. That felt really good."

Selected discography

Hard Luck Woman (Don Dokken solo), Hard Records, 1980.
Breaking the Chains, Carrere, 1982, Elektra, 1983.
Tooth and Nail, Elektra, 1984.
Under Lock and Key, Elektra, 1986.
Back for the Attack, Elektra, 1987.
Beast from the East (live double album), Elektra, 1989.
Up from the Ashes, Geffen, 1990.
Dysfunctional, Geffen, 1995.

Sources

Amusement Business, May 22, 1995.
Billboard, October 22, 1983.
Chicago Tribune, May 11, 1986; November 19, 1990.
Guitar Player, February 1985.
Los Angeles Times, November 29, 1987; January 31, 1988.
People, November 19, 1984, p. 30; January 13, 1986.
Rolling Stone, February 9, 1989.
Washington Post, June 23, 1995.

—Carol Brennan

Steve Earle

Singer, songwriter, guitarist

Photograph by David Corio, MICHAEL OCHS ARCHIVES/Venice, CA

Steve Earle's career has been derailed several times, primarily because of the singer-songwriter's prickly, rebellious attitude and destructive off-stage habits. But with Earle's larger-than-life persona comes a tremendous talent. "He didn't write no bad songs," country music legend Waylon Jennings told *Spin* writer Mark Schone. "And if he did, he hid 'em." Earle spent several years as a songwriter for other country musicians, finally earning acclaim with his 1986 major-label debut, *Guitar Town.* Still showered with accolades a decade after its release, the work blended an old-time country sound with a rock and roll sensibility.

Earle's subsequent albums veered more toward rock and did not receive the critical praise accorded his debut. His career began to head downhill. Personal problems—drug use, several tumultuous marriages, brushes with the law—combined with a sharp tongue helped undo what some felt was assured crossover stardom in country and rock. Almost miraculously, Earle reappeared in 1995 with a new album. "The music business has left Earle for dead so many times that no one really expects him to bounce back anymore," wrote *Newsweek's* Karen Schoemer in 1995. "So in his utmost ornery fashion, that's exactly what he's doing."

Music and Drugs Marked Teenage Years

Earle was born in Virginia in 1955 but grew up just outside of San Antonio, Texas, the son of an air-traffic controller. Seduced by music at an early age—Earle claims he remembers seeing Elvis Presley on television at the age of three—he dropped out of school at fourteen and eventually moved to Houston. He had already begun playing guitar, as well as experimenting with controlled substances, and by the age of sixteen he was performing in local coffeehouses. It was during these early years that he befriended Townes Van Zandt, the legendary Texas singer-songwriter who would become a mentor of sorts to Earle (and, himself a heavy drinker, a bad influence).

Earle left Texas around 1974 to follow Van Zandt to Nashville, Tennessee, the creative and business hub of the country music industry. In between construction jobs, Earle hustled to make an inside industry connection; by 1975 he had become a staff songwriter for a record label. He penned countless songs, though few of them ever made it onto vinyl. By the early 1980s, however, some of his songs had been recorded by artists like rock and roll pioneer Carl Perkins. Earle nonetheless remained frustrated by his lack of success.

Around 1982 Earle recorded a rockabilly-style album, *Pink and Black,* for an independent label. The LP

For the Record . . .

Born Stephen Fain Earle, January 17, 1955, in Fort Monroe, VA; son of an air traffic controller and a homemaker; first wife's name, Sandie (divorced); second wife's name, Cynthia (divorced); third wife's name, Carol (divorced, 1985); married Lou-Anne Gill, 1987 (divorced, 1987; remarried, 1993); married Teresa Ensenat (a music industry executive), 1988 (divorced, 1992); children: (with third wife) Justin Townes, (with Gill) Ian.

Staff songwriter for country music label, Nashville, TN, late 1970s-early 1980s; released debut album, *Pink and Black,* on an independent label, c. 1982; signed with MCA Records, 1986, and released *Guitar Town;* signed with Winter Harvest Records, 1994, and released *Train A Comin',* 1995.

Selected Awards: Named best country music artist, *Rolling Stone* critics' poll, 1986.

Addresses: *Home*—Fairview, TN. *Record company*—E-Squared, 1815 Division St., Ste. 101, Nashville, TN 37203.

attracted some attention. Country music's popularity had waned, forcing industry decision-makers to seek out and introduce more unconventional artists. Earle seemed to fit the bill. A contract with MCA, then the most powerful label in country music, led to the release of *Guitar Town* in 1986. It catapulted Earle to instant stardom, winning critical acclaim and earning him big-name fans, including rock idol Bruce Springsteen. Many of the songs on *Guitar Town* reflected a life lived on the edge; they were comprised of vignettes he had collected for years and had worked into poignant tunes about the underbelly of American life. Both country and rock fans loved *Guitar Town;* it quickly went platinum, selling over one million units.

Raves for *Guitar Town*

"In a voice that recalls the wry, plaintive sparseness of John Prine and the tender tough-guy bravado of [John] Mellencamp, Earle moves through the personal sagas of small-town dreamers, big-love losers, and day-to-day existers hanging on by their fingernails and praying for change," wrote *Stereo Review* critic Alannah Nash. Jay Cocks of *Time* noted, "Earle's tunes do not have the sentimentality of mainstream country. They have older echoes: the scarred spirit and lonesome heart of Hank

Williams, the grittiness of Johnny Cash, the Bull Run rhythmic charge of another Texas boy, Buddy Holly." In 1986 Earle was named best country singer in *Rolling Stone's* critics' poll, snatching the honor from soon-to-be country giants Dwight Yoakam and Randy Travis, both of whom had released lauded debuts that year. A decade later *Guitar Town* was still called one of the most influential records of the 1980s.

Yet success brought out demons. "Thrilled with the comparisons and lured by the wide world of rock, Earle plunged into the no-man's-land" between country music and rock and roll, wrote Schone in *Spin.* "He lined up Gibsons [guitars] across the stage, played Boss [Springsteen]-like three-hour shows, and awed an audience of hipsters, hicks, punks, and metalheads. But just as he was threatening to go platinum on his own contrarian terms, his bad-boy pose destroyed him." Bourbon, cocaine, heroin, and intravenously self-administered painkillers were Earle's preferred substances of choice, and his blatant use of these coupled with his outlaw attitude cost him supporters in the conservative, company town of Nashville.

Continues Departure from Country

Exit 0, Earle's sophomore studio effort, was released in the summer of 1987. It was his first record with his backing band the Dukes. The work was even edgier than *Guitar Town,* evidence that Earle, perhaps at the direction of MCA, was leaning toward mainstream rock acceptance. The record reached the Top 20 of *Billboard's* country chart while *Guitar Town* continued as a force in the Top 50. Yet Earle's personal and professional lives were becoming increasingly chaotic. When a record company executive had suggested putting Earle's face on the cover of *Exit 0* during dinner, Earle had tossed a steak at him. Executives also suggested a haircut, which Earle refused for four years. He began to use his new affluence and public platform to champion causes important to him, supporting American Indian rights, playing the Farm Aid benefit, and speaking out against the death penalty and the policies of Republican president Ronald Reagan; many of these positions were unpopular in the frequently right-wing world of country music.

By this time Earle's marriage to his third wife had ended; when girlfriend Lou-Anne Gill became pregnant, she became wife number four. Divorce papers were served three months later (though the couple would remarry in 1993). Earle next became involved with Teresa Ensenat, a talent scout affiliated with MCA's Geffen Records imprint. It was also at this time that he asked the label to transfer him out of its country division and into the pop and rock division, where Ensenat worked. MCA executives granted his request, and his new wife—who had helped launch rock powerhouse Guns 'N' Roses—became increasingly involved in his career.

In 1988 Earle released *Copperhead Road,* a full-fledged rock album. The cover bore a skull and crossbones insignia, and "the title cut, a broody tale of drug-running Vietnam vets, had a start-stop swagger closer to Led Zeppelin than [country great] Lefty Frizzell," noted Mark Blake in *Country Music International.* It also featured a song recorded with the Irish folk-punk band the Pogues. *Copperhead Road* received little promotional support from MCA, and album sales headed south. Poor sales, combined with company frustration over Earle's notoriously difficult behavior, effectively spelled his doom within the industry.

> *"If I had known I was going to live this long, I would have taken a lot better care of myself."*

Earle's personal life began sliding even further downhill, and by the time *The Hard Way* was released in 1990, Earle was playing hockey rinks in Canada in between sojourns overseas for dates in British clubs. *Newsweek* referred to *The Hard Way* as "dark, scary, [and] inconsistent." It was dismissed by some as one of Earle's worst albums, though it turned up in *Stereo Review*'s "best recordings of the month" in the fall of that year. Noted country music critic Nash praised its evocation of the seedier side of small-town America with its songs of go-nowhere teens, death-row injustice, and corrupt televangelists. She remarked, "Earle's songs of corruption, greed, outlaws, drink, and dope are so rooted in reality that they show up the kind of commercial country music that attempts to deal with the same subjects as the empty, smarmy dreck it is. It's no wonder that Earle's name is seldom spoken in Nashville anymore."

Earle's last record for MCA was *Shut Up and Die Like an Aviator,* a 1991 live release of new material. He was released from his contract with the label shortly thereafter. When his marriage to fifth wife Ensenat broke up in 1992, Earle's surrender to drug abuse—now including crack cocaine—and alcoholism became even more pronounced. "Earle sightings became a morbid sport in Nashville," reported Schone in *Spin.* "He began to hit up acquaintances for money as rumors began circulating about his guitars turning up in pawn shops." The once hefty performer became thinner and thinner and was arrested several times in the rougher areas of Nashville and charged with drug possession. Occasionally he played unannounced gigs at small clubs. MCA released a greatest hits package in 1993 called *The Essential Steve Earle.*

Clean, Sober, and Successful

A car accident in the spring of 1994 nearly finished what was left of Earle's physical presence, but it was not showing up for a court date that spelled the true end of his wayward ways. A judge sentenced the singer to nearly a year in prison. Earle managed to spend a month of that time cleaning up in a rehab center. He returned to prison for a few more months before being released on probation in November of 1994. From there, in what seemed like a million-to-one shot, Earle began to turn his life around. He was signed to a one-record deal with a small, independent label in Nashville called Winter Harvest. In January of 1995, Earle spent three days in a recording studio, leaving it with a new album of acoustic songs.

Train A Comin' appeared later in 1995 to critical accolades. The work was modeled after Emmylou Harris's *Roses in the Snow,* and Harris, one of Earle's heroes, guested on two of the tracks. One of Van Zandt's songs was also covered, as well as the Beatles' "I'm Looking Through You." Other material on the record had first been recorded as demos two decades before. By April of 1995 *Train A Comin'* was making a run at the alternative rock charts. Nashville, however, seemed loath to accept a record so out of step with the polished, often soulless sound then emanating from Music City—especially one from Earle, despite his turnaround. *Newsweek*'s Schoemer described *Train A Comin'* as "a spare, beautifully tender acoustic effort recorded in loose back-porch jamboree fashion."

In 1996 Earle was back with a new album on a new record company—his own. *I Feel Alright* was the first release on E-Squared (partner Jack Emerson is the other *E*), a Nashville based production company/label to be marketed and distributed by Warner Brothers. "Basically, we're a freestanding independent bringing things to Warner Brothers when it makes sense to go thorough them," Emerson told *Billboard*'s Jim Bessman. Earle added that he wanted to be a Nasville label that does other things besides country music. A clear example of those words could be *I Feel Alright.* A departure from the acoustic bluegrass sound of *Train,* the new release combined a driving acoustic sound with electric guitars that *Entertainment Weekly*'s Alanna Nash says, "regulary crash into the mix like turbo-charged chainsaws."

Earle's plethora of other songs, written over his topsy-turvy 20-year career, began finding welcome homes on other country music releases, including the 1995 effort from country supergroup the Highwaymen. Also, with his new record and company Earle appeared to be leading a healthy, clean-and-sober lifestyle. "If I had known I was going to live this long,"he told *Newsweek's* Schoemer, "I would have taken a lot better care of myself."

Selected discography

Pink and Black, c. 1982.
Guitar Town, MCA, 1986.
Early Tracks, Epic, 1987.
Exit 0, MCA, 1987.
Copperhead Road, MCA, 1988.
The Hard Way, MCA, 1990.
Shut Up and Die Like an Aviator, MCA, 1991.
The Essential Steve Earle, MCA, 1993.
Train A Comin', Winter Harvest, 1995.
(Contributor; with Marty Stuart) "Cryin, Waiting, Hoping," *notfadeaway: remembering buddy holly*, Decca, 1996.
(Contributor)*Dead Man Walking* (soundtrack), Columbia, 1996.
I Feel Alright, E-Squared/Warner Bros, 1996.

Sources

Books

The Penguin Encyclopedia of Popular Music, edited by Donald Clarke, Viking, 1989.

Periodicals

Billboard, January 6, 1996.
Country Music, March/April 1993; January/February, 1996.
Country Music International, March 1995.
Entertainment Weekly, March 8, 1996.
Guitar Player, November 1993.
Newsweek, April 17, 1995.
People, August 10, 1987.
Pulse!, November 1993.
Spin, May 1995.
Stereo Review, November 1986; October 1990.
Time, September 8, 1986.
USA Today, April 11, 1995.

Additional information for this profile was obtained from Winter Harvest Entertainment publicity materials, 1995.

—*Carol Brennan*

Roky Erickson

Singer, songwriter

AP/Wide World Photos

Roky Erickson's music is, "refracted invariably through the prism of legend," ventured *Spin* reviewer Jason Cohen. "As with kindred spirits Skip Spence and Syd Barrett, Erickson's notoriety combines equal parts mis-understood genius and acid-fried loon." Like Spence and Barrett—the most adventurous members of the psychedelically inspired 1960s incarnations of Moby Grape and Pink Floyd, respectively—Erickson helped forge the mind-bending sound of the era but was also a casualty of its excess. Periodically imprisoned and institutionalized and usually dependent on his mother and a handful of friends, he has lost the rights to his trailblazing material and has expressed a feeling of disconnection from songwriting generally; even so, he has continued to release records periodically and in 1995 emerged with a new album.

With the Texas-based group the 13th Floor Elevators and as a solo artist, Erickson served as a decided influence on the development of punk and alternative rock. As Peter Buck, guitarist for rock superstars R.E.M., told Richard Leiby of the *Washington Post,* Erickson's songs "hold up better than any other music from that period" and "are concise and terrifying in their power."

Roger Kynard Erickson—"Roky" came from the first two letters of his first and middle names—was born in Dallas, Texas, in 1947; his family moved to Austin when he was quite young. At age two, his mother recollected in the interview with Leiby, Roky learned to sing the Christmas novelty song "Rudolph the Red-Nosed Reindeer," and he was studying piano "when he was 5, before he could really read." A few years later he picked up the guitar; he began writing songs and playing in bands as a teenager.

Drugs As Inspiration and Impediment

A model early-60s rebel, Erickson grew his hair over his ears, which led to his expulsion before he could complete his senior year at Travis High School. He recorded a single, "You're Gonna Miss Me"—an edgy, pumped-up rock song that Leiby described as "a prototypical punk record"—with his group the Spades. The fledgling artist's songwriting skills and vocal range so impressed a University of Texas anthropology student named Tary Owens that Owens decided to introduce him to his neighbor, Tommy Hall. Hall had little musical experience, but he had vision, charisma, and access to psychotropic drugs. Soon he and Erickson had co-founded a band, which they called the 13th Floor Elevators; the name referred to the floor skipped by superstitious building planners and thus implied that only the band's music could take the listener to such a place. Erickson played guitar and sang—with ferocious energy—while Hall played an amplified jug, producing a sound variously described as "psychedelic" and "irritating."

The band's entire sensibility, it seemed, was founded on LSD and other hallucinogenic substances. What's more, as Owens himself averred in an interview John Morthland of the *L.A. Weekly*, "Tommy was the first person I ever saw use acid to manipulate people. He did that to Roky and all the band." At Hall's urging, band members dropped LSD on a daily basis; while such intensive mood alteration no doubt inspired material such as "Reverberation (Doubt)" and "Roller Coaster," it also took a profound toll.

Yet the band's distinctive sound landed them a deal with International Artist Records, which released their debut album *The Psychedelic Sounds of: The 13th Floor Elevators* in 1966. According to Billy Gibbons of Texas hitmakers ZZ Top, the album was enormously influential. Indeed, it "revealed something far deeper than a frantic version of rock-and-roll," he explained to Leiby. "Here we had some intellectual sensibilities that suggested some real serious thinking. That it came out of this little Texas town was truly amazing." By most accounts, the group would have preferred to stay in their little Texas town; their manager, Lelan Rogers, said they declined high-profile tours. Even so, they played regularly in San Francisco and gained a rabid following in the burgeoning hippie culture with their intense, wigged-out live performances.

Legal and Emotional Troubles

The group released a follow-up album in 1967 and replaced its original rhythm section; Tommy and Roky continued using vast quantities of acid. Leiby quoted Erickson's 1960s declaration that he found tripping on the drug "so beautiful because it's an art. It's like being an artist." Yet such "artistic" behavior interfered with such fundamentals as remembering song lyrics. Erickson spent a year in San Francisco with Dana Morris, whom he would later marry, and returned to Texas in a state of physical and emotional disrepair. His mother sent him to a psychiatrist, who tried to cure him with legal drugs, and then to another doctor, who attempted to undo the damage done by the first. Ironically, Erickson was later arrested for marijuana possession—apparently for a single joint.

Fearing a jail term, Erickson feigned insanity and earned a stay at a hospital prior to his hearing; he fled with Morris a short time later and was arrested when he resurfaced at an Elevators gig. Erickson's flight from justice and a diagnosis of schizophrenia landed him in the Hospital for the Criminally Insane in Rusk, Texas; his three-year tenure there inspired, among other things, his song "I Walked with a Zombie." He also wrote a book of poems called *Openers* under the moniker "the Rev. Roger Roky Kynard Erickson."

After his release, Erickson tried to assemble a new incarnation of the Elevators; when this failed, he moved on and led a band called Bleib Alien—"Bleib" being an anagram for "Bible." In 1977 he put out the single "Starry Eyes," backed with "Red Temple Prayer (Two Headed Dog)." *Rolling Stone* praised the latter song as the kind of radical departure that could save rock from choking on its own mediocrity. Later, Erickson fronted a pick-up group calling itself the Bizarros and featuring, among others, Sterling Morrison (a founding member of New York's avant-rock trailblazers the Velvet Underground). By the late 1970s, Erickson had joined the Aliens, found management, and landed a U.K. record deal with CBS. He released an album in 1980, a revised version of which appeared domestically as *The Evil One*. Erickson's songs, reported Morthland of the *L.A. Weekly*, "are startling, bone-crushing rock & roll with satanic and monster-movie themes."

Erickson's marriage to Morris ended in the early 1980s. His second album was turned down by CBS but ultimately came out in 1986 on the Enigma label. He continued playing with various bands but was clearly impaired by the medication that kept him relatively lucid. In 1989 Erickson was arrested for mail theft—he apparently thought that he should still be collecting the mail for a neighbor who'd long since departed from his housing complex—and sent to an institution in Missouri and then back to the Hays County Correctional Institute near Austin for 60 days.

1990s Revival

In the meantime, some of Erickson's admirers decided to raise money to help him and settled on the idea of a tribute album. Enlisting musician fans like R.E.M., ZZ Top, and John Wesley Harding, among many others, to record versions of his songs, they assembled *Where the Pyramid Meets the Eye*, which was released in 1990. Proceeds went to Erickson's trust fund. Unfortunately, the record didn't sell tremendously well; the seminal singer-songwriter still depended on welfare and the ministrations of his mother and friends to survive. It did, however, increase interest in Erickson's work.

Ultimately, King Coffey—drummer for Texas underground rockers and *Pyramid* participants the Butthole Surfers—signed Erickson to his Trance Syndicate label and put together some older tracks with some new ones for the 1995 release *All That May Do My Rhyme*. "This is sincerely the most excited thing I've ever been associated with," Coffey exclaimed in the *Austin American-Statesman*. "I"m honored and I'm humbled. This guy is a hero of mine, and he's turned from someone I've worshipped from afar into a friend." *Rolling Stone* praised the new album as "a brilliant trip through a variety of pop-music genres," while *Spin* deemed it "a poignant, even tasteful work befitting a sweet, sensitive man a few years shy of 50." The track "We Are Never Talking" was named "Single of the Week" by the British publication *Melody Maker* upon its U.K. release. Meanwhile, rocker-writer Henry Rollins announced the publication of a book of Erickson's lyrics called *Openers II*.

Roky Erickson's reputation as an influence on the development of psychedelia and punk rock is assured. Unfortunately, he has yet to see much financial reward from his work, and his mental instability has cast a dark shadow over most of his adult life. Yet he has returned from the abyss several times before, against seemingly insurmountable odds, and now has the opportunity to reach a new generations of listeners hungry for musical thrills.

Selected discography

With the 13th Floor Elevators

The Psychedelic Sounds of: The 13th Floor Elevators (includes "You're Gonna Miss Me," "Reverberation (Doubt)," and "Roller Coaster"), International Artist, 1966.
Easter Everywhere, International Artist, 1967.
Live, 1968.
Bull of the Woods, 1969.

Solo recordings

"Starry Eyes"/"Red Temple Prayer (Two Headed Dog)," 1977.
The Evil One, 415, 1981.
Clear Night for Love (EP), New Rose (France), 1985.
Don't Slander Me, Enigma, 1986.
All That May Do My Rhyme (includes "We Are Never Talking"), Trance Syndicate, 1995.

Other

Various artists, *Where the Pyramid Meets the Eye* (tribute album), Sire, 1990.

Selected writings

Openers, 1972.
Openers II: The Lyrics of Roky Erickson, 2.13.61 Publications, 1995.

Sources

Austin American-Statesman, July 21, 1992; August 11, 1994.
Austin Chronicle, July 22, 1994.
Billboard, August 27, 1994.
Daily Texan, February 20, 1987.
L.A. Weekly, November 16, 1990.
Rolling Stone, May 18, 1995.
Spin, April 1995.
Third Coast, November 1984.
Village Voice, June 19, 1990; January 6, 1994.
Washington Post, June 23, 1991.

Additional information for this profile was taken from Trance Syndicate publicity materials, 1995.

—*Simon Glickman*

Melissa Etheridge

Singer, songwriter

AP/Wide World Photos

When he reviewed rocker Melissa Etheridge's debut album for *Melody Maker* in May of 1988, Kris Kirk dubbed the work a "very brave album." Etheridge chose the title *Brave and Crazy* for her second album. And her rise to rock stardom has included much courage, as well: in general, challenging the male-dominated world of traditional rock to accept a female vocalist and guitarist; and more specifically, challenging that same world to accept her as a lesbian. But Etheridge's courage has ultimately been worthwhile: she rose to major rock star status by the mid-1990s.

Born in Leavenworth, Kansas, around 1961, Etheridge's roots provided a powerful affinity between herself and an audience hailing largely from working-class middle America. Although her father, John, had a white-collar job—he taught psychology and coached in the local high school—and her mother, Elizabeth, was a homemaker, the family had little money; they lived at the same level as their neighbors, most of whom worked at the Hallmark factory or in the nearby federal prison, which once housed infamous gangster Al Capone. "I'm glad I grew up in a small town," she told *Rolling Stone*'s Rich Cohen. "I grew up with television and radio. I grew up with huge dreams, and yet I had this sort of small-town sensibility. I had what I call values. But they're certainly not what I mean by morality. You learn to treat people good. There was a real work ethic. And I can't help but be very open and very straightforward."

Early Life Inspired Writing

Etheridge has credited her home environment with the motivation that made her a musician, citing both negative and positive influences. She has described both of her parents as loving, but emotionally closed, especially reluctant to express anger or sadness. "So I grew up in a house where everything was just fine," she told Cohen. "I wasn't abused. If I needed something, I had it. But there was no feeling. There was no joy, there was no sadness or pain. And then if there was pain, it was just a nod. So I would go into the basement—where we had a rec room—and write. I would put down all these feelings I had. The songs I was writing in adolescence were very intense because here I am going through all this, feeling all these things, but they're totally denied, and there's nothing there, you know?"

Although Etheridge's parents, who both came from alcoholic homes, discouraged emotional expression, they welcomed it in young Melissa's music. "I was raised ... by parents who were good parents," she told Stacey D'Erasmo when the reporter interviewed her for *Rolling Stone* in 1994, "but all they wanted was for everything to be OK and not to talk about anything. As

I went into my adolescence and was also gay, I could take all this crazy energy, all this 'I m going mad' energy, and play it, sing it, yell, scream, and people would applaud."

"I always wanted to perform," Etheridge recalled in *Rolling Stone* to Cohen. "I remember being 3 years old—one of the first memories I had—and there was a bunch of people over at the house, and I was dancing around in the middle of them, and they were saying, 'Oh, look at her, isn't she cute!' I was like, 'Yeah, this is it, man.' Later, I would organize the neighborhood kids and do, you know, 'Let's play rock band.' And I'd pull the tennis rackets out and the pots and pans just like lots of kids do. I'd always play the tennis racket." Naturally, Etheridge coupled that love of performing with her love of music—something else her family encouraged.

She received her first guitar, from her father, when she was only eight, and soon became dedicated to it, supplementing a year of lessons with a lot of practice. By the time she was ten, Etheridge had written her first song and decided that she wanted to be a musician. She told *Musician's* Scott Benarde in 1989, 'My song-

writing developed before I did. Writing has become part of my life process. When things happen to me they go through this filter." When Etheridge was 11, she performed one of her own compositions, a song called "Lonely as a Child," at a talent contest. During her high school years, she toured the Leavenworth area with a band that played at local bars, where audiences were often engaged more in fighting than in the music, and at the nearby prison.

Leavenworth, Boston, Los Angeles

In an effort both to escape Leavenworth and to become a professional musician, Etheridge moved to Boston in 1980 to study at the Berklee College of Music. She left Berklee after a quick two semesters, dissatisfied with the academic approach to music. Her other education, which she felt was more valuable, came from performing: she played five nights a week at a city restaurant, and could take part in a burgeoning contemporary folk movement permeating Boston's coffee houses. Nonetheless, she felt limited, and came to believe that her true musical home would be Los Angeles.

Of course, when Etheridge arrived in Los Angeles, she discovered that the current there was largely the same as in Boston: heavy metal, punk, and the beginnings of new wave reigned. She secured regular work playing at a gay club, called the Executive Suite, in Long Beach only after much dedicated footwork. Her venues increased over the years, but they remained within the lesbian bar circuit. It was in this arena, nonetheless, that she secured her manager and her record contract.

In 1983 Etheridge shared her demo tape with a woman from one of the bars she played in; the woman passed the tape on to a friend on her softball team. The friend's husband was manager Bill Leopold, who promptly decided to promote Etheridge. He brought a string of record executives into Que Sera Sera, one of Etheridge's regular stages at the time. "I was almost being signed at Capitol Records," Etheridge told Cohen, "almost being signed at A&M, Warner Bros., EMI, all of them coming out." Finally, in 1986, Leopold brought in Chris Blackwell, the founder and head of Island Records, who was so enchanted that he asked Etheridge to sign a contract on the spot.

Despite Blackwell's enthusiasm, Etheridge still had one obstacle to overcome: the difficulty of translating her one-woman-and-a-guitar performance sound into a professional recording. When she first went into the studio with her newly acquired back-up band, they produced ten tracks that Blackwell hated; the layers of studio-polished sound had nothing to do with the spare voice and guitar he had heard in the club. Kevin McCormack, Etheridge's new bass player, discerned the problem and encouraged Etheridge to ask Blackwell for another chance. This time, the singer went into the studio with only the bassist and the drummer, and they managed to capture on tape in four days the distinctive sound that Etheridge had been honing over the years. Blackwell loved it, and preparations for releasing the first album began.

The critical response to *Melissa Etheridge* proved Blackwell right. Critics loved the album's minimalism, especially for the way it showcased the singer's unusual vocals. Kris Kirk, in his *Melody Maker* review, defined his love for the album as a paradox. He declared that "there's something about this ... singer ... that can set teeth on edge, induce foaming at the mouth and spark off migraines. Needless to say, I'm beginning to like Melissa Etheridge and her highly unapproachable LP." Responding both to the production quality and Etheridge's lyrics, Kirk noted, "Raw is the key word, and this is the rawest of albums. As in callow. And as in cold, bleak, rawness of emotion." It sounded as if Blackwell's instinct was just right. A few months later, Paul Mathur blessed the singer in *Melody Maker* with the statement that "the promise is tantalisingly great."

"The Female Bruce Springsteen"

"Bring Me Some Water" made its way onto the airwaves and earned Etheridge a Grammy nomination for best female rock vocal performance. Her musical appearance at the award presentation introduced her to a huge and receptive audience. The reviewer for *People* initiated one of the fundamental comparisons of Etheridge's career, suggesting that the vocalist could be "the female Bruce Springsteen." Despite this kind of coverage and critical interest, which should have placed Etheridge firmly in the midst of the mounting excitement over female musician contemporary folk, Etheridge remained at the fringes of the mainstream.

Used to working hard at her craft, Etheridge threw herself into an expanded performance schedule. She traveled Britain as an opener for another musician and had her own major cities tour of clubs in the United States, including her New York debut in Greenwich Village. She also returned to the studio, turning out *Brave and Crazy* within a year and *Never Enough* in the spring of 1992.

Although the sophomore effort met with some uncertainty, the old enthusiasm resurfaced for *Never Enough*. Ralph Novak greeted the album for *People* as "another triumph," noting the strength of Etheridge's image—

"she is no run-of-the-video pop rock cookie." While conceding that "musically, *Never Enough* is rather conventional," *Rolling Stone*'s Jim Cullen declared Etheridge's voice "as passionate as ever, but used with greater subtlety than before." *Stereo Review* found that the album "positively shines," arguing that "overall this is an impressive, fully rounded album, one that sacrifices no emotional intensity or cut-to-the-bone playing in helping Etheridge show the full range of her writing and performing skills. A stunner." C.M. Smith described the album for *Guitar Player*, writing that Etheridge "spits venomous leads and cranks out grooves so thick you could trip over them."

Coming Out

As massive as the critical response to her music was, it was still eclipsed by a public fascination with her sexual orientation, which she expressed early in 1993. When Bill Clinton was inaugurated as U.S. president in 1993, events were held all over Washington D.C., including the Triangle Ball: the first-ever gay and lesbian inaugural ball. It was here that Etheridge "came out," telling the public what everyone in the music industry already knew—that she was a lesbian.

Although the actual announcement was a spontaneous one, the decision wasn't; Etheridge had long considered the pros and cons of coming out. "You think there's some big black hole you're going to fall into and that all of a sudden people who have loved you all your life aren't going to love you anymore," she told the *Advocate*'s Judy Wieder in a 1994 interview. Nonetheless, her need to be honest overcame that fear, as she told Cohen: "It was something that I felt uncomfortable not talking about. I never lied about it. I never tried to do anything else, but it just would stop there. And as my career went on, and I became more successful, it felt really uncomfortable."

Etheridge's particular value as an "out" musician was, precisely, her mainstream audience: she could make lesbianism less demonic to people who, otherwise, would believe they didn't know any lesbians. As Barry Walters observed in his April, 1993, *Advocate* article, "No other gay or lesbian rock musician is as mainstream as Etheridge. Go to her shows and you'll see a combination of fans that's unlike any other—teased-hair rock chicks with rock-dude boyfriends draped around their shoulders, stray straight-male rockers that wouldn't be out of place at a Bon Jovi show, and packs of highly identifiable lesbians dressed to impress."

Of course, that audience was also one of the reasons Etheridge hesitated about coming out. "I have always been the working woman's singer," she told Wieder. "I come from the Midwest. Mine is heartland music. My audiences are very mixed. So I worried, if I come out, will it make me strange?" But it didn't seem to, and Etheridge remained dedicated to keeping her music accessible, telling Wieder that "I like that my music reaches not just gay but straight fans—men and women both."

Cohen raised the possibility that, after Etheridge came out, straight fans might "have trouble relating to openly gay lyrics." Etheridge responded, "They know it comes from a gay person, but the music talks about the human experience. I mean, I knew that Joni Mitchell was singing about a guy. But I—even as a lesbian—related to her songs and made them my own.... So I hope that any straight listener could just feel the music and feel the words as human experience."

> "My audiences are very mixed. So I worried, if I come out, will it make me strange?....[But] I like that my music reaches not just gay but straight fans—men and women both."

Once Etheridge came out, of course, the press focused on her sexual orientation in interviews, wanting to hear her life story retold in this new light. She placed her initial coming out—the point at which she admitted her orientation to herself—in her mid-teens, while she still made the effort to be or appear straight, dating the occasional boy. "But they were boring," she told Kennedy, "there was never that heart-pounding thing." But she first fell in love, as she told many interviewers, at age 17, when she and her best friend became involved. The relationship, of course, remained a secret from everyone. "It's bad enough being *straight* and dealing with adolescent sexuality," she told *People*'s Peter Castro in 1994, adding that this was "very hard, very lonely."

The decision to leave Leavenworth for Boston became a very different story: musical opportunities awaited in the big city, but so did a large women's community. There, as she told Wieder, she "met all these gay women. I wasn't alone. There were people just like me." After leaving Boston, Etheridge came out to both of her parents on separate occasions and was pleased with both of their responses. Recalling the experience for Castro, Etheridge's mother admitted that, although at first she "didn't quite know how to deal with it," she

eventually "saw how lovely her friends were and how happy she was," which had always been her "main concern."

By the time she came out, Etheridge was in a very committed relationship with director Julie Cypher. "I'd do anything for her," Etheridge told Wieder. "If I had to choose, the career would be the thing I'd give up." The two had met in 1988 when Cypher served as assistant director on Etheridge's "Bring Me Some Water" video. Despite an immediate attraction, they remained friends only, since they were both in long-term relationships, with Cypher in a four-year marriage to actor Lou Diamond Phillips. But both of these partnerships were already troubled, and by 1990 Cypher was separated from Phillips and dating Etheridge. When Etheridge came out, the two shared a home together in the Hollywood Hills and a life that the "Couples" writer for *People* portrayed as idyllic, marking a change in public opinion that Etheridge's bravery helped to bring about.

All this time, Etheridge seemed poised to break through into true rock stardom. She spent much of her year on the road, in the United States and overseas, building an ever-more-devoted fan base. By 1993 she had collected four Grammy nominations; *Never Enough*'s "Ain't It Heavy" finally came through for her that year, winning her the award for best female rock vocal performance. Into this atmosphere, in late 1993, Island released *Yes I Am*, apparently catalyzing the musician's rise as a household name. This new status had many manifestations. She carried the bill in her first major U.S. tour as well as a guest spot in the highly celebrated Eagles tour, and she won a coveted place on the Woodstock '94 roster. She also sold out Madison Square Garden, one of New York City's largest performance spaces. Cohen supplied *Rolling Stone*'s seal of approval with his determination that "Etheridge has solidified her reputation as one of rock's most dynamic performers."

Yes I Am Goes Quadruple Platinum

By the summer of 1994, all of Etheridge's albums had achieved platinum status, and *Yes I Am* eventually went quadruple-platinum. Probably most important in terms of moving Etheridge from the fringes to the center, three of the album's singles—"Come To My Window," "I'm the Only One," and "If I Only Wanted To"—broke into Top 40 radio, and the album spent over a year in the Billboard 200. By 1995 they all had reached the Top Ten. "Come To My Window" provided Etheridge with her second Grammy for best female rock vocal performance.

Although she had always been an "outsider" at MTV, Etheridge became VH1's darling. "VH1 ... rotates her videos so much she might as well be their official mascot," Dana Kennedy wrote in *Entertainment Weekly*. The cable station proved it a month later, when it sponsored—with a massive publicity campaign—Etheridge's 1995 tour. It was, in the words of *Billboard's* Deborah Russell, the "most comprehensive tour sponsorship, promotional campaign, and direct marketing effort in its history." The station's 40,000 concert tickets were gone to callers in two-and-a-half minutes. Further proving Etheridge's megastar status, the station began running promotional videos chronicling the performer's life and career.

Also in 1995, the performer experienced her own greatest sign that she had "arrived"—the opportunity to sing with her lifelong idol and one of the most enduring names in American rock, Bruce Springsteen. He accepted her invitation to sing "Thunder Road" with her at a taping of *MTV Unplugged,* recorded at the Brooklyn Academy of Music's Opera House. In *Time,* Christopher John Farley called the performance "magical ..., spontaneous, liberating, passionate," and declared it the "best and most transporting performance in the new series."

The end of 1995 saw the release of Etheridge's fifth album, *Your Little Secret.* Although berated by critics as being too similar to her previous work, fans eagerly withdrew themselves to her bluesy vocals and emotional delivery. Still, the momentum couldn't carry the album to the multi-platinum levels of *Yes I Am*, but she continued to pack arenas with her full force stage presentation.

Selected discography

On Island
Melissa Etheridge (includes "Bring Me Some Water"), 1988.
Brave and Crazy, 1989.
Never Enough (includes "Ain't It Heavy"), 1992.
Yes I Am (includes "Come To My Window," "I'm the Only One," and "If I Only Wanted To"), 1993.
Your Little Secret, 1995

Sources

Advocate, April 20, 1993; September 21, 1993; July 26, 1994.
Billboard, November 11, 1989; April 4, 1992; December 10, 1994; April 15, 1995.
Detroit Free Press, June 9, 1995.
Entertainment Weekly, March 17, 1995; November 17, 1995.
Guitar Player, November 1989; October 1992.
Melody Maker, May 28, 1988; July 2, 1988.
Musician, June 1989.
Out, May 1995.
People, August 8, 1988; May 15, 1989; May 4, 1992; September 5, 1994.
Rolling Stone, May 14, 1992; June 2, 1994; December 29, 1994; June 1, 1995; November 30, 1995.
Stereo Review, June 1992; January 1994.
Time, March 27, 1995.

Additional information for this profile was obtained from Shock Ink.

—*Ondine Le Blanc*

Tommy Flanagan

Pianist

Archive Photos/Frank Driggs Collection

One of the consummate members of Detroit's post-World War II jazz scene, pianist Tommy Flanagan career has taken him from gifted sideman to critically acclaimed solo artist. A reticent man who reserves few words concerning his own art, Flanagan expresses instead through his music depth and articulation unequaled by most contemporary jazz pianists. As Stuart Nicholson observed in *Jazz: The Modern Resurgence,* "Flanagan is one of the few artists in jazz able to make a convincing statement every time he recorded." With over forty years of experience accompanying gifted singers and instrumentalists, Flanagan has helped elevate modern jazz into high musical art form.

Born in the Detroit neighborhood of Conant Gardens on March 16, 1930, Tommy Lee Flanagan grew up the youngest child of Johnson Sr., a postman, and Ida Mae Flanagan. Both admirers of music, Flanagan's father sang in a quartet and his mother taught herself to read music. A strict disciplinarian, Flanagan's father instilled in his children the importance of character and personal values. "He kept us in check," recalled Flanagan in Whitney Balliet's *American Musicians: Fifty-Six Portraits in Jazz.* "He had a way of sending us to the basement, of taking privileges away. But he showed us all the things of how to be a good person." At age six Flanagan was given a clarinet as a Christmas present; after learning to read music on the instrument, he performed in a family band. Failing to develop an affinity for the woodwind, he sat down at the family piano, and by age ten began to imitate the playing of his older brother, Johnson Jr., a professional pianist. Around this time, he also began taking formal piano lesson from Gladys Dillard. Flanagan spoke with David Rosenthal for the book *Hard Bop: Jazz and Black Music 1955-1965* about this first musical instructor, who, he recalled, taught him "correct pianist attack—how to finger correctly and use the tips of my fingers."

Though Mrs. Dillard taught him the music of Bach and Chopin, the young Flanagan remained drawn to the sound of jazz. From recordings his brothers brought home, he heard the piano styles of Fats Waller, Teddy Wilson, Art Tatum, and Bud Powell. Without the knowledge of his parents, he accompanied his brother on nightclub dates, performing on clarinet and saxophone, and spent evenings listening to jazz outside local nightspots. By invitation of bebop pianist Phil Hill, he entered Detroit's legendary Blue Bird Inn at age sixteen, sitting in with Hills' house band on piano—until being chased out of the club by owner Robert Du Bois.

In the 1940s Flanagan benefitted from the excellent music programs of the Detroit public schools. At Northern High School, his peers included such noted area musicians as alto saxophonist Sonny Red and pianist

Born Tommy Lee Flanagan on March 16, 1930, in Detroit, MI; son of Johnson, Sr. (a postal worker) and Ida Mae Flanagan; married, 1960; wife's name, Ann (divorced, early 1970s); married, 1976; wife's name, Diana; children (first marriage): Tommy, Jr., Rachel, Jennifer, Ann (deceased, 1980).

At age six learned to read music on the clarinet; age ten began formal keyboard training; six years later performed dates and sat in at local clubs in Detroit; became a professional musician after graduating from high school; performed with the band of Rudy Rutherford and subsequently backed singer Bobby Caston; around 1947, co-founded a trio with guitarist Kenny Burrell and bassist Alvin Jackson; 1953 performed in Billy Mitchell's house band at Blue Bird Inn; drafted into the U.S. Army and served overseas in Korea; returned to Detroit and played local clubs until leaving for New York City in 1956; recorded first date under own name 1956; performed trombonist J.J. Johnson's band 1956-1957; recorded with John Coltrane 1959, and Coleman Hawkins and Wes Montgomery in 1960; pianist with Ella Fitzgerald's band, 1963-1965; performed a year with Tony Bennett, mid-1960s; rejoined Fitzgerald as pianist and music director, 1968-1978; pursued solo career, 1980—.

Selected Awards: *Thelonica* was voted by the *Village Voice* as one the best albums of 1982; *Billboard* selected *Jazz Poet* as one of the ten best records of 1990; Flanagan also won first place in the readers' polls of *Down Beat* and *Jazz Times* in 1990; American Jazz Master fellowship from the National Endowment of the Arts, 1996.

Address: *Record company*—Verve Records, 825 Eighth Ave., New York, NY 10019.

Roland Hanna. In an interview with author Michael Ullman for *Jazz Lives: Portraits in Words and Pictures*, Flanagan recalled the impact of his school music instructors: "They took an interest in kids who showed talent. They pushed them on. They would teach you basics. There were even good teachers in the intermediate schools."

After graduating from high school, Flanagan ended his formal training with Gladys Dillard and turned to performing as a regular member of Detroit's vibrant jazz scene. He played dates with the band of Rudy Rutherford at the Parrot Lounge, and accompanied his first singer, Bobby Caston, through whom he met pianist Art Tatum. Around 1947, Flanagan formed a Nat King Cole-style trio with guitarist Kenny Burrell and bassist Alvin Jackson. With Burrell doubling on vocals, the trio performed at dances and parties. When not playing parties or clubs, Flanagan practiced at the family homes of Burrell, Hugh Lawson, and fellow pianist Barry Harris.

Bebop Disciple

Though he listened to various styles of jazz piano, Flanagan's primary musical influence emerged from the modernist sounds of Charlie Parker and Dizzy Gillespie. "We were crazy about Charlie Parker and Dizzy at that time," explained Flanagan in *Jazz Spoken Here: Conversations with Twenty-Two Musicians*. "They came to Detroit quite a bit. It was like we religiously went to see them." "Parker and Gillespie," he added, in *Jazz Times*, "opened our ears to what was new." Years earlier he had stood outside the screen door of the El Sino Club to hear the sound of Parker's horn. Influenced by Parker's innovative single lines, Flanagan later developed what he termed a Parker horn style of piano. A fervent follower of the Parker school, Flanagan, unlike many other aspiring jazzmen, refused to play side jobs which required the performance of commercial music. Because of the popularity of barrelhouse blues and other forms of stage entertainment, many clubs did not cater to the more obscure sounds of bebop. In 1949, the *Michigan Chronicle* announced "Tommy is laid off...How can a man with his ability not find work." Detroit saxophonist George Benson described Flanagan, in a private interview, as a "brilliant musician, an extremist, who opposed any form of entertainment which demeaned his modernist artistry."

In 1953 Flanagan performed with numerous Detroit jazzmen including trumpeter Thad Jones and saxophonist Billy Mitchell at the Blue Bird Inn. Describing his experience at the Blue Bird in the *Detroit News*, Flanagan stated that "it was a great time. Thad was writing all these original things. The music was played such a high caliber of musicianship. The people that used to visit there were important people." That same year, his musical career was interrupted by his induction into the U.S. Army. After training at Fort Leonard, Missouri, he received instruction as a motion-picture operator, and was sent to the Korean port city of Kunsan. With no desire to join the military, he described the experience in Balliet's *American Musicians* as a "nightmare time."

Returning to Detroit, Flanagan resumed his career playing in local clubs like Klien's Showbar, the Crystal Show Bar, and the Rouge Lounge. He also attended Tuesday night concerts held by a private musician's collective, the New World Music Society. The society's rented Woodward Avenue location, the New World Stage, was an upstairs room which featured the finest musicians in the city such as Kenny Burrell (the organization's president), Yusef Lateef, Donald Byrd, and Barry Harris.

By the mid-Fifties, Flanagan sought to further his career outside the local scene. As he explained in *Down Beat,* "Most of the opportunities had been exhausted in Detroit and it was time for a change." Invited to travel to New York City by Burrell, who had made a number of connections with prominent New York-based musicians, Flanagan left for the East Coast in 1956. In a live interview with Detroit radio host Ed Love, Burrell recalled the occasion: "I called my friend Tommy Flanagan one day and said, 'Look, I'm going to move to New York in a couple of weeks and if you want to go let me know.' He called me back in a few days. He said, 'ok.' So we drove to New York together."

New Horizons in New York City

Arriving in New York in the spring of 1956, Flanagan began attending jam sessions held at renowned jazz spots Club 125, Count Basie's, and Small's. After a few weeks, he sat in on his first recording session, which produced the Blue Note LP *Detroit—New York Junction* with Burrell, Oscar Pettiford, and Shadow Wilson. On Flanagan's twenty-sixth birthday, he, along with saxophonist Sonny Rollins and bassist Paul Chambers, appeared on Miles Davis' *Miles Davis All Stars.* Two months later, he backed Rollins on the saxophonist's landmark solo recording *Saxophone Colossus.* In the LP's liner notes, Ira Gitler observed that "the impeccable Tommy Flanagan is as fluid as ever and fiery in a more overt manner than usual." By the end of July, he performed his first date with Ella Fitzgerald, replacing the group's ailing pianist, Don Abney. Landing the job through the recommendation of Ella's cousin E.V. Perry and Detroit saxophonist Billy Mitchell of Dizzy Gillespie's big band, Flanagan joined Fitzgerald's group in Cleveland. Quoted in Stuart Nicholson's biography *Ella Fitzgerald,* Flanagan recalled the occasion: "[Ella] had charts for everything, a lot of stuff, she had a large book there. Not only did she have a trio book but she had a book for band arrangements...To begin with I don't think she had much confidence in me, I was recommended, I just tried to do my job."

After his brief stint with Fitzgerald, Flanagan went on to perform with several of the era's most influential modern jazz artists. Between 1957 and 1959, he toured Europe with trombonist J.J. Johnson's band, a group that included trumpeter Nat Adderly and drummer Elvin Jones. During a 1957 European tour, Flanagan recorded his first album as a leader: *The Tommy Flanagan Trio Overseas.* "The record contains," wrote Rosenthal in *Hard Bop,* "at least one example of Flanagan's silky, caressing approach to ballads: 'Chelsea Bridge,' the beginning of a long love affair on wax with Billy Strayhorn tunes. But in general it is a rocking, kicking session booted along by Jones's busily interweaving, loose-jointed brushwork." In May of 1959, he appeared on John Coltrane's first Atlantic recording, *Giant Steps* (a year earlier he performed on the outstanding collaborative effort *Kenny Burrell & John Coltrane*). On "Giant Steps" and "Cousin Mary," Flanagan provided a refined backdrop to the arrangement's complex chord changes and vertical improvisatory patterns.

In early 1960, Flanagan attended a session that produced guitarist's Wes Montgomery's critically acclaimed second album, *Wes Montgomery: The Incredible Jazz Guitar.* "Well, we had heard a lot about Wes, even before we started to record," stated Flanagan in *Jazz Spoken Here,* "He'd chord just chorus after chorus and not repeat himself...He was that incredible." A day following Montgomery's session, he stepped into the studio again to perform on tenor saxophonist Coleman Hawkins's album, *At Ease With Coleman Hawkins.* A set of ballads, the recording is a timeless showcase of lyricism. "Tommy has a flowing style that rolls along," wrote Ron Eyre in the liner notes. "He does not pound or abuse, in fact he does none of the the things that are of the 'hardsell' variety."

After a stint with Coleman Hawkins' band, Flanagan was approached by promoter Norman Granz in the summer of 1963 to take over the piano chair in Ella Fitzgerald's group. As Flanagan admitted in *Ella,* "I guess I had a better reputation the second time I worked with her...I was available. I had been working with Coleman Hawkins and he wasn't doing all that much and it was a chance for some steady work." With the addition of Flanagan, the group comprised guitarist Les Spann, bassist Jimmy Hughart, and drummer Gus Johnson. Upon the departure of Spann, Granz often featured trumpeter Roy Eldridge with Fitzgerald's trio. In November 1965, Flanagan left Fitzgerald's group; after moving to California he performed a year with singer Tony Bennett.

Back With Ella

Upon her return from touring Europe in 1968, Fitzgerald re-hired Flanagan, who remained her music director for the next decade. "We worked forty to forty-five weeks a year," related Flanagan in *Ella,* "There wasn't much time for anything else. She would take a few weeks at Christmas and a month in summer." With Fitzgerald's trio, he performed jazz festivals and appearances throughout Europe, and backed the famous singer for a performance at Louis Armstrong's funeral in 1971. His accompaniment on Fitzgerald's live *Montreux 1975* has been critically recognized for its superb musical approach and inventive wit.

In the fall of 1978, years of a demanding schedule and ill health prompted Flanagan to leave Fitzgerald's trio. "I finally left Ella," explained Flanagan in *American Musicians,* "because the traveling got to be too much for me and because in 1978 I had a heart attack." By the early 1980s, Flanagan was back on track His 1982 tribute to the music of Thelonious Monk, *Thelonica,* was voted by the *Village Voice* as one the best albums of the year. In 1990, *Billboard* selected his album *Jazz Poet* as one of the ten best records of the year; both *Down Beat* and *Jazz Times* awarded him first place in their readers' poll categories that year as well. Flanagan's 1991 release, *Beyond the Blue Bird* brought him together once again with Kenny Burrell in a tribute to the two artists' early musical roots. Unlike so many recent collaborations, it seems less an article of nostalgia, more a reaffirmation of artistry. In the album's liner notes, jazz scholar Dan Morganstern described Flanagan's ability to maintain a level of vibrant creative expression: "There are certain artists—a blessed few—who, having already reached the pinnacle, continue to surpass themselves. Tommy Flanagan is such an artist."

Selected discography

Solo LPs

Moodsville, Original Jazz Classics, 1960.
Jazz at the Santa Monica Civic Center '72, Pablo, 1972.
Tokyo Recital, Pablo, 1975.
The Best of Tommy Flanagan, Pablo, 1977.
Eclypso, Enja, 1977.
Ballads and Blues, Enja, 1978.
Something Borrowed, Something Blue, Galaxy, 1980.
Super Session, Enja, 1980.
A Little Pleasure, Reservoir, 1981.
The Magnificent, Progressive, 1981.
In Memory of John Coltrane, Enja, 1982.
Thelonica, Enja, 1982.
Alone Too Long, Denon.
More Delights, Galaxy.
Jazz Poet, Timeless, 1989.
Beyond the Blue Bird, Timeless, 1990.
Lady Be Good...For Ella, Verve, 1994.

Has also recorded the LPs *The Complete Overseas* (DIW), *Plays the Music of Rodgers and Hammerstein* (Savoy), *Let's Play the Music of Thad Jones* (Enja), *Confirmation* (Enja), and *Super Session* (Enja).

With Others

(With Sonny Rollins) *Saxophone Colossus,* Prestige, 1956.
Miles Davis All Stars, Prestige, 1956.
Kenny Burrell: All Day Long, Prestige, 1957.
Kenny Burrell & John Coltrane, Prestige, 1958.
(With John Coltrane) *Giant Steps,* Atlantic, 1959.
The Incredible Guitar of Wes Montgomery, Riverside, 1960.
At Ease With Coleman Hawkins, Prestige, 1960.
Coleman Hawkins: The Jazz Version "No Strings", Moodsville, 1962.
(With Hank Jones) *Our Delights,* Original Jazz Classics, 1979.
(With Red Mitchell) *You're Me,* Phontastic, 1980.
(With Pepper Adams) *The Adams Effect,* Uptown, 1988.
(With Mark Whitfield) *7th Ave. Stroll,* Verve, 1996.

Has also recorded *I'm Still All Smiles* (with Hank Jones; piano duets) for Verve; *Together: Tommy Flanagan/Kenny Barron* for Denon; and *Kenny Burrell Jazzmen From Detroit* for BYG.

Sources

Books

Balliet, Whitney, *American Musicians: Fifty-Six Portraits in Jazz,* Oxford University Press, 1986.
Chambers, Jack, *Milestones Vol. I: The Music and Times of Miles Davis to 1960,* University of Toronto Press, 1983.
Enstice, Wayne and Paul Rubin, *Jazz Spoken Here: Conversations With Twenty-Two Musicians,* Louisiana Press, 1992.
Nicholson, Stuart, *Ella Fitzgerald,* Victor Gollancz, 1993.
Nicholson, Stuart, *Jazz: The 1980s Resurgence,* Da Capo, 1995.
Rosenthal, David, *Hard Bop: Jazz and Black Music 1955-1965,* Oxford University Press, 1992.
Ullman, Michael, *Jazz Lives: Portraits in Words and Pictures,* New Republic Books, 1980.

Periodicals

Detroit Free Press, March 14, 1996.
Detroit News, September 26, 1992.
Down Beat, October 15, 1970.
Jazz Times, October, 1992.
Michigan Chronicle, July 30, 1949; January 3, 1953.

Information for this profile was also obtained via a radio interview with Kenny Burrell conducted by Ed Love on WDET-FM, Detroit, and a private interview with saxophonist George Benson in Detroit on November 22, 1990.

Liner notes from *At Ease With Coleman Hawkins* (Prestige, 1960), written by Dan Eyre; *Saxophone Colossus* (Prestige, 1956), written by Ira Gitler; and *Beyond the Blue Bird* (Timeless, 1991), written by Dan Morganstern, were also used in compiling this profile.

—John Cohassey

Rosie Flores

Singer, songwriter, guitarist

Reviewing a Rosie Flores concert, Neil Strauss of the *New York Times* referred to her as "a spinning wheel of American roots music." While Flores has amassed her fan base outside of the country music mainstream, she has demonstrated consistent growth and increasing ambition as a guitarist, singer, and writer. After a disappointing experience with a major label, she signed on with the "indie" label Hightone and recorded a series of well-regarded albums that fused the song smarts of the Austin, Texas scene with the rambunctious energy of early rock and roll. In 1995 she wowed critics and fans alike with *Rockabilly Filly,* an unabashed celebration of her roots and a chance to collaborate with some of her idols.

Flores was born in San Antonio, Texas; early rock icon Elvis Presley and pop crooner Brenda Lee fueled her interest in music. Her father was able to record Rosie and her siblings singing together when she was 7, and a snippet of one such session was included on *Rockabilly Filly.* When she was 12 her family moved to San Diego, California, where a variety of burgeoning pop forms influenced her tastes as well as her decision to form Penelope's Children, an all-female band, at 16. In a *Guitar Player* profile, Flores recalled a back-handed compliment she received for her fretwork: a male audience member said, "You're pretty good for a girl." Far from rearing up in feminist outrage, Flores noted, "I remember thinking, 'Yeah, I *am* pretty good for a girl, aren't I?,' because back then very few girls were playing lead guitar. I felt like I was breaking new ground. But whenever some guy said that, he'd always follow by saying, 'No, I mean, you're pretty good for a guy too— I mean, you're just pretty good—*period.*'"

"Wow, Girls Can Do it Too"

It was partly the work of trailblazing singer Wanda Jackson that nudged Flores in this direction. "I had heard Elvis and [1950s hitmaker and rock pioneer] Buddy Holly," she told the *Boston Globe.* "But I kinda didn't think of it as something a woman could perform until I heard her records, and then I went, 'Wow, girls can do it too.'" Flores later formed the band Rosie and the Re-boppin' Screamers and in 1984 joined the country-punk outfit Screamin' Sirens; according to *Nashville Scene* "she was the only musically adept member" of that group.

She earned a record deal with Warner Bros. as a solo artist in 1986, releasing her debut album the following year. Unfortunately, opined *Guitar Player*'s Kevin Ransom, "she was pigeonholed as a C&W chick singer by Nashville types who didn't care much about her genre-bending guitar playing," which draws on hard blues and riff rock as well as the twang of country. *Musician* noted that while her Warner bow "did a nice job of showcasing Flores' smoky, out-of-breath delivery and her knack for milking the dickens out of a country lyric, she seemed somewhat boxed in by Dwight Yoakam producer Pete Anderson's heavy-handed direction."

Flores later acknowledged the contradictions of her major-label experience. "This friend of mine helped me make some demos that we sent to Warners in Nashville," she told *Request* writer Susan Hamre. "I was really surprised that the demos we made caught the attention of the A&R [talent scout] people over there. It was an even bigger surprise when they dropped me two years later because I had been told that they didn't want to change me. But my uniqueness had them a little mind-boggled, so they said go find a label that understands you."

Artistic Control, Critical Praise

She continued to soldier on, however, moving to Austin, Texas in 1988. That town's alternative-country scene relied on folk-influenced songcraft and was in general more tolerant of stylistic eccentricity than Nashville. Flores played on the well-regarded television series *Austin City Limits* and rapidly earned cult status as a performer and songwriter. In 1989 she had a chance to sing backup with Wanda Jackson; the two became fast friends and would later collaborate in the studio. And ultimately Flores found a label that understood her, the

California indie company Hightone, which she described to Hamre as "the easiest place to go to be able to do my music creatively the way that I'd like to do it." Unburdened by the conservative nature of corporate country music, which tends to distrust women who seem unusual or too eclectic, Flores could indulge her wide-ranging musical passions completely. Even if the label wasn't wild about every song she wrote, "they don't stop me from putting them on, and that's the freedom of artistic control."

In 1992 Flores released *After the Farm*, which she recorded with her band The Bad Boys. On this album, *Musician* reviewer Peter Cronin noted, "Flores is playing more guitar and writing better songs" than on her ill-fated Warner Bros. debut. "Most importantly, the singer sounds like she's having a blast." Ransom of *Guitar Player* called the record "a tough-minded three-guitar country-rock showcase that uses [1960s country-influenced rockers] The Byrds and The Buffalo Springfield as musical touchstones." With the aid of Wayne "DJ" Jarvis on electric and slide guitars and the versatile Greg Leisz on pedal steel, lap steel, dobro, and other guitars—along with a solid rhythm section—Flores finally had a band that could showcase the range of her talents. At the same time, her talented sidemen scarcely overshadowed her own playing. "Rosie's solos flow instinctively from her melodies and rhythms," wrote Ransom, "while her lines weave in and out of the tough-but-tasteful textures laid down by Jarvis and Leisz." The album made the year-end Top 10 lists of several magazines, including *Pulse!* and *Request*.

"Robo Rosie" Recovers

More praise came with her 1993 set *Once More With Feeling*. In a *Musician* review, Chris Willman managed to compare Flores to a number of her primary influences in one fell swoop: "Imagine the pre-adolescent Brenda Lee grown up and matured without losing any of her spunk and pluck, and you've got a good idea of Flores' appeal—though her assured songwriting and aggressively rocky lead guitar bring to mind less demure forerunners like Wanda Jackson and Bonnie Raitt." John Morthland of *Country Music*, meanwhile, heard "this unique, and endlessly effective, breathy 'pull' in her voice that is reminiscent of the smoky Mountain sound of early Dolly Parton"; while complaining about some aspects of the production, Morthland felt she had great potential. The album's single "Honky Tonk Moon" received a fair amount of attention, thanks to a frequently played clip on the video stations CMT and VH-1.

During a 1994 world tour, Flores suffered a major setback. Running down a wet London street with her laundry, she slipped and landed on her right hand. She performed that night with her arm in a cast, leaving the guitar playing to others, and the show went well. Back in the states, however, increased pain sent her to a specialist who warned she might need surgery. She cancelled her tour and headed for her parents' home in San Diego. "I couldn't cook, I couldn't write, I couldn't hardly do anything," she recalled to *Pulse!* Since it was necessary for her arm to heal correctly, she had the surgery, which involved fusing the bones with metal screws. Her arm was also placed in an external device to keep it from moving the wrong way. "For eight weeks, I was Robo Rosie," she quipped to *Nashville Scene.* "It was so painful, I kept telling them, 'If I'm having to put up with this much pain, this is going to have to work.' But we didn't know how it was going to affect my guitar playing. The screws were right where I use my wrist the most. The only way I could get through it was to stay positive. I put every bit of mental positive framework into it I could. I thought, 'This is going to heal. It's going to.'"

Her positive thinking paid off. After some physical therapy, she was able to perform, and even appeared on a TNN country music special, *Live at the Ryman Auditorium,* with Jackson, alternative-country singer Iris DeMent, and country superstar Pam Tillis. Performing behind Jackson on the song "Let's Have a Party" was a particular thrill for Flores. During her guitar solo, she told *Nashville Scene,* she heard Jackson let out "this wild rockabilly scream. She said, 'Oh yeah! WOOOOOO!' It was an incredible thing." The charge of this experience, as well as some gigs on the re-emerging Nashville and Los Angeles rockabilly scenes, influenced her decision to undertake the project that would be *Rockabilly Filly.*

Rosie Reinvigorates Rockabilly

Released in 1995 and featuring guest vocals by Jackson and veteran wailer Janis Martin, *Rockabilly Filly* allowed Flores to expand her instrumental range. "My approach was more low-down and dirty," she explained to the *Boston Globe.* "Now I'm learning how to play more jazzy and that's so much a part of rockabilly," she added, noting that exploring these stylistic tributaries was "what I'm working on now, trying to make myself grow and incorporate that into my playing." The album earned a number of glowing reviews. According to Eric Levin of *People,* Flores "reinvigorates rockabilly, mixing in dabs of country steel guitar, doo-wop, boogie-woogie and swinging blues. It's all breathless fun, and the slow tunes are sexy enough to alarm a chaperone." *New Country* critic Geoffrey Himes enthused that after three

albums that failed to capture the electricity of her live shows, Flores had at last "figured out how to bottle that lightning on a recording," adding that she "has come up with a handful of new rockabilly songs as exciting as anything Jackson or Martin ever recorded."

It seemed that with her travels into pure rockabilly, Flores had found a way to communicate her musical essence. And though it was clear she had always been better than just "pretty good for a girl," she commented to the *Boston Globe* about the importance of being an influence herself. "A lot of women have come up to me, and their eyes are on fire and they say 'You've really inspired me,'" she noted. "You know there's not very many of us out there playing lead. Bonnie Raitt's a role model for me, and if I can be that by playing rockabilly, I think it's neat. I inspire more girls to get out and play."

Selected discography

Rosie Flores, Warner Bros., 1987.
After the Farm, Hightone, 1992.
Once More With Feeling (includes "Honky Tonk Moon"), Hightone, 1993.
Rockabilly Filly, Hightone, 1995.

With others

(Dave Alvin) *King of California,* (appears on "Goodbye Again"), Hightone, 1994.
Tulare Dust, (Merle Haggard tribute album, appears on "My Own Kind of Hat"), Hightone, 1994.

Sources

Boston Globe, December 8, 1995.
Color Red, November 1995.
Country Music, November 1993.
Guitar Player, September 1992.
Musician, July 1992; February 1994; February 1996.
Nashville Scene, December 7, 1995.
New Country, December 1995.
New York Times, July 26, 1995.
People, December 11, 1995.
Pulse!, December 1995.
Request, November 1993.
Rolling Stone, October 29, 1992.

Additional information was provided by Hightone Records publicity materials, 1995.

—*Simon Glickman*

Radney Foster

Singer, songwriter

Courtesy of Fitzgerald Hartley Co.

ountry singer and songwriter Radney Foster began making a name for himself in the late 1980s as half of the duo Foster & Lloyd. Later, Foster shone on his own as one of a bright new generation of country stars raised as much on the Beatles and the Rolling Stones as on Merle Haggard and Hank Williams. Coming from a pop-country background and wearing glasses instead of the requisite cowboy hat, Foster was nonetheless embraced by a Nashville not known for bucking trends. But Foster's country roots are beyond reproach and that's something the folks in Music City appreciate.

Born in Del Rio, Texas, in 1959, Foster recalled in an Arista Records press biography, "I remember the first time I heard Waylon [Jennings] sing 'The Only Daddy That'll Walk the Line.' I mean, I had to pull the car over. It was like, 'Maaaaaannnn, that's the hippest thing I ever heard.'" As a student majoring in forestry and geology at the University of the South in Sewanee, Tennessee, Foster performed as part of an acoustic duo. When a friend found out that Foster was the one writing the twosome's material, he invited a producer from Nashville to hear Foster play. The producer was impressed.

So Foster told his folks that he wanted to quit school to pursue music. They were appalled, but they struck a compromise with him stipulating that if he didn't have a publishing or record deal in a year, he'd leave Nashville and finish college. "Hell, I was 20 years old, full of fire and way too much energy," he recounted in the Arista bio. "I thought I was gonna be the next Elvis by the time I was 21. It didn't work out that way." Foster returned from Nashville, finished school, and married his college sweetheart. He then moved back to Nashville to give it another shot.

Joined Forces With Bill Lloyd

In 1985 Foster was signed as a staff songwriter by MTM and began writing with Holly Dunn and Bill Lloyd. With Lloyd he wrote Sweethearts of the Rodeo's first Top Ten hit, "Since I Found You." He and Dunn wrote several songs that she would eventually record, including her first Number One single, "Love Someone Like Me." Foster also wrote the T. Graham Brown/Tanya Tucker hit "Don't Go Out With Him" and has contributed songs to a range of other artists, including Guy Clark, the New Grass Revival, and the reunited Poco. In 1987 Foster and Lloyd were signed as performers by RCA Records.

Their pop-country mix was well received. Together they recorded three albums: *Foster & Lloyd, Faster & Llouder*, and *Version of the Truth*. The pair's initial single, "Crazy Over You," was the first debut effort by a duo ever to reach the Number One position on *Billboard's*

For the Record . . .

Born July 20, 1959, in Del Rio, TX; son of John (a lawyer) and Bette Foster; married a woman named Mary-Springs, early 1980s (divorced, 1995); children: a son. *Education:* Graduated from the University of the South.

Staff songwriter, MTM, Nashville, TN, beginning in 1985; began writing songs with Bob Lloyd, 1985; as part of duo Foster & Lloyd, signed with RCA Records, 1987; released *Foster & Lloyd,* 1987; Foster & Lloyd disbanded, 1991; signed by Arista Records, c. 1991; released first solo album, *Del Rio, Texas, 1959,* 1992.

Addresses: *Record company*—Arista Records, 7 Music Circle North, Nashville, TN 37203. *Management*—Fitzgerald-Hartley Co., 1212 16th Ave. South, Nashville, TN 37212.

country chart. Boasting a wide appeal, their records crossed over from country radio to the alternative and college rock formats. *Stereo Review* offered this of their sound: "If the Byrds and the Beatles were to have lunch at the Everly Brothers' house and listen to Hank Williams, Sr., records, the music would sound like Foster & Lloyd." In a similar vein, *Guitar Player* wrote, "These guys are either two of country's hottest rockers or two of rock's hottest country players." But some reviewers found the music derivative. An *Entertainment Weekly* scribe opined that Foster & Lloyd 'seemed merely to be grafting pop elements to country lyrics, or country instrumentation to pop attitude."

"We'd get reviews," Foster recalled in his press bio of his days with Lloyd, "and it would always be, 'This country guy from Texas and this pop-rock kind of guy,' and I turned to my wife after reading the fifth one of those, and said, 'Why do I always have to be the *'billy* in the band?' And she turned right back around to me and said, 'Because you are.' I think that's the point at which I accepted the fact that I may write with other influences for other people or even for myself, but as a singer and as a person, that's who I am. I'm a Southern kid from a small town in West Texas who grew up liking country and rock records."

In 1991—after placing four Top Ten hits and a total of nine singles on *Billboard's* Hot Country Singles & Tracks chart—Foster & Lloyd found themselves going in different directions. "We did things the right way," Foster told *CMA* contributor Mandy Wilson. "It was an amicable split. Both of us knew what we wanted, and we went after it."

Foster promptly went looking for a solo deal. He started talking with Arista president Tim DuBois, who had once managed Foster & Lloyd. DuBois knew that Foster was talented, but he wasn't sure the bespectacled singer had the sound Arista was looking for. After hearing Foster's set at Nashville's famed Bluebird Cafe, however, DuBois realized that what Foster was doing was much more traditionally country than the Foster & Lloyd material had been. They shook hands on a deal in the restaurant's kitchen.

At DuBois's suggestion, Foster concentrated on songwriting before jumping back into recording. He also spent some months opening for country stars like Mary-Chapin Carpenter, Alan Jackson, and Vince Gill with just his guitar as accompaniment. "It was really good for me," he explained in his Arista biography. "There's a different feel you get when you're writing things you can do with just a guitar. It really influenced what I was writing and what I wanted to say."

In 1992 Foster released *Del Rio, Texas, 1959.* "This record," he noted in the press materials heralding its arrival, "is about learning how to two-step at the 4-H barns in Del Rio. It has to do with growing up in a little tiny town and cruising the Sonic on Saturday nights, and with all of the records that accompanied that—the Waylon Jennings, the old Beatles, the Buddy Holly and Rodney Crowell and Emmylou Harris—there was life-changing stuff for me in there." *Del Rio* spawned three Top 10 singles, "Just Call Me Lonesome," "Nobody Wins," and "Easier Said Than Done," and sold roughly 350,000 copies.

Fans *and* Critics Wooed by *Del Rio*

Critics were delighted by Foster's musical approach, even with its eclectic pop influences. A *Country Fever* reviewer called the disc "one of the freshest I've heard." In the *Edmonton Journal* Peter North said, "Foster could very well become one of the finest songwriters in the history of country music." Observers were especially impressed that Foster had written or cowritten every cut on the album, which is not often the case in country music.

Foster toured extensively for *Del Rio,* greatly broadening his fan base. He also contributed songs to several compilations, including an all-star tribute to Merle Haggard, *Mama's Hungry Eyes,* and the AIDS benefit album *Red Hot & Country.* Then, in 1995, Foster released his own second album, *Labor of Love. Country Music's* Bob Allen called it "an intelligently wrought, inspired work, full of earnestness and bravado, with near-seamless arrangements and precious few weak spots." A *Bill-*

board writer reported that Foster had "developed into one of country music's more substantive singer/songwriters, capable of turning out songs that are as hookladen as they are thought-provoking." And *Country Music International* averred that *Labor of Love* "showcases Foster's vocal thump, every song delivered with earnest passion and polished to near perfection.... Foster has produced an accomplished, intelligent and very listenable slice of progressive country."

Despite the "progressive" tag, a nod to his pop sensibilities, Foster has not strayed far from his roots. "If you're in country music," he told *Billboard*'s Peter Cronin, "you're traditional, and I love traditional country. But there's always something creative and different that comes along in country music and shakes the trees. It may make things easier on me, or tougher, but that's my goal."

Selected discography

Solo releases; on Arista Records

Del Rio, Texas, 1959, 1992.
Labor of Love, 1995.

Also contributed to *Red Hot & Country,* Arista, *Flaco Jimenez,* Arista, the *Maverick* soundtrack, Icon/Atlantic, and *Mama's Hungry Eyes: A Tribute to Merle Haggard,* Arista, all 1994.

With Foster & Lloyd; on RCA Records

Foster & Lloyd, 1987.
Faster & Llouder, 1989.
Version of the Truth, 1990.

Sources

Billboard, November 14, 1987; September 3, 1988; April 22, 1989; October 31, 1992; July 16, 1994; March 25, 1995.
CMA, September 1993.
Country Fever, September 1994.
Country Music, March 1988; July 1989; March 1990; November 1992; January 1995; March 1995.
Country Music International, October 1994.
Edmonton Journal (Alberta, Canada), February 10, 1995.
Entertainment Weekly, December 18, 1992; June 17, 1994; November 18, 1994.
Guitar Player, December 1990.
People, April 17, 1995; June 27, 1994.
Rolling Stone, January 14, 1988.
Stereo Review, January 1988; July 1989; September 1990.

Additional information for this profile was obtained from Arista Records publicity materials, 1992, 1995.

—*Joanna Rubiner*

Michael Franti

Rap artist

Michael Franti emerged as one of the most provocative and talented members of the crowded rap/hip-hop universe in the early 1990s. A musician with a chameleonlike ability to reshape his musical style from album to album, Franti first garnered attention with an avant-garde funk outfit known as the Beatnigs. He then moved on to the Disposable Heroes of Hiphoprisy, a fiery, politically charged group drenched in a booming industrial rap sound. After the Disposable Heroes folded, Franti reinvented his sound once again and in 1994 founded the group Spearhead. Critics and fans alike were bowled over when their first effort, *Home,* was released. As reviewer Ken Capobianco remarked in *The Tab,* "Nothing in Disposable [Heroes of Hiphoprisy] prepares you for Franti's new brain-child, Spearhead, a diverse mix of organic hip-hop, pop and Franti's vivid verse filled with both potent politics and a newfound warmth and whimsy."

Michael Franti was born in 1968 in Oakland, California. Put up for adoption as an infant, he spent his first months of life in a number of foster homes. When he was still a toddler, he was adopted by a white family that moved around to various California locales throughout his childhood. Years later Franti searched for and found his birth parents—his mother was white, his father black—but he recognized that "when it's all over, it's the people who raised me who are my parents. You know what I'm saying? They loved me and looked

after me all those years," he said in an interview with Mike Greenblatt for *Right On!* "So as I've gotten older, digested the information, thought about it, talked about it, written about it, I have an understanding about who I am as an individual and where I fit in with my feelings."

After completing high school in northern California, Franti ambled down to San Francisco. He attended college at the University of San Francisco, having secured a scholarship to play basketball. A rangy, six-and-a-half footer who loved to play the game, Franti nonetheless found himself drifting increasingly to music. He soon picked up a bass guitar from an area pawn shop and began doodling around. At the same time, Franti became acquainted with Dr. Harry Edwards, a sociologist at the Berkeley campus who, back in 1968, had organized the politically motivated protests by African American athletes at the Olympics in Mexico City. Edwards urged Franti to study and investigate the world around him.

Franti subsequently quit the university's varsity team, on which he was a starter, devoting his energies instead to his newfound passions for music and social issues. He eventually became part of a band called the Beatnigs, which recorded an album on Jello Biafra's Alternative Tentacles label. "We started throwing these underground parties in abandoned warehouses," recalled Franti in a *Musician* interview with Mark Rowland. "We were combining African drums with poetry and African and hip-hop dancers, garbage-can stuff." The group attracted some critical attention, but it eventually broke up.

Birth of Disposable Heroes

As memory of the Beatnigs faded, Franti and another member of that band, Rono Tse, formed the Disposable Heroes of Hiphoprisy. The new group began releasing singles in 1991, and it quickly became clear that Franti and Tse were a twosome that demanded to be heard. *Westword* reviewer Michael Roberts recalled that "their opening blast, 'Television, the Drug of the Nation,' was an immensely powerful warning shot fired across popular culture's bow—and there were plenty more to follow."

The hip-hop duo received almost universal critical accolades from reviewers who hailed Franti's "articulate, politically provocative and subtly nuanced raps," wrote Rowland. The Detroit *Metro Times* summarized the critical buzz around the band, noting, "Whereas other rap artists indulge the genre in all its gangsterish trappings, the Heroes use their dense, dense rhythms as an accessible and confrontational platform for their dense,

For the Record . . .

Born in 1968 in Oakland, CA, to an interracial couple; adopted and raised by white parents; children: Cappy (son). *Education:* Attended University of San Francisco, late 1980s.

Formed Beatnigs with fellow musicians and released album on Alternative Tentacles label, late 1980s; formed Disposable Heroes of Hiphoprisy with ex-Beatnig Rono Tse; released *Hypocrisy Is the Greatest Luxury,* 1992; opened for Arrested Development and U2 on concert tours, then disbanded; formed Spearhead, 1994, with Mary Harris (vocals), Ras I Zulu (vocals), Liane Jamison (keyboards), Keith McArthur (bass), James Gray (drums), and David James (guitar); released *Home,* 1995.

Addresses: *Record company*—Capitol Records, 1750 N. Vine St., Hollywood, CA 90028.

dense politics," which included uncompromising stands against the Gulf War, racism, anti-gay violence, and other issues.

After the release of their album *Hypocrisy Is the Greatest Luxury* on the 4th & Broadway label, Franti and Tse further consolidated their standing with a series of memorable concerts. Soon the Disposable Heroes of Hiphoprisy were asked to tour with music giants Arrested Development and U2. Ultimately, though, the Heroes fell by the wayside. "When I started Disposable Heroes, it wasn't intended to be a group. It was just a concept. The truth is that Disposable Heroes wasn't even a record I would listen to at home," Franti told *Rolling Stone* contributor David Wild. "The big problem with Disposable Heroes was that it was a record people listened to because it was good for them—kind of like broccoli."

After lending a songwriting assist to Hal Wilner in the creation of William Burroughs's Island Red label release *Spare Ass Annie and Other Tales,* Franti and Tse got together to record their second album. They soon realized, though, that the musical paths they wished to explore had diverged. The Disposable Heroes of Hiphoprisy, a group that had blasted into the music world like a comet, thus disappeared with similar speed, leaving a trail of incendiary and challenging music behind.

After the Disposable Heroes disbanded, Franti turned for inspiration to the music he'd listened to while growing up—acts like Marvin Gaye, Earth, Wind & Fire, Bob Marley, and Parliament. His next project, Spearhead,

reflected those influences. "This time around," he explained to *URB Magazine* contributor Jazzbo, "I wanted to make music that you could bounce your head to, that you could enjoy putting on and chill with at your house." Still, Franti's desire to comment on the world around him had not waned. "It wasn't that I didn't want to make statements anymore," he told Roberts. "But when I was a kid, I got into the music first, and then later, after I'd listened to the songs for awhile, I started hearing what the artists had to say. And that's what I wanted to do."

Spearhead Finds a *Home*

Franti gathered together a diverse range of musical talent to form Spearhead. He recruited Mary Harris and Ras I Zulu to share the vocal chores, then rounded out the group's lineup with instrumentalists Liane Jamison, Keith McArthur, James Gray, and David James. The new group then entered the studio to record their first album, *Home,* a work that Jazzbo called "vibrant and aware seventies soul for today, a sound that is as powerful as it is seductive." The 13 songs on the album run the gamut both stylistically and lyrically. A seamless fusion of hip-hop, funk, reggae, and jazz, *Home* features pointed political commentary next to easygoing affirmations of the simple pleasures of home and family. Critics note that party songs of a decidedly funky bent, such as "Red Beans and Rice," complement rather than neutralize powerful militant numbers like "Dream Team."

Other tracks were hailed as well, among them "Positive," a song described by *Vibe* columnist Tricia Rose as "the tension-ridden, soul jazz journey of a young man who's finally decided to be tested for AIDS," and "Hole in the Bucket," Franti's intriguing version of a bouncy Jamaican folksong popularized by Harry Belafonte a generation before.

Franti's Topical Brand of Hip-Hop

Home enjoyed almost universal critical praise upon its release. *West County Times* reviewer Tim Goodman wrote, "When you come across an album of this magnitude, there's a danger of slipping around in the critical slobber." He added, "Consider *Home* to be the nineties version of Marvin Gaye's classic, *What's Going On.* It's that great." *New York Newsday's* Ira Robbins agreed, calling Spearhead's debut album "smart, funny, funky, and glowing with humanity."

Other critics focused on Franti's insights into what it means to be a black man in America in the 1990s. "*Home* explores a range of ways to be a black man by going where vulnerability, fire, rage, and love hide out," commented Rose. "Michael Franti and Spearhead get around sermons and government statistics to present a masculinity infused with political passion, exorcised pain, earthy pleasure, and the strength we gain from taking risks, again and again."

Ironically, a chief strength of *Home*—the album's diverse mix of soul, hip-hop, and jazz—hindered its acceptance by the niche-oriented radio industry, which was unable to pigeonhole Spearhead into a single musical category. But while Franti wanted Spearhead to be heard, his primary concern was being true to his musical vision.

"When I write songs, I write about human emotion and feelings which everybody has. It doesn't matter if you're black, white or brown," Franti told *extreme* writer Chris Sanderson. "We live in a time and place where my generation has to deal with AIDS, violence, police brutality and death." Other musical artists shy away from such topics, but Franti told Jazzbo, "I feel as an artist you have some responsibility to elevate the consciousness of your listener. I know that not everybody feels that way. Some artists felt that their motivation is to make people dance and that's cool. But for my music, I feel I have responsibility."

Franti also acknowledges the role that his son Cappy, who was born in 1988, has had on his lyrics. "I want to be able to make records that Cappy can listen to 15 years from now and see that they weren't just records of me holding my dick, no matter how much money it makes," Franti told Rowland in *Musician.* "I want to say, here's a record that has some ideas. So that's how I gauge the decisions I make in the music."

Clearly, Franti's decisions have been on target. As Goodman indicated in the *West County Times,* "Franti is the complete package. In fact, he shouldn't be lumped in as strictly a bright light in the hip-hop scene—he's an intellectual wordsmith towering above most in the current pop-rock world."

Selected discography

With the Disposable Heroes of Hiphoprisy

Hypocrisy Is the Greatest Luxury, 4th & Broadway, 1992.

With Spearhead

Home, Capitol, 1994.

Sources

Atlanta Journal, March 3, 1995.
Billboard, June 17, 1995.
Black Beat, May 1995.
Boston Globe, March 16, 1995.
California Aggie, December 6, 1994.
extreme, April 1995.
Hip Hop Magazine, March 1995.
Metro Times (Detroit, MI), September 2, 1992.
Musician, January 1993.
New York Newsday, December 24-25, 1994.
Right On!, May 1995.
Rolling Stone, January 26, 1995.
Spin, November 1994.
The Tab, March 14, 1995.
URB Magazine, February 1995.
Vibe, November 1994.
West County Times, March 12, 1995.
Westword, March 1, 1995.

Additional information for this profile was obtained from Capitol Records press material, 1995.

—*Kevin Hillstrom*

Peter Gabriel

Singer, songwriter, record company executive

On the surface, singer-songwriter Peter Gabriel seems full of contradictions. A shy Englishman with a penchant for rock spectacle, a fiercely cerebral writer who champions the liberation of the body and the emotions, and a gatherer of ancient international music who also works on the frontier of interactive technology, Gabriel embraces an array of seemingly incompatible pursuits. Yet the clarity of his vision reconciles his differing impulses. Since his departure from the progressive rock band Genesis in the mid-1970s, he has produced an ambitious—and at times tremendously successful—body of work as a solo artist. He has also founded his own production facility and record label, campaigned for a bevy of worthy causes, and made strides toward the establishment of the first digital theme park.

Gabriel was born in Cobham, a town in the English county of Surrey, in 1950. His father, an Italian-born electrical engineer, was something of a visionary whose interests prefigured many of his son's technological passions. The singer told *Los Angeles Times* writer Amy Harmon that Gabriel senior "was campaigning for electronic democracy, for home shopping, films on demand and education and entertainment accessible to anyone." These concepts may have seemed outlandish in the days when the novelty of television hadn't yet worn off, but Gabriel noted, "I listened to him and championed the idea since I was old enough to understand what he was saying. And in some ways I've tried to carry it on."

Formed Genesis at School

He took an indirect route to this path. Gabriel's earliest preoccupation was rock music; at Charterhouse, a reputable English boarding school, he cofounded a band with some friends. After signing to a record label and having their name changed to Genesis, they began recording in 1968. With their arty themes and elaborate, classically influenced arrangements, the band fit into the "progressive" rock school; main songwriter and frontman Gabriel often sported outlandish costumes and turned Genesis concerts into unpredictable spectacles. Yet despite a number of ambitious recordings—most notably their swan song, the concept album *The Lamb Lies Down on Broadway*—Genesis didn't get much airplay until long after Gabriel's departure. Vocal chores were then taken up by drummer Phil Collins, whose simpler, radio-friendly tunes piloted the band to mainstream superstardom in the 1980s.

Gabriel also met a woman named Jill Moore at Charterhouse, and it wasn't long before they married. They had a daughter, Melanie, toward the end of his tenure with reflective song about a mystical experience; the album reached Number Seven on the UK charts.

Worked for World Causes, World Music

Robert Fripp—guitarist and leader of the progressive rock band King Crimson, among many other projects—produced Gabriel's second solo outing, which is known to the faithful as "Fingernails." It charted in the UK and the States. Next came the album known as "Melting Face," a particularly challenging collection of songs that was rejected by Gabriel's record company, Atlantic. It was released by Mercury in 1980. Veering from the surrealistic politics of "Games without Frontiers" to the disturbing "Intruder" to the powerfully uplifting celebration of the life of slain South African activist "Biko," the album still stands as a quantum leap for Gabriel as a songwriter. "Biko" reappeared throughout the decade on recordings and film soundtracks supporting the struggle for racial justice in South Africa, and Gabriel participated in numerous all-star concerts for this cause.

In the early 1980s, Gabriel was a motivating force behind the establishment of the World of Music, Arts and Dance (or WOMAD) Festival. Debuting in Somerset, England, in 1982, WOMAD became an annual gathering for artists from all over the world. Though the venture initially lost money for Gabriel—so much, in fact, that he agreed to participate in a Genesis semireunion concert—it figured prominently in the growth of so-called "World Music" and in his subsequent projects. He next signed to Geffen Records and released *Security*, another eclectic, challenging collection; powered in part by the single "Shock the Monkey," the album was certified gold. Gabriel's tour in support of the album provided material for the 1983 double-disc *Plays Live*.

"Sledgehammer" Success with *So*

Gabriel's soundtrack for the Alan Parker film *Birdy* was released in 1985. This highly personal, emotionally charged record was followed in 1986 by the breakthrough success of his album *So*. Thanks to barnstorming singles like "Sledgehammer" (the imaginative video to which earned scores of awards on its own and was dubbed the best of all time by *Rolling Stone*), "Big Time," "In Your Eyes," and a duet with alternative rock heroine Kate Bush called "Don't Give Up," the recording reached the Number Two chart position and achieved triple-platinum sales in the United States. "Sledgehammer," with its melding of rock hooks and dance rhythms, earned three Grammy nominations, and the album was nominated for album of the year. Gabriel also earned two BRIT awards, including one for best British male artist.

Genesis. She was born with a serious infection that nearly claimed her life, and Gabriel spent as much time with her as he could. Melanie survived, but her father's relationship with the band was irreparably impaired by his absence. Gabriel left in 1975 and took a hiatus—apart from recording a cover version of a song by the Beatles for a film soundtrack—before working on the first of several albums that bore the same title: *Peter Gabriel*. Fans have since given these recordings nicknames inspired by their cover art. His solo debut, released in 1977, is known as "Rainy Windshield" and contains the enduring single "Solsbury Hill," a folky,

Those who had followed Gabriel's career were not surprised that the singer-songwriter didn't issue some kind of "sequel" that sought to copy *So's* formula. Instead, he composed the score for Martin Scorsese's controversial film *The Last Temptation of Christ.* The Grammy-winning soundtrack album, titled *Passion,* was the first release on Real World, a label that the artist had formed in conjunction with WOMAD. With his Real World studios near Bath, England, Gabriel was able to record international artists in a state-of-the-art, independent facility and then release these recordings through his own company. His anthology *Shaking the Tree: Sixteen Golden Greats* followed in 1990; Real World has also released recordings by Sufi devotional singer Nusrat Fateh Ali Khan, among many others.

Therapy Influenced Songwriting

It wasn't until 1992, however, that Gabriel resurfaced with a new studio album. Unlike the commercial supernova *So,* his next effort, *Us,* is a somewhat more understated recording; *People* magazine praised it as a "well-conceived and carefully crafted album" that conveys "anger, pain, and finally self-knowledge." Indeed, the album reflects some sobering changes in the performer's life. After a painful divorce from Jill Moore and a brief but turbulent relationship with actress Rosanna Arquette, Gabriel found himself exploring his difficulties in relationships. "I started with twenty-three different lyric ideas, on a range of subjects," he related to Rob Tannenbaum of *GQ* in describing the process of creating *Us.* "But the personal stuff seemed to dominate the songwriting, as it had done in my life for the past five or six years. I did couples' group therapy and single group therapy for about five years, to try and understand what was going wrong in the relationships." Ultimately, he noted, the painful "look inside was central for me, and not to have written about it would have been a denial." Perhaps most importantly, this introspection helped him get closer to his second daughter, Anna-Marie.

The album's first single, "Digging in the Dirt," describes the difficult process of therapeutic self-examination. The video that accompanied that song features Gabriel hitting his female companion, and when asked what affect this might have on his image as an international do-gooder, he replied, "Ah, I'm sick of that. I don't think I'm Mr. Nice Guy. There's an aggressive, mean bastard and a playful, humorous character in my makeup, and I don't get to show those faces so often." Many of his friends corroborated this self-description, noting that Gabriel had often been difficult to get close to; yet the artist's positive experiences in therapy made him something of a convert. It also helped shed light on some of his past work and piqued a renewed interest in the

theatricality that he'd set aside after leaving Genesis. "The mask, which people see as an instrument with which to hide," he mused to Tannenbaum, "is seen in most other cultures as a way of releasing parts of the personality or soul that don't normally get expressed."

With renewed vision, Gabriel mounted his most ambitious tour yet, with a cast of international musicians, high-tech visuals, and a handful of "concepts" guiding a career retrospective that included not big hits but personal favorites. Renowned Canadian theater and opera director Robert Le Page contributed to the realization of the enormous set, which occupied two opposing spaces; *Billboard's* Zenon Schoepe described these as "a square 'male, urban, water' stage and a circular 'female, rural, fire' stage connected by a conveyer belt." This thematic division guided the entire production. "We tried to analyze the songs in terms of whether they belonged to the 'male' or 'female' or represented a journey between the two," Gabriel told Schoepe. A video recording of the concert made in Modena, Italy, was released in 1994 with a double-CD, both titled *Secret World Live. People* claimed, "The video is not the companion piece to the recording. It is the true, indispensable text."

> "Interactive technology is going to open up in the form of this whole big communication, entertainment, information and education soup."

"It's a rare moment when an artist takes his established, even iconic work and makes it still stronger," raved Susan Richardson in her *Rolling Stone* review, adding that *Secret World Live* is "just such a moment." Meanwhile, Gabriel went on to pursue still grander dreams. True to his commitment to interactive technology, he helped develop a CD-ROM called *Xplora 1.* In addition to permitting users to remix his songs with their computers, *Xplora* provides video footage from Gabriel's career, a sampling of international music and information about the non-Western instruments that create it, and a virtual tour of Real World studios.

Not content to dwell on music, Gabriel introduced a political dimension to his CD-ROM by adding footage from his Witness Project, which handed out video cameras to document human rights abuses worldwide. Some highly disturbing footage of violent incidents is included to jar participants into actively supporting human rights. Gabriel told *Musician's* Martin Townsend that *Xplora* and related ventures would pose a stark alternative to the fantasy violence of video games. "The shoot-'em-up esthetic is going to be challenged," he insisted. "Interactive technology is going to open up in the form of this whole big communication, entertainment, information and education soup."

Eager to be in the soup himself, Gabriel set to work designing an interactive theme park with fellow music-performance visionaries Brian Eno and Laurie Anderson. Set to open in Barcelona, Spain, the park would differ from mainstream amusement parks. "We want to create a beautiful, natural environment with lots of water, trees and gardens," he informed Townsend, "and then bury the experiences. It would be like the Greek underworld. You would come up to the surface, where it's calm and relaxing; then, when you're ready for another big adventure, you go down."

Plenty of big adventures remain in store for Gabriel. Dedicated, as he declared to Harmon of the *Los Angeles Times,* to the "issue of democratizing technology," he seems to have found a way to merge his eclectic musical vision, his fascination with multimedia development, and his hope for enhancing communication and freedom worldwide. Indeed, he predicted to Harmon, the new media "will break down this ridiculous barrier that exists between supposedly 'creative' people and the rest of the population." Whether or not this turns out to be true, Gabriel's own creative spark will now reach an even greater audience.

Selected discography

Solo

Various artists, *All This and World War II* (soundtrack; appears on "Strawberry Fields Forever"), 1975.
Peter Gabriel (aka "Rainy Windshield"; includes "Solsbury Hill"), Atlantic, 1977.
Peter Gabriel (aka "Fingernails"), Atlantic, 1978.
Robert Fripp, *Exposure* (appears on "Here Comes the Flood"), 1979.
Peter Gabriel (aka "Melting Face"; includes "Games without Frontiers," "Intruder," and "Biko"), Mercury, 1980.

Security (includes "Shock the Monkey"), Geffen, 1982.
Plays Live, Geffen, 1983.
Against All Odds (soundtrack; appears on "Walk through the Fire"), 1984.
Birdy (soundtrack), Geffen, 1985.
So (includes "Sledgehammer," "Big Time," "In Your Eyes," and "Don't Give Up"), Geffen, 1986.
Passion: Music from the Last Temptation of Christ (soundtrack), Real World/Geffen, 1989.
Various artists, *Rainbow Warriors* (appears on "Red Rain"), Geffen, 1989.
Shaking the Tree: Sixteen Golden Greats, Real World/Geffen, 1990.
Us (includes "Digging in the Dirt"), Real World/Geffen, 1992.
Secret World Live, Real World/Geffen, 1994.

With Genesis

"The Silent Sun," Decca, 1968.
"A Winter's Tale," Decca, 1968.
From Genesis to Revelation, Decca, 1969.
"Where the Sour Turns to Sweet," Decca, 1969.
Trespass, Impulse, 1970.
Nursery Cryme, Charisma, 1971.
Foxtrot, Charisma, 1972.
Selling England by the Pound, Charisma, 1973.
The Lamb Lies Down on Broadway, Atlantic, 1974.

Sources

Books

Rees, Dafydd, and Luke Crampton, *Rock Movers & Shakers,* ABC/CLIO, 1991.

Periodicals

Billboard, August 20, 1994.
GQ, December 1992.
Los Angeles Times, March 8, 1995.
Musician, June 1994.
People, November 2, 1992; October 3, 1994.
Rolling Stone, August 19, 1993; October 20, 1994.

—Simon Glickman

Diamanda Galás

Vocalist, pianist, composer, performance artist

Photograph by Rotem, Courtesy of Mute Records

Trained in avant-garde, jazz, and opera music, Diamanda Galás reaches deep into the heart of her emotions and broadcasts her feelings to her audiences. Unlike many popular artists, she explores and expresses the depths of the angst and pain within herself and the world around her. "With astounding vocal abilities spanning three octaves, three languages, and a wider sonic palette than most synthesizers, there's little in Heaven, Earth, or Hell that she can't put forth in song," declared Ernie Rideout in *Keyboard*. As Galás told Martin Johnson in *New York Newsday*, "All my work has been about a schizophrenic state of mind induced by incredible pain."

Galás's style elicits strong responses—good or bad—similar to those evoked by masters of the horror genre. Brian Cullman wrote in *Rolling Stone*, "The talented Diamanda Galás has a vision of the world that makes the horror-stricken likes of Edgar Allan Poe and H.P. Lovecraft seem like pink-cheeked Pollyannas."

Born in San Diego, California, the daughter of Greek immigrants, Galás began studying the piano at the age of five. During her childhood, she often accompanied the gospel choir led by her father. As a result, when she was 13 years old, he asked her to play with his own New Orleans-style band. "My father, who plays bass and trombone, was my first teacher," Galás noted in *Keyboard*. "I played in his jazz band when I was very young, long before I could read music.... He comes from that New Orleans tradition that says, 'You play whatever you hear.'"

By the time Galás was 14 years old, she had performed Beethoven's *Piano Concerto No. 1* as a soloist with the San Diego Symphony. She went on to study music performance at the University of California at San Diego, where she received both her bachelor's and master's degrees. In graduate school, Galás began exploring avant-garde music.

Asylums Led to International Tours

During the early 1970s, Galás played piano around San Diego and Los Angeles with improvisational musicians like David Murray, Butch Morris, and Bobby Bradford. She kicked off her solo career and further developed her talent by performing in mental institutions and underground theaters. In 1979, after hearing one of her tapes, composer Vinko Globokar invited Galás to play the lead in his opera *Un Jour comme une autre* at the Festival Avignon. Globokar had based the opera on Amnesty International documentation of the arrest and torture of a Turkish woman for alleged treason.

For the Record . . .

Born c. 1953 in San Diego, CA; daughter of James (a musician) Galás. *Education:* Received B.A. and M.A. in music performance from University of San Diego.

Performed as a soloist with San Diego Symphony at age 14; played lead in *Un Jour comme une autre*, Festival Avignon, 1979; released debut album, *The Litanies of Satan*, Y Records, 1982; released *Diamanda Galás*, Metalanguage Records, 1984; signed with Mute Records, 1986, and released *The Divine Punishment*.

Addresses: *Record company*—Mute Records, 584 Broadway, Suite 1008, New York, NY 10012-3253.

The theme fit right in with Galás's own topical style. "All the work I've done has to do with issues of extreme oppression, various mental states that happen when a person is being put in a black box and being squeezed, or strangled, and has no visible way out, and what a human being will do to survive—people losing their minds and creating a new voice simply because another one doesn't exist," Galás told Derk Richardson in the *Bay Guardian*. "Isolation is something that will kill people, and that's the theme of most of my stuff."

From Avignon, Rene Gonzales, the director of the Theatre Gerard Phillippe Saint-Denis, invited Galás to perform in Paris. She performed her solo works *Wild Women with Steak Knives*, about battered women, and *Tragouthia Apo to Aima Exour Fonos* (translated as "Song from the Blood of Those Murdered"), based on the victims of the 1967 coup in Greece. The performances launched her solo tour throughout Europe during the early 1980s.

"We Are All HIV-Positive"

Galás released her first album, *The Litanies of Satan*, on Y Records in 1982. The work includes a vocal adaptation of a poem by nineteenth-century French writer Charles Baudelaire and a rendition of the earlier "Wild Women with Steak Knives." Two years later, she released her self-titled album on Metalanguage Records, featuring "Tragouthia Apo to Aima Exoun Fonos" and "Panoptikon," based on British law theorist Jeremy Bentham's proposal for a prison where inmates could be kept under constant observation by unseen captors.

During that same year, 1984, Galás went to San Francisco and began developing a three-record set dedicated to those dead and dying of AIDS. The continually evolving work, titled *Plague Mass*, was launched before Galás learned that her brother, playwright and performer Philip-Dimitri Galás, was HIV-positive. She discussed her motivations with Johnson in *New York Newsday*. "[Some people] believe that I'm doing this out of hysteria, not cold, clinical interest. The Greek tradition is not about whimpery tears of sorrow; it's a vendetta culture. You're never going to see me get up and sing, 'Oh, the suffering of my people, isn't it awful.'" Galás spent 1985 traveling throughout Europe to discuss the evolution of *Plague Mass* and its political intent. The following year, AIDS claimed the life of Philip-Dimitri. As part of her message, Galás put a tattoo on the fingers of her left hand that reads: "We are all HIV-positive."

Galás released *The Divine Punishment* and *Saint of the Pit* in 1986 on Mute Records. The latter sets French decadent poetry by authors such as Baudelaire, Nerval, and Corbiere to her own wild style of singing, accompanied by keyboards ranging from subtle atmospherics to horror-movie organ.

Two years later, Galás conducted a one-woman performance tour of *Plague Mass*. The tour began with workshops in the United States, then moved on to performances in Australia, Sweden, Yugoslavia, Holland, Italy, Spain, and Bavaria. On New Year's Day of 1989, *Plague Mass* premiered in England at Queen Elizabeth Hall. Galás followed with a performance at Lincoln Center in New York. Later in the year, she released *Masque of the Red Death*, a trilogy of *The Divine Punishment*, *Saint of the Pit*, and 1988's *You Must Be Certain of the Devil*.

As her stand in the fight against AIDS continued, Galás decided to stage a revised and expanded version of *Plague Mass (1984—End of the Epidemic)*, featuring a new section titled *There Are No More Tickets to the Funeral*. Her first performance took place in October of 1990 at the Cathedral Saint John Divine in New York, the second largest cathedral in the world. When she walked across the stage half-naked and dripping in cow's blood, many of the shocked members of the audience walked out. Galás recorded the performance and released it as the live album *Plague Mass*. After she performed the composition at the Festival delle Colline in Italy, she was censured and banned for committing blasphemy against the Roman Catholic Church.

Galás took her style to yet another level in 1992's *The Singer*, a compilation of blues and gospel influences. "As always, it is an extension of my earlier work," she told Richardson in the *Bay Guardian* interview. "I have intentionally reappropriated these blues, gospel, and spiritual pieces in the context of the AIDS community.... My appropriation of this music is in service of those voices who are crying in the darkness, who are actually saying these things. What people are going through now is hardly a remembrance of past misery, hardly a vague abstraction of pain."

Also in 1992, Galás's *Vena Cava,* a companion to *Plague Mass* that deals with clinical depression and AIDS dementia, premiered at the Kitchen in New York. The next year, she performed *Insekta* (translated as "Insignificant")—a story about a survivor who encounters repeated traumas within an inescapable enclosed space—at the Serious Fun! Kitchen Residency Program Festival at Lincoln Center.

Living *The Sporting Life*

On September 5, 1994, Galás released *The Sporting Life* on Mute Records. She recorded the LP with former Led Zeppelin bass and keyboard player John Paul Jones and Attractions drummer Pete Thomas. Jones also joined Galás on an international tour following the album's release.

Galás has contributed music to several films, including *Last of England, The Serpent and the Rainbow, Silence=Death,* and *Lord of Illusions,* and she provided sound effects and voice-overs for Francis Ford Coppola's 1992 remake of *Bram Stoker's Dracula.*

In 1995 Galás developed *Schrei X,* an intimate theater piece exploring the use of silence and high density speech and sounds performed in darkness. Her music continues to delve into the universe of intense emotion, pain, and suffering while pushing the creative limits of composition. Greg Kot summed up Galás's technique in the *Chicago Tribune* when he wrote, "Galás combines a prodigious, multi-octave voice with a dramatic sense of theater. She's a major talent, but not for everyone; her albums are almost claustrophobic in their intensity."

Selected discography

The Litanies of Satan, Y Records, 1982, reissued, Mute Records, 1988.

Diamanda Galás, Metalanguage Records, 1984.
The Divine Punishment, Mute Records, 1986, reissued, 1989.
Saint of the Pit, Mute Records, 1986, reissued, 1989.
You Must Be Certain of the Devil, Mute Records, 1988.
Masque of the Red Death, Mute Records, 1989.
Plague Mass, Mute Records, 1991.
The Singer, Mute Records, 1992.
Vena Cava, Mute Records, 1993.
The Sporting Life, Mute Records, 1994.

Sources

Books

The Trouser Press Record Guide, edited by Ira A. Robbins, Collier, 1992.

Periodicals

Artweek, September 17, 1992.
Bay Guardian (San Francisco, CA), April 8, 1992.
Billboard, July 23, 1994.
Buffalo News (Buffalo, NY), October 16, 1993.
Chicago Tribune, November 18, 1994.
CMJ Music Report, April 1992.
Details, May 1992.
Entertainment Weekly, September 23, 1994.
Interview, March 1992.
Keyboard, August 1992; December 1994.
Mondo 2000, issue no. 8.
Musician, October 1984; November 1994.
New York Newsday, February 19, 1992.
New York Times, February 25, 1992; July 4, 1993.
Paper Magazine, June 1993.
Philadelphia Daily News, January 6, 1993.
Rolling Stone, June 25, 1992; October 5, 1994.
San Diego Union Tribune, October 28-November 3, 1993.
San Francisco Chronicle, April 17, 1992.
Seattle Times, December 9, 1994; December 12, 1994.
Village Voice, March 10, 1992; July 20, 1993.

Additional information for this profile was obtained from Mute Records press material, 1995.

—*Sonya Shelton*

Danny Gatton

Guitarist

AP/Wide World Photos

The music world lost one of its most talented, yet chronically underexposed members when Danny Gatton died of a self-inflicted gun blast on October 4, 1995. His blazing virtuosity combined with a love of country, bluegrass, jazz, rock, and rockabilly to produce technically complex compositions infused with a soulful expression reminiscent of guitar legends Eric Clapton and the late Les Paul. Though major labels waited 20 years to release a Gatton record, the Washington, D.C. native built a cult following among other musicians who remain awed by his incredible abilities. Longtime friend and bandmate Evans Johns remarked to *Guitar Player,* "Danny had God's hands. I heard God come out of his amp."

After years of major-market obscurity, Gatton released two albums on Elektra Records in the early 1990s. *88 Elmira Street,* released in 1991, captured critical attention and a Grammy nomination, though sales were modest. With critical praise and major-label support, the future looked very bright for Gatton. However, management changes at Elektra two years later left Gatton suddenly without a contract even though he had recorded only two of the seven records his deal stipulated. Contributing to Elektra's decision to drop Gatton was the fact that he played so many styles of music so well. From a marketing standpoint, his records are nearly impossible to categorize and difficult to promote to any single demographic. *Rolling Stone* editor David Fricke told the *Baltimore Sun,* "He was so well-versed in so many genres that he was almost the classic outsider who didn't fit into any category." For his part, Gatton told *Guitar Player,* "I never understood why certain players would limit themselves to just one style."

Born in the Anacostia section of Washington, Gatton grew up in a home where music was a constant. His father was a professional guitarist who played in big bands around Washington, D.C. in the 1930s, while his grandfather and great-grandfather were fiddlers. Gatton knew music would be his career at a surprisingly early age. "I must have been two years old because I was lying in a crib. The sun was shining, and I started hearing this beautiful improvisational music," he told *Guitar Player.* "To this day, I don't know what it was; it sounded like something from heaven. After that I knew I was going to have to play, and I've been hooked on music ever since." After two years of lessons, Gatton's instructor told his parents that no more training was necessary—the 11-year-old could sight read just about any composition and imitate guitar licks after hearing them only once.

After a brief stint with a Washington teen-club band, the Lancers, in 1957, Gatton was well on his way toward a musical profession. At 14, and with the help of a clever

Born Daniel Gatton, Jr., September 4, 1945, in Anacostia section of Washington, D.C.; died of a self-inflicted gunshot wound, October 4, 1995, Newburg, Maryland; son of Daniel Gatton, Sr. (a guitar player in big bands in the Washington, D.C. area) and Norma (operates NRG Records of Alpharetta, Georgia); brother, Brent; married wife, Jan, 1968; daughter, Holly, born in 1981.

Began taking guitar lessons at age seven; professional career started at age 14, playing in Washington, D.C. teen-club band, the Lancers; joined the Offbeats shortly thereafter; played in and around Washington for many years with occasional New York performances; recorded *American Music,* 1975, on Aladdin Records, then released *Redneck Jazz* in 1978 on NRG Records; left for Nashville, c. 1968, to work as a session guitarist, returned to Washington six months later; after a hiatus in his musical career, returned to eventually record *Unfinished Business* in 1987; signed first major-label contract in 1990 with Elektra; released *88 Elmira Street* and *Cruisin' Deuces* before being dropped by label; recorded jazz album, *New York Stories,* 1992, for Blue Note Records; signed to Big Mo Records of Vermont; released *Relentless,* 1994; toured Europe and the United States, summer 1995.

Selected awards: Grammy nomination in 1991 for *88 Elmira Street;* received over 70 Washington Area Musician's Awards (WAMMIES) over the course of his career; named best country guitarist by *Guitar Player,* 1989-93.

fake I.D., Gatton began playing in Washington clubs with several bands and quickly built a solid reputation as an outstanding young guitarist. According to Jack Casaday, who eventually played with Jefferson Airplane but started on the Washington nightclub circuit with Gatton in a band known as the Offbeats, "If you had Danny in your band that night, then you had a good band," reported *Rolling Stone.* His notoriety soon landed opportunities to join other acts in New York and the rest of the country, but the acutely modest Gatton preferred to remain in his hometown. It was his modesty and some simple bad luck that joined together to leave Gatton a regional legend, but nationally unknown.

Gatton continued honing his talents in the 1960s, spending time studying the jazz guitar styles of Wes Montgomery and Howard Roberts, and maintained his Washington club schedule. The Offbeats played constantly around the D.C. area and managed to find gigs in New York and other East Coast cities. Looking to finally make a name for himself outside his familiar Washington surroundings, Gatton met up with fellow Washingtonian and rockabilly guitarist Roy Buchanan in Nashville in the late 1960s and worked as a session musician. Only six months later, a homesick Gatton returned to work in Washington cover bands. Offered a job with pianist Robert Scott for a steady New York City gig, Gatton declined in favor of his hometown. Gatton felt that if Buchanan—who claimed in 1970 that he was asked to join the Rolling Stones—could carve out a well-respected career from Washington, then its clubs could propel him toward the same. "[Buchanan] didn't have to go anywhere to be discovered," Gatton said to *Rolling Stone.*

Gatton formed Danny and the Fat Boys in the early 1970s after a respite from performing, during which period he managed a guitar shop in suburban Maryland. The group's reputation grew quickly as Gatton dazzled audiences with Fender Telecaster wizardry, marked by his beer-bottle slide-guitar technique. Sparked by mounting regional interest, Gatton and the band released *American Music* in 1975. The album and its successor, *Redneck Jazz,* received some critical attention and today rate as collector's items, but sales were low. Based on the band's popularity with critics and musicians, more than one major label showed interest in signing the band and re-releasing *Redneck Jazz.* After bringing Gatton to New York for a private performance, the label reportedly decided against his band based on a single label executive's vote against them in final negotiations.

While Gatton's decision to remain around Washington contributed to his lack of major-market success, his career is also marked by an occasional bad turn of fate. Once offered a job playing with former Little Feat guitarist Lowell George, Gatton accepted, only to learn of George's untimely death due to a heart attack the following day. Years later, an agent called to see if Gatton would be interested in supporting John Fogarty, formerly of Creedence Clearwater Revival, in an early 1980s solo tour. After telling the agent he would call the next day to confirm plans, Gatton forgot to make the call, distracted by his second passion, restoring old cars. He told *Rolling Stone,* "I just plum forgot about it. I went back to screwing the grill on the car and didn't think about it anymore."

Though the record-buying public remained largely unaware of his gift, music professionals never ignored Gatton's talent. Asked by Blue Note records to play in a jazz quartet in 1992, Gatton's work on the album, *New York Stories,* again found critical praise. He appeared on albums by Chris Isaak and Arlen Roth, and with the release of *Relentless* in 1994 or Vermont's Big Mo Records, Gatton was at his highest point yet on the commercial scale. American and European tours in 1995 accompanied growing sales and ever-present critical support, raising only more questions as to why he chose to end his life. "He was more of a person than a musician," Dave Elliot, former band-member and longtime friend, told the *Washington Post.* "Danny's whole approach didn't have anything to do with being a star—he played for his soul and his guitar. I guess being a regular guy and a musician just doesn't work."

Gatton's reputation among his peers was cemented with feature articles in *Guitar Player, Rolling Stone, Guitar World,* and *Musician.* Gatton was constantly hailed as one of the biggest talents in contemporary music. A 1989 issue of *Guitar Player* claimed Gatton to be "the world's greatest unknown guitarist." Gatton supported both Robert Gordon and Roger Miller in session work and his technique was chronicled on instructional video and the pages of guitar magazines. In recognition of Gatton's musical innovations, Fender Guitars issued a limited edition Danny Gatton signature model Telecaster with the custom fixtures Gatton built into his vintage 1953 model. The guitar featured a solid steel tail piece and hot-rodded pick-ups, upgrades Gatton used to create blazing arpeggios and rhythms built on his unique finger-picking style. It was a style Gatton himself termed "redneck jazz."

Selected discography

American Music, Aladdin Records, 1975.
Redneck Jazz, NRG, 1978.
Unfinished Business, NRG, 1987.
88 Elmira Street, Elektra, 1991.
(Contributor)*New York Stories,* Blue Note, 1992.
Cruisin' Deuces, Elektra, 1993.
Blazing Telecasters, Sky Ranch Records, 1993.
(With Joey DeFrancesco)*Relentless,* Big Mo Records, 1994.

Sources

Baltimore Sun, October 6, 1994.
Dallas Morning News, June 25, 1993.
Down Beat, January 1995; December 1994.
Guardian (London), October 14, 1994.
Guitar Player, January 1995; November 1994; July 1993.
Los Angeles Times, October 11, 1994.
New York Times, October 7, 1994.
Rolling Stone, May 18, 1989.
Sacramento Bee, July 2, 1993.
St. Louis Post-Dispatch, September 4, 1993; August 26, 1993.
Record (Bergen Co., New Jersey), October 7, 1994.
Washington Post, October 6, 1994
Washington Times, October 11, 1994; October 9, 1994; October 6, 1994.

—*Rich Bowen*

The Goo Goo Dolls

Rock band

In early 1995 the Goo Goo Dolls were dubbed "America's best unknown band" in their record company biography. They had released several albums, each of which garnered ample critical acclaim and expanded their loyal fan base, yet full-blown commercial success eluded the Dolls until late 1995, when their song "Name" became a huge hit at modern rock radio. While the band has often been compared to the post-punk garage pop of the Replacements, *Huh* magazine's Dave Kendall described the band as, "poppy punk rockers, just like the Buzzcocks and 999."

The Goo Goo Dolls, comprised of singer-guitarist Johnny Rzeznik, singer-bassist Robby Takac, and drummer Mike Malins (who replaced drummer George Tutuska in 1995) formed in Buffalo, New York, in 1985. Before choosing the name Goo Goo Dolls, the band was briefly known as Sex Maggot. Takac and Rzeznik decided on the name Goo Goo Dolls when they spotted an ad for a doll with a moveable, rubber head in *True Detective* magazine.

Early musical influences for the band include the Sex Pistols, the Damned, Devo, the Plasmatics and other punk rock pioneers of the late 1970s and early 1980s. Rzeznik told *Huh*'s Kendall, "The first wave of punk stuff that came from England just blew me away when I heard it.... The Damned and the Buzzcocks, all that was amazing. Then there was the East Coast American stuff ... the Ramones and the Dead Boys. And some of the West Coast stuff ... Fear and the Dickies and those bands were great."

Rzeznik was born in 1965 to a postal clerk and his wife. He has four older sisters. His grandparents arrived in the U.S. from Kraków, Poland, in 1913. After moving to Buffalo when Rzeznik was a child, his family opened a neighborhood bar. As a teenager, he decided he wanted to become a plumber. His father died of complications from alcoholism when Rzeznik was 15. His mother died six months later. Rzeznik told *Billboard*'s Timothy White, "My mom was gone six months later 'cause she was so lonely. If it hadn't been for my sisters, I wouldn't have made it."

Rzeznik worked as an assistant plumber for one day before quitting to enroll in Buffalo State University. At the time he was playing in a band called the Beaumonts, a hardcore punk outfit. Rzeznik's cousin played in a heavy metal band of which Takac was a member. The two met through this connection and became fast friends and, not long after, musical collaborators.

Rzeznik shared his band's philosophy with *Billboard*'s White, allowing, "Our music is saying that it's best to keep yourself more process-oriented than outcome-

Members include **Mike Malins** (replaced **George Tutuska**, 1995), drums; **Johnny Rzeznik** (born December 5, 1965, in Buffalo, NY; son of Joseph [a postal clerk and bar proprietor] and Edith Pomeroy Rzeznik), vocals, guitar; and **Robby Takac,** vocals, bass.

Group formed in 1985 in Buffalo, NY; known briefly as Sex Maggot; released debut album, *Goo Goo Dolls,* Mercenary/Celluloid, 1987; signed with Death/Enigma and released *Jed,* 1989; signed with Metal Blade/ Warner Bros. and released *Hold Me Up,* 1990.

Addresses: *Record company*—Warner Bros. Records, 3300 Warner Blvd., Burbank, CA 91505; 75 Rockefeller Plaza, 20th floor, New York, NY 10019.

oriented.... If you can somehow do things from the bottom of your soul, but not get hung up dwelling on them, then it's a good, unselfish feeling."

The Goo Goo Dolls started out covering songs by artists as diverse as Prince, Creedence Clearwater Revival, and the Plimsouls, adding their own twist of homespun humor. The band had to rent performance spaces in order to play. Matt Ashare of the *Boston Phoenix* described their early original material as "loud, raucous songs that combined Ramones-style buzz-saw guitars with Cheap Trick hooks and a lot of rock-and-roll heart."

The band's debut album, *Goo Goo Dolls,* released on the independent Mercenary label, was picked up in 1987 by a larger indie, Celluloid Records. Takac told *Rolling Stone's* Chris Mundy of the band's relationship with the label, "I'll give the guy at Celluloid Records one thing—he put out our record.... But we'd say, 'We need twenty dollars for gas,' and he'd say, 'What the f—k are you calling me for?' They were making 90 percent of the profit, we paid all of the bills."

The Goo Goo Dolls then decided to try their hand in Los Angeles, where they struggled mightily, surviving on peanut butter sandwiches. They signed with the Death/ Enigma label and released the album *Jed* in 1989. The band discovered major-label media visibility with their next album, 1990's *Hold Me Up,* issued on Metal Blade, an imprint of Warner Bros. The album's title is a tribute to the faith of the Catholic-raised bandmembers, though it is meant more as a general statement about spirituality than Catholicism specifically.

The release of 1993's *Superstar Car Wash,* which included the lauded singles "Fallin' Down" and "Already There," served to underscore the artistry, dedication, and talent of the Goo Goo Dolls. By 1993 the Dolls were being heralded as the next Replacements. Paul Westerberg, the leader of that band, even wrote the lyrics to one of the songs on *Superstar Car Wash.* But *A Boy Named Goo,* released in 1995, would mark the band's crossover to mass appeal, sparked by their song "Name."

A Boy Named Goo was produced by Lou Giordano, whose credits include albums by Hüsker Dü, Sugar, the Smithereens, and Pere Ubu and who is credited by Rzeznik with imparting a raw, rough, power-pop sound to the album. Rob Cavallo, who earned his reputation working with Green Day, also produced. Both Rzeznik and Takac contributed songs to *A Boy Named Goo.*

The Goo Goo Dolls still consider Buffalo home. *Guitar World's* Tony Gervino called the city a place where "a pitcher of beer is pocket change and everybody owns their own bowling shoes." Rzeznik's father was, in fact, a three-time bowling champion, and each band member owns his own bowling ball. Rzeznik told *New York Newsday's* Ira Robbins, "I have a great life. I get to sleep till noon. I get to scream and yell and run around and drive around in a bus and have people talk to me about myself. Wow!"

Selected discography

Goo Goo Dolls, Mercenary/Celluloid, 1987.
Jed, Death/Enigma, 1989.
Hold Me Up, Metal Blade/Warner Bros., 1990.
Superstar Car Wash, Metal Blade/Warner Bros., 1993.
A Boy Named Goo, Metal Blade/Warner Bros., 1995.

Sources

Billboard, February 25, 1995; April 15, 1995.
Boston Globe, April 13, 1995.
Boston Phoenix, April 7, 1995.
Guitar World, July 1995.
New York Newsday, March 24, 1995.
RIP, August 1995.
Spin, June 1993.

Additional information for this profile was obtained from Warner Bros. Records publicity materials, 1995.

—B. Kimberly Taylor

Morton Gould

Composer, conductor

Despite receiving no formal education in orchestration or conducting, Morton Gould became one of the most prominent American composers and conductors of the twentieth century. His works have been hailed for their accessibility to the general listener and are included in the standard repertory of bands and orchestras throughout the U.S and Europe. As a conductor he had over 100 recordings and a dozen Grammy nominations to his credit, and he had served as a guest conductor for most top American orchestras. Joseph McLellan wrote in the *Washington Post* in 1994, "The first thing you notice about the music of composer Morton Gould is how easy it is to enjoy."

Gould was best known for his orchestral works and has written music in many genres. According to *The New Grove Dictionary of Music,* "Gould has promoted serious music for symphonic band through his own compositions" and is "a master of orchestration." Max Harrison wrote in the *Contemporary Composers,* "There is also great rhythmic freedom in his [Gould's] music, fluent counterpoint and highly effective orchestration." While many of Gould's compositions are renowned for satisfying a wide range of musical tastes, his symphonic works have been acclaimed by such titans of serious music as Reiner, Toscanini, Stokowski, Mitropoulos, and Rodzinski.

Revealed Talent at Early Age

A musical prodigy, Gould was an accomplished pianist by the age of five. A year later he published his first composition, "Just Six." When he earned a scholarship to the Institute for Musical Art at the age of eight, he was the youngest person to train at the school. However, his experience at the Institute proved disappointing. "I wanted to study theory, and they wouldn't let me," he told *Musical America* about his stint at the Institute. "They said I was too young. It was an old-fashioned, dogmatic kind of approach, and I was miserable." Gould left the school after a year of study to pursue other training, and by age thirteen was learning theory as well as performing. He studied composition with Vincent Jones and piano with Abby Whiteside, and Whiteside became his long-time coach, advisor, and friend. "She [Whiteside] believed that music is all-embracing, that you did not isolate technique from music-making," Gould noted in *Musical America.* "Much of what she taught me has stood me in good stead over the years."

As a teenager Gould gave piano recitals in the New York City area, often improvising on themes contributed by the audience. His improvisations demonstrated his love for jazz, and many of his future compositions revealed jazz influences. Gould also played piano for silent films,

For the Record . . .

Born December 10, 1913, in Richmond Hill, NY; died February 22, 1996, in Orlando, FL; son of James and Frances (Arkin) Gould; married twice; four children. Education: Richmond Hill High School, Institute of Musical Art, New York, New York.

Played piano and composed music at the age of four; was staff pianist, Radio City Music Hall, 1931–1932; was composer, arranged, and conductor in charge of "Music for Today" broadcasts, Mutual Radio Network (WOR), New York, NY, 1935–1942; was composer, arranger, conductor, for CBS-sponsored radio broadcasts, 1942–1945; has served as guest conductor of many major symphony orchestras; has recorded many albums for RCA, Columbia, and other labels; made concert and radio appearances in Europe, 1956, Australia, 1977, and Japan, 1979; has composed numerous works, including three symphonies, ballets, and a score for a television miniseries.

Selected Awards: Numerous Grammy-Award nominations; Grammy Award, Best Classical Record (*Symphony Number One*, Charles Ives) 1966; Gold Baton Award, American Symphony Orchestra League, 1983; Elected to the American Academy of Arts and Letters, 1986; Gold Medal, National Association of American Composers and Conductors; Kennedy Center Honor, 1994; Pulitzer Prize for "Stringmusic," 1995.

in jazz bands, and as part of a two-piano duo on the local vaudeville circuit. His compositions were first heard in concert when he was just sixteen.

When Gould was seventeen, a friend set up an audition for him with famed conductor Fritz Reiner. Reiner was impressed, and said that he would recommend Gould for a scholarship to the prestigious Curtis Institute. But his father's failing health and financial difficulties in the family during the Depression prevented Gould from taking advantage of the opportunity, and he had to quit school in order to help his parents pay the rent. Gould thinks that his lack of academic training in music may have helped him in other ways "I don't know whether formal training would have been for the better," he said in *Musical America.* "Maybe a lot of the positive things that have happened during my career would not have happened if I had gone another route."

In 1931 the still teenage Gould became the pianist at the newly opened Radio City Music Hall, where he per-

formed solos as well as played with the Hall orchestra. At age 21 he began a lifelong affiliation with radio when he was hired to compose, arrange, and conduct weekly orchestra programs for WOR. His programs drew from many musical genres, mostly American, that included jazz, folk, and modern classical.

Making A Name

At age 24 Gould composed his famous *Second Symphonette,* which contained his highly melodic and popular "Pavanne" segment. His light compositions were popular with millions of radio listeners, giving him a national exposure that accelerated his career. Soon he was in demand by orchestras around the country, and he was also invited into the recording studio. Many of his compositions and orchestrations became staples for high school orchestras and bands in the U.S., most notably his *American Salute.*

Some critics wrote off Gould as being too lightweight, and at first the composer was upset at the labeling. Later he changed his opinion, and became a champion of "popular" music. He said in the *Washington Post,* "I was very embarrassed when I was young — put out by the fact that people liked my music." "It bothered me that because my music was popular it couldn't be important," he added in *Musical America.* "But in those days, the feeling was that you did one kind of music or the other. The idea of crossing over was not accepted."

One of Gould's greatest talents was his ability to place popular standards into a symphonic context. His *Cowboy Rhapsody* transferred melodies such as "Home on the Range" into the symphonic realm, and works such as *American Ballads, Classical Variations on Colonial Themes* and *Spirituals for Orchestra* drew heavily on Americana. According to Harrison in *Contemporary Composers,* "In fact Gould has been more successful than some more renowned figures in applying classical procedures to jazz, folk and pre-rock popular idioms."

After leaving his post at WOR in 1942, Gould took on similar responsibilities for NBC and other radio stations. He provided music for shows such as the "Cresta Blanca Carnival" program and "The Chrysler Hour" on CBS. Gould soon branched out into music for theater and film. He was commissioned to score ballet music for Agnes DeMille's *Fall River Legend* in 1949, George Balanchine's *Clarinade* in 1964, and for Jerome Robbins's tribute to Fred Astaire, *I'm Old Fashioned,* in 1983. He also provided scores for the Broadway musicals *Billion Dollar Baby* in 1945 and *Arms and the Girl* in 1952.

Gould has always considered himself an eclectic composer who eagerly embraces new musical influences. As he said in *Contemporary Composers*, "I am not a purist and espouse no dogma but am curious and fascinated by the infinite variety of all kinds of musical sounds." A prime example of his innovativeness is 1952's *Tap Dance Concerto*, a piece that integrated the sound of a solo tap dancer with music played by an orchestra.

Fused Orchestra and Rap at 80

Gould satisfied his interest in jazz with pieces such as *Derivations* in 1956, which he composed especially for clarinetist Benny Goodman. He was also praised for his compositions for two or more pianos, especially his *Two Pianos* that he composed for the first Murray Dranoff Foundation's International Two Piano Symposium in 1987. Showing he could still adapt to changing musical tastes when he was past 80, Gould wrote a concert piece for children in the 1990s called "The Jogger and Dinosaur" that featured a rap musician with orchestra, dancers and visuals.

Dedicated to fostering music appreciation, Gould lectured on the art of composing, served as a musical commentator on television, and conducted student orchestras and bands. A board member of the American Society of Composers, Authors, and Publishers (ASCAP) beginning in 1959, he was its president from 1986 to 1994. In 1986 Gould was elected to the American Academy of Arts and Letters and received a prestigious Kennedy Center Honor in 1994 for his lifetime achievements in music. In 1995 Gould was awarded a Pulitzer Prize for "Stringmusic," a 30-minute work commissioned by the National Symphony in Washington, D.C., as a tribute to conductor Mstislav Rostropovich.

Morton Gould died February 21, 1996, at the age of 82. He was in Orlando, Florida at the time as artist-in-residence at the Disney Institute. The night before his death, he attended a concert by the U.S. Military Academy Band which performed all Gould compositions. Slated to conduct the concert, he was advised not to because he was feeling ill. Upon hearing of his death, songwriter and ASCAP presidential successor Marilyn Bergman told Heidi Waleson of *Billboard,* "America has lost one of its most distinguished composers and conductors, and the creative community has lost one of its great leaders." She added, "His vigor, his wit, and his spirit led us to believe he would live forever. And in fact, through his music and the legacy he left us, he will."

Selected compositions

Second American Symphonette (with *Pavanne*), 1935.
Latin American Symphonette, 1941.
Cowboy Rhapsody, 1942.
American Salute, 1942.
Billion Dollar Baby (musical), 1945.
Delightfully Dangerous (film score), 1945.
Fall River Legend (ballet), 1947.
Arms and the Girl (musical), 1952.
Derivations, 1956.
Windjammer (film score), 1958.
Clarinade (ballet), 1964.
Concerto Grosso, 1968.
Holocaust: Suite (score for television program), 1978.
Two Pianos, 1987.
Minute and Waltz Rag, 1990.
Stringmusic, 1995.

Sources

Books

Anderson, E. Ruth, compiler, *Contemporary American Composers,* G.K. Hall, 1982.
Burbank, Richard, *Twentieth Century Music,* Facts On File, 1984.
Hitchcock, H. Wiley, and Stanley Sadie, editors, *The New Grove Dictionary of Music, Volume Two,* Macmillan, 1986.
Morton, Brian, and Pamela Collins, editors, *Contemporary Composers,* St. James Press.
Sadie, Stanley, editor, *The New Grove Dictionary of Music and Musicians, Volume Seven,* Macmillan, 1980.

Periodicals

American Record Guide, March 1995.
Billboard, March, 2 1996.
Musical America, January 1989.
Washington Post, December 4, 1994.

—Ed Decker

Grant Lee Buffalo

Rock band

In a *Rolling Stone* profile Grant Lee Phillips, singer, guitarist, and songwriter for the Los Angeles trio Grant Lee Buffalo admitted, "I've always been fascinated by American history...But when I write songs it's more like a tornado came through history and picked everything up and spun it around. And when it landed, it wasn't history anymore, it was something else." With songs that "combine the simple structure of pop, the lyrical intimacy of folk and the pure passion of punk," according to Paul Zollo of *Musician,* the band has carved a rare niche for itself in alternative pop.

Phillips was raised in Stockton, California. Several of his ancestors were Pentecostal preachers. He grew up with an eclectic set of influences, as he revealed to Zollo: "I was listening to artists like [English rock chameleon and "glam" hero David] Bowie and [bubblegum-metal champions] KISS on the radio, and at the same time I was loving the music my grandmother loved— singers like [country legends] Buck Owens and Merle Haggard. So my vision of the ideal band at the time was kind of like [bluegrass icon] Bill Monroe meets [1970s

Photograph by Dennis Keeley, © 1994 Slash Records

shock rocker] Alice Cooper. I dreamed of banjos and mandolins and fiddles and all, but with a lot of explosions." By 13 Phillips was playing guitar; it wasn't long before he tried his hand at writing songs. He later joined a band called Bloody Holly. "We'd get our PA system out of a country church and rehearse almost every night in my friend's garage," he recollected to Neil Strauss of *Rolling Stone.*

Hot Tar and Shiva Burlesque

At age 19 Phillips left home and headed south. "I roofed houses for ten years," he told Judy Jade Miller in the *Los Angeles Village View.* "I was mopping hot tar in the day, going to film school at night, and on weekends, I was trying to put a band together." The Los Angeles music scene was still reverberating from the punk revolution, and Phillips's musical ideals were shaped by what he saw in tiny clubs like the Cathay De Grande. Though he would soon drop out of film school, his one-time goal of fusing the musical fantasy *The Wizard of Oz* with the true-life murder tale *In Cold Blood,* as he told Richard Cromelin of the *Los Angeles Times,* could be seen as a blueprint for his lyrical approach.

Drummer Joey Peters moved to Los Angeles in 1985 from Santa Cruz, a coastal university town to the north. He and Phillips met soon thereafter and joined a neo-psychedelic rock band called Shiva Burlesque. Multi-instrumentalist Paul Kimble—who would settle into bass, keyboard, and production duties in Grant Lee Buffalo—had driven to California from Freeport, Illinois, having allowed the outcome of a baseball game determine his destination.

Kimble caught a Shiva Burlesque gig some time later and expressed to a friend his desire to "get in this band and steal the guitarist and drummer and start a band." Shiva Burlesque put out a couple of records independently, but the group split in 1989 and Phillips, Peters, and Kimble struck out on their own. Phillips noted to the *Village View*'s Miller that in the waning days of Shiva, "I had amassed a whole slew of songs that I knew would never see the light of day in the context of that band. Joey and Paul were really excited about those songs, and they too knew that those songs could never happen in Shiva Burlesque."

A "Fuzzy" Period

Though the chemistry among the three musicians allowed them to accomplish a great deal in a short time, they were at a loss to find a name for the project. They went under a variety of monikers, including the Machine Elves and Mouth of Rasputin, changing their name with each early gig. The handle they settled on in 1991 reflected both Phillips's own name and his favorite themes. "Grant Lee Buffalo was sort of a character," he told *Huh* magazine. "A composite of Buffalo Bill and Harry Houdini and a whole lot of history and a whole lot of nightmares." Critics have been unable to resist pointing out that placing Grant and Lee—names of the two most famous generals of the Civil War—alongside the name of an animal extinguished by the settlement of the West also points out the nightmare side of history itself.

The band's weekly gig at West Hollywood's Cafe Largo helped Grant Lee Buffalo gradually amass a following. Meanwhile, they sent their demo tape to Singles Only, a label run by Bob Mould, founder of the influential alternative bands Hüsker Dü and Sugar; the song "Fuzzy" was picked up by the label and released as a single in 1992. Mould later called the song "one of the strongest singles" in his label's catalog, according to Miller. The group continued to record and began drawing larger crowds; Slash Records executive Randy Kaye had been following the band's progress, as he told Miller. "The first couple of times I went [to Largo]," he recalled, "there was hardly anyone there and I just watched it build and build until I was waiting 45 minutes in line to get in—even when we were about to sign 'em."

The group finally agreed to sign with Slash and released its debut album, also called *Fuzzy,* in 1993. The album "was made under the most horrific conditions in many ways," noted Peters, who left the sessions to go on tour with alternative rockers Cracker for eight months. "It was a really stressful thing. It was the first record and I don't know that we entirely knew what we were doing." Critics took to the band even in its relatively undeveloped state; Thom Jurek of the Detroit *Metro Times* called *Fuzzy* "an embarrassingly naive, refreshingly brave collection of provocative songs that offer glimpses of possibility and irritation in their quirkiness."

Superstar rockers Pearl Jam, meanwhile, were so taken by *Fuzzy* that they invited Grant Lee Buffalo on tour with them. The band had to turn the offer down, though, as they'd already committed to touring with Paul Westerberg, founder of post-punk giants the Replacements. Pearl Jam—impressed that Grant Lee Buffalo honored its commitments even when it meant less exposure—later gave them another shot. Phillips told Strauss of *Rolling Stone* that watching Pearl Jam from the wings "was inspiring," especially given the group's preference for changing its show from night to night. Grant Lee Buffalo, too, has "always been into the idea that you don't come to a show to recite something, you come to share in something that's bigger than any one of us."

It was live performance that solidified the group's identity. Touring intensively in support of *Fuzzy*, as Peters told *Strobe*, "expanded our idea of what the band could sound like." With Phillips on amplified twelve-string acoustic guitar, Kimble alternating between his punkified bass playing and elegant turns at the keyboard, and Peters lending subtlety to the trio's considerable rhythmic drive, the emphasis is on dynamics. When Phillips and Kimble simultaneously stomp on distortion pedals, the group can change from delicate folk to explosive rock in the blink of an eye. "It's like a complete change of scenery when that happens," Phillips observed in *Musician*. "Suddenly, out of nowhere, we've got on new costumes, and there's different lighting."

Turned Disaster into Art for *Moon*

Fuzzy didn't fare especially well commercially—except for the title song's inclusion on a film soundtrack—but the band continued to build a cult following. 1994 saw them at work on a new album after an exhausting and at times exasperating period on the road that included being stranded in various parts of Europe and having equipment and CD masters stolen from their tour bus. "Once we started touring, everything I had known up to that point was shattered, and we were all forced to think about life in a completely different way," Phillips told *Pulse!* writer Jon Wiederhorn. "Basically it was like we were kidnapped by the carnival."

The January 17, 1994, earthquake in Los Angeles destroyed both Kimble's house and Phillips's trailer; the two temporarily set up camp in the backyard of Peters's

home. "They were both living out in the tent, and the crows that live out there would wake them up every morning at six after we'd been up working on the album until three," Peters explained to Alan Benson of *The Boston Phoenix*. "That went on for quite a few weeks." Yet Phillips turned the wreckage of his former digs and the upstart noise of the birds into the ballad "Mockingbirds," which would serve as the first single from the 1994 release *Mighty Joe Moon*. Produced by Kimble, the album expanded the scope of the band in terms of its sound and its subject matter. "We were able to try things and push the boundaries of what we'd done before," Peters told Benson, while Kimble pointed out that the band had so many ideas that they "thought it was more essential to sort them all out and get what we wanted on tape than to have some big-name producer."

Featuring the raucous, expansive "Lone Star Song," such encounters with the canvas of American myth as "Sing Along" and "Lady Godiva and Me," and incorporating cellos and other eclectic instruments, *Mighty Joe Moon*—supposedly named for a recording engineer who regaled the band with stories—was a bold next step for an already ambitious troupe. "As great as it is, Grant Lee Buffalo's debut merely signaled the arrival of a songwriting genius," opined *Raygun* critic Robert Levine. "*Mighty Joe Moon* shows what he can do." *College Music Journal* (*CMJ*) agreed: "Once again, the L.A.-based trio's songs are tenderly intimate, yet grand, juxtaposing an astrally high, lonesome sound with concrete, earthly fortitude."

Despite critical acclaim, *Mighty Joe Moon* failed to achieve impressive sales; its subtlety no doubt prevented it from competing with the "New Punk" and other aggressive music then dominating *Billboard*'s Modern Rock chart. Grant Lee Buffalo went on tour with top-grossing rockers R.E.M. on that group's first road trip in five years; when R.E.M. drummer Bill Berry suffered an aneurysm during a show, Peters finished the set. Though that tour was put on hold, the L.A. trio struggled on. "I'm aiming for the transcendent," Phillips declared to Ann Powers in *Rolling Stone*. "A lot of people, I fear, have given up on that."

Selected discography

"Fuzzy," Singles Only, 1992.
Fuzzy, Slash, 1993.
Mighty Joe Moon (includes "Mockingbirds," "Lone Star Song," "Sing Along," and "Lady Godiva and Me"), Slash, 1994.
(Contributors) *If I Were a Carpenter*, ("We've Only Just Begun"), A&M, 1995.
Copperopolis, Slash, 1996.

Sources

Billboard, April 17, 1993.

Boston Herald, November 3, 1994.

Boston Phoenix, September 23, 1994.

College Music Journal (CMJ), November 1994.

Detroit Free Press, April 23, 1993.

Huh, October 1994.

Los Angeles Times, November 19, 1994.

Los Angeles Village View, September 23, 1994.

Metro Times (Detroit), April 21, 1993.

Musician, April 1994.

Pulse!, October 1994.

Raygun, October 1994.

Rolling Stone, August 19, 1993; December 1, 1994; April 18, 1996.

Spin, October 1994.

Strobe, September 1994.

—*Simon Glickman*

Denyce Graves

Opera singer

Unlikely diva Denyce Graves has brought new life to international opera circles. Her rich mezzo soprano vocal style, characterized by the *American Record Guide* as a "full and voluptuous instrument," has made her famous in Europe and the United States, carrying her far beyond her tough, inner-city beginnings. Graves grew up in turbulent southwest Washington, D.C., a neighborhood littered with nondescript tenement buildings and plagued by drugs and violence, a long way from the celebrated opera houses of Europe and the United States. In her signature role as Carmen in Bizet's classic opera of the same name, Graves has performed in Paris's Bastille Opera, Vienna's State Opera, and New York's Metropolitan Opera. Graves travels nine months of the year performing around the globe and has portrayed Carmen, the Spanish cigarette girl, in over 30 productions. With her Met debut, Graves distinguished herself as one of opera's rising stars and, in addition to her prodigious talent and dramatic flair, she is known as one of the friendliest of mezzo sopranos in international music. Her Met performance in January of 1996, documented by the CBS television news program, *60 Minutes,* returned generally positive critical reviews, though the 100 Graves family members in attendance would argue that there has never been a more dazzling Carmen.

But while her life today may be the stuff of dreams, her youth was anything but. In a story recounted in the *Washington Post,* a teenaged Graves came face to face with the kind of tragedy that all too often destroys the aspirations of urban children. She was on her way to a Washington, D.C., vocal competition when, as her bus rolled to a stop, a gunshot rang out and its victim fell against the door. In the panic, the driver and passengers fled the gruesome scene. "I remember leaping over that body out into the night and the rain, and just running and running and running in the dark," she told the *Washington Post.* "I didn't know where I was, I didn't know where I was going. I just knew I had to get away from there. As far away as I could get." Under the firm wing of a loving mother, Graves and her two siblings managed to escape their Galveston Street neighborhood. While her mother, Dorothy, worked as a typist at Federal City College (now the University of the District of Columbia), Graves, her older brother, and younger sister were given chores and productive projects to complete to keep them from the streets. Popular music was forbidden in the house and television viewing had to meet the strict standards of their mother. "She didn't want her babies to be lost to the streets, like so many," Graves told the *New York Times.*

The Graveses were active members of a D.C. baptist church, attending services two or three times a week, and integral members of the choir. Thursday nights in

Born c. 1965 in Washington, D.C. to Dorothy (a registrar at University of the District of Columbia) and Charles (a Baptist minister) Graves (Dorothy remarried to Oliver Kenner, a maintenance worker, after Charles left family, c. 1967); married David Perry (a classical guitar importer, born c. 1950) c. 1990.

Began vocal training singing in church choirs; formal training began at the Duke Ellington School for the Performing Arts in Washington, D.C.; studied at Oberlin Conservatory at Oberlin College in Ohio; studied at the New England Conservatory, Boston; after nearly a year away from music due to vocal problems, took an apprenticeship with the Houston Grand Opera, 1988-90; performed Verdi's *Otello* opposite tenor Placido Domingo; performed lead role in Bizet's Carmen with the Minnesota Opera, 1991; launched successful European audition tour, 1992; has since played the role of Carmen in over 40 productions, notably at London's Covent Garden, Paris's Bastille Opera, and the Vienna Opera.

Selected awards: Received Grand Prize in 1990's Concours International de Chant de Paris given by Union Femmes Artistes et Musiciennes (Paris International Voice Competition, Union of Female Artists and Musicians).

Addresses: *Home*—Resides in Leesburg, Virginia.

the Graves household was music night and the children formed a gospel group their mother dubbed "The Inspirational Children of God." The children traveled to churches around Washington to perform and Denyce gradually developed into the group's soloist. "I was very shy," she told the *Houston Chronicle*, "and my mother didn't want me to be shy. So she would give me solos to sing. She would push me in front and say, 'You have to get over this, Denyce.'" Graves became known to the other kids in the neighborhood as "Hollywood" because she did not pursue the same activities as they did—she spent her time buried in books of poetry or doing homework. Through all her days at Patterson Elementary and then at Friendship Junior High, Graves was an outsider. "I was one of the weird kids, one of those who was not 'in,'" she remarked to *Ebony*.

At the suggestion of junior high teacher Judith Grove, Graves auditioned for admission to Washington's Duke Ellington School for the Performing Arts. Though she initially planned to study theater, faculty members encouraged her to pursue music. Graves studied under voice teacher Helen Hodam and progressed quickly. It was at the Ellington School that Graves realized that opera was her true calling. A class trip to the Kennedy Center in 1980 to view a rehearsal of Beethoven's *Fidelio* triggered Graves's operatic ambitions and after a teacher loaned her a copy of Marilyn Horne singing arias from *Cavalleria Rusticana,* Graves pinned her hopes on such a career. "I thought it was beautiful. I listened to it over and over and over again, and the more I heard it, the more I said, 'Yea, this is me. This is what I want to do,'" she remarked to the *Washington Post.*

Graves worked hard at singing in French, German, and Italian and caught a break when, at a recital, a member of the Washington Opera chorus heard her sing and remarked to Graves that her singing was wonderful. "I had always known how my singing made me feel, but it had never occurred to me that it might provoke the same sort of emotions in others," she told the *Washington Post*. When teacher Helen Hodam left the Ellington School and moved on to Oberlin College in Ohio, Graves followed. Despite offers for full scholarships elsewhere, Graves chose to study with her high school mentor. At Oberlin Conservatory Graves worked several jobs to pay the private school's tuition, cleaning dormitories and working in the cafeteria to get herself through. She performed her first full-length opera at Oberlin, singing in *Eros and Psyche,* a work commissioned in celebration of the college's sesquicentennial. When Hodam left Oberlin for the New England Conservatory, Graves again followed, still working diligently at both her craft and odd jobs to support herself. Eventually Graves progressed through the ranks and became known as one of the conservatory's top prospects.

Poised for success, Graves auditioned at the conservatory for the Metropolitan Opera's Young Artist Program. She passed the opening rounds and was set to perform at the final round in New York. "I had to win. I was four months behind in my rent. I couldn't pay for the rented dress I was wearing," she confessed to the *New York Times.* The stress from working long hours as a hotel desk clerk in Boston and her rigorous vocal training caught up with her, however, and her performance in New York was less than representative of her talents. Crushed by her lackluster performance and experiencing severe vocal problems, Graves visited doctor after doctor to find successful treatment. When none presented itself, she gave up singing entirely and resigned herself to a job as a secretary in a Boston hospital. When a doctor whom she had previously visited reported that her condition was nothing more than a treatable thyroid problem, Graves hesitantly decided to give singing another try. The Houston Grand Opera called her three times before she would accept an apprenticeship in 1988.

In Houston, Graves had the opportunity to work with the legendary Placido Domingo in a production of *Otello* by Verdi. Domingo, engaged by her abilities, became a strong supporter and helped launch her career in earnest. He told the *New York Times*, "What impressed me immediately about her, aside from her obvious vocal and physical beauty, was an aura of the dramatic about her." After completing the apprenticeship in 1990, she offered her distinct take on the role of Carmen with the Minnesota Opera in a modern production of the classic, set in 1950s America rather than 19th-century Spain. Choosing not to listen to previous versions of the opera, Graves opened herself to a new interpretation of the beloved character. "I loved the new concept," she remarked to the *Washington Times*, "staging the opera as a kind of 1950s drama with hoods and street toughs."

Though she established herself professionally in the role of Carmen, Graves looks to complement her repertoire with other roles. She told the *Houston Chronicle*, "It's a popular opera. This is a problem for my career. I want people to come to the theater because I'm singing, not because it's Carmen." Though Graves is booked by opera companies around the world through 1998, many of her roles will be as Carmen due to her unique vocal character and dramatic presence. Former Washington Opera director Martin Feinstein commented to *People*, "She's the definitive Carmen. She has a beautiful voice with great range. She's beautiful and sexy. Not only that, she's very nice."

Selected discography

Hamlet (singing the role of Gertrude), EMI, 1994.
Heroines of Romantic French Opera, FNAC Music (France), 1995.
Otello (singing the role of Emilia), DG Records, 1995.

Sources

Ebony, February 1996.
Evening Standard (London), January 19, 1996.
Houston Chronicle, October 23, 1994; October 29, 1994.
Houston Post, November 7, 1994.
Los Angeles Times, January 26, 1996.
New York Times, October 14, 1995.
Opera News, December 25, 1993; March 5, 1994; February 18, 1995; January 6, 1996.
People, October 23, 1995.
Washington Post, February 10, 1994; March 26, 1995; October 9, 1995.
Washington Times, March 24, 1995.

—*Rich Bowen*

Green Day

Punk band

In the early 1990s Green Day helped bring a new brand of punk rock to the forefront of mainstream music. Bratty and bored, Green Day appealed to the so called "Generation X" crowd—the twentysomethings who were getting bored with the slow-moving angst of grunge music. Green Day's youthful vigor made their pop punk radio friendly and fun for a range of people, many of whom hadn't discovered punk before. The fact that they were genuinely nice, articulate guys also gave their career a boost.

Green Day began in the dreary town of Rodeo, California just 15 miles north of Berkeley. There, ten-year-olds Billie Joe Armstrong and Michael Pritchard—who later changed his last name to Dirnt—met in the school cafeteria. Neither had had a good home life. When he was ten, Armstrong's jazz musician father died, fragmenting his family. Armstrong found solace in his new friend and in music. Dirnt, born to a heroin-addicted mother, was adopted by a Native American mother and a white father who divorced when he was seven. When his mom moved north when Dirnt was 15, he rented a room off Armstrong's house.

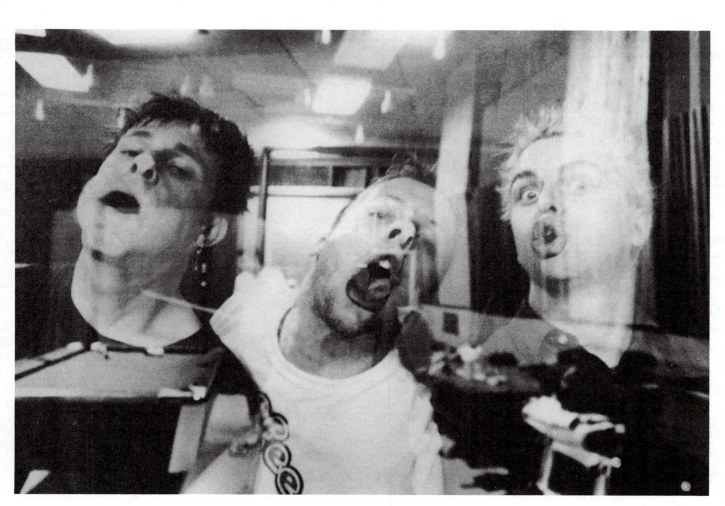

Photograph by Eva Janey, © 1995 Reprise Records

Even if either boy had had enough money to buy records, there wasn't a record store in town. They learned about music from their older siblings and friends. They listened to early punk progenitors the Replacements, the Ramones, and the earliest works of British punkers the Sex Pistols and the Buzzcocks. They were finally able to scrape together enough cash by the time they were 11 to buy their own guitars. That's when Armstrong got his beloved Stratocaster, which he plays to this day.

In 1987 the boys formed the band Sweet Children, with John Kiftmeyer (aka Al Sobrante) on drums. By then Dirnt had switched to the bass. Soon they became consumed by their weekend lives at the Gilman Street Project in Berkeley. This unassuming-looking caning-and-wicker shop housed a major underground punk club on the weekends. "That place and that culture saved my life," Armstrong told *Rolling Stone's* Chris Mundy. "It was like a gathering of outcasts and freaks. It wasn't about people moshing in a pit and taking their shirt off. That's one thing I hate about the new mainstream thing: blatant violence.... To me punk rock was about being silly." Both boys tried their best juggling music, jobs, and school—virtually raising themselves.

Green Day recorded their first EP, *1,000 Hours*, in 1987 and by 1989 had enough steam behind them to begin lobbying Lookout! Records for a deal. They also changed their name to Green Day, the title of one of their songs. Lawrence Livermore, head of this independent punk label, signed the band immediately upon hearing them. Green Day began touring in earnest after they released their first album *39/Smooth* in 1990. Just the week before that Armstrong gave up the ghost at school, dropping out the day before his eighteenth birthday. Dirnt struggled through and got his diploma. Lack of brains hadn't been the problem for either student, it was trying to earn a living and make music that took the toll on their school work.

Broke into the Big Time

Meanwhile, deep in the Mendocino mountains of California, Frank Edwin Wright III lived with his family in near isolation. Wright's nearest neighbor was Livermore, and when his band the Lookouts! needed a drummer they called on 12-year-old Wright, renaming him Tre Cool. When Green Day got back from their first van tour in 1990, Kiftmeyer jumped ship. Cool, Kiftmeyer's drum teacher, took over where his student left off. *39/Smooth* gained the band national attention, allowing them to garner packed houses in most places they played. In 1991, with their new flamboyant drummer on board, Green Day released *Kerplunk*. *Kerplunk* quickly broke sales records for Lookout! and several successful tours ensued.

In early 1993 Green Day left Lookout! on friendly terms and began searching for a label that would be able to give them the promotion and tour support that an independent couldn't. Against the odds, Green Day had managed to cut three 7-inch singles, book seven U.S. tours plus two European jaunts, and sell 30,000 copies of both of their LPs all before they turned 21; the major labels had a feeding frenzy trying to sign them. It was Rob Cavallo, the young producer/A & R representative from Warner Bros.'s Reprise Records, who convinced the guys to choose Warner. Also convincing was that Warner had been the label of the Sex Pistols and the Ramones.

Dookie

In 1993 Green Day released their major-label debut, *Dookie*, which is slang for excrement. The music blended raw punk force with pop melodies. The songs were short and catchy. They were also funny and irreverent, highlighting lives of boredom, pot smoking, and masturbation. *Rip* wrote: "14 whirlwind tunes sweep you up in guitar-drenched sentiments, leaving barely enough time between tracks to catch your breath. Like their musical forbears, the Who and the Ramones, they aren't afraid of melodies, and there are some downright pretty ones here, which they tackle boldly, armed with Billie Joe's bracing power chords, Dirnt's agile bass lines and the dynamic drumming of Tre picked up playing with his jazz buddies." *Time* called it "a cathartic punk explosion and the best rock CD of the year so far." MTV put Green Day's videos in heavy rotation and the boys graced the cover of nearly every music magazine. Bringing down the house during their mud-drenched performance at Woodstock 94, Green Day solidified their super stardom.

With stardom came cries of sellout. Suddenly, along with punkers the Offspring and Rancid, Green Day had brought underground punk rock into the mainstream. Assuredly, it was a new 1990s punk, much more positive and born from a different kind of angst. But it was still punk, English accents and all. Green Day responded to naysayers with reasonable thinking. To *Rip* Dirnt explained that they couldn't survive to play music without help from the big labels. "Selling out is compromising your musical intentions. And we don't know how to do that." Armstrong put it even more simply. *People* reported him telling a friend, "I don't come from that world where you can afford to turn down cash."

Practiced Responsible Punk

Green Day has a lot going for them. Besides being so radio friendly, their live performances are electrifying. Because they consider their brand of punk to have a strong silliness component, they are *very* silly. And, as one Berkeley club promoter put it in *People,* "they're just a bunch of nice guys. They're polite. They never put holes in the wall. Never vomited on stage." Despite their angry stage posturing and immature antics, they're three newly married guys who just want to be able to raise the good healthy families that they never had. Armstrong and Cool, in fact, already have a baby each. In addition to being responsible parents, Green Day does their best to be a responsible band. They defy ticket company service charges by cutting their touring costs—often sleeping on the tour bus—and taking a smaller cut to keep ticket and t-shirt prices under $15. They made sure that 100 percent of the sales of their Lookout! albums go to Lookout! in order to keep that independent scene alive. Proceeds of several of their shows have gone to charity.

No matter how hard they try, first-time fatherhood and a demanding life in the spotlight takes its toll. 1995's *Insomniac* was a darker, somewhat less accessible album than *Dookie.* Sales were still good—700,000 in less than three months—although not as brilliant as *Dookie,* which had a sold over 8 million copies by the time *Insomniac* came out. Reviewers didn't come down hard as they often do on a follow-up album. In *Spin,* Eric Weisbard wrote, "The Green Day three have never crunched as powerfully as they do on *Insomniac....* One or two moments excepted, the rest is a sustained thrill." *People* said, "On their visceral follow up, Green Day is intent on gaining punk credibility among hard-core denizens of the mosh pit—even at the risk of diminished sales." Risky or no, *Spin* voted *Insomniac* number 15 out of 20 of the best albums of 1995.

One thing that even the band realizes, according to their 1995 press materials, is that trends are fleeting. "When the punk rock craze dies an ugly mainstream death next year (just for the record, it died in the underground two years ago) Green Day will still be standing and they'll be making great records." Or, as Armstrong mused in *Rip,* "Here today, gone later today." But for now, Green Day's got a Grammy, they've helped out their struggling families, and they're the biggest selling punk band in history. They did all that before they were 25.

Selected discography

1,000 Hours (EP), 1987.
39/Smooth, Lookout! Records, 1990.
Kerplunk, Lookout! Records, 1992.
Dookie, Reprise Records, 1993.
(Contributors) *Angus* (soundtrack), 1995.
Insomniac, Reprise Records, 1995.

Sources

BAM, January 12, 1996.
Billboard, June 25, 1994.
Details, September 1994.
Entertainment Weekly, June 10, 1994; December 23, 1994; October 20, 1995.
Guitar Player, July 1994.
Musician, September 1994; June 1995.
People Weekly, March 20, 1995; October 30, 1995.
Raygun, April 1994.
Rip, June 1994; March 1995.
Rolling Stone, September 22, 1994; November 17, 1994; December 15, 1994; January 26, 1995; December 28, 1995.
Spin, September 1994; November 1994; March 1995; November 1995; December 1995; January 1996.
Time, June 27, 1994.

Additional information for this profile was provided by Reprise Records press materials, 1993 and 1995.

—*Joanna Rubiner*

Andre Harrell

Record company executive

When Andre Harrell was touring the legendary Hitsville U.S.A. building, the birthplace of Motown, shortly after becoming the company's president and CEO, he told Brian McCollum of the Detroit Free Press, "This is so much bigger than just being president of a record company. It's like being inducted into some kind of musical royal family." As one of the reigning kings of black entertainment, it's an appropriate analogy. "I am a lifestyle entertainment entrepreneur," he said in *Upscale* magazine while president of his own Uptown Entertainment. "I'm promoting the whole spectrum of black lifestyles, from the teenage street hip-hop lifestyle to an adult, upwardly mobile black lifestyle." While heading Uptown Records, Harrell promoted the "black lifestyle" by catapulting former unknowns Jodeci, Heavy D and The Boyz, Mary J. Blige, and Al B. Sure! to stardom. *Upscale* magazine noted that Harrell quickly gained a reputation as having a "golden finger on the pulse of what's hot in the music industry," and left the entire entertainment industry "standing at rapt attention, waiting for his next successful move."

Born Andre O'Neal Harrell to a supermarket foreman and a nurse's aid, Harrell grew up in the housing projects of the Bronx, New York. While both of his parents labored for their meager existence, young Harrell was somehow confident of a promising future. Though he was a self described poor, inner-city kid, he explained that, "I grew up thinking wonderful things could happen, I always believed I'd have a wonderful life."

Harrell's 16th year was a watershed period in his life. While his parents were divorcing, he teamed up with high-school buddy, Alonzo Brown to form the successful rap duo, Dr. Jekyll (Harrell) and Mr. Hyde (Brown). For their first performance, the duo stood atop chairs and rapped for a crowd of 40 that had gathered at the DeWitt Clinton Housing Project. Harrell said he turned to rapping because, "I couldn't play basketball well enough to be on the starting team, but I could rap well enough." In fact, Harrell and Brown rapped so well that Dr. Jekyll and Mr. Hyde enjoyed three top 20 hits: "Genius Rap," "Fast Life," and "AM/FM."

The duo became popular weekend rappers, but having set his sights on becoming a newscaster, Harrell went on to study communications and business management at the Bronx's Lehman College. After three years, however, he dropped out and went to work selling air time for a local radio station. In 1983, Harrell met Russell Simmons, the founder of Rush Management, a company that launched the careers of cutting-edge black "street" artists. In time, Simmons persuaded Harrell to come to work for Rush at a mere $200 per week. Within his two years at Rush, Harrell became vice-president

For the Record . . .

Born Andre O'Neal Harrell, c. 1962. *Education:* Attended Lehman College.

With Alonzo Brown, formed Dr. Jekyll and Mr. Hyde (rap duo); Rush Management, New York City, vice president and general manager, c. 1985; Uptown Records, New York, NY, founder and president, 1987-92; Uptown Entertainment, New York, NY, president, 1992-95; Motown Record Company, President and CEO, 1995-.

Addresses: *Office*—Motown Record Company, 5750 Wilshire Blvd., Ste. 300, Los Angeles, CA 90036.

and general manager, playing a pivotal role in building the careers of artists like Run DMC, LL Cool J, and Whoodini.

Filled the Urban Void

While at Rush, Harrell became increasingly aware of "a void in the marketplace for a certain black lifestyle—a very urban, young adult, cool vibe." Rush did a phenomenal job of promoting the raw, black street sound, but Harrell saw another black sound being overlooked: the more subtle sound coming from the marriage of rhythm and blues with hip-hop. The black lifestyle, Harrell saw, was being expressed in extremes: in the street culture of many cutting edge black musicians and in the bourgeois culture represented, somewhat unrealistically, in television's *Cosby Show.*

Harrell felt he could bridge the gap between "street" and middle to upper class. "I had more of an understanding of what this vibe was all about than any other major label executive I knew," he commented. He left Rush Management to launch Uptown Records, a company that would fill the void in urban black music. Longtime friend tag Nelson George explained that Harrell made music for the type of people he knew growing up, "the black bus driver from Queens [New York] who wears suits on weekends and goes to clubs to pick up girls." Harrell argued that the media—especially white critics—"think it is boring when black people sing about being in love or paying bills." Uptown was created to market music reflective of a more mainstream black lifestyle.

Harrell took Uptown through a series of successes. By 1988, MCA was courting Harrell and offered him a $75,000 label deal. His first release under MCA, a compilation of works by then-unknown artists, was a huge success. Harrell followed up this surprise hit by producing Heavy D's platinum album, *Livin' Large.* He built on these first successes with hit albums from Al B Sure! and Guy. It became almost commonplace to see Uptown releases go gold or platinum, as the enterprise became a major force in the music industry.

Joined With MCA

With the growing popularity of its artists, Uptown's success continued multiplied until 1992, when MCA offered Harrell a $50 million multimedia deal. The nearly unprecedented arrangement opened up Harrell's creative vistas to include film and television. Uptown Records thus was renamed Uptown Entertainment. For the next seven years Harrell would have the power to produce albums with MCA Music Entertainment Group and to feature his recording artists in film and television productions for Universal Pictures and Universal Television respectively.

With the power to produce for music, film, and television, Harrell's mission remained the same: "I want to tell stories about everyday black people that will have a wide reaching appeal—experiences that are African American, but feelings that are universal." Working with MCA/Universal allowed Harrell to nearly triple Uptown's staff and to set up satellite offices in Los Angeles.

With ever increasing responsibilities and less time for being "in the mix," Harrell staffed both his New York City and Los Angeles Uptown offices with young producers and vice-presidents who could keep him connected to the pulse of the urban African American lifestyle. The swell of funds and staff also allowed Uptown to thrive with the incorporation of in-house video, publicity, and marketing departments.

In the Game

Uptown Entertainment immediately launched development of a full slate of film and television projects, many featuring Uptown recording artists. For example, it was not long before Uptown Entertainment sold a pilot to Fox Television starring Heavy D as a rapping dad. A drama called *Flavor,* a variety/comedy show similar to *In Living Color,* and a feature film starring the soulful singers of En Vogue were also soon in the works.

Uptown's musical prowess was celebrated in 1993, when Music Televisions (MTV) showcased Uptown recording artists Mary J. Blige, Father MC, Heavy D, Christopher Williams, and Jodeci on the cable network's popular acoustic show, *Unplugged.* Not surprisingly, this was the first time that the popular show had devoted its entire timeslot to artists of a single record label. The show was such a success that it was released as a video.

In addition to creating overwhelming pressures to keep increasing profits, Harrell's success reaped the financial rewards necessary to build the lifestyle he dreamed of during his childhood in the housing projects of the Bronx. In 1988, Harrell recalled. "I was rollin'. I was in the game. I was coming into spots and it was going on. I was all over the country, all over the world. I was 20 years old. The dough was flowing. I bought a house. Bought a BMW. Two. Was Happy. It was the beginning of the game. I was crazy happy. Crazy happy." He enjoyed his success thoroughly, earned a reputation as the premiere party-giver on the east coast. However, he realized that with success came a responsibility, for, as he told "I want to show kids what can be achieved if they never take no for an answer."

Harrell's extraordinary rise from the housing projects of the Bronx to his leadership role in the music, film, and television industries prompted the inevitable reflection on just what accounts for such success. In large part he credited his success with being both a rap artist and an entrepreneur. As a former performer Harrell gained a rapport with musicians that some industry executives are lacking. He has been perceived as a peer of musicians, an approachable ally.

From Uptown to Motown

Harrell's entrepreneurial savvy may have also found its roots in his youth in the Bronx. Chris Albrecht of Home Box Office (HBO) Independent Productions told *Vanity Fair* that Harrell's business edge was reflective of his street-fighter sense of survival. In essence, Harrell's success stemmed from fierce determination. As he told *Vanity Fair,* "I can do just about anything I want. It's a matter of will. Yeah, I guess you have to be talented and smart and stuff, and I hope I've proven that. But I know, at this point in my career, the doors of opportunity are open. As long as I have the desire and the will to want to do it, a lot of different things will get ready to happen."

One door of opportunity was to the president's office of Motown Records. In October of 1995 Harrell was appointed president/CEO of Motown, a deal reportedly worth some $20 million, in an effort to update that labels image and utilize Harrell's considerable skills in spotting new talent. Alain Levy, head of Motown parent PolyGram, told *Billboard*'s J. R. Reynolds, "The music business is driven by A&R (artists and repertory), especially at Motown. Andre has shown that he knows how to build artists." As for Harrell's liberal use of corporate funds and relative inexperience in running a major company, Levy told Ronald Grover of *Business Week,* "His job is to find the acts, ours is to give him the boundaries."

As for Harrell, he knew his job was to put Motown back on the musical map. "I'm gonna bring back *real* soul music," he told *New York*'s Kiki Mason. "I want young people with old voices that reek of life experience, of pain." Steps Harrell planned on taking were to move Motown's headquarters from Los Angeles to New York, and to open A&R offices in Atlanta and Detroit, the home of Motown from its founding in 1958 until 1972. Harrell also said he was planning to go back to the streets to find the next generation of black artists. "I've created stars and celebrities," he told Mason. "Now I want to make superstars."

Sources

Billboard, May 11, 1991; December 12, 1992; June 20, 1992; October 14, 1995.
Black Enterprise, August 1993.
Business Week, November 6, 1995.
Detroit Free Press, March 24, 1996.
Ebony, November 1991; October 1993.
Gentlemen's Quarterly, April 1993.
New York, October 23, 1995.
Upscale, September/October 1993.
Vanity Fair, September 1993.
Vibe, December/January 1994.

Additional information for this profile was obtained from press materials from Uptown Entertainment and Motown Record Company.

—Lisa Fredricks

Fletcher Henderson

Bandleader, composer, pianist

Fletcher Henderson, a figure whose place in music history continues to arouse debate and critical discussion, occupied a unique position in the development of jazz. A classically trained pianist, he helped bridge the world of the formal written arrangement with the African-American art of improvisation, creating a new orchestral style in jazz known as "swing." The dominant exponent of the New York, or "eastcoast," style, Henderson launched his career as part of the society orchestra and dance band craze of the 1920s and emerged, by the 1930s, as the leader of a model jazz ensemble.

Born on December 18, 1897, in Cuthbert, Georgia, James Fletcher Henderson was the son of a middle-class school principal and a music teacher who demanded that their three children receive a formal musical education. Henderson began to study piano at age six; he was often locked in a room and forced to practice. After seven years of classical instruction he developed a proficient sense of pitch and an ability to sight read music. As Richard Hadlock wrote in *Jazz Masters of the 20s*, "Fletcher did well by his demanding father, performing in small classical recitals and avoiding the 'undesirable' influence of the blues."

Viewed as part of a well-rounded education, Henderson's musical training did not immediately inspire a career in the arts. In 1916 he attended Atlanta University to study mathematics and chemistry. Occasionally taking a job in music, he devoted most of his time to science and sports, particularly baseball. It was in reference to his batting average and his singular habit of smacking his lips that Henderson's university colleagues gave him the nickname "Smack."

Reading Skills Valued at Pace and Handy

In 1920 Henderson, intent on further pursuing his education and finding work in science, arrived in New York City. He was soon confronted, however, by the lack of job opportunities for black chemists. He then began work as a pianist with the Pace & Handy publishing house, demonstrating and promoting songs. Because music publisher W. C. Handy, often called the Father of the Blues, emphasized musically correct scores and sheet music, rather than traditional interpretations of the blues, Henderson's musical reading skills were held in high regard at the company.

In 1921 Handy's partner Harry Pace left the firm and founded Black Swan Records, a black-owned company boasting such distinguished directors as educator and writer W. E. B. Du Bois and New York real estate giant John E. Nail. Because of Pace's disinterest in blues and other non-classical forms, he employed Hend-

For the Record . . .

Born James Fletcher Henderson, December 18, 1897, in Cuthbert, GA; wife's name, Leora. *Education:* Attended Atlanta University, 1916-20.

Began studying piano at age six; pianist with the Pace & Handy publishing company, New York City, 1920; musical director, Black Swan Recording Company, 1921-23; became leader of eight-piece orchestra, 1924; disbanded orchestra, 1935; arranger for Benny Goodman, 1936; led band at Grand Terrace, Chicago, 1936; rejoined Goodman, 1939; toured with own band, 1944; appeared at Rhumboogie Room and Club Delisa, Chicago, 1945; toured as pianist with Ethel Waters, 1949; led band at Bop City and Cafe Society, New York City, 1950.

erson—a respected college graduate and formally trained musician—to become the company's musical director. At Black Swan Henderson led small bands, organized recording sessions, and played piano for numerous vaudeville-style blues singers. Clarinetist/saxophonist Garvin Bushell, in his memoir *Jazz from the Beginning,* recalled how "Fletcher was in charge of the recording dates. He might pick the numbers in the office, present them to vocalists, then we'd have rehearsal and get it together. Often there were only two pieces of music, one for the piano and one for the trumpet (or violin)."

Creating A New Style

Since Henderson's upbringing and musical training had not brought him in direct contact with the blues, his musicianship was received with little enthusiasm by singers like Ethel Waters, who, in her first meeting with the erudite pianist, found him priggish and without real knowledge of, or feeling for, blues music. As a remedy, Waters insisted Henderson listen to James P. Johnson piano rolls.

In the studio Henderson and his core of musical sidemen were extemporaneously developing a new style, incorporating the looseness and improvisation of the blues with standard European musical forms. Though this style did not have the distinctively loping and relaxed feel of the New Orleans or Chicago styles, it clearly contributed to the melding of African-American and European musical traditions. "Fletcher Henderson's reputation for over-orchestrated jazz and blues," wrote Ted Vincent in *Living Blues,* "has to be seen in light of the understandable attempt to display structure ... as can be seen in the complex introductions and breaks in the classic blues that was the product of Bessie Smith, Ethel Waters, Rosa Henderson, Ida Cox, Ma Rainey, and the other recorded singers of the '20s."

By mid-1923 Henderson was one of the most in-demand session men in New York, recording for the Black Swan, Columbia, Paramount, and Edison labels. It was around that time that he assembled an eight-piece group, which landed a job at the Club Alabam, a cellar club on West 44th Street and Broadway. He was reluctant to lead the band, but the ensemble urged him on. As bandmember Don Redman recalled in *Jazz Panorama,* "We decided to make Fletcher the leader because he was a college graduate and presented a nice appearance." Since the band sought work in high-paying white clubs, Henderson's sophisticated appearance and musical knowledge was vital to its commercial success. "Smack was a man of imposing stature," wrote trumpeter Rex Stewart in *Jazz Masters of the 1930s,* "about six feet two or so. His complexion was that of an octoroon, and in his youth he could be mistaken for Italian.... He could be frivolous or serious, according to mood. However, even in his zany moments, there would be overtones of gentility. His greatness also lay in his impeccable selection of sidemen."

Henderson's band included banjoist Charlie Dixon, drummer Kaiser Marshall, tuba player Ralph Escudero, saxophonist Coleman Hawkins, and trumpeters Elmer Chambers and Joe Smith. But it was his arranger, saxophonist Don Redman, who proved to be his most vital asset. Reared as a musical prodigy, Redman was largely responsible for the modern character and development of the Henderson band. As Lewis Porter wrote in *Jazz from its Origins,* Redman "learned to write passage-work in the style of jazz solos. He left space for jazz solos, and he began opposing the band's sections, reeds against brass, in a way that would become cliché of the era."

Enter Armstrong

While on tour with Ethel Waters in 1921, Henderson heard a young New Orleans trumpet player named Louis Armstrong. In 1924 Armstrong joined Henderson as third chair in the band's new three-man trumpet section. Armstrong's fourteen-month stay had a profound impact on the band—his horn stimulating the stylistic sensibility of his bandmates and inspiring Redman to make additional solo space in his arrangements. At the same time, the band helped hone Armstrong's reading skills. "The band gained a lot from Louis, and he learned a lot from us," explained Henderson in *Record Changer*. "He influenced the band greatly, by making the men really swing ... with that New Orleans style of his." An excellent example of Armstrong's sway was captured on the band's 1925 recording "Sugar Foot Stomp." A reworking of King Oliver's "Dippermouth Blues," the arrangement, as Dan Morganstern observed in the liner notes to *Louis Armstrong: Portrait of an Artist*, "is smoothed out to an Armstrongian 4/4 feel; the sections phrase much more smoothly," with a fitting solo in tribute to Armstrong's ex-leader, King Oliver.

With the departure of Armstrong in 1925, Henderson continued on the path of commercial success. Since establishing residency at the Roseland Ballroom on Broadway in 1924, the Henderson band had secured a stable economic base. The band's live radio broadcasts from Roseland and seasonal eastern tours brought it nationwide fame. "All the musicians hung around front of our bandstand at the Roseland," recalled Stewart in *Jazz Masters of the 30s*, "eager to hear (and borrow) from Smack."

Artistic Resurgence, Commercial Decline

But Henderson's economic and artistic success proved short-lived. The first setback came with Redman's departure in 1927. The following year, a car accident in Kentucky left Henderson with a broken collar bone and facial lacerations. During his recovery, he fell into a dark depression. Henderson's wife, Leora, recalled in *Hear Me Talkin' to Ya*, "Fletcher was never the same after he had that automobile accident.... He never did have much business qualities anyhow, but after the accident he had even less." The constant changing of sidemen and the inability to find an arranger of Redman's caliber resulted in a period of artistic lull for the Henderson band.

Though the subsequent addition of drummer Walter Johnson and tuba-player John Kirby, along with the arranging contributions of saxophonist Benny Carter, contributed to artistic resurgence in 1930, the band continued to struggle financially. The great bandleader and composer Duke Ellington observed, as quoted in *Hear Me Talkin to Ya*, "Smack's band was beginning to find the going a little tough around '32 and '33. Work was scarce, but the band was so fine, and the guys so attached to it, that nobody had the heart to quit." Traveling by "classy car caravan" across the country, the Henderson band continued to play theaters coast to coast.

Ultimately, though, the lack of steady employment led to the break-up of Henderson's famed orchestra in 1935.

"How utterly frustrating it must have been," wrote Gunther Schuller in *The Swing Era*, "at [a time of such development], in such pieces as 'Down Home Camp Meetin' and "Wrappin' It Up," that his orchestra's fortunes had sunk so low it was forced to disband!"

In 1936 Henderson took a job as staff arranger for swing clarinetist and bandleader Benny Goodman. Within a few months he'd formed a new band featuring soloists like trumpeter Roy Eldridge, saxophonist Chu Berry, and drummer Sid Catlett. Also that year, Henderson established his band at the Grand Terrace in Chicago and landed his first hit with Berry's "Christopher Columbus," arranged by the bandleader's brother Horace Henderson. But as Schuller noted in *The Swing Era*, "The Henderson band was closing in on itself, cutting off its own vital circulation. The band's final demise— except for five more sides cut in 1941 by a temporarily reorganized band—was sad indeed, when one considers that the band could hardly manage even a well-known vintage piece like 'Moten Stomp.'"

Following stints at Chicago's Rhumboogie Room and Club Delisa in 1945, Henderson worked periodically with Goodman and toured as an accompanist for Ethel Waters. In 1950 he led a sextet at Cafe Society in New York. That same year, while a member of the Jazz Train show at New York's Bop City, he suffered a stroke that left him partially paralyzed. Henderson died on December 28, 1952, after collapsing in the street. His wife somberly recalled in *Hear Me Talkin' to Ya*, "He was really trying to make a comeback—working days and nights on arrangements and rehearsals. But all of it came to nothing."

Despite his many years of struggle and lack of long-term commercial success, Henderson has emerged as a man, who, in the second and third decades of the 20th century, stood at the crossroads of modern musical development. His contribution to the art form," wrote Max Harrison in *The New Grove Gospel, Blues and Jazz*, "was not only ultimately an orchestral one; rather, he and his [sidemen] showed that improvisation could flourish within the context of written scores, that spontaneity and careful preparation were not incompatible." In a recent *Down Beat* review of Henderson's music, critic Kevin Whitehead measured the enduring impact of Henderson's contribution to American musical history by boldly expressing: "If you consider yourself culturally literate you better know your Fletcher Henderson."

Selected discography

Rarest Fletcher, Vol. 1, 1923-24, MCA.
Fletcher Henderson: 1924/1927, Zeta Records.

First Impressions (1924-1931), MCA.
Fletcher Henderson and the Dixie Stompers, 1925-1928, DRG.
Jazz Age: 1925-1928, ABC.
Fletcher Henderson: 1927, Classics.
Fletcher Henderson: 1927-1931, Classics.
Swing 1929-1937, ABC.
Swingin' the Thing, 1931-34, MCA.
Hocus Pocus, Classic Big Band Jazz, RCA/Bluebird.
Tidal Wave, Decca.
Under a Harlem Moon, ASV.
A Study in Frustration: The Fletcher Henderson Story, The-saurus of Classic Jazz, Columbia/Legacy, 1994.

Sources

Books

Bushell, Garvin, as told to Mark Tucker, *Jazz from the Begin-ning,* University of Michigan Press, 1990.
Hadlock, Richard, *Jazz Masters of the 20s,* Da Capo, New York.
Hear Me Talkin' to Ya: The Story of Jazz as Told by the Men Who Made It, edited by Nat Shapiro and Nat Hentoff, Dover Publications, 1955.

Hennessey, Thomas J., *From Jazz to Swing: African-Ameri-can Musicians and Their Music 1890-1935,* Wayne State University Press, 1994.
Jazz Panorama: From the Pages of the Jazz Review, edited by Matin T. Williams, Da Capo, 1979.
The New Grove Gospel, Blues and Jazz, with Spirituals and Ragtime, edited by Paul Oliver and Max Harrison, Norton, 1980.
Porter, Lewis, and Michael Ullman, with Edward Hazell, *Jazz from its Origins to the Present,* Prentice Hall, 1993.
Schuller, Gunther, *The Swing Era: The Development of Jazz 1930-1945,* Oxford University Press, 1989.
Stewart, Rex, *Jazz Masters of the 30s,* Da Capo, 1972.

Periodicals

Down Beat, January 1995.
Living Blues, May/June, 1989.
Record Changer, July/August 1950.

Additional information for this profile was obtained from liner notes by Dan Morganstern to *Louis Armstrong: Portrait of the Artist as a Young Man 1923-1934,* Columbia/Legacy.

—John Cohassey

Incognito

Acid jazz group

By the mid-1990s, musical boundaries had become less and less restrictive and the term "crossover"—used to describe musicians who ventured beyond their own genre—carried less and less meaning. Rap, soul, country, rock, and alternative music have all appeared at one time or another, sometimes simultaneously, on *Billboard*'s Top Ten chart. Vintage crooner Tony Bennett found fame in MTV circles while country music, once relegated to rural America and the urban South, entered the mainstream. Even the solid institution of jazz has seen a change in its scope, particularly in the way that acid jazz has blurred the distinctions between jazz, hip-hop, and R&B. As Island Records executive Peggy Dold explained to *Billboard*, "You can't define acid jazz with one particular record or artist. There are nuances and differences in the music, which is very healthy." Enter England's Incognito. Comprised of Jean-Paul "Bluey" Maunick, Joy Malcolm, Pamela Anderson, and Simon Hale, Incognito began making records in the early Eighties that took jazz and soul as a starting place, but arrived somewhere entirely different by way of street-smart creativity and experimental yet solid musicianship.

Photograph by David Corio, MICHAEL OCHS ARCHIVES/Venice, CA

For the Record . . .

Formed in 1979 in London, England by leader Jean-Paul "Bluey" Maunick (born c. 1957 in Mauritius; emigrated to England, c. 1967). Other core members include vocalists Pamela Anderson and Joy Malcolm and musician Simon Hale. Joined by others for recordings and tours to form a 12- to 15-member band, often featuring an orchestra section.

First recording *Jazz Funk* released in the U.K., 1980; signed with Verve's Talkin' Loud label, 1991; released *Inside Life*, 1992; single "Always There" from *Inside Life* hits Top Ten, 1992; vocalist Maysa Leak joins group for recording of *Tribes, Vibes + Scribes*, 1993; recorded and released *Positivity*, 1994; single "Still a Friend of Mine" from *Positivity* achieves highest commercial success for group, 1994; released *100@ and Rising* featuring Barry Stewart, 1995.

Addresses: *Record company*—Talkin' Loud/Verve Forecast, 825 8th Avenue, New York, N.Y. 10019.

Incognito delivers Seventies-style R&B dressed up in Nineties garb with definite jazz underpinnings, a mood that follows the musical vision of the band's leader, Bluey Maunick. An adolescence in London, where R&B, funk, and jazz were tremendously popular, ensured that Maunick developed a strong affinity for artists such as Herbie Hancock, Stevie Wonder, and Earth, Wind & Fire. "Jazz-funk [in the '70s] gave British kids a tremendous sense of freedom," Maunick told *Newsday.* "It loosened them up on the dance floor in a way that no other music had previously, bringing together black and white for the first time. The lyrics suggested the positivity of life; it was an optimistic, life-affirming vibe."

Sounds of Seventies for Nineties Ears

Though the band's soulful rhythms usually escape criticism and attract listeners, their detractors point to the jazz element in their sound as a source of weakness. The venerable chronicle of the jazz scene, *Down Beat,* critiqued the band's 1994 album *Positivity* and found that "Maunick's bland, laid-back tunes are no jazzier than, say, Sade's." Elsewhere, Howard Reich of the *Chicago Tribune* said of a 1994 performance, "Evidently, Incognito believes its horn players' riffs constitute jazz, though these simplistic little melodic hooks, repeated ad nauseum, are pale imitations of the real thing." In his defense of his inspirations, Maunick declared in an interview with the *Los Angeles Times,* "I dug Roberta Flack and Chaka Khan, but I equally dug Joni Mitchell. When you grow up in a society where music wasn't pigeonholed, you have an advantage. It was all just music in those days."

While Maunick plays the guitar and his compositions rely on steady percussion and occasional horn flurries, the attention generally falls on the band's vocalists. Singers Pamela Anderson and Joy Malcolm both demonstrate well-trained abilities to deliver sultry sounds reminiscent of Anita Baker. Critics generally agree that Incognito's jazz heritage is largely present in its lyrical delivery. *Positivity,* the band's 1994 album, made use of vocalist Maysa Leak of Baltimore, Maryland. Maunick hired Leak to appear on the group's 1993 release after an audition conducted over the telephone. Leak's alto voice so powerfully filled the record that the *Tribune*'s Reich termed her vocals rife with "voluptuousness."

London's Music Scene Inspired Eclectic Sound

As Incognito's founder and leader, the band's history begins—and will presumably end—with Maunick's own. Born on Mauritius Island, near Madagascar in the Indian Ocean, Maunick moved with his mother to London at age ten. Inspired by the city's rich music scene, he formed Light of the World, an R&B/jazz band noted for the fact that they were one of the first black bands in London to receive critical attention. When that band came to a demise, Maunick formed Incognito in 1979. The band released *Jazz Funk* in 1980 and the record found its way to the British Top 30, where it remained for two months.

The record's success notwithstanding, musical tastes in Britain, and London especially, shifted from the lush and soulful to the sparse and erratic. Punk bands began to consume the charts and clubs looked to new bands such as the Clash and the Buzzcocks to occupy their stages. Seemingly a casualty of music's evolution, Maunick held firm to his style and found work producing other acid jazz bands that continued to forward the genre. Maunick told London's *Guardian,* "I was still searching for my place in the scheme of things, but trying to stay true to music."

Signed With Talkin' Loud

Maunick's fortunes took a dramatic turn for the better in 1991. A well-respected club DJ, Giles Peterson, took control of a newly formed Verve Records division, Talkin' Loud Records. Talkin' Loud, affiliated with Verve, itself a division of Polygram, was charged with signing bands that fell beyond the boundaries of its more traditional corporate parents. With Peterson—a veteran of London's thriving club scene—at the helm, Talkin' Loud sought out Maunick and gave Incognito a second life. Maunick surrounded himself with the core group of Joy Malcolm, Pamela Anderson, and Simon Hale, but for each of Incognito's four Talkin' Loud releases, he added several additional musicians to make for a bigger, more orchestral sound.

A string of successful albums and a few high-scoring singles solidified Incognito's place in acid-jazz circles. "Still a Friend of Mine," from 1994's *Positivity* was the band's commercial high-water mark until the release of 1995's *100@ and Rising*. Maunick brought in singer Barry Stewart to record on the album, which features a bit of flamenco guitar in addition to Incognito's trademark blend of Seventies rhythm with jazzed-up vocals. Because Maunick prides himself on his ability to meld diverse musical styles into a single coherent groove, it comes as no surprise that in discussing the record he told the *Los Angeles Times*, "I'm like a musical vampire. I need the fresh blood to give me that musical life source, the feeding source, to inject into my new ideas."

In addition to scouring the musical landscape for sonic rejuvenation, Maunick busies himself at the producer's console, working with big-name artists like Stevie Wonder, Chaka Khan, and George Benson. The transition for Maunick from behind the mic to behind the board for artists of such caliber comes as a singular thrill for the 38-year old. "...Why, it's like getting a call from God," he told the *Los Angeles Times* of his work with such platinum artists. Incognito, in all its line-up permutations,

has built a solid club following and with Maunick's experience as a producer and his inexhaustible quest for fertile territory, critics and fans envision only bigger and better things for one of Britain's top acid-jazz ensembles.

Selected discography

Inside Life, Verve Forecast/Talkin'Loud, 1992.
Tribes, Vibes + Scribes, Verve Forecast/Talkin'Loud, 1993.
Positivity (contains the single "Still a Friend of Mine"), Verve Forecast/Talkin'Loud, 1994.
100@ and Rising, Verve Forecast/Talkin'Loud, 1995.

Also recorded and released the LP *Jazz Funk in the United Kingdom*, 1980.

Sources

Billboard, December 17, 1995.
Chicago Tribune, May 8, 1994.
Down Beat, August 1994.
Guardian, (London), June 2, 1995.
Journal and Constitution (Atlanta), June 9, 1995; June 12, 1995.
Los Angeles Times, June 7, 1995; June 9, 1995.
Newsday (New York), May 22, 1994.
Rolling Stone, June 16, 1994; October 19, 1995.
Schwann Spectrum, Winter 1995.
Sun-Sentinel (Fort Lauderdale), July 30, 1995.
Vibe, August 1995.
Washington Times, May 14, 1994.

—*Rich Bowen*

Janet Jackson

Singer, songwriter

Photograph by Yuri Elizondo, courtesy of Virgin Records

Rolling Stone praised Janet Jackson's 1993 album *janet.* as "irrefutably the work of a woman of substance." With that release—which the magazine dubbed her "erotic rite of passage"—the singer sought to shed the girlish, cutesy image with which she had been saddled throughout her career; she also demonstrated a longing to stretch out artistically.

Having grown up in America's most celebrated musical family—and notably in the shadow of her megastar brother, Michael—Jackson has nonetheless demonstrated a willingness to veer at least briefly from the assured path of mainstream pop. "My concepts are never bright ideas; they're never notions I think will sell or be trendy or attract new fans," she insisted to *Rolling Stone's* David Ritz. "I don't think that way. All I can do is sing from my life." In addition to establishing herself as a fixture in the firmament of pop music, Jackson has also pursued an acting career—though with decidedly mixed results.

Jackson was born in 1966 to Joseph and Katherine Jackson in Gary, Indiana, the youngest of nine children. When five of her brothers—known as the Jackson 5 and led by the charismatic Michael—achieved pop stardom in the early 1970s, the family moved to Encino, California, an affluent section of the San Fernando Valley. In the interview with Ritz, Jackson recalled her upbringing in the Jackson home there, "with peacocks and llamas and giraffes in the back yard." When asked if she was lonely, she replied, "At times, yes," but added, "On certain days, I felt like the luckiest kid in the world." She called "Hot Fun in the Summertime" by soul-rock sensations Sly and the Family Stone "one of the biggest musical influences of my life," noting, "I was only 3 years old when that song had me jumping up and down. It made me so happy." Similarly, 1960s anthems by the Turtles, Simon and Garfunkel, and the Association "are all precious moments to me. They're about just plain feeling good."

Jackson's debut stage appearance was in a Jackson 5 revue at the MGM Grand Hotel in Las Vegas; she was seven. Unlike her brothers, however, she made her way into the public eye through acting. At 11—after capturing the attention of influential television producer Norman Lear—she landed the role of the abused child Penny on the situation comedy *Good Times.* Parts on the series *Diff'rent Strokes* and *Fame* followed, as Janet Jackson grew up before the nation's eyes. It was at the urging of her father that she ventured into music.

Her solo recording debut came with *Janet Jackson,* which A&M Records released in 1982. Although the album's highest-charting single failed to reach the Top Forty, the young singer established her own tradition by

For the Record . . .

Born May 16, 1966, in Gary, IN; daughter of Joseph (a music manager) and Katherine (a homemaker and sales clerk) Jackson; married James DeBarge (a musician), September 1984 (marriage annulled, 1985).

Actress on TV series *Good Times, Diff'rent Strokes,* and *Fame,* beginning c. 1977; recording and performing music artist, 1982—; signed with Virgin Records, 1991; coproducer of own album *janet.,* 1993; actress in film *Poetic Justice,* 1993; performed at several Grammy Award shows and at the 1995 MTV Video Music Awards.

Selected awards: Platinum records for *Control,* 1986, *Rhythm Nation 1814,* 1989, and *janet.,* 1993. Voted top R&B artist, top pop singles artist female, top dance sales artist, top dance club play artist, and top R&B singles artist, all 1986, by *Billboard;* seven American Music Awards, 1987, 1990, and 1991; Grammy Award for best music video (long form), 1990; three Soul Train Awards, 1990; awarded star on Hollywood "Walk of Fame" as part of "Janet Jackson Week," Los Angeles, 1990; *Billboard* Sterling Award, 1990; 1990 BMI Pop Award for songwriter of the year; MTV Video Music Award for best female video, 1991 and 1994; NAACP Chairman's Award, 1992; Sammy Davis Jr. Award for Entertainer of the Year, 1992.

Addresses: *Record company*—Virgin Records, 338 N. Foothill Rd., Beverly Hills, CA 90210. *Management*—Levine/Schneider Public Relations, 8730 Sunset Blvd., 6th Floor, Los Angeles, CA 90069.

touring high schools to promote it. She shocked the Jackson clan in the summer of 1984, however, when she eloped with singer James DeBarge. The couple contacted the family from Michigan to announce they'd married, though the wedding was annulled the following spring and Jackson ended up returning to her family's home in Encino. After the annulment, she was comforted by longtime friend Rene Elizondo, with whom she would later develop a romantic relationship.

A Desire For *Control*

November of 1984 saw the release of Jackson's sophomore effort, *Dream Street.* Despite the participation of producers Giorgio Moroder and Jesse Johnson and a duet with pop legend Cliff Richard, the record didn't

exactly set the charts ablaze. "I didn't quite know how to sing from my life," she told Ritz. Though it was painful, she told her father she didn't want him to manage her any longer: "I couldn't say the words—I was bawling like a baby—and finally he just said: 'You don't want me involved in your career. Isn't that it?' "'Yes,' I finally had the nerve to say, 'that's it.'"

With her 1986 release, *Control,* Jackson at last gave an indication of her potential. The project teamed her with hot R&B producers Jimmy Jam and Terry Lewis, who cowrote much of the material. Sales of the album surged after the release of the single "What Have You Done for Me Lately," which moved to the top of the R&B chart. It eventually reached the peak spot on the album chart and achieved platinum status. The twenty-year-old Jackson became the youngest artist to reach the U.S. Number One position since Stevie Wonder reached it at age thirteen.

Control went on to sell eight million copies. Jackson performed at the 1987 Grammy Awards but didn't take home any trophies. She did, however, win an armload of American Music Awards and came up the favorite in several categories of *Billboard* magazine's 1986 year-end survey. A&M soon released *Control—The Remixes,* a collection of eight alternate versions of Jackson's hits.

Greater Success with *Rhythm Nation*

Janet Jackson's Rhythm Nation 1814, released in 1989, demonstrated even greater pop ambition. "*Control* was an album about what I went through in my life when I was 19 and the self-discovery that resulted," reads a quote in a Virgin Records biography. "*Rhythm Nation* contained my views about what was going on in the world and the problems we have in trying to educate the kids—the idea was to give them hope." Working again with Jam and Lewis, Jackson proved that *Control's* success was no accident. *Rhythm Nation* topped the U.S. charts four weeks after its release and produced a string of hits. The album's long-form video won a Grammy, and Jackson received her fair share of tributes. These included a Los Angeles "Janet Jackson Week," a star on Hollywood's "Walk of Fame," a meeting with then-President George Bush, and an array of *Billboard* Music Awards, American Music Awards, and Soul Train Awards. BMI honored her as songwriter of the year in 1990.

Rhythm Nation 1814—the number refers to the year "The Star-Spangled Banner" was written—became the first album ever to have seven of its singles on the *Billboard* Top Five; four of those singles reached Number One. Jackson's 1990 World Tour was an enormous success, and some of its profits helped the Cities in Schools program, which encourages students to stay in school. After the tour ended, she gave the United Negro College Fund a "Rhythm Nation Scholarship" to the tune of a half-million dollars.

In 1991 Janet Jackson signed a huge recording contract with Virgin Records. "A Rembrandt rarely becomes available," went a quote from Virgin head Richard Branson cited in *Rock Movers & Shakers.* "When it does, there are many people determined to get it. I was determined." The deal, at $50 million, stood as the most lucrative in history—for about a week, after which time it was surpassed by her brother Michael's new deal with Sony. Janet Jackson has admitted to a friendly rivalry with her brother, but her adoration of him is obvious in every interview she gives. It was he, she noted, who gave her the most important early encouragement when she began singing: "Michael told me to 'just practice, always have confidence in yourself, and never give up,'" she recalled in *Jet.*

> "My concepts are never bright ideas; they're never notions I think will sell or be trendy or attract new fans. I don't think that way. All I can do is sing from my life."

In 1992 the National Association for the Advancement of Colored People (NAACP) gave Jackson its Chairman's Award for her public service work, especially on behalf of young people. As she addressed these large issues, however, she found increasing public attention focused on conflicts within her family. Public acrimony between her sister LaToya—also a performer—and the rest of the Jackson clan gained considerable publicity, and Janet was forced to comment, admitting the rift; she later remarked that she found it impossible to communicate with her sister.

Meanwhile, she and Michael appeared together on the 1993 Grammy Awards, where he jokingly stated that their dual appearance put to rest rumors that they were the same person. Michael's own public troubles—especially public accusations that he had molested a young fan—placed even greater stress on the Jackson clan. During Janet's 1994 concert tour, reported Robert Christgau in the *Village Voice,* she asked the crowd to "bow our heads and say a silent prayer for my brother Michael."

Director John Singleton wrote the central role of his 1993 film "Poetic Justice" specifically for Jackson, but her much-hyped return to acting was something of a disappointment. The film fared poorly at the box office, and reviewers were less than kind to its star. "Jackson isn't an inept actress," reasoned Owen Gleiberman of *Entertainment Weekly,* "yet there are no more edges to her personality than there are to her plastic Kewpie-doll visage." Yet this relatively unsuccessful detour hardly dented Jackson's meteoric career.

Celebrated Sexuality

Jackson's 1993 album *janet.* announced her arrival as an adult pop figure, openly celebrating her sexuality. "I love feeling deeply sexual—and don't mind letting the world know," she told Ritz in the *Rolling Stone* profile. "For me, sex has become a celebration, a joyful part of the creative process." She added that what "excites me isn't becoming a bigger star but a better artist, deeper, truer to the things I find exciting." The album's guest appearances by opera singer Kathleen Battle and rapper Chuck D. of the celebrated rap group Public Enemy attested to her expanded musical palette.

Some critics considered Jackson at the top of her form with *janet. Rolling Stone's* year-end roundup of major releases found her in "more versatile voice than ever," adding that she "perches atop the rhythmic percolations—cool, not exactly calm, but collected." Yet while many applauded Jackson's newly bold persona, reviewers like *Entertainment Weekly's* David Browne felt she sounded "tentative" and found the album "a mess—period." Even so, it was enormously successful, as was her 1994 tour. "I've never seen an arena spectacle to match it," enthused *Village Voice* writer Christgau. *Rolling Stone* criticized its almost mechanical perfection, noting that sometimes "it seemed like the audience was eavesdropping on a shoot for a long-form video rather than being engaged by a performer."

Jackson contributed a song to the soundtrack of the 1994 fashion industry flick *Ready-to-Wear (Pret-a-Porter).* She also appeared on her brother Michael's 1995 single "Scream" and in its innovative video, which was nominated for several awards. *Entertainment Weekly* complained that her voice was "buried deep in the [song's] mix—too bad, since her sweet croon adds what little swing the record has."

Later that year Jackson's former label, A&M, released a greatest-hits package which featured selections from *Control, Rhythm Nation 1814,* her Virgin release, *janet.,* and two new singles, including "Runaway." Entitled *Design Of A Decade 1986-1996,* an accompanying home video and laserdisc were also released. At this time there was much speculation that Jackson would return to A&M, or perhaps make a move to another label. All theories were silenced, however, when at the beginning of 1996, Jackson signed a four-album, $80 million deal with Virgin, ensuring future decades of Janet Jackson hits.

Selected discography

Janet Jackson, A&M, 1982.
Dream Street, A&M, 1984.
Control, A&M, 1986.
Control—The Remixes, A&M, 1987.
(Contributor) Herb Alpert, *Diamonds*, 1987.
Janet Jackson's Rhythm Nation 1814, A&M, 1989.
janet., Virgin, 1993.
Various artists, *Ready-to-Wear (Pret-a-Porter)* (soundtrack; appears on "70s Love Groove"), Columbia, 1994.
Michael Jackson, *HIStory, Volume 1: Past, Present, and Future* (appears on "Scream"), Epic, 1995.
Design Of A Decade, A&M, 1995.

Sources

Books

Rees, Dafydd, and Luke Crampton, *Rock Movers & Shakers*, ABC/CLIO, 1991.

Periodicals

Billboard, August 26, 1995; September 2, 1995.
Entertainment Weekly, May 21, 1993; July 23, 1993; December 16, 1994; June 9, 1995; January 26, 1996.
Jet, August 8, 1994.
Rolling Stone, September 16, 1993; December 23, 1993; January 27, 1994.
Village Voice, January 4, 1994.

Additional information for this profile was taken from Virgin Records publicity materials, 1994.

—Simon Glickman

James P. Johnson

Pianist

MICHAEL OCHS ARCHIVES/Venice, CA

Acknowledged as the "Grandfather of Hot Piano," jazz pianist James P. Johnson emerged during the transitional period between ragtime—a music performed strictly from written scores—and the improvisatory and rhythmically more relaxed foundations of shout piano, or what became known as stride piano. Bringing together elements of ragtime, blues, African American religious music, and classical themes, Johnson originated a piano style that dominated New York City's African American musical world during the early decades of the twentieth century. Though his composition "Charleston" became the anthem for the "flaming youth" of the 1920s, his musical ability extended beyond the writing of popular songs. In his 37-year career, he also wrote 19 symphonic works, scored 11 stage musicals, and contributed to numerous stage productions.

A forefather of the stride style, Johnson brought the idiom into its most complex form. Opposed to the two-beat configuration of ragtime, stride piano accentuated a more steady, loping four-four feel, exhibiting a left-hand "oom-pah" bass pattern. As Frank Kappler pointed out in the liner notes to *Giants of Jazz,* "The left hand is the motor in stride, providing propulsion, leaving the right to create the characteristic rhythm." As one of stride's greatest practitioners, Johnson "played more quickly and accurately than his peers," commented Mike Lipskin in the notes to *The Fats Waller Piano Solos.* "[He] was capable of the most spontaneous improvising, with a singular anachronistic inventiveness that still amazes listeners today."

Beginnings of a Jazz Giant

James Price Johnson was born on February 1, 1894, in New Brunswick, New Jersey. His mother, Josephine, sang in the Methodist choir and held Saturday night dance parties, where James heard the playing of guitars, mandolins, and jew's harps (tiny lyre-shaped instruments held between the lips and played with a finger). With money she earned working as a maid, she bought an upright piano from her employers and soon taught herself to play popular tunes. As a small child, wrote Kappler in *Giants of Jazz,* Johnson "played with the pedals until he grew tall enough to reach the keyboard, then starting picking out 'Little Brown Jug' and other tunes he had heard his mother play."

When James was eight, the Johnson family moved to a Jersey City neighborhood near a railroad stop lined with gambling houses and nightspots. Around this time, he played his first gig, earning 25 cents from a woman who invited him to play in her parlor. Told to perform with his back to the guests, Johnson entertained for several hours, playing popular tunes, hymns, and nursery

For the Record . . .

Born James Price Johnson, February 1, 1894, in New Brunswick, NJ; died November 17, 1955; son of William (a hardware store assistant) and Josephine (a maid; maiden name, Harrison) Johnson; married Lillie Mae Wright. *Education:* Attended Jersey City and New York City public schools.

Performed at house parties, c. early 1900s; during high school years played clubs and summer resorts; left high school, 1912, and became professional musician; toured the South, then established residencies at New York clubs; performed at Jungles Casino and studied under Bruno Giannini, 1913; recorded piano rolls for several companies, 1917; worked in touring show *Dudley's Smart Set,* 1918; recorded first side, "Harlem Strut," 1921; scored music for 1923 stage show *Runnin' Wild;* scored music for stage show *Keep Shufflin'* and completed extended work *Yamekraw,* both 1928; wrote programmatic work *Harlem Symphony,* 1932; periodically led own orchestra in early 1930s; performed with Fess Williams, 1936-37; collaborated with poet Langston Hughes to complete blues opera *De Organizer* and performed in Carnegie Hall concert *From Spirituals to Swing,* both 1938; recorded for Blue Note, 1942-44; played Eddie Condon's New York club, mid-1940s; worked on California production of *Sugar Hill,* 1949.

rhymes. Once exposed to the opulently dressed ticklers (the name given to ragtime and stride keyboardists), he decided to become a first-class pianoman.

In 1908 the Johnsons relocated to the San Juan section of New York City on Manhattan's West Side. Attending P.S. 69, he performed in school assemblies and sang soprano in the choir under the direction of Frank Damrosch. Though he attended concerts of the New York Philharmonic Orchestra, his main musical interest remained with the uptown cabaret pianomen.

In 1911 Johnson made his way to a 100th Street cellar club owned by an able ragtime pianist. At 2:00 each morning, the owner reportedly pulled the club's piano to the middle of the floor and, after displaying his own talents, allowed Johnson to take over at the keyboard. "He'd let me play and hit the piano until 4:00 A.M.," recalled Johnson, as quoted in *Ragtime: Its History, Composers, and Music.* "I kept my schoolbooks in the coal bin and went on to school after a little sleep." While still a youth in short pants, the fledgling musician gained entrance to Barron Wilkins's famed Harlem nightclub,

where he marveled at the rakish clothes and finger-stylings of New Orleans piano great Jelly Roll Morton. During the summer of 1912, he took his first professional job at Far Rockaway, a resort cabaret.

From Student to Master

Instead of returning to school that fall, Johnson landed a gig at a Jersey City nightclub owned by Freddie Doyle. Jobs at Jim Allen's cellar club on 61st Street and the Jungles Casino followed. Licensed as a dance school, the Jungles Casino drew Southern stevedores and Gullahs (people of color living along the coast and on the sea islands of South Carolina, Georgia, and northern Florida) who danced so-called "Geechie dances" and unique steps like the "Metropolitan Glide." From these dances, Johnson composed eight Charlestons, one of which would emerge as his famous stage hit.

Johnson's first formal piano lessons came in 1913, when his friend's mother arranged for him to study under symphonically trained Bruno Giannini, an Italian voice and music instructor. Under Giannini's tutelage, Johnson learned harmony, counterpoint, and formal finger positions. To master his instrument, Johnson often practiced in the dark or with a sheet over the keyboard. Like earlier pianomen, he learned to "rag" the classics by imitating the string sections and incorporating melodies of such European concert masters as Franz Lizst, Edvard Grieg, and Sergei Rachmaninoff.

But Johnson soon tired of Giannini's exercises and resumed his system of self-study, observing New York's finest stride pianists—keyboardists like the exponent of the "backward 10th" Freddie Bryant and Richard "Abba Labba" McLean. "When you heard James P. at his best," recalled clarinetist Garvin Bushell in *Jazz from the Beginning,* "you were hearing Abba Labba's style, except that James P., who had studied, played with a little more finesse and taste." Other musicians of great influence included flamboyant "finger-stretcher" Charles Luckeyeth ("Luckey") Roberts, and Yiddish World War I veteran Willie "The Lion" Smith.

By 1916 Johnson had taken his place within the vanguard of New York's finest pianomen. A year later, he entered the profitable world of recording piano rolls for Imperial, Perfection, Universal, Metro-Art, and QRS. "The piano rolls of this period," related Scott E. Brown in *James P. Johnson,* "show Johnson to be a ragtime player of great proficiency. At times, his playing sounds restless as he tries to break from the rhythmic and melodic formalisms of ragtime. His [style was] becoming increasingly sophisticated, enabling him to convey the full intensity and range of expression of the shout dances."

Upon America's entry into World War I in 1917, Johnson contributed to President Woodrow Wilson's preparedness campaign by composing the march fantasia *Liberty*. After the Allied victory, he performed in a band led by Happy Rhone and in the ensembles assembled by the Clef Club, the prestigious New York-based African American musician's union. In 1918 Johnson and his wife, Lillie Mae Wright, worked with the all-black touring show *Dudley's Smart Set*.

The Roaring Twenties

Sparked by the Harlem Renaissance and the popularity of African American music, Johnson's career took off. He earned great praise within New York's musical world. As Kappler put it in *Giants of Jazz*, "The roaring '20s saw the flowering of musical talent in jazz, but few, perhaps only [George] Gershwin and [Duke] Ellington, could match James P. Johnson for the quality, quantity and variety of musical output." In 1921 Johnson recorded his first side, "Harlem Strut," followed by the classic stride numbers "Keep off the Grass" and "Carolina Shout"—a composition which, since its first appearance on piano roll, emerged as a test piece for aspiring ticklers, including young Edward Kennedy "Duke" Ellington.

In 1923 Johnson traveled to England as musical director for the production of *Plantation Days* and scored the music for the stage show *Runnin' Wild*. After opening on October 29, 1923, to generally favorable reviews, two hits emerged from *Runnin' Wild*—"Old Fashioned Love" and the legendary "Charleston." With this success, Johnson turned to writing extended stage and symphonic works. In the winter of 1928, he penned the score to *Keep Shufflin'*. Later that year, Johnson's first extended work, *Yamekraw*—dedicated to Savannah, Georgia's colorful waterfront section—was performed at Carnegie Hall. (When the producers of *Keep Shufflin'* refused to allow Johnson to leave the show to perform his work *Yamekraw*, he had his young understudy, Fats Waller, take his place at the Carnegie Hall concert.) In 1929 Johnson directed the orchestra for *St. Louis Blues*—a film by blues singer Bessie Smith, who two years earlier had recorded "Preachin' the Blues" and "Back Water Blues" backed by Johnson's solo piano.

New Directions and a New Decade

Aside from recording piano numbers such as the 1930 classics "Jingles" and "You Got to Be Modernistic," Johnson spent the next decade concentrating on composing symphonic pieces and extended works. Though he sought to elevate jazz into a higher written form,

economic depression and the wane of the Harlem Renaissance had devastating effects on the support and funding of his work. As Brown observed in the liner notes to *Victory Stride*, "Johnson applied for fellowships to support his studies, and he wrote to many conductors and musical benefactors for his pieces to be given a performance. His scrap books are filled with rejection letters."

Nevertheless, Johnson spent the 1930s producing a number of symphonic pieces. In 1932 he wrote a four-movement programmatic work called *Harlem Symphony*, which was performed at the Brooklyn Museum seven years later. He also collaborated with lyricist Andy Razaf to compose the stage show *Harlem Hotcha*, featuring the piece "Drums—A Symphonic Poem." In 1934 he completed a piano concerto titled *Jassamine* and *American Symphonic Suite—St. Louis Blues*, based on W. C. Handy's 1914 blues hit. The following year he wrote *Symphony in Brown*.

By 1938 Johnson was collaborating with legendary black poet Langston Hughes to produce the one-act blues opera *De Organizer*, which received a performance at Carnegie Hall in 1940. And in December of 1938, record producer and promoter John Hammond invited Johnson to appear in the Carnegie Hall concert *From Spirituals to Swing*, dedicated to the memory of Bessie Smith.

Stride Slowed by A Stroke

Johnson led his own bands at the Elks Rendezvous and Cafe Society until he suffered a mild stroke in 1940. He spent the rest of the year relaxing with his family. Returning to music after his recuperation, he became musical director for *Pinkard's Fantasies*. In 1942 and 1943 he recorded for the Blue Note label with a core group, the "Blue Note Jazzmen"—an ensemble led by Johnson, with clarinetist Edmund Hall, trumpeter Sidney DeParis, and big band trombonist Vic Dickerson. Under his leadership, Johnson and the Blue Note Jazzmen recorded the 1944 side "Victory Stride," a 16-bar arrangement featuring Duke Ellington's saxophonist Ben Webster. The Blue Note sessions also yielded Johnson's first recorded version of his solo piano number "Carolina Balmoral."

In the mid-1940s, Johnson performed at guitarist Eddie Condon's New York Town Hall concerts. He later returned to scoring the music for theater productions, including the California production of his revue *Sugar Hill*. After suffering a serious stroke in 1951, he spent his remaining years bedridden at his home. On November 17, 1955, Johnson died in Queens Hospital.

Looking back on New York City's early jazz musicians, Duke Ellington noted, as quoted in *Hear Me Talkin' to Ya,* that "the king at that time was James P. Johnson." The New Jersey-born pianist is part of a musical legacy whose strains can be heard in artists from Ellington to Thelonious Monk. His solo piano recordings still awe listeners with their profound sense of mastery. In 1987 New York's Concordia Orchestra restored Johnson's symphonic repertory—much of which had been lost for decades—and performed the scores at a 1992 concert at Lincoln Center. Johnson's music will remain forever interwoven in the creative fabric of jazz music.

Selected discography

Giants of Jazz: James P. Johnson, Time-Life, 1981.
James P. Johnson: Snowy Morning Blues, Decca, 1991.
Victory Stride: The Symphonic Music of James P. Johnson, Music Masters, 1994.

Sources

Books

Brown, Scott E., *James P. Johnson: A Case of Mistaken Identity,* Scarecrow Press and the Institute of Jazz Studies, 1986.
Bushell, Garvin, and Mark Tucker, *Jazz from the Beginning,* University of Michigan Press, 1990.
Hadlock, Richard, *Jazz Masters of the Twenties,* Da Capo, 1988.
Ragtime: Its History, Composers, and Music, edited by John Edward Hasse, Schirmer Books, 1985.
Shapiro, Nat, and Nat Hentoff, *Hear Me Talkin' to Ya: The Story of Jazz As Told by the Men Who Made It,* Dover Publications, 1955.

Additional information for this profile was taken from liner notes by Scott E. Brown to *Victory Stride: The Symphonic Music of James P. Johnson,* 1994; notes by Frank Kappler to *Giants of Jazz,* 1981; and notes by Mike Lipskin to *The Fats Waller Piano Solos: Turn on the Heat,* 1991.

—John Cohassey

Philly Joe Jones

Drummer

Archive Photos/Frank Driggs Collection

Joseph Rudolph Jones is remembered as one of the most innovative drummers in jazz, particularly in the area of bebop. To avoid being mistaken for Count Basie's most famous drummer, "Papa Jo" Jones, he dubbed himself "Philly Joe" after his hometown of Philadelphia. In a *Musician* tribute, Chip Stern wrote, "Philly Joe was a consummate student of drum history; an urbane and witty man, knowledgeable and well-read. And on the drums, in a word, *slick.*"

Jones was born on July 15, 1923. His musical training, part of a family tradition, began at an early age. "Drums have always been my choice of instrument," he explained to *Modern Drummer*'s Rick Mattingly. "I had an opportunity to pick several instruments because my maternal grandmother made all of her daughters take music, and [they] really got into it deeply." Jazz heritage played a key role in Jones's musical life as well. He was inspired by classic swing drummers like Baby Dodds, Sid Catlett, and Chick Webb. Throughout his career, he continually revisited these idols' music and reflected upon it. "If any drummer tells me he can't go back and listen to Chick and Dave Tough and Baby and Sid ... [or tells] me that's not drums, I'll break up the drums and forget it!" he told *Down Beat* writer Ralph J. Gleason.

Jones's drumming aspirations were interrupted between 1941 and 1947 by his engagement in the army. Soon after leaving the service, he moved to New York City and joined Joe Morris's rhythm and blues band, which featured up-and-comers like Johnny Griffin on tenor sax, pianist Elmo Hope, and bassist Percy Heath. One night during his stint with Morris, Baby Dodds was playing in a club across the street. Philly Joe reminisced in a *Down Beat* interview, "I went into the Onyx, and Baby was playing in there with a bass drum, and a snare drum, and *one* cymbal.... He was swingin' *so much* I was late an entire set!"

Early in the 1950s Jones became one of the most sought-after session drummers. He joined Duke Ellington's Orchestra in 1952, but he left that organization to concentrate on studio work rather than touring. As he told *Modern Drummer*'s Mattingly, "Playing with Duke was an honor, but I thought it would be better for me to stay in New York and play and make records with all the different giants."

In 1954 Jones began his fruitful association with Miles Davis. Both men held each other in high regard. In his autobiography, Davis said of Jones, "Philly Joe was the fire that was making a lot of [things] happen. See, he *knew* everything I was going to do, everything I was going to play; he anticipated me, felt what I was thinking.... Philly Joe was the kind of drummer I knew my music had to have." In an interview with *Down Beat*'s

For the Record . . .

Born Joseph Rudolph Jones, July 15, 1923, in Philadelphia, PA; died of a heart attack, August 30, 1985, in Philadelphia.

Played professionally in Philadelphia, c. 1947; toured and recorded with rhythm and blues bands led by Joe Morris, Bull Moose Jackson, and Tiny Grimes, late 1940s; member of Tadd Dameron's band; 1951-53; member of Duke Ellington Orchestra, 1952; member of Miles Davis Quintet, 1954-57; leader and session player, 1958-85; wrote pamphlet "Brush Artistry" for Premier Drum Co., 1969; led bands Le Grand Prix, 1972-75, and Dameronia, 1981-85. *Military service:* U.S. Army, 1941-47.

Gleason, Jones displayed a similar attitude about Davis, remarking, "The greatest experience of my life was with Miles, of course.... I could get with Miles and go into *anything,* just like he does with me.... He would know the amount of time that I had to be playing, and I'd come out right, and it would bring him right back, and he'd come right back where *I* was ... and it was always beautiful."

The Miles Davis Quintet, featuring saxophonist John Coltrane, pianist Red Garland, bassist Paul Chambers, and Philly Joe Jones on drums is considered Davis's "classic" quintet. In *Jazz on Record,* Brian Priestley asserted, "The musicians in this henceforth legendary quintet exerted an enormous influence in the coming years—not only John Coltrane ... but Philly Joe Jones and Paul Chambers immediately became the most in-demand drummer and bassist for free-lance recording sessions."

Despite their close friendship, Davis fired Jones in 1957. A heroin habit was making the drummer unreliable. Jones eventually kicked his habit, though. He later put his problem in perspective in *Down Beat,* commenting, "Well, that was a phase of my life. Fortunately for me, I wasn't playing bad when I was getting high.... But I feel now that I would have played better, and I think that I'm playing better today than I've ever played."

During the 1950s and 1960s Jones recorded several albums as a leader. He nonetheless continued session work for other musicians, especially those recording for the Riverside label, for which he practically became the house drummer. In a 1959 *Down Beat* feature, Riverside owner Orrin Keepnews attested, "[Philly Joe] has appeared on our LPs more than any other drummer and mostly because leaders ask for him or assume they'll

get him. And he's wonderful at a session. He has the knack of knowing how to play for whatever we're doing."

Jones moved to London during the late 1960s. But because English union laws kept him from playing there, he relocated to Paris. He left Paris and returned to the United States in 1972. Still, he would visit Europe regularly for the rest of his life. He told *Modern Drummer* contributor Mattingly, "I enjoy playing in Europe more than I do playing the States. The people over there are better recipients of the music—they love it and they come out. If you open in a club there, that club will be crowded *every* night."

During the early 1980s Jones fulfilled one of his life's ambitions by forming Dameronia, a repertory group dedicated to the music of his former associate, arranger Tadd Dameron. According to *The Penguin Guide to Jazz,* Dameron's compositions "[combine] the broad-brush arrangements of the big band and the advanced harmonic language of bop." Dameronia, which consisted of musicians who had worked with Dameron, re-leased two critically acclaimed albums, one after the death of Jones.

Jones died on August 30, 1985, at the age of 62. The body of work he left behind includes his contributions to more than 500 albums. He never stopped playing. Jones explained in *Modern Drummer,* "I feel good when I hear people go out saying, 'Man, I really enjoyed myself tonight.'... It is profound fulfillment to know that you are contributing to someone's happiness—even your own."

Selected discography

(With Miles Davis), *Cookin',* Prestige, 1956.
(With Davis), *Relaxin',* Prestige, 1956.
(With Davis), *Workin',* Prestige, 1956.
(With Davis), *Steamin',* Prestige, 1956.
(With Davis), *Miles Davis and the Modern Jazz Giants,* Prestige, 1956.
(With Davis), *Round about Midnight,* Columbia, 1956.
(With Sonny Rollins), *Tenor Madness,* Prestige, 1956.
(With John Coltrane), *Blue Trane,* Blue Note, 1957.
(With Nat Adderley and Johnny Griffin) *Blues for Dracula,* Riverside/OJC, 1958.
(With Davis) *Milestones,* Columbia, 1958.
(With Davis and Coltrane), *Miles & Coltrane,* Columbia, 1959.
(With Davis), *Porgy and Bess,* Columbia, 1959.
(With Art Pepper), *Art Pepper Meets the Rhythm Section,* 1959.
Showcase, Riverside, 1959.
Drums around the World, Riverside, 1959.
Mo'Joe, Black Lion, 1968.
The Big Beat, Milestone.

Philly Joe's Beat, Atlantic.
Trailways Express, Black Lion.
(With Elvin Jones) *Philly Joe Jones and Elvin Jones Together,* Atlantic.
(With Freddie Hubbard) *Goin Up,* Blue Note.
(With Donald Byrd) *The Cat Walk,* Blue Note.
(With Bill Evans) *Bill Evans,* Milestone.
(With Jackie McLean) *Jackie's Bag,* Blue Note.
(With Kenny Durham) *Whistle Stop,* Blue Note.
(With Bud Powell) *Time Waits,* Blue Note.

Sources

Books

Balliett, Whitney, *The Sound of Surprise,* Dutton, 1959.
Cole, Bill, *Miles Davis: A Musical Biography,* Morrow, 1974.
Cook, Richard, and Brian Morton, *The Penguin Guide to Jazz,* Penguin, 1994.
Davis, Miles, with Quincy Troupe, *Miles: The Autobiography,* Simon & Schuster, 1989.
Long, Daryl, *Miles Davis for Beginners,* Writers and Readers, 1992.
Priestley, Brian, *Jazz on Record,* Billboard, 1991.
Taylor, Arthur, *Notes and Tones,* Coward, McCann & Geoghegan, 1977.

Periodicals

Down Beat, September 19, 1957; March 5, 1959; March 3, 1960 (article reprinted, November 1994); March 30, 1961; September 9, 1976; December 1985.
Jazz Journal International, November 1985.
Jazz Review, February 1959.
Modern Drummer, February/March 1982.
Musician, December 1985.
New Yorker, November 4, 1985.

—Jim Powers

Sonny Landreth

Singer, songwriter, guitarist

Photograph by Dennis Keeley, © 1994 Zoo Entertainment

Singer-songwriter-guitarist Sonny Landreth brings together blues, jazz, Cajun, zydeco, and rock music, creating a style that's increasingly appealing to a wide array of listeners. The Mississippi-born recording artist employs a slide technique praised by critics from *Guitar Player* magazine to the *Vancouver Sun.* Each of Landreth's two solo albums is woven from the various musical styles he picked up in southern Louisiana, his home since the age of two. His ability to meld these loosely associated deep South genres has earned him a broad following, and, with twenty years as a professional musician, his résumé packs important contacts. He has worked with the likes of John Hiatt, Mark Knopfler, and the late king of zydeco, Clifton Chenier and his Red Hot Louisiana Band.

After spending time as a sought-after session player, Landreth quickly moved from the shadows to the spotlight. With *South of I-10,* his 1995 Zoo/Praxis release, Landreth finally dispelled the sideman image, utilizing the talents of Knopfler and definitive New Orleans musician Allen Toussaint to do so. Critics applauded the album's meticulously produced displays of guitar ability and the conviviality among its many elements. The release also found new fans with Adult Album Alternative radio, a format that offers an outlet for musicians whose material falls outside conventional formats. Landreth noted in a Zoo/Praxis publicity release: "I wanted the listeners to feel like they spent part of their summer with me in Louisiana and this album would reflect the stories they took back home with them."

Picked Up Strong Southern Accent

A childhood spent in Lafayette, Louisiana, in the 1950s and 1960s brought Landreth in contact with the blues, jazz, Cajun, and zydeco artists whose styles influenced his music. "Growing up in southwest Louisiana with a really rich cultural heritage, I got a lot of influences," Landreth explained in the *Chicago Tribune.* "I really feel fortunate to have that as a backdrop. One's roots really are inspiring and they remain, to this day." With New Orleans and its jazz just a short drive away, a grandfather living in the Mississippi Delta with its blues, and Cajun and zydeco flourishing around his hometown, the self-taught guitarist almost had no recourse other than to become a musician.

In elementary school, Landreth began playing the trumpet, though he soon found the guitar to be the most direct vehicle for his musical expression. "By the time I was 13, I knew I wanted to play guitar, and I knew I wanted to play in a band," he told the *Houston Chronicle.* Landreth's first experience with a guitar was with a toy Elvis Presley model belonging to his brother. Unfortunately, the family dog chewed off its neck while the budding rock and roll stars were in school one day.

Quick to overcome that setback, Landreth acquired another guitar and learned to play it by listening to Chet Atkins, appropriating his finger-picking style. The Ventures and Scotty Moore, who backed Elvis, were other influences, though the biggest impact on Landreth's early career would come from zydeco master Clifton Chenier. "I must have been no more that 16, 17 years old the first time I saw him play. Me and a friend wandered into the Blue Angel Club, and he was up there on the bandstand. The guy just blew me away. We were the only white people in the place, but Clifton, he came right over and took us under this wing," he recalled in an interview for the *Sante Fe New Mexican.*

Emerged with an In-Demand Technical Style

Also important to Landreth's style was the slide mastery of Robert Johnson. By combining Chet Atkins's picking with Johnson's technique of pressing the slide directly on the guitar's fretboard, Landreth honed his own method of playing. Describing the evolution of his guitar style, he told the *Los Angeles Times,* "I had been learning the guitar as a solo instrument, where Chet would play the melody, rhythm and bass line at the same time. And then to hear Robert Johnson doing it with a bottleneck so many years before was a real

influence." This fusion begat a musical career that has taken the guitarist around the globe.

Record label interest began as early as 1973 with Columbia Records. Landreth recorded a full-length album for the label that went unreleased. Columbia, at that time, was unsure of the record's audience and how to reach it. Combining session work with gigs as a backing musician, Landreth was eventually asked to perform with Chenier's Red Hot Louisiana Band. Of the experience, Landreth told the *Los Angeles Times,* "I figure that to be the highlight of my career, and that was in 1979." By that time, he had also formed Bayou Rhythm with David Ransom on bass and Gregg Morrow on drums. With limited gig work, the trio released two albums in the early 1980s.

After a short break from music, Landreth reemerged in 1988 playing with noted folk-rock performer John Hiatt. When Hiatt needed a touring band to take on the road in support of his *Bring the Family* album, he turned to Landreth and the Bayou Rhythm band, renaming them the Goners. Successfully recreating the guitar tracks laid down on the album by Ry Cooder, Landreth and his energetic playing provided solid backing for Hiatt's songwriting.

Sideman Stepped in Front

The combination worked so well that Hiatt recorded his following release, *Slow Turning,* with the Goners after label-recruited session musicians failed to meet his expectations. The album was a success for Landreth both critically and personally. "That was pretty much a once-in-a-lifetime thing. We all knew it was something special," he commented in the Seattle *News Tribune.* The exposure was just enough to create label interest in a solo project. The result was *Outward Bound,* released on Zoo/Praxis in 1992. The album received mostly positive critical attention, though a few reviewers felt that Landreth sometimes put his technical displays before his songwriting. *Outward Bound* made appearances on some critics' Top Ten lists and fueled the development of Landreth's solo career.

The move from backing musician to frontman is known to be difficult, with some artists unable to make the switch, but Landreth knew the ropes. "There's obviously more responsibility, but I did a lot of that stuff before with John Hiatt, and I had my own band before that. All of that helped me scope out the fire without being in the middle of it," he told the *Los Angeles Times.* His *Outward Bound* has a blues feel, highlighted by sounds coaxed patiently from the best in electric and resonator guitars— names like Fender, Gibson, and National. Landreth's seamless bottleneck slide provides an often vaporous undercurrent to the solo record.

The same formula of blues, zydeco, and roots-rock produced *South of I-10* in 1995, much to the delight of critics. Landreth went back home to Louisiana to make the record. In his native South, he apparently found it easier to pull together his musical influences. The guitarist worked at a recording studio on an 11-acre estate along the forested Vermilion River. "I'd be recording at all hours of the night, so I'd have less distraction," he noted in the *Los Angeles Times.* "Then about three or four in the morning ... these tugboats barging shale from the gulf would be going by 30 feet away, with these lights cutting through the fog. It was an ethereal experience." Landreth told Andy Ellis of *Guitar Player* that he hopes *South of I-10* will take him one step closer to reaching his life's goal of "turning people on to Cajun music."

Selected discography

Solo recordings; on Zoo/Praxis

Outward Bound, 1992.
South of I-10, 1995.

Sources

Books

The Rolling Stone Encyclopedia of Rock & Roll, edited by Jon Pareles and Patricia Romanowski, Rolling Stone Press/ Summit Books, 1983.

Periodicals

Chicago Sun-Times, October 14, 1992.
Chicago Tribune, February 26, 1993.
Guitar Player, April 1995.
Houston Chronicle, September 8, 1992.
Kansas City Star, June 23, 1995.
Los Angeles Times, March 27, 1995; March 30, 1995.
News Tribune (Seattle, WA), April 11, 1995.
Orlando Sentinel Tribune, August 28, 1992.
Plain Dealer (Cleveland, OH), April 14, 1995.
St. Louis Post-Dispatch, February 10, 1995.
Sante Fe New Mexican, June 16, 1995.
Vancouver Sun, April 13, 1995.

Additional information for this profile was provided by Zoo/ Praxis, 1995.

—*Rich Bowen*

Yusef Lateef

Saxophonist, flutist, oboist, educator

Multi-instrumentalist, educator, poet—Yusef Lateef emerged, in the 1940s, as one of the first jazz musicians to study the music of Afro-Asian cultures and to embrace the traditional teachings of Islam. Since his early musical career in Detroit, Yusef Lateef has traveled the world and various creative avenues. A contributor to the development of the flute and oboe as mainstream jazz instruments, Lateef is a serious student of ethnic instruments from around the world, for which he has emerged as a time-honored mentor among jazzmen and the post-bebop cultural avant garde.

Yusef Lateef was born William Evans in Chattanooga, Tennessee, on October 9, 1920. At age three Lateef moved with his parents to Lorraine, Ohio, and later relocated to Detroit. The Evans family resided in an apartment above the Arcade Theatre on Hastings Street—the cultural and business center of the city's crowded eastside ghetto. In the liner notes of the *Yusef Lateef Anthology*, Lateef recalled his early exposure to music: "My parents were innately musical. Both of them sang, and my mother also played piano. I can recall my mother and her siblings getting together every week to sing spirituals while my grandmother played one of those organs you pump with your feet." At a Pentecostal Church near his grade school, he stood by the building's painted-black windows to hear the musical sounds of the congregation.

Early Musical Education

Lateef's formal music education began at Miller High School under the instruction Louis Cabrara and Mr. Goldberg, who influenced Lateef's classmate Milt Jackson to take up the study of the vibraphone. At venues around Hastings Street, Lateef watched stage shows and on Monday nights attended big band performances at the Graystone Ballroom and the Paradise Theatre on Woodward Avenue. After taking up alto saxophone, Lateef switched to tenor, and by 1939 found work in the four-man sax section of "Matthew Rucker and His 13 Spirits of Swing." In 1941 a friend introduced him to Charlie Parker's alto saxophone solo on Jay McShann's recording "Hootie Blues." As he stated, in the *Yusef Anthology,* "We never heard the alto saxophone played that way, and were very impressed."

In 1944 one of Lateef's early musical associations, Detroit-born tenor saxophonist Eli "Lucky" Thompson, helped him land a job with trumpeter Erskine Hawkins' Bama State Collegians. When the Bama State Collegians broke up in Chicago in 1946, Lucky Thompson recommended Lateef to bandleader Lucius "Lucky" Millinder and later to trumpeters Oran "Hot Lips" Page and Roy Eldridge, all of whom employed Lateef until he

For the Record . . .

Born William Evans, Chattanooga Tennessee, October 9, 1920; education: B.A. Music Wayne State University; B.A. Music Education M.A. Manhattan School of Music; Doctorate Music Education University of Massachusetts, 1975; Senior Research Fellowship in Zaria, Nigeria, 1980-84.

Took up alto-saxophone late 1930s; studied music at Detroit's Miller High School; performed with Matthew Rucker and His 13 Spirits of Swing 1939; joined Bama State Collegians 1944; 1946-1948 performed with Lucky Millinder, Oran "Hot Lips" Page, and Roy Eldridge; performed with Dizzy Gillespie big band 1949; returned to Detroit 1950 to play local clubs; formed own group in 1954; recorded for Savoy label 1956-58; moved to New York 1960 and joined Charles Mingus; performed with Olatunji 1961-62; recorded for Riverside 1960 and Prestige 1961; performed with Cannonball Adderly 1962-64; reformed group 1964; recorded for Impulse! 1963-66; signed with Atlantic Records 1967; formed new working quartet 1971; stopped playing nightclubs 1981; taught and played festivals 1981 to present; instructor at University of Massachusetts at Amherst and Hampshire College.

Addresses: *Record company*—Atlantic Records, 75 Rockefeller Plaza, New York, NY 10019.

---

went on the road with Oklahoma bandleader Ernie Fields. Tenor saxophonist Jimmy Heath recalled, in *Swing to Bop*, hearing Fields' ensemble: "That's the first band I saw Bill Evans playing in—Yusef Lateef—but he was Bill Evans then. He came to Wilmington, North Carolina, where I was going to high school. I remember that big tone, even then." Upon leaving Fields' band, Lateef performed with alto saxophonist Sonny Stitt and tenor saxophonist Gene Ammons in Chicago. He recorded with the band of bassist Gene Wright for the Aristocrat label—a 1948 session which included pianist Sun Ra.

In 1949 Lateef joined Dizzy Gillespie's big band in Chicago. In April, Gillespie took the band to New York and cut several sides for Bluebird/Victor including Gil Fuller's "Swedish Suite," Bud Johnson's arrangement of "St. Louis Blues," and numbers featuring vocalists Johnny Hartman and chief scatter Joe "Bebop" Carroll. On "Jump Did-La Ba," recorded in a May session for Victor, Carroll's vocals are accompanied by the solos of Gillespie and Lateef. In following month, Lateef returned to the studio with Gillespie's band to record such bebop vocal sides as "Hey Pete! Let's Eat Mo' Meat, "Jumpin' With Symphony Sid," and Mary Lou Williams' "In the Land of Ooo-Bla Dee."

Path To Islam

According to the most reliable sources, William Evans changed his name to Yusef Lateef (an Arabic name which translates to Joseph who is gentle or who is kind) late in 1949, the time of his stint with the Gillespie band. As jazz writer Ira Gitler pointed out in the liner notes to *Dizzy Gillespie: The Complete RCA Victor Recordings*, on Gillespie's 1949 April-May recording session sheets Lateef's name is still listed as "W. Evans"—a reference which sheds some light on the time of his conversion to Islam (some scholars have placed several years earlier). In his memoir, *To Be or Not to Bop*, Gillespie stated, "Yusef told us how a Muslim missionary, Kahil Ahmed Nasir, had converted many modern jazz musicians in New York to Islam and how he read the Quran daily and strictly observed the prayer and dietary regulations of the religion." Years of devout study of orthodox Islam inspired Lateef to learn to speak, read, and write in arabic, the orthodox language of the holy Quran.

Following his departure from Gillespie's band, William Evans—now known formally as Yusef Lateef—arrived back in Detroit in 1950 to be reunited with his family and to pursue an academic musical education. A year later, influenced by guitarist Kenny Burrell who studied music composition at Wayne State University, he enrolled in the school's music program, pursuing a bachelor's degree in music as well as taking up the study of the flute. During his early years in Detroit, he also studied flute with Larry Teal at the Teal School of Music.

While in Detroit, Lateef helped Burrell and trumpeter Donald Byrd establish the New World Music Society, a musicians collective headquartered in a second floor venue, the New World Stage. Apart from serving on a three man organizing panel, Lateef eventually became vice president of the society. His musical participation at the New World Stage was represented on Donald Byrd's recording, *First Byrd* (recently reissued as *First Flight*), featuring Lateef on tenor sax, Barry Harris on piano, Bernard McKinney on euphonium, Alvin Jackson on bass, and Frank Gant on drums. The session, recorded live at the New World Stage on August 23, 1955, features, along with several standards, Barry Harris' tribute composition, "Yusef."

Beginning in 1953 Lateef often led the house band at a popular westside jazz club, the Blue Bird Inn. At this time he began to attract notice among local Detroiters for his incorporation of Eastern musical and cultural influences. In 1953 a local black newspaper, the *Michigan Chronicle*, published a semi-sensational photograph of him at a local club entitled, "The Man With The Turban."

In 1954 Lateef took up the formal study of the oboe, and formed his own group, a quintet comprising trombonist Curtis Fuller, pianist Hugh Lawson, bassist Ernie Farrow, and drummer Louis Hayes. By 1955 the band became a fixture at George Kliers' Kleins Show Bar, a westside club. Lateef's drummer Oliver Jackson, recalled, in the liner notes for *Yusef Lateef*, the creative interaction at Klein's: "I learned control from Teefski and I learned what swing was all about."

> "No one record is better; each is unique, and if I can relate my sense of concepts to all of them, I'll become that much more complete."

In 1955 Savoy record producer Ozzie Cadenza invited Lateef and his group to record for the New York-based label. "We were working six nights a week in Detroit," recalled Lateef in *The Yusef Anthology*, "and when a record session came up, we would finish the Sunday night performance, immediately drive to Hackensack, New Jersey, record in Rudy Van Gelder's studio on Monday, then drive back on Monday night, which was our off night." Many compositions from Lateef's first 1956 Savoy session, recently reissued as *Jazz Moods*, featured original Lateef compositions augmented by the sound of a one-stringed instrument, the rabat, finger cymbals, the scraped gourd, castanets, and the argol, described as a flute-like wooden oboe-sounding instrument. Lateef's other early Savoy sides included such Detroit musicians as fluglehornist Wilbur Harden, pianist Terry Pollard, and drummer Oliver Jackson.

Orchestral Settings And African Roots

By 1960 Lateef and his band moved to New York. That same year he left his own ensemble to join the band of bassist and composer Charles Mingus. An orchestral jazz session, Mingus' 1960 LP, *Pre-Bird* reissued in 1965 as *Mingus Revisited*, featured Lateef's saxophone solos above the large brass section, and twin-flute performances with Eric Dolphy. After leaving Mingus' band in 1961, Lateef performed a year with the drum ensemble of Nigerian-born Babatunde Olatunji—a Yoru-

ba singer, composer, and percussionist whose artistry reflected the high cultural tradition of the Yoruba royal court. (Though it never materialized, Lateef entered into an informal agreement with Olatunji and Coltrane in 1968 to form an independent booking agency). In 1961 Lateef also appeared as a guest on guitarist Grant Green's critically acclaimed LP *Grantstand*. The album's classic number, "Blues in Maude's Flat," observed Tom Evered, in the liner notes to *The Best Of Grant Green Vol. 1*, "offers plenty of playing space to all involved, starting with a priceless Yusef Lateef performance over the moody and rich support of [organist] Jack McDuff and Green.

In 1962 Lateef joined alto-saxophonist Julian "Cannonball" Adderly's band. Added to the group through the connections of Adderly's pianist Joe Zawinul, Lateef's membership expanded the group to a sextet. During his two year stay with Adderly many of Lateef's original compositions appeared on Adderly's albums. *The Cannonball Adderly Sextet in New York* spotlighted the Lateef originals "Syn-anthesia" and "Planet Earth"—a number which Orrin Keepnews described in the album's liner notes as "lusty number that displays how well the band now uses its three-horn status to construct effective background for the soloists." Another acclaimed live recording, the 1963 LP *Nippon Soul*, contained the Lateef compositions "The Weaver" and "Brother John," dedicated to John Coltrane. As Keepnews pointed out, in the album's liner notes, "Brother John" offered a "fascinating performance on oboe, what can only be called a brilliant emulation (certainly not an imitation) of Coltrane's soprano work."

Around 1964 Lateef left Adderly to reform his own group—once again recruiting former sidemen Hugh Lawson and Ernie Farrow. Aside from a varied repertoire of standards and original compositions, Lateef introduced the group to various avant garde harmonic conceptions. "One of Yusef's were very free," recalled pianist Lawson in *Thinking Jazz*. "We had to improvise using classical composition technique he had gotten from [Karl] Stockhausen like a twelve-tone row. Yusef wouldn't tell what to play, but he might ask you to project a certain kind of mood." At various intervals, Lateef's group featured such drummers as James Black, Lex Humphries, and Detroiter Roy Brooks. Bassist Farrow was eventually replaced by Coltrane veteran Reggie Workman, and later New Zealand-born Mike Nock took over for Lawson at the piano. These various combinations of Lateef's early 1960s working groups were captured on several LPs on the ABC/Impulse label between 1963 and 1966.

Signing with Atlantic in 1967, Lateef recorded albums that explored various Third World and African American musical elements. His 1968 release, *The Blue Yusef Lateef*, brought together a number of former Detroit jazzmen such as guitarist Kenny Burrell, saxophonist Sonny Red, and Hugh Lawson. His effort to incorporate modern soul and funk-oriented sounds emerged in a 1969 tribute album to the local landmarks of his former home: *Yusef Lateef's Detroit: Latitude 42 30'-Longitude 83*. His creative relationship with Atlantic allowed him to continue to pursue the use of non-Western instruments— shanai, argol, rabat, and self-made bamboo flutes, modeled after those played by Nigerian Falani herdsmen. Though Lateef experienced criticism concerning his experimental forays, he stated in *Down Beat* that his "attempts to experiment with new instruments grew out of the monotony of hearing the same old sounds played on the same horns." He added, "If you're recording two albums a year, you can't keep giving the audience the same thing."

His 1971 release, *Suite 16*, included his seven-movement work, "Symphonic Blues Suite." Drawing upon the influences of J.S. Bach and modernist composer Karl Stockhausen, the suite, described by Lateef as "Neo-Concerto Grosso," was performed with Cologne Radio Orchestra and conducted by William S. Fischer. In his *Down Beat* review, Larry Ridley wrote that "this album is a must, and shows the ever-expanding musical language of a truly great artist." Lateef's long tenure at Atlantic brought forth a 1989 Lateef keyboard album, *Nocturne*. Accompanied by several wind instruments, Lateef's solo work on electronic keyboards delved into bi-tonal harmonic explorations.

On Stage In The 1970s

In 1971, Lateef recruited pianist Kenny Barron who, along with bassist Bob Cunningham and drummer Albert Heath, made up an exceptional working quartet. In a 1975 *Down Beat* article, Barron, who first met Lateef a decade earlier at age 17, described the band's fifty-five year old leader: "Yusef amazes me," commented Barron, "I hope I have that kind of energy when I'm his age. And naturally, we draw on that; everyone sort of feeds off another. This is one of the most enjoyable bands I've ever been in." The holder of M.A. from the Manhattan School of Music and a Doctorate in Education from the University Of Massachusetts, Lateef inspired Barron and his fellow bandmates to resume their formal education at the Borough of Manhattan Community College, where he held a position as an associate professor of music.

In 1973 the band published the collective work *Something Else: Writings of the Yusef Lateef Quartet*. Lateef's skills as an instructor and educator took him to Nigeria

in 1980 where, for the next four years, he occupied a position as Senior Research Fellow at the Center for Nigerian Cultural Studies at Ahmadu Bello University in the city of Zaria. Returning in 1986 he took teaching positions at the University of Massachusetts and Amherst College. Presently, he continues to teach at the University of Massachusetts at Amherst and Hampshire College in western Massachusetts.

In 1981 Lateef stopped performing in venues which sold alcohol, and directed his live appearances to more conducive concert settings. In 1992 he appeared as a guest at the John Coltrane Memorial Concert, and in July of the following year, performed in Verona, Italy, and Stockholm, Sweden. In November of 1993, he premiered his "African-American Suite" in Cologne, Germany.

"Auto Physio-Psychic Music"

For Yusef Lateef art is a reflection of one's individual spirituality and personal identity. When asked by writers to rate music by numerical system, he refuses to employ such criticism on the premise that, as he explained in a *Down Beat* "Blind Fold Test," "No one record is better; each is unique, and if I can relate my sense of concepts to all of them, I'll become that much more complete." Like his contemporaries Max Roach and Sonny Rollins, Lateef opposes the use of the word "jazz" in defining his music. He prefers, instead, to describe his genre of expression as "auto-physio-psychic" music. "If an artist paints a picture," related Lateef in *Down Beat*, "he has a right to say what it is. No critics or Councils For the Arts have a right to define it for him." In the 1970s he requested that his listing not appear in Leonard Feather's *Encyclopedia of Jazz*, because the work was not, as Feather noted in the text, "an encyclopedia of music." Nevertheless, Feather included Lateef, explaining, as he noted in the text, that Lateef's "wide-ranging" contributions were too important to be omitted from the volume.

Lateef's emphasis on the value of individual expression and world cultures, served as the inspiration for the title of his 1994 Rhino Records anthology *Every Village Has a Song*, a comprehensive musical retrospective of his career spanning a half century. A primogenitor of the current world music trend, Lateef's study of third world music preceded the creative paths of John Coltrane and subsequent musicians who looked beyond the African-American musical, religious, and cultural roots. Over the last two decades, Lateef has composed symphonic suites, three-one act plays, numerous pieces of poetic verse, a work of vignettes entitled *Spheres*, and books of musical arrangements. Recognized throughout several continents, Lateef has earned himself a place as a talent of individual vision. "There are some musicians who have a natural, innate, soulful, bluesy feeling, and sound," observed Larry Ridley in *Down Beat*. "Yusef's artistry is of this natural breed."

Selected discography

Jazz Moods, Savoy, 1957.
Other Sounds, Prestige, 1957.
Cry-Tender, Prestige, 1960.
The Three Faces of Yusef Lateef, Milestone, 1960.
The Centaur and the Phoenix, Riverside, 1960.
Eastern Sounds, Moodsville, 1961.
Into Something, Prestige, 1961.
Live at Pep's, Impulse!, 1964.
The Complete Yusef Lateef, Atlantic, 1968.
Yusef Lateef's Detroit: Latitude 42 35 -Longitude 83, Atlantic, 1969.
Yusef Lateef, Prestige.
The Diverse Yusef Lateef, Atlantic, 1970.
Suite Sixteen, Atlantic, 1971.
The Gentle Giant, Rhino, 1972.
Reevaluations: The Impulse Years, Impulse!, 1973.
Hush 'N' Thunder, Atlantic, 1973.
The Doctor Is In ... And Out, Atlantic 1976.
Yusef Lateef's Little Symphony, Rhino, 1987.
Nocturne, Atlantic, 1989.
Meditations, Rhino, 1990.
Yusef Lateef's Encounters, Rhino, 1991.
Every Village Has a Song: The Yusef Lateef Anthology, Rhino, 1994.

With Others

(With Donald Byrd) *First Flight,* Delmark.
(With Charles Mingus) *Mingus Revisited,* Polygram, 1960.
(With Grant Green) *Grantstand,* Blue Note, 1961.
(With Cannonball Adderly) *The Cannonball Adderly Sextet In New York,* Riverside, 1963; *Nippon Soul,* Riverside, 1963.
(With Louis Hayes) *Louis Hayes With Yusef Lateef & Nat Adderly,* Vee Jay.
(With Doug Watkins) *Doug Watkins Quintet: Soulnik,* Original Jazz Classics.

Also appears on the compilations *Atlantic Jazz 60s: Vol. 2,* Atlantic; *Atlantic Jazz 70s,* Atlantic; and *Impulse Jazz: 30 Year Celebration,* Impulse!

Publications

Stage And Band Arrangements

Trio For Flute, Piano, & Cello.
Duet For Two Flutes.
Flute Book Of Blues #2.

Books

Something Else: The Writings of the Yusef Lateef Quintet.
Spheres.

Sources

Books

Berliner, Paul F., *Thinking Jazz: The Infinite Art,* University of Chicago Press, 1994.
Feather, Leonard, and Ira Gitler, *The Encyclopedia of Jazz in the Seventies,* Horizon, 1976.
Gillespie, Dizzy, with Al Fraser, *To Be Or Not to Bop: Memoirs,* Doubleday & Co., 1979.
Gitler, Ira, *Swing to Bop: An Oral History of the Transition of Jazz in the 1940s,* Oxford University Press, 1985.
Thomas, J.C., *Chasin' The Trane: The Music and Mystique Of John Coltrane,* Da Capo, 1976.

Periodicals

Michigan Chronicle, March 28, 1953.
Down Beat, October 1, 1970.
Down Beat, April, 1971.
Down Beat, November 6, 1975.
Down Beat, March, 1978.
Keyboard Magazine, November, 1989.

Additional information for this profile was obtained from the liner notes to: *Nippon Soul* by Orrin Keepnews, 1963; notes to *The Cannonball Adderly Sextet in New York,* by Orrin Keepnews, 1963; notes to *Lateef,* by Ira Gitler; notes to *The Best Of Grant Green Vol. 1,* by Tom Evered, 1993; notes to *Every Village Has a Song: The Yusef Lateef Anthology,* by Bob Blumenthal, 1994; notes to *Dizzy Gillespie: The Complete RCA Victor Recordings,* by Ira Gitler, 1995.

—John Cohassey

Madonna

**Singer, songwriter, record company
executive**

Photograph by Patrick DeMarchellier, © 1994 Maverick Recording Company

The career of pop music superstar Madonna has lasted longer than most of her detractors ever predicted. She has become a kind of modern-day, multimedia *ueber*-celebrity who dabbles in film, theater projects, and the occasional publishing venture in addition to her recording endeavors. But Madonna's most impressive feat may be her ability to sell millions of records around the world regardless of what the music press says about her. Rock critic Robert Christgau summed up Madonna's magic touch in *Vogue*, calling the singer-songwriter "a trailblazer in a raceless dance music with discernible roots in postpunk and Eurodisco, who is also on flirting terms with such white-bread subgenres as Vegas schlock, show tune, and housewife ballad." Christgau further described the accomplished performer's million-selling efforts as rife with "corny cool, postfeminist confidence, [and] pleasure-centered electronic pulse."

Off stage, Madonna demonstrates considerable business acumen as chief executive of her own company and record label. Her skills in guiding her career and the "Madonna" persona have, in the space of a decade, made her one of the world's wealthiest women.

Madonna was born Madonna Louise Ciccone in Bay City, Michigan, in 1958. The "Veronica" that is commonly cited as one of her birth names is really her confirmation name, chosen for the religious ceremony when she was in her early teens. Her family—Madonna is the third of eight children—was living in Pontiac, Michigan, at the time of her birth, but they were visiting relatives in Bay City when her then-very-pregnant mother went into labor. Tragically, Mrs. Ciccone died of cancer when Madonna and her siblings were quite young. The children lived for a while with various relatives until her father settled down in Rochester Hills, a suburb of Detroit, and reunited the family.

Madonna's father, an engineer by profession, eventually married the family's housekeeper. Being the eldest daughter of a large brood meant that a greater share of household and emotional responsibilities fell on Madonna's young shoulders. "Sometimes growing up I felt like the unhired help," she admitted to *Time* writer Carl Wayne Arrington. Of her strict, Italian American, Roman Catholic upbringing, she recalled, "My family life at home was very repressive, very Catholic, and I was very unhappy. I was considered the sissy of the family because I relied on feminine wiles to get my way. I wasn't quiet at all. I remember always being told to shut up."

Interested in dance from an early age, Madonna studied with local instructors as a teenager. In high school, she was an honor roll student and a cheerleader. She

Born Madonna Louise Ciccone (pronounced "Chick-one"), August 16, 1958, in Bay City, MI; daughter of Silvio (an engineer) and Madonna (Fortin) Ciccone; married Sean Penn (an actor), August 16, 1985 (divorced, January 1989). *Education:* Attended University of Michigan for two years; studied dance in New York City with Alvin Ailey American Dance Theater and with Pearl Lang.

Singer, songwriter, record company executive, and actress. Backup singer and drummer for the Breakfast Club (a dance band), 1980; backup singer for disco star Patrick Hernandez, 1980-81; singer in a number of New York-based dance bands, including the Millionaires, Modern Dance, and Emmy, 1981-83; solo performer, 1983—; signed with Sire Records (a division of Warner Bros.), 1983; released first album, *Madonna,* 1983; had first Top Ten hit, "Borderline," 1984; signed with Time-Warner, 1991; head of own record label (Maverick), 1992—. Actress in feature films, including *Desperately Seeking Susan,* 1985, *Shanghai Surprise,* 1986, *Who's That Girl?,* 1987, *Dick Tracy,* 1990, *A League of Their Own,* 1992, *Shadows and Fog,* 1992, *Body of Evidence,* 1993, *Dangerous Game,* 1993, *Blue in the Face,* 1995, *Four Rooms,* 1996, *Girl 6,* 1996; *Evita,* slated for release in 1996; also the subject of a documentary titled *Truth or Dare,* 1991. Has made several world tours in conjunction with album releases.

Selected Awards: Grammy Award nomination for best female pop performance, 1986, for "Crazy for You."

Addresses: *Home*—New York, NY; Los Angeles, CA; and Miami, FL. *Record company*—Maverick Records, 8000 Beverly Blvd., Los Angeles, CA 90048.

graduated early and attended the University of Michigan for two years, continuing her dance training, then dropped out and moved to New York City in the late 1970s. There she attempted to get her foot in the show business door. While working in a series of low-wage jobs—including a stint as an artist's model—she took more dance classes and eventually won a spot in the third company of Alvin Ailey's American Dance Theater.

Next, Madonna hooked up with disco performer Patrick Hernandez. She moved with him to Paris for a short time but then returned to New York City and became a part of burgeoning music scene that was combining post-

punk-rock shock with the quick-tempoed beats left over from the disco era. She played drums and sang for a number of New York-based ensembles, including Emmy, the Millionaires, and the Breakfast Club.

An Ambitious Streak

Around 1981 Madonna teamed up with boyfriend Steve Bray to form her own band, simply called Madonna. It was also around this time that she first picked up a guitar and started writing songs herself. Playing in New York City clubs, Madonna soon garnered attention with her new act. She found herself a respected manager and began leaning toward a more funky, rhythm-and-blues-tinged sound, which went over well in the dance clubs she played. New York club disc jockey Mark Kamins, who had extensive contacts in the music business, helped win her a recording contract with Warner Bros. in 1982. "I was very impressed with how determined she was," remembered recording executive Seymour Stein in an interview with *Vogue* writer David Handelman. "I don't want to use the word *ruthless;* at the time, I said, 'She's somebody who would take a shortcut through a cemetery at night to get somewhere.' You could tell it in her eyes."

The contract with Warner Bros. led to the release of Madonna's self-titled debut album in 1983; cuts from *Madonna* slowly became underground dance club hits. When the first single, "Holiday," got extensive airplay, many listeners were surprised to find that the voice belonged to a white woman. Stardom quickly followed when the singles "Borderline" and "Lucky Star" began climbing the charts. By early 1985 Madonna had become a household name, but her second album, *Like a Virgin,* did even more for her budding career. The record quickly went platinum, buoyed by the hits "Material Girl," "Into the Groove," and the title track.

At one point, two singles from *Like a Virgin* were in the Top Five at the same time, and it seemed Madonna was now turning up everywhere in the media. She launched her first tour in the spring of 1985, initially in small venues, but as the shows began selling out in less than an hour, the dates were switched into larger arenas— with the Beastie Boys opening for her on some nights. That spring also saw the release of *Desperately Seeking Susan,* a movie she had made in 1984 when she was still relatively unknown. The low-budget film, directed by Susan Seidelman, became a commercial hit.

The showy "Like a Virgin" tour catapulted Madonna into a very public eye, and it was also during this period that she started to become a sort of icon for fans of her pop music. Teenaged—and even younger—girls began adopting the mid-'80s Madonna look of messy, badly-dyed hair, neon rubber bracelets, black lace bras, white lace gloves, a "Boy Toy" belt buckle, and other sartorial signifiers. The cult of Madonna even spawned the term "wannabe"—as in youngsters who "wanted to be" like the star.

Early in her career, Madonna was already becoming an accomplished songwriter—*Like a Virgin* included five cuts that she wrote herself. Her next effort, the 1986 release *True Blue,* was another success, best remembered for the "Papa Don't Preach" dilemma-of-teen-pregnancy track. Shortly thereafter, in 1987, Madonna landed another major film role in *Who's That Girl?,* a light comedy that was panned by critics. An uneven soundtrack album accompanied the film, followed the next year by *You Can Dance,* a series of remixes of her best-known hits.

By this time, Madonna's personal life was attracting about the same amount of attention as her music and film performances. Her homes had become bastions of high-tech security measures designed to keep an increasingly frenzied fan base and similarly persistent paparazzi out of her hair. In 1985 she had married actor Sean Penn to much media hoopla, and the ups and downs of their marriage were well-chronicled by the press. By early 1989 the marriage was on the rocks, divorce papers had been filed, and her next full-length studio album, *Like a Prayer,* was released.

Continued to Provoke Controversy

Like a Prayer was especially notable for the racy videos to both the title cut and another track titled "Express Yourself." Prior to its release, Madonna had inked a $5 million deal with Pepsi for some commercials and sponsorship of an upcoming tour, but the religious symbolism in the "Like a Prayer" video made the cola giant wary; the company canceled the deal, although the increasingly savvy businesswoman kept the money.

During the late 1980s, Madonna took intermittent breaks from her music to work in film and theater. Her role opposite Warren Beatty in 1990's *Dick Tracy* garnered major media attention as much for her performance as for her off-camera relationship with the film's star. *The Trouser Press Record Guide* panned *I'm Breathless,* the album that was released in conjunction with the movie, calling its best-known single, "Vogue," "just an empty shell of a song, style sans substance."

Yet the "Vogue" single was another example of Madonna's ability to capitalize on a still-underground pop culture phenomenon. "Vogueing" had been a flourishing dance trend on the New York gay discotheque scene for a number of years, where men—sometimes dressed as women—posed and strutted to a high-energy beat. Madonna's video carried this trend into living rooms from Iowa to Omaha. Her next album, *The Immaculate Collection,* was also released in 1990, but it was mainly an assemblage of her biggest hits to date, including "Vogue."

Late in 1990 Madonna became embroiled in yet another controversy, this time surrounding the video to "Justify My Love," the only new track on *The Immaculate Collection.* The steamy images of slightly sado-masochistic situations and multiple partnerships, shot with Madonna's then-boyfriend Tony Ward, provoked MTV to initially ban it from airplay. The furor only boosted sales and prompted *Time* reporter Jay Cocks to point out that the flap made "MTV look an organization of aging church elders, and [Madonna] a champion of feminism and free expression in the process."

> *"It's not my nature to just kick back. I am not going to be anybody's patsy. I am not going to be anybody's good girl. I will always be this way."*

Madonna blended her interest in film and music in the concert documentary *Truth or Dare.* Shot during her 1990 "Blond Ambition" tour by video director Alex Keshishian, the work had a *cinema-verite,* "you-are-there" feel to it as it chronicled pre-show backstage prayer sessions with her dancers and followed the performer around both her L.A. abode and Manhattan apartment. *Time* reviewer Richard Corliss called it "raw, raunchy and epically entertaining ... pure, unadulterated Madonna." In another issue of *Time,* Carl Wayne Arrington described it as "a panoramic, emetic, beauty-marks-and-all" work that "draws its substance from the dark well of Madonna's life."

That dark well of Madonna—especially the out-there sexuality that seemed to unnerve most of her critics—was further explored in her first book, a hefty volume titled *Sex.* The 1992 tome contains racy images shot by fashion photographer Steven Meisel, along with intermittent text of Madonna's musings on sex and love written under the name of her alter ego, Dita Parlo. The $50 book was released to much fanfare, especially when some of the photographs appeared in the media prior to publication—leaked or perhaps sold by insiders.

The metal-jacketed *Sex* came tightly wrapped in Mylar to guard against bookstore peekers and was roundly condemned by more conservative elements in the media. The photographs—among them, one of Madonna hitchhiking nude and several others involving other people and bondage gear—seemed to be calculatingly titillating. Once again, Madonna was at the forefront of a new trend, opined *Newsweek* writer John Leland, who wrote: "Call it the new voyeurism: the middlebrow embrace, in the age of AIDS, of explicit erotic material for its own sake." The book was a sell-out across the country.

Multimedia Mogul

Madonna reportedly received an advance of $5.5 million for the *Sex* book from media giant Time-Warner, and the conglomerate also engineered an almost-unheard-of contract with the singer in 1991. (A year earlier, Madonna had appeared on the cover of the staid financial magazine *Forbes* under the banner "America's Smartest Business Woman?") The seven-year multimedia contract with Time-Warner, reportedly worth $60 million, gave her almost complete artistic control over her music—including her own label, Maverick—and supposedly included $5 million advances for each forthcoming album. Included in the package were deals for cable-TV specials and any film projects she wished to develop.

The *Sex* book coincided with the release of Madonna's 1992 album *Erotica*. Again, a steamy video accompanied the title track, but this time the video easily made it onto MTV playlists—albeit in the wee hours of the night. Much of the material, as in the *Like a Prayer* effort, was written by Madonna with the help of producers Shep Pettibone and Andre Betts. First, they developed the rhythm section for each song, which Madonna would listen to while paging through a journal she keeps for songwriting purposes. The early vocal takes she recorded usually wound up on the final mix, a quirk explained by Pettibone in the *Vogue* interview: "As soon as she comes up with a melodic idea, we record it, because it has that *feeling*, which usually gets watered down the more you sing it." In addition to *Erotica*'s bestselling title song, the record also contains "In This Life," a track about people close to the singer who have died of AIDS, as well as "Goodbye to Innocence," a wistful look at the nature of celebrity.

The *Erotica* album was followed by another film release, a mediocre murder mystery titled *Body of Evidence*, in which Madonna starred opposite Willem Dafoe. She also embarked on yet another world tour, this one entitled "The Girlie Show." It featured topless women

and more racy vignettes set to her music—and helped earn her condemnation from the Roman Catholic church authority in Rome.

After a short hiatus, Madonna made a splash in the spring of 1994 when she appeared on *Late Night with David Letterman*. The show was memorable for the antagonism between the host and guest and the audience's apparent willingness to see Letterman skewer her mercilessly. It was a battle of wits, with Madonna using a certain banned word 13 different times—a stunt that drew her severe media criticism the next day. *Entertainment Weekly* writer Ken Tucker saw it as an attention-getting ploy, "a way to keep her name in the papers in lieu of actually producing some sort of creative work," and noted that by 1994, "as a feminist culture hero," she was fading from the spotlight.

But Madonna showed another side of her complex persona with the late 1994 release of *Bedtime Stories*. The record featured quieter, more soul-tinged numbers, and reaction was favorable, although sales were not as brisk as for her previous records. "The eroticism she hints at on *Bedtime Stories* is actually sexier than that of her more wanton songs and videos," observed *Time* reviewer Christopher John Farley. The critic added that as "one of the pop-music giants of the 1980s ... she has risked becoming an artifact of that era," but pointed out that her collaborative efforts with some groundbreaking performers of the 1990s—songs either written or performed with the likes of Me'Shell Ndege-Ocello, Björk, and producer Kenneth "Babyface" Nelson—were quite impressive.

In addition to her work with Nelson, Madonna teamed with a trio of other producers specializing in the contemporary black sounds of R&B. When *Rolling Stone* writer Zehme asked Madonna if she ever felt black, she replied "Oh, yes, all the time.... When I was a little girl, I wished I was black. All my girlfriends were black. I was living in Pontiac, Michigan, and I was definitely the minority in the neighborhood.... I used to make cornrows and everything.... If being black is synonymous with having soul, then, yes, I feel that I am."

By the mid-1990s, Madonna had become an active chief executive of the Maverick label. Maverick's roster includes Me'Shell NdegeOcello—who performed on *Bedtime Stories*—heavy grunge rockers Candlebox, and Bad Brains. There is also a separate film production company, not attached to Time-Warner, that allows Madonna to develop film projects, among them *Farewell My Concubine* and *Dangerous Game*.

With a contract with Time-Warner that stretches into the very end of the twentieth century, Madonna's musical career—and celebrity status—shows no signs of abating. Yet the unwanted attention brought on by her fame may be the most difficult part of her life. *Newsweek* reporter David Ansen once queried, "Do you ever get sick of being Madonna?," and she replied, "Yes, I do. I do. Sometimes, I just want to go to a movie and not have someone pull on my shirt, you know what I mean? I mean, I can't go grocery shopping, and a lot of times, my secretaries don't get me what I want. And I think, 'God, if I could just go myself, I'd get the right kind of cereal.'"

In a 1995 interview with ABC news correspondent Forest Sawyer for *PrimeTime,* Madonna showed a softer side, ruminating over the loss of her mother, its impact on her life, and her desire to settle down and start a family. Still, she exhibits a philosophical and balanced attitude about her image, her career, and her future. "I see what has happened to me as a blessing because I am able to express myself in many ways that I never would have if I hadn't had this kind of career," she told Arrington in the *Time* interview. "I am lucky to be in the position of power that I am in and to be intelligent. Most people in my position say, 'Listen, you don't have to do any of that. Just kick back, man. Just enjoy your riches. Go get a house in Tahiti. Why do you keep getting yourself into trouble?' It's not my nature to just kick back. I am not going to be anybody's patsy. I am not going to be anybody's good girl. I will always be this way."

Selected writings

Sex, edited by Glenn O'Brien, photographs by Steven Meisel, Warner Books, 1992.

Selected discography

Madonna, Sire, 1983.
Like a Virgin, Sire, 1985.

True Blue, Sire, 1986.
Who's That Girl?, Sire, 1987.
You Can Dance, Sire, 1988.
Like a Prayer, Sire, 1989.
I'm Breathless: Music from and Inspired by the Film Dick Tracy, Sire, 1990.
The Immaculate Collection, Sire, 1990.
Erotica, Maverick, 1992.
Bedtime Stories, Maverick, 1994.
Something to Remember, Maverick, 1995.

Also contributed cuts to the soundtracks for the films *VisionQuest,* 1985, and *Desperately Seeking Susan,* 1985.

Sources

Books

The Trouser Press Record Guide, 4th edition, edited by Ira Robbins, Collier Books, 1991.

Periodicals

Entertainment Weekly, April 15, 1994.
Esquire, August 1994.
Nation, June 8, 1992.
Newsweek, November 2, 1992.
Rolling Stone, March 23, 1989; October 15, 1992; November 11, 1993; December 15, 1994.
Stereo Review, February 1995.
Time, May 27, 1985; December 17, 19904; May 8, 1991; May 20, 1991; November 7, 1994.
Vogue, October 1992.

Additional information for this profile was obtained from a *PrimeTime* interview with Forest Sawyer broadcast on December 6, 1995, on ABC-TV.

—Carol Brennan

Herbie
Mann

Flutist

Courtesy of Kokopelli Records, inc.

Not many musicians can claim to have single-handedly created the style of music for which they are famous. Among the select group who legitimately can is Herbie Mann, a seminal figure in the American jazz scene of the 1960s and '70s. Largely on the strength of his talent for improvisation and willingness to experiment, Mann formulated a jazz style for the flute, raising to the rank of lead an instrument which prior to his arrival had been limited to a minor role in the jazz pantheon. In the process, he was to garner a reputation as one of the most eclectic figures in the music world, readily mixing a wide range of styles from African to Brazilian, from Charlie Parker to disco, to create music that crossed boundaries in every sense of the word. Although his experiments did not always endear him to jazz critics, the result was a musical style that was indisputably his own.

Mann was born Herbert Solomon on April 16, 1930 in Brooklyn, New York, the son of Harry and Ruth Solomon. Musically inclined from an early age, his first concerts took the form of raucous banging on the kitchen pots and pans. His parents, driven to distraction, decided that young Herbert's energies would be channeled in a more fruitful direction by exposure to popular music; in 1939, his mother took him to see the then-reigning master of swing jazz, clarinetist Benny Goodman. The concert had the desired effect, as Mann, fascinated by the atmosphere and excitement of live performing, left off his drumming and took up the clarinet with enthusiasm.

Mann's talent for performing was immediately evident to his teachers and he progressed rapidly. As a teenager, he branched out into playing the tenor saxophone, an instrument that would come to dominate the post-World War II American music scene. For good professional measure, he also learned how to play the flute, a instrument used largely in studios as a backing double. Since flute playing was found almost solely on Latin jazz records, Mann gravitated toward listening to the luminaries of the Latin music scene like Tito Puente, Machito, Charlie Palmieri, or American stars who recorded with Latin musicians such as Charlie Parker.

But the tenor saxophone was Mann's first love, and his guide and inspiration was the dominant figure in the New York jazz scene of the late Forties, Lester Young. As was the case for many other young musicians of his generation, Mann was enthralled by Young's cool, almost low-key, highly melodic approach to rhythm and harmony. Mann carried his passion with him into the U.S. Army, serving overseas from 1948 to 1952, certain that upon returning to civilian life he would make an immediate name for himself as a tenor sax player. But when Mann arrived back in New York, he found that many others had had the same idea and the field was

<blockquote>
</blockquote>

overcrowded with hungry young saxophonists roaming from gig to gig.

Pretended to Play the Flute

It was at this point that Mann's career took the left turn that would change his and many others' ideas about jazz permanently. In early 1953, a friend of his approached him with the news that a Dutch accordionist, Mat Matthews, was forming a group to record with a then-unknown singer named Carmen McRae, and needed a jazz flute player. Mann convinced the friend to put his name forward, even though Mann knew next to nothing about jazz flute playing—a style which had virtually no precedents in the American music scene up until then. In a neat bit of chicanery, in person Mann convinced Matthews to take him on, explaining that his flute was being repaired and he would learn the arrangements on the saxophone. By drawing on Latin music he had absorbed earlier, as well as imitating on the flute the mannerisms of such up-and-coming trum-

pet players such as Miles Davis and Dizzy Gillespie, Mann quickly improvised a playing style that would give him a distinct stage presence.

Following a two-year stint with Matthews, Mann's career slowly took off. Over the course of the 1950s, he passed through a succession of groups, recording extensively as a sideman while enlarging and embellishing his creative mastery of the flute. Just as his style had originally developed out of Latin jazz, he found himself more and more drawn to that idiom's percussive rhythms and raw emotive power, tendencies running counter to the prevailing trend in jazz of the time toward intellectualized, distant compositions. As he explained in a 1973 *New York Times* interview, "The audience I developed wasn't listening intellectually; they were listening emotionally." Eager to tap into this current, Mann formed an Afro-Cuban sextet in 1958 that featured, among other developments, four drummers backing him. For the next several years, a steady parade of some of the best drummers of the era, such as Candido, Willie Bobo, Carlos "Patato" Valdes, and the Nigerian phenomenon Michael Olatunji, would pass through Mann's group.

Discovered Bossa Nova

With this innovative new sound, Mann began to make a name for himself in the jazz world. His percussion-heavy ensembles, apart from the audience excitement they generated, also proved to be an excellent counterpoint to his flute, the drums creating a wall of background noise against which his solos stood out in sharp relief. It didn't hurt that he was performing in a style that was totally new to most of his listeners; as Mann put it in a *Down Beat* interview, "... there wasn't really anybody for the people to compare me to... anytime I'd run out of ideas, the drums got it." After recording several albums for Verve Records, Mann signed with a major label, Atlantic, releasing his first album, *Common Ground,* with them in 1960. In 1962, his live album *Herbie Mann at the Village Gate* was his first major hit, selling over half a million copies; a song from that release, "Comin' Home Baby," would place in the Top 30 on the pop charts.

In spite of success that most musicians would envy, Mann was still not completely satisfied. Latin music with its dominant two-chord harmonies proved monotonous and ultimately constricting; he wanted a style that would allow him to explore a wider range of melodic possibilities. In 1961, he became interested bossa nova—a musical phenomenon then little known outside of its native Brazil—after seeing the movie *Black Orpheus.* His curiosity aroused, Mann persuaded his manager to include him in an all-star tour heading down to Rio de

Janeiro, Brazil's cultural center, and began jamming with local musicians almost from the moment he stepped off the plane. In this and subsequent tours, he would come in contact with some of the giants of Brazilian music, including Sergio Mendes, Baden Powell, and Antonio Carlos Jobim.

Brazilian music, with its combination of pulsing rhythms and beautiful, varied melodies and harmonies, was a revelation for Mann. Here was the style he was looking for that would allow his solos to soar through elaborate ranges of melody backed by multiple rhythm parts. On his return to the United States, his band became one of the first groups to play bossa nova and went on to record a number of albums with Brazilian musicians. One of these included an English version of the famed hit "One Note Samba," featuring the singing debut of the tune's composer, Jobim. Brazilian music, although not as commercially successful as some of the other musical idioms Mann would work in, remained an undercurrent to which he returned throughout the rest of his career; one of his most recent albums *Opalescence,* recorded in 1988, is a lyrical and evocative revisiting of contemporary Brazilian music.

Perhaps as important in terms of Mann's artistic horizons, his plunge into bossa nova seemed to have liberated him from the necessity of being associated with one specific "sound." From the early Sixties on, he would explore a wide variety of musical styles, grafting elements of Middle Eastern, pop, rock, R&B, reggae, soul, and disco music onto jazz to reach a wide audience. Although this approach did not please jazz critics, who often dismissed his work as lacking substance, Mann would string together a spectacular run of commercial successes. In the period 1962-1979, 25 of his recordings placed on the Top 200 pop charts; in 1970 alone, five of the 20 top-selling jazz albums bore the name Herbie Mann on the cover, an unprecedented convergence of hits for a jazz artist.

Ventured Into R&B and Disco

After bossa nova, the next style Mann gravitated toward was rhythm and blues. Fascinated by its improvisational possibilities, he went south to record in Memphis, Tennessee and Muscle Shoals, Alabama, exchanging ideas with and drawing inspiration from some of the greatest R&B studio musicians of the time. The result was *Memphis Underground,* a 1969 album that was to prove his second great hit of the decade. In 1971, Mann recorded another hit, *Push Push,* with guitarist Duane Allman, who, as was often the case for Mann, he had met during an impromptu jam in New York's Central Park. Mann's approach to recording and performing in this period was highly eclectic; he would throw together as many musicians with different backgrounds as possible in the hope that something interesting would emerge. At times the result, as one critic writing in *Down Beat* noted, was a jumble of sound that "looked like fun to do, but wasn't very pleasant to listen to."

In 1972, Mann stabilized his musical entourage by forming the group the Family of Mann, based around David Newman on tenor sax and flute, Pat Rebillot on keyboards, and a floating lineup of New York session players. Although in the first half of the decade he continued to explore jazz/rock fusion and dabbled in reggae, the burgeoning dance craze inevitably began to impact Mann's career. In 1974, his disco single "Hi-Jack," recorded with Cissy Houston and released 24 hours later, was a massive hit. Pressured by profit-minded executives at Atlantic to keep up the winning formula, Mann was deprived of his cherished freedom to experiment and found himself compelled to release records in a style he found more and more distasteful. As the decade progressed, he grew so disenchanted with the direction his career was taking that he began to preface concert appearances with the announcement that he would not be playing any of his disco hits. Finally in 1980, Atlantic and Mann went their separate ways, ending an almost twenty-year association.

Founded His Own Label

In the 1980s, Mann entered something of a lean period. While he still toured and played clubs such as the Blue Note in New York City, his recording output, enormous in the prior two decades, withered away to virtually nothing and he disappeared from the position of public prominence he had enjoyed since the late Fifties. His fortunes rebounded in 1991, however, when he founded Kokopelli Records, a small independent jazz label of the sort with which he had always wanted to record. The company is based in Mann's hometown of Santa Fe, New Mexico. As of the mid-1990s, he was continuing to perform and record, while working full-time overseeing the production of jazz albums by such artists as David "Fathead" Newman and Jimmy Rowles. The release by Rhino Records in 1994 of an anthology of his recorded work, *The Evolution of Mann,* has brought the flutist some measure of the attention his work merits.

Herbie Mann's career does not lend itself to easy characterization. His most popular recordings, as critics were quick point out, were often imbued with a heavy commercial sound bordering on the formulaic. At the same time, though, his recorded work speaks volumes about his ability to merge widely-varying forms into a coherent and appealing style that was accessible to the average listener. Mann could also be described as one of the first "world" musicians; his sensitivity for non-Western musical forms, evidenced by his ability to integrate them into work that could be easily appreciated by a largely Western audience while still retaining the essential characteristics of its origin, has few parallels among the other musicians of his generation. In the final assessment, however, Mann's impact on jazz music does not need to be evoked in words; it can be heard issuing from clubs across North America and the world in musical form, the form that Herbie Mann created, a soaring flute solo floating above the low grind of the drums and the hum of the bass.

Select Discography

Herbie Mann Plays, Bethlehem, 1955.
Mann in the Morning, Prestige, 1956.
The Magic Flute of Herbie Mann, Verve, 1957.
Herbie Mann With the Wessel Ilcken Trio, Epic, 1958.
Flautista: Herbie Mann Plays Afro-Cuban Jazz, Verve, 1959.
The Common Ground, Atlantic, 1960.
The Family of Mann, Atlantic, 1961.
Sound of Mann, Verve, 1962.
Herbie Mann at the Village Gate, Atlantic, 1962.
Do the Bossa Nova With Herbie Mann, Atlantic, 1963.
Herbie Mann Live at Newport, Atlantic, 1963.
Nirvana, Atlantic, 1964.
Latin Mann: Afro to Bossa to Blues, Columbia, 1965.
My Kinda Groove, Atlantic, 1965.
Standing Ovation at Newport, Atlantic, 1965.
Herbie Mann and Joao Gilberto, Atlantic, 1966.
Big Band Mann, Verve, 1966.
Today, Atlantic, 1966.
Our Mann Flute, Atlantic, 1966.
The Herbie Mann String Album, Atlantic, 1967.
The Beat Goes On, Atlantic, 1967.
St. Thomas, Solid State, 1968.
Memphis Underground, Atlantic, 1969.
Muscle Shoals Nitty Gritty, Embryo, 1970.
Push Push, Embryo, 1971.
Turtle Bay, Atlantic, 1973.
Et Tu Flute, MGM, 1973.
London Underground, Atlantic, 1974.
Discotheque, Atlantic, 1975.
Bird in a Silver Cage, Atlantic, 1976.
Gagaku & Beyond, Finnadar, 1976
Surprises, Atlantic, 1976.
Super Mann, Atlantic, 1978.
Mississippi Gambler, Atlantic, 1978.
Brazil Once Again, Atlantic, 1978.
Mellow, Atlantic, 1981.
Astral Island, Atlantic, 1983.
See Through Spirits, Atlantic, 1985.
Glory of Love, A&M, 1986.
Herbie Mann & Jasil Brazz, RBI, 1987.
Opalescence, Gaia, 1989.
Caminho de Casa, Chesky, 1990.
Deep Pocket, Kokopelli, 1992
The Evolution of Mann: The Herbie Mann Anthology, Rhino, 1994.

Sources

Down Beat, November 28, 1969; April 30, 1970; December 10, 1970; December 1980; January 1995.
High Fidelity, April 1989.
Houston Chronicle, April 23, 1995.
Jazz Times, January/February 1995.
New York Times, November 11, 1973.
Stereo Review, April 1988.

Additional source material was obtained from Kokopelli Records press release, 1995, Atlantic Records press release, 1975, and from Rhino Records liner notes for The Evolution of Mann, 1994.

—Daniel Hodges

Mississippi Fred McDowell

Singer, guitarist

Photograph by Michael Dobo, MICHAEL OCHS ARCHIVES/Venice, CA

Although he was born in Tennessee, folks called Fred McDowell "Mississippi Fred" because he was a master practitioner of the Mississippi Delta blues. McDowell "was one of the greatest rural blues performers to be discovered by folklorists in the 1950s," wrote one correspondent in *Cadence. Frets Magazine* called him "one of the greatest traditional bottleneck guitarists who ever lived." In liner notes to the first volume of *Mississippi Delta Blues Jam in Memphis*, Pete Welding described McDowell as "a singer and guitarist of such commanding, gripping power and originality that he must be numbered among the leading exponents of the pure country blues, now or anytime."

McDowell was born just east of Memphis, near Rossville, Tennessee, on January 12, shortly after the turn of the twentieth century. (Oldtimers who remember him as a youngster put the year at about 1904.) Because he was orphaned early, his older, married sister took him to live with her in Mississippi. Blues afficionado Tom Pomposello reminisced about McDowell in *Frets Magazine*. He quoted McDowell as saying, "When I was a boy, the first blues record I ever heard was Blind Lemon Jefferson singing 'Black Snake Moan.' *'O-oh ain't got no mama, now.'* Man, I tell you, I thought that was the prettiest little thing I'd ever heard."

The Road to Becoming a Guitar Master

McDowell played bottleneck guitar, which in his case meant that he wore part of a bottleneck—less than an inch wide—on the third finger of his chording hand, making it possible to play melody and rhythm with both hands. He fashioned the bottlenecks himself, working them down until they fit his fingers perfectly. McDowell remembered his uncle Gene Shields as the first guitarist he ever saw playing in the bottleneck style.

Shields's rather unorthodox method involved filing down the beef bone from a steak until it was smooth and playing with it placed on his little finger. The first time McDowell tried it, he used a pocket knife to recreate the sound his uncle made. He quickly realized that he would have to switch to a glass bottleneck to get the volume and clarity he was looking for. McDowell used one just about an inch long from a Gordon's gin bottle.

Shields played in a trio with a harmonica player named Cal Payne, who introduced McDowell to the blues classic "John Henry." Payne's son Raymond was a good guitar player, McDowell told Pomposello, "but if you'd walk into the room he'd put the guitar down so you couldn't see what he was doing. Then he'd make some kind of excuse, 'I'm tired now' or 'My fingers hurt.'" Pomposello thought this was one reason McDowell was always so open about his own playing. "Other musicians might try to lose you when they play with you, to make themselves look better than you," he'd say, "but they don't know how bad it makes *them* look."

In 1926 McDowell moved back to Memphis for work. He stacked sacks of yellow corn bigger than himself for the Buck-Eye Feed Mill, and in 1929 returned to Mississippi to pick cotton. He'd begun hearing records by Blind Lemon Jefferson and Charlie Patton that impressed him. While at a work camp near Cleveland, Mississippi, he went to a juke joint—a music and gambling club for rural blacks where many famous jazz and blues musicians got their starts—and saw Patton, Sid Hemphill, and Eli "Booster" Green perform. These legendary players had a great influence on McDowell. He learned from everyone he could, but he'd often say, according to Pomposello, "Even if you'd be showing me, I'd have to go off on my own and get it my way. They'd all be playing ball or something and I'd be practicing on Booster Green's guitar." McDowell's progress as a musician was seriously hindered by the fact that he didn't actually own his own guitar until he received one as a gift in 1941.

The first song McDowell ever learned was Tommy Johnson's "Big Fat Mama (With the Meat Shakin' on Your Bones)." "I learned it on one string," he told Pomposello, "then two, note by note. Man, I about worried that first string to death trying to learn that song." This method later became a major part of McDowell's technique. In the liner notes to *This Ain't No Rock N' Roll*, Welding described McDowell's sound as "one of the most inventive, gripping, sensitive and rhythmically incisive bottleneck styles to be heard on record. His command of the idiom was literally without parallel in the blues, for he had developed an approach which was both unique and wholly brilliant in design and execution. Playing in the open-chord tunings favored by country guitarists, McDowell supports his dark-hued, melancholy singing with rhythmic patterns of great tensile strength, subtlety and resilience."

The Sounds of Mississippi

It was in Mississippi where McDowell truly began to refine his sound, adapting Patton's style to his own. He played around a lot and met with many different bluesmen, incorporating all of their styles into his own. He also began to soak up the sounds of the Mississippi Delta blues, acquiring his nickname. In traditional blues, the lyric is everything, and it was particularly pleasing to McDowell to let his guitar do some of the talking. He would say, according to Pomposello, "When you hear me play, if you listen real close, you'll hear the guitar say the same thing I'm saying, too." Although "Mississippi Fred" did not originate the Delta blues, as *Guitar Player* put it, "his feel and field-holler voice were his and his alone."

In 1959 folklorist Alan Lomax traveled around the southern United States recording the music he heard in the fields. He was the first to capture Fred McDowell on tape, including a few of McDowell's songs on an Atlantic Records LP and thus introducing McDowell's sound to a huge audience. Suddenly, at age 55, the guitarist was lauded as a great "new" discovery in the blues world. When Chris Strachwitz of Arhoolie Productions heard the Atlantic record in 1964, he immediately contacted Lomax in order to find McDowell. Strachwitz traveled to Como, Mississippi, where McDowell lived with his wife, Annie Mae, and began a long friendship with them that included a great deal of recording. With each recording, and with every appearance at a major folk or blues festival, McDowell's status as a blues hero grew.

Although most of McDowell's early work was performed on acoustic guitars, he made blues history in Great Britain when he recorded an album there using an electric guitar. The Chicago blues was played on electric, but the Delta blues had always been played on acoustic. Reaction to his electric bottleneck was mixed, but McDowell was so tickled by the electric slide that he never went back to his acoustic guitar.

Legendary Inspiration

McDowell learned what he knew studying the Mississippi bluesmasters who came before him in the late 1920s and early 1930s: Charlie Patton, Son House, Big Joe Williams, and Robert Johnson. His own music became part of the folk blues revival of the 1960s, and it was

McDowell and those like him who passed the sounds on to the next generation. Legendary rockers the Rolling Stones were impressed with McDowell's early recording of "You Gotta Move." Strongly influenced by his style, they recorded their own version of the track on their *Sticky Fingers* album. When McDowell received his first substantial royalties from the song, it was the most money he had ever seen.

Even more important to McDowell was the fact that his music had inspired and found new life in another generation of performers. His work had great bearing on the style of northwest blues guitarist and vocalist Mike Russo, and singer Phoebe Snow felt she learned from McDowell's entire musical approach. But McDowell was perhaps closest to blues guitarist and vocalist Bonnie Raitt and is said to have treated her like his own grandchild. Raitt opened for many of McDowell's final gigs and eventually recorded several of his songs. McDowell died of cancer in 1972.

Selected discography

On Arhoolie, except where noted

Mississippi Delta Blues, 1990.
(Contributor) *Mississippi Delta Blues Jam in Memphis*, Volume 1 (recorded 1969), 1993.

Good Morning Little School Girl (recorded 1964-65), 1994.
You Gotta Move (recorded 1964-65), 1994.
Amazing Grace, Hightone, 1994.
This Ain't No Rock N' Roll (recorded 1968-69), 1995.
(Contributor) *Mississippi Delta Blues: Blow My Blues Away*, Volume 1.
(Contributor) *Shake 'Em on Down*.

Sources

Cadence, February 1989.
Down Beat, December 1989; May 1995.
Frets Magazine, April 1988.
Guitar Player, September 1981; May 1990; June 1991; April 1994; October 1994.
Jazz Journal International, April 1985.
Nation, April 16, 1990.
Playboy, December 1993.

Additional information for this profile was taken from Arhoolie Productions liner notes to *Mississippi Delta Blues Jam in Memphis*, Volume 1, 1993; *Good Morning Little School Girl*, 1994; *You Gotta Move*, 1994; and *This Ain't No Rock N' Roll*, 1995.

—Joanna Rubiner

McKinney's Cotton Pickers

Jazz band

In 1931 McKinney's Cotton Pickers were voted the second-most popular jazz dance band in the country, as was determined in a nationwide poll by the African American newspaper *The Pittsburgh Courier*. Though the Cotton Pickers placed second to Duke Ellington's Orchestra, the band's ranking nevertheless reflected the coast-to-coast popularity of the Detroit-based ensemble. "There was a lot of talk about McKinney's Cotton Pickers up in Detroit," recalled Ellington in *Hear Me Talkin' To Ya*. "That bunch...made a gang of musical history, and their recordings had everybody talking about them." Despite its long list of famous personnel—arrangers Don Redman and Benny Carter and trumpeters Joe Smith and Rex Stewart—this once top midwestern regional band has faded from popular history. Recent scholarship by jazz scholars and historians, however, has began to resurrect the legacy of this talented ensemble, which drew thousands of listeners in the years preceding the swing era.

McKinney's Cotton Pickers emerged from the small African American community of Springfield, Ohio. In

For the Record . . .

Members included **Cuba Austin** (drums, tap dancing; joined band early 1920s); **Benny Carter** (saxophone, arrangements, musical direction; bandmember 1931-32); **Adolphus "Doc" Cheatam** (trumpet; joined band 1931); **Ed Cuffee; Langston Curl; Roy Eldridge** (trumpet; bandmember 1934); **Wardell Gray** (saxophone; bandmember 1934); **Edward Inge** (saxophone; joined band 1930); **Quentin Jackson** (trombone, vocals; joined band 1930); **Claude Jones** (trombone; joined band early 1920s); **Buddy Lee; William McKinney** (drums, management; bandmember beginning 1921); **John Nesbitt** (trumpet, arrangements; joined band mid-1920s); **Don Redman** (saxophone, arrangements; bandmember 1927-31); **Todd Rhodes** (piano; bandmember beginning 1921); **Prince Robinson; Milton Senior** (saxophone; bandmember beginning 1921); **Joe Smith** (trumpet; bandmember 1930-31); **Rex Stewart** (cornet, trumpet; joined band 1931); **George "Fathead" Thomas** (saxophone, vocals; bandmember mid-1920s-1930); **Dave Wilborn** (banjo, joined band early 1920s); and others.

Formed as Synco Trio by William McKinney, Todd Rhodes, and Milton Senior, Springfield, OH, 1921; performed annually at Manitou Beach resort, MI; expanded and adopted name the Synco Band; performed at Arcadia Ballroom, Detroit, MI, 1926; resident band at Graystone Ballroom, Detroit, 1927; recorded for RCA/Victor, 1928-29, and Okeh, 1928; toured West Coast, 1931; formally disbanded, 1934; McKinney led guest bands under the Cotton Pickers name, 1934-1941.

1921 ex-circus drummer and World War I veteran William McKinney, Springfield-born saxophonist Milton Senior, and pianist Todd Rhodes, who had studied at the Springfield School of Music and the Erie Conservatory, formed the Synco Trio. Expanding its membership, the band became the Synco Septette and eventually took the name the Synco Band. The ensemble soon became the most popular show-style band touring Indiana, Kentucky, Michigan, Virginia, and West Virginia. Between 1922 and 1923, the band recruited Springfield banjo player and singer Dave Wilborn, trombonist Claude Jones, and drummer Cuba Austin, who was also a tap dancer. Ceding his drum stool to Austin, McKinney set out to become the band's full-time manager. Most members welcomed the addition of West Virginia-born Austin, whose skillful musicianship freed the unit from McKinney's "stiff" rhythmic technique.

Over the next few years the Synco Band toured widely, including dates in Charleston, West Virginia, where, in 1924, the "ragged" ensemble performed for England's visiting Prince Edward III, who sat in with the group on drums. The band's annual summer resort engagement at Manitou Beach, in southern lower Michigan, became crucial to its development. Away from the demands of downtown ballrooms, the stint at the resort allowed more time for members to rehearse and work on new arrangements. During one of the band's Manitou engagements of the mid-1920s, the unit added trumpeter John Nesbitt and vocalist-saxophonist George "Fathead" Thomas. One of the only members with formal skills, Nesbitt spent hours writing arrangements and teaching his fellow bandmates to read music.

Became McKinney's Cotton Pickers

Like many bands of the period, the Synco Band was a combination dance and show band with a repertoire centering around tap dancing and comedic stage routines that often included the wearing of paper hats and the use of whistles. Despite its reliance on such histrionic novelties, the unit did not lack musical ability. Bill Coleman recalled, as quoted in *McKinney's Music*, that the Cotton Pickers ensemble "was the first Negro orchestra to blend high-class playing and musicianship with showmanship. The dancers loved them and so did all the people 'round the edge of the dance-floor. The band had fantastic numbers. They would suddenly put on moustaches, funny hats, women's dresses, and false faces, but they'd continue to play very rhythmic music."

After performing in the Ohio cities of Toledo and Dayton, the Synco Band would travel north to play dates in Michigan, notably venues in Flint, Bay City, and Saginaw. In 1926 the group took a job at Detroit's Arcadia Ballroom, a fifteen hundred-seat establishment on the main artery of Woodward Avenue. The band's immediate success brought them several contract extensions, which resulted in a nearly five-month stay at the ballroom. From Arcadia the Synco Band moved north along the avenue to one of the city's most prestigious jazz dance establishments, the Graystone Ballroom. Under the proprietorship of the National Amusement Corporation (N.A.C.)—owned by its president, Charlie Horvath, and French-born bandleader Jean Goldkette—the Graystone, with its marble fountain, lavish garden, and spring-supported dance floor, accommodated two thousand dancers. Invited to perform at the Graystone in 1927 by Goldkette, the band was met by immediate acclaim.

At the insistence of the Graystone's management, the Synco Band took a new name. In an era when dance bands and nightclubs were imbued with plantation and riverboat themes of the antebellum South, the band was given the name McKinney's Cotton Pickers. Despite opposition by bandmembers who disdained the moniker's racist connotations, the name persisted, and the band took up residence at the Graystone as the N.A.C.'s first featured black orchestra.

Transformed by Arranger Don Redman

The Cotton Pickers' recruitment of saxophonist-arranger Don Redman in 1927 marked one of the most significant events in the history of the unit. Just as he had almost single-handedly transformed the band of his former employer, Fletcher Henderson, Redman's tenure with the Cotton Pickers, 1927 to 1931, brought the ensemble its greatest period of critical and commercial acclaim. A native of West Virginia, Redman was a child prodigy who went on to become a brilliant, conservatory-trained multi-instrumentalist. His work with the Henderson band produced the model jazz arrangements of the period. As Richard Hadlock wrote in *Jazz Masters of the Twenties,* Redman consigned "to paper what King Oliver and Louis Armstrong had already proved could be created by ear—thematic variations performed by two or more horns in close harmony without loss of rhythmic freedom." Along with arrangements contributed by trumpeter John Nesbitt, Redman built the Cotton Pickers' band book (collection of arrangements) into one of the finest in the country. Less than five feet tall but possessed of a charismatic stage presence, Redman replaced the dour McKinney as the band's master of ceremonies.

Through the connections of Goldkette, the Cotton Pickers acquired a recording contract with RCA/Victor. In July 1928 the band boarded a train for its Chicago recording session. In *Hear Me Talkin' To Ya,* drummer Cuba Austin recounted how "the boys were wild with excitement about recording, and on the train to Chicago for (our) first date there was a lot of drinking, laughing, talking, and everybody was in great spirits. We were just walking and cutting up the length of the train through the entire night—most of us didn't even go to bed or get any sleep." The next day in the studio, the band's timekeeping practice of foot-tapping frustrated engineers who worked to deaden the noise. To remedy the problem, the engineers placed pillows under the feet of the musicians. Despite several ruined takes caused by the pillows slipping out from under the feet of bandmembers, the Cotton Pickers produced a number of excellent sides: "Four or Five Times," "Milenberg Joys," "Cherry," and "Shim-Me Sha-Wabble." Nesbitt's arrangements of "Put It There" and "Stop Kidding," wrote Gunther Schuller and Martin Williams in the liner notes to the compilation *Big Band Jazz,* were the products of

"an unflagging imagination ... brilliantly unusual numbers filled with ingenious elaboration."

According to Schuller and Williams, the fast tempo and use of various time signatures in "Stop Kidding" was the result of "prodigious rehearsing" and was "(in 1928) beyond the means of almost all other jazz orchestras." Three months later, in October 1928, the band took part in a New York session for the Okeh label under the pseudonym the Chocolate Dandies. With guest guitarist Lonnie Johnson the band cut the sides "Paducah," "Star Dust," "Birmingham Breakdown," and a new version of "Four or Five Times."

> "That bunch ... made a gang of musical history, and their recordings had everybody talking about them."
> —Duke Ellington

In 1929 the band's popularity inspired RCA/Victor to arrange a recording date in New York City. Because of intense demand for the Pickers at the Graystone, however, Redman was prohibited by Goldkette from taking the entire band to New York. Needing a steady four-four banjo beat for the sessions, Redman took along Dave Wilborn. In New York Redman filled out the band with a stellar list of talent that numbered saxophonists Coleman Hawkins and Benny Carter, pianist Fats Waller, and trumpeter Joe Smith. "Compared to the [Fletcher] Henderson band of 1929," wrote John Chilton in *The Song of the Hawk,* "this edition of the Cotton Pickers was a superior unit. The tonal blends are better, as is the section phrasing and the use of dynamics; above all, the band has more rhythmic vitality than Henderson's." From these sessions came "Miss Hannah," "I'd Love It," "The Way I Feel," and one of the band's biggest hits, "Gee Baby, Ain't I Good to You."

Not long after the New York recording date, Joe Smith officially joined the Cotton Pickers. A former sideman with Bessie Smith and Fletcher Henderson, Smith possessed a smooth trumpet style. As Gunther Schuller observed in *Early Jazz,* "Joe Smith is one of the most interesting trumpet players of the twenties in that he combined sovereign technical mastery with a sensitivity and lyrical style unknown in those early rowdy days of jazz." In *A History of Jazz,* Barry Ulanov noted the importance of Smith's membership in the Cotton Pickers, asserting, "When Joe Smith joined, the band assumed importance, ranking with the bands of Duke [Ellington] and Fletcher [Henderson]."

In November 1930 Smith borrowed the car of drummer Kaiser Marshall, the band's temporary replacement for the ailing Cuba Austin. On his trip from Springfield, Massachusetts, to Bridgewater, Connecticut, Smith took along singer George Thomas. Behind schedule, he increased his speed as he attempted to pass through the closing gates of a railroad crossing. He lost control of the car and crashed. Though Smith escaped the accident unharmed, Thomas died in a nearby hospital. The death of Thomas left an indelible impact on Smith, who eventually entered New York's Bellevue psychiatric facility, where he died in 1937. As author Kaiser Marshall explained in *Hear Me Talkin' to Ya*, "I really think that it was that accident that put Joe where he spent his last few years, as Joe and Fat Head [Thomas] loved each other."

Though the entire band was devastated by Thomas's death, they kept a scheduled recording date for Victor, using replacement musicians Rex Stewart on trumpet and Benny Carter on sax, as well as free-lance vocalists. Thomas's place was filled by two new members, singer-trombonist Quentin Jackson and saxophonist Edward Inge. Performing intermittently with the band, Smith left in 1930 and was temporarily replaced; he rejoined in 1931.

Due to the severe economic impact of the Depression, McKinney's Cotton Pickers' Detroit fans found it difficult to patronize big halls and nightclubs. In contrast to Detroit's industrial blight, though, Los Angeles's film industry supported a number of bustling nightclubs. To take advantage of this vibrant West Coast scene, William McKinney booked the Cotton Pickers for an engagement at Sebastian's Cotton Club in Culver City. On the way west, the band played several other dates, including stops in Kansas City, where it battled the band of Bennie Moten.

Stress of "Endless Travel" Led to Disbanding

The Cotton Pickers' stay at Sebastian's and several other California clubs, from April through July of 1931, caused mass dissension among members. Low wages, poor management, and long hours of travel began to take their toll. Temporarily pacified by a vacation in Salt Lake City, Utah, the band resumed its western tour, appearing at cities along the California coast. The band's protestations, however, flared once more as it was booked into a last-minute string of one-nighters. As it traveled by car to play stops in cities across the Midwest and the upper South, the band, accustomed to

traveling by bus, began to voice its anger over the lack of suitable accommodations. "There isn't anything that can ruin a band quicker than a booker who keeps jumping it all over the country for one-nighters," recounted Dave Wilborn, as quoted in *McKinney's Music*. "We were all so tired of this endless traveling. Right there the boys voted to break up the band."

Following the end of that difficult tour, Don Redman left to form his own unit. From McKinney's ranks Redman's New York band eventually culled Prince Robinson, Ed Cuffee, Ed Inge, Buddy Lee, and Langston Curl. McKinney's remaining members soon formed a new orchestra under the direction of Benny Carter, an ace arranger in addition to his role as saxophonist. Members of the 1931 incarnation included cornetist Rex Stewart and trumpeter Adolphus "Doc" Cheatam. In December of that year the outfit took part in a battle of the bands with its chief rival, the Duke Ellington Orchestra; a month later the Pickers were in the studio to record once more for Victor.

However, following that date, Victor failed to renew the Cotton Pickers' contract. Another major setback occurred with the departure of Carter in 1932. Within two years, the band was devoid of its original, Ohio-based members. Lacking an able arranger and suffering from the apathetic management of McKinney, the band performed with numerous guest musicians until its official breakup in 1934. Throughout the decade McKinney periodically resurrected the Cotton Pickers in the form of guest bands, which he booked under the Cotton Pickers name. After 1941 McKinney left music and took a job at Ford Motor Company's River Rouge plant; he subsequently worked as a bellhop in a Detroit hotel.

The only black regional band to attain national prominence during the 1920s, McKinney's Cotton Pickers was a product of long years on the road and a musical camaraderie that transformed an unknown band into a top box-office attraction. The ensemble's "recordings and memories of the period," wrote Thomas J. Hennessey in *From Jazz to Swing*, "indicate the Cotton Pickers were a tight ensemble playing straight-ahead dance music that pleased its white dance audience and also impressed scores of Midwestern musicians," including young instrumentalists like swing drummer Gene Krupa. Indeed, the Cotton Pickers had a mighty impact on the swing musicians who followed them. Remembered Krupa, as quoted in *Hear Me Talkin' To Ya*, "One night in Chicago ... I stood open-mouthed, completely awed and fascinated. I'll never forget the Cotton Pickers."

Selected discography

The Band That Don Redman Built (1928-1930), Bluebird, 1990.

Don Redman: Doin' What I Please, Living Era, 1993.
Great Alternatives, Classics, 1993.

Also appear on the compilations *Big Band Jazz: From the Beginnings to the Fifties* (Smithsonian Collection of Recordings), RCA, 1983; and *Early Black Swing*, RCA.

Sources

Chilton, John, McKinney's Music, *Bloomsbury Book Shop, 1978.*

Chilton, John, Song of the Hawk: The Life and Recordings of Coleman Hawkins, *University of Michigan Press, 1990.*

Chilton, John, Who's Who of Jazz: Storyville to Swing Street, *Chilton Book Company, 1972.*

Hadlock, Richard, Jazz Masters of the Twenties, *Da Capo, 1988.*

Hennessey, Thomas J., From Jazz to Swing, *Wayne State University Press, 1994.*

Schuller, Gunther, Early Jazz: Its Roots and Early Development, *Oxford University Press, 1986.*

Shapiro, Nat, and Nat Hentoff, Hear Me Talkin' To Ya: The Story of Jazz by the Men Who Made It, *Dover, 1955.*

Ulanov, Barry, A History of Jazz, *Viking Press, 1952.*

Additional information for this profile was obtained from liner notes by Gunther Schuller and Martin Williams to *Big Band Jazz: From the Beginnings to the Fifties* (Smithsonian Collection of Recordings), RCA, 1983.

—John Cohassey

MC 900 Foot Jesus

Rap artist, songwriter

The oddly named act is a front for Mark Griffin, a musician who has developed a quirky sound that blends rap rhythms with socially conscious lyrics and bits of classic jazz. "To the eccentric hip-hop fan," attested *Vibe's* Joseph V. Tirella, "MC 900 Ft. Jesus is a messianic rapper-poet who shatters musical barriers and time-honored cliches." With occasional partner DJ Zero, Griffin has released several albums that made waves on the alternative and college radio charts. Laden with the "sampled" work of other artists and instrumentation that includes everything from trumpet to tabla (the hand drums used in Indian music), the discs are multi-layered affairs with dense lyrical content; state-of-the-art mixing technology is responsible for the final effect. Early in his career, Griffin preferred anonymity and little was known about the artist—press releases sometimes even featured a picture of Jesus. Yet he seems to have become more comfortable talking about his music as it has gained wider recognition on its own merits.

Writing in *Keyboard,* Mark Dery declared that MC 900 Ft. Jesus has "created a musical electroencephalogram of the American religious mind—epilepsy, ecstasy, and all." This hybrid form is defined by Griffin's fascination with the seamier aspects of late-twentieth-century life in the United States; the unbalanced and the devout are of special interest. The peculiar zealotry of fundamentalist religion in contemporary America even provided Griffin with his pseudonym. Evangelist Oral Roberts became infamous for a mid-1980s incident in which he spoke publicly of a vision he'd had: God had instructed him to build a 900-foot-tall statue of Jesus Christ.

Formal Musical Education

Born in the late 1950s, Griffin grew up in relatively middle-class surroundings, the son of an army officer. He studied trumpet at Kentucky's Morehead State University, receiving a B.A. in the late 1970s, and relocated to Texas to earn an advanced degree in music at North Texas State University in Dallas. It was there that he began playing in local rock bands, eventually becoming a member of a group called White Man. As part of this ensemble he began honing his medium—literate, laconic rapping over heavily sampled background noise. He later teamed up with DJ Zero, also known as Patrick Rollins, a recording artist who had worked with rap phenomenon Vanilla Ice.

The first release by MC 900 Ft. Jesus was an EP entitled *Born with Monkey Asses* recorded on Griffin's own label and released in the late 1980s. The name of the disc was derived from the title track, which samples a paranoid schizophrenic patient discussing his theories on what the doctors in the psychiatric facility were doing to the

Born Mark Griffin, c. 1957, in Kentucky; son of an army officer. *Education:* B.A. in music, Morehead State University, late 1970s; graduate study in music, North Texas State University, early 1980s.

Member of band White Man and worked in alternative record store, Dallas, TX, early 1980s; released debut EP, *Born with Monkey Asses,* on own label, late 1980s; signed with Nettwerk/I.R.S., 1989, and released *Hell with the Lid Off,* 1990.

Addresses: *Record company*—American Recordings, 3500 West Olive Ave., Ste. 1550, Burbank, CA 91505.

research animals at night. "I'm fascinated by the way the insane build up a picture of the world based on whatever information they get and assemble it in a completely unique way," Griffin told Dery in *Keyboard.* Another source of inspiration for Griffin's rantings were the people he encountered while working in a Dallas alternative record store for several years.

Explores Celebrity, Fundamentalism, Lunacy

Hell with the Lid Off was the first full-length release for MC 900 Ft. Jesus and the first time Griffin had appeared on a major record label. It was issued in 1991 on the Nettwerk/I.R.S. label. Its title is a reference to a fire-and-brimstone sermon delivered by Marjoe Gortner, once a child evangelist. Sampled artists on *Hell* include rappers Public Enemy, jazz ensemble the Weather Report, and Nigerian singer and political activist Fela Kuti. Griffin again pokes fun at the interrelated American cults of personality and do-it-yourself religion; actor and New Age doyenne Shirley MacLaine is skewered on "Truth Is out of Style" as Griffin conducts a talk show interview with himself. Another track, "I'm Going Straight to Heaven," is based on a street-corner preacher prone to ventriloquism. "Spaceman" was inspired by a man who approached Griffin in Los Angeles and began screaming at him, "like I was the source of a major problem in his life," the singer told *Rolling Stone's* Melissa Morrison. "My songs are ... about mental infirmity that makes you see things in apocalyptic terms," he explained.

Griffin often distorts his voice with electronic gadgetry, sending it through a Quadraverb synthesizer and a guitar overdrive. "If you have a wimpy white voice like mine," he told *Keyboard's* Dery, "then you have to use electronics." The backbone of beat supporting the work is composed by Griffin and laid out on digital audio tape. His vocals are added later, as are samples fed through another synthesizer. DJ Zero is responsible for the scratchy stylus emissions that provide the distinctive hip-hop sound. "I view Zero as an instrumental soloist," Griffin ventured in *Keyboard.* "When I write the tunes, I envision four bars where I want him to do something, and I leave the what he's going to do in that space up to him."

Reviewing *Hell with the Lid Off* for *Melody Maker* in 1990, Jonathan Selzer called it "the most subversive thing that's happened to rap yet." In describing its sound he asserted that "the music surrounds you. It's a frantic rhythm repeated over and over, unable to break out of its perpetual motion, its perpetual NOW, often with an underflow of late night, narcissistic sleaze."

Broadens Electronic Wizardry with Jazz Instrumentation

In 1992 MC 900 Ft. Jesus followed *Hell* with *Welcome to My Dream,* which marked a shift toward a more jazzy sound. One track, "Falling Elevators," seemed a direct homage to legendary jazz trumpeter Miles Davis; it utilized a trumpet and congas. Other cuts were also notable for more traditional instrumentation, including the use of bass clarinet. In a *Down Beat* review writer Bill Milkowski noted that *Welcome to My Dream's* musical configurations "are grounded in funk but far more ambitious than the average hip-hop fare."

Another track from *Welcome to My Dream,* "The City Sleeps," inspired a media controversy in Baltimore, Maryland. The song is presented from the first-person viewpoint of a compulsive arsonist who lights random fires at night. A local television news reporter used it as the soundtrack for a report on arson, then queried the city's fire chief as to whether he saw a connection between the song and local incidents of arson. The chief answered in the affirmative, though he had never heard the song before. The reporter then began an effort to have the song banned from local radio stations, arguing that it could increase the likelihood of arson in Baltimore. "Quite frankly, the impression I get is that it was a slow news day," Griffin said of the flap to *Washington Times* writer Jeff Alan Hewitt. Citing the First Amendment's protection of free speech, Griffin quipped, "It's really ironic that a journalist would be going around trying to get a song banned."

One Step ahead of the Spider was the next release for MC 900 Ft. Jesus and his first on American Recordings. Musicians such as Living Colour guitarist Vernon Reid joined Griffin in the studio for this 1994 opus. Reviewers commented on the continued use of Miles Davis-inspired musical threads, some pointing out *Spider's* similarities to Davis's seminal work *Bitches Brew,* an early example of the jazz-rock style known as fusion. Many of the tracks from *Spider* are several minutes long, and as the album progresses the music becomes more avant-garde. Reid plays guitar on "Stare and Stare," a song originally recorded by soul star Curtis Mayfield; "New Year's Eve" is based on a short story Griffin admired; he raps in Spanish on "Gracias Pepe." *Vibe* contributor Tirella called the record "a delightful blend of psychedelia, jazz-rock fusion, and [Griffin's] own Beat-like disembodied poetry recited over groove-saturated hip-hop beats."

Not surprisingly, Griffin claims a wide range of musical influences, from aforementioned jazz and soul greats to classical composers. He is also inspired by the writings of novelists such as Jim Thompson and Flannery O'Connor. "People who write very grotesque and difficult but beautiful books are as much an influence on my music as any musician," he told *Washington Times* contributor Hewitt. He views his chosen form as "something an individual can do on his own with whatever technology is around," remarking "It offers a lot of latitude lyrically." Griffin concluded of his creative method, "What I try to do is take the best aspects of what's happening now and combine [them] with what motivates me."

Selected discography

Hell with the Lid Off, Nettwerk/I.R.S., 1990.
Welcome to My Dream, Nettwerk/I.R.S., 1992.
One Step Ahead of the Spider, American, 1994.
Born with Monkey Asses (EP).

Sources

Books

Trouser Press Record Guide, fourth edition, Collier, 1991.

Periodicals

Down Beat, March 1992.
Guitar Player, March 1995.
Keyboard, April 1991.
Melody Maker, March 17, 1990; February 15, 1992.
Metro Times (Detroit, MI) August 3, 1994.
Rolling Stone, October 18, 1990; September 8, 1994.
Vibe, August 1994.
Washington Times, January 30, 1992.

—*Carol Brennan*

Eddie Money

Singer, songwriter

Photograph by Richard McCaffrey, MICHAEL OCHS ARCHIVES/Venice, CA

Rock singer Eddie Money's personal life has garnered him almost as much attention as his successful albums of the late 1970s and early 1980s. Seeming to come out of nowhere with his 1977 self-titled debut, Money had actually been a fixture around the San Francisco rock scene for several years. With the assistance of a big name concert promoter, he attained major-label stardom. But the temptations of such notoriety almost caused the singer to join that pantheon of young dead rock stars whose ranks had grown rapidly during the drug-fueled '70s. After staging a comeback with his successful 1982 album *No Control,* Money's career again seemed to grind to a halt during the rest of the 1980s as his forceful, edgy rock songs got lost in the shuffle of the burgeoning new music scene. Then, in 1995, the middle-aged rocker's career was resurrected once more.

Money was born Edward Mahoney on March 21, 1949, in New York City. His father, a police officer, relocated the family from Brooklyn to Long Island when Money was just a youngster. To the dismay of his parents, he began singing in rock bands while still in high school. He stayed out of the Vietnam War by enrolling in the New York Police Academy and continued to sing in local combos while serving as a police cadet. Soon, however, Money's antiestablishment philosophy and growing interest in the world of rock and roll clashed with the beliefs of his parents' generation. "I grew up with respect for the idea of preserving law and order, and then all of a sudden cops became pigs and it broke my heart," Money told *Rolling Stone* reporter Mikal Gilmore in 1978. "It was just a goddamn shame that getting high was illegal." One day he typed up a written defense of a certain unnamed drug on police stationery and found himself booted out of the academy.

Changed Mahoney into Money

Deciding to make a go of a career in music, Money relocated to the San Francisco Bay area, where he was finally free to grow his hair long. He sold blue jeans and got his first big break when he joined Big Brother and the Holding Company, singer Janis Joplin's backing band, shortly after her demise. In 1975, after singing for a number of years in different bands—and rearranging the Mahoney surname into "Money"—he became involved with popular Bay Area concert promoter Bill Graham's management company. The two had met after Money performed in a battle of the bands at one of Graham's venues, and the elder statesman of rock quickly became a friend, manager, and mentor to Money. Graham helped him negotiate a recording contract with Columbia Records. The singer's first release, 1977's *Eddie Money,* catapulted him to overnight stardom.

Money's gravelly voice and the accessible, hard rock sound of the self-titled debut spelled AOR success. His backing band featured musicians fresh from their work with the Steve Miller Band, best known for their hit "Keep On Rocking Me, Baby." The first two singles from Money's first record, "Baby, Hold On" and "Two Tickets to Paradise," reached Number 11 and Number 22 on the 1978 charts respectively. Heavy touring followed, including opening dates for the legendary rock band Santana, but the excesses of the rock and roll lifestyle seemed to lead Money into some well-publicized trouble. After recording and touring for two follow-up albums, *Life for the Taking* and *Playing for Keeps,* Money finished a late 1980 tour, was admitted to a Bay Area hospital, and then disappeared from the public eye for over a year. Initial press accounts reported that the singer was suffering from food poisoning, but rumors soon circulated that his affliction was drug-related.

In 1982, nearly a year and a half later, Money discussed the entire incident with *Rolling Stone* reporter Greg Hoffman. At a party one night back in 1980, after drinking heavily, the singer snorted a substance on a mirror that was being passed around the room. Money assumed it was cocaine, but it was really a synthetic barbiturate. He nodded off and spent the next 14 hours lying on his leg, severely damaging a nerve. The incident also brought temporary impairment of his kidney function. The ordeal helped Money look at his lifestyle a bit more closely. "I can't believe I was hanging out with and respecting people who let me lay dying for fourteen hours," he told Hoffman.

Came Back with *No Control*

Money's recuperation and hiatus from the public eye was spent working on a fourth album, released in the summer of 1982. Titled *No Control,* many of the tracks explore the demons that had led him down the wrong path. "You know why this record is so good?" he queried Hoffman in the *Rolling Stone* interview. "It's so good because I worked my balls off and because I almost killed myself. Half the people in the country probably think I'm dead, but I'm not dead. I'm *back*!" Of the album's best-known single, "Think I'm in Love," *High Fidelity* contributor Chuck Eddy opined that the song's "traction comes from how the initial mythological acoustica lures you siren-style toward the hard-boiled fuzz riff, which comes and goes." Another track, "Shakin'," features guitar work as "murderous as anything radio has accepted this decade," asserted Eddy.

In the *Rolling Stone* interview with Hoffman, Money attempted to explain the problems in his recent past as a split between who he was originally—Eddie Mahoney, working-class kid from Brooklyn—and who he became after overwhelming success—the rock star known as Eddie Money. He showed Hoffman his still-damaged leg. "Eddie Mahoney didn't do this to himself, Eddie Money did this to Eddie Mahoney. The big rock star with the Mercedes and the half a million dollars in the bank almost ruined what I really am. It took me a lot of years and a lot of work to get what I wanted, but it took Eddie Money only a couple of days to almost throw it away."

Personal Renewal

Money recorded a series of albums for Columbia during the 1980s, including 1984's *Where's the Party,* the 1986 effort *Can't Hold Back,* and *Nothing to Lose,* released in 1988. A greatest hits package followed the next year, but Money had taken a break to concentrate on family life. He got married, and within a few years he and his wife were expecting a fifth child. This period of Money's life was also marked by tragedy, however, when longtime friend Bill Graham died in a 1991 helicopter accident. An eighth studio album, *Right Here,* arrived in the same year, with the track "I'll Get By" dedicated to the late Graham. In 1992 Money released an acoustic effort entitled *Unplug It In.* Reviewing the work for *Entertainment Weekly,* David Browne declared that its "clunky, heartfelt renditions" of Money's best-known songs emit "more charm and warmth" than most pop acts. The singer also began playing small club dates of acoustic sets.

Money's career took an unexpected turn in 1995 when Graham's surviving namesake management company reactivated the Wolfgang Records label (a defunct imprint of Columbia originally started by Graham)—and Money became the first artist in their repertoire. Issuing *Love & Money* in the spring of 1995 heralded a comeback of sorts for Money. The record's first single, "After

This Love Is Gone," was lauded as "a chugging, rock-edged pop ballad" by *Billboard* magazine. Two other tracks—"Died a Thousand Times" and a cover of '70s soul singer Isaac Hayes's "Run Your Hurt Away," with its lyrics about resurrecting one's life—seemed to best reflect the renewal of Money's career and personal life.

Selected discography

Eddie Money, Wolfgang/Columbia, 1977.
Life for the Taking, Wolfgang/Columbia, 1978.
Playing for Keeps, Wolfgang/Columbia, 1980.
No Control, Wolfgang/Columbia, 1982.
Where's the Party, Columbia, 1984.
Can't Hold Back, Columbia, 1986.
Nothing to Lose, Columbia, 1988.
Greatest Hits: The Sound of Money, Columbia, 1989.
Right Here, Columbia, 1991.
Unplug It In (EP), Columbia, 1992.
Love & Money, Wolfgang, 1995.

Sources

Books

The Rolling Stone Encyclopedia of Rock & Roll, edited by Jon Pareles and Patricia Romanowski, Rolling Stone Press/Summit Books, 1983.

Periodicals

Billboard, April 8, 1995; May 6, 1995.
Entertainment Weekly, December 18, 1992.
High Fidelity, July 1989.
Rolling Stone, May 4, 1978; August 19, 1982.

Additional information for this profile was provided by Suzan Crane Public Relations.

—*Carol Brennan*

Morphine

Rock band

With "sheer originality, slow-burning intensity, excellence of songcraft, and pure fun," ventured *Billboard*'s Chris Morris, "Morphine is at the head of the pack among alternative rock bands." The moody, evocative sound of the Boston group has inspired rock critics to try to outdo one another in describing it: words like "noir" suggest its vibe, while "smoky" is usually the adjective of choice for bassist-singer Mark Sandman's voice. Inevitable references to the narcotic properties of the trio's music usually follow.

Morphine's striking aesthetic—so unlike the assaultive directness of most rock—derives from its unique instrumentation. Sandman's bass has usually sported only two strings, and he often plays with a slide; saxophonist Dana Colley generally plays a baritone, and drummer Billy Conway leaves lots of space for the music to breathe. With no guitar, apart from subtle touches in the studio, Morphine creates a spacious and surprisingly heavy musical environment. Their 1995 album *yes* saw them turning the cult success of the group's previous effort, *Cure for Pain,* into a prolonged stay on the charts.

Photograph by Pauline St. Denis, courtesy of Rykodisc.

For the Record . . .

Members include **Dana Colley**, baritone saxophone; **Billy Conway** (joined group 1993), drums; **Jerome Deupree** (left group 1993), drums; and **Mark Sandman**, bass, vocals.

Formed in Boston, MA, c. 1992; released debut album, *Good,* Accurate/Distortion, 1992; signed with Rykodisc and released *Cure for Pain,* 1993; appeared on soundtrack of film *Spanking the Monkey,* 1993.

Selected Awards: *Good* named Independent Album of the Year at Boston Music Awards, 1992.

Addresses: *Record company*—Rykodisc, 27 Congress St., Salem, MA 01970.

Sandman, a native of Newton, Massachusetts, grew up "a normal kid" listening to "adolescent cock rock," as he told *Option.* Yet he also revealed that his adult experience was somewhat more offbeat, including tuna fishing in the Aleutian islands, construction work in the Rocky Mountains, driving a Boston taxi, and gadding around Rio de Janeiro, Brazil. He and Conway formed part of the sultry blues-rock band Treat Her Right; Yale University alumnus Colley played with the group Three Colors.

"This Is Different"

Treat Her Right disbanded in 1990. Sandman then embarked on a period of musical experimentation, inviting various musicians to jam with him and looking for new sonic opportunities outside the overworked repertoire of guitar rock. Influenced by the ambitious soundscapes of jazz bassist and composer Charles Mingus, the single-string expressiveness of Middle Eastern music, the gritty intensity of Mississippi Delta blues, the bleak themes of classic country music, and the atmospheric pop of groups like the Police, he began to hone in on the Morphine concept. "I listen to a lot of tapes I pick up at ethnic grocery stores," he informed Steve Morse of the *Boston Globe.* "I like things that aren't necessarily coming from Western sources, that have phrasings that don't begin and end where you expect them to."

But it wasn't until Sandman played a one-stringed bass with a slide—inspired in part by seeing a bassist in a club do the same—against Colley's saxophone that the concept began to gel. "It wasn't like 'Eureka!' or any-

thing like that," he insisted to *Billboard's* Morris. "It was, 'This is different—let's try a gig and see if it flies.'" And, he remarked to Morse, "If the band didn't work, it would have been no great matter. We would have just tried something else another day."

Jazz-rock drummer Jerome Deupree originally rounded out the trio. Their maiden gig was well received, encouraging them to carry on. In 1992 Morphine recorded their debut album, *Good,* on the independent Accurate/Distortion label. It quickly became clear that the group's sound, which allows the confluence of saxophone and slide bass to work within the space normally filled by guitar, had found an audience. "It just seems like the guitars are there," Sandman mused in *Pulse!* "They're just sort of imaginary." Of the saxophone—usually relegated to brief solos in pop music—Colley noted in an interview with Randee Dawn Cohen of *Alternative Press* that he "always felt it had a lot more potential than that and could succeed in becoming part of the music, part of the rhythm and bass." *Pulse!* called *Good* a "surprisingly accessible" effort that "transcends petty genre distinctions in favor of timeless emotional truths." It was named "Independent Album of the Year" at the 1992 Boston Music Awards.

Dark, Sexy Themes

Sandman's lyrics and vocals evoked for many listeners the dark, jaded narratives of *noir* or "pulp" fiction and film—stories of crime, obsession, and betrayal. Reading off a list of his thematic preoccupations to *Option's* Bob Gulla, he cited "perseverance, disadvantage, lust, despair, international love, self-delusion." At the same time, of course, these often seedy tales are dangerously sexy, lending credence to Sandman's description of Morphine—solicited by Patrick Bryant of Detroit's *Metro Times*—as "f— rock."

Nonetheless, Sandman has argued that the *noir* element in his songwriting has been exaggerated. "I mean, I read a lot of those books," he admitted in *SF Weekly,* referring to such standards of the genre as the novels of Raymond Chandler, "but I don't read them over and over." Indeed, as he remarked to *Alternative Press* contributor Cohen, his compositions "are probably autobiographical, but it's hard to tell." In fact, he lamented not having "disguised" these elements as well as he'd intended.

The promise displayed by *Good* prompted the Rykodisc label, another independent, to sign Morphine and re-release the album. In the meanwhile, the trio set to work on a follow-up; during this period Deupree left the group and Conway took his place. *Cure for Pain* came out in 1993 and was a hit with both critics and underground music fans. "Morphine evoke the zonked swing of lounge jazz and the grind of dirty blues while maintaining rock & roll convictions," asserted *Rolling Stone* reviewer Arion Berger, who felt that Sandman displayed "no imagination" as a singer but conceded, "If his vocals can be faulted," his "songwriting can't." Songs like "Thursday," a tense story of lust and peril, the rocking "Mary Won't You Call My Name," and the plaintive, grooving title track—on which Sandman deadpans, "Someday there'll be a cure for pain/That's the day I'll throw my drugs away"—took the record's sales far beyond expectations. Five tracks from the album appeared on the soundtrack for the acclaimed independent film *Spanking the Monkey.*

Morphine toured relentlessly in support of *Cure for Pain;* Colley's tour diary—excerpts from which appeared in *Raygun*—preserved some of the immediacy of their international travels. After experiencing the massive earthquake in Los Angeles in January of 1994, the group broke the citywide curfew and played a show there the next night. Colley also wrote of the "surprise and terror" of a packed gig in Brest, a town in the French countryside: "By the time 'Mary won't you call my name' begins, all hell breaks loose. People are flying back and forth in one group of twisted limbs and bobbing heads. The monitors are the first to go, followed by mike stands, speaker stacks and light rigs." The hapless soundman was pinned against a wall, unable to improve the mix—which was being broadcast on the radio."

Continued Success with yes

Morphine's next release was 1995's *yes.* Rykodisc confidently issued the leadoff track, "Honey White," as a single, and the trio promptly hit the road again. The record earned more rave reviews—*Billboard* deemed it "one of the year's best releases," while *USA Today* gave the album 3 1/2 stars out of four and called it the group's "best album to date"—as did the band's now well-honed live act. "Morphine has developed from a surprisingly strong unit into a unique force in modern rock music," marveled Phil Gallo of *Daily Variety.* "There's no compromise within Morphine's caringly original songs that challenge notions of rhythm melody and even the use of instrumentation as the band bounces off tuneful skeletons from the closets of rockabilly, improvisational jazz, punk and blues."

yes also demonstrated significant, if not truly mainstream, commercial viability, debuting at the top of the *Billboard* Heatseekers chart and, despite losing some ground, remaining on the chart for months. As a Los Angeles record retailer told *Billboard,* "It's a rock thing, but it's not a rock thing—it's a *moody* rock thing, and there always seems to be a market for that stuff." Sandman expressed an eagerness to do "residencies" in the band's favorite cities—several gigs at the same small venue, rather than one in a larger space—as a way of offsetting the wear of nonstop touring. "It's a way to not have to travel every single day, and a way to get to see some of the cities we're interested in."

The members of Morphine have also had a hand in other projects—Sandman has played with the Pale Brothers, Hypnosonics, Supergroup, and Candybar, for example—and this freedom has allowed them, as Colley told *Alternative Press,* "to keep our chops up" and try different things. Resisting formula is a top priority for the band, as Sandman pointed out in *SF Weekly:* "We're trying to keep the definition of 'what's a Morphine song' pretty flexible. Pretty soon it's going to be just about anything. We've been holding back a lot of the stranger things. We're feeling braver now. It's a big cosmos out there."

Selected discography

Good, Accurate/Distortion, reissued by Rykodisc, 1992.
Cure for Pain (includes "Thursday," "Mary Won't You Call My Name," and "Cure for Pain"), Rykodisc, 1993.
yes (includes "Honey White"), Rykodisc, 1995.

Sources

Alternative Press, May 1995.
Billboard, February 12, 1994; February 11, 1995; March 25, 1995; April 15, 1995.
Boston Globe, May 20, 1994.
Boston Phoenix, March 17, 1995.
College Music Journal, April 1995.
Daily Variety, April 3, 1995.
Entertainment Weekly, March 17, 1995.
Metro Times (Detroit, MI), March 2, 1994.
New Yorker, April 10, 1995.
Option, March 1995.
Pulse!, November 1992; December 1993.
Raygun, April 1995.
Request, April 1995.
Rolling Stone, March 24, 1994; July 14, 1994; March 23, 1995.
SF Weekly (San Francisco, CA), March 29, 1995.
USA Today, April 3, 1995.

Additional information for this profile was obtained from Rykodisc publicity materials, 1995.

—Simon Glickman

Mudhoney

Rock band

Mudhoney set the stage for the emergence of grunge rock in the late 1980s. While other bands like Pearl Jam, Nirvana, and Soundgarden may have become better known faster, Mudhoney was getting the music out there before anyone. As Elizabeth Wurtzel put it in *Musician,* "When Kurt Cobain [of Nirvana] was still living in Olympia [WA], and still finding graffiti on his bathroom wall informing him that he smelled like Teen Spirit deodorant, Mudhoney was gigging around and laying down the tracks that would comprise the band's dazy, zoned-out, distortion-pedaled sound—which eventually became the Seattle scene's trademark."

It all began in the mid-1980s with Green River, Seattle's seminal grunge unit. Around 1988 Mark Arm—Mudhoney's rhythm guitarist and lead singer—quit Green River and hooked up with singer-guitarist Steve Turner. Turner had quit Green River a year earlier to attend college and study anthropology; Arm had already received his degree in English. (Jeff Ament and Stone Gossard—both of whom went on to play with Mother Love Bone and later to form Pearl Jam—were also

Photograph by Charles Peterson, © 1995 Reprise Records

199

Green River alumni.) Meanwhile, Arm and Turner joined with bass player Matt Lukin, who had just been kicked out of the Melvins, and drummer Dan Peters, who had drummed for many a band, including Nirvana. The band took the name "Mudhoney" from a Russ Meyer film. "We never meant to make an album," Turner told Wurtzel.

Not only did they make an album, they helped form an entirely new genre of music. Daniel Fidler described it in *Spin*: "The band's powerful combination of '60s garage rock and '70s-'80s punk ... has all but paved the way for Seattle bands to grow their hair out, take off their shirts, soak up the Zeppelin, and make moves toward the majors." *Rolling Stone* contributor Jason Fine declared, "Mixing '70s metal riffing and a no-frills punk sensibility, the Mudhoney sound echoes their name: It's dense, sloppy, distorted and full of disaffection." But the group's members have also been called goofballs and wiseasses. When asked why the bands who followed in their stead have had so much mass appeal, Arm suggested to Fidler, "They're good-looking.... But as soon as people see the plastic surgery we're getting, then things will change."

The Only True Grunge Band

Issues like looks *do* matter in the music industry, but the lack of major mainstream popularity for Mudhoney involved many factors. For one thing, according to Mudhoney, *true* grunge is not what really got so big. *Detour Magazine's* Jon Regardie suggested that "Mudhoney's oceans of feedback and distorted wah-wah

mess have never produced the palatable pop hooks that canonized Nirvana." Bandmember Turner noted in *Musician*: "I don't think [Nirvana's kind of success] is going to happen to us.... We don't play their kind of songs." He commented further in *CMJ*, "We knew we weren't a pop band. From the moment Nirvana hit, it made sense. We always thought they'd be huge, because it was their natural inclination. We're a grunge band; we're the only one left." Turner suggested that the bands that have become more popular did so because their music, no matter how alternative, still contained classic pop hooks and melodies. "In the end," a *Musician* contributor wrote, "grunge was just a catchy way to market punk rock. But without Arm's assorted bands ... there would have been little to market."

Until Nirvana's debut album broke all previous sales records, Mudhoney's 1991 effort, *Every Good Boy Deserves Fudge,* was the small, independent Sub Pop label's bestselling title. Sub Pop Records co-mogul Bruce Pavitt told *Spin* that "Mudhoney really set the stage for Nirvana. If *Superfuzz Bigmuff* [Mudhoney's first EP] hadn't been on the U.K. charts for a year and [the band] hadn't been a big sensation, who knows what would have happened to Nirvana?"

"Touch Me, I'm Sick," Mudhoney's first single, sold out its first three pressings. *Superfuzz Bigmuff* and their first LP, 1989's *Mudhoney*, won the band national acclaim in the independent rock world and got the group cited in an '89 *Rockpool* as the most preferred band by college radio programmers nationwide. Turner likes to describe their sound as "life-affirming, but a big f——you to society," he told Wurtzel. *Rolling Stone's* Trent Hill had this to say: "The group's brilliant early records ... mine a peculiar tension between sexual longing and a disgust with the possibility that that longing might be realized.... On those indie records, Mark Arm ... always sounds as though he's surprised and a little upset to find that he has somehow gained the cultural authority to deliver songs about the glories of sex, drugs and slutty women from the point of view of a newly slutty man."

Hungry for a Major Label Deal

With the release of *Every Good Boy Deserves Fudge,* the band grew hungry for a major label deal. "We keep thinking we'll get free meals from all these record companies trying to impress us," Turner told *Spin*. Arm continued, "We're really paying our dues. But everyone out there is stealing our moves. These young punks are just plugging themselves into the grunge computer and getting rich off it with lots of money in their pockets. And they're not sharing." Still, they wanted to make it clear that they didn't begrudge the guys in the big three—

Nirvana, Pearl Jam, and Soundgarden—any of their success. They're friends with those bands and are happy to ride in on their coattails.

When Nirvana put grunge through the roof, the major labels scrambled to sign like bands. Naturally they came sniffing after Mudhoney. The band didn't mind—they were sick of the money troubles their independent label Sub Pop was having. They nearly signed with Epic Records but insist that they chose not to because they weren't getting any free boxed sets—Warner Bros./ Reprise Records gave the band all the Jimi Hendrix reissues they wanted.

Mudhoney's first record for Reprise was *Piece of Cake*. Hill wrote in *Rolling Stone* that he felt "most of the record skitters between competent reworkings of the band's signature Stooges-meet-Blue Cheer sound and formulaic rock & role-playing that nobody, least of all Mudhoney, believes in anymore. As the band itself says on "Acetone": 'Oh, lord, what have we become? / We're not fooling anyone.'" Hill didn't think the album was completely without merit, however. "When Arm and company hit it," he continued, "as on 'Living Wreck,' 'Make It Now,' and the single "Suck You Dry," they go a long way toward making their new-found blues-metal vocabulary their own." *Musician* thought that *Cake* "sounds a lot like all the other Mudhoney albums, except that it's tighter and stronger, with more crunch and speed.... It's become increasingly clear that these guys couldn't sell out if they wanted to—*Piece of Cake* harks back to early Mudhoney, when the band's sound was crazier, crankier and far more instinctual."

The First and Last in Grunge

Just before recording *Cake*, Mudhoney contributed a song to writer-director Cameron Crowe's 1992 movie *Singles*. In an article for *Rolling Stone*, Tom Sinclair wrote, "[Mudhoney] offers a sardonic look at Seattle's sudden notoriety and the major-label race to snag the next big rock act with 'Overblown': 'Everybody loves us / Everybody loves our town / That's why I'm thinking lately / To be leavin' now.... It's so overbloowwwnn,' sings Mark Arm in his trademark bratty whine, before concluding, with venomous sarcasm, 'Long live rock & roll!'"

Singles and a few other mainstream films, along with the music, helped to spread grunge culture everywhere. Suddenly the garb of Pearl Jam's Eddie Vedder and Nirvana's Kurt Cobain was all the rage. Fashion runways saw models decked out in unkempt hair, cut-off army pants, and flannel flannel flannel. And, as often happens with media hype and fashion overkill, grunge

was suddenly a dirty word. In fact, it died. The capper came with Cobain's devastating suicide in 1994.

Grunge music didn't actually disappear, especially when the movement was just blossoming; they just stopped calling it by that name. The Seattle sound had become so mainstream it wasn't necessary to distinguish it from other forms of alternative rock and roll. Commenting on the release of Mudhoney's 1995 album *My Brother the Cow*, *Rolling Stone* contributor Grant Alden put it this way: "The first great grunge band from Seattle have composed the last great grunge record. That this has been accomplished so long after the fashion for flannel has expired is a delicious irony Mudhoney seem uniquely equipped to savor." Alden went on to say, "Mudhoney got by for years on a riff and a phrase, delivered with piercing intensity but tossed off as if the quality of their work were irrelevant.... [This time,] for the first time, the band entered the studio with more songs than were absolutely required. The result is stunning.... Grunge is dead. Long live grunge."

People magazine contributor Andrew Abrahams predicted the band's 1995 album might signal a crossover to the pop charts. "Mudhoney has injected *My Brother the Cow* with enough of the right elements—memorable choruses and tight grooves—to make it as commercially viable as the music of their friends and Seattle compatriots Pearl Jam.... By the time '1995' brings the record to a screeching, dissonant halt, the listener feels exhausted but satisfied. Leave the brooding anthems to Pearl Jam. Mudhoney delivers pure grunge—messy music that casts a powerful spell."

Pure grunge—perhaps that's the ticket. Many listeners and industry observers believe that Mudhoney invented it and are the only ones still doing it. Fame took the members of the Seattle music scene by surprise. Some have complained bitterly, some have taken long hiatuses; Cobain took his own life. But fame, Arm told *Rolling Stone* in 1995, "is not really a concern. I don't think we're in any danger of it happening to us." Mudhoney could well be much better off not rising to the top too quickly. Whether they like it or not, though, some critics feel they may get there eventually.

Selected discography

Superfuzz Bigmuff (EP), Sub Pop, 1988.
Mudhoney, Sub Pop, 1989.
Every Good Boy Deserves Fudge, Sub Pop, 1991.
(Contributors) *Soundtrack: Singles* (appear on "Overblown"), Epic Soundtrax, 1992.
Piece of Cake (includes "Acetone," "Living Wreck," "Make It Now," and "Suck You Dry"), Reprise, 1992.

(Contributors) *Freedom of Choice: Yesterday's New Wave Hits as Performed by Today's Stars,* Caroline, 1993.
Five Dollar Bob's Mock Cooter Stew (EP), Reprise, 1993.
My Brother the Cow (includes "1995"), Reprise, 1995.

Sources

Anti-Matter, November/December 1992.
CD Review, April 1995.
CMJ, April 1995.
Detour Magazine, March 1995.
Entertainment Weekly, August 21, 1992; October 23, 1992; November 19, 1993.
Guitar Player, February 1992; January 1993; January 1994.
Hits, April 17, 1995.
Melody Maker, February 11, 1989; March 11, 1989; March 24, 1989; April 8, 1989; May 20, 1989; June 10, 1989; August 19, 1989; October 28, 1989; December 2, 1989; December 9, 1989.

Musician, January 1993; June 1995.
New Times, March 9, 1995.
New York Times, October 31, 1992; April 20, 1994.
People, October 26, 1992; May 8, 1995.
Playboy, November 1992.
Request, April 1995.
RIP, July 1995.
Rolling Stone, August 20, 1992; January 7, 1993; January 21, 1993; January 26, 1995; April 6, 1995; June 1, 1995.
Spin, July 1991; February 1993.
Stereo Review, December 1992; May 1994.
Strobe, April 1995.
Village Voice, November 8, 1988.

Additional information for this profile was provided by Warner Bros./Reprise Records publicity materials, 1995.

—*Joanna Rubiner*

Gerry Mulligan

Saxophonist, arranger, composer

One of the most widely respected and admired jazz musicians of our time, Gerry Mulligan was the undisputed king of the baritone saxophone. He played a significant role in the evolution of jazz as a player, arranger, and composer, working with such legendary figures as Louis Armstrong, Count Basie, Duke Ellington, Billie Holliday, Lester Young, Miles Davis, and Jack Teagarden. High points of his career included the experimental group conceived in the late 1940s with Gil Evans, which led to the landmark recording *Birth of the Cool* under the leadership of Miles Davis. Having written and arranged 11 pieces for the seminal album, Mulligan then played a role in ushering in the laid-back sound known as West Coast Jazz in the early 1950s; his California-based quartet was renowned for both its lack of a piano and the presence of trumpeter Chet Baker. Mulligan also helped foster renewed interest in big band jazz with outfits that he formed in the 1960s.

Although making his reputation first as an arranger, Mulligan eventually earned widespread kudos for his playing. "As an improviser [Mulligan] was slower to

Photograph by Franca Rota, courtesy of Gerry Mulligan Productions

Born Gerald Joseph Mulligan, April 6, 1927, in New York, NY; son of an engineer; died of complications after surgery for a knee infection, January 20, 1996, in Darien, CT.

Played alto saxophone and arranged for dance bands, Philadelphia, PA, early 1940s; sold arrangements to WCAU-CBS radio orchestra director Johnny Warrington, Philadelphia, mid-1940s; arranged for Tommy Tucker's band and Elliott Lawrence at WCAU; composed music for Gene Krupa and Claude Thornhill orchestras, mid-1940s; played with Kai Winding and others, late 1940s; began focusing exclusively on baritone saxophone, 1947; wrote scores for Stan Kenton band, late 1940s; joined Miles Davis Nonet, late 1940s; formed pianoless quartet with Chet Baker, 1951; formed thirteen-piece Concert Jazz Band, 1960; toured with Dave Brubeck, 1968; wrote score for film version of Broadway comedy *Luv* and the French film *La Menace;* began playing soprano saxophone, mid-1970s; artist-in-residence, Miami University, 1974; led sextet, 1974-1977; formed 14-piece band, 1978; wrote symphonic music for baritone saxophone, 1980s; experimented with 20-piece band and electronic instruments, early 1980s; formed quintet with Scott Hamilton and Grady Tate, 1986; served as artistic director for series of summer jazz concerts in Chicago area, 1991; assembled Gerry Mulligan Tentet, 1992; toured Japan with Gerry Mulligan Quartet, 1993; taught jazz history, University of Bridgeport, Bridgeport, CT, beginning in 1994.

Selected awards: Grammy Award for best jazz instrumental performance by a big band 1982, for *Walk on the Water;* Connecticut Arts Award, 1982; became Duke Ellington Fellow, Yale University, 1988; elected to American Jazz Hall of Fame, 1991; elected to *Down Beat* Hall of Fame, 1994; won 29 consecutive *Down Beat* readers poll awards.

Mulligan was born in New York, but his father's work as an engineer demanded many job transfers, so the family moved frequently. Gerry began taking piano lessons at age seven, then learned to the play the clarinet. As a teenager he focused mostly on the saxophone. He loved the big band sound and developed an early interest in arranging. "I have a feeling that no matter what era I lived in, a hundred years ago or a hundred years from now, I'd always be interested in orchestration," he told *Down Beat* in 1989.

Early Knack For Arranging

Mulligan was encouraged in his arranging efforts by his music teacher. After his family moved to Philadelphia, he began selling arrangements to Johnny Warrington, musical director of the WCAU-CBS radio orchestra. In 1944 he arranged for and toured with Tommy Tucker's band, but Tucker lost interest when Mulligan's work became too jazzy. Playing alto sax, Mulligan performed with various dance bands around Redding and Philadelphia. He got his first taste of the limelight as a performer in the mid-1940s when he played baritone sax at Philadelphia's Academy of Music in a concert that showcased some of the hot new jazz performers of the day, including Charlie Parker, Dizzy Gillespie, and Sarah Vaughan. Mulligan performed well enough to earn an invitation from Parker to play in a jam session after the concert.

In 1946 Mulligan shifted his base of operations to New York City, where he concentrated on writing and arranging. His skill as an arranger was increasingly defined by his creation of "intricate inner parts, careful balance of timbres, and light swing," as described in *The New Grove Dictionary of Jazz.* "Mulligan was among the first to attempt to adapt the language of [bebop] for big band," asserted the *The Guinness Encyclopedia of Popular Music.* At age 19 he was writing, arranging, and sometimes playing for the orchestras of Gene Krupa and Claude Thornhill. His "Disc Jockey Jump," which he wrote for Krupa in 1947, was especially praised. According to the *New Grove Dictionary of Music and Musicians,* the arrangement for "Disc Jockey Jump" was particularly notable for "pitting a small group against the full ensemble, [foreshadowing] the resourcefulness of ... later, more personal works."

Developed Style on Baritone

The baritone saxophone became Mulligan's main instrument in 1947. His style of play was influenced by Harry Carney, though he ultimately moved away from Carney's mode. In a 1989 issue of *Down Beat* Mulligan

develop," allowed *The New Grove Dictionary of Music and Musicians,* "but [he] then established himself as an outstanding baritone saxophonist with a style that convincingly wed the harmonic and melodic characteristics of his own generation to a more traditional rhythmic discipline." In fact, Mulligan began improvising at age six. His piano teacher , a nun, told his mother not to waste her money on piano lessons, as he would always improvise a written tune.

attested, "I never tried to sound like Carney. I couldn't, impossible, but the fact was that any band that used the instrument well, the baritone had an effect on the sound." Mulligan's playing was also influenced by Deane Kincaide of Ozzie Nelson's band, as well as by Ernie Caceres, Serge Chaloff, Leo Parker, and Adrian Rollini. "It's quite possible that as a kid I heard Adrian Rollini [on radio]," he told *Down Beat* in 1994. "It's quite possible that that influence was stuck in my memory banks even though I wasn't aware of what or who it was."

Within a short span of time Mulligan became the top baritone sax player in jazz. "I came to the baritone with an idea of what I wanted to sound like, and then proceeded to try to do it," he explained in *Down Beat* in 1994. "It meant experimentation until I found a mouthpiece that would do what I want. Once I found that, I was on my way to being able to get out of the horn what I wanted."

Mulligan performed in groups with trombonist Kai Winding and other top musicians. He further honed his talent by studying with Gil Evans, whose place was a hangout for arrangers, and by spending time with artists such as John Lewis, Charles Mingus, Lee Konitz, Thelonius Monk, Miles Davis, Jack "Zoot" Sims, and others. A big step in his musical career was playing in the legendary Nonet, which featured Davis, Evans, Konitz on alto saxophone, J. J. Johnson or Winding on trombone, and Lewis on piano, among others. The group spent a remarkable residency at the Royal Roost in New York city in 1948. It was during 1949 and 1950 that Mulligan participated in the nonet's recording of its landmark *Birth of the Cool*. These sessions resulted in a groundbreaking album that would be elected to the Grammy Hall of Fame in 1982.

Contributed to *Birth of the Cool*

Heralding a new direction in jazz, *Birth of the Cool* emphasized improvisation in an orchestra setting. Mulligan's involvement was distinguished by a shift away from fast playing toward a more mellow style. His compositions and arrangements for the this ensemble resulted in heralded performances of songs such as "Jeru," "Boplicity," and "Godchild." Discussing these three songs, Barry McRae said in *The Jazz Handbook*, "[Mulligan's] gruff-toned but melodically uncomplicated baritone was well featured in all of them and it remained a style that was ageless."

Despite his artistic successes, Mulligan had trouble making ends meet during the late 1940s. He decided on a change of scene, and in 1951 he hitchhiked to California. On the West Coast Mulligan worked with his own ten-piece combo, then formed his legendary quartet without piano in 1952. This first quartet included Chet Baker on trumpet and Chico Hamilton on drums. Later members numbered Bob Brookmeyer, Zoot Sims, Art Farmer, and Red Mitchell. Some jazz mythology claims that there was no piano simply because one wasn't available when the group first got together.

The pianoless quartet proved to be an innovation that would influence musicians for decades to come. With this combo Mulligan thrived in a lower-volume setting than could groups with piano, which allowed the wind players to showcase themselves in a mellow, two-part counterpoint. The style became known as "cool" jazz; it offered an alternative to the more frenetic bebop of the era. The quartet became a perfect environment for displaying Mulligan's talent at countermelody, his saxophone and Baker's trumpet almost "talking" to each other. Improvisation was a hallmark of the group, and often Mulligan would play in a two-beat, dixieland style that made his solos quite danceable.

Touring frequently with the enormously popular Duke Ellington Orchestra, Mulligan's pianoless quartet was a major success. Though Mulligan and Baker did not get along personally, the former often said that playing with Baker was one of the more rewarding experiences of his career. The twosome worked together for only a year, but they generated a number of memorable recordings.

Mulligan played with various other groups during the 1950s, continuing to arrange on a free-lance basis. Some of his scores were performed by Stan Kenton's band. In 1960 he formed his Concert Jazz Band, which appeared with considerable fanfare at the famed Village Vanguard in New York City. This 13-piece ensemble also had no piano; it featured a percussion section, five reeds, and six brass instruments. Mulligan's new band "set the tone for big-band jazz into the '60s and continues to be an influence today," stated Mitchell Seidel in *Down Beat*. Mulligan wrote a number of highly praised scores for the band, managing to keep the sound intimate despite the larger number of instruments. The unit recorded five albums for the Verve label and toured the U.S. with the Woody Herman Orchestra and clarinetist Pete Fountain.
Mulligan played in small groups during the mid-1960s. He toured frequently with jazz pianist Dave Brubeck later in the decade. In 1972 his love of trains inspired him to create *The Age of Steam*, which featured a five-piece rhythm section of piano, guitar, bass, drums, and percussion. He expanded his playing range in the mid-1970s by taking up the soprano saxophone; he indulged his love of dixieland on clarinet.

From 1974 to 1977 Mulligan headed a sextet, and in 1978 he formed a 14-piece band that appeared at the Newport Jazz Festival in New York City. Over the next two years he coproduced "The Great Songs" show for the festival along with singer Mel Tormé. During this time and until 1988, he toured around the world alternating with the Concert Jazz Band and the quartet. Mulligan put together a 20-piece unit in the early 1980s that featured electronic instruments. But he returned to a smaller format by the middle part of the decade, working with a quintet for one recording in 1986.

Tackled Symphonic Music

Proving his versatility yet again, Mulligan began building a repertory of symphonic music for baritone saxophone in the 1980s. His long-standing affiliation with conductor Zubin Mehta led Mehta to invite him to play solo soprano saxophone in a performance of Ravel's "Bolero" with the New York Philharmonic in 1982. Two years later Mulligan completed his first symphonic composition for solo saxophone entitled "Entente for Baritone Saxophone and Orchestra." The work had its premiere in Italy. Mulligan and a new quartet later appeared with the New York Philharmonic in a highly praised concert series at Lincoln Center. His "Octet for Sea Cliff," a work for chamber orchestra, was released in 1990.

By 1992, yet another Mulligan band, a tentet christened "Re-Birth of the Cool," was on the road. The ensemble appeared at the JVC Jazz Festival at New York City's Carnegie Hall, then performed at European jazz festivals. Later that year Mulligan played with other top saxophonists at ceremonies celebrating President (and sax player) Bill Clinton's inauguration. His last quartet featured Ron Vincent on drums, Ted Rosenthal on piano, and Dean Johnson on bass.

Gerry Mulligan died of complications after surgery for a knee infection at his home in Darien, Connecticut, in 1996. He was 68. Over the course of his long career—he was still touring in 1995 and released a disc, Dragonfly, in October of that year—Mulligan compiled a list of achievements rivaled by few in the world of music. From composing movie scores to arranging works for big bands to playing everything from cool jazz to classical music, he mastered all aspects of the baritone saxophone. His unique musical adaptability never wavered. Record producer Todd Barkan saw Mulligan perform numerous times during his tour of Japan in 1993. He reported in Billboard, "[Mulligan] would play every night with as nonstop a stream of creative improvisations as I have ever heard from any jazz musician. He virtually never repeated himself."

Selected discography

Mulligan Plays Mulligan, Fantasy, 1951.
Funhouse, 1951.
Walkin' Shoes, 1952.
Gerry Mulligan and His Ten-tette, Capitol, 1953.
California Concerts, Volumes 1 and 2, Blue Note, 1954.
Gerry Mulligan Quartet at Storyville, Pacific Jazz, 1956.
Gerry Mulligan Meets Paul Desmond, Verve, 1957.
Gerry Mulligan and the Concert Band on Tour, Verve, 1960.
The Age of Steam, A&M, 1971.
Walk on the Water, DRG, 1982.
Little Big Horn, GRP, 1983.
Soft Lights and Sweet Music, Concord, 1986.
Symphonic Dreams, Intersound, 1987
Lonesome Boulevard, A&M, 1990.
Dream a Little Dream, Telarc Jazz, 1994.
Re-Birth of the Cool, GRP, 1992.
Dragonfly, Telarc Jazz, 1996.
Gerry Mulligan and the Concert Jazz Band En Concert, Europe 1, 1996.
The Gerry Mulligan Songbook, Pacific Jazz, 1996.

Sources

Books

The Blackwell Guide to Recorded Jazz, edited by Barry Kernfeld, Blackwell, 1991.
Cook, Richard, and Brian Morton, The Penguin Guide to Jazz on CD, LP and Cassette, Penguin, 1992.
The Guinness Encyclopedia of Popular Music, vol. 3, edited by Colin Larkin, Guinness Publishing, 1992.
McRae, Barry, The Jazz Handbook, G.K. Hall & Co., 1987.
Morgan, A., and R. Horricks, Gerry Mulligan: A Biography, Appreciation, Record Survey and Discography, London, 1958.
The New Grove Dictionary of Jazz, vol. 2, Macmillan, 1988.
The New Grove Dictionary of Music and Musicians, vol. 12, edited by Stanley Sadie, Macmillan, 1980.
The Oxford Companion to Popular Music, edited by Peter Gammond, Oxford University Press.

Periodicals

Billboard, February 3, 1996.
Down Beat, January 1989; December 1992; January 1994.
Musician, February 1996.
New York Times, June 30, 1992; June 22, 1993; March 5, 1994.

Additional information for this profile was obtained from Telarc International publicity materials, 1994, and Gerry Mulligan Productions.

—Ed Decker

Mystic
Revealers

Reggae band

The Mystic Revealers burst onto the global reggae music scene in 1985 with their first major single, "Mash Down Apartheid." Produced by reggae legend Jimmy Cliff, the song equates political revolution with personal spiritual upheaval in a potently mystical manner. Proceeds from its sale were donated to South Africa's African National Congress (ANC) to assist in that nation's struggle for racial, social, and political equality. This philanthropic gesture, unusual for a first-time success, accurately reflects the convictions, sensibilities, perspectives, and priorities of the Rastafarian, politically-oriented Mystic Revealers.

The Mystic Revealers were formed in the early 1980s in a rural village in the St. Andrew Parish of Jamaica. They draw upon Jamaica's rich, established reggae tradition of outspoken political awareness when writing and performing their original material. The band's four founding members form the heart of the group and include Kingston-born vocalist, guitarist, and songwriter Billy "Mystic" Wilmot; former Jalan and Earth Disciples drummer and record producer Nicholas "Drummie" Henry,

Courtesy of RAS Records

For the Record . . .

Original founding members include **Steve Davis** (born in Montego Bay, Jamaica), lead guitarist and vocalist; **Leroy "Lion" Edwards** (born in Kingston, Jamaica), bass guitarist; **Nicholas "Drummie" Henry** (born in the U.K.'s Shropshire region), drummer; and **Billy "Mystic" Wilmot** (born in Kingston), vocalist, guitarist, and songwriter. Later members include **William "Willigan" Cocking** (born in Kingston), percussionist; **Winston "Metal" Stewart**, keyboard player and lead guitarist; and **Robert "Patch" Walters**, keyboard player.

Group formed in the early 1980s in the St. Andrew Parish of Jamaica; hit global reggae music scene in 1985 with their first major single, "Mash Down Apartheid," produced by Jimmy Cliff; toured Japan, the United Kingdom, and Europe, 1985-91; performed at the Reggae Sunsplash Festival, 1988; released debut album, *Young Revolutionaries*, 1992; toured 17 American cities to promote the single and video "Religion" and the single "Remember Romeo"; performed at the EXPO 1992 in Seville, Spain; participated in the 1993 Reggae Sunsplash tour and the 50th birthday celebration concert for Bob Marley in Jamaica, 1995.

Addresses: *Record company*—RAS Records, P.O. Box 42517, Washington, D.C. 20015.

who hails from the Shropshire region of the United Kingdom; lead guitarist and vocalist Steve Davis of Montego Bay, Jamaica; and bass guitarist Leroy "Lion" Edwards of Kingston. Kingston-born percussionist William "Willigan" Cocking, keyboard player Robert "Patch" Walters, and keyboard player-lead guitarist Winston "Metal" Stewart were later additions to the band.

Authentic Approach to Reggae

In the early 1970s, when Wilmot, Henry, Davis, and Edwards were teenagers in Bull Bay, Jamaica—which is eight miles east of Kingston—they were surrounded by Rastafarians (followers of a complex set of mystical religious beliefs). Like the Rastas, they grew their hair into dreadlocks. Wilmot told *Vibe* magazine's Rob Kenner, "We were all awed by the magnificence of Rastafari. And at that time, it was what was hip. Them [sic] more look at you as a religious fanatic now if you tell them 'bout Rasta." *Caribbean News* contributor Jamie Lee Rake

noted, "There is a true Rastafarian spirit which lives and moves within [the Mystic Revealers], the first roots reggae band to emerge from the island of Jamaica in years."

Part of what distinguishes the Revealers from their more traditional counterparts is the fact that they utilize contemporary rap, hip-hop, and even disco sounds in their songs. Although the band is as conscientious and as roots-oriented as the older vanguard of reggae stars—such as Bob Marley and Peter Tosh—they have established their own style and sound, combining traditional reggae, dancehall, folk, and pop music. Kenner called the Mystic Revealers, "one of the few traditional roots bands still writing original songs that move the heart and the hips."

Reggae Show Stealers

Between 1985 and 1995 the Mystic Revealers played with such notable artists as Burning Spear, the Neville Brothers, Joan Baez, and Big Mountain. When the band performed at the Reggae Sunsplash Festival in 1988, they attracted international attention. Japanese producer Shinjiro Kanazawa of CHUKYO-TV featured the Revealers on Japanese television, deeming them the future of reggae music, and Canadian record producer Bob King lauded them as musicians with a universal appeal. They also performed at the EXPO 1992 in Seville, Spain. But the band garnered the most U.S. exposure and recognition from participating in the 1993 Reggae Sunsplash tour.

At a 50th birthday celebration concert held in Jamaica in honor of Bob Marley in February of 1995, the Mystic Revealers performed along with reggae greats the Wailers, Rita Marley, actress Vanessa Williams, vocalist Judy Mowatt, Toots Hibbert, Ziggy Marley, DJ Tony Rebel, and the veteran roots group Wailing Souls. *Billboard* contributor Garry Steckles, who attended the show, wrote, "The most solid and satisfying performance of the evening was provided by the Mystic Revealers, one of the few serious roots groups to emerge in Jamaica in recent years." Their rendition of "Natural Mystic," "We and Dem," and "Religion" won over numerous new fans that evening, including other respected reggae musicians.

Slow Start in the United States

Although the Mystic Revealers released their first single, "Mash Down Apartheid," in 1985, and the single was popular, they did not release their first album, *Young Revolutionaries*, until 1992. Between 1985 and

1991 the band toured Japan, the United Kingdom, and Europe. Then, in 1992, they toured 17 American cities to promote their singles "Religion" and "Remember Romeo." Their second album, *Jah Works*, was released in 1993 and their third, *Space and Time*, came out two years later.

The Mystic Revealers' songs reflect the band's commitment to basic human values. The single "Religion" is a straightforward reggae song, preaching love and protesting injustice, enhanced by Wilmot's sweetly lyrical voice. And singles such as "Young Revolutionaries" and "Living in Kingston" from the album *Young Revolutionaries* are a tribute to life in Kingston, a contribution to class consciousness, and a means for the Mystic Revealers to extol the virtues of a simple, honest life. The group's songs have also exerted a considerable influence on top-selling contemporary artists. Rake, writing in *Option*, suggested that the Revealers' track "Rasta Man" "provides a clue to where Seal might have picked a couple of his ideas."

The cover art for the band's album *Jah Works* features symbols from ancient Ethiopian scrolls, which highlight the performers' mystical, ancient Rastafarian perspective. The '93 release was listed at Number Two on the *Planet Reggae* Top 40 Chart. Meanwhile, their '95 effort, *Space and Time*, steadily gained popularity in the States. Video exposure in the United States—especially on the Black Entertainment Television (BET) cable network—is helping to spread word of the Mystic Revealers to mainland American listeners.

Selected discography

Singles

"Mash Down Apartheid," Gong Sounds, 1985.
"Gotta Be a Better World," Uni/MCA, 1993.
"Religion/Remember Romeo," RAS Records, 1994.

Albums

Young Revolutionaries, Gong Sounds, 1992.
Jah Works, RAS Records, 1993.
Space and Time, RAS/REP Records, 1995.

Sources

Billboard, June 4, 1994; February 25, 1995.
Caribbean News, June 7, 1994.
CMJ, February 28, 1992.
New Music Report, February 28, 1992.
New York Review of Records, July 1992.
Option, May/June 1992.
Santa Barbara Independent (Santa Barbara, CA), August 30, 1993.
Tahoe World (Tahoe City, CA), August 14, 1993.
Vibe, September 9, 1994.

Additional information for this profile was taken from RAS Records press materials.

—*B. Kimberly Taylor*

Oasis

Rock band

Big Picture/Archive Photos

Noel Gallagher, lead guitarist, songwriter and musical director of the English band Oasis declared, "I could say to any band member from any era, 'Pick your best song. Give me the best song you think you've written, and I'll pick mine.' And I think the best of ours would be above the best of theirs." This pronouncement from an interview with *Spin's* Neil Strauss gives a fair indication of Gallagher's confidence. Yet unlike many other U.K. hopefuls, Oasis managed with their first two records to match their voluminous hype with large-scale success. After a critically lauded debut and a couple of strong radio singles, they returned with an even more popular sophomore album; and despite alienating some listeners with their foul-mouthed, cocksure behavior and often lackadaisical live shows, they showed every indication of continued growth. And unlike many of their American compatriots, these self-proclaimed "lads" embraced stardom unequivocally. "I can't stand sniveling rock stars who complain about being famous," Noel groused to *Entertainment Weekly.* "Why not just work at a car wash or a McDonalds? There's no point in starting a band unless you wanna be famous."

The story of Oasis begins in the industrial, northern English town of Manchester, where Noel and his younger brother grew up. Their father poured concrete floors by day and worked parties at night as a country and western disc jockey. Though Noel was introduced to some classic country artists through his father, he discovered classic rock on his own. The crafted, eclectic pop of the Beatles, Led Zeppelin's thunderously adventurous rock, the glam-rock opuses of T. Rex, and punk standard-bearers the Sex Pistols' sneering iconoclasm all melded in his mind. He received his first guitar at age 13 and learned the Beatles' "Ticket to Ride"; soon he was writing his own songs. Though he shared his music with no one for many years, little else interested him. He gave up on school early on, as did many of his working-class peers. "As soon as I learned to read and write," he revealed to Jason Cohen of *Rolling Stone,* "I didn't even bother turning up half the time. I can't even spell, but who needs to spell? There was just nothing there for the musician in me." A period of rootlessness and petty crime followed.

"So I Started Me Own Band"

Liam Gallagher played soccer, which most of the world calls "football," and didn't gravitate toward music until the end of the 1980s, when Manchester became England's hot music town. Hosting a variety of successful bands that mixed post-punk energy with dance beats, "Madchester," as it was briefly known, swirled with excitement. Liam got together with some of his "mates," Paul "Bonehead" Arthurs and Paul McGuigan, and started up a band. McGuigan told Liam he couldn't play anything, he informed *Musician,* to which the younger Gallagher replied "'Then play bass, 'cause you only have to play the top string if you want.' So I said okay." They enlisted the only drummer they knew, Tony McCarroll, to round out the lineup. "We had f— all else to do," guitarist Arthurs recollected to *Rolling Stone.* "It was either get in a band or get drunk every night." The two pursuits turned out not to be mutually exclusive.

Noel, meanwhile, became the "guitar tech" for the band Inspiral Carpets, accompanying them on the road to keep their instruments and other equipment in shape. "I knew how to change strings, how to tune a guitar, and change a fuse or a plug, and that's about it, really," he told *Musician.* Though other guitar technicians he met possessed all manner of arcane knowledge about the gear, he admitted, "I haven't got a clue, mate. Not a clue. I just lied when I got the job."

Going on tour with the Inspirals was frustrating for him, since "they didn't treat us well at all, and I didn't like the music. They had a couple of good tunes, but they didn't have any spirit. They were just going through the motions for the money. And then, well, I'd be looking at them and thinking, 'F—ing hell, if they can get away with it, I can.' So I started me own band." In reality, he offered to take over Liam's band. Having written a number of songs during the Inspirals tour, he felt that his kid brother's group had little to offer beyond Liam's surprisingly powerful, sneering voice. He therefore announced that he would join—provided they stand aside and play his songs according to his exacting instructions. In

Rolling Stone he reported having said, "I can only do this one way: with me in complete control of it."

Definitely Wowed Critics, Fans

Oasis began working far more intensively. "All our friends would say, 'Let's get drunk, let's chase some women, let's take some drugs,'" Noel recounted in *Musician.* "We'd say, 'No, no, we have to practice.' They all thought we were mott [crazy] for quite a while." After spending the requisite period learning to play Noel's songs exactly as he wanted to hear them, Oasis talked themselves onto a bill at a Glasgow, Scotland club. Closing their set with an earsplitting rendition of the Beatles' "I Am the Walrus," they got a record offer from a member of the audience, Creation Records founder Alan McGee. "It was agreed that we were going to sign [a contract] that night," Noel told *Rolling Stone,* "but we didn't sign until two or three months later."

Their debut album, *Definitely Maybe,* was released in 1994 and synthesized the pop, glam-rock and punk influences that had informed Noel's youth. The band immediately became the darlings of the passionately fickle British music press. Thanks in part to singles like the evanescent ballad "Live Forever," the album rocketed up the English charts. Their status as darlings of U.K. rock scribes certainly derived in large part from their way with a pop tune, but the band's bad-boy attitude also contributed. "We always knew we were going to be good," Noel said with characteristic immodesty in *Guitar Player,* "because you don't write a song like 'Live Forever' and disappear. We weren't surprised that the album reached #1 in England and went gold. It was just surprising how fast it got there."

Unfazed By Skeptical Yanks

Things took a bit longer in the United States, where audiences and reviewers scarcely took Oasis' purported Godhead on faith. Despite largely glowing reviews for the album, the band's live shows often drew fire. Julia Rubiner complained about their "lackluster live set" in *Music Connection,* faulting Liam's "unvaried vocal presentation" and tendency to stand still with his hands behind his back most of the time. "Maybe delusions of grandeur pass for entertainment in England," Rubiner wrote, likening the band's performance to "the fulfillment of a contractual obligation." Onstage, Jason Cohen wrote in *Rolling Stone,* "Oasis act completely oblivious to the rich nuances and joyous, thudding impact of their music," and described their performance as "frustratingly passive-aggressive." A disgruntled concert-goer interviewed by *Musician's* Charles M. Young, meanwhile, dismissed the band as "a very loud version of [1970s bubblegum popsters] The Bay City Rollers." Yet the record fared quite well, thanks in large part to the airplay earned by "Live Forever."

Oasis very loudly replied to such criticism that they didn't care. They toured relentlessly—so much so that McGuigan had to take a break from the band, citing "exhaustion," and was briefly replaced—and proudly indulged in classic rock and roll pursuits like drinking, drugs and the trashing of hotel rooms. They also engaged in a very public feud with fellow Brit band Blur and derided most other bands, especially American ones. Their acerbic *esprit de corps* had its limits, of course; Liam and Noel quarrelled constantly. "Some days we get on really well," Noel reported to *huH*'s Mark Blackwell. "Other days we f—ing ate the sight of each other. But that's life." And the band's high opinion of itself was recorded faithfully in a stream of interviews. "I'm always sayin', 'We're the best band in the world,'" Liam informed Blackwell. "The reason I say it is because we jus' f—ing *are*. I don't say it for the sake of just sayin' it. I *believe* it, man. Every band should be able to go, 'Yeah, we're the best band in the world,'" though he added that not many bands could say so with conviction.

Morning Glory Showed Growth

While the band's meteoric rise and unflinching arrogance invited many a prediction—and no doubt a fervent wish or two—that they would wind up as one-hit wonders, Oasis instead came back stronger on their sophomore effort. They replaced McCarroll with Alan White before going back in to the studio, however. "Tony's a nice guy and all that," Noel explained to Elysa Gardner of *Rolling Stone*. "But the band is moving on, and he wasn't really up to standards." McCarroll would later file suit against the band for firing him wrongfully. The new album, *(What's the Story) Morning Glory?*, showed greater songwriting depth, according to reviewers like *Rolling Stone*'s Jon Wiederhorn, who called

it "more than a natural progression; it's a bold leap forward that displays significant personal growth."

Morning Glory stormed up the American charts on the strength of "Wonderwall," another anthemic ballad. By its fourteenth week in release it had reached the number-eighteen position on the *Billboard* 200 album chart, and was dubbed the week's "pacesetter" disc. Such triumphs hardly stunted Noel Gallagher's already towering self-regard. If Oasis had existed at the same time as the Beatles, he told *Spin*, "I think we'd *be* the Beatles." He described his band, "an unstoppable ball that is rolling down a mountain, and when it gets to the end, that's it. It's finished. I don't think any of us will be able to go off and do something else and have it be as big as that." In *Musician* he proclaimed, "I just want a back catalog, something for the kids to plagiarize. I'll have done my service to rock 'n' roll. So long as I have my music and I feel enthusiastic, that's all I want. I want to realize my own potential."

Selected discography

Definitely Maybe (includes "Live Forever"), Creation; reissued on Epic, 1994.
(What's the Story) Morning Glory? (includes "Wonderwall"), Epic, 1995.

Sources

Billboard, January 20, 1996.
Entertainment Weekly, March 10, 1995.
Guitar Player, March 1995.
huH, April 1995.
Music Connection, March 6, 1995.
Musician, September 1995.
Rolling Stone, December 15, 1994; May 18, 1995; August 5, 1995; October 19, 1995.
Spin, January 1995; November 1995; December 1995; February 1996.

—Simon Glickman

The Ohio Players

Rhythm and blues/soul band

The Ohio Players combine funk, disco, country, jazz, soul, and rock to create a uniquely danceable, multilayered, and memorable sound. The band reached an apex of popularity in the 1970s during the funk and disco era and with the advent of rap and hip-hop, has enjoyed an enthusiastic renaissance since the mid-1990s.

The brainchild of guitarist Robert Ward, the group began as the Ohio Untouchables in Dayton, Ohio, in 1959. Bassist Marshall Jones, saxophonist and flutist Clarence "Satch" Satchell, and trumpeter Ralph "Pee Wee" Middlebrook comprised the unchanging core of the group over the decades. Apart from this trio, the band's membership changed countless times over the course of almost four decades. Guitarist and vocalist Leroy "Sugarfoot" Bonner, keyboardist and percussionist William "Billy" Beck, conga player Robert "Kuumba" Jones, trumpeter Marvin "Merv" Pierce, percussionist James "Diamond" Williams, and rhythm guitarist and vocalist Clarence "Chet" Willis completed the band in the 1990s.

MICHAEL OCHS ARCHIVES/Venice, CA

As the Ohio Untouchables, the group worked backup in Detroit for the Falcons—whose lead singer was the young and incomparable Wilson Pickett—on their 1962 hit single "I Found a Love." Five years later, in 1967, the Untouchables changed their name to the Ohio Players, moved back to Dayton, and performed as a funky, soulful octet.

Debut Album Released in 1971

The group then moved to Los Angeles and remained there until the end of the 1960s before relocating once again back to their home state of Ohio. The funk and rhythm and blues music of the early 1970s was heavily influenced by bands like Sly & the Family Stone—bands that fused rock with funk and soul. The Ohio Players were eager to experiment as well, and their funky sound grew more progressive and distinctive. "Sugarfoot" Bonner added a nasal, almost comical quality to the band's vocal sound, rendering their singles danceable and catchy.

The Ohio Players released their debut album, *Pain*, in 1971 on Detroit's Westbound Records, a label shared

by George Clinton's Funkadelic band. They followed their debut with *Pleasure* a year later, then *Ecstasy* in 1973. The albums were only moderately successful, but the recording experience was invaluable for the band to hone its signature trademarks: large horn-powered tracks, odd background sounds such as whistles and alarms, and absurd, salacious lyrics. In 1974 the Ohio Players signed with Mercury Records; by then the band's fluctuating membership had finally stabilized.

Southern Ohio a Seminal Spot for Music

The Ohio Players' southern Ohio environment shaped their diverse tastes and the breadth of their musical knowledge. James Brown recorded many of his greatest hits in Cincinnati's King Records studio in the 1950s and 1960s, the soulful Isley Brothers and funk superstar Bootsy Collins were both products of the Cincinnati music scene, and during the 1970s and 1980s dance groups such as Lakeside, the Deele, Midnight Star, and Slave also emerged from the southern Ohio region.

There were no radio stations in southern Ohio that played strictly black music in the early and mid-1970s, so the Ohio Players would cover whatever was on the radio, which was usually an eclectic mix such as Peter, Paul & Mary, Grand Funk Railroad, Tower of Power, and the Jazz Crusaders. To attract the attention of record store browsers, the band became known for its racy album jackets, usually featuring an undressed woman in a suggestive pose. When they switched over to Mercury Records, the risque cover tradition continued; for example, one album pictured a nude woman covered in honey. In time, even people who did not purchase the Ohio Players' albums began to look forward to the band's next album jacket.

Hit Their Stride in Mid-1970s

In 1974 the Ohio Players released their first album for Mercury, *Skin Tight,* and ushered in a three-year run at the top of the R&B and dance music charts. The singles "Skin Tight" and "Jive Turkey" were both Top Ten R&B hits. The Ohio Players were adding more and more sound effects with each album, and when *Fire* was released in 1974, it pushed the envelope even further with sirens, high-pitched squeals, and space bleeps.

Fire is arguably the crown jewel in the Ohio Players' collection of albums. The bandmembers listened to the LP's tracks—without the vocals—in Los Angeles with Stevie Wonder, and they each knew even then that the album was going to be a tremendous hit. The title track was created out of a high-octane instrumental jam session, fusing funk, rock, and fiery drums. It became the band's first Number One single on the pop charts.

Fire also included a rare stab at social commentary with the single "I Want to Be Free." Aside from this album, the Ohio Players avoided heavy or moralistic lyrics, preferring a lighthearted, silly, almost nonsensical approach to their music. The band's next Number One single was "Love Rollercoaster" on the *Honey* album in 1975, followed by "Who'd She Coo?" in 1976 on *Contradiction;* then the string of hit singles ended. "O-H-I-O," released on *Angel* in 1977, was the band's last major single to become a hit, but the Ohio Players continued to tour well into the 1990s.

The influence of the Ohio Players is obvious in the music of the 1990s. Their songs have been heavily sampled by West Coast rap and hip-hop groups, most notably Dr. Dre and his "G-Funk" sound. Primus, the Red Hot Chili Peppers, and Soundgarden have all borrowed stylistically from the Ohio Players, and Soundgarden covered their single "Fopp" note for note.

With an extensive touring schedule and the 1995 release of the Mercury/Chronicles "Funk Essentials" collection—a seven-album overview of 1970s funk-rock-soul music that includes a compilation of the Ohio Players' material called *Funk on Fire!*—the band remained in the musical limelight two decades after the release of their best-known songs.

Selected discography

Pain, Westbound Records, 1971.
Pleasure, Westbound Records, 1972.
Ecstasy, Westbound Records, 1973.
Skin Tight, Mercury, 1974.
Fire, Mercury, 1974.
Honey, Mercury, 1975.
Contradiction, Mercury, 1976.
Gold, Mercury, 1977.
Angel, Mercury, 1977.
Mr. Mean, Mercury, 1977.
Jass-Ay-Lay-Dee, Mercury, 1978.
Funk on Fire!, Mercury/Chronicles, 1995.

Sources

The Aquarian, July 5, 1995.
Billboard, May 20, 1995.
Boston Globe, June 22, 1995.
Boston Phoenix, June 23, 1995.
Camden Courier-Post (New Jersey), June 20, 1995.
Charleston Post and Courier (South Carolina), June 15, 1995.
Philadelphia Inquirer, June 23, 1995.

Additional information for this profile was taken from the liner notes to *Funk on Fire!,* written by Alan Light, editor-in-chief of *Vibe* magazine.

—B. Kimberly Taylor

Johnny Otis

Singer, bandleader, producer

Courtesy of Johnny Otis

Johnny Otis, son of Greek immigrants, grew up in an ethnically mixed neighborhood in Vallejo, California during the 1920s. Even before falling in love with the black musical traditions, Otis identified with the culture of his black childhood friends and came to think of himself as black. As he wrote in the preface to his 1968 book *Listen to the Lambs*—penned largely in reaction to the Watts riots of 1965—"I reacted to the way of life, the special vitality, the atmosphere of the black community. . . this difficult to describe quality. . . popularly known as 'soul.'"

Johnny Otis lived the life of soul at the center of black music for starting in the 1940s. In 1939, having quit high school, Otis heard Count Basie at the San Francisco World's Fair and became interested in music. After taking up the drums, Otis played boogie-woogie and blues with a local Berkeley band, gradually moving on to regional bands and playing throughout the west. By this time he had married a black woman named Phyllis Walker, a sweetheart since high school and in 1943, Otis organized a group named after himself and partner Preston Love, the Otis Love Band.

The Otis Love Band worked at a club in Nebraska for a while but Otis soon left to play drums for Harlan Leonard at Los Angeles' Club Alabam. By 1945, Otis formed his first big band (sixteen pieces) to serve as the club's house ensemble. Otis also worked as a studio drummer, making recordings with various artists including Lester Young and Charles Brown. In 1946 Otis had his first hit record with a version of Earle Hagen's "Harlem Nocturne." That same year Otis' big band toured the country with the Inkspots.

By the time Otis' band returned home in 1947, the heyday of the big band had already passed while audiences rushed to listen to the blues. Otis, losing no time, trimmed down his crew to a smaller combo but kept the trombone, trumpet, and two saxes. "What you had was a small big band playing blues and that sound became R&B," Otis stated in an interview for the *Encyclopedia of Pop, Rock & Soul*. In 1948, Otis' band opened the Barrel House Club in the Watts section of Los Angeles. From the many black R&B acts at that club, Johnny Otis put together what eventually became known as "The Johnny Otis Show." This group, on the power of singers like Little Esther Phillips, Mel Walker, Devonia "Lady Dee" Williams and others, hit the R&B top forty charts an impressive 15 times between 1950 and 1952.

Otis' knowledge of R&B music, his connections and his popularity made him a natural promoter of the music he loved. Prompted by his desire to spend more time with his family, Otis quit touring in 1955. He became a Los Angeles disc jockey with an immensely popular radio

Born John Veliotes, December 28, 1921, in Vallejo, California, the son of Greek immigrants; married; wife's name, Phyllis; children: John, Jr. (Shuggie); Nicky; Daryl Jon; Janice; and Laura.

Co-founder of the Otis-Love Band, 1943.formed first big band in 1945; recorded first hit record, "Harlem Nocturne," 1946; formed the Johnny Otis Show, 1948; quit touring in 1955 and became a disc jockey and began a record label, Dig Records; signed with the Capitol label in the late 50s and wrote and recorded his biggest hit, "Willie and the Hand Jive"; appointed deputy chief of staff for California congressman, Mervin Dymally; founded and ministered at his Landmark Community Church in Los Angeles; continues to record and tour.

Address: *Office*—7105 Baker Ln., Sebastopol, CA 95472.

show which led to a television show, and later started his own record label, Dig Records. He ran both the television and radio show out of an office building where, as George Lipsitz noted in an introduction to Otis' 1993 book *Upside Your Head*, Otis "continued to record hit records himself and to serve as a talent scout for other labels such as Don Robey's Peacock Records from Houston."

As the racial climate of the 1950s and the aversion to rock and roll began to merge in Los Angeles, rock and roll shows were eventually forced from the city by police pressure. The El Monte Legion Stadium, outside the city limits, became the site of a series for legendary rock and roll concerts by Otis and other performers. But in the overtly racist and frightened atmosphere of the times, this too proved intolerable to the powers that be; they revoked a stadium dance license granted to Otis' then partner Hal Zeiger, only relenting thanks to pressure from the ACLU and the NAACP.

At the same time attempts were made to crush the live performances, major labels recognized the profit potential and moved into the R&B arena. Otis succumbed to the money offered and signed with Capitol Records. There he recorded the song "Willie and the Hand Jive" in 1958, possibly the biggest hit of his career. Yet Otis professed to be generally unhappy with this move to Capitol, having abandoned his black roots in favor of making "contrived rock and roll shit" as he told Lipsitz. Other forces, namely that of the British rock invasion, spelled the end of the R&B era.

During the subsequent decade, Otis served his chosen community in non-musical ways. For ten years he acted as deputy chief of staff to a politician named Mervin Dymally. Dymally served in the California State legislature and eventually U.S. Congress. Otis also ministered, via his nondenominational Landmark Community Church, in south central Los Angeles. This church would remain active until the mid-1980s. In the late 1960s Otis, together with his guitar-playing son Johnny Jr. (called "Shuggie"), began making records again starting with *Cold Shot*. During the 1970s Otis also continued to produce, efforts of this time including albums of Louis Jordan and T-Bone Walker.

The late 1980s and early 1990s found Otis as active as ever: selling an organic line of fruit juice, making radio broadcasts, and painting and sculpting works that reflected his love of African American culture. Further, Otis continued to tour with a 13 person band whose attraction was no doubt in part nostalgic. A revival of interest in 1950s R&B prompted Capitol Records to reissue Otis' work for that label, and Arhoolie, a record company long-interested in preserving American music, put out Otis' *Spirit of the Black Territory Bands* in 1993. Through this album, listeners may get a sense of Otis' music during the 1940s and visit a vanished era.

Selected discography

Singles

"Harlem Nocturne," Excelsior, 1945.
"Mistrustin' Blues," Savoy, 1950.
"Cupid's Boogie," Savoy, 1950.
"Deceivin' Blues," Savoy, 1950.
"Freight Train Boogie," Regent, 1950.
"Love Will Break Your Heart," Savoy, 1951.
"Gee Baby," Savoy, 1951.
"All Night Long," Savoy, 1951.
"Call Operator 210," Mercury, 1952.
"Willie and the Hand Jive," Capitol, 1958.
"Country Girl," Kent, 1968.

Albums

Harlem Nocturne Excelsior, 1946.
Rock and Roll Hit Parade, Dig, 1957.
The Johnny Otis Show, Capitol, 1958.
Cold Shot Kent, 1969.
Cuttin' Up Epic, 1970.
The Johnny Otis Show Live at Monterey, Epic, 1971.
The New Johnny Otis Show, Alligator, 1981.
The Capitol Years, Capitol, 1988.
Spirit of the Black Territory Bands (Johnny Otis and His Orchestra) Arhoolie, 1992.
Too Late to Holler, Night Train/City Hall, 1995.

Sources

Books

Hildebrand, Lee and Mary Lovelace O'Neal, *Colors and Chords: The Art of Johnny Otis,* Pomegranate Artbooks, 1995.

Otis, Johnny, *Listen to the Lambs,* Norton & Co., 1968.

Otis, Johnny, *Upside Your Head,* Wesleyan University Press, 1993.

Pareles, Jon and Patricia Romanowski, *The Rolling Stone Encyclopedia of Rock & Roll,* Rolling Stone Press/Summit Books, 1983.

Stambler, Irwin, *Encyclopedia of Pop, Rock & Roll,* St. Martin's Press, 1989.

Periodicals

DownBeat, March, 1993.

—*Joseph M. Reiner*

Twila Paris

Singer, songwriter

Courtesy of Sparrow Media Relations

Often compared to famed songwriter Fanny Crosby for her musical homage to God, Twila Paris is among "modern inspirational music's most prolific singer-songwriters," according to Thom Granger in the *All Music Guide.* She has frequently been referred to as "the modern-day hymn-writer" and has written and recorded many charting singles in Christian music since the early 1980s, including over 15 Number One hits. Her songs are gentle prayers put to music, with an up-tempo soft rock sound that closes the gap between traditional and contemporary inspirational music.

Virtually every Paris song focuses on relationships of a spiritual nature rather than earthly intimacy between two people. While not overly powerful, her voice has an ethereal quality that is well-suited to her choice of musical genre. In discussing Paris's *Sanctuary* album in 1992, Robert L. Doerschuk wrote in *Keyboard* that Paris has a "beautiful vocal timbre, which compensates for an apparently limited range."

Many Paris recordings have enjoyed long stays on the Christian music charts, and their success has made her a perennial nominee for the annual Gospel Music Association (GMA) Dove Awards. A number of her compositions are printed in hymnals used in churches around the world, among them "We Will Glorify," "Lamb of God," "How Beautiful," and "Faithful Men."

Comes from Religious Family

Devotion to God runs deep in the Paris family, with a dedication to ministry going back four generations. Her great-grandparents were itinerant preachers in Arkansas and Oklahoma who held outdoor revival meetings and established churches. Paris recounted this experience in "Seventy Years Ago," a song on her *Beyond a Dream* album. Musical talent also runs in the Paris family. When Twila Paris was a little girl, her grandmother wrote religious songs that were passed out at evangelical meetings. And her father, Oren Paris, is a minister as well as an accomplished musician and songwriter.

Paris sang at church before she was old enough to attend school. She began developing her instrumental talent at the age of six, when she started taking piano lessons. By the time she was performing in her high school choir, Paris was determined to become a choral teacher. She began to consider songwriting after attending a Christian discipleship school, where she decided that music would be a perfect way to express her feelings about God. Paris spent two years working full time with Youth with a Mission (YWAM), a project directed by her father and founded by her uncle, Loren

Born in 1958; daughter of Oren (a minister, musician, and songwriter) Paris; married Jack Wright.

Began singing in church choir as a preschooler; spent a year at a Christian discipleship school; served two years as staff member with Youth with a Mission (YWAM); recorded first album, *Knowin' You're Around,* 1981; wrote "Carry the Light," theme song for world evangelism project Target 2000: "The Great Commission Torch Run," 1989; worked with producers Brown Bannister and Richard Souther, 1990s; began serving as spokesperson for the Parable Group stores, 1993; joined Young Messiah Tour, 1993; began work on the Chapel of the Air radio program, 1994; performed at the White House, 1994; released *Beyond a Dream,* 1994.

Selected Awards: Gospel Music Association (GMA) Dove Award and Praise & Worship Album of the Year Award for *Sanctuary,* 1992; GMA Dove Award for female vocalist of the year, 1993 and 1994.

Addresses: *Management*—Sparrow Communications, P.O. Box 5010, Brentwood, TN 37024-5010.

Cunningham. "I began to realize how much hollowness and self-righteousness there had been in my Christianity, growing up as a preacher's kid," she said in the *Wall Street Journal.* "It was like God was doing major surgery on my heart.... With all that happening so fast, I needed an outlet. As a musician, I very naturally began to write songs."

Musical success was not instant for Paris. She needed to take out a bank loan to pay for her first recording; it took four years of selling cassettes to pay it off. Before long, however, her message had begun to break through. Starting in 1984, she received a string of nominations for Gospel Music Association female vocalist of the year—a hefty nine nominations in all. Her first album, *Knowin' You're Around,* was released in 1981 on Milk & Honey Records, and from that point on she averaged about an album a year into the mid-1990s. Every one of her songs celebrates love of God, and her continuing dedication to Christian missions led her to write the theme song "Carry the Light" for Target 2000 "The Great Commission Torch Run" in 1989. Paris has also performed a number of times with the Young Messiah Tour.

After a string of triumphs in the 1980s, a high point for Paris came in 1990 with the release of *Cry for the Desert.*

Her first album produced by Brown Bannister, this release on the Star Song label helped to spark new development in her musical creativity. As she told *Billboard* in 1992, "Things changed with 'Cry for the Desert.' My own musicality was involuntarily awakened. For the first time, I was on the road a lot when I'd usually write. I began to write more than ever, but it was away from the piano.... I began writing things I never would have written at the piano because I've been afraid to use the full range of my imagination at the piano—mostly because I'm such a limited pianist!"

Hit Career High with Souther

In the early 1990s, Star Song's Darnell Harris introduced Paris to musician-producer Richard Souther at Paris's Arkansas home. The meeting led Souther to produce, arrange, and play on Paris's 1991 album *Sanctuary,* which many critics considered her best to date. In *Billboard,* Bob Darden called the album "one of 1991's best," adding, "It is a brilliant, haunting piece of work." Critics made note of Souther's important "new age" influence. Granger wrote in the *All Music Guide* that the album "set new musical standards in the inspirational field for arrangement and production ideas." And Doerschuk asserted in *Keyboard,* "Throughout *Sanctuary,* Souther's wispy fills, beautifully designed and unerringly placed, never fail to shine." Paris herself praised Souther's contribution to the work. "It is difficult to say enough about Richard's arrangements and production," she told *Billboard.* "[*Sanctuary*] is more accurately called a collaboration between us than a solo project of my own."

Paris's goal in recording *Sanctuary* was to create "a worship album for people who like 'Cry for the Desert.'" As she explained in *Billboard,* "I thought, 'What have I done for people who want to be in a contemplative frame of mind?' 'Sanctuary' is for them, whether they're listening in their car on a country road or listening while they read their Bible. At the same time, we wanted it to be something artistically that could inspire and challenge people who like contemporary music or cutting-edge music."

Hot Name at the Gospel Music Association Awards

After years of extensive touring and album production, Paris retreated from performing and recording during the first half of 1992 so that she could spend more time with her husband, Jack Wright. That year she was nominated for seven Dove Awards, and her *Sanctuary* album became the top-selling album of her career. She won the coveted Dove Award for female vocalist of the year in both 1993 and 1994. Paris helped spread the gospel even more by joining up with the Chapel of the Air radio program in 1994. The program featured her songs in 70 nationwide conferences, as well as in videos and printed materials meant to enrich the worship experience through music.

In 1994 Paris also performed at the White House with Michael English, Steve Green, Carman, Daryl Coley, and other Gospel Music Association performers. That same year she released *Beyond a Dream,* which continued her trend toward "modernization." "Paris spun a few heads with this one, featuring her most contemporary material to date, and a bit of a new and more confident vocal approach to match it," wrote Granger of the album in the *All Music Guide.* "This album is very current," said Paris of *Beyond a Dream* in a Sparrow Communications press release. "It talks about how to face what's going on in the world, not from the point of me being some sort of an authority, but from the struggles that I'm going through and writing as I go through them. It was also the biggest stretch for me so far, artistically." Many of the album's songs assure Christians of their security in a world of confusion, emphasize God's mercy, and address other religious themes. Other songs pay homage to Paris's spiritual, ethnic, and geographic roots.

Paris has appeared on numerous magazine covers and television programs showcasing her talents as a performer of Christian music. By 1995 she was continuing to chart on the Contemporary Christian Top 40, never wavering from her musical praise of the Lord. "We sing about the Atonement, but it cost the Lord something to give us that," she said in the press release. "We can have fun with the music; that's okay. But on another level, that respect should always be there—concern for

the message, and concern for those to whom we would deliver the message."

Selected discography

Knowin' You're Around, Milk & Honey, 1981.
The Warrior Is a Child, Milk & Honey, 1984.
The Best of Twila Paris, Milk & Honey, 1985.
Cry for the Desert, Star Song, 1990.
Sanctuary, Star Song, 1991.
Beyond a Dream, Star Song, 1994.

Selected writings

(With Robert Webber) *In This Sanctuary,* Star Song Communications, 1993.

Sources

Books

Erlewine, Michael, Chris Woodstra, and Vladimir Bogdanov, editors, *All Music Guide: The Best CDs, Albums & Tapes,* Miller Freeman Books, 1994.

Periodicals

Billboard, February 22, 1992; March 21, 1992; February 25, 1995.
Keyboard, March 1992.
Wall Street Journal, January 6, 1993.

Additional information for this profile was obtained from Sparrow Communications publicity materials.

—Ed Decker

Don Pullen

Pianist, composer

Hailed as "one of the major jazz pianists of his generation" by Peter Watrous in his 1995 *New York Times* obituary, Don Pullen was known for his innovative free jazz that synthesized influences ranging from modern European classical compositions to American gospel to Brazilian jazz.

An accomplished organist as well as pianist, Pullen's trademark was a highly aggressive attacking of the keyboard. He often used his knuckles, backs of hands, and even elbows to generate his distinctive sound. As Watrous noted, "Pullen was one of the most percussive pianists in jazz. His improvisations brimmed with splashed clusters, hammered notes and large two-handed chords." Also incredibly versatile, Pullen was able to evoke both instantly likable songs as well as more dissonant ones. "He plays some of the most accessible melodies and tenderest ballads of any pianist around," noted Kevin Whitehead in *Down Beat.* "But at other times, he'll give the piano the back of his hand—literally—rolling his wrist 180 degrees or so and running lightning-stroke glisses up the treble register with his knuckles."

Photograph by Tom Copi, MICHAEL OCHS ARCHIVES/Venice, CA

For the Record . . .

Born December 25, 1941, in Roanoke, VA; died of lymphoma, April 22, 1995, in East Orange, NJ; children: Andre, Don, Keith, Tracey. *Education:* Attended John C. Smith University, Charlotte, NC.

Played piano in a church and local bands; studied with Muhal Richard Abrams in Chicago; made first recordings, early 1960s; led first band, 1965-70; played piano and organ for Ruth Brown, Big Maybelle, Arthur Prysock, and other R&B singers, 1960s; worked with Nina Simone, 1970-1971; collaborated on recordings with Charles Mingus, 1973-1975; played with Art Blakey, 1974; appeared in festivals at Umbria, Italy, 1974-1975, and Montreux, Switzerland, 1975; began recording as solo artist, 1975; led 360 Degree Music Experience with Beaver Harris, late 1970s; formed quartet with Charles Adams, 1979; worked with Brazilian, African, and Native American musicians, 1990s.

Pullen began his playing career as a church pianist, an experience that would factor heavily into his later jazz style. During this period he studied classical music to help with his gospel training, while also playing in small bands in his hometown of Roanoke, Virginia. Later, as a college student in North Carolina, he immersed himself in the recordings of Art Tatum, Ornette Coleman, Eric Dolphy, and pianist Clyde "Fats" Wright, who was also his cousin. The young Pullen was especially impressed with Coleman's *This Is Our Music* and Dolphy's *Live at The Five Spot.*

While on his way to New York City in 1964, Pullen made a stop in Chicago and studied with Muhal Richard Abrams, an experience that had a major impact on his developing talent. "It was only two weeks," said Pullen of that stopover in *Down Beat,* "but it was a very important two weeks, because at that time I was still struggling with questions like, 'Do I sound right, do I sound okay?' I had no one, no criteria to go by." By that time Pullen was already poised to venture beyond the standard range of his instrument. "I remember having ambitions to make the piano be able to bend notes, like horns can bend," he added in *Down Beat.*

In the early Sixties began Pullen playing with Hugh Masekela and Miriam Makeba. His first recordings were with a quartet that featured reed player Giuseppe Logan, bassist Eddie Gomez, and drummer Milford Graves. He also did musical arrangements for the King Records label in New York City. Although he frequently played organ as well as piano for R&B singers such as Ruth Brown, Big Maybelle, and Arthur Prysock, his chief interest by mid-decade was free jazz, and he became closely associated with the jazz avant-garde. Sometimes he fused his experimental piano work into his R&B organ playing. By the end of the Sixties Pullen was playing an extremely percussive, freewheeling piano with Logan, Graves, and others, while also working steadily as an organist for lounge singers. "People who knew me as an organ player did not know me as a piano player, and vice versa," he told Whitehead in *Down Beat.*

Mingus Collaboration Proved Pivotal

Pullen led his own combo from 1965 to 1970, and did some recording work with soul singer Nina Simone in the early Seventies. When he began playing with noted bluesman Charles Mingus in 1973 after being recommended by Mingus's drummer, Roy Brooks, his talent became recognized by a much larger audience. Pullen was invited into the Mingus ensemble because of his "knack for negotiating the brawny side of the blues and the protracted expressionism of the avant-garde," according to Jim Macnie in *Billboard.* In the *New York Times,* Watrous added that "Mingus prized what Mr. Pullen had to offer: a church-driven power, a blues sensibility and a harmonic sophistication." In his initial recording with Mingus, 1974's *Mingus Moves,* Pullen clearly displayed the musical voice that would define him in the years to come. The two-year musical association between Mingus and Pullen also resulted in two seminal jazz albums, *Changes 1* and *Changes 2.*

After a collaborative stint with Art Blakey in 1974, Pullen began his solo career in 1975 with a series of recordings on the Canadian Sackville label that dramatically showcased his unique percussive piano style. His solos would begin in a traditional manner, then seem to expand and almost explode in new directions as they progressed. Pullen developed his innovative technique of rolling his wrists across the keyboard as a result of slashing at the keys with his knuckles one day because he wanted to get a fuller and faster sound. "That just sort of happened," Pullen told *Billboard.* "It was the only method by which I could play what I was hearing." During this decade Pullen also expanded the horizons of jazz organ. Macnie called his 1978 LP *Milano Strut* "one of the key documents of the organ entering the progressive jazz realm."

His extremely physical style made Pullen appear to be dancing at the piano. He would sometimes wear an ankle bell on one cuff of his pants, so he could stamp his foot and create a tambourine-like sound. Pullen's music was often used in conjunction with dance performances, including in collaboration with Eva Anderson's Baltimore Dance Theater, Diane McIntyre's Sounds in Motion, and performance artist Jana Haimsohn, also Pullen's companion at the time of his death.

Quartet Received Critical Acclaim

When Mingus died in 1979, Pullen formed a combo with saxophonist George Adams, drummer Dannie Richmond, and bass player Cameron Brown, all of whom had played with Mingus. He and Adams were the mainstays of a quartet that recorded ten highly praised albums over the next decade, first on various foreign labels and then with Blue Note starting in 1986. Later, Pullen and drummer Beaver Harris led a group called 360 Degree Music Experience in the late 1970s and early 1980s that featured steel drums and saxophonist Ricky Ford.

Pullen performed steadily on the club scene during the Eighties. By this time his sound had become refined, and he began showing a preference for solo and trio combos. Jazz critics praised his solo work, especially 1983's *Evidence of Things Unseen,* and *The Sixth Sense,* released two years later, both done for Italy's Black Saint label. He also came out with a series of albums for Blue Note Records that showcased his diverse talents in R&B, pop, and jazz as well as his unique improvisational talent.

Despite his tremendous ability at improvisation, Pullen eventually retreated back somewhat from his free-wheeling ways. "It's always fascinating to sit down and play without any written music," he told Macnie in *Billboard,* "but it also has limitations. One of them is that it all begins to sound alike. I found constantly playing free did lead to a bit of a dead end. Good writing gives you direction." As a composer, Pullen said that he got some of his best ideas from his dreams. His performance style was often trance-like, with his eyes frequently closed as he played.

Embraced Other Cultures

Music of different cultures attracted Pullen during the Nineties. He worked frequently with a group of African and Brazilian musicians known as the African-Brazilian Connection, performing and recording songs that sometimes featured traditional African instruments and themes. In a 1992 review of Pullen's performance with this group, *New York Times* critic Jon Pareles noted that "in the quintet's music, melody and rhythm, passion and propulsion are inseparable." A 1993 *Vibe* review of the pianist's *Ode to Life* album—a collaboration with the

African-Brazilian Connection—the critic Watrous described Pullen as "a master at writing simple, bright melodies."

Just weeks before he died in 1995, Pullen had been in the studio working on an album with the Chief Cliff Singers, a drum and voice ensemble from the Salish and Kootenai Native American tribes of Montana. This emerged as *Sacred Common Ground,* about which Chip Deffaa of *Entertainment Weekly* stated, Pullen "makes music that can dance with life or invite awareness." He left behind a diversified legacy of both ensemble and solo playing, with an exceptional ability to synthesize many different elements into his keyboard virtuosity. Pullen described it best in the 1989 *Down Beat* when he said, "I can just play whatever I want to."

Selected discography

Piano Album, Sackville, 1974.
Capricorn Rising (quartet), Black Saint, 1975.
Five to Go, Horo, 1976.
Healing Force, Black Saint, 1976.
Tomorrow's Promises (10-piece combo), Atlantic, 1976.
Montreaux Concert (quintet), Atlantic, 1977.
Warriors (quartet), Black Saint, 1978.
Milano Strut (duet), Black Saint, 1978.
The Magic Triangle (trio), Black Saint, 1979.
Evidence of Things Unseen, Black Saint, 1983.
Ode to Life (with the African-Brazilian Connection), Blue Note, 1993.
Live...Again (with the African-Brazilian Connection), Blue Note, 1995.
Sacred Common Ground, Blue Note, 1996.

Sources

Books

Clarke, Donald, editor, *The Penguin Encyclopedia of Popular Music,* Viking, 1989.
Feather, Leonard, and Ira Gitler, *Encyclopedia of Jazz in the Seventies,* Horizon Press, 1976.

Periodicals

Billboard, May 6, 1995.
Down Beat, November 1989.
Entertainment Weekly, January 26, 1996.
Los Angeles Times, November 21, 1993.
New York Times, February 6, 1992; April 24, 1995.
People, June 12, 1995.
Vibe, September 1993.

—*Ed Decker*

Collin Raye

Singer

Noted for his poignant ballads, Texas-bred vocalist Collin Raye has tested his warm, smooth tenor on everything from hard-core country to hard-driving rock and roll. Securing his niche as one of the most popular "contemporary country" vocalists in Nashville, Raye defends his eclectic taste in music. "Critics jump on me for singing those non-country songs—asking how can a true country artist sing those songs," he noted in a *Los Angeles Times* interview. "[But] country has changed so much in the past few years that a country artist can sing anything." Raye's three platinum albums, as well as the ever-growing crowds of hatted and booted fans that continue to flock to his stage performances, seem to confirm his belief.

Raye was born Floyd Collin Wray in DeQueen, Arkansas, on August 22, 1959. He was raised across the border in Texas, where he soon picked up the nickname "Bubba." It was virtually inevitable that music would figure prominently in Raye's life: his father was a bass player and his mother sang backup vocals for Sun Records greats like Jerry Lee Lewis and Carl Perkins when they came to town.

Along with his brother, Scott, Raye started his own band while still in his teens. By 1980 they had moved to the northwestern United States and eventually came to roost in Reno, Nevada. As part of the brothers' lounge act—called, not surprisingly, the Wray Brothers—Collin got some of the most valuable training of his career, and he ranks it more highly than working the dance-hall circuit, the traditional training ground for country artists. "In Nevada, all you were looking at was people sitting there," he told *Country Music*'s Bob Millard. "I always had a great band, but we had to go that extra mile. We had to make 'em laugh. We had to give them songs that would make 'em want to hold each other's hands. We had to make 'em get up and have some fun."

On His Own—and on to Nashville

After recording several singles for local fans, Collin and Scott parted ways; Collin Raye then went solo and made tracks to Nashville, where he was signed to Epic Records in 1990. His debut album, *All I Can Be*, was released in 1991. "Love, Me" hit the Number One spot on the country charts and hung on for three weeks in 1992, eventually garnering the singer a Country Music Association (CMA) song of the year nomination. Helped by the momentum of several other chart-topping ballads, *All I Can Be* went gold and then platinum, beginning a trend that would continue for Raye's first three albums.

Raye's second effort, *In This Life*, reached million-seller status with the help of its title cut, a Number One hit that

For the Record . . .

Born Floyd Collin Wray, August 22, 1959, in De-Queen, AR; divorced; children: Jake Wray, Brittany Wray.

Formed a lounge act with his brother, Scott Wray; performed as the Wray Brothers, Reno, NV, mid-1980s; recorded several singles on Mercury before dissolving act; went solo and signed with Epic Nashville, 1990; released solo debut album, *All I Can Be,* 1991; released *Extremes,* 1994; appeared in film *Street Justice,* 1994.

Addresses: *Record company*—Epic Nashville, 34 Music Square East, Nashville, TN 37203.

quickly became one of the most popular wedding ballads of the early 1990s. The album's success proved to Raye that he was on the right track, especially in his selection of material. "When I'm looking for songs for my records, I'm looking for songs that are about things I've felt or I've seen," he explained in an Epic press release. "But I also want those songs to be the kind of song that people will feel are their own. When you get out on the road and people start telling you all these stories about what the songs have meant to them, *that's* when those songs really take on a deeper meaning."

Extremes Marks Changes

Raye's third album, 1994's *Extremes,* made fans see a more socially aware side of their favorite singer. The single "Little Rock," a song about the life of a recovering alcoholic, not only reached the Number One spot on the charts and the final cut in the contest for CMA song of the year but also reached out to many listeners who had been touched by alcoholism. After the release of "Little Rock," Raye used the accompanying music video to promote Al-Anon, a support group for children of alcoholic parents. The song was also the momentum behind a series of public service announcements he later filmed. Raye's public-mindedness was further broadened by his son, Jake, who was diagnosed with mild cerebral palsy. "My son's disability matured me a great deal," he confessed to Millard. In addition to spending a great deal of time with both his children—he also has a daughter, Brittany—Raye devotes time to several charities, including the annual Special Olympics and the Emily Harrison Foundation for children.

Extremes signalled a shift for the well-known country balladeer. The soulful devotion that resonated through-

out most of his first two albums was replaced by the rowdy buffoonery of the Lyle Lovett-penned "That's My Story" and the saucy Number One hit "My Kind of Girl." "I knew early I was tagged 'a balladeer,'" Raye explained to Millard, "which is wonderful for people to say 'boy, this guy can really sing a ballad,' but that's not all that I am about." To prove that there's more to the singer than a sad, slow song, *Extremes* also contains a cover of Waylon Jennings's "Dreaming My Dreams," which Raye told *Country Song Roundup* contributor Jennifer Fusco-Giacobbe is his "favorite song of all time." He added, "It's my way of thankin' Waylon Jennings ... because without Waylon, I probably wouldn't have a career. He laid the foundation, he made me do what I wanted to do."

Bringing New Fans to Country Music

In fact, Raye names Highwaymen alumni Waylon Jennings, Willie Nelson, and Johnny Cash among his greatest influences. "Waylon and Willie and George [Jones] and them guys, they basically built the foundation for this thing," he asserted in the interview with Millard. "They brought a lot of people to the table." And Raye's fourth album, *I Think About You,* brought more fans to his own table, as the album's first single—the musical fairy-tale "One Boy, One Girl"—hit airwaves across the country. But the release also finds Raye in a more realistic state of mind in the thought-provoking "What If Jesus Comes Back Like That," a song that ponders the form the Second Coming might take in today's hard-edged, urban world. Critics have predicted that *I Think About You* will follow in the tracks of its three predecessors on its way to platinum status.

In contrast with his continuing reputation as a country balladeer, Raye puts on shows noted for their high energy, and he often adds country spins to tunes by such notable rockers as Rod Stewart, Elton John, and the Eagles. "Our obligation as artists is not only to ourselves, but to the industry, to bring more people to country music," Raye explained to Fusco-Giacobbe. "If we give them a good show we might capture the people who went to see a country artist to take a look at this 'country thing.' But if they come and see a guy standing there, just strumming a guitar, they can go, 'I can listen to that on tape. There's nothing there.' So if we go out there and really break our necks, they're gonna go, 'I like this stuff.'"

Selected discography

All I Can Be, Epic, 1991.
In This Life, Epic, 1992.

Extremes (includes "Little Rock" and "That's My Story"), Epic, 1994.
I Think About You, Epic, 1995.

Sources

Country Music, September/October 1994; November/December 1995.
Country Song Roundup, July 1994.
Country Weekly, June 14, 1994.
Los Angeles Times, February 13, 1994; October 10, 1995.
Music Row, April 8, 1994.

Additional information for this profile was provided by Epic Nashville, 1995.

—*Pamela Shelton*

Lou Reed

Singer, songwriter

AP/Wide World Photos

A 1995 story in *Interview* declared, "Since the 1960s, Lou Reed has arguably been one of the most influential figures in rock 'n' roll." The mercurial Reed—whose group The Velvet Underground may have been the first art-rock band and was certainly crucial to the development of today's "alternative" rock—has pursued a very personal path in his solo career. Experimenting with everything from glam rock to pop to all-out noise, he has disregarded commercial considerations in the name of his own truths. "Sometimes the definition of what rock and roll is caused me to be thought of in ways that are too confining," he commented in a 1992 Sire Records press biography, "so sometimes it becomes easier to just think of it as 'Lou Reed Music.'"

Reed was born in 1942 and raised on Long Island, New York. He became infatuated with rock and roll and rhythm and blues during his teens. He wrote his own songs and performed with bands like the Shades during the 1950s; he also frightened his parents with his behavior. According to Victor Bockris's 1995 biography *Transformer: The Lou Reed Story*—excerpted in *Interview*—the teenager turned his family's world upside down: "Tyrannically presiding over their middle-class home, he slashed screeching chords on his electric guitar, practiced an effeminate way of walking, drew his sister aside in conspiratorial conferences, and threatened to throw the mother of all moodies if everyone didn't pay complete attention to him." The Reeds sent Lou to a mental institution, believing that treatment there would cure their son of his attitude problems and apparent homosexuality. At Creedmore State Psychiatric Hospital, the troubled teen underwent electroshock therapy; the trauma of this "cure" would never entirely leave him.

Velvet Tones

Reed attended Syracuse University and later worked as a songwriter for Pickwick Records, gulping amphetamines and trumping up and recording tracks like the alleged dance sensation "The Ostrich." Yet even as he penned these no-brainers, he was absorbing the most lurid works of literature—including the writings of the notorious Marquis de Sade and Leopold von Sacher-Masoch, the namesakes of sadism and masochism, respectively. Reed's dark romanticism was profoundly influenced by a unique combination of highbrow underground writings such as these and the yearning teenaged plaint of early rock and roll—not to mention his own painful experiences.

This feverish sensibility drove The Velvet Underground, the band Reed helped form in the early 1960s with multi-instrumentalist and musical avant-gardist John Cale, guitarist Sterling Morrison, and drummer Moe Tucker.

Born March 2, 1942, in Brooklyn, NY (some sources say Freeport, Long Island, NY); son of Sidney Joseph (an accountant) and Toby (Futterman) Reed; married Betty (a waitress), 1973 (divorced); married Sylvia Morales, 1980 (divorced). *Education:* B.A., Syracuse University, 1964.

Songwriter, Pickwick Records, New York City, 1965; singer, guitarist, and songwriter for The Velvet Underground, 1965-70; solo recording artist, 1971—; acted in film *One Trick Pony,* 1980; participated in Amnesty International and Farm Aid benefit concerts, 1985; appeared on television commercials, 1980s; published *Between Thought and Expression,* Simon & Schuster, 1991; reunited with Velvet Underground for concerts and album, 1993; appeared in film *Blue in the Face,* 1995.

Selected Awards: Received Best New Poet award, Council of Small Literary Magazines, 1977; Velvet Underground inducted into Rock and Roll Hall of Fame, 1996.

Addresses: *Home*—New York, NY. *Record company*—Warner Bros., 75 Rockefeller Plaza, New York, NY 10019-6908.

Thanks to artist-impresario Andy Warhol, the Velvets were able to hone their vision in shows around New York City before recording their debut album with the frosty German chanteuse Nico. Reed songs such as "Venus in Furs" (a fetishistic odyssey that took its title from a Sacher-Masoch novel), "Femme Fatale," "Heroin," "I'm Waiting for My Man," "White Light/White Heat," "Sweet Jane," and many others limned experiences other rock bands wouldn't touch.

The Velvet Underground's music, meanwhile, incorporated brutal, primitive rock, aching melodies, experimental noise, spoken-word pieces, and even country-western. Yet the Velvets saw little real success; a cliché of rock has it that only a thousand people listened to the group during its career, but every one of the thousand formed a band. Though exaggerated, this anecdote reflects the influence the band had on the subsequent movements of glam-rock, punk, and alternative rock.

The Velvet Underground disbanded in 1970, and Reed went home to his parents' house in Long Island. He spent some time recuperating from his tumultuous years with the Velvets—which were marked by drug addiction and sexual anarchy—and worked in an office;

eventually, though, he decided to accept a solo recording contract. He released his solo debut in 1972; the following year he married for the first time and released a more successful sophomore effort, *Transformer.* Produced by Reed devotee and emerging glam-rock phenom David Bowie, the album included the smash hit "Walk on the Wild Side," a deceptively mellow, jazzy pop song narrating a variety of sexual transformations. "Walk" is undoubtedly Reed's most commercially successful offering; it became something of an anthem for the decade. The album *Sally Can't Dance,* meanwhile, was his most successful in terms of chart action, reaching the Top Ten in the U.S.

Reed released a number of other glam-rocking albums in the 1970s, but he outraged his critics, fans, and especially his record company with *Metal Machine Music,* a double disc filled with shrill sounds and no songs. Often viewed as an elaborate attempt to get out of his contract with RCA—for which company he released the melodious *Coney Island Baby* the following year—the 1975 opus stands as one of the more perverse recordings of the modern era, at least by a mainstream artist. In any event, Reed left RCA and signed with Arista; though his albums didn't sell terribly well, most managed to chart at least briefly.

Challenging His Audience

Having divorced his first wife, Reed married Sylvia Morales in 1980 (they would later divorce as well). After several years of output that thrilled neither critics nor many fans, he assembled a new band—which included guitarist Robert Quine, late of the innovative punk-era band Television, and the virtuosic Fernando Saunders on bass—and released *The Blue Mask.* According to *Nation* critic Gene Santoro, the album "chronicles Reed's genuinely harrowing descent into the hells of sex- and drug-driven terror, rage and violence, a place nobody else can plumb with his scarred power." Yet, Santoro lamented, Reed squandered the force of his group and blunted the edge of his writing. "By the time of *New Sensations* in 1984, Reed had become a self-parodic name-dropper," the critic averred.

In addition to his solo work, Reed appeared on a multi-artist tribute to German songwriter Kurt Weill, whose dark, often carnivalesque melodies strongly influenced his own work. He also lent his voice to another all-star vehicle, a benefit for the struggle against the racist Apartheid system of South Africa called *Sun City.* A duet with R&B legend Sam Moore on a remake of the 1960s hit "Soul Man" for the 1987 movie of the same name and an appearance on bassist-producer Rob Wasserman's anthology recording, *Duets,* followed.

Yet even as Reed lost some of his credibility among the hipsters who'd been emulating him for years by filming television commercials for motor scooters and credit cards, he created a strong impression with his 1989 album *New York,* a meditative collection that showed a renewed vitality. He also reunited with Cale for a series of concerts in New York. The death of Warhol, an inspiration and friend to both Reed and Cale, spurred the two to write a suite of songs; this culminated in the 1990 recording *Songs for 'Drella.* Reed's contributions emphasized, among other issues, Warhol's intense work ethic—and proposed the artist's need to escape his small-town origins as a partial explanation for his ambition.

Loss, Recovery, Reunion

The deaths of two other friends, Reed's Syracuse roommate Lincoln Swados and songwriter extraordinaire Doc Pomus, motivated another album, 1992's *Magic and Loss.* (Reed would be dealt another blow in 1995 when his Velvet Underground mate Sterling Morrison succumbed to cancer.) Although its meditations on illness and mortality might seem depressing on the surface, Reed insisted in his press bio, "I think *Magic and Loss* is a very 'up' album. It makes you feel better because what I gained from what happened to my friends is really very inspirational." *Rolling Stone* noted of the disc, "[It] couples Reed's bravest and most self-revelatory writing with his sparest and least-developed music. Highly charged prose writing, not songwriting, is now his focus." No doubt some fuel for this hypothesis was provided by the 1991 publication of *Between Thought and Expression,* an anthology of Reed's writings.

Esteemed music journalist Kurt Loder, catching up with the singer-songwriter for a 1991 *Esquire* piece, noted that Reed's "still-astonishing cult band, The Velvet Underground, has been nominated for the Rock & Roll Hall of Fame ('Can we campaign?' he asks), but there'll be no big reunion." It may have been further reflection on life's brevity that proved this statement untrue, but whatever the reason, Reed reunited with Cale, Morrison, and Tucker for a series of European concerts in 1993. Sire Records released an undoctored recording of a Paris show titled *Live MCMXCIII* before the year's end; David Browne of *Entertainment Weekly* lauded it as "that rare, and wonderful, beast a nostalgia-free return to old glories that both recaptures and expands on the tension and beauty that made the Velvet Underground so monumental so long ago." The album includes "Coyote," a new Reed-Cale collaboration that *Rolling Stone's* Don McLeese felt "could have fit just fine on that third Velvets album while sounding reflective of the maturity these writers have gained over the years."

Nonetheless, McLeese asserted, "*MCMXCIII* sidesteps the question of where the Velvets go from here, of what a band that embodied so much experimentation might mean in the middle age of both its members and rock & roll." The answer came shortly thereafter: true to form, the Velvets broke up again immediately after re-establishing their immense potential. Just as personality conflicts motivated the first breakup, the "maturity" bestowed by the intervening years couldn't prevent old conflicts from resurfacing. "It was a volatile brew," Reed noted in *Musician.* "I was happy it made it through Europe in the first place."

Reed contributed a track to *Sweet Relief,* a benefit-tribute anthology for Victoria Williams, a singer-songwriter afflicted with multiple sclerosis, and also appeared onstage with her during several of her subsequent performances. "Vic is easily one of the most talented people I've ever come in contact with in my life," he gushed in *Musician.* He also lent his rendition of the classic Doc Pomus song "This Magic Moment" to the 1995 tribute album *Till the Night Is Gone.* The following year saw the publication of Bockris's *Transformer* biography; *Spin's* Mark Schone noted that the book "tries to answer the question: What makes the father of punk, führer of rock's most important Underground, such an unmitigated asshole?" According to Schone, Bockris portrays Reed—who cooperated with him—as a manipulative dissembler.

Hall of Fame and *Reeling*

In 1996 the Rock and Roll Hall of Fame at last inducted The Velvet Underground, an event considered long overdue by many in the rock intelligentsia. In February of 1996 Reed released *Set the Twilight Reeling,* which was notable in part for having been written entirely on a computer. Reed said of the record in *Billboard,* "I just wanted to rock after 'Magic and Loss.' I didn't want to put the burden of it having to be thematic on myself, so I told myself, 'Just write whatever.' And if it was connected in any way, that's OK." Reed went on to remark of *Reeling's* content, much of which continues his exploration of the idea of transformation, "We're all growing. When we stop growing, that's the end of it. I'm happy I'm even walking on two legs. Making rock records is kind of too good."

Lest one despair that Reed had lost some of his trademark malcontent ire, the album featured a track called "Sex with Your Parents (Motherf—er) Part II," which *Billboard's* Melinda Newman described as "a diatribe against right-wing Republicans that postulates that the reason many of them are so uptight is that they had improper liaisons with their parents." Said Reed of the song, "I hope 'Sex with Your Parents' works its way into the [1996 presidential] election somehow, if nothing else, to mock and ridicule the right-wing Republican fundamentalists who are so abhorrent to every principle of freedom of expression. Nothing could disgust me more."

Lou Reed's eccentric career has embraced numerous styles, but his distinctive writing voice has been a constant. Whether pushing the envelope of noise-rock or musing over hushed guitar chords, he has followed only his own inclinations. "I write the albums for myself and I try to make it something I would listen to," he insisted in his press biography. "I operate under the idea that I'm not unusual. And if I try to do it really well for myself, other people can relate to it, too. But I don't really know how to write *for* other people so I can't do that."

Selected discography

With the Velvet Underground; on MGM/Verve, except where noted

The Velvet Underground & Nico (includes "Femme Fatale," "I'm Waiting for My Man," "Venus in Furs," and "Heroin"), 1966.
White Light/White Heat (includes "White Light/White Heat"), 1967.
The Velvet Underground, 1969.
Loaded (includes "Sweet Jane"), Cotillion, 1970.
The Velvet Underground Live at Max's Kansas City, Atlantic, 1972.
1969: The Velvet Underground Live, Mercury, 1974.
VU, Polydor, 1985.
Another View, Polydor, 1986.
Live MCMXCIII (includes "Coyote"), Sire, 1993.
Peel Slowly and See, Polydor Chronicles, 1995.

Solo releases; on RCA, except where noted

Lou Reed, 1972.
Transformer (includes "Walk on the Wild Side"), 1973.
Berlin, 1973.
Rock 'N' Roll Animal, 1974.
Sally Can't Dance, 1974.
Lou Reed Live, 1975.
Metal Machine Music, 1975.
Coney Island Baby, 1976.
Walk on the Wild Side: The Best of Lou Reed, 1977.
Rock and Roll Heart, Arista, 1976.
Street Hassle, Arista, 1978.

Take No Prisoners, Arista, 1979.
The Bells, Arista, 1979.
Growing Up in Public, Arista, 1980.
Rock and Roll Diary, 1967-80, Arista, 1980.
The Blue Mask, 1982.
Legendary Hearts, 1983.
New Sensations, 1984.
Mistrial, 1986.
New York, Sire, 1989.
Magic and Loss, Sire, 1992.
Set the Twilight Reeling (includes "Sex with Your Parents (Motherf—er) Part II"), Warner Bros., 1996.

Other

"September Song," *Lost in the Stars: The Music of Kurt Weill*, A&M, 1985.
Artists United Against Apartheid, "Sun City," Manhattan, 1985.
Rob Wasserman, *Duets*, 1988.
(With John Cale) *Songs for 'Drella*, Sire, 1990.
"Tarbelly and Featherfoot," *Sweet Relief: A Benefit for Victoria Williams*, Chaos/Sony, 1993.
"This Magic Moment," *Till the Night Is Gone: A Tribute to Doc Pomus*, Rhino, 1995.

Sources

Books

Rees, Dafydd, and Luke Crampton, *Rock Movers & Shakers*, Billboard, 1991.

Periodicals

Billboard, January 27, 1996.
Entertainment Weekly, October 29, 1993.
Esquire, November 1991.
Interview, August 1995.
Musician, August 1993; January 1994.
Nation, February 27, 1989.
Rolling Stone, December 10, 1992; April 1, 1993; August 5, 1993; November 25, 1993; January 26, 1995; April 20, 1995.
Spin, September 1995.

Additional information for this profile was obtained from Sire Records publicity materials, 1992.

—Simon Glickman

Dianne Reeves

Singer

Photograph by Paula Ross, Archive Photos/Frank Driggs Collection

With jazz as the base of her vocal stylings, Dianne Reeves freely mixes in pop, African and South American influences as well as her own vision, a combination that has led to her acclaim as a unique contemporary songstress. However, Reeves' albums have met with mixed receptions, with *I Remember* at the top of the jazz charts for weeks and *Art and Survival* critically acclaimed but rarely played. Occasionally criticized by jazz purists for straying from the straight-and-narrow or for indulging in pop-like schmaltz, Reeves has nevertheless attracted a strong following for her vocal interpretations.

Born in Detroit, Michigan, in 1956, Reeves grew up in Colorado, and at an early age her talent brought her to the attention of professional musicians. While performing at a National Association of Jazz Educators convention as a featured singer in her high school's big band, Reeves was heard by trumpeter Clark Terry. He took an interest in the young performer and invited her to sing with his big band. Reeves performed with Terry's group for several years, continuing even while still attending the University of Colorado.

When Reeves completed her studies at the University of Colorado in 1976, she moved to Los Angeles to further her career and her musical education. She worked as a studio artist, recording with Lenny White, Stanley Turrentine, and Alphonos Johnson. She also began working with Billy Childs, developing a musical relationship that would continue for a decade. In the late Seventies Reeves performed with the group Night Flight; their gigs took them throughout southern California on the "beach circuit." These various experiences—session recordings, live performances, and musical experimentation with Childs—all made this period a richly educational one for Reeves.

Toured with Sergio Mendes

In 1980 Reeves continued this education by taking on studies with vocal coach Phil Moore. The following year Reeves embarked on an important new experience: she auditioned for and won a spot with Sergio Mendes' world tour group. Fresh from performing for international audiences with Mendes, Reeves recorded her first album in 1982, *Welcome to My Love.* She produced it with Billy Childs and included several of her own compositions. One of these original Reeves pieces was "Better Days," which made it onto the jazz charts.

Although Reeves had already tempered her jazz origins with pop and fusion influences from the likes of Stanley Turrentine, George Duke, and Mendes, she further expanded her musical repertoire through the influence

Born 1956 in Detroit, MI. *Education:* Attended the University of Colorado in the mid-1970s.

Began performing with trumpeter Clark Terry while still in high school; recorded sessions with Lenny White, Stanley Turrentine, and Alphonso Johnson in the mid- to late 1970s; performed with the group Night Flight in southern California, late 1970s; joined the world tour of Sergio Mendes, 1981; recorded debut album, *Welcome to My Love,* in 1982; performed with Harry Belafonte, 1983-1986; formed a trio with Billy Childs and toured the United States in 1986; recorded *Dianne Reeves* in 1987 and toured the United States and Asia for the next two years; recorded the jazz hit album *I Remember* in 1991 and the critically acclaimed *Art and Survival* in 1993; recorded *Quiet After the Storm* in 1995 and toured in support of the album.

Addresses: Home—Denver, CO. *Record company*—Blue Note Records, 1290 Avenue of the Americas, 35th Floor, New York, NY 10104.

of Harry Belafonte. After moving the New York in 1983, Reeves began performing with Belafonte and has credited these mid-Eighties performances for her introduction to the rhythms of West Africa and the West Indies. She continued this exploration by experimenting with music from Brazil and Cuba, as well as venturing into the rhythms of early African-American folk music such as field hollers and slave songs.

Added World Rhythms to Album

Reeves' next album, *For Every Heart,* reveled in the new knowledge she had gained with Belafonte. Mixing reggae and world rhythms into jazz, Reeves took what she had learned under Belafonte's tutelage and made it her own. Reeves acknowledged Belafonte's influence when she noted in her artist biography for the Blue Note label that "Harry's always been an artist who mentors others. He has respect for that folk tradition." The album also featured many of the world musicians Reeves met while working with Belafonte.

In 1986 Reeves returned to the West Coast and formed a trio with Billy Childs, which they took on the road throughout the United States. The next year, after a Grammy-nominated performance at the "Echoes of Ellington" concert captured the attention of Blue Note

president Bruce Lundvall, Reeves began recording *Dianne Reeves* for the eminent jazz label. The 1987 album benefited from her collaboration with George Duke, Herbie Hancock, Freddie Hubbard, Tony Williams, and Stanley Clarke. As Reeves' most successful recording effort to date, it garnered attention from critics and fans alike. Will Friedwald described the various influences on the self-titled LP in *Jazztimes,* noting that "on one hand, in [Reeves'] pan-cultural voyages she strives for a degree of authenticity, but at the same time she feels a strong obligation to the tenets of jazz and fusion, and also to her own idiosyncracies."

When criticized by jazz purists for the pop leanings of the album, Reeves defended her experimentation with various styles. As she explained to Peter Keepnews in *Billboard,* "Jazz is my foundation. . . . I come from Sarah Vaughan, Ella Fitzgerald, Billie Holiday. They set a standard of excellence; nobody sounds like them. And people forget that they also did albums that could have been considered pop albums."

Climbed the Jazz Charts

Still exploring new genres, Reeves added an R&B component to her next album, *Never Too Far.* Released in 1989, the album sold well and attracted more fans to her sound. However, Reeves chose to return to a more purely jazz format in her 1991 release, *I Remember.* Remaining for 12 weeks at the top of the *Billboard* jazz chart, this album was her most popular yet. Reeves also continued to gather fans through her live performances in the U.S., Europe, and Japan.

Reeves' next recording evoked an unusual response from her audience. *Art and Survival,* released in late 1993, was acclaimed by critics but little received little promotion from EMI and little exposure on the radio. Reeves attributes this reaction to the emotionally charged topics she explored on the album, including her condemnation of female circumcision in "Endangered Species." Although the album did not sell well and was criticized by some fans as too emotional, Reeves has said it was an important album for her personal growth.

Rallying after *Art and Survival*'s poor sales, Reeves quickly began work on her next album, *Quiet After the Storm.* After the emotional storm and controversial topics of her previous album, Reeves said she wanted to simply sing on this one. It was completed in two weeks. "I feel with this album I have become a *real* storyteller," Reeves told Zan Stewart in *Down Beat.* "It was done with a great deal of ease, because I have an understanding of a lot of life-related things, and it's easy for me now to translate that into music and tell a story." Some of those stories were her own; Reeves peppered the album with original songs, including "Smile" and the autobiographical "Nine." The album rose to the top ten of the jazz charts and solidified Reeves position as one of the more important jazz divas of the late twentieth century.

Selected discography

Welcome to My Love, Palo Alto Jazz, 1982.
For Every Heart, Palo Alto Jazz, 1985.
Dianne Reeves, Blue Note, 1987.
Never Too Far, EMI, 1989.
I Remember, Blue Note, 1990.
Art and Survival, EMI, 1994.
Quiet After the Storm, Blue Note, 1995.

Sources

Billboard, June 18, 1988; March 11, 1995; June 17, 1995.
Down Beat, September 1991; November 1995.
Jazztimes, January 1988.

Additional information for this profile was provided by Blue Note Records publicity materials, 1995.

—Susan Windisch Brown

Esa-Pekka Salonen

Conductor, composer

Esa-Pekka Salonen is the boy wonder of symphony conducting. The music director of the Los Angeles Philharmonic, Salonen is young, handsome, and going out of his way to revitalize the 200-year-old European symphonic tradition. *Los Angeles Magazine*'s Richard Pietschmann called Salonen "a mesmerizing conductor with catlike moves on the podium; a crowd pleaser with looks, charisma and flair; and a musician's musician who enjoys a profound rapport with his orchestra.... He's experimental, flexible, creative, approachable and understanding of his role [in LA] as head cheerleader, top fund raiser and reluctant matinee idol. Most of all, perhaps, he possesses that rare ability to pack 'em in no matter what's on the program."

Born in Helsinki, Finland, in 1958, Salonen was the only child of two loving and nurturing parents. His father, a banker, and his mother, a homemaker, were encouraging but not domineering. Salonen's godfather, who didn't know a great deal about children, taught the young boy to read at the ripe age of three. That changed Salonen's life. Not interested in the piano, which his

AP/Wide World Photos

For the Record . . .

Born in 1958 in Helsinki, Finland; son of a banker and a homemaker; married Jane Price (a violinist), 1991; children: two daughters. *Education:* Attended the Sibelius Academy, Helsinki, beginning c. 1973; studied with private teachers in Italy.

Made conducting debut with the Finnish Radio Symphony, 1979; gained international attention guest conducting the London Philharmonia Orchestra, 1983; made American debut with the Los Angeles Philharmonic, 1984; principal conductor, Swedish Radio Symphony Orchestra, 1985-94; principal guest conductor, Philharmonia of London, 1985—; music director and conductor, Los Angeles Philharmonic, 1992—.

Selected awards: Grammy Award, Cecilia Prize, Koussevitzky Award, and the 1986 Gramophone Award for best contemporary record for Lutoslawski's *Symphony #3*, 1986; Gramophone Award for Sibelius and Nielsen *Violin Concertos*, 1989; his original composition, *Floof*, chosen as best work at the 39th Annual International Rostrum of Composers in Paris, 1992; first conductor ever to win the Siena Prize of the Accademia Chigiana, 1993.

Addresses: c/o Los Angeles Philharmonic Association, The Music Center, 135 North Grand Ave., Los Angeles, CA 90012.

mother started him on a year later, he waited and tried the recorder at age nine. Salonen's home was always filled with the sounds of music, and he kept trying different instruments until one stuck. After the recorder, he tried the French horn; then he gave the piano another chance—his mother had been smart enough not to push it on him in the first place.

At age 15, Salonen became a horn and composition student at the Sibelius Academy in Helsinki, and later with private teachers Franco Donatoni and Niccolò Castiglioni in Italy. The self-professed troublemaker resisted authority but was eventually given the opportunity to lead a student performance of Humperdinck's *Hänsel und Gretel.* Critics predicted big things from the 17-year-old conductor.

His true conducting debut came with the Finnish Radio Symphony in 1979. He was soon leading concerts and opera performances throughout Scandinavia. It was just a few years later, in 1983, that the break came that would catapult him to fame. With five days' notice, and as a virtual unknown in England—although rumors about a Finnish wonder preceded him—Salonen was asked to replace the ailing Michael Tilson Thomas in a major concert with the London Philharmonia.

Trial By Fire

The piece to be performed that evening was Gustav Mahler's extremely difficult *Symphony #3.* As Martin Bernheimer put it in the *Los Angeles Times Magazine,* "Salonen at 25 had not yet learned the meaning of fear." "I had never seen the score, so I went to the library and looked through it," Salonen told Bernheimer. He recalled thinking, "If it turns out not to be a major disaster, at least I could say I have conducted the Philharmonia once and go back to composing.... That was five days before the concert and three before the first rehearsal. I had never studied the piece. I had never conducted the orchestra. It was dangerous, like diving into a pool where one didn't know if there was water or not."

There *was* water, and Salonen made a huge splash. His success in London made him a star, and he garnered regular positions in Stockholm and Oslo as well as recording contracts and guest engagements with important orchestras throughout Europe. In fact, Ernest Fleischmann, executive vice president and managing director of the Los Angeles Philharmonic Association, was so bowled over by the London performance that he immediately signed Salonen for a guest conducting appearance the following year.

"The Great White Hope"

Fleischmann had big plans for Salonen. He wanted him to become music director of the LA Philharmonic. Although talented, the young conductor was extremely inexperienced at the time, so André Previn took up the orchestra's reigns instead. But the relationship with Previn was never a good one. Salonen signed on as music director beginning with the 1992-93 season. It was the LA Philharmonic's hope that he would breathe much-needed life into the orchestra. Having been led by nothing but guest conductors since Previn's departure in 1989, the Philharmonic had suffered. "But the case can also be made that the Philharmonic has lacked the passion of a world-class symphony longer than that," wrote Pietschmann in *Los Angeles Magazine,* "indeed, since [Zubin] Mehta left [in 1978]."

The media hype over Salonen's tenure in Los Angeles was huge. Teasing billboards were pasted all over the city. Newspaper headlines read "The Great White Hope," "The Maestro of Change," "LA's Fair-Haired Finn," and the like. Esa-Pekka Salonen was expected to be the Philharmonic's savior—and a breath of fresh air. Far from the usual maestro, Salonen could often be seen in jeans and a polo shirt. And he went out of his way to loosen up and vary the orchestra's repertoire, broadening the range of music accepted in LA as "classical." As he explained to Pietschmann, "I'll see how challenging I can get. The variety of things that we offer must be great. It's not always giving what we're expected to give.... [On the other hand,] I don't think we can win by calling classical music anything but what it is. This is f—-ing classical music—and that's it. Either you like it or you don't." To Bernheimer, he insisted, "The task of our generation is to introduce new repertory, to let the repertory go forward. To perform our grandfathers' repertory is really not that interesting."

The risks that Salonen took paid off, even with the more rigid European audiences. According to various press releases, German reviewers praised the Philharmonic's 1994 European tour. "Since Salonen, this top-class orchestra from California is more brilliant than ever. Perfectionism reigns without any loss of identity. Virtuosity strikes sparks on every strand," gushed Berlin's *Tagesspiegel*. A writer for *Die Welt* noted: "It was obvious that Esa-Pekka Salonen radiated to his musicians a special inner tension that inspired them to veritable peak achievements." A contributor to the *Rheinische Post* of Düsseldorf suggested, "Since the engagement of Esa-Pekka Salonen, the orchestra has finally and deservedly entered the champion's league." And Cologne's *Kölnische Rundschau* offered, "The Los Angeles Philharmonic belongs to the best in the country, and among the leading orchestras in the world. Only a few top European orchestras can bear comparison with its exquisite tonal culture.... And ... their young Finnish music director Esa-Pekka Salonen [ranks among] the most sought-after podium stars of our time."

Risks Rewarded with Praise

Salonen continually receives kudos for his performances—both live and recorded. He is one of the few living maestros who can sell a recording of standard repertoire on the strength of his name alone. He has made a point, however, of being sure his own compositions are not overshadowed by his conducting. As Bernheimer put it, "He carefully divides his professional time between his two callings. Most listeners find his colorful, often-witty compositions both orderly and accessible. Although the musical language—like the man—does not shrink from dissonance, it strives to balance the cerebral and the dramatic."

Salonen was indeed a savior to the Los Angeles Philharmonic, and although he himself would bristle at the term—he shies away from the hype—he spends his time spreading the gospel about symphony music as far and as wide as he can. When not conducting the LA Philharmonic or guest conducting elsewhere, Salonen works with children from California's Santa Monica High School to Mexico's Tepoztlan Youth Symphony Orchestra. He is a hero to many; he even has groupies, but he is not doing all this for the publicity. "I'm concerned about the future because I have to be," he told *Los Angeles Times* contributor Mark Fineman. "[Today] Madonna is mainstream and classical music has gone underground and counterculture. I don't want to be the last generation of conductors, and [working with children] is the best way to guarantee continuity of interest." To Bernheimer he suggested, "Young people see sissy conductors in stupid posters and think, 'This is nothing for me.'... What music needs is a sense of danger."

Selected discography

On CBS/Sony Classical

(New Stockholm Chamber Orchestra; Los Angeles Philharmonic) Messiaen: *Turangalila Symphonie*/Lutoslawski: *Symphony #3*, 1986.

(Philharmonia Orchestra; with trumpeter Wynton Marsalis) Jolivet/Tomasi: *Trumpet Concertos*, 1986.

(Swedish Radio Orchestra) Nielsen: *Symphony #4; "Inextinguishable,"* 1986.

(New Stockholm Chamber Orchestra) Nielsen: *Symphony #1; Little Suite*, 1987.

(Philharmonia Orchestra) Sibelius: *Symphony #5*, 1987.

(London Sinfonietta; with pianist Paul Crossley) Messiaen: *Des canyons aux etoiles*, 1988.

(Philharmonia Orchestra) Stravinsky: *Firebird; Jeu de Cartes*, 1988.

(Swedish Radio Orchestra) Nielsen: *Symphony #5; "Maskarade"* (excerpts), 1988.

(New Stockholm Philharmonic) R. Strauss: *Metamorphosen, etc.*, 1989.

(Swedish Radio Orchestra) Nielsen: *Symphony #2; Aladdin Suite*, 1989.

(Swedish Radio Orchestra; with Cho-Liang Lin) Sibelius: *Violin Concerto*/Nielsen: *Violin Concerto*, 1989.

(London Sinfonietta; with pianist Paul Crossley) Stravinsky: *Works for Piano and Orchestra*, 1990.

(London Sinfonietta) Stravinsky: *Pulcinella* (complete ballet); *Rag-time; Renard; Wind Octet*, 1991.

(London Sinfonietta; with guitarist John Williams) Takemitsu: *To the Edge of Dream*, 1991.

(Stockholm Chamber Orchestra) Haydn: *Symphonies #22, #78, and #82*, 1991.

(Stockholm Chamber Orchestra) Stravinsky: *Apollon Musagete; Concerto in D; Cantata*, 1991.

(Swedish Radio Orchestra) Nielsen: *Symphonies #3 and #6*, 1991.

(Swedish Radio Orchestra) *A Nordic Festival*, 1991.

(Los Angeles Philharmonic) Sibelius: *Lemminkrainen Legends, Op. 22; En Saga, Op. 9*, 1992.

(Los Angeles Philharmonic; with Barbara Hendricks) *Symphony #4*, 1992.

(The Philharmonia; with pianist Yefim Bronfman) Rachmaninov: *Piano Concertos #2 and #3*, 1992.

(Swiss Radio Orchestra; with Otter, Cole, Estes, Gedda) Stravinsky: *Oedipus Rex*, 1992.

(Berlin Philharmonic) Prokofiev: *Romeo and Juliet* (excerpts), 1993.

(Los Angeles Philharmonic) Sibelius: *Kullervo*, 1993.

(Oslo Philharmonic) Grieg: *Peer Gynt Suite*, 1993.

(The Philharmonia; with pianist Emanuel Ax) Schoenberg: *Piano Concerto, Op. 42/*Liszt: *Piano Concertos #1 and #2*, 1993.

(The Philharmonia) Stravinsky: *Petrouchka* (1947 version); *Orpheus*, 1993.

(Swedish Radio Orchestra) Nielsen: *Flute Concerto; Clarinet Concerto*, 1993.

(Los Angeles Philharmonic Orchestra; with soprano Dawn Upshaw, mezzo-soprano Paula Rasmussen, and the Women of the Los Angeles Master Chorale) Debussy: *Nocturnes, La Damoiselle élue, and Le Martyre de Saint Sébastien*, 1994.

(Los Angeles Philharmonic; with Shirley Quirk) Lutoslawski: *Symphonies #3 and #4; Les Espaces du sommeil*, 1994.

(Los Angeles Philharmonic; with Cho-Liang Lin) Prokofiev/Stravinsky: *Violin Concertos*, 1994.

Sources

American Record Guide, January 1988; July 1988; May 1989; September 1989; November 1989; January 1990; March 1990; July 1990; January 1991; September 1991; November 1991; March 1992; July 1992; September 1992; November 1992; January 1993; March 1993; May 1993; July 1993; November 1993; January 1994; May 1994; July 1994; November 1994; January 1995.

Audio, December 1988; March 1994.

Chatelaine, June 1990.

Consumers' Research Magazine, April 1988; September 1988; March 1989; August 1989; November 1992.

High Fidelity, December 1988.

Los Angeles Daily News, April 21, 1995.

Los Angeles Magazine, September 1992.

Los Angeles Times, October 9, 1992; March 7, 1994; November 24, 1994; February 1, 1995; April 27, 1995.

Los Angeles Times Magazine, October 4, 1992.

Musical America, March 1988; July 1989; March 1990; May 1990; July 1990; January 1991.

New York, July 25, 1988.

New Yorker, August 8, 1988; December 12, 1994.

New York Times, November 27, 1994; November 30, 1994; February 9, 1995.

Opera News, October 1992; December 5, 1992.

Ovation, December 1985.

Stereo Review, January 1988; October 1988; June 1989; August 1989; October 1989; February 1990; September 1991; January 1992; March 1992; August 1992; December 1992; January 1993; September 1993; May 1994; August 1994; September 1994.

Time, October 30, 1989; March 15, 1993.

Additional information for this profile was obtained from Los Angeles Philharmonic press materials, 1995, and Sony Classical press materials, 1995.

—Joanna Rubiner

Pharoah Sanders

Saxophonist

Photograph by Ton Copi, MICHAEL OCHS ARCHIVES/Venice, CA

Pharoah Sanders declared in a 1971 *Down Beat* interview, "I play for the Creator...And my music talks for me." The jazz saxophonist's prodigious body of work—including, but not limited to, his work with trailblazer John Coltrane—encompasses a wide variety of styles, yet it has always been a reflection of his spiritual searching. With his mastery of "circular breathing" and a variety of other techniques, Sanders has helped to expand the range of his instrument as well as the parameters of "free" or avant-garde jazz. "I don't separate what I do musically from my spiritual life," he insisted to *Boston Phoenix* columnist Ted Drozdowski. "I can't. So it's always about what's most pure, always striving for perfection."

Sanders was born in Little Rock, Arkansas, to a very musical family. "My grandfather was a schoolteacher; he taught music and mathematics," he related to Martin Williams of *Down Beat.* "My mother and her sisters used to sing in clubs and teach piano. For myself, I started playing drums in the high school band. Then I played tuba and baritone horn, clarinet and flute. In 1959, I started playing tenor saxophone, still in the school band." It was the sound of the tenor sax that most captivated him, though at first he played primarily rhythm and blues, not jazz. His school band teacher, Jimmy Cannon—whom he has always credited as a major influence—introduced him to jazz. Even so, Sanders envisioned a career not in music but in commercial art. It was to this end that he headed off to California to study at Oakland Junior College.

Seduced by Burgeoning Jazz Scene

It soon became clear to Sanders that his heart was in music. As he told *Down Beat,* "I had fallen in love with the tenor." He moved to nearby San Francisco and began playing any gig he could get, most of them rock and roll or blues jobs. At the same time, he gravitated toward the burgeoning jazz scene; it was a particularly exciting period for the form, which had expanded upon the free-form possibilities suggested by bebop, venturing into even more sonically adventurous territory. Saxophone innovators Sonny Rollins, John Coltrane, Eric Dolphy, Ornette Coleman and others presented new possibilities for jazz, and Sanders wanted in. He started to expand his technique. "When I was living in Oakland," he told *Seconds,* "there was a guy who taught at a music school and he taught me a whole lot about the overtones, how to play more than one note at a time. I practiced how to control that for years and years, and a lot of the time I can just about tell what's going out before I play it."

Eventually, Sanders decided to go to New York City, where most of the jazz innovation of the period was

For the Record . . .

Born October 13, 1940, in Little Rock, AR; married women named Thembi (divorced) and Shukuru. *Education:* Studied music with Jimmy Cannon, mid-1950s; attended Oakland Community College, Oakland, CA, late 1950s.

Played with Sun Ra Arkestra, early 1960s; recorded solo debut, *First Album,* ESP, 1964; recorded and performed with John Coltrane, 1965-67; signed with Impulse! label and released *Tauhid,* 1967; released one album on India Navigation label, 1976; signed to Arista and released *Love Will Find a Way,* 1977; signed to Theresa and released *Journey to the One,* 1980; signed to Evidence and released *Shukuru,* 1992; collaborated with Maleem Mahmoud Ghania on *The Trance of Seven Colors,* Axiom, 1994.

Addresses: *Record company*—Evidence Music, Inc., 1100 East Hector St., Ste. 392, Conshohocken, PA 19428. Axiom/Island, 400 Lafayette St., 5th Floor, New York, NY 10003; 8920 Sunset Blvd., 2nd Floor, Los Angeles, CA 90069.

taking place. On his arrival in 1962 he hoped to phone John Coltrane but found out that his number had changed. Though he played gigs with some notables, including Don Cherry, Coleman, and Sun Ra's Arkestra, he was impoverished. While playing with Ra's band, he recollected to Martin Johnson of *Down Beat,* "I didn't have my own place, so when I left [the Arkestra], I was out on the streets. It was hard times. Everyone who stayed in New York City struggled till daylight came. I used to give blood to make five dollars. Since a slice of pizza was only 15 cents and a candy bar cost a nickel, if I had a dollar, that would take care of you and me all day long!" Sanders also held short-term restaurant jobs for little or no pay, slept on subway cars or under tenement stairwells, and often ate only the wheat germ he kept in a jar in his saxophone case. He reflected to Johnson that he "should have waited to come to New York, but I came and waited it out."

Explored "Out" Jazz with Trane

He found Trane—as tenorist John Coltrane was known—playing at a club called the Half Note in 1963. Despite his destitute condition, he was invited to play with his idol. The two musicians, both devout Muslims, also became friends, as Sanders informed Martin Williams in a 1968 *Down Beat* profile: "He would call me and we would talk about religion and about life. He was also concerned about what he wanted to do next in his music, about where he was headed." Coltrane famously described Sanders as "very strong in spirit and will"; together they began exploring the outer reaches of "out" jazz, utilizing dissonance and otherwise shattering the established rules of what constituted "music" in the name of emotional truth; they often outraged purist critics and fans in the process. "If Trane was well on his way out of this world before he met Sanders," opined *Vibe* writer Greg Tate, "the two of them boldly took African-American improvisational music where no music had gone before." Some of their stops along the way were Coltrane's albums *Ascension, Meditations,* and *Expression.*

Tate further noted that Coltrane was rumored to have put down his sax and screamed at times during gigs, as if the instrument couldn't adequately vent his feelings. Yet "Sanders never had to do that because his sound—which involved heavy use of multiphonics, a technique in which several tones are blown simultaneously, creating a dense, squealing sound like a thousand pigs being gutted at once—was such that no single human voice could match its intensity." Coltrane died in 1967, and with him died a great deal of critical interest in the avant-garde; even so, Sanders was only beginning his own odyssey. He had recorded his debut solo release, *First Album,* on the avant-garde label ESP in 1964; beginning in 1967 he recorded a slew of albums for ABC's cutting-edge Impulse! label. Among his most celebrated work during this period was "The Creator Has a Master Plan," from the 1970 disc *Karma.*

"My playing has a lot of energy," Sanders averred to *Jazziz* magazine. "Some people ask why my tunes are so long," he said, adding, "I don't think the tunes are long enough." He has employed a number of special techniques to find unique sounds. After hearing a record recorded at the Taj Mahal—an ornate, ancient mausoleum in India—and marvelling at its echoes, Sanders told Drozdowski of the *Boston Phoenix,* "I had a dream of trying to get that effect—of playing in a big cathedral or something—by circular breathing." This tactic allows him to fill his sax with air and continue to work the valves and produce sound even when he removes his mouth.

Drozdowski complained that in the 1980s Sanders "made a string of albums so lightly arranged and jazz-pop flavored, so easily digestible, they seemed like pablum." Yet Sanders himself has never expressed concern about pleasing those who expect "out" experimentalism in every recording. Indeed, he refuses even more general labels. "I have never said I was a jazz player; I'm just a player," he asserted to Johnson of

Down Beat. "I get jobs with whoever calls me, you know, and I perform in whatever the situation may be." Even so, many fans of his more venturesome work saw Sanders's contributions to *Ask the Ages*—the 1992 album by guitarist Sonny Sharrock, who'd played on some of the sax player's early solo work—as a return to form.

Recorded with Gnawa Musicians in Morocco

In 1994 Sanders revisited his debt to Coltrane with the album *Crescent with Love,* though he has been cautious about dwelling on this part of his career; he also contributed a track to the *Red Hot + Cool* AIDS benefit album. When offered an opportunity to travel to Morocco to record an album with native musicians there, he jumped at the chance. Producer Bill Laswell set up the date for his experimental fusion label Axiom; Sanders would meet and record with Gnawa musicians, descendents of West Africans who were brought to Morocco as slaves. The Gnawa specialize in music as a healing ritual; this particular group was led by singer-musician Maleem Mahmoud Ghania. Just before Sanders departed for North Africa, he heard that his friend Sharrock had died; as a result, one piece on the album—the elegiac "Peace in Essaouira"—was dedicated to his memory. "I felt like he was there when we were making the record," Sanders told Drozdowski.

"Ever since I first listened to Pharoah years ago," Laswell recalled in *Pro Sound News,* "I heard tones that go back very far, beyond time. I always felt his sound came from somewhere else, and that relates to Gnawa music. He's always had that presence. He sounded very old when he was really young. I never thought of it as jazz or as the saxophone: it was another kind of energy; it was spiritual music." The result of Sanders's collaboration with the Gnawa players, *The Trance of Seven Colors,* was released late in 1994. "Highly improvisational and daring," the recording "goes beyond jazz, roots and folk music into a territory charted more by spiritual movement than physical moment," enthused *College Music Journal,* concluding by calling it "simply brilliant." While a *Down Beat* reviewer felt that the project yielded "mixed results," *Trance* was named Disc of the Month by *CD Review,* which ventured, "Ghania and Sanders achieve a musical collaboration that sounds very old, yet entirely new."

Pharoah Sanders has never garnered the recognition that many of his colleagues have, yet he has continued to explore the possibilities offered by free-form jazz for over three decades. Practicing yoga daily and experimenting with boxes of mouthpieces in search of just the right sound, he still seemed—at the age of 55—an enthusiastic youngster. "I'm just trying to get my music where it's supposed to be and not worry about other things," he affirmed to *Jazziz.* "I believe in one God but have no formal affiliation with religion. Nor with politics. I'm musically involved with all cultures. I think everyone has something to say musically."

Selected discography

With John Coltrane; on Impulse!

Ascension, 1965.
Meditations, 1966.
Expression, 1967.

Solo releases; on Impulse! except where noted

First Album, ESP, 1964.
Tauhid, 1967.
Izipho Zam, 1969.
Karma (includes "The Creator Has a Master Plan"), 1970.
Thembi, 1970.
Black Unity, 1971.
Live at the East, 1971.
Wisdom Through Music, 1972.
Village of the Pharoahs, 1972.
Elevation, 1973.
Love Is in Us All, 1973.
Harvest Times, India Navigation, 1976.
Love Will Find a Way, Arista, 1977.
Beyond a Dream, Arista, 1978.
Journey to the One, Theresa, 1980, reissued, Evidence, 1994.
Rejoice, Theresa, 1981, reissued, Evidence, 1992.
Heart Is a Melody, Theresa, 1982, reissued, Evidence, 1993.
Live, Theresa, 1982.
Welcome To Love: Pharoah Sanders Plays Beautiful Ballads, Timeless, 1991, reissued, Evidence, 1996.
(With New York Unit) *Naima,* King Records (Japan), 1992, reissued, Evidence, 1995.
Shukuru, Evidence, 1992.
A Prayer Before Dawn, Evidence, 1993.
Ed Kelly & Pharoah Sanders, Evidence, 1993.
Crescent with Love, Evidence, 1994.
(Contributor) "This Is Madness," *Stolen Moments: Red Hot + Cool,* 1994.
(With Maleem Mahmoud Ghania) *The Trance of Seven Colors* (includes "Peace in Essaouira"), Axiom, 1994.

Has also contributed to recordings by Sonny Sharrock, Alice Coltrane, the Elvin Jones-McCoy Tyner Quintet, Idris Muhammad, the Franklin Kiermyer Quartet, Ornette Coleman, Don Cherry, and others.

Sources

Boston Phoenix, December 16, 1994; April 28, 1995.

CD Review, April 1995.

College Music Journal (*CMJ*), October 10, 1994; October 24, 1994.

Down Beat, May 16, 1968; May 13, 1971; August 1991; March 1995; April 1995.

Jazziz, June 1995.

Pro Sound News, October 1994.

Seconds, November 1994.

Vibe, November 1994.

Additional information for this profile was provided by Evidence and Axiom Records publicity materials, 1994.

—*Simon Glickman*

Selena

Singer

AP/Wide World Photos

The undisputed "Queen of Tejano," Selena Quintanilla-Pérez rocketed meteorically into the spotlight in the late 1980s. Within a few years, the artist, known simply as Selena, won a Grammy Award for her album *Selena Live.* Selena sold six albums between 1987 and 1994. By the age of 19, she was a millionaire; by the age of 21, she could draw crowds of 20,000 at the fairgrounds at Pasadena, Texas. Music critics proclaimed she would be the next Madonna, i.e. a mega-star of music and movies. Tragically, however, Selena's career was cut short at the age of 23, when she was murdered by the president of her fan club.

Selena and her band performed Tejano music—Mexican *ranchera* style music mixed with German polka sounds owing influence to pop, country and western, and Caribbean music. Tejano traditionally meant music by Texans of Mexican descent. But Selena, among others, modernized the traditional accordion-based Tejano or Tex-Mex music with country twangs, techno-pop beats, dance mixes, and international influences. More than 70 radio stations playing the uniquely, Latino-styled tunes form a corridor from south Texas through California.

Selena Quintanilla was born April 16, 1971, in Lake Jackson, Texas, a small industrial town near Houston. Her father Abraham Quintanilla, Jr. worked as a shipping clerk at the Dow Chemical plant. Abraham and his wife Marcela had three children: Abraham III, Suzette, and Selena, the youngest. In his own youth, Quintanilla had performed as a vocalist with Los Dinos ("the boys") a popular South Texas band. When Quintanilla heard his daughter sing at six years of age, he knew Selena was destined for a musical career and encouraged the musical talents that she revealed. In a 1995 *People* article, Quintanilla affirmed that Selena's "timing and [her] pitch were perfect. I could see it from day one."

Early Love of Music

Selena practiced with the music she enjoyed, a wide range of music from the soul music of Little Anthony and the Imperials to country and western music and even the stylized R&B of Michael Jackson. Through her love of all different kinds of music and early jam sessions with her brother on bass and her sister on drums, Selena demonstrated her passion for the musical arts.

After years of working for others, Abraham Quintanilla opened his own Tex-Mex restaurant in Lake Jackson. There Selena first performed in public with her brother and sister as members of her band. But the economic recession of the early 1980s delivered a knockout blow that closed the family restaurant, forcing them to leave their home and sell all their belongings. Selena's talent would save them.

While the rest of the Quintanilla's relocated in Corpus Christi, Selena and her siblings hit the road, performing throughout southern Texas as Selena y Los Dinos ("Selena and the Boys"). They played at weddings and in cantinas and honky-tonks to very small audiences—oftentimes less than ten people. In a dilapidated van with one foldout bed in the back, the troupe traveled and performed. In 1979, eight-year-old Selena recorded her first tune—a country song sung in Spanish; her Tex-Mex band was in full swing by 1980.

Selena left school in the eighth grade to spend more time travelling with the band and earning money for her family, but she eventually completed her high school equivalency requirements through a correspondence course. The band started playing larger venues, including ballrooms. They also recorded nearly one dozen albums for a small regional label. In 1987, Selena—then 15-years-old—won Tejano Music Awards for best female vocalist and performer of the year. This was the big break that Selena and the band had worked for years to achieve. Two years later, the Latin division of the EMI Records Group signed the band to a record deal.

Though Selena was the rising star of Latino pop, she was still very much a Texan. She could not speak Spanish and learned the Spanish lyrics for her lively

songs and romantic ballads phonetically, coached by her brother, who wrote the songs. At the advice of her father, turned manager, she began taking Spanish lessons in the early 1990s, so that she could project a more genuine Latino image during interviews on Spanish-language radio.

In 1992 Selena Quintanilla married the band's guitarist Chris Pérez. The union did not hamper Selena's sexy image. Rather, Selena became known as the "Tex-Mex Madonna" because of her sexy bustiers and provocative smiles on-stage though off-stage she remained a wholesome, married woman who was devoted to her family.

Hired Fan Club President

Selena had repeatedly refused offers for fan clubs, keeping her career a family project. But then came Yolanda Saldivar who expressed interest in founding and running Selena's fan club. She was an aunt of one of Selena's childhood friends, but beyond that she was a stranger. Saldivar lived near San Antonio, working as a registered nurse, and caring for three children abandoned by her brother. Despite Saldivar's remote connection to the Quintanillas, Selena and her family appointed Saldivar as the president of the Selena fan club, an unpaid position. In just four years, Selena's fan club attracted 9000 members.

When speaking of her desire to work for Selena, Saldivar told the *Dallas Morning News* in 1994 that she became a devoted Selena fan after seeing a San Antonio concert in 1989. "Selena just inspired me—with her talent, her motivation. She gives her whole to you." The two developed a close friendship. Though Saldivar did not receive an official salary, Selena often bestowed the woman with gifts and indulged Saldivar's penchant for spotted cows with cow-patterned rugs and phones. Saldivar reciprocated by transforming her apartment into a Selena shrine, laden with Selena photos and memorabilia, including a life-size cardboard pop-up of the singer.

In 1993 *Selena Live* received a Grammy Award for best Mexican American album. Selena's 1994 album, *Amor Prohibido* (*Forbidden Love*)—recipient of a Grammy nomination—sold 600,000 copies in the United States. The fourth single from the album, "Fotos y Recuerdos" ("Photographs and Memories"), reached the top ten on *Billboard* magazine's Latino charts.

By 1995, Selena's albums had sold a combined total of 3 million copies. Twice, she played to record crowds of 60,000 at Houston's annual Livestock Show and Rodeo. Selena's "Bidi Bidi Bom Bom" won the singer a song of the year award at the Tejano Music Awards in early

1995. She also won five more of the 15 awards presented at the 1995 Tejano Music Awards ceremonies, including best female entertainer; best female vocalist; album of the year; Tejano crossover song; and record of the year. An amazed Selena was quoted as saying in *Time* magazine, "Never in my dreams would I have thought I would become this big. I am still freaking out."

In 1994, Selena promoted Saldivar to a paid position as head of Selena Etc. Inc., a company devoted to overseeing two Selena boutiques/salons—one in Corpus Christi and one in San Antonio—and to marketing a line of Selena fashions to be sold in the boutiques as well as in other retail venues. But things began falling apart rapidly. First, fashion designer Martin Gomez quit, claiming that he could not work with Saldivar, who he accused of being "mean and manipulative." The problem escalated with reports of other lapses by Saldivar involving misuse of funds.

Meanwhile, fans were not receiving t-shirts and other Selena items that they had paid for, and money was disappearing from one of the salons. Selena and her father both confronted Saldivar about the reported abuses. Saldivar protested claiming that she had documentation to prove her innocence, and offered to show Selena the alleged papers.

Gone Too Soon

Selena and Saldivar were supposed to meet alone at the Days Inn where Saldivar was staying. Instead Selena brought her husband; Saldivar proved not to have the papers she'd claimed to possess. The next day Selena went to the Days Inn sometime before noon to talk with Saldivar. At 11:50 a.m., the Corpus Christi police received a 911 call of a shooting at the motel.

Police detailed that Saldivar met Selena at the door of her motel room with a .38-caliber revolver, shooting the singer in the back and shoulder. Selena staggered to the lobby before collapsing, though she remained conscious until paramedics arrived. Response teams rushed Selena to the hospital. Despite blood transfusions, Selena died a few hours after being shot, on March 31, 1995. Saldivar was charged with Selena's murder.

But the ordeal did not end with Selena's death. Saldivar holed up with the revolver in the cab of a pickup truck in the Days Inn parking lot. For hours she threatened to shoot herself while negotiating with police via a cellular car phone. As the news of Selena's murder spread, the singer's fans stood vigil at the Days Inn. Saldivar finally surrendered at 9:30 p.m.

In the wake of Selena's murder, grieving fans swamped the Quintanilla family with remembrances, including bouquets, rosaries, and votives. Condolences were sent to the Quintanillas by Julio Iglesias, Gloria Estefan, Madonna, and La Mafia, a well-known Latino group. Local radio stations devoted their programming to Selena's music, and more than 1000 Selena tapes and compact discs were sold at a frenzied pace during the next couple of weeks.

Fifteen hundred mourners attended a vigil for the singing star at the Bayfront Plaza and Convention Center prior to her funeral held at Corpus Christi's Memorial Coliseum, the arena where she had recorded her smash hit *Selena Live*. 10,000 people flooded Corpus Christi to pass by Selena's coffin. In Los Angeles, 4000 people gathered at the Sports Arena Memorial to honor the slain singer. Mourners also gathered in San Antonio, the capital of Tejano music, at two separate sites.

> "She was about to take center stage as the first Tejano performer to attempt a full-scale crossover, and she was robbed of that opportunity."
> —Cameron Randle

Selena was killed just as her career was about to skyrocket in new directions. She had recorded six songs for an English-language album, her first with EMI's SBK division, making her only the third Latino performer to ever cross from the Latin division to the more mainstream part of the record company. In addition, she had made her film debut as herself in *Dos Mujeres, Un Camino*, a Latino Television soap. In 1995, she continued to advance her film career as a mariachi singer in the film *Don Juan DeMarco*, and she had collaborated with former Talking Heads leader David Bryne on the song "God's Child" for the film *Blue in the Face*.

Cameron Randle, a recording industry executive specializing in Tex-Mex music, voiced his opinions of Selena in a retrospective of her career published in *Entertainment Weekly* in April of 1995. "Selena was not merely forging an exceptional career, she was defining a new genre as uniquely American as Delta blues or New Orleans jazz. There's every indication she would have been as enormously popular as [fellow Latinos] Jon Secada or Gloria Estefan. She was about to take center stage as the first Tejano performer to attempt a full-scale crossover, and she was robbed of that opportunity."

Selena's posthumous release *Dreaming of You* entered the *Billboard* 200 at number one—the second-highest chart debut after Michael Jackson's *HIStory*—and was also a number one album on the *Billboard* Latin 50. The jump into the top pop slot made Selena one of the fastest selling female artists of all time, second only to Janet Jackson. An amazing 175,000 copies of the compact disc were sold on the first day of release.

Selected discography

On Capitol/EMI Latin

Entre A Mi Mundo, 1992.
Mis Mejores Canciones, 1993.

Selena Live, 1993.
Amor Prohibido, 1994.
Dreaming of You, 1995.

Sources

Billboard, February 25, 1995.
Entertainment Weekly, April 14, 1995.
Hispanic, December 31, 1994.
Los Angeles Times, April 1, 1995; April 2, 1995; April 3, 1995.
La Prensa de San Antonio, June 11, 1993; November 19, 1993; April 29, 1994.
New York Times, April 2, 1995; April 3, 1995.
People, April 17, 1995; July 10, 1995.
Time, April 10, 1995.

—*Christopher B. Tower*

Paul Simon

Singer, songwriter, guitarist

Newsweek's Jeff Giles—in a 1993 profile celebrating Paul Simon's three-disc career retrospective—referred to the veteran performer as "the only songwriter of his generation still curious, bent on change and utterly awake." Tony Scherman of *Life* seconded this view: "Few longtime pop-music idols have steered their careers so gracefully into the present." Simon's recipe for long-term career vitality, it would seem, contains equal parts insatiable passion for musical growth and lingering insecurity.

After turning his partnership with singer Art Garfunkel into a hit pop act, Simon went on to become one of the premier solo singer-songwriters of the 1970s. Though he experienced a slump of sorts in the ensuing decade, he came roaring back with *Graceland,* which garnered critical raves and multi-platinum sales. Even then, however, he was forced to fend off claims of musical imperialism for his use of South African song forms and employment of African musicians; his subsequent album relied on Brazilian music in a similar way and received the same criticism.

AP/Wide World Photos

For the Record . . .

Born October 13, 1941, in Newark, NJ; son of Louis (a former musician and college professor) and Belle (a schoolteacher) Simon; married Peggy Harper, 1969 (divorced, 1975); married Carrie Fisher (an actress), 1983 (divorced, 1983); married Edie Brickell (a singer-songwriter), 1992; children: (first marriage) Harper, (third marriage) Adrian. *Education:* B.A. in English, Queens College; attended Brooklyn Law School.

With Art Garfunkel, performed as Tom and Jerry, 1957-59, recording "Hey Schoolgirl," Big, 1958; recorded as "Jerry Landis" and "Tico & the Triumphs," among other names, for labels including MGM and Warwick, and recorded demos for music publishers, 1959-63; reunited with Garfunkel and, as Simon and Garfunkel, signed with Columbia and released debut album *Wednesday Morning, 3 A.M.,* 1964; released solo album *The Paul Simon Songbook,* 1965; with Garfunkel, provided songs for soundtrack to film *The Graduate,* 1968; split from Garfunkel and released solo album *Paul Simon,* 1972; appeared in film *Annie Hall,* 1977; performed at Inaugural Eve Gala for President Jimmy Carter, 1977; wrote, starred in, and provided songs for soundtrack of film *One-Trick Pony,* 1980; signed with Warner Bros. and released *Hearts and Bones,* 1983; appeared on *MTV Unplugged,* 1992; collaborated with poet Derek Walcott on musical *Capeman,* 1990s.

Selected awards: With Garfunkel, Grammy awards for best album and best performance by a pop vocal group, 1969, for *The Graduate;* Grammy awards for best album, for *Bridge over Troubled Water,* and for best single and best performance by a pop vocal group, for "Bridge over Troubled Water," all 1970; inducted into Rock and Roll Hall of Fame, 1990. As solo artist, Grammy awards for best album, 1975, for *Still Crazy after All These Years,* and 1987, for *Graceland.* Emmy Award, 1977, for television special *Paul Simon.*

Addresses: *Record company*—Warner Bros., 75 Rockefeller Plaza, New York, NY 10019; 3300 Warner Blvd., Burbank, CA 91510.

Yet Simon has steadfastly defended all of his work, arguing that foreign musical territory has both helped him grow and built enduring international relationships. Still, his artistic and commercial growth have not seemed to alleviate the insecurity that keeps him on edge. "He's particularly vulnerable when he's writing," noted Simon's friend Lorne Michaels, best known as producer of the TV program *Saturday Night Live.* "Sometimes he'll play you a song and you'll go, 'That's great!' and he seems genuinely surprised you like it. He's pretty rough on himself."

Words and Music

A quintessential Manhattanite in adulthood—his urbane lyrics are rivaled in sophistication only by his nuanced melodies—Simon was born in Newark, New Jersey, and grew up in Queens, New York. His mother was a schoolteacher; his father worked as a jazz bassist for many years before becoming a college professor. The anti-Semitic tenor of the late 1940s moved the elder Simon to disguise his Jewish surname: "He used the name Lou Sims," Simon told *Life.* Further reminiscing about his father, he revealed, "When I was five or six, he would bring me to Manny's [music store] on 48th Street, where he bought his bass strings and rosin. So I knew a world that was pre-rock and roll." Ultimately, however, his father became bored with the musician's life and entered academia, receiving a doctorate in semantics—the study of language. "The older I get," Simon ventured, "the more I realize that my thing is so much like my father's. I'm his kid, more and more interested in words."

What caught his fancy at first, however, was a sound—the sound of early rock and roll. During the 1950s he and his pal Arthur Garfunkel formed a duet called Tom and Jerry—camouflaging their Jewish names just as Simon's father had—and became stars while still in high school, thanks to the hit single "Hey Schoolgirl." Though Tom and Jerry saw no further chart action, Simon soon found himself working with another promising young singer-songwriter. "Carole King and I made a lot of demos—Carole Klein, from Brooklyn," he recollected in *Life.* "She'd play piano and drums, I could play bass and guitar, and we sang all the parts. That's where I learned how to stack [overlay] voices and do overdubs—how to make records. One moment we were making demos; the next she was making $150,000 a year writing Number One hits. It was very demoralizing to me."

Simon recorded a number of solo singles as "Jerry Landis" and saw some of them recorded by other acts. He attended Queens College while Garfunkel was at Columbia. He then tried Brooklyn Law School. Finally, the two decided to work together again and began performing in local clubs.

By the dawn of the 1960s, "ethnic"—including ethnic-sounding names—was in vogue and folk music was catching the national ear; the duo became Simon and Garfunkel. Their first album, *Wednesday Morning, 3 A.M.,* fared poorly, and Simon went to England for a time to play the folk scene there. But on its re-release in 1966—following a retooled pop version of their single "The Sounds of Silence" that featured drums—the record became a hit. Merging the evocative, lyrically dense folk-rock popularized by Bob Dylan with their own radio-friendly pop hooks, Simon and Garfunkel would send a score of singles up the charts, including "The Sounds of Silence," "The Boxer," "Mrs. Robinson," "The 59th Street Bridge Song (Feelin' Groovy)," the traditional "Scarborough Fair/Canticle," and "Bridge over Troubled Waters." They won five Grammy awards in 1969 and 1970. Their vocal harmonies were peerless, but their partnership became rocky; Simon felt his musical ambition was hampered by Garfunkel's conservatism and acting aspirations. The pair split in 1971. They would reunite occasionally, however—as on Simon's "My Little Town," various Garfunkel projects, and a couple of extremely successful live engagements—and in 1990 would be inducted jointly into the Rock and Roll Hall of Fame.

Going Solo

"Going solo was my decision," Simon pointed out in a *Time* magazine profile. "But I was nervous about it." He was met with profound skepticism from industry types who were loath to part with the duo's proven formula, yet he persevered. "I thought, if Simon and Garfunkel is all about the voices and not the songs, so much for my career," he remembered in *Newsweek.* "But if it's about the songs *as well as* the voices, then I'm going to be fine."

He needn't have worried; he proceeded to score hits throughout the 1970s, including "Mother and Child Reunion," "Me and Julio down by the Schoolyard," "Kodachrome," "Slip Slidin' Away," "Loves Me Like a Rock," "50 Ways to Leave Your Lover," and many others. His 1975 disc, *Still Crazy after All These Years,* took a best album Grammy; in 1977 he won an Emmy award for a TV special. Noted modern composer Phillip Glass, interviewed in *Life,* called Simon "a great artist," adding, "Yes—why not? The only music that counts is the music we love, the records in our collections that keep coming to the top. And for a quarter century now, Paul has generated a tremendous amount of music we love."

But Simon's ambitions weren't limited to songwriting. He was a frequent host of *Saturday Night Live,* once lampooning his sincere image by donning a turkey suit for a Thanksgiving episode and crooning his way, deadpan, through "Still Crazy." His friend Woody Allen cast him—comically—as a slick L.A. show biz figure in the

1977 film *Annie Hall,* and 1980 saw the release of *One-Trick Pony,* a semi-autobiographical feature written by and starring Simon. Of course, he also wrote and performed the songs on the soundtrack.

As the 1980s dawned, Simon reunited with Garfunkel for a concert in New York's Central Park, the recording of which sold vigorously upon its release in 1981. His personal life was less rosy; he divorced his first wife, Peggy Harper, in 1975, then married actress-writer Carrie Fisher in 1983. That union foundered within a year. The dissolution of this marriage coincided with Simon's least commercially successful album (and his first for Warner Bros.), *Hearts and Bones.* Many prophesied the end of his career.

Graceland

Yet in 1986, Simon—after traveling to South Africa and working with a large group of musicians there and at home—emerged with *Graceland,* a pop album at once epic and personal. The record filtered a panoply of styles, including South African township jive, zydeco, and rock, through Simon's distinctive lyrical perspective. It garnered rave reviews; *Life's* Scherman quoted a *New York Times* critic who called it "an album-length song cycle that far transcends the normal pop record for complexity and richness."

Among the guest artists on the record were the South African vocal group Ladysmith Black Mambazo, L.A. rockers Los Lobos, pop diva Linda Ronstadt, and guitar experimentalist Adrian Belew. The title song refers to the Memphis, Tennessee, home of rock idol Elvis Presley as though it were a haven for the weary faithful: "I have reason to believe," Simon sings, "we all will be received in Graceland." The album snagged a Grammy for best album; the single "You Can Call Me Al" was among the hits that took *Graceland* past the ten million sales mark. Simon later wrote a piece for *Musician* magazine about the process of writing "Al": "At its best," he concluded, "songwriting for me means peeling back layers. It's discovery, and that's the truth."

Simon's path to musical discovery, however, was also something of a mine field. Many political activists objected to his work in South Africa, since that country at the time was in thrall to a system of racial inequality known as apartheid and was thus being boycotted by artists around the world. They argued that Simon, as a rich white musician, was exploiting oppressed Third World musicians and doing nothing about their plight. Even worse, these critics maintained, he used their musical styles merely to sing about his own life. His attempts to explain himself rarely assuaged such attacks. "I suppose someone could say, 'Well, that's very nice for you, Paul Simon, and congratulations. But there's a whole suffering continent there.' Which is valid," he reflected in *Life*. "But my answer is, 'Was I supposed to solve things in a song?'" Furthermore, the bridges that Simon built with African musicians have had their own impact; the leader of Ladysmith Black Mambazo gave him the Zulu name Vutlendela, "the man who opened the door."

"At its best, songwriting for me means peeling back layers. It's discovery, and that's the truth."

Simon's work on *Graceland* altered his songwriting process. A new emphasis on rhythm was particularly evident, and this continued on his 1990 follow-up, *The Rhythm of the Saints*. Born of his work with Brazilian musicians and requiring $1 million and 2 years to complete, *Rhythm* was a trickier beast than *Graceland*; though it sold some four million copies, it was less than a smashing success when compared to its predecessor. "The world hasn't gotten it yet," he averred to Scherman some three years after the album's release. "It's taking a while for people to realize that it's more interesting than *Graceland*." More interesting, perhaps, but less sunny: "There are aspects of my personal life and my family's personal life that are more grave than they were four years ago," he noted in a *Time* interview. "And that's in there. It was on my mind, it had to be in there."

By 1993, the various strands of Simon's career began to look less like detours and more like parts of a cohesive musical vision. This was demonstrated in part by the valedictory three-disc boxed set *Paul Simon, 1964/1993* and a performance on the popular acoustic showcase *MTV Unplugged*, but also by a series of mammoth stage shows billed as "The Concert Event of a Lifetime" and featuring Garfunkel, Ladysmith, a coterie of Brazilian musicians, and even a cameo by comedian Steve Martin. Audiences at these concerts saw Simon run through everything from "Feelin' Groovy" to revamped material from *Graceland* and *Rhythm*. The perceptive among them also saw the elements in his early work that prefigured his Third World wandering. Simon, observed composer-producer Quincy Jones to *Newsweek*, is "smart enough to understand the African motor, which has driven pop music for so long."

Life on the home front had stabilized a bit in the meantime. Simon married singer-songwriter Edie Brickell,

and the two had a child in 1993. He built a studio in his Manhattan home and continued exploring new ground. "I'm at the peak of my career," he insisted to Scherman. "In terms of creativity, in terms of fame, in terms of drawing power, in terms of—you just name anything." Simon next undertook a collaboration with acclaimed poet Derek Walcott on a musical, *The CapeMan*. Due in 1996 and based on a true story of a teenager who murdered two 16 year-olds while wearing a nurse's cape, it was clear from various interviews that this new project tapped some old insecurities. Nonetheless, venturing into uncharted territory has been a key source of Simon's continued vitality as an artist. "The thing that happens to musicians in middle age," he mused to David Gates of *Newsweek*, "especially if you've had a lot of success, a lot of attention, is that there comes a point where you either rediscover why you love music or it just becomes slick." For over 30 years, Simon has transformed his discoveries into musical treasures.

Selected discography

Simon and Garfunkel; on Columbia, except where noted

(As Tom and Jerry) "Hey Schoolgirl," Big, 1958.
(As Tom and Jerry) "Don't Say Goodbye," Big, 1958.
(As Tom and Jerry) "Our Song," Big, 1958.
Wednesday Morning, 3 A.M. (includes "The Sounds of Silence"), 1964, reissued, 1966.
The Sounds of Silence (includes "The Sounds of Silence" and "I Am a Rock"), 1966.
Parsley, Sage, Rosemary & Thyme (includes "Scarborough Fair/Canticle" and "59th Street Bridge Song [Feelin' Groovy]"), 1966.
The Graduate (soundtrack; includes "Mrs. Robinson"), 1968.
Bookends, 1968.
Bridge over Troubled Waters (includes "Bridge over Troubled Waters" and "The Boxer"), 1970.
Concert in Central Park, Warner Bros., 1981.

Solo releases

(As Jerry Landis) "Anna Belle," MGM, 1959.
(As Jerry Landis) "I Want to Be the Lipstick on Your Collar," Warwick, 1961.
(As Jerry Landis) "Play Me a Sad Song," Warwick, 1961.
(As Tico & the Triumphs), "Motorcycle," Amy, 1962.
(As Jerry Landis) "The Lone Teen Ranger," Amy, 1963.
The Paul Simon Songbook, Columbia, 1965.
Paul Simon (includes "Mother and Child Reunion" and "Me and Julio down by the Schoolyard"), Columbia, 1972, reissued, Warner Bros., 1988.
There Goes Rhymin' Simon (includes "Kodachrome"), Columbia, 1973, reissued, Warner Bros., 1988.

Live Rhymin': Paul Simon in Concert, Columbia, 1974, reissued, Warner Bros., 1988.

Still Crazy after All These Years (includes "Still Crazy after All These Years," "50 Ways to Leave Your Lover," "Slip Slidin' Away," and "My Little Town"), Columbia, 1975.

Greatest Hits, Etc., Columbia, 1978.

One-Trick Pony (soundtrack), WEA, 1980.

Hearts and Bones, Warner Bros., 1983.

Graceland (includes "Graceland" and "You Can Call Me Al"), Warner Bros., 1986.

Negotiations and Love Songs, 1971-1986, Warner Bros., 1988.

The Rhythm of the Saints, Warner Bros., 1990.

Paul Simon, 1964/1993, Warner Bros., 1993.

Sources

Books

Rees, Dafydd, and Luke Crampton, *Rock Movers & Shakers*, Billboard, 1991.

Periodicals

Life, November 1993.

Musician, January 1994.

Newsweek, January 14, 1991; October 11, 1993.

Time, November 12, 1990; June 12, 1995.

Additional information for this profile was obtained from Warner Bros. publicity materials, 1993.

—Simon Glickman

Special Ed

Hip-hop artist

Photograph by Michael Benabib, courtesy of Profile Entertainment

At the age of 16, Brooklyn's Special Ed found himself a rising star in hip-hop's often tumultuous skies. His 1989 album, *Youngest in Charge,* released on Profile Records, drew praise from critics and fans alike. Special Ed throws out line after line of flowing lyrics with a rapid-fire delivery often used to describe the sights and sounds of his native Flatbush, a borough in Brooklyn. Slick with late-Eighties style and possessed of devilish rhymes, Ed became wildly popular among rap fans— younger female fans in particular. His fame precipitated a 1990 appearance on *The Cosby Show,* as well as a cameo appearance in Omar Epps' 1992 film *Juice.* Despite this success, Ed struggled with his management and his career lost its momentum. After a four-year absence from the hip-hop scene, Ed rebounded with his 1994 album, *Revelations* and reclaimed his mantle as one of hip-hop's most innovative leaders.

Born Edward Archer to parents of Jamaican descent, Ed was the youngest of five boys and the only one born in the United States. His vibrant Flatbush neighborhood is sprinkled with West Indian and Jamaican influences that often find their way into Ed's music. He first started writing rhymes in public school and rapping followed soon after. "... School put me on to rapping, and vocabulary, you can't rap without a vocabulary. So throughout the years I gathered vocabulary, I learned [words] and I put it all to use," Ed told *The Flavor,* a prominent East Coast hip-hop journal.

Ed's big break would come through a meeting with respected hip-hop DJ and producer Howie Tee. One of Ed's cousins lived across the street from Tee and persuaded Ed to present his material at a club where the local star was spinning records. Tee liked Ed's style and took the 15-year-old into a studio to lay down some demo material, an unexpected outcome for Ed who held almost reverential feelings for the successful producer. He told *The Flavor,* "I was surprised 'cause I thought I was going to be wasting my time." After shopping the tape for several months, Profile offered Ed a contract and, with Howie Tee producing much of *Youngest in Charge,* his career rocketed.

Following the wildly successful *Youngest in Charge,* Special Ed's second album, *Legal,* was released in 1990. While Ed retained control over his material and its production, Profile executives took the lead in marketing the product. The record was graced by a *GQ*-ish photo of Ed dressed in colorful garb more typical of a shopping mall devotee than an innovator in hip-hop. Even with Profile's heavy marketing push, the record fell quickly from the charts, along with much of Ed's celebrity. Gangster and house rap emerged to become the dominant styles in the genre and Ed suffered through management disputes with his record company. As often happens in the music business, and rap in particular, the spotlight vanished just as suddenly as it arrived. Despite these setbacks, Special Ed had delivered several solid hits. "I Got It Made," from *Youngest in Charge*, achieved "classic" status in the hip-hop community and was covered by Shaquille O'Neal of the Orlando (Florida) Magic on the basketball star's 1994 foray into the recording business, *Shaq Fu.*

Not every day does a gold-selling performer undergo a four-year hiatus between records, raising the eyebrows of critics and fans alike. In response, Ed offered to reporter Chris Smith of the New York City scene-chronicler *Paper*, "For all those who had their doubts, it wasn't a music thing. It was a business thing." noted that Ed's "sophomore effort, *Legal*, was a bit of a disappointment, and after four years of silence, the self-proclaimed 'Youngest in Charge' was rerouted to the relic heap in the minds of many."

The down-time gave Ed the chance to reflect on his early career, and he reflected back on those days in an interview with Chris Wilder of *The Source*. "Back when I got my record deal, in the '80s, at the age I was, I would have took anything. I just wanted to hear myself on the radio," Ed explained. "But when I *realized* what I had got into I stepped back, looked at everything and was able to deal with the hand I had been dealt in a real way." Reportedly, Ed feuded with Profile's president over their management style while Profile chided Ed over a perceived lack of effort during his performances. The dispute was settled when Profile changed leader-

ship, inviting Steve Plotnicki to run the show, much to Ed's delight.

After *Legal*, Special Ed's next musical appearance came on the soundtrack to Spike Lee's 1994 film *Crooklyn*. Fresh from that work, Ed began his next project: 1995's *Revelations*. On it, Special Ed continued his tradition of free-flowing rhymes but added heavier beats, staying current with changes in rap. On "Just a Killa," Ed combined his artful rhymes and unique meter with reggae's steady beat in a formula he has employed with some success throughout his career. The track was recorded in Kingston, Jamaica, with noted reggae/hip-hop artist Bounty Killer as well as DJ Akshun. On "Neva Go Back," Ed rejoined his long-time associate Howie Tee, who produced the song which became *Revelations'* first single. The video for "Neva Go Back" was directed by Omar Epps, whose movie credits include 1995's *Higher Learning* in addition to *Juice*.

In addition to his performing career, Special Ed owns and runs Dolla Cab Lab, a recording studio in Brooklyn. The studio's name comes from the alternative transportation network that spans through many of New York's boroughs. Though technically illegal, this system offers a choice to users of public transportation just as Ed's "Lab," as it is known, opens doors for local talent. The Lab reflects his ambition to remain close to his neighborhood while boosting his career, and to make music independent of interference from heavy-handed label executives. The studio makes use of a 32-track digital recording set-up and is frequented by talented young artists who look to Special Ed for not only creative guidance, but also business know-how.

With his 1994 album *Revelations*, Ed stepped back into the limelight, re-emerging as one of rap's most in-demand MCs. After suffering through the trials of a serious management dispute, Ed is now more astute in the business aspects of hip-hop. Never short of self-confidence, Special Ed told *Black Beat's* Cynthia Rivera, "I'm finally being appreciated in the way that I should be, 'cuz I work hard at this and deserve the praise."

Selected discography

On Profile

Youngest in Charge (contains the single "I Got It Made"), 1989.
Legal, 1990.
Revelations (contains the singles "Neva Go Back" and "Just A Killa"), 1995.

Sources

Billboard, June 17, 1995.
Black Beat, October 1995.
College Music Journal, June 5, 1995; July 10, 1995.
The Flavor, July 1995.
Hits, May 29, 1995.
Muzik, August 1995.
Paper, Summer 1995.
The Source, August 1995.
Tafrija, August 1995.
Vibe, August 1995.

Additional information for this profile was obtained from Profile publicity materials, 1995.

—*Rich Bowen*

The Stone Roses

Rock band

Photograph by Pennie Smith, © 1994 Geffen Records, Inc.

The Stone Roses burst onto the pop music scene in Manchester, England, in the late 1980s, personifying the popularity of "rave" clubs, house music, and the "feel good" drugs of the era. Their flared, baggy pants, loose-limbed stage antics, confident lyrics, and neo-psychedelic stance defined their style.

At the time, Manchester was dubbed "Madchester" because of its "rave" clubs—like the infamous Hacienda Club—where patrons could spend a full 24 hours dancing, and the Stone Roses were quickly deemed the best of Manchester's club bands by devotees of the rave movement. Robert Hilburn of the *Los Angeles Times* wrote, "The Roses expressed youthful independence and innocence in ways that suggested a new generation awakening."

The popularity of the Stone Roses is also attributed to the wide-ranging and creative musical tastes of its members. The band became known for blending psychedelic '60s sounds reminiscent of the Byrds, '70s American funk music, hard-edged punk influences such as the Sex Pistols, danceable '80s-style house music, and the innocent, sugary sounds of standard pop music. The band is a classic four-man British pop formation—like the Beatles—and is comprised of singer Ian Brown, guitarist and songwriter John Squire, bassist Gary "Mani" Mounfield, and drummer Alan "Reni" Wren. Brown and Squire were raised in the same suburb of Manchester, and Reni and Brown met at a fair when they were about ten years old.

The Stone Roses started out by playing a series of shows in Sweden after a chance meeting with a promoter. Then they began playing illegally in abandoned warehouses, created a burgeoning underground fan base. Their first single, "So Young," was released in 1985, followed by "Sally Cinnamon" in 1987 and "Elephant Stone" in 1988. "Made of Stone" came out just prior to their album debut in April of 1989.

First Album Skyrockets

The band's first album, *Stone Roses,* was released to much acclaim both in England and abroad. It sold 300,000 copies in the U.K. (where 200,000 signifies platinum certification) and stayed near the top of the U.S. alternative charts for several months—primarily by word of mouth—in spite of the fact that the Stone Roses had never performed in the States.

In November of 1989 the single "Fool's Gold" reached the Top Ten on the U.K. indie charts, and "She Bangs the Drums" reached the Top 40. "Fool's Gold" became the bestselling independent-label single of the year, and the *Stone Roses* album was *Sounds'* pick for the best of '89. *Melody Maker* even included *Stone Roses* in their list of "Top 20 Albums of the Decade." *Rolling Stone* contributor David Wild described the band's debut as "an eponymous opus that winningly married '60s tinged folk rock with contemporary dance beats—upon the altar of a community still mired in the decade's slickness and decadence. The musical community promptly worshipped."

The Stone Roses staged a performance on Britain's Spike Island in May of 1990, attracting 30,000 fans. Still, the next single the band released—"One Love" in 1990—seemed like a recycled version of "Fool's Gold," and it was not received half as well as their first popular single. The Stone Roses struggled to maintain the popularity they had enjoyed in 1989, but a series of legal and organizational mishaps worked against them for a while.

Lapsed into a Downswing

In 1990, dissatisfied with their Silvertone label contract, the band went to court to resolve their contractual complaints. The time-consuming legal battle left them unable to record music or release new material until May of 1991. After the Stone Roses were finally released from their contractual obligation with Silvertone, they imme-

diately signed on with Geffen Records. However, Silvertone appealed the court's verdict and successfully paralyzed the band once again until 1992.

In the years that the Stone Roses had been tied up in litigation, Manchester's rave club scene had shifted into a more violent and less cohesive musical mode. Guns began appearing in the beltloops of concertgoers, and heroin was added to previously popular drugs like Ecstacy. Soon concert venues like the Hacienda were forced to install metal detectors at their entranceways. The Stone Roses, disillusioned by the change in the club culture, isolated themselves from the new music scene.

The band spent 1992 and much of 1993 traveling throughout Europe, savoring quiet time in the countryside and enjoying the financial windfall that accompanied their switch to Geffen Records, a deal said to be worth $20 million for five albums.

In the summer of 1993 the Stone Roses began working on their second album, only to be derailed again by unforeseen events, including a series of untimely deaths and the responsibilities of fatherhood. The new manager for the Stone Roses was one of the people close to the band who had died in 1993, and his death jarred the band's psyche and sapped their drive. John Squire had a daughter that year, Ian Brown had a son, and drummer Alan "Reni" Wren had two sons, leaving each of them with less time for the band.

The Stone Roses had problems with producers in 1993 as well. John Leckie, producer of their debut album, quit working with the band that year because their creative pace was excruciatingly slow. For example, one studio session required six weeks of work, cost $60,000, and produced only one three-minute song. The band eventually required 347 ten-hour days to produce 75 minutes of music, an extravagance that they felt they could afford.

At Last, a *Second Coming*

Second Coming, the band's dramatically-titled sophomore album, was finally released in December of 1994. This constituted an unusual five-year gap between a debut and sequel album and created a lot of curiosity in the music world. Many of the album's singles reveal the mentality, musical influences, and politics of the band's members. "Love Spreads" is a feminist tribute to the strength of women, "Good Times" is a bluesy rock song tinged with metallica, "Your Star Will Shine" is a Beatles-inspired folk song, "Daybreak" is an anti-European ode to African civilization, and "How Do You Sleep" is an unveiled barb at warmongering politicians.

The Stone Roses' debut album was created and patched together by both Squire and Brown, but *Second Coming* was created primarily by Squire. He wrote all but three of the album's songs, and he dominates its sound with his fiery solos, explosions, manic speed, and Zeppelin-inspired riffs. The influences of the Sex Pistols, Led Zeppelin, the Beach Boys, and the Beatles are all easily detected on *Second Coming*.

British pop fans had a mixed reaction to *Second Coming,* but most reviewers deemed the album excellent. A downturn in the political and economic climate in the U.K. may have had something to do with the tepid response of listeners; politics and a shared sense of hope had been dramatically altered in Britain in the five years between records for the Stone Roses. In the United States, though *Second Coming* reached Number 47 on *Billboard*'s pop charts in its first week.

In 1995 the Stone Roses chose Doug Goldstein, the manager for Guns n' Roses, to take over their management reins. They obtained A&R direction from Tom Zutaut, who worked with Motley Crue and Guns n' Roses, and their second album was mixed by Bill Price, who had previously lent his expertise to efforts by the Sex Pistols, the Clash, and Guns n' Roses. With Geffen behind them, the Stone Roses were poised to take the United States by storm in the late 1990s.

Selected discography

Singles

"So Young," Silvertone, 1985.
"Sally Cinnamon," Silvertone, 1987.
"Elephant Stone," Silvertone, 1988.
"Made of Stone," Silvertone, 1989.

Albums

Stone Roses, Silvertone, 1989.
Turns Into Stone, Silvertone, 1992.
Second Coming, Geffen, 1994.
The Complete Stone Roses, Silvertone, 1995.

Sources

Alternative Press, May 1995.
Entertainment Weekly, March 10, 1995.
Los Angeles Times, January 15, 1995; February 5, 1995.
Musician, January 1995.
New York Newsday, January 15, 1995.
People, January 23, 1995.
Rolling Stone, April 20, 1995.
Spin, May 1993; May 1995.

—*B. Kimberly Taylor*

Sunnyland Slim

Blues pianist, singer

Photograph by James Fraher, © James Fraher Photography

Blues legend Sunnyland Slim made music over the course of eight decades, from the hard-luck Deep South of the 1920s to the enduring grit of Chicago's South Side in the 1990s. One of the great singer-piano players of the century, Slim worked with blues greats like Ma Rainey and Little Brother Montgomery and fostered the careers of many others, most notably Muddy Waters.

In a recording career stretching from 1947 to 1985, Slim chalked up an impressive catalog of over 250 songs, or "sides," as they're known in blues parlance. Informing the feats of Slim the musician, though, was the heart of a man "who reveled in the hardscrabble, often profane blues life, yet could see—and taught others to see—the handiwork of God in people from church sisters to streetwalkers; a man whose faith enabled him to travel the hard, dangerous road of a bluesman and yet never fall prey to bitterness, self-destruction or despair," as was revealed in the liner notes to the album *Sunnyland Train.*

Practiced on a Shoe Box

The grandson of slaves, Sunnyland Slim was born Albert Luandrew on a farm in rural Mississippi in 1907. His early musical experiences included playing an organ owned by a church friend; he used a shoe box with keys drawn on it to practice his fingering between sessions on the actual instrument. He ran away from home at the age of 13—his mother had died of pneumonia and his stepmother was abusive. He made his way by doing odd jobs, like carrying water for a railroad gang and driving a doctor's car, until he finally landed a piano gig two nights a week at a juke joint (a small, inexpensive club) in rural Mississippi. Blues chronicler Dave Whiteis, in the liner notes to Slim's 1994 *Decoration Day* CD, described a typical sawmill juke joint scene of the 1920s: "Hard-working men, calloused and with rippling muscles, quaffed whiskey and danced with pretty women who'd been made available for the occasion. A high-stakes card game of Georgia skin was going on, dice were rolling, money moved from hand to hand. Most of it would end up in the coffers of the company that owned the mill, the juke, and—for all intents and purposes—most of the workers as well."

Such was the setting of Slim's first significant collaboration—with Little Brother Montgomery, a major southern blues pianist of the 1920s and 1930s. In 1923 Slim was traveling with a gambler-pimp friend and his party of prostitutes when an overnight jail stay followed by a car breakdown led him by chance to a juke where Montgomery was performing.

Born Albert Luandrew, September 5, 1907, near Vance, MS; died of complications stemming from kidney failure, March 17, 1995, in Chicago, IL; married Big Time Sarah (a blues singer), c. 1974 (marriage dissolved); second wife's name, Geraldine; children: Gregory Perkins.

Worked at odd jobs, including water carrying and chauffeuring; began playing piano professionally, c. 1922; played at cafés and gambling houses, Memphis, TN, c. 1923; performed in juke joints along Mississippi River, 1920s-30s; also worked as a cook, barber, pipe fitter, and electrician; recorded with Muddy Waters, 1946-47; began solo recording career, 1947; worked as house pianist at J.O.B. label, which he co-owned; became bandleader, Chicago, 1940s-50s; released album debut, *Slim's Shout*, Bluesville/Prestige, 1960; toured Canada and Europe, 1960s; recorded over 250 songs and numerous albums; founded Airway label, 1974; performed regularly in clubs and at festivals until his death.

Awards: City of Chicago Medal of Merit, 1987; National Heritage Foundation Award, National Endowment for the Arts, 1988; Sunnyland Slim Memorial Piano Set, Chicago Blues Festival, established in 1995.

Slim's playing and singing impressed Montgomery, and the two men soon made their way to Memphis, where piano players could get decent work in cafés and gambling houses. This was preferable to the fate of country blues guitarists, who played for change in parks, but not as lucrative and prestigious as gigs in vaudeville theaters, which required an ability to read music and improvise jazz. "Memphis used to be a barrelhouse town," Slim told *Deep Blues* author Robert Palmer. "It was the greatest town in the world for pimps and hustlers. That's where a whole lot of people got killed, you know." Palmer cites a 1916 insurance company report documenting a murder rate of 90 per 100,000 inhabitants, higher than that of Washington, D. C. in the 1990s.

Rather than stay in Memphis, though, Slim decided to travel the Mississippi River, shifting between river towns and lumber and turpentine camps. He picked up a number of skills while working to supplement his performance income, including cooking, barbering, pipe fitting, and electrical wiring—not to mention the more crafty talents associated with professional pool, dice, and card playing. Up to this point he was known by his given name; he acquired the moniker "Sunnyland Slim"

in the 1930s when he wrote a song recounting the deaths of two families that occurred in the span of a week on the tracks of the Sunnyland train. The train ran from Memphis to St. Louis, Missouri, and would often catch people unawares as they crossed the tracks, which ran right through the fields of the flat Mississippi Delta plains. "Seein' those little ... kids killed, that given me my tender heart. That rested on my mind and it given me a tender heart," Slim told *Down Beat* 60 years later.

These years of constant traveling and playing introduced Slim to a number of important southern blues musicians of the time. Among them were fellow pianists Roosevelt Sykes and Memphis Slim, harmonica players Sonny Boy Williamson and Snooky Pryor, the guitarist Honeyboy Edwards and—if Slim is to be taken at his word—even blues legend Robert Johnson himself. The fruit of these early experiences was a distinctive piano style that, according to Whiteis in the liner notes to *Sunnyland Train,* combined early Delta roots with newer urban energy: "Sunnyland's signature riff was a shimmering treble cascade—beginning with a chiming upper-register flurry, he'd ease back into the melody with a complex descent through the registers. But, at any given moment, he might also unfurl a driving boogie flagwaver, or ease into a melodic stride; listeners might hear anything from the high, lonesome tones of field hollers to a super-charged rendition of the standard 'Rollin' and Tumblin'."

Though his first studio experience may have been as far back as 1929, Slim did not join the musicians union until the late 1940s; his earliest recordings date from 1947. It was that year that he recorded eight sides for the RCA Victor label as "Dr. Clayton's Buddy." The pseudonym was an attempt to capitalize on his prior association with the late Peter Cleighton, who had attained some measure of success before drinking himself to death following the loss of his wife and two children, again in the path of a speeding train. He also recorded a few songs as "Delta Joe" on the Opera label.

Settled in Chicago, Played with Waters

Slim's traveling days wound to a close when he moved to Cairo, Illinois, in the late 1930s. In 1939 he settled down for good in Chicago, where he met Muddy Waters, who went on to become one of the most successful and perhaps most widely known of all blues musicians. About five years after moving to town, Slim joined a band at the Flame Club on Chicago's South Side that featured Waters's country-style guitar picking. That band didn't last long, but Slim and Waters formed a mutual respect based on musicianship and professionalism. When Slim was asked to play piano on a Columbia Records session in late 1946, he brought Waters along. Though the label released nothing from that session, Slim arranged another the following year with Aristocrat Records (later Chess), which began a long association between Waters and the label's owners, Leonard and Phil Chess. The relationship, and Chess Records, would make musical history.

Throughout the 1940s and 1950s Slim continued his collaboration with top musicians like guitarists Lonnie Johnson, Hubert Sumlin and Robert Jr. Lockwood, harp player Big Walter Horton, and tenors Red Holloway and Ernest Cotton. Many of these would perform at Slim's after-hours "parties" at his home, which brought in a fair amount of cash—even after local authorities were paid off. Slim was proud of his efforts to help younger musicians get their start, modeling his mentor role on that of Big Bill Broonzy, who had done the same for him when Slim first arrived in Chicago. "It's not a day goes past that I don't think about somethin' Slim said," singer Zora Young recalled in *Living Blues*. "When you left Sunnyland's finishing school, you were ready for the world."

Slim's varied collaborations were matched by the large number of labels for which he recorded, including Hytone, Mercury, Apollo, Regal, Chance, Blue Lake, Cobra, and J.O.B. (which he co-owned). His album debut came in 1960 with the release of *Slim's Shout* on Bluesville (a subsidiary of Prestige), featuring a New York band that boasted the tenor sax talents of King Curtis.

Played Eastern Europe, Started Own Label

In the late 1950s and 1960s the blues enjoyed a "revival" as increased attention was paid to the uniquely American musical form. Musicians like Slim became highly sought after for Canadian and European tours. Traveling with the American Folk Blues Festival in Europe in 1964, Slim was among the first blues musicians to play in Eastern Europe. Back home in Chicago, years of peddling records out of the trunk of his car when conventional distribution proved inadequate gave way to more refined methods—Slim started his own Airway label in 1974. Another example of his grandfatherly role in the Chicago blues scene, the label featured a host of local talent, as well as Slim's own recordings, the first of which was *Sunnyland Slim Live in Europe, 1975.*

Beginning in the early 1980s and continuing for over ten years, until his health failed him, Slim was a regular Sunday night feature at Chicago's B.L.U.E.S. club. But the effects of a stroke and a broken hip, among other infirmities, took their toll in these last years and moved one observer to describe Slim hunched over his piano as resembling an ancient question mark. His performances were nevertheless strong to the end. "He flies over the furiously swinging ensemble with singing so powerful as to give the lie to his eight and a half decades of life," John Brisbin wrote in *Living Blues*. "Twisting a long sweet note into a lemony falsetto howl, he sheds years and ailments like a faith-healed believer." Slim died of complications stemming from kidney failure on March 17, 1995.

Like so many other blues musicians, Slim never achieved a level of mass appeal in accord with his stature in American music history. He played featured sets in the annual Chicago Blues Festival, however, and honors bestowed on him in his later years include a 1987 City of Chicago Medal of Merit and a 1988 National Endowment for the Arts National Heritage Foundation Award. The 1995 Chicago Blues Festival, mounted two months after Slim's death, showcased the first annual Sunnyland Slim Memorial Piano Set, and the city's mayor declared the final day of the festival "Sunnyland Slim Day in Chicago." Perhaps the most telling reflection of Slim's legacy, though, was a four-hour musical tribute undertaken by his fellow musicians and attended by many of his earnest fans—beneficiaries one and all of his conviction that "you can't have it all. You gotta spread some of it around."

Selected discography

Singles

As Doctor Clayton's Buddy; on Victor, 1947

"Nappy Head Woman."
"Broke and Hungry."
"Illinois Central."

With Muddy Waters; on Aristocrat (later Chess), c. 1947-48

"Johnson Machine Gun."
"Fly Right, Little Girl."
"She Ain't Nowhere."
"My Baby, My Baby."

On Hytone, 1949

"Jivin' Boogie."
"The Devil Is a Busy Man."
"Mud Kicking Woman."

On Constellation, 1953

"Bassology."
"When I Was Young."
"Living in the White House."

With Lefty Bates and Willie Dixon; on Cobra, 1956

"It's You Baby."
"Highway 51."

Also recorded for Opera label as "Delta Joe."

Albums

Slim's Shout, Bluesville/Prestige, 1960.
Sunnyland Slim Live in Europe, 1975, Airway, 1975.
Be Careful How You Vote (includes "You Can't Have It All" and "Johnson Machine Gun"), Airway, 1981, reissued, 1983, reissued on Earwig, 1989.
Sunnyland Train (includes "Sunnyland Train" and "Highway 61"), Red Beans, 1983, reissued, Evidence, 1995.
Chicago Jump (includes "You Used to Love Me" and "Chicago Jump"), Red Beans, 1985, reissued, Evidence, 1995.
Sunnyland Slim Blues Band, Red Beans, 1986.
Decoration Day (recorded in 1980; includes "Rock Little Daddy" and "Dust My Broom"), Evidence, 1994.
(With Koko Taylor) *Off the Record*, Chess.

With others, also recorded *Sunnyland Slim* (from sessions as J.O.B. Records house pianist), Flyright.

Sources

Books

The Blackwell Guide to Blues Records, edited by Paul Oliver, Basil Blackwell, 1989.
Blues Records, January 1943 to December 1966, edited by Mike Leadbitter, Oak Publications, 1968.
Nothing But the Blues, edited by Mike Leadbitter, Hanover Books, 1971.
Palmer, Robert, *Deep Blues*, Penguin, 1982.

Periodicals

Down Beat, September 1984; December 1985; April 1986; February 1991; May 1991; June 1995.
Living Blues, May/June 1995.
New York Times, March 20, 1995.

Additional information for this profile was obtained from liner notes by Dave Whiteis, John Brisbin, and Bill Dahl to the Evidence and Earwig releases cited above.

—*John Packel*

Irma Thomas

Singer

AP/Wide World Photos

The story of R&B singer Irma Thomas seems the ideal candidate for a film biography, one that would pick its leading lady from the younger generation of soul divas that carry on Thomas's legacy. "Honey, my story sounds like a black version of the Loretta Lynn story," Thomas joked with a writer from the *New Yorker* once. A native of New Orleans, Thomas cut her first record while a teen single mother in the late 1950s, and went on to have a nominally successful recording career—although she never made as much money from it as those behind the scenes. The British Invasion and cataclysmic weather put her career under water in New Orleans, so she packed up her four children and moved to California, alternating performing gigs with her sales clerk job. Returning to New Orleans in the mid-1970s was the beginning of a change of fortune for Thomas, and since then she has enjoyed a successful recording career on Rounder Records as well as the support of a loyal local fan base. A celebrity in her hometown, Thomas puts her good Grammy-nominated name to use in charity work and as the proprietor of her own club.

Thomas's launch into the music business seems a veritable rags-to-riches tale. A mother at 15, to support her family—one that grew to four children by the time she was 20—Thomas found employment in restaurants around New Orleans, usually as a cook or dishwasher. However, one job had her waiting tables in an R&B club, and when famed bandleader Tommy Ridgely played there one night, the seventeen-year-old Thomas boldly asked if she could sing a number. "I do know I was a ham," Thomas recalled about herself to *Advocate* writer John Wirt, in part because of her years of experience singing gospel in her church. "I didn't have any problems with standing up and singing in front of an audience."

Became a Minor Success

Thomas's performance with Ridgely went over well with the audience and she soon began splitting up her singing and waitressing shifts, much to the annoyance of the manager; he made her choose one or the other, and she chose the microphone. Soon Thomas began playing in other New Orleans clubs and along the Gulf Coast. She cut her first record, "You Can Have My Husband (But Don't Mess With My Man)," in 1959; it was an immediate hit. Soon she signed to Minit Records and began collaborating with local producer and writer Allen Toussaint. The songs released during this era—"It's Raining," "I Done Got Over It," and "I Wish Someone Would Care," achieved "a modern soul sound, but with a powerful blues interest," noted *Down Beat* writer Terri Hemmert. Almost all of them made the R&B charts—with "I Wish Someone Would Care," reaching Number 17—although Thomas was certainly not getting rich off

Born c. 1941 in New Orleans, LA; married Emile Jackson (a music business manager), late 1970s; four children.

Worked as a restaurant cook; began performing in New Orleans clubs in 1958; released first single, "You Can Have My Husband (But Don't Mess With My Man)," 1959; signed to Minit Records, late 1950s; during the early 1960s recorded "Time Is On My Side," a song subsequently recorded by the Rolling Stones to great success; recording career sidelined by other trends in music; worked as a sales clerk in a Montgomery Ward department store in Los Angeles, CA; signed with Atlantic Records, early 1970s; also recorded for the Cotillion label, mid-1970s; began performing again in New Orleans in the late 1970s; signed to Rounder Records, mid-1980s; released comeback album, *The New Rules,* 1986.

Selected awards: *Simply the Best: Live* was nominated for a Grammy Award, 1991; recipient of numerous humanitarian awards for public-service work in New Orleans.

Addresses: *Record company*—Rounder Records, One Camp St., Cambridge, MA 02140.

the proceeds. "That was the scheme of things when I got into this business," she recalled for the *Advocate,* referring to the raw deals young African American artists were sometimes signed to in exchange for their talent. "It had nothing to do with my being young and naive.... That was a situation where what you didn't know did hurt."

Another song Thomas recorded during the early 1960s was not as successful for her as her other releases, but it went on to bigger fame when covered by another act. Back then, a young, undiscovered English rock band called the Rolling Stones were devotees of American soul and R&B music; their early repertoire consisted of covers of songs by the likes of Muddy Waters, B.B. King—and Irma Thomas. When the Stones recorded her "Time Is On My Side," it became their first big hit. Thomas continued to perform it for a number of years, but eventually ceased because fans thought she was paying homage to *them.*

Thomas's recording career suffered further at the hand of fate. She performed the New Orleans/Gulf Coast circuit for the rest of the 1960s, but unfortunately the popularity of her particular brand of R&B had waned in favor of British acts and the Motown sound (and later the Philly sound and disco); when a hurricane wiped out all the clubs at which she had been booked along the Gulf Coast in 1969, Thomas packed up her children and moved to Los Angeles.

Attempt at Major-Label Career Failed

From the start, things were difficult for Thomas in California. "It was a very cliquish situation," she said in the *Advocate* interview with Wirt. "It wasn't what you knew and how good you were, it was who you know. I didn't know anybody." She took a job as a lingerie sales associate at a Montgomery Ward department store, and she performed in local clubs as well as farther north around San Francisco and Oakland. Eventually Atlantic Records offered her a deal, and she went into the studio to record, with disastrous results. "The producers wanted me to sound like Diana Ross," Thomas recalled for *St. Petersburg Times* reporter Tony Green. "I have no idea why because I have my own voice, which I feel is just as strong as hers. To me the whole session was a joke." The studio work in L.A. went nowhere, but Thomas did eventually land steady work performing around the Oakland and San Francisco environs. After a time she relocated her family farther north and even got herself transferred to a Montgomery Ward store there.

During the 1970s, Thomas recorded some material for the Cotillion label, and when visiting home found that New Orleans audiences were again eager for her particular brand of soul. She began traveling back and forth between California and Louisiana, and when she found herself spending more time on the road than at home, she moved back to New Orleans in 1976. Performing in the plethora of blues and R&B clubs that her hometown has to offer, Thomas also found love there when she met Emile Jackson one night. A year after they were married, Thomas made him her business manager. She had been dissatisfied with her previous one, and as she told the *New Yorker* in 1988, "I figured [my husband] would be the best judge if whether I wanted to do something or didn't want to do it. And I figured he'd have my financial interests at heart, because they'd be his financial interests, too."

Career Resurrected in Mid-1980s

When a New Orleans writer saw Thomas perform one night, he recommended her to the famed jazz, R&B, gospel and soul label Rounder Records for their forthcoming compilation *New Orleans Ladies.* The record company liked her work so much they offered her a contract, and her comeback began in earnest with the 1986 LP *The New Rules.* Throughout the 1990s other recording efforts followed, such as *The Way I Feel* and *True Believer.* "Thomas now joins ranks with Tina Turner and Ruth Brown, women who have made significant contributions to the r&b scene of the '50s and '60s and have returned decades later with fresh energy and maturity," *Down Beat's* Hemmert wrote.

Rounder sent Thomas on tour, and one particular gig at a club in San Francisco owned by 1970s musician Boz Scaggs was put down on tape. The result was *Irma Thomas Live: Simply The Best,* released in 1992 and earning her a Grammy Award nomination. The new label also offered the singer a chance to explore another facet of her musical abilities on vinyl: gospel. Back in New Orleans Thomas had become the featured soloist in her church's gospel choir, despite a busy secular recording and performing career. This house of worship, the First African Baptist Church of New Orleans, is the city's oldest African American congregation. In 1994 she used this experience and love of the form when recording *Walk Around Heaven: New Orleans Gospel Soul.* Two big names in the city's gospel scene, Sammy Berfect and Dwight Franklin, collaborated with Thomas on the record. It was her first pure gospel effort, and as the singer explained to Green in the *St. Petersburg Times,* she refuses to "mix the two; when I'm on stage I basically sing R&B and blues. I was raised in the church, so I know mixing the two is wrong." Ron Wynn reviewed *Walk Around Heaven* for *CD Review* and asserted that "Thomas simply sings God's music with the same passion, power, and integrity she's always brought to her own."

Thomas also tours extensively, and does not shy away from performing "Time Is On My Side" any longer in her well-attended club appearances. Contemporary singer Bonnie Raitt convinced her to start singing it again one night at the Hard Rock Cafe in New Orleans. "Go ahead on and sing it regardless of what people think," Thomas recalled Raitt saying when she spoke with the *Advocate.* "Just sing it! You do it better than they do anyway." Thomas also began a venture that hearkened back to her early years when she opened her own club, the Lion's Den—she cooks food at home and carts it in for the audience. The singer also uses her local celebrity-hood in New Orleans for various good causes, in particular as an advocate for at-risk youth. Happy to have

such a rich life after so many years of hard work, Thomas claims to feel more comfortable with her voice at a later age. "It has matured, yes," she told Wirt in the *Advocate.* "I can hear a major difference in the voice of the 17-year-old and the voice of the 54-year-old. My voice has deepened somewhat. I have a better grasp and understanding of music and how to perform it than when I was younger."

Selected discography

Singles; on Minit

"You Can Have My Husband (But Don't Mess With My Man)," 1959.
"I Wish Someone Would Care," 1964.

Also recorded "It's Raining," "I Done Got Over It," and "Time Is On My Side."

LPs; on Rounder except where otherwise noted

Wish Someone Would Care, Imperial, 1964.
The New Rules, 1986.
The Way I Feel, 1988.
Ruler of Hearts, Charly, 1989.
Something Good: The Muscle Shoals Sessions, Chess, 1990.
True Believer, 1992.
Irma Thomas Live: Simply The Best, 1991.
Time Is On My Side: The Best of Irma Thomas, Vol. 1, EMI/America, 1992.
Walk Around Heaven: New Orleans Gospel Soul, 1994.

Sources

Advocate (Baton Rouge, LA), May 5, 1995.
Chicago Tribune, June 16, 1994.
CD Review, July 1994.
Daily World (Helena, AR), October 4, 1995.
Down Beat, May 1990.
New Yorker, July 11, 1988.
Rolling Stone, June 16, 1994.
St. Petersburg Times, October 21, 1994.

Additional information for this profile was obtained from Rounder Records publicity materials, 1995.

—Carol Brennan

Too $hort

Rap artist

MICHAEL OCHS ARCHIVES/Venice, CA

The "acknowledged West Coast master of the pimp rhyme," Jonathan Gold wrote in the *Los Angeles Times,* "Oakland rapper Too $hort built a hip-hop empire on the vulgar street-corner snap, clever though rudimentary litanies of profanity and mayhem." Todd Shaw created the rap persona Too $hort out of the tradition of the "pimp," which was popularized in the 1970s by a fad for "blaxploitation," exemplified in films like *Shaft.* The character is one that has a mixed reception among black audiences. Some listeners see him as an insult to black women and as a degrading caricature of black masculinity; others have flocked to the record stores, embracing what they believe to be an image of a powerful, defiant black man. Both sides have made Too $hort an important phenomenon, as they argue about what he "means" in his rapped narratives about sex and "bitches"—and drive up his record sales, despite the fact that most of his songs are too sexually explicit for radio airwaves.

Shaw comes from a background that bears little resemblance to the film heroes he imitates. Born in Los Angeles in the mid-1960s, he grew up in a solidly middle-class home. Both of his parents were accountants, and his mother spent 30 years working for the IRS before retiring in the 1990s when her son built her a home in Atlanta. Contradicting the attitude about women deployed in his music, $hort has maintained a strong and respectful relationship with his mother. He told *Vibe* contributor Laura Jamison, "We're good friends, always have been. We never had a strain in our relationship at all." Nonetheless, his mother is offended by his "mouth." "I get really uncomfortable when I know my mother's in the crowd," he confessed to Jamison. "She'll come to me after and say, 'You got a foul mouth.'"

Created Pimp Persona

The pimp character, then, is one Shaw actively had to seek out. The move from Los Angeles to Oakland, California, helped make it accessible to him, especially as he chose to immerse himself in the city's "street" life. In 1992 $hort described Oakland to *Billboard*'s Havelock Nelson as "a pimp town. That vibe started to fade in the '80s, but in '92 it's still here." Nelson determined that $hort's "pimp stance is the result of having read blaxploitation books by authors Iceberg Slim and Donald Goines, and [absorbed] the mood of his Bay-area surroundings." *The Source*'s Ronin Ro, writing in 1995, reported that $hort's image "was inspired by Richard Pryor's early comedy routines and by the pimps in '70s films and TV shows." $hort told him that "back then, everybody was just interested in pimps! I used to wanna wear big pimp hats in old photos I took as a kid! I learned how to pimp-walk before I could walk straight!" Shaw

For the Record . . .

Born Todd Shaw, c. 1966, in Los Angeles, CA; raised in Oakland, CA; son of accountants.

With friend Freddy B., began producing tapes of his raps, comprised largely of "Freaky Tales" of sexual escapades; sold the tapes on the streets while in high school before producing albums through independent label 75 Girls Records, 1983-88; developed own production company, Dangerous Music; signed by Jive, a subsidiary of RCA, 1987.

Three albums attained platinum status by 1995: *Life Is ... Too Short, Short Dog's in the House,* and *Get In Where You Fit In.*

Addresses: *Record company*—Jive, 137-139 West 25th St., New York, NY 10001.

earned his street nickname in high school, when his growth seemed to have halted at 5 feet 2 inches.

Jeff Chang, writing in *Vibe,* set down the fundamental truth of $hort's career, recalling that the rapper "built his seemingly unshakable fan base with the 'Freaky' songs and others like them." The "Freaky Tales" Chang refers to were the staple of $hort's high school raps—strung together vignettes of his alleged sexual escapades with a seemingly endless supply of insatiable women. Shaw didn't have the naiveté or the patience to wait and be "discovered." Instead, he and friend Freddy B. produced and manufactured their tapes at home and then sold them on the sidewalks in Oakland.

For almost three years, from 1981 to 1983, Freddy and $hort were self-supporting musical entrepreneurs, doing a brisk business selling $hort's x-rated rhymes. He released three albums under the auspices of a small independent label, 75 Girls Records, between 1983 and 1988. Concurrently, beginning in 1986, he pursued one of his primary dreams by founding his own record label, Dangerous Music. The label's first release, of course, was a collection of $hort's rhymes called *Born to Mack,* which he sold, in his traditional manner, from the trunk of his car. *Born to Mack* sold 20,000 copies—an impressive feat for a tiny label— before Jive, a subsidiary of RCA, took note and signed $hort in 1987.

While this new home provided $hort with major label security, it also agreed not to limit the content of his raps. $hort remained as prolific as ever, providing Jive with

the material for a new album every year. Jive's first step was to rerelease *Born to Mack* in 1989, quickly turning it into a gold record. The label brought out *Life Is ... Too Short* in 1989 and *Short Dog's in the House* in the fall of 1990. The latter album brought $hort some crossover attention, mainly because of a song called "The Ghetto." The single not only tackled issues more serious than his usual "Freaky Tales," it was also clean enough for DJs to spin on the air, bringing the rapper attention that otherwise eluded him—and a Number 20 position on *Billboard*'s Top Pop Albums chart.

Mixed Reviews

$hort had a piece included in the soundtrack for *New Jack City* in 1991 before he prepared *Shorty the Pimp* for release in 1992. Picking up on the tale end of *Short Dog*'s momentum, this album entered *Billboard*'s Top 200 in the Number Six position and rose through the numbers in the R&B albums chart. Of course, national sales also brought national opinion—not all of it warm. In her review for *Rolling Stone,* Danyel Smith described the '92 album as "a female-hating string of songs pulsing with $hort's usual blend of nonchalance, heavy bass lines and disdainful lyrics. His rhymes ... flow so effortlessly, and $hort's delivery is so laid-back and listless, you'd think he was rhyming by accident if it weren't for the calculated coldness of his words." Nelson described the album as vintage Too $hort, filled with unbleeped cursing and outrageous tales from "da hood."

Like *Short Dog, Shorty the Pimp* had its serious side, inspired by the police beating of Rodney King in Los Angeles. A track called "I Want to Be Free" ends with the line, "I ain't mad / I'm just black," which inspired quotation in many reviews. This piece aside, $hort had already decided to step back from the crossover potential of "The Ghetto." "I was at a point in my career," he told Nelson, "where I had to ask myself, 'Where should I go?' I am a platinum artist who has decided to be hardcore." The choice also had a market motive, since $hort faced the loss of his primary fan base if he was perceived as catering to mainstream tastes. Barry Weiss, an executive at Jive, explained to Nelson that although they "were hoping for another 'The Ghetto' ..., to be honest, we're glad that we didn't get one. Too $hort's appeal is at the street level. With an artist like him, the worst thing to have is the perception that he's selling out."

But he was selling, and very consistently; even 1986's *Born to Mack* was still holding its own in music store bins in 1992. "Oddly enough," Chang concluded in *Vibe,* "$hort's formula works. He and his music make people part with hard-earned cash for some ill-satisfaction."

When Toure reviewed *Get In Where You Fit In* for *Rolling Stone* in the fall of 1993, he pegged $hort as one of the definitive elements in the Oakland rap sound, which he saw as the "home of a nascent hip-hop explosion." "He's been recording for years," Toure noted about $hort, "but he's still got an underground flavor, meaning he's got the skill to put his ghetto on tape.... $hort makes no attempt at accessibility.... He just shows you a door into his world: Press play, and suddenly you're a young black boy cruising East Oaktown at about 15 mph on a hot ... Saturday, watching the girls pass in shorts."

Writing for *The Source*, Allen Gordon saw *Get In Where You Fit In* as a "back to basics" album for Too $hort, arguing that after eight albums, "at this stage of his life what is there left for him to do? He is too set in his ways to start jumping on any trends and bandwagons that might come his way. He's not about to chase after the elusive crossover audience." Gordon was happy with what he found on the recording, praising both the rapper's rhymes—"it is a delight to see $hort on top of his mackin' game"—and his music—"it is even better to listen to his beats, triple helpings of pure uncut, un-looped funk." The album took the top of the R&B chart and rose into the Top Ten in pop. *Get In Where You Fit In* eventually reached platinum status, along with *Life Is ... Too Short* and *Short Dog*, while *Shorty the Pimp* went gold.

Dangerous Music

In 1994 Jive also backed $hort's independent label, giving Dangerous Music some solid resources and strength. By the 1990s Dangerous was developing its own roster of rap talent, beginning to fulfill $hort's ambition for the outfit. It was created as "an outlet for the many talented artists in the Bay with no outlet," $hort told Nelson. By that time, both Pooh Man and Ant Banks were part of the production company. Soon after, $hort moved Dangerous Music to Atlanta. In 1995 he told Ronin Ro that the "whole move to Atlanta was about money. [Two years ago] Dangerous Music was outgrowing its location in Oakland, which was a three bedroom home." He did add, however, that it was also about finding a safer home for his mother and brother.

Cocktales came out in 1995 to good reviews. Chang called it "his most musically seductive ever," noting that the artist "values easy rhymes, phat bass, and explicit sex" because those "are the skills that pay his bills." Reviewing the release for the *New York Times*, S. H. Fernando, Jr., referred to it as "vintage Too $hort ..., stuffed with more machismo and misogyny than a porn movie. But behind the raunch are thoughtful, melodic grooves, custom-made for cruising on a sunny after-noon." Even Frank Owen's critique, which appeared in *New York Newsday*, ended with a slap on the back, admitting that the rapper's "sometimes lackluster delivery, limited vocabulary and the often plodding musical arrangements can't stop [the album] from impressing with sheer cheek."

Wet Dream Rap—The Misogynist Element

Despite all the critical and popular success of his work, Too $hort has faced ongoing backlash for his unabashedly antifemale lyrics. In her piece for *Rolling Stone*, Smith voiced much of the frustration with Too $hort's persistent misogyny, finding it represented fully in the 1992 release *Shorty the Pimp*. Describing the lyrics as "stuffed to busting with lines about sluts and girls riding on $hort's 'snoopy,'" Smith determined that the "album is a byproduct of his angry, warranted nightmares (the police) and his angry wet dreams (the bitches)." She argued further that despite "all its deftly drawn urban male realities, *Shorty the Pimp* lacks the immediacy necessary to make its he-man poetry jolting. $hort's songs momentarily empower the disfranchised Young Black Male and the fascinated Young White Male but move any self-respecting female to press EJECT—firmly." She concluded that "his misogyny, which used to be bewildering, more taunting than challenging, has gone from insulting to scary."

Although he admits that young men "listen to my words and wanna start calling their women 'Bee-atch!'" as he told Ronin Ro, $hort has tried to defuse his malevolent image by detaching it from his off-stage personality. "See, I know a lot of guys listen to Too $hort and wanna be like me," he explained to Ro. "But I ain't no 'super-pimp,' all invincible and shit. I'm a normal human being and a businessman doing what I gotta do." When Jamison visited $hort in Oakland to interview him for a 1994 issue of *Vibe*, she discovered not a pimp at all, but a "preoccupied inner-city businessman who's got deals—not wheels or women—on his mind." In fact, the rapper explained to Jamison that he sees his tales about women in a very matter-of-fact light: they are the way he makes his living. "Rap was always my hustle," he told her, "the way I made money. You can't call it a work of genius—the shit is so lame. I grab the smallest part of the funk and ride it for eight minutes."

Selected discography

Born to Mack (contains "Freaky Tales"), Dangerous Music, 1986, reissued, Jive, 1989.
Life Is ... Too Short, Jive, 1989.
Short Dog's in the House (includes "The Ghetto"), Jive, 1990.

(Contributor) *New Jack City* (soundtrack), 1991.
Shorty the Pimp (includes "I Want to Be Free"), Jive, 1992.
Greatest Hits, Volume 1, In a Minute, 1993.
Get In Where You Fit In, Jive, 1993.
Cocktales, Jive, 1995.
Paystyle (maxi single), Jive, 1995.

Sources

Billboard, December 22, 1990; August 22, 1992; January 14, 1995.
Los Angeles Times, January 22, 1995.
New York Newsday, January 22, 1995.
New York Times, March 12, 1995.
Rolling Stone, February 7, 1991; December 12, 1991; September 17, 1992; November 25, 1993.
The Source, December 1993; December 1994; February 1995.
Vibe, February 1994; February 1995

Additional information for this piece was obtained from Jive.

—*Ondine Le Blanc*

Junior Vasquez

Producer, DJ

Occasional club disc jockey and record producer Junior Vasquez has become one of the key forces in dance music with his seamless mixing skills and intuitive knack for knowing exactly what his audiences want. People who frequented New York City's Sound Factory in the early and mid-1990s knew Vasquez as the innovative musical ringleader of the nightclub and a link to what was looming on the musical horizon.

As the influential club's resident DJ, Vasquez would spin records from late Saturday night through Sunday brunch, tirelessly and enthusiastically presenting the sounds of the moment; his gift for mixing tracks was soon in great demand. Record company executives took a keen interest in what Vasquez played and contemplated how he could reshape the music of their artists. Vasquez's playlist was usually comprised of music only available on promotional test pressings; other material came from tapes whisked directly out of studios. Whether or not a particular single moved the crowd could be crucial to a musician's career or a record company executive's.

Born Donald Mattern in the early 1950s, Vasquez was raised in Lancaster, Pennsylvania, a small town in the eastern part of the state. He spent endless hours as a child listening to records and dancing. His father, a butcher, sometimes took young Donald to his workplace; there Vasquez once watched his father kill a cow with a sledgehammer. "I've blocked it from my mind," he told *Rolling Stone*'s Rich Cohen, claiming only to remember the wooden ramp that led to the slaughterhouse.

Vasquez's interest in both music and dance seemed odd to his family and neighbors, and as a result, the young man felt out of place in Lancaster. He told Cohen, "I knew I was on my way somewhere else. It had to be a big city and far from Lancaster."

After Vasquez arrived in Manhattan in 1971, he adopted a new name—simply because he liked the sound of it. He drifted from job to job, uncertain of where his dreams would lead him. In the meantime, he took college courses in art, fashion, design, and hairdressing.

Almost ten years after his arrival in New York City, Vasquez walked into a music store in the 42nd Street subway station to look for a Chaka Khan album. He suddenly experienced what Cohen described as "a moment of clarity." He told the journalist, "All those records overwhelmed me. I knew this was my future."

Vasquez began making tapes of his favorite music during this period, which led him to do the same for local radio stations. He started working as a DJ for small

For the Record . . .

Born Donald Mattern, August 24, c. 1952, in Lancaster, PA; son of a butcher. *Education:* Courses in art, fashion, design, and hairdressing.

Began making mix tapes for radio stations and working as a DJ for small parties, New York City, 1986; DJ at the Sound Factory, 1989-95; began remixing singles, 1989, and coproducing tracks for various artists; released own singles "Get Your Hands off My Man," "X," and "Drag Queen," Tribal/IRS, 1995.

Addresses: *Office*—This Beats Workin' Inc., 254 West 54th St., New York, NY 10019.

Lauper's 1994 *Hat Full of Stars* album, produced four tracks on Lauper's *Twelve Deadly Cyns* disc in 1995, and was asked to produce an album for John Mellancamp that year. He also produced and cowrote "Brand New Love" and "Behind the Scenes" for J. Quest's album *The Quest Is On* and produced the Tom Jones single "She's a Lady" in 1995.

In addition to his high-profile work with other artists, Vasquez has released his own singles: 1995's "Get Your Hands off My Man," "X," and "Drag Queen," all on the Tribal/IRS label. He told *Rolling Stone*'s Cohen of his creative method, "I'm an abstract artist. I take a whole lot of sound, put it in a barrel, shake it up like paint, and out come these wild designs." Another area in which Vasquez has achieved great acclaim is in post-production and remix work. He has been known to completely transform a song—frequently making it more dance-friendly—by electronically manipulating its various components. He has provided this type of service to over one hundred musicians, including Janet Jackson, Annie Lennox, Paula Abdul, Elton John, Madonna, Duran Duran, Mavis Staples, Cher, Prince, Mellancamp, Naomi Campbell, Queen, The Time, Sheena Easton, and Hammer.

Clearly, the future looks promising for Vasquez in spite of the closing of the revered Sound Factory, which may eventually reopen in another location. Vasquez told Flick at the time of the club's shuttering, "I keep telling myself that this is all happening for a good reason. Hey, maybe it's time for me to go and reinvent myself—or to explore a new part of myself." This attitude has continued to serve him, helping him to explore new territory in his work. According to Flick, it's very likely that Vasquez's most impressive and passionate output as a writer, producer, mixer, and DJ is yet to come.

parties and eventually branched out to increasingly larger Manhattan nightclubs as word of his talents began to spread. Described by Cohen as "wary and aggressive ... austere and forbidding ... with the rough-hewn features and cocky gait of an old-time boxer" and sporting numerous tattoos, Vasquez said of his break into the business, "I was never one of the pretty people. So I had to be a bulldog."

In 1989 Richard Grant, owner of the Sound Factory, approached Vasquez and asked him if he would oversee the music end of his new venture. By 1990 the Sound Factory had far exceeded anyone's expectations; more than a dance club and showcase for new music, it had become a marathon Saturday night blowout, a place of sanctuary where twisting torsos and happily sweating bodies let loose, and where a week's culmination of repressed primal energy came to life through Vasquez's grooves. Said *Billboard* dance music columnist Larry Flick, "For many, the Sound Factory was a primary lifestyle component."

Madonna recruited dancers for her "Vogue" video at the sparsely decorated club, and Prince was so enthralled with Vasquez after checking him out at the club that he hired him to remix his 1990 release, *Graffiti Bridge*. When the Sound Factory closed in 1995 due to conflicts over its hours of operation and New York liquor license laws, it marked the end of an era. "Where do they go?" Vasquez asked Cohen of the club crawlers," remarking, "I feel sorry for them. I gave them so much but now can give to them no more."

By the time the club closed down, however, Vasquez had developed numerous other creative outlets. He had produced and co-written Lisa Lisa's "When I Fell in Love" single in 1993, produced six cuts from Cyndi

Selected discography

Singles; on Tribal/IRS, 1995.

"Get Your Hands off My Man."
"X."
"Drag Queen."

As producer

Lisa Lisa, "When I Fell in Love," Pendulum, 1993.
Cyndi Lauper, "Lies," "Feels Like Christmas," "Like I Used To," "A Part Hate," and "Someone Like Me," *Hat Full of Stars*, Epic, 1994.
Cyndi Lauper, "Hey Now ... Girls Just Wanna Have Fun," "Who Let in the Rain," "Sally's Pigeons," and "That's What I Think," *Twelve Deadly Cyns*, Epic, 1995.

J. Quest, "Behind the Scenes" and "Brand New Love," *The Quest Is On,* Mercury, 1995.

Tom Jones, "She's a Lady," *To Wong Foo, Thanks for Everything, Julie Newmar* (soundtrack), MCA, 1995.

Wild Orchid, "Talk to Me," RCA, 1995.

Sources

Billboard, March 11, 1995.
Rolling Stone, April 20, 1995.
Genre, September 1995.

—*B. Kimberly Taylor*

Chris Whitley

Singer, songwriter, guitarist

Creating an original musical language that blends Delta-based blues with innovative rock, Chris Whitley has etched out a unique place for himself as a songwriter and performer. He has been heralded as one of the greatest slide guitarists of the 1990s and as a vocalist and musician who has both mastered and reinvented the blues. "[Whitley's] lyrics approach poetry, his playing would shame some jazz musicians, and his singing stretches from the lower chakras to a higher reach of reason no one would call blue," wrote Sean Elder in *Vogue.*

Whitley's music derives from many influences, ranging from the legendary Robert Johnson and Thelonious Monk to Jimi Hendrix, Iggy Pop, Erik Satie, and even the sounds of Moroccan and Tibetan music and jug bands. He has also professed a great love of rhythm and blues, especially as performed by Al Green. Although known for his blues sensibility, Whitley uses the blues in a fashion that is all his own. "I never wanted to do traditional music," he told *Vogue.* "Maybe that was why I got a lot out of it: I got the essence of what I wanted from it and kept looking for something else. When I was listening to Robert Johnson I was also listening to things like Gary Numan [the synth master best known for 'Cars']."

Whitley's musical restlessness reflects his nomadic youth. His family moved often, setting up residences in Texas, Oklahoma, and Connecticut before he was a teenager. After his parents divorced, he moved with his sister and mother to Mexico. A year later the family moved to Vermont, where Whitley began to immerse himself in music and spend a lot of time racing motorcycles. His first record purchase was Jimi Hendrix's *Smash Hits,* and he also found musical inspiration in Johnny Winter, Led Zeppelin, and Muddy Waters.

By age eleven, Whitley was playing harmonica in a dance band. He first picked up a guitar at age fifteen and then formed the short-lived group Faded Glory. Whitley was so disillusioned by the experience that he sold all his equipment after the group's demise and purchased a Dobro™ so he could pursue his growing passion for blues music.

Found Success Abroad

Eager to move on musically, Whitley dropped out of high school and moved to New York City. He got a job at a deli and began performing his blues-based Dobro™ and guitar music wherever he could in public, often in city parks and on piers at night after work. Eventually he became a house musician at a club called Studio 10. Then a friend who worked in a travel agency helped him land a few gigs in Belgium.

Photograph by Paul S. Howell, Gamma-Liaison Network

For the Record . . .

Born c. 1961, in Houston, TX; married; children: one daughter.

Played harmonica in dance band, early 1970s; began playing guitar, 1976; formed Faded Glory, late 1970s; performed in small clubs in New York City, late 1970s; played solo and with Noh Rodeo in Belgium, early to mid-1980s; returned to New York City and began playing in blues clubs, late 1980s; recorded *Living with the Law*, 1991; performed on *Trios* with Les Claypool; recorded "I Can't Stand the Rain," a duet with Cassandra Wilson; recorded *Din of Ecstasy*, 1995.

Addresses: *Record company*—The WORK Group, 2100 Colorado, Santa Monica, CA 90404.

After returning to the United States, Whitley reassessed his musical path. "I was working as a bike messenger," he said in a WORK Group press release. "It didn't seem like the kind of music I was making fit in anywhere. Everything was either new wave or really slick and I just felt out of place. In Belgium, I knew I could at least make a living just playing music, so I saved up enough money to go back, and wound up staying there off and on for almost six years."

Although he established a local fame abroad that contrasted sharply with his relative obscurity back in New York, Whitley lost his musical direction while in Belgium. He began trying to polish his music with synthesizers and a drum machine and found his creative efforts being homogenized while playing with a band called Noh Rodeo. As he told Mike Baker in *Guitar Player*, "I was in Belgium studying how many beats per minute people dance to and trying to write accessible tunes. I almost raped myself creatively doing that, and I finally asked myself, 'Why are you still playing music? You might as well work for IBM.'" He added in *Rolling Stone*, "It was sort of an attempt to slickify what I was doing, to make myself fit in somewhere."

Whitley stopped playing slide guitar for about four years and recorded an album that he didn't especially care for on a small Belgium label. After breaking up his band, he willingly derailed himself from a commercial path and focused on blues music again. By the time he returned to the States in 1986, blues music had gained considerable popularity. Numerous new blues clubs opened the door for Whitley's style of music, and he landed a weekend gig at Mondo Cane in New York City that lasted eight months. Meanwhile, he continued to write songs such as "Living with the Law" and "Phone Call from Leavenworth"—both rallying cries for the down and out.

First Solo Album Acclaimed

While playing at Mondo Cane, Whitley was spotted by Daniel Lanois, a record producer who had worked with the Neville Brothers and U2. Whitley had built up an impressive selection of songs, and Lanois got him into the studio to record them for his major-label debut album, *Living with the Law*. Other artists contributing to the album included drummer Ronald Jones, bassist Daryl Johnson, and guitarist Bill Dillon.

Both underground and mainstream critics praised *Living with the Law*, which reveals Whitley's many influences from blues and country rock while still seeming fresh and new. The album also showcases his ability to sing in a variety of styles, from a low and rumbling growl to an eardrum-piercing falsetto. *Rolling Stone* called it "the most impressive debut album of [1991], a cohesive collection of songs that turns the rather neat trick of making bluesy material—mostly played on an open-tuned National steel guitar—sound simultaneously contemporary and as old as the hills." David Patrick Stearns wrote in *Stereo Review* that Whitley's "netherworldly blues poetry, alternately graphic and opaque, casts a spooky spell, an eerie ghost-town glow."

Seemingly overnight, Whitley was a hot act in music. The raves for his album helped him land a spot as the opening act on a major North American tour with Tom Petty and the Heartbreakers. After the tour, he went into relative seclusion and assembled a new band with Alan Gaevert on bass, Dougie Bowen on drums (who had played with the Lounge Lizards and Iggy Pop), and other top musicians.

Shifted Emphasis to Electric Music

Whitley spent the better part of six months recording songs for his next album. The final result was *Din of Ecstasy*, released in early 1995. Reviews were mixed for the album, which depends much more on electric music than *Living with the Law*. It draws on sources ranging from the free-flowing playing of Jimmy Page, Jimi Hendrix, and Neil Young to the 12-bar progressions of Robert Johnson and other bluesmen. In *Guitar Player*, Baker praised its "haunting bottleneck shivers over spacious, overdriven chords that angle out in unexpected directions underneath emotive singing and powerful lyrics." According to *Time* contributor Christopher John Farley, the album's "Narcotic Prayer" was "one of the better rock songs released [in '95]." However, John Milward opined in *Rolling Stone*, "The songs are thick with gnarly guitar lines and six-string orchestrations of Jimi Hendrix but largely lack the melodies to make them matter. And the often nonsensical Beat-style poetry of the lyrics doesn't help."

Homage to Jimi Hendrix on *Din of Ecstasy* is especially evident in the churning guitar licks of "O God My Heart" and "Ultraglide," and the smoky and steamy vocals of "God Thing." Songs such as "WPL" show tinges of psychedelic rock within a blues rock mix. Refusing to be predictable, Whitley set aside the noise on some his numbers, even offering an unpolished blues number with a sound that's straight from the Delta—called "New Machine"—on which he plays the slide guitar. As on *Living with the Law,* Whitley's lyrics on *Din of Ecstasy* reveal a preoccupation with living on the edge and groping desperately to feel alive, often courting danger. Jon Pareles noted in the *New York Times,* "They are troubled songs, testifying to struggles that have not been resolved." Whitley sings in "Never": "I stood all night out there waiting for the Ark / Gasoline all in my hair to tempt a spark."

Although *Din of Ecstasy's* title track has a polished power-pop sound and a more defined melodic line that may qualify it for release as a single, Whitley maintains a staunch attitude against going mainstream and still considers his talent to be evolving. As he told *Guitar Player* in 1995, "I can describe my guitar playing in two words. Clumsy and pragmatic. I still just make up the chords, and I'm as illiterate as hell."

Selected discography

Living with the Law, Columbia, 1991.
Din of Ecstasy, Chaos/Columbia, 1995.

Sources

Guitar Player, May 1995.
New York Times, January 21, 1992; January 14, 1995.
Rolling Stone, September 5, 1991; April 20, 1995.
Stereo Review, November 1991.
Time, April 17, 1995.
Vogue, January 1993.

Additional information for this profile was obtained from the WORK Group publicity materials. (The WORK Group is a trademark of Sony Music Entertainment Inc.)

—*Ed Decker*

LaMonte Young

Composer, saxophonist, pianist

Called "the grandfather of minimal music" by Brooke Wentz in *Down Beat,* La Monte Young has been a key figure in the musical avant-garde since the early 1960s. He evolved from a jazz and blues saxophonist in the 1950s to a minimalist pianist, composer, and performance artist who is still active in the 1990s. Musicians influenced by his theories include Terry Riley, a former classmate of his, and modern composers Steve Reich and Philip Glass.

Young is known for keyboard pieces stripped down to bare essentials, with extended meditations on just one chord and frequent shifts from consonance to dissonance. A prime example is his "Dorian Blues in G," in which each chord of a six-chord progression is played for a solid 20 minutes. Some of Young's pieces last for hours, and his compositions have been known to evolve over many years.

The blues has been a major influence on his work. "Young's blues are unlike any you've heard before, and at the same time they're as pure a musical illumination

Photograph by Marian Zazeela, courtesy of MELA Foundation, Inc.

of the form as you're ever likely to hear," wrote Glenn Kenny in *Spin.* Thom Jurek claimed in the *Detroit Metro Times* that Young's compositions "are loosely related in *concept* to those of blues masters Robert Johnson, Son House and John Lee Hooker, who employed certain guitar strings as drones to lay their improvisations over."

Young's masterwork as a composer is "A Well-Tuned Piano," a piece that has developed over nearly 25 years, since the early 1960s. According to Neil Strauss in a 1994 issue of the *New York Times*, this composition has been called "one of the most important musical works of this quarter century." In *Down Beat* Wentz deemed it "a major documentation—a documentation that seems to end an era, or at least closes another chapter in modern music." Edward Rothstein opined in the *New York Times*, "With the creation of such works as 'The Well-Tuned Piano,' [Young] became an almost archetypal figure of the musical counterculture, devoted to varieties of Indian music while acting as a pioneer of Western Minimalism."

Learned the Blues from Jazz Musicians

Born into what he called a "hillbilly' family in *Pulse!*, Young's first exposure to music was cowboy music. He began singing and playing guitar at about age three

and learned to play the harmonica soon afterwards. His father taught him to play the saxophone when Young was seven. Blues as played by jazz musicians held a strong appeal for him early on as well. "My first experience with the blues that I can consciously recall was listening to the recording of Charlie Parker and Thelonious Monk playing 'Bloomdido,'" he told *Pulse!* Young listened to that recording many times as a high school student, gaining both education and inspiration from the naturalness of Parker's playing. "What's important to me about the blues," he explained, "is that even though I learned it through this very specific format of jazz, it always represented something to me that was very big and powerful that went outside of any particular style."

Young became very active on the jazz underground scene in Los Angeles in the 1950s. He frequently jammed with forward-thinking musicians like Billy Higgins, Don Cherry, Eric Dolphy, and Ornette Coleman, and became a highly accomplished alto saxophone player. Early in the decade he composed his first song, "Annod (To Donna Lee)," which he recorded with Higgins. Young later earned a spot as second chair in saxophone in the Los Angeles City College Dance Band, winning out over Dolphy.

Throughout the 1950s Young's saxophone playing evolved from jazz improvisation to more harmonically static music. By 1957 he had begun teaching himself to play the piano. Before long, he was a highly skilled pianist and was composing pieces in a minimalist style that would become a major influence on works by Philip Glass and Steve Reich.

Advanced Avant-Garde with Fluxus Movement

In the late 1950s Young embraced the Fluxus movement, a group of artists and musicians who attempted to break free from conventional standards of art and music. Young was attracted to the Fluxus notion that the focus should be on the music-making process itself, and that music should be considered an evolutionary event. Young's involvement with Fluxus marked a shift away from jazz and contemporary classical composition and toward the realm of art music. He began staging Fluxus events in New York City. This Chambers Street Series featured exhibitions by leading performance artists of the day, including Yoko Ono. Many bright lights of the New York avant-garde attended these often bizarre exhibitions.

By the early 1960s Young had begun implementing "just intonation" in his musical works, a system that defied the long-standard method of tuning instruments.

Just intonation is an ancient tuning system that rejects the equally tempered spacing of notes on the scale. "With the standard equal-tempered scale, the 12-note limitation makes for expedience," he told Down Beat. "There are only 'X' number of tones to deal with. But in just intonation, the fundamental frequencies of [a stringed] instrument are tuned one-to-one with the pitches that mirror the full harmonic content of the strings themselves. Since everything reinforces everything else, the nuances you get are natural rather than exaggerated. There is both simplicity and a wealth of possibilities." Employing this system allowed Young to tap into a wider span of sound options with each play of a piano key.

Around this time Young formed the Theater of Eternal Music, which became a key ensemble of the minimalist music boom. With this group he became known for his marathon piano playing and works that were continually transforming themselves, apparently with no end in sight. The group included John Cale, then a student of Young's who later became part of the pioneering rock band The Velvet Underground. With the Theater of Eternal Music, Young devoted himself to exploring the musical potential of staying on each chord change for an extended period. He became known for his trademark use of minor sevenths and slightly dissonant chords. According to Down Beat's Wentz, Young created "a masterful dialectic between the multiplicity of sounds and silence."

Explored Indian Music

By 1962 Young had switched from alto saxophone to soprano, an instrument with a higher pitch. Some years later, though, he stopped playing saxophone altogether and took up singing. Throughout the 1960s and in the decades that followed, Young often performed at the Kitchen, a famed haven for avant-garde musicians in New York City. His performances there afforded him increasing visibility and helped move minimalism toward mainstream acceptance. Starting in 1970, Young began studying with noted raga singer Pandit Pran Nath. Since then he has amassed a vast collection of Indian instruments in his continuing exploration of raga.

Long fearful of recording or distributing his works due to an intense fear of being plagiarized, Young finally overcame his reluctance in 1987 and recorded a five-record version of The Well-Tuned Piano. The recording represented 23 years of work on a single harmonic theme, and it merged the ideas behind Young's 1960s jazz improvisation experiments with his sustained tone works of the late 1970s. "What appears to be repetitive and simple evolves into complex, entangled cadences," said Wentz in his Down Beat review of Piano. Wentz went on to say that Young "continually plays with the structuring of tempo, duration, and pitch, holding the listener's attention and always tricking him with surprising discordant interjections.... Every section is paced and moves succinctly from one to the next, repeating phrases until their dissonance fades to familiarity."

Many of Young's performances in the 1990s have been with the Forever Bad Blues Band, which, as of 1993, consisted of Jon Catler on guitar, Brad Catler on bass, and Jonathan Kane on drums. Describing this band in Down Beat, Young said, "It's a lot like a rock band, but we play one song for two hours." In an interview with Martin Johnson in Pulse!, he noted that working with the band helped him regain his enthusiasm for performing, which he had come to miss. Young told Johnson, "The Forever Bad Blues Band came out of the fact that in my bigger works ... I had set up the situation that was very difficult for sponsors to produce, whereas this band can go in, we can do the sound check at 3:00 and do the concert and pack up and go on to the next situation."

> "My whole life has been devoted to music because nothing else ever gave me that spiritual inspiration, that sense I was doing the right thing with my life."

"The playing seemed to create an auditory space with its own dimension and depth, within which the music took place," reported New York Times contributor Edward Rothstein about a performance of Young and the Forever Bad Blues Band at the Kitchen. "As in Mr. Young's other works, the listener was always discovering something about the sound, the way it shimmered around the edges or seemed to change color." Rothstein concluded, "The music emerged as an intriguing combination of blues, 1960's happening, Eastern esthetic, rock and Minimalism."

Young has performed on a regular basis in New York City in recent years, often adding a touch of performance art to his concerts. A typical example was his appearance at Merkin Concert Hall in 1993, when he placed his musicians around the hall as if beckoning members of the audience to be a part of the performance. Many of his concerts have featured lighting designed by Marian Zazeela, his wife and collaborator, that imbues the stage with a New Age aura.

Young recorded *Just Stompin': Live at the Kitchen* with his band in 1993. Clearly influenced by the blues of John Lee Hooker and John Coltrane, he album also somewhat resembled the work of the Velvet Underground and modern rock experimentalists Sonic Youth. David Fricke gave the album four stars n his review in *Rolling Stone.* "Two hours, one song (never mind 'song,' one chord progression), no break—and zero boredom," noted Fricke. In his review of *Just Stompin'* in the Detroit *Metro Times,* Jurek said, "The band plays dynamically, from soft to hard and back, gradually building in both intensity and tension, laying back just enough—without letting the air out—to allow the musicians (and listeners) to breathe and start again, until he music reaches an unbearable pitch [that] shatters all divisions between blues, Indian classical music, punk, heavy metal, grunge, modal jazz and noise, because it's all of them and none of them at once."

Adding another chapter to his explorations of sound and space, Young created an interactive sound-and-light installation in a room above his loft in the TriBeCa section of New York City in 1994. The layout featured six speakers arranged around the room that droned continuously; magenta lighting designed by Zazeela further defined the environment. Listeners would hear a different sound mix according to how they moved in the room, thus enabling them to create new note sequences with a mere tilt of the head. "I started thinking about the possibility of doing tuned rooms in the 1960's," Young told the *New York Times.* "But this is one of my most advanced and far-reaching creations yet."

Young's pursuit of new musical territory in the realm of minimalism remained unabated as the 1990s wore on, and he has no regrets about his chosen path. As he said in *Pulse!,* "My whole life has been devoted to music because nothing else ever gave me that spiritual inspiration, that sense I was doing the right thing with my life."

Selected discography

The Well-Tuned Piano 81 X 25, Gramavision, 1987.
Fluxtellus: 89 VI 8 c. 1:45-1:52 AM Paris Encore from Poem for Tables, Chairs and Benches, etc., Tellus, 1990.
The Melodic Version of The Second Dream of The High-Tension Line Stepdown Transformer from The Four Dreams of China, Gramavision, 1991.
(With the Forever Bad Blues Band) *Just Stompin': Live at the Kitchen,* Gramavision, 1993.
Just West Coast/Microtonal music for Guitar and Harp, Bridge, 1993.

Sources

Down Beat, August 1987; August 1993.
Metro Times (Detroit), July 28, 1993.
New York Times, November 4, 1991; January 12, 1993; April 14, 1993; June 15, 1994.
Pulse!, November 1993.
Rolling Stone, November 11, 1993.
Spin, July 1993.

—Ed Decker

Cumulative Indexes

Cumulative Subject Index

Volume numbers appear in **bold**.

Kronos Quartet **5**
Lemper, Ute **14**
Levine, James **8**
Liberace **9**
Ma, Yo-Yo **2**
Marsalis, Wynton **6**
Masur, Kurt **11**
McNair, Sylvia **15**
McPartland, Marian **15**
Mehta, Zubin **11**
Menuhin, Yehudi **11**
Midori **7**
Nyman, Michael **15**
Ott, David **2**
Parkening, Christopher **7**
Perahia, Murray **10**
Perlman, Itzhak **2**
Phillips, Harvey **3**
Rampal, Jean-Pierre **6**
Rota, Nino **13**
Rubinstein, Arthur **11**
Salerno-Sonnenberg, Nadja **3**
Salonen, Esa-Pekka **16**
Schickele, Peter **5**
Schuman, William **10**
Segovia, Andres **6**
Shankar, Ravi **9**
Solti, Georg **13**
Stern, Isaac **7**
Sutherland, Joan **13**
Takemitsu, Toru **6**
Toscanini, Arturo **14**
Upshaw, Dawn **9**
von Karajan, Herbert **1**
Weill, Kurt **12**
Wilson, Ransom **5**
Yamashita, Kazuhito **4**
York, Andrew **15**
Zukerman, Pinchas **4**

Composers
Adams, John **8**
Allen, Geri **10**
Alpert, Herb **11**
Anka, Paul **2**
Atkins, Chet **5**
Bacharach, Burt **1**
Beiderbecke, Bix **16**
Benson, George **9**
Berlin, Irving **8**
Bernstein, Leonard **2**
Blackman, Cindy **15**
Bley, Carla **8**
Bley, Paul **14**
Braxton, Anthony **12**
Britten, Benjamin **15**
Brubeck, Dave **8**
Burrell, Kenny **11**
Byrne, David **8**
    Also see Talking Heads
Cage, John **8**
Cale, John **9**
Casals, Pablo **9**
Clarke, Stanley **3**
Coleman, Ornette **5**

Cooder, Ry **2**
Cooney, Rory **6**
Copeland, Stewart **14**
Copland, Aaron **2**
Crouch, Andraé **9**
Davis, Chip **4**
Davis, Miles **1**
de Grassi, Alex **6**
Dorsey, Thomas A. **11**
Elfman, Danny **9**
Ellington, Duke **2**
Eno, Brian **8**
Enya **6**
Foster, David **13**
Frisell, Bill **15**
Galás, Diamanda **16**
Gillespie, Dizzy **6**
Glass, Philip **1**
Gould, Glenn **9**
Gould, Morton **16**
Grusin, Dave **7**
Guaraldi, Vince **3**
Hamlisch, Marvin **1**
Hancock, Herbie **8**
Handy, W. C. **7**
Hargrove, Roy **15**
Harris, Eddie **15**
Hartke, Stephen **5**
Henderson, Fletcher **16**
Herrmann, Bernard **14**
Hunter, Alberta **7**
Isham, Mark **14**
Jarre, Jean-Michel **2**
Jarrett, Keith **1**
Johnson, James P. **16**
Jones, Hank **15**
Jones, Quincy **2**
Joplin, Scott **10**
Jordan, Stanley **1**
Kenny G **14**
Kern, Jerome **13**
Kitaro **1**
Kottke, Leo **13**
Lateef, Yusef **16**
Lee, Peggy **8**
Lewis, Ramsey **14**
Lincoln, Abbey **9**
Lloyd Webber, Andrew **6**
Loewe, Frederick
    See Lerner and Loewe
Mancini, Henry **1**
Marsalis, Branford **10**
Marsalis, Ellis **13**
Masekela, Hugh **7**
McPartland, Marian **15**
Menken, Alan **10**
Metheny, Pat **2**
Mingus, Charles **9**
Monk, Meredith **1**
Monk, Thelonious **6**
Morricone, Ennio **15**
Morton, Jelly Roll **7**
Mulligan, Gerry **16**
Nascimento, Milton **6**
Newman, Randy **4**

Nyman, Michael **15**
Ott, David **2**
Palmieri, Eddie **15**
Parker, Charlie **5**
Peterson, Oscar **11**
Ponty, Jean-Luc **8**
Porter, Cole **10**
Previn, André **15**
Puente, Tito **14**
Pullen, Don **16**
Reich, Steve **8**
Reinhardt, Django **7**
Ritenour, Lee **7**
Roach, Max **12**
Rollins, Sonny **7**
Rota, Nino **13**
Salonen, Esa-Pekka **16**
Sanders, Pharoah **16**
Satriani, Joe **4**
Schickele, Peter **5**
Schuman, William **10**
Shankar, Ravi **9**
Shaw, Artie **8**
Shorter, Wayne **5**
Solal, Martial **4**
Sondheim, Stephen **8**
Sousa, John Philip **10**
Story, Liz **2**
Strayhorn, Billy **13**
Summers, Andy **3**
Sun Ra **5**
Takemitsu, Toru **6**
Talbot, John Michael **6**
Taylor, Billy **13**
Taylor, Cecil **9**
Thielemans, Toots **13**
Threadgill, Henry **9**
Tyner, McCoy **7**
Washington, Grover, Jr. **5**
Weill, Kurt **12**
Weston, Randy **15**
Williams, John **9**
Wilson, Cassandra **12**
Winston, George
Winter, Paul **10**
Worrell, Bernie **11**
Yanni **11**
York, Andrew **15**
Young, La Monte **16**
Zimmerman, Udo **5**
Zorn, John **15**

Conductors
Bacharach, Burt **1**
Bernstein, Leonard **2**
Britten, Benjamin **15**
Casals, Pablo **9**
Copland, Aaron **2**
Domingo, Placido **1**
Fiedler, Arthur **6**
Gould, Morton **16**
Herrmann, Bernard **14**
Jarrett, Keith **1**
Jones, Hank **15**
Levine, James **8**

Mancini, Henry **1**
Marriner, Neville **7**
Masur, Kurt **11**
Mehta, Zubin **11**
Menuhin, Yehudi **11**
Previn, André **15**
Rampal, Jean-Pierre **6**
Salonen, Esa-Pekka **16**
Schickele, Peter **5**
Solti, Georg **13**
Toscanini, Arturo **14**
von Karajan, Herbert **1**
Welk, Lawrence **13**
Williams, John **9**
Zukerman, Pinchas **4**

Contemporary Dance Music
Abdul, Paula **3**
Aphex Twin **14**
Bee Gees, The **3**
B-52's, The **4**
Brown, Bobby **4**
Brown, James **2**
C + C Music Factory **16**
Cherry, Neneh **4**
Clinton, George **7**
Deee-lite **9**
De La Soul **7**
Depeche Mode **5**
Earth, Wind and Fire **12**
English Beat, The **9**
En Vogue **10**
Erasure **11**
Eurythmics **6**
Exposé **4**
Fox, Samantha **3**
Gang of Four **8**
Hammer, M.C. **5**
Harry, Deborah **4**
    Also see Blondie
Ice-T **7**
Idol, Billy **3**
Jackson, Janet **16**
    Earlier sketch in CM **3**
Jackson, Michael **1**
    Also see Jacksons, The
James, Rick **2**
Jones, Grace **9**
Madonna **16**
    Earlier sketch in CM **4**
M People **15**
New Order **11**
Peniston, CeCe **15**
Pet Shop Boys **5**
Prince **14**
    Earlier sketch in CM **1**
Queen Latifah **6**
Rodgers, Nile **8**
Salt-N-Pepa **6**
Simmons, Russell **7**
Summer, Donna **12**
Technotronic **5**
TLC **15**
Vasquez, Junior **16**
Village People, The **7**
Was (Not Was) **6**

Waters, Crystal **15**
Young M.C. **4**

Contemporary Instrumental/New Age
Ackerman, Will **3**
Clinton, George **7**
Collins, Bootsy **8**
Davis, Chip **4**
de Grassi, Alex **6**
Enigma **14**
Enya **6**
Hedges, Michael **3**
Isham, Mark **14**
Jarre, Jean-Michel **2**
Kitaro **1**
Kronos Quartet **5**
Story, Liz **2**
Summers, Andy **3**
Tangerine Dream **12**
Winston, George **9**
Winter, Paul **10**
Yanni **11**

Cornet
Armstrong, Louis **4**
Beiderbecke, Bix **16**
Cherry, Don **10**
Handy, W. C. **7**
Oliver, King **15**

Country
Acuff, Roy **2**
Alabama **1**
Anderson, John **5**
Arnold, Eddy **10**
Asleep at the Wheel **5**
Atkins, Chet **5**
Auldridge, Mike **4**
    Also see Country Gentlemen, The
    Also see Seldom Scene, The
Autry, Gene **12**
Bellamy Brothers, The **13**
Berg, Matraca **16**
Black, Clint **5**
Bogguss, Suzy **11**
Boone, Pat **13**
Brooks, Garth **8**
Brooks & Dunn **12**
Brown, Junior **15**
Brown, Marty **14**
Brown, Tony **14**
Buffett, Jimmy **4**
Byrds, The **8**
Cale, J. J. **16**
Campbell, Glen **2**
Carpenter, Mary-Chapin **6**
Carter, Carlene **8**
Carter Family, The **3**
Cash, Johnny **1**
Cash, June Carter **6**
Cash, Rosanne **2**
Chesnutt, Mark **13**
Clark, Roy **1**
Cline, Patsy **5**
Coe, David Allan **4**

Collie, Mark **15**
Cooder, Ry **2**
Cowboy Junkies, The **4**
Crowe, J. D. **5**
Crowell, Rodney **8**
Cyrus, Billy Ray **11**
Daniels, Charlie **6**
Davis, Skeeter **15**
DeMent, Iris **13**
Denver, John **1**
Desert Rose Band, The **4**
Diamond Rio **11**
Dickens, Little Jimmy **7**
Diffie, Joe **10**
Dylan, Bob **3**
Earle, Steve **16**
Flatt, Lester **3**
Flores, Rosie **16**
Foster, Radney **16**
Ford, Tennessee Ernie **3**
Frizzell, Lefty **10**
Gayle, Crystal **1**
Gill, Vince **7**
Gilley, Mickey **7**
Gilmore, Jimmie Dale **11**
Greenwood, Lee **12**
Griffith, Nanci **3**
Haggard, Merle **2**
Hall, Tom T. **4**
Harris, Emmylou **4**
Hartford, John **1**
Hay, George D. **3**
Hiatt, John **8**
Highway 101 **4**
Hinojosa, Tish **13**
Howard, Harlan **15**
Jackson, Alan **7**
Jennings, Waylon **4**
Jones, George **4**
Judd, Wynonna
    See Wynonna
Judds, The **2**
Kentucky Headhunters, The **5**
Kershaw, Sammy **15**
Ketchum, Hal **14**
Kristofferson, Kris **4**
Lang, K. D. **4**
Lawrence, Tracy **11**
LeDoux, Chris **12**
Lee, Brenda **5**
Little Feat **4**
Little Texas **14**
Louvin Brothers, The **12**
Loveless, Patty **5**
Lovett, Lyle **5**
Lynn, Loretta **2**
Lynne, Shelby **5**
Mandrell, Barbara **4**
Mattea, Kathy **5**
Mavericks, The **15**
McBride, Martina **14**
McClinton, Delbert **14**
McCoy, Neal **15**
McEntire, Reba **11**
Miller, Roger **4**

Milsap, Ronnie **2**
Monroe, Bill **1**
Montgomery, John Michael **14**
Morgan, Lorrie **10**
Murphey, Michael Martin **9**
Murray, Anne **4**
Nelson, Willie **11**
   Earlier sketch in CM **1**
Newton-John, Olivia **8**
Nitty Gritty Dirt Band, The **6**
Oak Ridge Boys, The **7**
O'Connor, Mark **1**
Oslin, K. T. **3**
Owens, Buck **2**
Parnell, Lee Roy **15**
Parsons, Gram **7**
   Also see Byrds, The
Parton, Dolly **2**
Pearl, Minnie **3**
Pierce, Webb **15**
Price, Ray **11**
Pride, Charley **4**
Rabbitt, Eddie **5**
Raitt, Bonnie **3**
Raye, Collin **16**
Reeves, Jim **10**
Restless Heart **12**
Rich, Charlie **3**
Robbins, Marty **9**
Rodgers, Jimmie **3**
Rogers, Kenny **1**
Rogers, Roy **9**
Sawyer Brown **13**
Scruggs, Earl **3**
Seals, Dan **9**
Skaggs, Ricky **5**
Sonnier, Jo-El **10**
Statler Brothers, The **8**
Stevens, Ray **7**
Stone, Doug **10**
Strait, George **5**
Stuart, Marty **9**
Sweethearts of the Rodeo **12**
Texas Tornados, The **8**
Tillis, Mel **7**
Tillis, Pam **8**
Tippin, Aaron **12**
Travis, Merle **14**
Travis, Randy **9**
Tritt, Travis **7**
Tubb, Ernest **4**
Tucker, Tanya **3**
Twitty, Conway **6**
Van Shelton, Ricky **5**
Van Zandt, Townes **13**
Wagoner, Porter **13**
Walker, Jerry Jeff **13**
Watson, Doc **2**
Wells, Kitty **6**
West, Dottie **8**
White, Lari **15**
Whitley, Keith **7**
Williams, Don **4**
Williams, Hank, Jr. **1**
Williams, Hank, Sr. **4**

Willis, Kelly **12**
Wills, Bob **6**
Wynette, Tammy **2**
Wynonna **11**
   Also see Judds, The
Yearwood, Trisha **10**
Yoakam, Dwight **1**
Young, Faron **7**

Dobro
Auldridge, Mike **4**
   Also see Country Gentlemen, The
   Also see Seldom Scene, The
Burch, Curtis
   See New Grass Revival, The
Knopfler, Mark **3**
Whitley, Chris **16**

Drums
   See **Percussion**

Dulcimer
Ritchie, Jean **4**

Fiddle
   See **Violin**

Film Scores
Anka, Paul **2**
Bacharach, Burt **1**
Berlin, Irving **8**
Bernstein, Leonard **2**
Blanchard, Terence **13**
Britten, Benjamin **15**
Byrne, David **8**
   Also see Talking Heads
Cafferty, John
   See Beaver Brown Band, The
Cahn, Sammy **11**
Cliff, Jimmy **8**
Copeland, Stewart **14**
Copland, Aaron **2**
Crouch, Andraé **9**
Dibango, Manu **14**
Dolby, Thomas **10**
Donovan **9**
Eddy, Duane **9**
Elfman, Danny **9**
Ellington, Duke **2**
Ferguson, Maynard **7**
Froom, Mitchell **15**
Gabriel, Peter **16**
   Earlier sketch in CM **2**
   Also see Genesis
Galás, Diamanda **16**
Gershwin, George and Ira **11**
Gould, Glenn **9**
Grusin, Dave **7**
Guaraldi, Vince **3**
Hamlisch, Marvin **1**
Hancock, Herbie **8**
Harrison, George **2**
Hayes, Isaac **10**
Hedges, Michael **3**
Herrmann, Bernard **14**

Isham, Mark **14**
Jones, Quincy **2**
Knopfler, Mark **3**
Lennon, John **9**
   Also see Beatles, The
Lerner and Loewe **13**
Mancini, Henry **1**
Marsalis, Branford **10**
Mayfield, Curtis **8**
McCartney, Paul **4**
   Also see Beatles, The
Menken, Alan **10**
Mercer, Johnny **13**
Metheny, Pat **2**
Morricone, Ennio **15**
Nascimento, Milton **6**
Nilsson **10**
Nyman, Michael **15**
Peterson, Oscar **11**
Porter, Cole **10**
Previn, André **15**
Reznor, Trent **13**
Richie, Lionel **2**
Robertson, Robbie **2**
Rollins, Sonny **7**
Rota, Nino **13**
Sager, Carole Bayer **5**
Schickele, Peter **5**
Shankar, Ravi **9**
Taj Mahal **6**
Waits, Tom **12**
   Earlier sketch in CM **1**
Weill, Kurt **12**
Williams, John **9**
Williams, Paul **5**
Willner, Hal **10**
Young, Neil **15**
   Earlier sketch in CM **2**

Flugelhorn
Sandoval, Arturo **15**

Flute
Anderson, Ian
   See Jethro Tull
Galway, James **3**
Lateef, Yusef **16**
Mann, Herbie **16**
Rampal, Jean-Pierre **6**
Ulmer, James Blood **13**
Wilson, Ransom **5**

Folk/Traditional
America **16**
Arnaz, Desi **8**
Baez, Joan **1**
Belafonte, Harry **8**
Black, Mary **15**
Blades, Ruben **2**
Bloom, Luka **14**
Brady, Paul **8**
Bragg, Billy **7**
Buckley, Tim **14**
Bulgarian State Female Vocal Choir,
   The **10**

Byrds, The **8**
Carter Family, The **3**
Chandra, Sheila **16**
Chapin, Harry **6**
Chapman, Tracy **4**
Chenille Sisters, The **16**
Cherry, Don **10**
Chieftains, The **7**
Childs, Toni **2**
Clegg, Johnny **8**
Cockburn, Bruce **8**
Cohen, Leonard **3**
Collins, Judy **4**
Colvin, Shawn **11**
Cotten, Elizabeth **16**
Crosby, David **3**
    Also see Byrds, The
Cruz, Celia **10**
de Lucia, Paco **1**
DeMent, Iris **13**
Donovan **9**
Dr. John **7**
Dylan, Bob **3**
Elliot, Cass **5**
Enya **6**
Estefan, Gloria **15**
    Earlier sketch in CM **2**
Feliciano, José **10**
Galway, James **3**
Gilmore, Jimmie Dale **11**
Gipsy Kings, The **8**
Griffith, Nanci **3**
Guthrie, Arlo **6**
Guthrie, Woody **2**
Hakmoun, Hassan **15**
Harding, John Wesley **6**
Hartford, John **1**
Havens, Richie **11**
Hinojosa, Tish **13**
Iglesias, Julio **2**
Indigo Girls **3**
Ives, Burl **12**
Khan, Nusrat Fateh Ali **13**
Kingston Trio, The **9**
Kottke, Leo **13**
Kuti, Fela **7**
Ladysmith Black Mambazo **1**
Larkin, Patty **9**
Lavin, Christine **6**
Leadbelly **6**
Lightfoot, Gordon **3**
Los Lobos **2**
Makeba, Miriam **8**
Masekela, Hugh **7**
McLean, Don **7**
Melanie **12**
Mitchell, Joni **2**
Morrison, Van **3**
Morrissey, Bill **12**
Nascimento, Milton **6**
N'Dour, Youssou **6**
Near, Holly **1**
Ochs, Phil **7**
O'Connor, Sinead **3**
Odetta **7**
Parsons, Gram **7**
    Also see Byrds, The

Paxton, Tom **5**
Peter, Paul & Mary **4**
Pogues, The **6**
Prine, John **7**
Proclaimers, The **13**
Redpath, Jean **1**
Ritchie, Jean, **4**
Rodgers, Jimmie **3**
Sainte-Marie, Buffy **11**
Santana, Carlos **1**
Seeger, Pete **4**
    Also see Weavers, The
Selena **16**
Shankar, Ravi **9**
Simon, Paul **16**
    Earlier sketch in CM **1**
Snow, Pheobe **4**
Story, The **13**
Sweet Honey in the Rock **1**
Taj Mahal **6**
Thompson, Richard **7**
Tikaram, Tanita **9**
Van Ronk, Dave **12**
Van Zandt, Townes **13**
Vega, Suzanne **3**
Wainwright III, Loudon **11**
Walker, Jerry Jeff **13**
Watson, Doc **2**
Weavers, The **8**

French Horn
Ohanian, David
    See Canadian Brass, The

Funk
Bambaataa, Afrika **13**
Brand New Heavies, The **14**
Brown, James **2**
Burdon, Eric **14**
    Also see War
Clinton, George **7**
Collins, Bootsy **8**
Fishbone **7**
Gang of Four **8**
Jackson, Janet **3**
Khan, Chaka **9**
Mayfield, Curtis **8**
Meters, The **14**
Ohio Players **16**
Parker, Maceo **7**
Prince **14**
    Earlier sketch in CM **1**
Red Hot Chili Peppers, The **7**
Stone, Sly **8**
Toussaint, Allen **11**
Worrell, Bernie **11**

Fusion
Anderson, Ray **7**
Beck, Jeff **4**
    Also see Yardbirds, The
Clarke, Stanley **3**
Coleman, Ornette **5**
Corea, Chick **6**
Davis, Miles **1**

Fishbone **7**
Hancock, Herbie **8**
Harris, Eddie **15**
Lewis, Ramsey **14**
McLaughlin, John **12**
MC 900 Ft. Jesus **16**
Metheny, Pat **2**
O'Connor, Mark **1**
Ponty, Jean-Luc **8**
Reid, Vernon **2**
Ritenour, Lee **7**
Shorter, Wayne **5**
Summers, Andy **3**
Washington, Grover, Jr. **5**

Gospel
Anderson, Marian **8**
Boone, Pat **13**
Brown, James **2**
Carter Family, The **3**
Charles, Ray **1**
Cleveland, James **1**
Cooke, Sam **1**
    Also see Soul Stirrers, The
Crouch, Andraé **9**
Dorsey, Thomas A. **11**
Five Blind Boys of Alabama **12**
Ford, Tennessee Ernie **3**
Franklin, Aretha **2**
Green, Al **9**
Houston, Cissy **6**
Jackson, Mahalia **8**
Kee, John P. **15**
Knight, Gladys **1**
Little Richard **1**
Louvin Brothers, The **12**
Oak Ridge Boys, The **7**
Paris, Twila **16**
Pickett, Wilson **10**
Presley, Elvis **1**
Redding, Otis **5**
Reese, Della **13**
Robbins, Marty **9**
Smith, Michael W. **11**
Soul Stirrers, The **11**
Sounds of Blackness **13**
Staples, Mavis **13**
Staples, Pops **11**
Take 6 **6**
Waters, Ethel **11**
Watson, Doc **2**
Williams, Deniece **1**
Williams, Marion **15**
Winans, The **12**
Womack, Bobby **5**

Guitar
Ackerman, Will **3**
Allman, Duane
    See Allman Brothers, The
Atkins, Chet **5**
Autry, Gene **12**
Baxter, Jeff
    See Doobie Brothers, The
Beck, Jeff **4**
    Also see Yardbirds, The

Belew, Adrian **5**
Benson, George **9**
Berry, Chuck **1**
Bettencourt, Nuno
    See Extreme
Betts, Dicky
    See Allman Brothers, The
Bloom, Luka **14**
Boyd, Liona **7**
Bream, Julian **9**
Brown, Junior **15**
Buck, Peter
    See R.E.M.
Buckingham, Lindsey **8**
    Also see Fleetwood Mac
Burrell, Kenny **11**
Campbell, Glen **2**
Chesnutt, Mark **13**
Christian, Charlie **11**
Clapton, Eric **11**
    Earlier sketch in CM **1**
    Also see Cream
    Also see Yardbirds, The
Clark, Roy **1**
Cockburn, Bruce **8**
Collie, Mark **15**
Collins, Albert **4**
Cooder, Ry **2**
Cotten, Elizabeth **16**
Cray, Robert **8**
Cropper, Steve **12**
Dale, Dick **13**
Daniels, Charlie **6**
de Grassi, Alex **6**
de Lucia, Paco **1**
Dickens, Little Jimmy **7**
Diddley, Bo **3**
Di Meola, Al **12**
Dokken, Don
    See Dokken
Earl, Ronnie **5**
    Also see Roomful of Blues
Eddy, Duane **9**
Edge, The
    See U2
Etheridge, Melissa **16**
    Earlier sketch in CM **4**
Feliciano, José **10**
Fender, Leo **10**
Flatt, Lester **3**
Flores, Rosie **16**
Ford, Lita **9**
Frampton, Peter **3**
Frehley, Ace
    See Kiss
Fripp, Robert **9**
Frisell, Bill **15**
Gallagher, Noel
    See Oasis
Garcia, Jerry **4**
    Also see Grateful Dead, The
Gatton, Danny **16**
George, Lowell
    See Little Feat
Gibbons, Billy
    See ZZ Top

Gill, Vince **7**
Gilmour, David
    See Pink Floyd
Green, Grant **14**
Green, Peter
    See Fleetwood Mac
Guy, Buddy **4**
Haley, Bill **6**
Harrison, George **2**
Hatfield, Juliana **12**
    Also see Lemonheads, The
Havens, Richie **11**
Healey, Jeff **4**
Hedges, Michael **3**
Hendrix, Jimi **2**
Hillman, Chris
    See Byrds, The
    Also see Desert Rose Band, The
Hitchcock, Robyn **9**
Holly, Buddy **1**
Hooker, John Lee **1**
Hopkins, Lightnin' **13**
Howlin' Wolf **6**
Iommi, Tony
    See Black Sabbath
Ives, Burl **12**
James, Elmore **8**
Jardine, Al
    See Beach Boys, The
Johnson, Robert **6**
Jones, Brian
    See Rolling Stones, The
Jordan, Stanley **1**
Kantner, Paul
    See Jefferson Airplane
King, Albert **2**
King, B. B. **1**
Klugh, Earl **10**
Knopfler, Mark **3**
Kottke, Leo **13**
Landreth, Sonny **16**
Larkin, Patty **9**
Leadbelly **6**
Lennon, John **9**
    Also see Beatles, The
Lindley, David **2**
Lockwood, Robert, Jr. **10**
Lynch, George
    See Dokken
Marr, Johnny
    See Smiths, The
    Also see The The
May, Brian
    See Queen
Mayfield, Curtis **8**
McClinton, Delbert **14**
McCoury, Del **15**
McDowell, Mississippi Fred **16**
McGuinn, Roger
    See Byrds, The
McLachlan, Sarah **12**
McLaughlin, John **12**
McReynolds, Jim
    See McReynolds, Jim and Jesse
Metheny, Pat **2**

Montgomery, Wes **3**
Morrissey, Bill **12**
Nugent, Ted **2**
Owens, Buck **2**
Page, Jimmy **4**
    Also see Led Zeppelin
    Also see Yardbirds, The
Parkening, Christopher **7**
Parnell, Lee Roy **15**
Pass, Joe **15**
Patton, Charley **11**
Perkins, Carl **9**
Perry, Joe
    See Aerosmith
Petty, Tom **9**
Phair, Liz **14**
Phillips, Sam **12**
Prince **14**
    Earlier sketch in CM **1**
Raitt, Bonnie **3**
Ray, Amy
    See Indigo Girls
Reed, Jimmy **15**
Reid, Vernon **2**
    Also see Living Colour
Reinhardt, Django **7**
Richards, Keith **11**
    Also see Rolling Stones, The
Richman, Jonathan **12**
Ritenour, Lee **7**
Robbins, Marty **9**
Robertson, Robbie **2**
Robillard, Duke **2**
Rodgers, Nile **8**
Rorschach, Poison Ivy
    See Cramps, The
Rush, Otis **12**
Saliers, Emily
    See Indigo Girls
Santana, Carlos **1**
Satriani, Joe **4**
Scofield, John **7**
Segovia, Andres **6**
Sharrock, Sonny **15**
Shines, Johnny **14**
Simon, Paul **16**
    Earlier sketch in CM **1**
Skaggs, Ricky **5**
Slash
    See Guns n' Roses
Springsteen, Bruce **6**
Stewart, Dave
    See Eurythmics
Stills, Stephen **5**
Stuart, Marty **9**
Summers, Andy **3**
Taylor, Mick
    See Rolling Stones, The
Thielemans, Toots **13**
Thompson, Richard **7**
Tippin, Aaron **12**
Townshend, Pete **1**
Travis, Merle **14**
Tubb, Ernest **4**
Ulmer, James Blood **13**

Vai, Steve **5**
Van Halen, Edward
    See Van Halen
Van Ronk, Dave **12**
Vaughan, Jimmie
    See Fabulous Thunderbirds, The
Vaughan, Stevie Ray **1**
Wagoner, Porter **13**
Waits, Tom **12**
    Earlier sketch in CM **1**
Walker, Jerry Jeff **13**
Walker, T-Bone **5**
Walsh, Joe **5**
    Also see Eagles, The
Watson, Doc **2**
Weir, Bob
    See Grateful Dead, The
Weller, Paul **14**
White, Lari **15**
Whitley, Chris **16**
Wilson, Nancy
    See Heart
Winston, George **9**
Winter, Johnny **5**
Yamashita, Kazuhito **4**
Yarrow, Peter
    See Peter, Paul & Mary
Young, Angus
    See AC/DC
Young, Malcolm
    See AC/DC
York, Andrew **15**
Young, Neil **15**
    Earlier sketch in CM **2**
Zappa, Frank **1**

Harmonica
Dylan, Bob **3**
Guthrie, Woody **2**
Lewis, Huey **9**
Little Walter **14**
McClinton, Delbert **14**
Musselwhite, Charlie **13**
Reed, Jimmy **15**
Thielemans, Toots **13**
Waters, Muddy **4**
Williamson, Sonny Boy **9**
Wilson, Kim
    See Fabulous Thunderbirds, The
Young, Neil **15**
    Earlier sketch in CM **2**

Heavy Metal
AC/DC **4**
Aerosmith **3**
Alice in Chains **10**
Anthrax **11**
Black Sabbath **9**
Blue Öyster Cult **16**
Cinderella **16**
Danzig **7**
Deep Purple **11**
Def Leppard **3**
Dokken **16**
Faith No More **7**

Fishbone **7**
Ford, Lita **9**
Guns n' Roses **2**
Iron Maiden **10**
Judas Priest **10**
King's X **7**
Led Zeppelin **1**
L7 **12**
Megadeth **9**
Metallica **7**
Mötley Crüe **1**
Motörhead **10**
Nugent, Ted **2**
Osbourne, Ozzy **3**
Pantera **13**
Petra **3**
Queensrÿche **8**
Reid, Vernon **2**
    Also see Living Colour
Reznor, Trent **13**
Roth, David Lee **1**
    Also see Van Halen
Sepultura **12**
Slayer **10**
Soundgarden **6**
Spinal Tap **8**
Stryper **2**
Suicidal Tendencies **15**
Whitesnake **5**

Humor
Coasters, The **5**
Jones, Spike **5**
Lehrer, Tom **7**
Pearl, Minnie **3**
Russell, Mark **6**
Schickele, Peter **5**
Shaffer, Paul **13**
Spinal Tap **8**
Stevens, Ray **7**
Yankovic, "Weird Al" **7**

Inventors
Fender, Leo **10**
Harris, Eddie **15**
Paul, Les **2**
Scholz, Tom
    See Boston
Teagarden, Jack **10**

Jazz
Adderly, Cannonball **15**
Allen, Geri **10**
Anderson, Ray **7**
Armstrong, Louis **4**
Bailey, Mildred **13**
Bailey, Pearl **5**
Baker, Anita **9**
Baker, Chet **13**
Baker, Ginger **16**
    Also see Cream
Basie, Count **2**
Beiderbecke, Bix **16**
Belle, Regina **6**
Bennett, Tony **16**
    Earlier sketch in CM **2**

Benson, George **9**
Berigan, Bunny **2**
Blackman, Cindy **15**
Blakey, Art **11**
Blanchard, Terence **13**
Bley, Carla **8**
Bley, Paul **14**
Blood, Sweat and Tears **7**
Brand New Heavies, The **14**
Braxton, Anthony **12**
Brown, Ruth **13**
Brubeck, Dave **8**
Burrell, Kenny **11**
Burton, Gary **10**
Calloway, Cab **6**
Canadian Brass, The **4**
Carter, Benny **3**
    Also see McKinney's Cotton Pickers
Carter, Betty **6**
Carter, Ron **14**
Charles, Ray **1**
Cherry, Don **10**
Christian, Charlie **11**
Clarke, Stanley **3**
Clooney, Rosemary **9**
Cole, Nat King **3**
Coleman, Ornette **5**
Coltrane, John **4**
Connick, Harry, Jr. **4**
Corea, Chick **6**
Davis, Miles **1**
DeJohnette, Jack **7**
Di Meola, Al **12**
Eckstine, Billy **1**
Eldridge, Roy **9**
    Also see McKinney's Cotton Pickers
Ellington, Duke **2**
Ferguson, Maynard **7**
Fitzgerald, Ella **1**
Flanagan, Tommy **16**
Fleck, Bela **8**
    Also see New Grass Revival, The
Fountain, Pete **7**
Frisell, Bill **15**
Galway, James **3**
Getz, Stan **12**
Gillespie, Dizzy **6**
Goodman, Benny **4**
Gordon, Dexter **10**
Grappelli, Stephane **10**
Green, Grant **14**
Guaraldi, Vince **3**
Haden, Charlie **12**
Hampton, Lionel **6**
Hancock, Herbie **8**
Hargrove, Roy **15**
Harris, Eddie **15**
Hawkins, Coleman **11**
Hedges, Michael **3**
Henderson, Fletcher **16**
Henderson, Joe **14**
Herman, Woody **12**
Hines, Earl "Fatha" **12**
Hirt, Al **5**
Holiday, Billie **6**

Horn, Shirley **7**
Horne, Lena **11**
Hunter, Alberta **7**
Incognito **16**
Isham, Mark **14**
Jackson, Milt **15**
James, Harry **11**
Jarreau, Al **1**
Jarrett, Keith **1**
Johnson, James P. **16**
Jones, Elvin **9**
Jones, Hank **15**
Jones, Philly Joe **16**
Jones, Quincy **2**
Jordan, Stanley **1**
Kennedy, Nigel **8**
Kenny G **14**
Kirk, Rahsaan Roland **6**
Kitt, Eartha **9**
Klugh, Earl **10**
Kronos Quartet **5**
Krupa, Gene **13**
Laine, Cleo **10**
Lateef, Yusef **16**
Lee, Peggy **8**
Lewis, Ramsey **14**
Lincoln, Abbey **9**
Israel "Cachao" Lopez **14**
Lovano, Joe **13**
Mancini, Henry **1**
Manhattan Transfer, The **8**
Mann, Herbie **16**
Marsalis, Branford **10**
Marsalis, Ellis **13**
Marsalis, Wynton **6**
Masekela, Hugh **7**
McFerrin, Bobby **3**
McKinney's Cotton Pickers **16**
McLaughlin, John **12**
McPartland, Marian **15**
McRae, Carmen **9**
Metheny, Pat **2**
Mingus, Charles **9**
Monk, Thelonious **6**
Montgomery, Wes **3**
Morgan, Frank **9**
Morton, Jelly Roll **7**
Mulligan, Gerry **16**
Nascimento, Milton **6**
Norvo, Red **12**
Oliver, King **15**
Palmieri, Eddie **15**
Parker, Charlie **5**
Parker, Maceo **7**
Pass, Joe **15**
Paul, Les **2**
Peterson, Oscar **11**
Ponty, Jean-Luc **8**
Powell, Bud **15**
Previn, André **15**
Professor Longhair **6**
Puente, Tito **14**
Pullen, Don **16**
Rampal, Jean-Pierre **6**
Redman, Joshua **12**

Reeves, Dianne **16**
Reid, Vernon **2**
    Also see Living Colour
Reinhardt, Django **7**
Rich, Buddy **13**
Roach, Max **12**
Roberts, Marcus **6**
Robillard, Duke **2**
Rodney, Red **14**
Rollins, Sonny **7**
Sanborn, David **1**
Sanders, Pharoah **16**
Sandoval, Arturo **15**
Santana, Carlos **1**
Schuur, Diane **6**
Scofield, John **7**
Scott, Jimmy **14**
Scott-Heron, Gil **13**
Severinsen, Doc **1**
Sharrock, Sonny **15**
Shaw, Artie **8**
Shorter, Wayne **5**
Simone, Nina **11**
Solal, Martial **4**
Strayhorn, Billy **13**
Summers, Andy **3**
Sun Ra **5**
Take 6 **6**
Taylor, Billy **13**
Taylor, Cecil **9**
Teagarden, Jack **10**
Thielemans, Toots **13**
Threadgill, Henry **9**
Torme, Mel **4**
Tucker, Sophie **12**
Turner, Big Joe **13**
Turtle Island String Quartet **9**
Tyner, McCoy **7**
Ulmer, James Blood **13**
Vaughan, Sarah **2**
Walker, T-Bone **5**
Washington, Dinah **5**
Washington, Grover, Jr. **5**
Webb, Chick **14**
Weston, Randy **15**
Williams, Joe **11**
Wilson, Cassandra **12**
Wilson, Nancy **14**
Winter, Paul **10**
Young, La Monte **16**
Young, Lester **14**
Zorn, John **15**

Keyboards, Electric
Aphex Twin **14**
Bley, Paul **14**
Brown, Tony **14**
Corea, Chick **6**
Davis, Chip **4**
Dolby, Thomas **10**
Emerson, Keith
    See Emerson, Lake & Palmer/Powell
Eno, Brian **8**
Foster, David **13**
Froom, Mitchell **15**

Hancock, Herbie **8**
Jackson, Joe **4**
Jarre, Jean-Michel **2**
Jones, Booker T. **8**
Kitaro **1**
Manzarek, Ray
    See Doors, The
McDonald, Michael
    See Doobie Brothers, The
McVie, Christine
    See Fleetwood Mac
Pierson, Kate
    See B-52's, The
Shaffer, Paul **13**
Sun Ra **5**
Waller, Fats **7**
Wilson, Brian
    See Beach Boys, The
Winwood, Steve **2**
Wonder, Stevie **2**
Worrell, Bernie **11**
Yanni **11**

Liturgical Music
Cooney, Rory **6**
Talbot, John Michael **6**

Mandolin
Bush, Sam
    See New Grass Revival, The
Duffey, John
    See Seldom Scene, The
Hartford, John **1**
Lindley, David **2**
McReynolds, Jesse
    See McReynolds, Jim and Jesse
Monroe, Bill **1**
Rosas, Cesar
    See Los Lobos
Skaggs, Ricky **5**
Stuart, Marty **9**

Musicals
Allen, Debbie **8**
Allen, Peter **11**
Andrews, Julie **4**
Andrews Sisters, The **9**
Bacharach, Burt **1**
Bailey, Pearl **5**
Baker, Josephine **10**
Berlin, Irving **8**
Brown, Ruth **13**
Buckley, Betty **16**
    Earlier sketch in CM **1**
Burnett, Carol **6**
Carter, Nell **7**
Channing, Carol **6**
Chevalier, Maurice **6**
Crawford, Michael **4**
Crosby, Bing **6**
Curry, Tim **3**
Davis, Sammy, Jr. **4**
Garland, Judy **6**
Gershwin, George and Ira **11**
Hamlisch, Marvin **1**

Professor Longhair **6**
Puente, Tito **14**
Pullen, Don **16**
Rich, Charlie **3**
Roberts, Marcus **6**
Rubinstein, Arthur **11**
Russell, Mark **6**
Schickele, Peter **5**
Sedaka, Neil **4**
Shaffer, Paul **13**
Solal, Martial **4**
Solti, Georg **13**
Story, Liz **2**
Strayhorn, Billy **13**
Sunnyland Slim **16**
Taylor, Billy **13**
Taylor, Cecil **9**
Tyner, McCoy **7**
Waits, Tom **12**
    Earlier sketch in **1**
Waller, Fats **7**
Weston, Randy **15**
Wilson, Cassandra **12**
Winston, George **9**
Winwood, Steve **2**
Wonder, Stevie **2**
Wright, Rick
    See Pink Floyd
Young, La Monte **16**

Piccolo
Galway, James **3**

Pop
Abba **12**
Abdul, Paula **3**
Adam Ant **13**
Adams, Bryan **2**
Alpert, Herb **11**
America **16**
Amos, Tori **12**
Andrews Sisters, The **9**
Armatrading, Joan **4**
Arnold, Eddy **10**
Astley, Rick **5**
Atkins, Chet **5**
Avalon, Frankie **5**
Bacharach, Burt **1**
Bailey, Pearl **5**
Basia **5**
Beach Boys, The **1**
Beatles, The **2**
Beaver Brown Band, The **3**
Bee Gees, The **3**
Belly **16**
Bennett, Tony **16**
    Earlier sketch in CM **2**
Benson, George **9**
Benton, Brook **7**
B-52's, The **4**
Blige, Mary J. **15**
Blondie **14**
Blood, Sweat and Tears **7**
BoDeans, The **3**
Bolton, Michael **4**

Boone, Pat **13**
Boston **11**
Bowie, David **1**
Boyz II Men **15**
Bragg, Billy **7**
Branigan, Laura **2**
Brickell, Edie **3**
Brooks, Garth **8**
Brown, Bobby **4**
Browne, Jackson **3**
Bryson, Peabo **11**
Buckingham, Lindsey **8**
    Also see Fleetwood Mac
Buckley, Tim **14**
Buffett, Jimmy **4**
Burdon, Eric **14**
    Also see War
Campbell, Glen **2**
Campbell, Tevin **13**
Carey, Mariah **6**
Carlisle, Belinda **8**
Carnes, Kim **4**
Carpenters, The **13**
Case, Peter **13**
Chandra, Sheila **16**
Chapin, Harry **6**
Chapman, Tracy **4**
Charlatans, The **13**
Charles, Ray **1**
Checker, Chubby **7**
Cher **1**
Cherry, Neneh **4**
Chicago **3**
Chilton, Alex **10**
Clapton, Eric **11**
    Earlier sketch in CM **1**
    Also see Cream
    Also see Yardbirds, The
Clayderman, Richard **1**
Clooney, Rosemary **9**
Coasters, The **5**
Cocker, Joe **4**
Cocteau Twins, The **12**
Cole, Lloyd **9**
Cole, Natalie **1**
Cole, Nat King **3**
Collins, Judy **4**
Collins, Phil **2**
    Also see Genesis
Colvin, Shawn **11**
Como, Perry **14**
Connick, Harry, Jr. **4**
Cooke, Sam **1**
    Also see Soul Stirrers, The
Cope, Julian **16**
Costello, Elvis **12**
    Earlier sketch in CM **2**
Cranberries, The **14**
Crash Test Dummies **14**
Crenshaw, Marshall **5**
Croce, Jim **3**
Crosby, David **3**
    Also see Byrds, The
Crowded House **12**
Daltrey, Roger **3**
    Also see Who, The

D'Arby, Terence Trent **3**
Darin, Bobby **4**
Dave Clark Five, The **12**
Davies, Ray **5**
Davis, Sammy, Jr. **4**
Davis, Skeeter **15**
Dayne, Taylor **4**
DeBarge, El **14**
Denver, John **1**
Depeche Mode **5**
Des'ree **15**
Devo **13**
Diamond, Neil **1**
Dion **4**
Dion, Céline **12**
Doc Pomus **14**
Donovan **9**
Doobie Brothers, The **3**
Doors, The **4**
Duran Duran **4**
Dylan, Bob **3**
Eagles, The **3**
Earth, Wind and Fire **12**
Easton, Sheena **2**
Edmonds, Kenneth "Babyface" **12**
Electric Light Orchestra **7**
Elfman, Danny **9**
Elliot, Cass **5**
Enigma **14**
En Vogue **10**
Estefan, Gloria **15**
    Earlier sketch in CM **2**
Eurythmics **6**
Everly Brothers, The **2**
Everything But The Girl **15**
Exposé **4**
Fabian **5**
Feliciano, José **10**
Ferguson, Maynard **7**
Ferry, Bryan **1**
Fiedler, Arthur **6**
Fisher, Eddie **12**
Fitzgerald, Ella **1**
Flack, Roberta **5**
Fleetwood Mac **5**
Fogelberg, Dan **4**
Fordham, Julia **15**
Foster, David **13**
Four Tops, The **11**
Fox, Samantha **3**
Frampton, Peter **3**
Francis, Connie **10**
Franklin, Aretha **2**
Frey, Glenn **3**
    Also see Eagles, The
Garfunkel, Art **4**
Gaye, Marvin **4**
Gayle, Crystal **1**
Geldof, Bob **9**
Genesis **4**
Gershwin, George and Ira **11**
Gibson, Debbie **1**
Gift, Roland **3**
Goodman, Benny **4**
Gordy, Berry, Jr. **6**

Springsteen, Bruce **6**
Squeeze **5**
Stansfield, Lisa **9**
Starr, Ringo **10**
Steely Dan **5**
Stevens, Cat **3**
Stewart, Rod **2**
Stills, Stephen **5**
Sting **2**
Story, The **13**
Streisand, Barbra **2**
Summer, Donna **12**
Supremes, The **6**
Sweat, Keith **13**
Sweet, Matthew **9**
SWV **14**
Talking Heads **1**
Taylor, James **2**
Tears for Fears **6**
Teenage Fanclub **13**
Temptations, The **3**
10,000 Maniacs **3**
The The **15**
They Might Be Giants **7**
Thomas, Irma **16**
Three Dog Night **5**
Tiffany **4**
Tikaram, Tanita **9**
Timbuk 3 **3**
TLC **15**
Toad the Wet Sprocket **13**
Tony! Toni! Toné! **12**
Torme, Mel **4**
Townshend, Pete **1**
    Also see Who, The
Turner, Tina **1**
Valli, Frankie **10**
Vandross, Luther **2**
Vega, Suzanne **3**
Vinton, Bobby **12**
Walsh, Joe **5**
Warnes, Jennifer **3**
Warwick, Dionne **2**
Was (Not Was) **6**
Washington, Dinah **5**
Waters, Crystal **15**
Watley, Jody **9**
Webb, Jimmy **12**
"Weird Al" Yankovic **7**
Weller, Paul **14**
Who, The **3**
Williams, Andy **2**
Williams, Deniece **1**
Williams, Joe **11**
Williams, Lucinda **10**
Williams, Paul **5**
Williams, Vanessa **10**
Wilson, Jackie **3**
Wilson Phillips **5**
Winwood, Steve **2**
Womack, Bobby **5**
Wonder, Stevie **2**
XTC **10**
Young, Neil **15**
    Earlier sketch in CM **2**
Young M.C. **4**

Producers
Ackerman, Will **3**
Albini, Steve **15**
Alpert, Herb **11**
Austin, Dallas **16**
Baker, Anita **9**
Benitez, Jellybean **15**
Bogaert, Jo
    See Technotronic
Brown, Junior **15**
Brown, Tony **14**
Browne, Jackson **3**
Burnett, T Bone **13**
Cale, John **9**
Clarke, Stanley **3**
Clinton, George **7**
Collins, Phil **2**
    Also see Genesis
Combs, Sean "Puffy" **16**
Costello, Elvis **2**
Cropper, Steve **12**
Crowell, Rodney **8**
Dixon, Willie **10**
DJ Premier
    See Gang Starr
Dr. Dre **15**
    Also see N.W.A.
Dolby, Thomas **10**
Dozier, Lamont
    See Holland-Dozier-Holland
Edmonds, Kenneth "Babyface" **12**
Enigma **14**
Eno, Brian **8**
Ertegun, Ahmet **10**
Foster, David **13**
Fripp, Robert **9**
Froom, Mitchell **15**
Grusin, Dave **7**
Holland, Brian
    See Holland-Dozier-Holland
Holland, Eddie
    See Holland-Dozier-Holland
Jackson, Millie **14**
Jam, Jimmy, and Terry Lewis **11**
Jones, Booker T. **8**
Jones, Quincy **2**
Jourgensen, Al
    See Ministry
Krasnow, Bob **15**
Lanois, Daniel **8**
Laswell, Bill **14**
Leiber and Stoller **14**
Lillywhite, Steve **13**
Lynne, Jeff **5**
Marley, Rita **10**
Martin, George **6**
Mayfield, Curtis **8**
Miller, Mitch **11**
Parsons, Alan **12**
Prince **14**
    Earlier sketch in CM **1**
Riley, Teddy **14**
Robertson, Robbie **2**
Rodgers, Nile **8**
Rubin, Rick **9**
Rundgren, Todd **11**

Shocklee, Hank **15**
Simmons, Russell **7**
Skaggs, Ricky **5**
Spector, Phil **4**
Sure!, Al B. **13**
Sweat, Keith **13**
Swing, DeVante
    See Jodeci
Too $hort **16**
Toussaint, Allen **11**
Vandross, Luther **2**
Vasquez, Junior **16**
Walden, Narada Michael **14**
Wexler, Jerry **15**
Willner, Hal **10**
Wilson, Brian
    See Beach Boys, The
Winbush, Angela **15**

Promoters
Clark, Dick **2**
Geldof, Bob **9**
Graham, Bill **10**
Hay, George D. **3**
Simmons, Russell **7**

Ragtime
Johnson, James P. **16**
Joplin, Scott **10**

Rap
Arrested Development **14**
Austin, Dallas **16**
Bambaataa, Afrika **13**
Basehead **11**
Beastie Boys, The **8**
Biz Markie **10**
Black Sheep **15**
Campbell, Luther **10**
Cherry, Neneh **4**
Combs, Sean "Puffy" **16**
Cypress Hill **11**
Das EFX **14**
De La Soul **7**
Digable Planets **15**
Digital Underground **9**
DJ Jazzy Jeff and the Fresh Prince **5**
Dr. Dre **15**
    Also see N.W.A.
Eazy-E **13**
    Also see N.W.A.
EPMD **10**
Eric B. and Rakim **9**
Franti, Michael **16**
Gang Starr **13**
Geto Boys, The **11**
Grandmaster Flash **14**
Hammer, M.C. **5**
Heavy D **9**
House of Pain **14**
Ice Cube **10**
Ice-T **7**
Jackson, Millie **14**
Kane, Big Daddy **7**
Kid 'n Play **5**

Sledge, Percy **15**
Stansfield, Lisa **9**
Staples, Mavis **13**
Staples, Pops **11**
Stewart, Rod **2**
Stone, Sly **8**
Supremes, The **6**
    Also see Ross, Diana
Sure!, Al B. **13**
Sweat, Keith **13**
SWV **14**
Temptations, The **3**
Third World **13**
Thomas, Irma **16**
TLC **15**
Tony! Toni! Toné! **12**
Toussaint, Allen **11**
Turner, Tina **1**
Vandross, Luther **2**
Was (Not Was) **6**
Waters, Crystal **15**
Watley, Jody **9**
Wexler, Jerry **15**
Williams, Deniece **1**
Williams, Vanessa **10**
Wilson, Jackie **3**
Winans, The **12**
Winbush, Angela **15**
Womack, Bobby **5**
Wonder, Stevie **2**

Rock
AC/DC **4**
Adam Ant **13**
Adams, Bryan **2**
Aerosmith **3**
Albini, Steve **15**
Alexander, Arthur **14**
Alice in Chains **10**
Allman Brothers, The **6**
America **16**
American Music Club **15**
Anthrax **11**
Babes in Toyland **16**
Bad Brains **16**
Baker, Ginger **16**
    Also see Cream
Band, The **9**
Basehead **11**
Beach Boys, The **1**
Beastie Boys, The **8**
Beatles, The **2**
Beaver Brown Band, The **3**
Beck, Jeff **4**
    Also see Yardbirds, The
Belew, Adrian **5**
Belly **16**
Benatar, Pat **8**
Berry, Chuck **1**
Björk **16**
    Also see Sugarcubes, The
Black Crowes, The **7**
Black, Frank **14**
Black Sabbath **9**
Blackman, Cindy **15**

Blondie **14**
Blood, Sweat and Tears **7**
Blue Öyster Cult **16**
Blues Traveler **15**
BoDeans, The **3**
Bon Jovi **10**
Boston **11**
Bowie, David **1**
Bragg, Billy **7**
Brickell, Edie **3**
Browne, Jackson **3**
Buckingham, Lindsey **8**
    Also see Fleetwood Mac
Buckley, Tim **14**
Burdon, Eric **14**
    Also see War
Burnett, T Bone **13**
Butthole Surfers **16**
Buzzcocks, The **9**
Byrds, The **8**
Byrne, David **8**
    Also see Talking Heads
Cale, J. J. **16**
Cale, John **9**
Captain Beefheart **10**
Cave, Nick **10**
Charlatans, The **13**
Cheap Trick **12**
Cher **1**
Chicago **3**
Church, The **14**
Cinderella **16**
Clapton, Eric **11**
    Earlier sketch in CM **1**
    Also see Cream
    Also see Yardbirds, The
Clash, The **4**
Clemons, Clarence **7**
Clinton, George **7**
Coasters, The **5**
Cocker, Joe **4**
Collective Soul **16**
Collins, Phil **2**
    Also see Genesis
Cooder, Ry **2**
Cooke, Sam **1**
    Also see Soul Stirrers, The
Cooper, Alice **8**
Cope, Julian **16**
Costello, Elvis **12**
    Earlier sketch in CM **2**
Cougar, John(ny)
    See Mellencamp, John "Cougar"
Cracker **12**
Cramps, The **16**
Cranberries, The **14**
Crash Test Dummies **14**
Cream **9**
Creedence Clearwater Revival **16**
Crenshaw, Marshall **5**
Crosby, David **3**
    Also see Byrds, The
Crowded House **12**
Cult, The **16**
Cure, The **3**
Curry, Tim **3**

Curve **13**
Dale, Dick **13**
Daltrey, Roger **3**
    Also see Who, The
Daniels, Charlie **6**
Danzig **7**
D'Arby, Terence Trent **3**
Dave Clark Five, The **12**
Davies, Ray **5**
    Also see Kinks, The
Dead Can Dance **16**
Deep Purple **11**
Def Leppard **3**
Depeche Mode **5**
Devo **13**
Diddley, Bo **3**
Dinosaur Jr. **10**
Doc Pomus **14**
Dokken **16**
Doobie Brothers, The **3**
Doors, The **4**
Duran Duran **4**
Dylan, Bob **3**
Eagles, The **3**
Eddy, Duane **9**
Einstürzende Neubauten **13**
Electric Light Orchestra **7**
Elliot, Cass **5**
Emerson, Lake & Palmer/Powell **5**
English Beat, The **9**
Eno, Brian **8**
Erickson, Roky **16**
Etheridge, Melissa **16**
    Earlier sketch in CM **4**
Eurythmics **6**
Extreme **10**
Faithfull, Marianne **14**
Faith No More **7**
Fall, The **12**
Ferry, Bryan **1**
fIREHOSE **11**
Fishbone **7**
Fleetwood Mac **5**
Flores, Rosie **16**
Fogelberg, Dan **4**
Fogerty, John **2**
    Also see Creedence Clearwater
    Revival
Ford, Lita **9**
Fox, Samantha **3**
Frampton, Peter **3**
Franti, Michael **16**
Frey, Glenn **3**
    Also see Eagles, The
Froom, Mitchell **15**
Fugazi **13**
Gabriel, Peter **16**
    Earlier sketch in CM **2**
    Also see Genesis
Gang of Four **8**
Garcia, Jerry **4**
    Also see Grateful Dead, The
Gatton, Danny **16**
Genesis **4**
Gift, Roland **3**
Goo Goo Dolls, The **16**

Wynette, Tammy **2**
Yoakam, Dwight **1**
Young, Angus
  See AC/DC
Young, Neil **15**
  Earlier sketch in CM **2**
Zappa, Frank **1**
Zevon, Warren **9**

Trombone
Anderson, Ray **7**
Dorsey, Tommy
  See Dorsey Brothers, The
Miller, Glenn **6**
Teagarden, Jack **10**
Watts, Eugene
  See Canadian Brass, The

Trumpet
Alpert, Herb **11**
Armstrong, Louis **4**
Baker, Chet **13**
Berigan, Bunny **2**
Blanchard, Terence **13**
Cherry, Don **10**
Coleman, Ornette **5**
Davis, Miles **1**
Eldridge, Roy **9**
  Also see McKinney's Cotton Pickers
Ferguson, Maynard **7**
Gillespie, Dizzy **6**
Hargrove, Roy **15**
Hirt, Al **5**
Isham, Mark **14**
James, Harry **11**
Jones, Quincy **2**

Loughnane, Lee **3**
Marsalis, Wynton **6**
Masekela, Hugh **7**
Mills, Fred
  See Canadian Brass, The
Oliver, King **15**
Rodney, Red **14**
Romm, Ronald
  See Canadian Brass, The
Sandoval, Arturo **15**
Severinsen, Doc **1**

Tuba
Daellenbach, Charles
  See Canadian Brass, The
Phillips, Harvey **3**

Vibraphone
Burton, Gary **10**
Hampton, Lionel **6**
Jackson, Milt **15**
Norvo, Red **12**

Viola
Dutt, Hank
  See Kronos Quartet
Jones, Michael
  See Kronos Quartet
Killian, Tim
  See Kronos Quartet
Menuhin, Yehudi **11**
Zukerman, Pinchas **4**

Violin
Acuff, Roy **2**

Anderson, Laurie **1**
Bush, Sam
  See New Grass Revival, The
Chang, Sarah **7**
Coleman, Ornette **5**
Daniels, Charlie **6**
Doucet, Michael **8**
Gingold, Josef **6**
Grappelli, Stephane **10**
Gray, Ella
  See Kronos Quartet
Harrington, David
  See Kronos Quartet
Hartford, John **1**
Hidalgo, David
  See Los Lobos
Kennedy, Nigel **8**
Krauss, Alison **10**
Lewis, Roy
  See Kronos Quartet
Marriner, Neville **7**
Menuhin, Yehudi **11**
Midori **7**
O'Connor, Mark **1**
Perlman, Itzhak **2**
Ponty, Jean-Luc **8**
Salerno-Sonnenberg, Nadja **3**
Shallenberger, James
  See Kronos Quartet
Sherba, John
  See Kronos Quartet
Skaggs, Ricky **5**
Stern, Isaac **7**
Wills, Bob **6**
Zukerman, Pinchas **4**

Cumulative Musicians Index

Volume numbers appear in **bold**.

Abba **12**
Abbruzzese, Dave
  See Pearl Jam
Abdul, Paula **3**
Abong, Fred
  See Belly
Abrahams, Mick
  See Jethro Tull
Abrantes, Fernando
  See Kraftwerk
AC/DC **4**
Ackerman, Will **3**
Acland, Christopher
  See Lush
Acuff, Roy **2**
Adam Ant **13**
Adams, Bryan **2**
Adamendes, Elaine
  See Throwing Muses
Adams, Clifford
  See Kool & the Gang
Adams, Craig
  See Cult, The
Adams, Donn
  See NRBQ
Adams, John **8**
Adams, Terry
  See NRBQ
Adcock, Eddie
  See Country Gentleman, The
Adderly, Cannonball **15**
Adderly, Julian
  See Adderly, Cannonball
Adler, Steven
  See Guns n' Roses
Aerosmith **3**
Afonso, Marie
  See Zap Mama
AFX
  See Aphex Twin
Ajile
  See Arrested Development
Alabama **1**
Albini, Steve **15**
Albuquerque, Michael de
  See Electric Light Orchestra
Alexander, Arthur **14**
Alexander, Tim
  See Asleep at the Wheel
Alexander, Tim "Herb"
  See Primus
Ali
  See Tribe Called Quest, A
Alice in Chains **10**
Allcock, Martin
  See Jethro Tull

Allen, April
  See C + C Music Factory
Allen, Dave
  See Gang of Four
Allen, Debbie **8**
Allen, Duane
  See Oak Ridge Boys, The
Allen, Geri **10**
Allen, Papa Dee
  See War
Allen, Peter **11**
Allen, Red
  See Osborne Brothers, The
Allen, Rick
  See Def Leppard
Allen, Ross
  See Mekons, The
Allman, Duane
  See Allman Brothers, The
Allman, Gregg
  See Allman Brothers, The
Allman Brothers, The **6**
Allsup, Michael Rand
  See Three Dog Night
Alpert, Herb **11**
Alston, Shirley
  See Shirelles, The
Alvin, Dave
  See X
Ament, Jeff
  See Pearl Jam
America **16**
American Music Club **15**
Amos, Tori **12**
Anastasio, Trey
  See Phish
Anderson, Al
  See NRBQ
Anderson, Emma
  See Lush
Anderson, Ian
  See Jethro Tull
Anderson, John **5**
Anderson, Jon
  See Yes
Anderson, Laurie **1**
Anderson, Marian **8**
Anderson, Pamela
  See Incognito
Anderson, Ray **7**
Anderson, Signe
  See Jefferson Airplane
Andersson, Benny
  See Abba
Andrews, Barry
  See XTC

Andrews, Julie **4**
Andrews, Laverne
  See Andrews Sisters, The
Andrews, Maxene
  See Andrews Sisters, The
Andrews, Patty
  See Andrews Sisters, The
Andrews Sisters, The **9**
Anger, Darol
  See Turtle Island String Quartet
Anka, Paul **2**
Anselmo, Philip
  See Pantera
Ant, Adam
  See Adam Ant
Anthony, Michael
  See Van Halen
Anthrax **11**
Anton, Alan
  See Cowboy Junkies, The
Antunes, Michael
  See Beaver Brown Band, The
Aphex Twin **14**
Appice, Vinnie
  See Black Sabbath
Araya, Tom
  See Slayer
Ardolino, Tom
  See NRBQ
Arm, Mark
  See Mudhoney
Armatrading, Joan **4**
Armstrong, Billie Joe
  See Green Day
Armstrong, Louis **4**
Arnaz, Desi **8**
Arnold, Eddy **10**
Arnold, Kristine
  See Sweethearts of the Rodeo
Arrau, Claudio **1**
Arrested Development **14**
Arthurs, Paul
  See Oasis
Ash, Daniel
  See Love and Rockets
Asleep at the Wheel **5**
Astbury, Ian
  See Cult, The
Astley, Rick **5**
Astro
  See UB40
Asuo, Kwesi
  See Arrested Development
Atkins, Chet **5**
Atkinson, Sweet Pea
  See Was (Not Was)

Berenyi, Miki
See Lush
Berg, Matraca **16**
Berigan, Bunny **2**
Berlin, Irving **8**
Berlin, Steve
See Los Lobos
Bernstein, Leonard **2**
Berry, Bill
See R.E.M.
Berry, Chuck **1**
Berry, Robert
See Emerson, Lake & Palmer/Powell
Best, Nathaniel
See O'Jays, The
Best, Pete
See Beatles, The
Bettencourt, Nuno
See Extreme
Betts, Dicky
See Allman Brothers, The
Bevan, Bev
See Black Sabbath
Also see Electric Light Orchestra
B-52's, The **4**
Big Mike
See Geto Boys, The
Big Money Odis
See Digital Underground
Bingham, John
See Fishbone
Binks, Les
See Judas Priest
Birchfield, Benny
See Osborne Brothers, The
Bird
See Parker, Charlie
Birdsong, Cindy
See Supremes, The
Biscuits, Chuck
See Danzig
Bishop, Michael
See Gwar
Biz Markie **10**
Bjelland, Kat
See Babes in Toyland
Björk **16**
Also see Sugarcubes, The
Black, Clint **5**
Black Crowes, The **7**
Black Francis
See Black, Frank
Black, Frank **14**
Black, Mary **15**
Black Sabbath **9**
Black Sheep **15**
Black Uhuru **12**
Black, Vic
See C + C Music Factory
Blackman, Cindy **15**
Blackmore, Ritchie
See Deep Purple
Blades, Ruben **2**
Blake, Norman
See Teenage Fanclub

Blakey, Art **11**
Blanchard, Terence **13**
Bland, Bobby "Blue" **12**
Bley, Carla **8**
Bley, Paul **14**
Blige, Mary J. **15**
Blondie **14**
Blood, Sweat and Tears **7**
Bloom, Eric
See Blue Öyster Cult
Bloom, Luka **14**
Blue Öyster Cult **16**
Blues, Elwood
See Blues Brothers, The
Blues, "Joliet" Jake
See Blues Brothers, The
Blues Brothers, The **3**
Blues Traveler **15**
Blunt, Martin
See Charlatans, The
BoDeans, The **3**
Bogaert, Jo
See Technotronic
Bogdan, Henry
See Helmet
Bogguss, Suzy **11**
Bolade, Nitanju
See Sweet Honey in the Rock
Bolan, Marc
See T. Rex
Bolton, Michael **4**
Bon Jovi **10**
Bon Jovi, Jon
See Bon Jovi
Bonebrake, D. J.
See X
Bonham, John
See Led Zeppelin
Bonner, Leroy "Sugarfoot"
See Ohio Players
Bono
See U2
Bonsall, Joe
See Oak Ridge Boys, The
Boone, Pat **13**
Books
See Das EFX
Booth, Tim
See James
Bordin, Mike
See Faith No More
Bostaph, Paul
See Slayer
Boston **11**
Bostrom, Derrick
See Meat Puppets, The
Bottum, Roddy
See Faith No More
Bouchard, Albert
See Blue Öyster Cult
Bouchard, Joe
See Blue Öyster Cult
Bouchikhi, Chico
See Gipsy Kings, The
Bowen, Jimmy
See Country Gentlemen, The

Bowens, Sir Harry
See Was (Not Was)
Bowie, David **1**
Boyd, Liona **7**
Boyz II Men **15**
Brady, Paul **8**
Bragg, Billy **7**
Bramah, Martin
See Fall, The
Brand New Heavies, The **14**
Branigan, Laura **2**
Brantley, Junior
See Roomful of Blues
Braxton, Anthony **12**
B-Real
See Cypress Hill
Bream, Julian **9**
Brickell, Edie **3**
Bright, Ronnie
See Coasters, The
Briley, Alex
See Village People, The
Britten, Benjamin **15**
Brittingham, Eric
See Cinderella
Brix
See Fall, The
Brockie, Dave
See Gwar
Bronfman, Yefim **6**
Brooke, Jonatha
See Story, The
Brookes, Jon
See Charlatans, The
Brooks, Garth **8**
Brooks, Leon Eric "Kix"
See Brooks & Dunn
Brooks & Dunn **12**
Broonzy, Big Bill **13**
Brown, Bobby **4**
Brown, Clarence "Gatemouth" **11**
Brown, George
See Kool & the Gang
Brown, Harold
See War
Brown, Ian
See Stone Roses, The
Brown, James **16**
Earlier sketch in CM **2**
Brown, Jimmy
See UB40
Brown, Junior **15**
Brown, Marty **14**
Brown, Mick
See Dokken
Brown, Norman
See Mills Brothers, The
Brown, Ruth **13**
Brown, Selwyn "Bumbo"
See Steel Pulse
Brown, Tony **14**
Browne, Jackson **3**
Also see Nitty Gritty Dirt Band, The
Brubeck, Dave **8**
Bruce, Jack
See Cream

Cavoukian, Raffi
   See Raffi
Cease, Jeff
   See Black Crowes, The
Cervenka, Exene
   See X
Cetera, Peter
   See Chicago
Chamberlin, Jimmy
   See Smashing Pumpkins
Chambers, Martin
   See Pretenders, The
Chambers, Terry
   See XTC
Chance, Slim
   See Cramps, The
Chandra, Sheila **16**
Chang, Sarah **7**
Channing, Carol **6**
Chapin, Harry **6**
Chapin, Tom **11**
Chapman, Steven Curtis **15**
Chapman, Tony
   See Rolling Stones, The
Chapman, Tracy **4**
Chaquico, Craig
   See Jefferson Starship
Charlatans, The **13**
Charles, Ray **1**
Chea, Alvin "Vinnie"
   See Take 6
Cheap Trick **12**
Checker, Chubby **7**
Cheeks, Julius
   See Soul Stirrers, The
Chenier, C. J. **15**
Chenier, Clifton **6**
Chenille Sisters, The **16**
Cher **1**
Cherone, Gary
   See Extreme
Cherry, Don **10**
Cherry, Neneh **4**
Chesnutt, Mark **13**
Chevalier, Maurice **6**
Chevron, Phillip
   See Pogues, The
Chicago **3**
Chieftains, The **7**
Childress, Ross
   See Collective Soul
Childs, Toni **2**
Chilton, Alex **10**
Chimes, Terry
   See Clash, The
Chopmaster J
   See Digital Underground
Christ, John
   See Danzig
Christian, Charlie **11**
Christina, Fran
   See Fabulous Thunderbirds, The
   Also see Roomful of Blues
Chuck D
   See Public Enemy
Chung, Mark
   See Einstürzende Neubauten

Church, Kevin
   See Country Gentlemen, The
Church, The **14**
Cinderella **16**
Clapton, Eric **11**
   Earlier sketch in CM **1**
   Also see Cream
   Also see Yardbirds, The
Clark, Dave
   See Dave Clark Five, The
Clark, Dick **2**
Clark, Gene
   See Byrds, The
Clark, Mike
   See Suicidal Tendencies
Clark, Roy **1**
Clark, Steve
   See Def Leppard
Clarke, "Fast" Eddie
   See Motörhead
Clarke, Michael
   See Byrds, The
Clarke, Stanley **3**
Clarke, Vince
   See Depeche Mode
   Also see Erasure
Clarke, William
   See Third World
Clash, The **4**
Clayderman, Richard **1**
Claypool, Les
   See Primus
Clayton, Adam
   See U2
Clayton, Sam
   See Little Feat
Clayton-Thomas, David
   See Blood, Sweat and Tears
Cleaves, Jessica
   See Earth, Wind and Fire
Clegg, Johnny **8**
Clemons, Clarence **7**
Cleveland, James **1**
Cliburn, Van **13**
Cliff, Jimmy **8**
Clifford, Douglas Ray
   See Creedence Clearwater Revival
Cline, Patsy **5**
Clinton, George **7**
Clivilles, Robert
   See C + C Music Factory
Clooney, Rosemary **9**
Coasters, The **5**
Cobain, Kurt
   See Nirvana
Cockburn, Bruce **8**
Cocker, Joe **4**
Cocking, William "Willigan"
   See Mystic Revealers
Cocteau Twins, The **12**
Coe, David Allan **4**
Coffey, Jeff
   See Butthole Surfers
Coffie, Calton
   See Inner Circle

Cohen, Jeremy
   See Turtle Island String Quartet
Cohen, Leonard **3**
Cohen, Porky
   See Roomful of Blues
Cole, David
   See C + C Music Factory
Cole, Lloyd **9**
Cole, Natalie **1**
Cole, Nat King **3**
Coleman, Ornette **5**
Collective Soul **16**
Colley, Dana
   See Morphine
Collie, Mark **15**
Collin, Phil
   See Def Leppard
Collins, Albert **4**
Collins, Allen
   See Lynyrd Skynyrd
Collins, Bootsy **8**
Collins, Judy **4**
Collins, Mark
   See Charlatans, The
Collins, Phil **2**
   Also see Genesis
Collins, Rob
   See Charlatans, The
Collins, William
   See Collins, Bootsy
Colomby, Bobby
   See Blood, Sweat and Tears
Colt, Johnny
   See Black Crowes, The
Coltrane, John **4**
Colvin, Shawn **11**
Combs, Sean "Puffy" **16**
Comess, Aaron
   See Spin Doctors
Como, Perry **14**
Conneff, Kevin
   See Chieftains, The
Connick, Harry, Jr. **4**
Conti, Neil
   See Prefab Sprout
Conway, Billy
   See Morphine
Cooder, Ry **2**
Cook, Jeff
   See Alabama
Cook, Paul
   See Sex Pistols, The
Cook, Stuart
   See Creedence Clearwater Revival
Cooke, Sam **1**
   Also see Soul Stirrers, The
Cool, Tre
   See Green Day
Cooney, Rory **6**
Cooper, Alice **8**
Cooper, Michael
   See Third World
Coore, Stephen
   See Third World
Cope, Julian **16**
Copeland, Stewart **14**

Desert Rose Band, The **4**
Des'ree **15**
DeVille, C. C.
See Poison
Destri, Jimmy
See Blondie
Deupree, Jerome
See Morphine
Devo **13**
Devoto, Howard
See Buzzcocks, The
DeWitt, Lew C.
See Statler Brothers, The
de Young, Joyce
See Andrews Sisters, The
Diagram, Andy
See James
Diamond, Mike
See Beastie Boys, The
Diamond, Neil **1**
Diamond "Dimebag" Darrell
See Pantera
Diamond Rio **11**
Di'anno, Paul
See Iron Maiden
Dibango, Manu **14**
Dickens, Little Jimmy **7**
Dickerson, B. B.
See War
Dickinson, Paul Bruce
See Iron Maiden
Diddley, Bo **3**
Diffie, Joe **10**
Difford, Chris
See Squeeze
Digable Planets **15**
Diggle, Steve
See Buzzcocks, The
Digital Underground **9**
DiMant, Leor
See House of Pain
Di Meola, Al **12**
DiMucci, Dion
See Dion
DiNizo, Pat
See Smithereens, The
Dinning, Dean
See Toad the Wet Sprocket
Dinosaur Jr. **10**
Dio, Ronnie James
See Black Sabbath
Dion **4**
Dion, Céline **12**
Dirks, Michael
See Gwar
Dirnt, Mike
See Green Day
Dittrich, John
See Restless Heart
Dixon, Willie **10**
DJ Domination
See Geto Boys, The
DJ Fuse
See Digital Underground
DJ Jazzy Jeff and the Fresh Prince **5**

D.J. Lethal
See House of Pain
D.J. Minutemix
See P.M. Dawn
DJ Muggs
See Cypress Hill
DJ Premier
See Gang Starr
DJ Ready Red
See Geto Boys, The
DJ Terminator X
See Public Enemy
Doc Pomus **14**
Dr. Dre **15**
Also see N.W.A.
Dr. John **7**
Doe, John
See X
Dokken, Don
See Dokken
Dokken **16**
Dolby, Thomas **10**
Dolenz, Micky
See Monkees, The
Domingo, Placido **1**
Domino, Fats **2**
Don, Rasa
See Arrested Development
Donelly, Tanya
See Belly
Also see Throwing Muses
Donovan **9**
Doobie Brothers, The **3**
Doodlebug
See Digable Planets
Doors, The **4**
Dorge, Michel (Mitch)
See Crash Test Dummies
Dorsey, Jimmy
See Dorsey Brothers, The
Dorsey, Thomas A. **11**
Dorsey, Tommy
See Dorsey Brothers, The
Dorsey Brothers, The **8**
Doucet, Michael **8**
Douglas, Jerry
See Country Gentlemen, The
Dowd, Christopher
See Fishbone
Downes, Geoff
See Yes
Downey, Brian
See Thin Lizzy
Downing, K. K.
See Judas Priest
Dozier, Lamont
See Holland-Dozier-Holland
Drayton, Leslie
See Earth, Wind and Fire
Dreja, Chris
See Yardbirds, The
Drew, Dennis
See 10,000 Maniacs
Drumdini, Harry
See Cramps, The
Dryden, Spencer
See Jefferson Airplane

Duffey, John
See Country Gentlemen, The
Also see Seldom Scene, The
Duffy, Billy
See Cult, The
Duffy, Martin
See Primal Scream
Dunbar, Aynsley
See Jefferson Starship
Also see Whitesnake
Dunbar, Sly
See Sly and Robbie
Duncan, Steve
See Desert Rose Band, The
Duncan, Stuart
See Nashville Bluegrass Band
Dunlap, Slim
See Replacements, The
Dunn, Holly **7**
Dunn, Larry
See Earth, Wind and Fire
Dunn, Ronnie
See Brooks & Dunn
Dupree, Champion Jack **12**
Duran Duran **4**
Dutt, Hank
See Kronos Quartet
Dylan, Bob **3**
E., Sheila
See Sheila E.
Eagles, The **3**
Earl, Ronnie **5**
Also see Roomful of Blues
Earle, Steve **16**
Earth, Wind and Fire **12**
Easton, Sheena **2**
Eazy-E **13**
Also see N.W.A.
Echeverria, Rob
See Helmet
Eckstine, Billy **1**
Eddy, Duane **9**
Edge, The
See U2
Edmonds, Kenneth "Babyface" **12**
Edwards, Dennis
See Temptations, The
Edwards, Gordon
See Kinks, The
Edwards, Leroy "Lion"
See Mystic Revealers
Edwards, Mike
See Electric Light Orchestra
Einheit
See Einstürzende Neubauten
Einstürzende Neubauten **13**
Eitzel, Mark
See American Music Club
Eldon, Thór
See Sugarcubes, The
Eldridge, Ben
See Seldom Scene, The
Eldridge, Roy **9**
Also see McKinney's Cotton Pickers
Electric Light Orchestra **7**
Elfman, Danny **9**

Foster, Paul
    See Soul Stirrers, The
Foster, Radney **16**
Fountain, Clarence
    See Five Blind Boys of Alabama
Fountain, Pete **7**
Four Tops, The **11**
Fox, Lucas
    See Motörhead
Fox, Oz
    See Stryper
Fox, Samantha **3**
Frampton, Peter **3**
Francis, Connie **10**
Francis, Mike
    See Asleep at the Wheel
Franke, Chris
    See Tangerine Dream
Franklin, Aretha **2**
Franklin, Larry
    See Asleep at the Wheel
Franklin, Melvin
    See Temptations, The
Franti, Michael **16**
Frantz, Chris
    See Talking Heads
Fraser, Elizabeth
    See Cocteau Twins, The
Frehley, Ace
    See Kiss
Freese, Josh
    See Suicidal Tendencies
Freiberg, David
    See Jefferson Starship
Freni, Mirella **14**
Frey, Glenn **3**
    Also see Eagles, The
Friedman, Marty
    See Megadeth
Friel, Tony
    See Fall, The
Fripp, Robert **9**
Frisell, Bill **15**
Frizzell, Lefty **10**
Froese, Edgar
    See Tangerine Dream
Froom, Mitchell **15**
Frusciante, John
    See Red Hot Chili Peppers, The
Fugazi **13**
Gabriel, Peter **16**
    Earlier sketch in CM **2**
    Also see Genesis
Gadler, Frank
    See NRBQ
Gahan, Dave
    See Depeche Mode
Gaines, Steve
    See Lynyrd Skynyrd
Gaines, Timothy
    See Stryper
Galás, Diamanda **16**
Gale, Melvyn
    See Electric Light Orchestra
Gallagher, Liam
    See Oasis

Gallagher, Noel
    See Oasis
Gallup, Simon
    See Cure, The
Galway, James **3**
Gambill, Roger
    See Kingston Trio, The
Gamble, Cheryl "Coko"
    See SWV
Gang of Four **8**
Gang Starr **13**
Gano, Gordon
    See Violent Femmes
Garcia, Dean
    See Curve
Garcia, Jerry **4**
    Also see Grateful Dead, The
Gardner, Carl
    See Coasters, The
Gardner, Suzi
    See L7
Garfunkel, Art **4**
Garland, Judy **6**
Garrett, Peter
    See Midnight Oil
Garrett, Scott
    See Cult, The
Garvey, Steve
    See Buzzcocks, The
Gaskill, Jerry
    See King's X
Gatton, Danny **16**
Gaudreau, Jimmy
    See Country Gentlemen, The
Gaye, Marvin **4**
Gayle, Crystal **1**
Geary, Paul
    See Extreme
Geffen, David **8**
Geldof, Bob **9**
Genesis **4**
Gentry, Teddy
    See Alabama
George, Lowell
    See Little Feat
George, Rocky
    See Suicidal Tendencies
Georges, Bernard
    See Throwing Muses
Gerrard, Lisa
    See Dead Can Dance
Gershwin, George and Ira **11**
Geto Boys, The **11**
Getz, Stan **12**
Gibb, Barry
    See Bee Gees, The
Gibb, Maurice
    See Bee Gees, The
Gibb, Robin
    See Bee Gees, The
Gibbons, Billy
    See ZZ Top
Gibbons, Ian
    See Kinks, The
Gibson, Debbie **1**

Gibson, Wilf
    See Electric Light Orchestra
Gifford, Peter
    See Midnight Oil
Gift, Roland **3**
Gilbert, Gillian
    See New Order
Gilbert, Ronnie
    See Weavers, The
Gilkyson, Tony
    See X
Gill, Andy
    See Gang of Four
Gill, Janis
    See Sweethearts of the Rodeo
Gill, Pete
    See Motörhead
Gill, Vince **7**
Gillan, Ian
    See Deep Purple
Gillespie, Bobby
    See Primal Scream
Gillespie, Dizzy **6**
Gilley, Mickey **7**
Gillian, Ian
    See Black Sabbath
Gilmore, Jimmie Dale **11**
Gilmour, David
    See Pink Floyd
Gingold, Josef **6**
Gioia
    See Exposé
Gipsy Kings, The **8**
Glass, Philip **1**
Glasscock, John
    See Jethro Tull
Glennie, Jim
    See James
Glover, Corey
    See Living Colour
Glover, Roger
    See Deep Purple
Gobel, Robert
    See Kool & the Gang
Godchaux, Donna
    See Grateful Dead, The
Godchaux, Keith
    See Grateful Dead, The
Golden, William Lee
    See Oak Ridge Boys, The
Goldstein, Jerry
    See War
Goo Goo Dolls, The **16**
Gooden, Ramone PeeWee
    See Digital Underground
Goodman, Benny **4**
Gordon, Dexter **10**
Gordon, Kim
    See Sonic Youth
Gordon, Mike
    See Phish
Gordy, Berry, Jr. **6**
Gore, Martin
    See Depeche Mode
Gorham, Scott
    See Thin Lizzy

Harris, Steve
　　See Iron Maiden
Harrison, George **2**
　　　Also see Beatles, The
Harrison, Jerry
　　See Talking Heads
Harrison, Nigel
　　See Blondie
Harry, Deborah **4**
　　　Also see Blondie
Hart, Lorenz
　　See Rodgers, Richard
Hart, Mark
　　See Crowded House
Hart, Mickey
　　See Grateful Dead, The
Hartford, John **1**
Hartke, Stephen **5**
Hartman, Bob
　　See Petra
Hartman, John
　　See Doobie Brothers, The
Harvey, Bernard "Touter"
　　See Inner Circle
Harvey, Polly Jean **11**
Hashian
　　See Boston
Haskins, Kevin
　　See Love and Rockets
Haslinger, Paul
　　See Tangerine Dream
Hassan, Norman
　　See UB40
Hatfield, Juliana **12**
　　　Also see Lemonheads, The
Hauser, Tim
　　See Manhattan Transfer, The
Havens, Richie **11**
Hawkins, Coleman **11**
Hawkins, Screamin' Jay **8**
Hay, George D. **3**
Hayes, Isaac **10**
Hayes, Roland **13**
Haynes, Gibby
　　See Butthole Surfers
Haynes, Warren
　　See Allman Brothers, The
Hays, Lee
　　See Weavers, The
Hayward, Richard
　　See Little Feat
Headliner
　　See Arrested Development
Headon, Topper
　　See Clash, The
Healey, Jeff **4**
Heard, Paul
　　See M People
Heart **1**
Heavy D **10**
Hedges, Michael **3**
Heggie, Will
　　See Cocteau Twins, The
Hellerman, Fred
　　See Weavers, The

Helm, Levon
　　See Band, The
　　　Also see Nitty Gritty Dirt Band, The
Helmet **15**
Henderson, Fletcher **16**
Henderson, Joe **14**
Hendricks, Barbara **10**
Hendrix, Jimi **2**
Henley, Don **3**
　　　Also see Eagles, The
Henrit, Bob
　　See Kinks, The
Henry, Nicholas "Drummie"
　　See Mystic Revealers
Herman, Maureen
　　See Babes in Toyland
Herman, Woody **12**
Herman's Hermits **5**
Herndon, Mark
　　See Alabama
Herrera, R. J.
　　See Suicidal Tendencies
Herrmann, Bernard **14**
Herron, Cindy
　　See En Vogue
Hersh, Kristin
　　See Throwing Muses
Hester, Paul
　　See Crowded House
Hetfield, James
　　See Metallica
Hewson, Paul
　　See U2
Hiatt, John **8**
Hickman, Johnny
　　See Cracker
Hicks, Chris
　　See Restless Heart
Hicks, Sheree
　　See C + C Music Factory
Hidalgo, David
　　See Los Lobos
Highway 101 **4**
Hijbert, Fritz
　　See Kraftwerk
Hill, Brendan
　　See Blues Traveler
Hill, Dusty
　　See ZZ Top
Hill, Ian
　　See Judas Priest
Hillman, Bones
　　See Midnight Oil
Hillman, Chris
　　See Byrds, The
　　　Also see Desert Rose Band, The
Hinderas, Natalie **12**
Hinds, David
　　See Steel Pulse
Hines, Earl "Fatha" **12**
Hines, Gary
　　See Sounds of Blackness
Hinojosa, Tish **13**
Hirst, Rob
　　See Midnight Oil

Hirt, Al **5**
Hitchcock, Robyn **9**
Hodo, David
　　See Village People, The
Hoenig, Michael
　　See Tangerine Dream
Hoffman, Guy
　　See BoDeans, The
　　　Also see Violent Femmes
Hogan, Mike
　　See Cranberries, The
Hogan, Noel
　　See Cranberries, The
Hoke, Jim
　　See NRBQ
Hole **14**
Holiday, Billie **6**
Holland, Brian
　　See Holland-Dozier-Holland
Holland, Dave
　　See Judas Priest
Holland, Eddie
　　See Holland-Dozier-Holland
Holland, Julian "Jools"
　　See Squeeze
Holland-Dozier-Holland **5**
Holly, Buddy **1**
Holt, David Lee
　　See Mavericks, The
Honeyman, Susie
　　See Mekons, The
Honeyman-Scott, James
　　See Pretenders, The
Hook, Peter
　　See New Order
Hooker, John Lee **1**
Hopkins, Lightnin' **13**
Hopwood, Keith
　　See Herman's Hermits
Horn, Shirley **7**
Horn, Trevor
　　See Yes
Horne, Lena **11**
Horne, Marilyn **9**
Hornsby, Bruce **3**
Horovitz, Adam
　　See Beastie Boys, The
Horowitz, Vladimir **1**
Hossack, Michael
　　See Doobie Brothers, The
House, Son **11**
House of Pain **14**
Houston, Cissy **6**
Houston, Whitney **8**
Howard, Harlan **15**
Howe, Steve
　　See Yes
Howell, Porter
　　See Little Texas
Howlin' Wolf **6**
H.R.
　　See Bad Brains
Hubbard, Greg "Hobie"
　　See Sawyer Brown
Hubbard, Preston
　　See Fabulous Thunderbirds, The
　　　Also see Roomful of Blues

Johnson, Daryl
  See Neville Brothers, The
Johnson, Gene
  See Diamond Rio
Johnson, Gerry
  See Steel Pulse
Johnson, James P. **16**
Johnson, Matt
  See The The
Johnson, Mike
  See Dinosaur Jr.
Johnson, Ralph
  See Earth, Wind and Fire
Johnson, Robert **6**
Johnson, Shirley Childres
  See Sweet Honey in the Rock
Johnson, Tamara "Taj"
  See SWV
Johnston, Bruce
  See Beach Boys, The
Johnston, Tom
  See Doobie Brothers, The
JoJo
  See Jodeci
Jolly, Bill
  See Butthole Surfers
Jolson, Al **10**
Jones, Booker T. **8**
Jones, Brian
  See Rolling Stones, The
Jones, Busta
  See Gang of Four
Jones, Claude
  See McKinney's Cotton Pickers
Jones, Davy
  See Monkees, The
Jones, Elvin **9**
Jones, Geoffrey
  See Sounds of Blackness
Jones, George **4**
Jones, Grace **9**
Jones, Hank **15**
Jones, John Paul
  See Led Zeppelin
Jones, Kendall
  See Fishbone
Jones, Kenny
  See Who, The
Jones, Marshall
  See Ohio Players
Jones, Maxine
  See En Vogue
Jones, Michael
  See Kronos Quartet
Jones, Mick
  See Clash, The
Jones, Philly Joe **16**
Jones, Quincy **2**
Jones, Rickie Lee **4**
Jones, Robert "Kuumba"
  See Ohio Players
Jones, Sandra "Puma"
  See Black Uhuru
Jones, Spike **5**
Jones, Steve
  See Sex Pistols, The

Jones, Tom **11**
Jones, Will "Dub"
  See Coasters, The
Joplin, Janis **3**
Joplin, Scott **10**
Jordan, Lonnie
  See War
Jordan, Louis **11**
Jordan, Stanley **1**
Jorgensor, John
  See Desert Rose Band, The
Joseph-I, Israel
  See Bad Brains
Jourgensen, Al
  See Ministry
Joyce, Mike
  See Buzzcocks, The
  Also see Smiths, The
Judas Priest **10**
Judd, Naomi
  See Judds, The
Judd, Wynonna
  See Judds, The
  Also see Wynonna
Judds, The **2**
Jukebox
  See Geto Boys, The
Jungle DJ "Towa" Towa
  See Deee-lite
Jurado, Jeanette
  See Exposé
Kabongo, Sabine
  See Zap Mama
Kahlil, Aisha
  See Sweet Honey in the Rock
Kakoulli, Harry
  See Squeeze
Kalligan, Dick
  See Blood, Sweat and Tears
Kaminski, Mik
  See Electric Light Orchestra
Kanawa, Kiri Te
  See Te Kanawa, Kiri
Kane, Big Daddy **7**
Kane, Nick
  See Mavericks, The
Kannberg, Scott
  See Pavement
Kanter, Paul
  See Jefferson Airplane
Karajan, Herbert von
  See von Karajan, Herbert
Kath, Terry
  See Chicago
Katz, Steve
  See Blood, Sweat and Tears
Kaukonen, Jorma
  See Jefferson Airplane
Kaye, Tony
  See Yes
Kay Gee
  See Naughty by Nature
K-Ci
  See Jodeci
Keane, Sean
  See Chieftains, The

Kee, John P. **15**
Keifer, Tom
  See Cinderella
Keith, Jeff
  See Tesla
Kelly, Kevin
  See Byrds, The
Kendrick, David
  See Devo
Kendricks, Eddie
  See Temptations, The
Kennedy, Nigel **8**
Kenner, Doris
  See Shirelles, The
Kenny G **14**
Kentucky Headhunters, The **5**
Kern, Jerome **13**
Kershaw, Sammy **15**
Ketchum, Hal **14**
Khan, Chaka **9**
Khan, Nusrat Fateh Ali **13**
Kibble, Mark
  See Take 6
Kibby, Walter
  See Fishbone
Kid 'n Play **5**
Kiedis, Anthony
  See Red Hot Chili Peppers, The
Kilbey, Steve
  See Church, The
Killian, Tim
  See Kronos Quartet
Kimball, Jennifer
  See Story, The
Kimble, Paul
  See Grant Lee Buffalo
Kincaid, Jan
  See Brand New Heavies, The
Kinchla, Chan
  See Blues Traveler
King, Albert **2**
King, B. B. **1**
King, Ben E. **7**
King, Bob
  See Soul Stirrers, The
King, Carole **6**
King, Ed
  See Lynyrd Skynyrd
King, Jon
  See Gang of Four
King, Kerry
  See Slayer
King, Philip
  See Lush
King Ad-Rock
  See Beastie Boys, The
Kingston Trio, The **9**
King's X **7**
Kinks, The **15**
Kinney, Sean
  See Alice in Chains
Kirk, Rahsaan Roland **6**
Kirkwood, Cris
  See Meat Puppets, The
Kirkwood, Curt
  See Meat Puppets, The

Lewis, Ramsey **14**
Lewis, Roger
    See Inner Circle
Lewis, Roy
    See Kronos Quartet
Lewis, Samuel K.
    See Five Blind Boys of Alabama
Lewis, Terry
    See Jam, Jimmy, and Terry Lewis
Libbea, Gene
    See Nashville Bluegrass Band
Liberace **9**
Lifeson, Alex
    See Rush
Lightfoot, Gordon **3**
Lilienstein, Lois
    See Sharon, Lois & Bram
Lilker, Dan
    See Anthrax
Lillywhite, Steve **13**
Lincoln, Abbey **9**
Lindley, David **2**
Linna, Miriam
    See Cramps, The
Linnell, John
    See They Might Be Giants
Lipsius, Fred
    See Blood, Sweat and Tears
Little, Keith
    See Country Gentlemen, The
Little Feat **4**
Little Richard **1**
Little Texas **14**
Little Walter **14**
Live **14**
Living Colour **7**
Llanas, Sammy
    See BoDeans, The
L.L. Cool J. **5**
Lloyd Webber, Andrew **6**
Lockwood, Robert, Jr. **10**
Loewe, Frederick
    See Lerner and Loewe
Loggins, Kenny **3**
Lombardo, Dave
    See Slayer
Lopes, Lisa "Left Eye"
    See TLC
Lopez, Israel "Cachao" **14**
Lord, Jon
    See Deep Purple
Los Lobos **2**
Los Reyes
    See Gipsy Kings, The
Loughnane, Lee
    See Chicago
Louris, Gary
    See Jayhawks, The
Louvin, Charlie
    See Louvin Brothers, The
Louvin, Ira
    See Louvin Brothers, The
Louvin Brothers, The **12**
Lovano, Joe **13**
Love, Courtney
    See Hole

Love, Gerry
    See Teenage Fanclub
Love, Mike
    See Beach Boys, The
Love and Rockets **15**
Loveless, Patty **5**
Lovering, David
    See Cracker
Lovett, Lyle **5**
Lowe, Chris
    See Pet Shop Boys
Lowe, Nick **6**
Lowery, David
    See Cracker
Lozano, Conrad
    See Los Lobos
L7 **12**
Luccketta, Troy
    See Tesla
Lucia, Paco de
    See de Lucia, Paco
Luke
    See Campbell, Luther
Lukin, Matt
    See Mudhoney
Lupo, Pat
    See Beaver Brown Band, The
LuPone, Patti **8**
Lush **13**
Lydon, John **9**
    Also see Sex Pistols, The
Lynch, George
    See Dokken
Lyngstad, Anni-Frid
    See Abba
Lynn, Loretta **2**
Lynne, Jeff **5**
    Also see Electric Light Orchestra
Lynne, Shelby **5**
Lynott, Phil
    See Thin Lizzy
Lynyrd Skynyrd **9**
Lyons, Leanne "Lelee"
    See SWV
Ma, Yo-Yo **2**
MacColl, Kirsty **12**
MacGowan, Shane
    See Pogues, The
MacKaye, Ian
    See Fugazi
Mack Daddy
    See Kris Kross
Madonna **16**
    Earlier sketch in CM **4**
Magoogan, Wesley
    See English Beat, The
Maher, John
    See Buzzcocks, The
Makeba, Miriam **8**
Malcolm, Joy
    See Incognito
Malins, Mike
    See Goo Goo Dolls, The
Malkmus, Stephen
    See Pavement

Malo, Raul
    See Mavericks, The
Malone, Tom
    See Blood, Sweat and Tears
Mancini, Henry **1**
Mandrell, Barbara **4**
Maness, J. D.
    See Desert Rose Band, The
Manhattan Transfer, The **8**
Manilow, Barry **2**
Mann, Herbie **16**
Manuel, Richard
    See Band, The
Manzarek, Ray
    See Doors, The
Marie, Buffy Sainte
    See Sainte-Marie, Buffy
Marini, Lou, Jr.
    See Blood, Sweat and Tears
Marley, Bob **3**
Marley, Rita **10**
Marley, Ziggy **3**
Marr, Johnny
    See Smiths, The
    Also see The The
Marriner, Neville
Mars, Chris
    See Replacements, The
Mars, Mick
    See Mötley Crüe
Marsalis, Branford **10**
Marsalis, Ellis **13**
Marsalis, Wynton **6**
Marshal, Cornel
    See Third World
Martin, Barbara
    See Supremes, The
Martin, Christopher
    See Kid 'n Play
Martin, Dean **1**
Martin, George **6**
Martin, Greg
    See Kentucky Headhunters, The
Martin, Jim
    See Faith No More
Martin, Jimmy **5**
    Also See Osborne Brothers, The
Martin, Phonso
    See Steel Pulse
Martin, Sennie
    See Kool & the Gang
Martin, Tony
    See Black Sabbath
Marx, Richard **3**
Mascis, J
    See Dinosaur Jr.
Masdea, Jim
    See Boston
Masekela, Hugh **7**
Maseo, Baby Huey
    See De La Soul
Mason, Nick
    See Pink Floyd
Masse, Laurel
    See Manhattan Transfer, The

Miller, Charles
    See War
Miller, Glenn **6**
Miller, Jacob "Killer" Miller
    See Inner Circle
Miller, Jerry
    See Moby Grape
Miller, Mark
    See Sawyer Brown
Miller, Mitch **11**
Miller, Rice
    See Williamson, Sonny Boy
Miller, Roger **4**
Miller, Steve **2**
Milli Vanilli **4**
Mills, Donald
    See Mills Brothers, The
Mills, Fred
    See Canadian Brass, The
Mills, Harry
    See Mills Brothers, The
Mills, Herbert
    See Mills Brothers, The
Mills, John, Jr.
    See Mills Brothers, The
Mills, John, Sr.
    See Mills Brothers, The
Mills, Sidney
    See Steel Pulse
Mills Brothers, The **14**
Milsap, Ronnie **2**
Mingus, Charles **9**
Ministry **10**
Miss Kier Kirby
    See Lady Miss Kier
Mitchell, Alex
    See Curve
Mitchell, John
    See Asleep at the Wheel
Mitchell, Joni **2**
Mizell, Jay
    See Run-D.M.C.
Moby Grape **12**
Modeliste, Joseph "Zigaboo"
    See Meters, The
Moginie, Jim
    See Midnight Oil
Molloy, Matt
    See Chieftains, The
Moloney, Paddy
    See Chieftains, The
Money B
    See Digital Underground
Money, Eddie **16**
Monk, Meredith **1**
Monk, Thelonious **6**
Monkees, The **7**
Monroe, Bill **1**
Montand, Yves **12**
Montgomery, John Michael **14**
Montgomery, Wes **3**
Monti, Steve
    See Curve
Moon, Keith
    See Who, The

Mooney, Tim
    See American Music Club
Moore, Alan
    See Judas Priest
Moore, Angelo
    See Fishbone
Moore, Melba **7**
Moore, Sam
    See Sam and Dave
Moore, Thurston
    See Sonic Youth
Morand, Grace
    See Chenille Sisters, The
Moraz, Patrick
    See Yes
Morgan, Frank **9**
Morgan, Lorrie **10**
Morley, Pat
    See Soul Asylum
Morphine **16**
Morricone, Ennio **15**
Morris, Kenny
    See Siouxsie and the Banshees
Morris, Nate
    See Boyz II Men
Morris, Stephen
    See New Order
Morris, Wanya
    See Boyz II Men
Morrison, Bram
    See Sharon, Lois & Bram
Morrison, Jim **3**
    Also see Doors, The
Morrison, Sterling
    See Velvet Underground, The
Morrison, Van **3**
Morrissey **10**
    Also see Smiths, The
Morrissey, Bill **12**
Morrissey, Steven Patrick
    See Morrissey
Morton, Everett
    See English Beat, The
Morton, Jelly Roll **7**
Morvan, Fab
    See Milli Vanilli
Mosely, Chuck
    See Faith No More
Moser, Scott "Cactus"
    See Highway 101
Mosley, Bob
    See Moby Grape
Mothersbaugh, Bob
    See Devo
Mothersbaugh, Mark
    See Devo
Mötley Crüe **1**
Motörhead **10**
Motta, Danny
    See Roomful of Blues
Mould, Bob **10**
Moulding, Colin
    See XTC
Mounfield, Gary
    See Stone Roses, The

Mouskouri, Nana **12**
Moyet, Alison **12**
M People **15**
Mr. Dalvin
    See Jodeci
Mudhoney **16**
Mueller, Karl
    See Soul Asylum
Muir, Mike
    See Suicidal Tendencies
Mullen, Larry, Jr.
    See U2
Mulligan, Gerry **16**
Murph
    See Dinosaur Jr.
Murphey, Michael Martin **9**
Murphy, Dan
    See Soul Asylum
Murray, Anne **4**
Murray, Dave
    See Iron Maiden
Musselwhite, Charlie **13**
Mustaine, Dave
    See Megadeth
        Also see Metallica
Mwelase, Jabulane
    See Ladysmith Black Mambazo
Mydland, Brent
    See Grateful Dead, The
Myers, Alan
    See Devo
Myles, Alannah **4**
Mystic Revealers **16**
Nadirah
    See Arrested Development
Nagler, Eric **8**
Nakamura, Tetsuya "Tex"
    See War
Nakatami, Michie
    See Shonen Knife
Narcizo, David
    See Throwing Muses
Nascimento, Milton **6**
Nashville Bluegrass Band **14**
Nastanovich, Bob
    See Pavement
Naughty by Nature **11**
Navarro, David
    See Jane's Addiction
Nawasadio, Sylvie
    See Zap Mama
N'Dour, Youssou **6**
Near, Holly **1**
Neel, Johnny
    See Allman Brothers, The
Negron, Chuck
    See Three Dog Night
Neil, Vince
    See Mötley Crüe
Nelson, Errol
    See Black Uhuru
Nelson, Rick **2**
Nelson, Willie **11**
    Earlier sketch in CM **1**
Nesbitt, John
    See McKinney's Cotton Pickers

Pavarotti, Luciano **1**
Pavement **14**
Paxton, Tom **5**
Payne, Bill
  See Little Feat
Payne, Scherrie
  See Supremes, The
Payton, Denis
  See Dave Clark Five, The
Payton, Lawrence
  See Four Tops, The
Pearl, Minnie **3**
Pearl Jam **12**
Pearson, Dan
  See American Music Club
Peart, Neil
  See Rush
Pedersen, Herb
  See Desert Rose Band, The
Peduzzi, Larry
  See Roomful of Blues
Peek, Dan
  See America
Peeler, Ben
  See Mavericks, The
Pegg, Dave
  See Jethro Tull
Pendergrass, Teddy **3**
Pengilly, Kirk
  See INXS
Peniston, CeCe **15**
Penn, Michael **4**
Penner, Fred **10**
Perahia, Murray **10**
Peretz, Jesse
  See Lemonheads, The
Perez, Louie
  See Los Lobos
Perkins, Carl **9**
Perkins, John
  See XTC
Perkins, Percell
  See Five Blind Boys of Alabama
Perkins, Steve
  See Jane's Addiction
Perlman, Itzhak **2**
Perlman, Marc
  See Jayhawks, The
Perry, Brendan
  See Dead Can Dance
Perry, Doane
  See Jethro Tull
Perry, Joe
  See Aerosmith
Peter, Paul & Mary **4**
Peters, Bernadette **7**
Peters, Dan
  See Mudhoney
Peters, Joey
  See Grant Lee Buffalo
Peterson, Oscar **11**
Petersson, Tom
  See Cheap Trick
Petra **3**
Pet Shop Boys **5**

Petty, Tom **9**
Pfaff, Kristen
  See Hole
Phair, Liz **14**
Phantom, Slim Jim
  See Stray Cats, The
Phelps, Doug
  See Kentucky Headhunters, The
Phelps, Ricky Lee
  See Kentucky Headhunters, The
Phife
  See Tribe Called Quest, A
Phil, Gary
  See Boston
Philips, Anthony
  See Genesis
Phillips, Chynna
  See Wilson Phillips
Phillips, Glenn
  See Toad the Wet Sprocket
Phillips, Grant Lee
  See Grant Lee Buffalo
Phillips, Harvey **3**
Phillips, Sam **5**
Phillips, Sam **12**
Phillips, Simon
  See Judas Priest
Phish **13**
Phungula, Inos
  See Ladysmith Black Mambazo
Piaf, Edith **8**
Picciotto, Joe
  See Fugazi
Piccolo, Greg
  See Roomful of Blues
Pickering, Michael
  See M People
Pickett, Wilson **10**
Pierce, Marvin "Merv"
  See Ohio Players
Pierce, Webb **15**
Pierson, Kate
  See B-52's, The
Pilatus, Rob
  See Milli Vanilli
Pilson, Jeff
  See Dokken
Pink Floyd **2**
Pinkus, Jeff
  See Butthole Surfers
Pinnick, Doug
  See King's X
Pirner, Dave
  See Soul Asylum
Pirroni, Marco
  See Siouxsie and the Banshees
Plakas, Dee
  See L7
Plant, Robert **2**
  Also see Led Zeppelin
Ploog, Richard
  See Church, The
P.M. Dawn **11**
Pogues, The **6**
Poindexter, Buster
  See Johansen, David

Pointer, Anita
  See Pointer Sisters, The
Pointer, Bonnie
  See Pointer Sisters, The
Pointer, June
  See Pointer Sisters, The
Pointer, Ruth
  See Pointer Sisters, The
Pointer Sisters, The **9**
Poison **11**
Poison Ivy
  See Rorschach, Poison Ivy
Poland, Chris
  See Megadeth
Polygon Window
  See Aphex Twin
Pomus, Doc
  See Doc Pomus
Ponty, Jean-Luc **8**
Pop, Iggy **1**
Popper, John
  See Blues Traveler
Porter, Cole **10**
Porter, George, Jr.
  See Meters, The
Porter, Tiran
  See Doobie Brothers, The
Posdnuos
  See De La Soul
Potts, Sean
  See Chieftains, The
Powell, Billy
  See Lynyrd Skynyrd
Powell, Bud **15**
Powell, Cozy
  See Emerson, Lake & Palmer/Powell
Powell, William
  See O'Jays, The
Powers, Congo
  See Cramps, The
Prater, Dave
  See Sam and Dave
Prefab Sprout **15**
Presley, Elvis **1**
Pretenders, The **8**
Previn, André **15**
Price, Leontyne **6**
Price, Louis
  See Temptations, The
Price, Ray **11**
Price, Rick
  See Electric Light Orchestra
Pride, Charley **4**
Primal Scream **14**
Primettes, The
  See Supremes, The
Primus **11**
Prince **14**
  Earlier sketch in CM **1**
Prince Be
  See P.M. Dawn
Prine, John **7**
Proclaimers, The **13**
Professor Longhair **6**
Propes, Duane
  See Little Texas

Roe, Marty
  See Diamond Rio
Roeder, Klaus
  See Kraftwerk
Roeser, Donald
  See Blue Öyster Cult
Rogers, Kenny **1**
Rogers, Norm
  See Jayhawks, The
Rogers, Roy **9**
Rogers, Willie
  See Soul Stirrers, The
Roland, Dean
  See Collective Soul
Roland, Ed
  See Collective Soul
Rolling Stones, The **3**
Rollins, Henry **11**
Rollins, Sonny **7**
Romm, Ronald
  See Canadian Brass, The
Ronstadt, Linda **2**
Roomful of Blues **7**
Roper, De De
  See Salt-N-Pepa
Rorschach, Poison Ivy
  See Cramps, The
Rosas, Cesar
  See Los Lobos
Rose, Axl
  See Guns n' Roses
Rose, Michael
  See Black Uhuru
Rosen, Gary
  See Rosenshontz
Rosen, Peter
  See War
Rosenshontz **9**
Rosenthal, Jurgen
  See Scorpions, The
Rosenthal, Phil
  See Seldom Scene, The
Ross, Diana **1**
  Also see Supremes, The
Rossi, John
  See Roomful of Blues
Rossington, Gary
  See Lynyrd Skynyrd
Rota, Nino **13**
Roth, David Lee **1**
  Also see Van Halen
Roth, Ulrich
  See Scorpions, The
Rotsey, Martin
  See Midnight Oil
Rotten, Johnny
  See Lydon, John
    Also see Sex Pistols, The
Rourke, Andy
  See Smiths, The
Rowe, Dwain
  See Restless Heart
Rubin, Rick **9**
Rubinstein, Arthur **11**
Rudd, Phillip
  See AC/DC

Rue, Caroline
  See Hole
Ruffin, David **6**
  Also see Temptations, The
Rundgren, Todd **11**
Run-D.M.C. **4**
Rush **8**
Rush, Otis **12**
Rushlow, Tim
  See Little Texas
Russell, Alecia
  See Sounds of Blackness
Russell, Mark **6**
Rutherford, Mike
  See Genesis
Rutsey, John
  See Rush
Ryan, David
  See Lemonheads, The
Ryan, Mick
  See Dave Clark Five, The
Ryder, Mitch **11**
Ryland, Jack
  See Three Dog Night
Rzeznik, Johnny
  See Goo Goo Dolls, The
Sabo, Dave
  See Bon Jovi
Sade **2**
Sager, Carole Bayer **5**
Sahm, Doug
  See Texas Tornados, The
St. Hubbins, David
  See Spinal Tap
St. John, Mark
  See Kiss
St. Marie, Buffy
  See Sainte-Marie, Buffy
Sainte-Marie, Buffy **11**
Salerno-Sonnenberg, Nadja **3**
Saliers, Emily
  See Indigo Girls
Salmon, Michael
  See Prefab Sprout
Salonen, Esa-Pekka **16**
Salt-N-Pepa **6**
Sam and Dave **8**
Sambora, Richie
  See Bon Jovi
Sampson, Doug
  See Iron Maiden
Samuelson, Gar
  See Megadeth
Samwell-Smith, Paul
  See Yardbirds, The
Sanborn, David **1**
Sanders, Pharoah **16**
Sanders, Steve
  See Oak Ridge Boys, The
Sandman, Mark
  See Morphine
Sandoval, Arturo **15**
Sanger, David
  See Asleep at the Wheel
Santana, Carlos **1**

Saraceno, Blues
  See Poison
Satchell, Clarence "Satch"
  See Ohio Players
Satriani, Joe **4**
Savage, Rick
  See Def Leppard
Sawyer Brown **13**
Saxa
  See English Beat, The
Saxon, Stan
  See Dave Clark Five, The
Scaccia, Mike
  See Ministry
Scaggs, Boz **12**
Scanlon, Craig
  See Fall, The
Scarface
  See Geto Boys, The
Schemel, Patty
  See Hole
Schenker, Michael
  See Scorpions, The
Schenker, Rudolf
  See Scorpions, The
Schenkman, Eric
  See Spin Doctors
Schermie, Joe
  See Three Dog Night
Schickele, Peter **5**
Schlitt, John
  See Petra
Schmelling, Johannes
  See Tangerine Dream
Schmit, Timothy B.
  See Eagles, The
Schmoovy Schmoove
  See Digital Underground
Schneider, Florian
  See Kraftwerk
Schneider, Fred III
  See B-52's, The
Schnitzler, Conrad
  See Tangerine Dream
Scholten, Jim
  See Sawyer Brown
Scholz, Tom
  See Boston
Schrody, Erik
  See House of Pain
Schroyder, Steve
  See Tangerine Dream
Schulze, Klaus
  See Tangerine Dream
Schuman, William **10**
Schuur, Diane **6**
Scofield, John **7**
Scorpions, The **12**
Scott, Ronald Belford "Bon"
  See AC/DC
Scott, George
  See Five Blind Boys of Alabama
Scott, Howard
  See War
Scott, Jimmy **14**

Ulvaeus, Björn
   See Abba
Unruh, N. U.
   See Einstürzende Neubauten
Upshaw, Dawn **9**
U2 **12**
   Earlier sketch in CM **2**
Vachon, Chris
   See Roomful of Blues
Vai, Steve **5**
   Also see Whitesnake
Valentine, Gary
   See Blondie
Valentine, Rae
   See War
Valli, Frankie **10**
Vandenburg, Adrian
   See Whitesnake
Vandross, Luther **2**
Van Halen **8**
Van Halen, Alex
   See Van Halen
Van Halen, Edward
   See Van Halen
Vanilla Ice **6**
Van Ronk, Dave **12**
Van Shelton, Ricky **5**
Van Vliet, Don
   See Captain Beefheart
Van Zandt, Townes **13**
Van Zant, Johnny
   See Lynyrd Skynyrd
Van Zant, Ronnie
   See Lynyrd Skynyrd
Vasquez, Junior **16**
Vaughan, Jimmie
   See Fabulous Thunderbirds, The
Vaughan, Sarah **2**
Vaughan, Stevie Ray **1**
Vedder, Eddie
   See Pearl Jam
Vega, Suzanne **3**
Velvet Underground, The **7**
Vettese, Peter-John
   See Jethro Tull
Vicious, Sid
   See Sex Pistols, The
   Also see Siouxsie and the Banshees
Village People, The **7**
Vincent, Vinnie
   See Kiss
Vinnie
   See Naughty by Nature
Vinton, Bobby **12**
Violent Femmes **12**
Virtue, Michael
   See UB40
Vito, Rick
   See Fleetwood Mac
Volz, Greg
   See Petra
Von, Eerie
   See Danzig
von Karajan, Herbert **1**
Vox, Bono
   See U2

Vudi
   See American Music Club
Wadenius, George
   See Blood, Sweat and Tears
Wadephal, Ralf
   See Tangerine Dream
Wagoner, Faidest
   See Soul Stirrers, The
Wagoner, Porter **13**
Wahlberg, Donnie
   See New Kids on the Block
Wailer, Bunny **11**
Wainwright III, Loudon **11**
Waits, Tom **12**
   Earlier sketch in CM **1**
Wakeling, David
   See English Beat, The
Wakeman, Rick
   See Yes
Walden, Narada Michael **14**
Walker, Colin
   See Electric Light Orchestra
Walker, Ebo
   See New Grass Revival, The
Walker, Jerry Jeff **13**
Walker, T-Bone **5**
Wallace, Sippie **6**
Waller, Charlie
   See Country Gentlemen, The
Waller, Fats **7**
Wallinger, Karl **11**
Wallis, Larry
   See Motörhead
Walls, Chris
   See Dave Clark Five, The
Walls, Greg
   See Anthrax
Walsh, Joe **5**
   Also see Eagles, The
Walters, Robert "Patch"
   See Mystic Revealers
War **14**
Ward, Bill
   See Black Sabbath
Warner, Les
   See Cult, The
Warnes, Jennifer **3**
Warren, George W.
   See Five Blind Boys of Alabama
Warren, Mervyn
   See Take 6
Warwick, Dionne **2**
Was, David
   See Was (Not Was)
Was, Don
   See Was (Not Was)
Wash, Martha
   See C + C Music Factory
Washington, Chester
   See Earth, Wind and Fire
Washington, Dinah **5**
Washington, Grover, Jr. **5**
Was (Not Was) **6**
Waters, Ethel **11**
Waters, Crystal **15**

Waters, Muddy **4**
Waters, Roger
   See Pink Floyd
Watkins, Tionne "T-Boz"
   See TLC
Watley, Jody **9**
Watson, Doc **2**
Watt, Ben
   See Everything But The Girl
Watt, Mike
   See fIREHOSE
Watts, Charlie
   See Rolling Stones, The
Watts, Eugene
   See Canadian Brass, The
Weaver, Louie
   See Petra
Weavers, The **8**
Webb, Chick **14**
Webb, Jimmy **12**
Webber, Andrew Lloyd
   See Lloyd Webber, Andrew
Weiland, Scott "Weiland"
   See Stone Temple Pilots
Weill, Kurt **12**
Weir, Bob
   See Grateful Dead, The
Welch, Bob
   See Fleetwood Mac
Welk, Lawrence **13**
Weller, Paul **14**
Wells, Cory
   See Three Dog Night
Wells, Kitty **6**
Welnick, Vince
   See Grateful Dead, The
West, Dottie **8**
West, Steve
   See Pavement
Westerberg, Paul
   See Replacements, The
Weston, Randy **15**
Wexler, Jerry **15**
Weymouth, Tina
   See Talking Heads
Wheat, Brian
   See Tesla
Wheeler, Audrey
   See C + C Music Factory
Whelan, Gavan
   See James
White, Alan
   See Oasis
White, Alan
   See Yes
White, Barry **6**
White, Billy
   See Dokken
White, Clarence
   See Byrds, The
White, Freddie
   See Earth, Wind and Fire
White, Lari **15**
White, Mark
   See Mekons, The

York, John
    See Byrds, The
Young, Angus
    See AC/DC
Young, Faron **7**
Young, Fred
    See Kentucky Headhunters, The
Young, Gary
    See Pavement
Young, Grant
    See Soul Asylum
Young, Jeff
    See Megadeth

Young, La Monte **16**
Young, Lester **14**
Young, Malcolm
    See AC/DC
Young, Neil **15**
    Earlier sketch in CM **2**
Young, Richard
    See Kentucky Headhunters, The
Young, Robert "Throbert"
    See Primal Scream
Young M.C. **4**
Yo Yo **9**

Yule, Doug
    See Velvet Underground, The
Zander, Robin
    See Cheap Trick
Zap Mama **14**
Zappa, Frank **1**
Zevon, Warren **9**
Zimmerman, Udo **5**
Zoom, Billy
    See X
Zorn, John **15**
Zukerman, Pinchas **4**
ZZ Top **2**